Buddhism and Asian History

Religion, History, and Culture
Readings from The Encyclopedia of Religion

Mircea Eliade
EDITOR IN CHIEF

EDITORS

Charles J. Adams
Joseph M. Kitagawa
Martin E. Marty
Richard P. McBrien
Jacob Needleman
Annemarie Schimmel
Robert M. Seltzer
Victor Turner

ASSOCIATE EDITOR

Lawrence E. Sullivan

ASSISTANT EDITOR

William K. Mahony

Buddhism and Asian History

EDITED BY

Joseph M. Kitagawa
and
Mark D. Cummings

Religion, History, and Culture
Readings from The Encyclopedia of Religion

Mircea Eliade
EDITOR IN CHIEF

MACMILLAN PUBLISHING COMPANY
New York
COLLIER MACMILLAN PUBLISHERS
London

MACMILLAN PUBLISHING COMPANY
866 Third Avenue, New York, N.Y. 10022

Collier Macmillan Canada, Inc.

Library of Congress Catalog Card Number: 89-8128

Printed in the United States of America

printing number
1 2 3 4 5 6 7 8 9 10

Library of Congress Cataloging-in-Publication Data

Buddhism and Asian history.

(Religion, history, and culture)
Includes readings from the Encyclopedia of religion.
1. Buddhism—History. I. Kitagawa, Joseph Mitsuo, 1915– . II. Cummings, Mark D. III. Series.
IV. Encyclopedia of religion.
BQ266.B833 1989 294.3'095 89-8128
ISBN 0-02-897212-0

CONTENTS

MAPS

PUBLISHER'S NOTE

Since publication of *The Encyclopedia of Religion* in 1987, we have been gratified by the overwhelming reception accorded it by the community of scholars. This reception has more than justified the hopes of the members of the work's editorial board, who, with their editor in chief, cherished the aim that it would contribute to the study of the varieties of religious expression worldwide. To all those who participated in the project we express again our deepest thanks.

Now, in response to the many requests of our contributors and other teachers, we take pride in making available this selection of articles from the encyclopedia for use in the classroom. It is our hope that by publishing these articles in an inexpensive, compact format, they will be read and reflected upon by an even broader audience. In our effort to select those articles most appropriate to undergraduate instruction, it has been necessary to omit many entries of interest primarily to the more advanced student and/or to those who wish to pursue a particular topic in greater depth. To facilitate their research, and to encourage the reader to consult the encyclopedia itself, we have thus retained the system of cross-references that, in the original work, served to guide the reader to related articles in this and other fields. A comprehensive index to the coverage of Buddhism may be found in volume sixteen of the encyclopedia.

Charles E. Smith
Publisher and President
Macmillan Reference Division

INTRODUCTION

The essays that appear in this volume are part of a larger collection of articles on Buddhism that originally appeared in *The Encyclopedia of Religion.* They are the product of a collaborative effort involving scholars of many intellectual backgrounds and disciplines, whose work on the encyclopedia was an attempt to provide an overview of the tradition from the perspective of late-twentieth-century scholarship. Our aim in the creation of this present work has been to preserve this perspective, while at the same time bringing together in a single volume those articles most useful for introductory and undergraduate instruction in Buddhism. The result is a collection that is broader than it is deep, but one that attempts to do credit to the sometimes astonishing variety of cultural forms that pass under the rubric *Buddhist.*

Buddhism began with a historical figure who lived in what is now northern India sometime around the fifth century before the beginning of the common era. The Buddha's actual words will forever remain a matter of some uncertainty, but we know that the Buddha claimed to have discovered a "truth" (Dharma) that, in the formula of the scriptures, is "independent of time, verifiable, fruitful, and capable of being personally discovered by the wise." This truth had, in contemporary language, both a historical and an ahistorical dimension. As a universal "law" of action and its causes, it was deemed timeless and immutable, but because the appearance and preservation of this law in the world is dependent upon human institutions—language, for instance—the Dharma as a social and historical phenomenon (i.e., as embodied in the teachings of the Buddha) was acknowledged to be subject to the same process of change, the same possibility of *interpretation,* as anything else.

This inability of the Dharma to be bound or exhausted by a single cultural form, and its ability to be independently discovered by discerning persons other than the Buddha, was to have a profound effect on the development of the religion. These factors lent to the tradition the virtue of portability; in other words, it could thrive in the language and idiom of cultures vastly different from the one in which it was born. Not only that, it could—indeed, was expected to—adapt over time to fit concrete historical situations. Just as the tradition looked back to the existence of enlightened beings who had proclaimed the Dharma in eons past, it also looked ahead to the appearance of other expositors of the same Truth, and to the eventual dissemination of these teachings to the widest possible audience under conditions that the founder could not have fully anticipated. Given these assumptions, the historical spread and development of the teachings of the Buddha was more or less assumed by even his earliest followers.

In the centuries following the death of the Buddha, the small group of religious mendicants who constituted the original Buddhist order (the *saṃgha*) grew to become a prominent part of the religious landscape of northern India. With the reign of the Mauryan monarch Aśoka (consecrated c. 270 BCE), the *saṃgha* forged links with polity that gave it not only a broad geographical base, one coincident with the boundaries of the Mauryan empire, but also an ideology by which it could cooperate with and flourish in the presence of civil authority. Contact with the empires at the fringes of Mauryan power led to its rapid expansion into what is now Pakistan and Afghanistan in the northwest, and into Sri Lanka in the south. Soon thereafter, by the first century of the common era, the religion had spread into the city-states of Central Asia and from there into the vast Chinese empire beyond. As Buddhism spread beyond the confines of India it gradually developed three secondary centers of diffusion. Sri Lanka became the site of a Theravāda tradition that was highly influential in the religious history of Southeast Asia, particularly during the classical period of the monarchical kingdoms. China served as the center of the Mahāyāna Buddhist culture that was transmitted to Korea, Japan, and Vietnam. Tibet, last of the three to be missionized, was heir to the Indian Tantric tradition, which it propagated in the trans-Himalayan region and in parts of Inner Asia. The result of this expansion was something without parallel in the history of Asia: the formation of a pan-Asian religious culture, a culture that was profoundly Buddhist.

Given the diversity of the cultures into which Buddhism was introduced, and the flexibility and adaptability of the tradition itself, we would scarcely expect to see a uniform expression of religious thought or practice in Buddhist Asia, and indeed, when we look at the variety of forms under which the religion has flourished, it is sometimes difficult to see what links them all together. The Buddhism of Japan (which is not itself homogeneous) is very far indeed from the Buddhism of Sri Lanka or Thailand; the Buddhism of Tibet, quite unlike that practiced in China or Vietnam. Even where there is uniformity of profession, it is often balanced by an amazing diversity of expression. From one Buddhist culture to the next, Buddhists recognize little by way of a common creed other than the most simple formula of faith in the Buddha, his teachings (Dharma), and the community he founded *(saṃgha),* or confidence in certain "fundamental" teachings universally associated with the Buddha but accepted by no one school as constituting his entire message. They observe no common liturgy or meditational regimen, and they fail to agree on what constitutes the authentic words of the founder. Even the Vinaya, the code of monastic discipline that notionally binds all Buddhist clergy in a common rule, regardless of sectarian stance or affiliation, was not universally observed.

Can we then identify elements that unify all those professing themselves to be Buddhists? Is it possible to speak of a Buddhist Asia, of Buddhist culture as a whole? As Professor Reynolds has noted in his opening chapter on Buddhist culture and civilization (chapter one), our attempts to define the tradition in terms of broad conceptual categories have thus far yielded useful but ultimately less than comprehensive results. They have been constrained by the need to establish definitions that are broad enough to account for all that calls itself Buddhist yet specific enough to generate meaningful categories of interpretation. Yet despite the diversity of the various Buddhist cultures, we can find among Buddhists themselves a simpler answer. However much the various regional traditions may differ with respect to what constitutes the core elements of the religious path, all Buddhists are united in their veneration of the figure of the Buddha, in the reverence and esteem they accord him as the founder of their way of life. It is in this "imagination of the Buddha," that is, in the recovery and reconstruction of his personality and experience, that the Buddhist tradition has achieved its unity and creative power. Sometimes this act of imagination was ideological, the assertion of this or that point of view regarding the "nature" of buddhahood and the path to it. More often, however, it expressed itself in the everyday fabric of religious practice, from the most formal meditational regimes of the clerical elites to the practices of laypersons of little or no theoretical sophistication. All of these expressions draw their inspiration from the personality of the "enlightened one" *(buddha)*. From his person and career are derived the symbols and values that contribute, in a fully elaborated form, to Buddhist meditation, liturgy, iconography, architecture, cosmology, ethics, even statecraft and social theory.

It is for these reasons that we have thought it important not merely to describe the elements of Buddhist doctrine that are intellectually crucial to the tradition, but also to include discussions of the way in which the religion has been practiced in different social and historical contexts. The work itself is divided into five parts. "Foundations of the Tradition" attempts to establish the ways in which we can speak meaningfully of a Buddhist religion; it includes a discussion of the Buddha and of buddhahood and gives an overview of the history of the tradition in the land of its origin. "The Pan-Asian Buddhist World" is devoted to the development of the religion throughout the rest of Asia, and includes articles on Buddhism in Southeast and Central Asia, China, Tibet, Korea, Japan, and Mongolia. "Buddhist Schools and Sects" focuses on the development of Buddhist doctrine, first in terms of the three great *yānas*, or vehicles to enlightenment, then on the regional development of Buddhist thought in East Asia and Tibet. The social forms assumed by the religion are the topic of the fourth section, "Dimensions of Religious Practice." Here, we have included chapters on the Buddhist *saṃgha,* the relation of the Buddhist church to the state, Buddhist cultic life in various areas of Asia, the role of meditation, the visual images that reinforce religious practice, and the way in which Buddhism interacts with other, purely local, traditions. Finally, in "The Path to Enlightenment," we return to the main theme of the religion, enlightenment, as articulated in the notion of its various ideal figures: *arhat, bodhisattva, mahāsiddha.* Taken as a whole, the essays in this book reveal the vast distances that separate the Buddhist cultures of Asia, but they also express something of the underlying community of symbolic structures that permeate all Buddhist discourse.

FEBRUARY, 1989 THE EDITORS

ONE

FOUNDATIONS OF THE TRADITION

1

BUDDHIST RELIGION, CULTURE, AND CIVILIZATION

FRANK E. REYNOLDS AND CHARLES HALLISEY

The concept of Buddhism was created about three centuries ago to identify what we now know to be a pan-Asian religious tradition that dates back some twenty-five hundred years. Although the concept, rather recent and European in origin, has gradually, if sometimes begrudgingly, received global acceptance, there is still no consensus about its definition. We can, however, identify two complementary meanings that have consistently informed its use. First, it groups together the thoughts, practices, institutions, and values that over the centuries have—to use a phrase coined by the French Buddhologist Louis de La Vallée Poussin—"condensed around the name of the Buddha." The implicit conclusion of this usage is that Buddhism is, in short, whatever Buddhist men and women have said, done, and held dear. Second, the concept suggests some unifying character or order in the overwhelming diversity encompassed by the first usage. The beginning of this ordering process has often been to consider Buddhism as an example of larger categories, and thus Buddhism has been variously labeled a religion, a philosophy, a civilization, or a culture. It must be admitted, however, that no single ordering principle has been found that takes full account of the data included within the first meaning. This admission stands as a rebuke of the limitations of our current understanding, and as a continuing challenge to go further in our descriptions and explanations.

When the first meaning of Buddhism, which emphasizes its encompassment of accumulated traditions, is placed in the foreground, the resulting conception is indeed comprehensive. The further scholarship proceeds, the more comprehensive this conception becomes, because Buddhists have done in the name of the Buddha almost everything that other humans have done. Buddhists have, of course, been concerned with living religiously, some with the aim of salvation, and they have created traditions of belief and practice that help to realize these aspirations. But they have been concerned with much more as well. Buddhists have built cities sanctified by monuments dedicated to the Buddha and they have cultivated their crops using blessings that invoke his name. They have written self-consciously Buddhist poems and plays as well as highly technical works of grammar and logic that begin with invocations to the Buddha. They have commended nonviolence, but they have also gone to war with the name of Buddha on their lips. They have valued celibacy, but have also written erotic manuals and rejoiced in family life, all in the name of

Buddha. Buddhists have created subtle philosophical concepts, such as the absence of self *(anātman),* which are contravened by other ideas and values they have held. Like other human beings, Buddhists have been inconsistent and even contradictory, and they have been both noble and base in what they have said and done.

Although most scholars have at some level accepted this first conception of Buddhism as a diverse cumulative tradition, few have been content to allow this encompassing notion to prevail. They have sought to discover what ideals and values have inspired Buddhists, or to formulate generalizations that will help us to see the behavior of individuals as distinctively Buddhist. Some scholars have singled out a pattern, an idea, or a cluster of ideas that they felt was important enough to provide continuity through Buddhist history, or at least sufficient to suggest a coherence to the variety. Important candidates for this "key" to Buddhism are the purported teaching of the founder of Buddhism, Gautama, which provides an essence that has unfolded over the centuries; the monastic organization *(saṃgha),* whose historical continuity provides a center of Buddhist practice and a social basis for the persistence of Buddhist thought and values; the closely related ideas of nonself and emptiness *(anātman, śūnyatā),* realized through insight, which are said to mold Buddhist behavior; and the goal of *nirvāṇa* as the purpose of life. While such patterns and notions are very important for Buddhist sociology and soteriology, they also omit a great deal. Moreover, we can see that the element that is singled out as important is often distictive to Buddhism only in comparison with other religions or philosophies and cannot serve as a core that informs the entire corpus of Buddhist beliefs, rituals, and values.

Scholars have also sought to identify the characteristic order of Buddhism by dividing the cumulative tradition into more manageable parts, whether by chronology, by school, or by country. Some scholars, following the Buddhist historians Bu-ston (1290–1364) and Tāranātha (1574–1608), have divided Buddhism into three periods, mainly along philosophical lines. A first phase, represented by the early Theravāda (Way of the Elders) and Sarvāstivāda (All Things Are Real) schools, emphasized the no-soul idea and the reality of the constituents (*dharmas*) of the world. A middle phase, represented by the Mādhyamika (Middle Way) school, introduced the idea of the ultimate emptiness *(śūnyatā)* of all phenomena. A third period, represented by the Vijñānavāda (Consciousness Only) school, was philosophically idealistic in character. The limitations of this philosophical division are severe in that it only touches certain aspects of Buddhism and acknowledges no significant development after the fifth century CE.

Other scholars have elaborated a schema based on polemical divisions within the Buddhist community. They have focused attention on three great Buddhist "vehicles" *(yāna)* that are characterized by different understandings of the process and goal of salvation. The Hīnayāna, or Lesser Vehicle, elaborated a gradual process of individual salvation, and in that context distinguished among the attainment of an *arhat,* the attainment of a *pratyekabuddha* (one who achieves enlightenment on his own but does not become a teacher), and the attainment of a fully enlightened Buddha who teaches others the way to salvation. The Theravāda and Sarvāstivāda schools mentioned above are two of the major schools that are included under the Hīnayāna rubric. The term *Hīnayāna* was in its origins a pejorative name coined by the adherents of a new movement, self-designated as the Mahāyāna, or Great Vehicle, which generated new texts and teachings that were rejected by the Hīnayānists.

Like the adherents of the Hīnayāna, the Mahāyānists elaborated a gradual path of salvation lasting over many lifetimes, but their emphasis was different in two very important and related respects. They held that an individual's soteriological process could be aided and abetted by what some Mahāyāna schools came to designate as "other-power," and they recognized, ultimately, only one soteriological goal—the attainment of fully realized Buddhahood. The Vajrayāna (Diamond Vehicle), which is also known as Mantrayāna (Sacred Sounds Vehicle), Esoteric Buddhism, or Tantric Buddhism, accepted the basic approach and goal of the Mahāyāna, but felt that individual realization could be accomplished more quickly, in some cases even in this present life. The Vajrayānists described the practices that lead to this attainment in texts called *tantras* that were not accepted by either the Hīnayāna or the Mahāyāna schools. Although this Hīnayāna/Mahāyāna/Vajrayāna schema is probably the most common one used by scholars to divide Buddhism into more manageable segments, it too has serious drawbacks. It underestimates the significance of developments after the first millennium of the common era and it tends to overemphasize certain traits therein as extreme differences, beyond what is warranted by history.

Finally, scholars have recognized that Buddhism has always been deeply shaped by its surrounding culture. The Buddhist tradition has been more accretive in its doctrine and practice than the other great missionary religions, Christianity and Islam. It has shown an enduring tendency to adapt to local forms; as a result we can speak of a transformation of Buddhism in various cultures. The extent of this transformation can be seen in the difficulty that the first Western observers had in recognizing that the religion they observed in Japan was historically related to the religion found in Sri Lanka. This cultural division of Buddhism into Tibetan Buddhism, Chinese Buddhism, and so forth has been most successfully applied to the more recent phases of Buddhist history, especially to contemporary developments. Its dangers are, of course, quite obvious: above all, it conceals the Buddhist tradition's capacity to transcend the boundaries of culture, politics, and nationality.

The general trends of scholarship on Buddhism in this century have been within such accepted divisions of the cumulative tradition, with the result that our sense of Buddhism's historical continuity has been greatly obscured. Theodore Stcherbatsky, a Soviet Buddhologist, is in this regard a representative example. He adopted Buston's tripartite "philosophical" division of Buddhist history and, in his *Conception of Buddhist Nirvāṇa* (Leningrad, 1927), commented on the transition between the first phase and the second phase as follows: "the history of religions has scarcely witnessed such a break between new and old within the pale of what nevertheless continued to claim common descent from the same religious founder" (p. 36). Similar statements pointing to radical discontinuity have been made from the perspective of the soteriological and cultural forms of Buddhism as well.

The investigation of each segment of the Buddhist cumulative tradition is now generally done in isolation from other segments. This strategy has had remarkable success in our discovery of the imprint of Buddhist thought and practice in areas far beyond the monasteries, beyond the level of elite groups. In small domains scholars have begun to see patterns in the full extent of phenomena grouped under the name of Buddhism. At the same time, contemporary scholarship often risks missing the forest for the trees. Our advances in particular areas of research may be at the price of the scholar's unique vision of Buddhism as a pan-Asian tradition.

As is often the case in the study of religion, however, the scale of investigation is decisive. This article will discuss Buddhism on a general level and will highlight continuities rather than disjunctions within the tradition. These continuities cannot be found in any static essence or core threading its way through all of Buddhist history. They will be traced here by following certain elements that have been preserved in a changing series of structures, expanded to meet new needs, and brought into relation with new elements that are continuously being introduced. We will, in other words, identify various elements and successive structures that have constituted Buddhism as it developed from a small community of mendicants and householders in northeastern India into a great "universal" religion associated with empire, civilization, and culture in various parts of Asia, and ultimately with "modernity" and the West as well.

Buddhism as Sectarian Religion

Buddhism began around the fifth or fourth century BCE as a small community that developed at a certain distance, both self-perceived and real, from other contemporary religious communities, as well as from the society, civilization, and culture with which it coexisted. Thus, we have chosen to characterize the Buddhism of this period as "sectarian."

It is quite probable that Buddhism remained basically a sectarian religion until the time of King Aśoka (third century BCE). Whether this was a period of approximately two hundred years, as some scholars, dating the death of the Buddha around 486 BCE, maintain, or of approximately one hundred years (accepting a death date around a century later) as others contend, it was by all accounts a crucial period in which many elements and patterns were established that have remained fundamental to subsequent phases of Buddhist thought and life. Despite the importance of this early phase of Buddhist history our knowledge about it remains sketchy and uncertain. Three topics can suggest what we do know: the source of authority that the new Buddhist community recognized, the pattern of development in its teaching and ecclesiastical structures, and the attitude it took toward matters of political and social order. In discussing these three topics we shall identify some of the main scholarly opinions concerning them.

One primary factor that both accounts for and expresses Buddhism's emergence as a new sectarian religion rather than simply a new Hindu movement is the community's recognition of the ascetic Gautama as the Buddha ("enlightened one") and of the words that he had reportedly uttered as a new and ultimate source of sacred authority. The recognition of the Buddha's authority was based on an acceptance of the actuality and relative uniqueness of his person and career, and of his enlightenment experience in particular. [*See* Buddha *and* Tathāgata.] It was based on the conviction that through his enlightenment he had gained insight into the Dharma (the Truth). [*See* Dharma, *article on* Buddhist Dharma and Dharmas.] This included the aspect of truth that he had formulated more "philosophically" as, for example, in the teaching concerning the dependent co-origination *(pratītya-samutpāda)* of the various elements that constitute reality, and also the aspect of truth he had formulated more soteriologically, as summarized, for example, in the classic delineation of the Four Noble Truths (that reality is permeated with suffering, that desire is the cause of suffering, that the cessation of suffering is a possibility, and that there is a path that leads to a cessation of suffering). [*See* Soul, *article on* Buddhist Concepts; Pratītya-samutpāda; Four Noble Truths; Eightfold Path; *and* Arhat.] Finally, the Buddha's authority was based on the confidence that the teachings and actions that had flowed from his enlightenment had been accurately transmitted by those who had heard and seen them. [*See* Saṃgha, *overview article, and* Vinaya.]

From certain stories preserved in the tradition it seems that there were some challenges to the Buddha's authority. For example, there are numerous reports that even during his own lifetime a more ascetically inclined cousin named Devadatta tried to take over leadership of the new movement. Such challenges were successfully met by the Buddha and by those who carried on the tradition. As a result, later controversies concerned not so much the authority of his teachings and actions as their content and correct interpretation.

There is less scholarly agreement concerning the more specific content of the early Buddhist teaching and about the closely related question of the structure of the early Buddhist community. Three conflicting interpretations have been set forth, each defended on the basis of detailed text-critical research. Some scholars have maintained that early Buddhism was a movement of philosophically oriented renouncers practicing a discipline of salvation that subsequently degenerated into a popular religion. A second group has contended that Buddhism was originally a popular religious movement that took form around the Buddha and his religiously inspiring message, a movement that was subsequently co-opted by a monastic elite that transformed it into a rather lifeless clerical scholasticism. A third group has argued that as far back as there is evidence, early Buddhist teaching combined philosophical and popular elements, and that during the earliest period that we can penetrate, the Buddhist community included both a significant monastic and a significant lay component. This argument, which is most convincing, has included the suggestion that the philosophical/popular and monastic/lay dichotomies should actually be seen as complements rather than oppositions, even though the understandings of the relative importance of these elements and their interrelationships have varied from the beginning of the Buddhist movement.

By the time of the Second Buddhist Council, held in the city of Vaiśālī probably in the fourth century BCE, the Buddhist community already encompassed two competing assemblies whose members espoused positions that correspond to the modern scholarly group of those who associate the "original" or "true" Buddhism with an elite monastic tradition, and those who associate it with a more democratic and populist tradition. [*See* Councils, *article on* Buddhist Councils.] A split occurred at or shortly after the Second Council: those who adhered to the former position came to be known in Sanskrit as Sthaviravādins (Pali, Theravādins; the proponents of the Way of the Elders), while those who adhered to the latter position came to be known as the Mahāsāṃghikas (Members of the Great Assembly).

The third area of discussion about early Buddhism has focused on its sectarian character. While it is not disputed that during the pre-Aśokan period the Buddhist community was a specifically religious community only tangentially involved with issues of political order and social organization, it is less clear whether this distance was a matter of principle or simply an accident of history. Some scholars have argued that early Buddhists were so preoccupied with individual salvation, and the early monastic order so oriented toward "otherworldly" attainments, that early Buddhism's sectarian character was intrinsic, rather than simply circumstantial. While individualistic and otherworldly strands played an important role in some segments of the early Buddhist community, there are balancing factors that must also be taken into account. Early Buddhists were concerned to gain royal patronage and were often successful in their efforts; they appropriated royal symbolism in their depiction of the Buddha and his career; they maintained their own explicitly anti-Brahmanic conception of kingship and social order, in the *Aggañña Sutta,* for example; and they encouraged a respect for authority and moral decorum conducive to civil order and tranquillity. Thus, within the sectarian Buddhism of the early period, there were a number of elements that prepared the way for the "civilizational Buddhism" that began to emerge during the reign of King Aśoka.

Buddhism as Civilizational Religion

Buddhism has never lost the imprint of the sectarian pattern that characterized its earliest history, largely because the sectarian pattern has been reasserted at various points in Buddhist history. But Buddhism did not remain a purely sectarian religion. With the reign of King Aśoka, Buddhism entered a new phase of its history in which it became what we have chosen to call a "civilizational religion," that is, a religion that was associated with a sophisticated high culture and that transcended the boundaries of local regions and politics. By the beginning of the common era Buddhism's civilizational character was well established in various areas of India and beyond. By the middle centuries of the first millennium CE, Buddhism as a civilizational religion had reached a high level of development across Asia. However, the signs of the transition to a new stage had already begun to appear by the sixth and seventh centuries CE.

HISTORY AND LEGEND OF THE AŚOKAN IMPACT

Aśoka (r. circa 270–232 BCE) was the third ruler in a line of Mauryan emperors who established the first pan-Indian empire through military conquest. In one of the many in-scriptions that provide the best evidence regarding his attitudes and actual policies, Aśoka renounced further violent conquest and made a commitment to the practice and propagation of Dharma. In other inscriptions Aśoka informs his subjects concerning the basic moral principles that form his vision of the Dharma; he mentions related meditational practices that he commends to his subjects as well as festivals of Dharma that he sponsored. He also tells of sending special representatives to ensure that the Dharma was appropriately practiced and taught by the various religious communities within his realm.

It would seem from Aśoka's inscriptions that the Dharma that he officially affirmed and propagated was not identical to the Buddhist Dharma, although it was associated with it, especially insofar as Buddhist teaching impinged on the behavior of the laity. However, the inscriptions give clear evidence that if Aśoka was not personally a Buddhist when he made his first commitment to the Dharma, he became so soon thereafter. His edicts indicate that he sponsored Buddhist missions to various areas not only within his own empire, but in the Greek-ruled areas of the northwest and in Sri Lanka to the south. They indicate that he maintained a special interest in the well-being and unity of the Buddhist *saṃgha,* that he was concerned to emphasize the importance of Buddhist texts that dealt with lay morality, and that he undertook a royal pilgrimage to the sites associated with the great events in the Buddha's life.

Aśoka's actual policies and actions represent only one aspect of his impact in facilitating the transition of Buddhism from a sectarian religion to a civilizational religion. The other aspect is evidenced in the legends of Aśoka that appeared within the Buddhist community in the period following his death. These legends vary in character from one Buddhist tradition to another. For example, the Theravādins present an idealized portrait of Aśoka and depict him as a strong supporter of their own traditions. Another widely disseminated Aśokan text, the *Aśokāvadāna,* composed in Northwest India probably in a Sarvāstivāda context, depicts an equally imposing but more ambivalent figure, sometimes cruel in behavior and ugly in appearance. But all of the various Aśokan legends present in dramatic form an ideal of Buddhist kingship correlated with an imperial Buddhism that is truly civilizational in character. [*See* Cakravartin; Saṃgha, *article on* Saṃgha and Society; Kingship, *article on* Kingship in Southeast Asia; *and the biography of Aśoka.*]

During the Aśokan and immediately post-Aśokan era there are at least three specific developments that sustained the transformation of Buddhism into a civilizational religion. The first, a realignment in the structure of the religious community, involved an innovation in the relationship and balance between the monastic order and its lay supporters. [*See* Monasticism, *article on* Buddhist Monasticism.] Prior to the time of Aśoka the monastic order was, from an organizational point of view, the focus of Buddhist community life; the laity, however important its role may have been, lacked any kind of independent institutional structure. As a result of the Aśokan experience, including both historical events and the idealized example he set as lay participant *par excellence* in the affairs of the *saṃgha,* the Buddhist state came to provide (sometimes as a hoped-for possibility, at other times as a socioreligious reality) an independent institution that could serve as a lay counterpoint and counterbalance to the order of monks. In addition, this realignment in the structure of the Buddhist community fostered the emergence of an important crosscutting distinction between monks and laypersons who were participants in the imperial-civilizational elite on the one hand, and ordinary monks and laypersons on the other.

The transformation of Buddhism into a civilizational religion also involved doctrinal and scholastic factors. During the Aśokan and post-Aśokan periods, factions within the monastic community began to formulate aspects of the teachings more precisely, and to develop those teachings into philosophies that attempted to explain all of reality in a coherent and logically defensible manner. As a result, the literature in which the community preserved its memory of the sermons of the Buddha (the Sūtras) and of his instructions to the monastic order (Vinaya) came to be supplemented by new scholastic texts known as Abhidharma ("higher Dharma"). [*The formation of the canon, the range of Buddhist texts, and the problems raised in their interpretation are treated in* Buddhist Literature.] Given the philosophical ambiguities of the received traditions, it was inevitable that contradictory doctrines would be put forward and that different religio-philosophical systems would be generated. This led to controversies within the community, and these controversies led to the proliferation of Buddhist schools and subschools, probably in conjunction with other more mundane disputes that we do not have sufficient data to reconstruct. Some sources list a total of eighteen schools without any consistency in names. The institutional and ideological boundaries between groups and subgroups were probably very fluid. [*See* Buddhism, Schools of, *article on* Hīnayāna Buddhism; Mahāsāṃghika; Sarvāstivāda; Sautrāntika; *and* Theravāda.]

Developments in the areas of symbolism, architecture, and ritual were also significant components in the transformation of Buddhism into a civilizational religion. Some changes were related to the support Buddhism received from its royal and elite supporters. For example, royal and elite patronage seems to have been crucial to the emergence of large monastic establishments throughout India. Such support was also a central factor in the proliferation of stūpas (Skt., *stūpas*), memorial monuments replete with cosmological and associated royal symbolism that represented the Buddha and were, in most cases, believed to contain a portion of his relics. These stupas were an appropriate setting for the development of Buddhist art in which the Buddha was represented in aniconic forms such as a footprint, a Bodhi ("enlightenment") Tree, a royal throne, the wheel of the Dharma, and the like. Merit making and related rituals proliferated and assumed new forms around these stupas. Pilgrimages to the sacred sites associated with the great events of the Buddha's life became more popular. The veneration and contemplation of stupas and other symbolic representations of the Buddha became increasingly widespread. Moreover, the notion of merit making itself was expanded so that it came to include not only merit making for oneself but the transfer of merit to deceased relatives and others was well. [*See also* Iconography, *article on* Buddhist Iconography; Pilgrimage, *article on* Buddhist Pilgrimage in South and Southeast Asia; Temple, *article on* Buddhist Temple Compounds; Stupa Worship; *and* Merit, *article on* Buddhist Concepts.]

IMPERIAL BUDDHISM REASSERTED AND TRANSCENDED

Despite the importance of Aśoka to the history of Buddhism, the imperial order that he established persisted only a short time after his death. Within fifty years of his death (i.e., by the year 186 BCE), the Buddhistoriented Mauryan dynasty collapsed and was replaced by the Śuṅga dynasty, more supportive of Brahmanic Hindu traditions. The Buddhist texts claim that the Śuṅgas undertook a persecution of Buddhism, although the force of any such persecution is rendered dubious by the fact that Buddhism and Buddhist institutions continued to flourish and develop within the territory ruled by the Śuṅgas. Moreover, Buddhism emerged as a dominant religion in areas outside northeastern India where the Śuṅgas were unable to maintain the authority and prestige that their Mauryan predecessors had enjoyed.

During the three centuries from the second century BCE through the first century CE Buddhism became a powerful religious force in virtually all of India, from the southern tip of the peninsula to the Indo-Greek areas in the northwest, and in Sri Lanka and Central Asia as well. [*See* Missions, *article on* Buddhist Missions.] New polities seeking to secure their control over culturally plural areas emulated Aśoka's example and adopted Buddhism as an imperial religion. This happened in Sri Lanka, probably when Duṭṭhagāmaṇī brought about the unification of the island kingdom in the mid-second century BCE. [*See the biography of Duṭṭhagāmaṇī.*] It happened in central India when the rising Sātavāhana dynasty became a supporter of the Buddhist cause. It happened to some extent in northwestern India when certain Greek and invading Central Asian kings converted to Buddhism. And it happened more fully in northwestern India during and after the reign of King Kaniṣka (first to second century CE), who ruled over a vast Kushan empire that extended from northern India deep into Central Asia. By this time Buddhism had also begun to penetrate into trading centers in northern China and to spread along land and sea routes across Southeast Asia to South China as well.

A major aspect of the transformation of Buddhism into a fully civilizational religion was the differentiation that occurred between Buddhism as a civilizational religion and Buddhism as an imperial religion. During late Mauryan times the civilizational and imperial dimensions had not been clearly differentiated. However, by the beginning of the common era Buddhism had become a civilizational religion that transcended the various expressions of imperial Buddhism in particular geographical areas. As a direct correlate of this development, an important distinction was generated within the elite of the Buddhist community. By this period this elite had come to include both a truly civilizational component that maintained close international contacts and traveled freely from one Buddhist empire to another and beyond, as well as overlapping but distinguishable imperial components that operated within the framework of each particular empire.

At this time Buddhist texts and teachings were being extended in a variety of ways. In some schools, such as the Theravāda and the Sarvāstivāda, canons of authoritative texts were established, but even after this had occurred new elements continued to be incorporated into the tradition through commentaries. In the case of the Sarvāstivādins, a huge collection of commentaries known as the *Mahāvibhāṣā* was compiled at a Buddhist council held by King Kaniṣka. In other schools the Piṭakas themselves were still being enriched by the incorporation of a variety of new additions and embellishments. There also began to appear, on the fringes of the established schools, a new kind of *sūtra* that signaled the rise of a new Buddhist orientation that came to be known as the Mahāyāna. [*See* Buddhism, Schools of, *article on* Mahāyāna Buddhism.] The earliest of these were the Prajñāpāramitā Sūtras, which put forward the doctrine of *śūnyatā* (the ultimate "emptiness" of all phenomena) and proclaimed the path of the *bodhisattva* (future Buddha) as the path that all Buddhists should follow. [*See* Bodhisattva Path.] Before the end of the second century CE the great Buddhist philosopher Nāgārjuna had given the perspective of these *sūtras* a systematic expression and thereby established a basis for the first of the major Mahāyāna schools, known as Mādhyamika. [*See* Mādhyamika; Śūnyam and Śūnyatā; *and the biography of Nāgārjuna.*]

This extension of Buddhist traditions of texts and teachings was accompanied by two other developments that also contributed to their civilizational efficacy. During this period the older Buddhist schools (hereafter collectively called the Hīnayāna) that had previously limited themselves to the oral transmission of tradition, and the newly emerging Mahāyāna fraternities as well, began to commit their versions of the Buddha's teaching to writing. Some Buddhist groups began to translate and write their most authoritative texts in Sanskrit, which had become the preeminent civilizational language in India.

The rapid development of Buddhism led to major changes in Buddhist ways of representing the Buddha and relating to him ritually. Some Hīnayāna schools produced autonomous biographies of the Buddha. The most famous of the biographies is the *Buddhacarita* (Acts of the Buddha), by Aśvaghoṣa, written in refined Sanskrit in a classic literary form *(kavya)*. The Hīnayāna schools provided the context for the production of anthropomorphic images of the Buddha, which became a major focal point for sophisticated artistic expression on the one hand, and for veneration and devotion on the other. These schools also made a place within the Buddhist system for a new and very important figure who became a focus for new forms of devotional practice and, in later phases of Buddhist history, new forms of religio-political symbolism and activity as well. This new figure was the future Buddha Maitreya ("the friendly one"), who was believed to be residing in the Tuṣita Heaven awaiting the appropriate time to descend to earth. [*See* Maitreya.] By the beginning of the common era other buddhological trends were beginning to surface that were exclusively Mahāyāna in character. For example, *sūtra*s were beginning to appear that focused attention on a celestial Buddha named Amitābha ("infinite light") and portrayed practices of visualization that could lead to rebirth in the western paradise over which he presided. [*See* Amitābha *and* Pure and Impure Lands.]

Closely associated developments were taking place at the level of cosmology and its application to religious practice. In the Hīnayāna context the most important development was probably the rich portrayal of a set of six cosmological *gati*s, or "destinies" (of gods, humans, animals, *asura*s or titans, hungry ghosts, and beings who are consigned to hell), which depicted, in vivid fashion, the workings of *karman* (moral action and its effects). [*See* Karman, *article on* Buddhist Concepts.] These texts, which were probably used as the basis for sermons, strongly encouraged Buddhist morality and Buddhist merit-making activities. Other Hīnayāna works of the period suggested the presence of a vast expanse of worlds that coexist with our own. In the new Mahāyāna context this notion of a plurality of worlds was moved into the foreground, the existence of Buddhas in at least some of these other worlds was recognized, and the significance of these Buddhas for life in our own world was both affirmed and described. [*See* Cosmology, *article on* Buddhist Cosmology.] Finally, there are indications that during this period both Hīnayāna and Mahāyāna Buddhists increasingly employed exorcistic rituals that depended on the magical power of various kinds of chants and spells (*paritta* in Pali, *dhāraṇī* in Sanskrit).

BUDDHISM AS PAN-ASIAN CIVILIZATION

From the second to the ninth century, Buddhism enjoyed a period of immense creativity and influence. Prior to the beginning of the sixth century, Buddhist fortunes were generally on the rise. Buddhism flourished in Sri Lanka, India, and Central Asia. Through already familiar processes involving its introduction along trade routes, its assimilation to indigenous beliefs and practices, and its adoption as an imperial religion, Buddhism became firmly entrenched in both northern and southern China and in many parts of Southeast Asia. After about 500 CE, these well-established dynamics of expansion continued to operate. Buddhism became the preeminent religion in a newly unified Chinese empire, it continued its spread in parts of Southeast Asia, and it was established in important new areas, first in Japan and then in Tibet. However, during this latter period its successes were coupled with setbacks, and by the middle of the ninth century the era of Buddhism as a pan-Asian civilization was rapidly drawing to a close.

The geographical expansion of Buddhism was both a cause and an effect of its civilizational character. But Buddhism's role as a pan-Asian civilization involved much more than a pan-Asian presence. Buddhist monasteries, often state supported and located near capitals of the various Buddhist kingdoms, functioned in ways analogous to modern universities. There was a constant circulation of Buddhist monks, texts, and artistic forms across increasingly vast geographical areas. Indian and Central Asian missionaries traveled to China and with the help of Chinese Buddhists translated whole libraries of books into Chinese, which became a third major Buddhist sacred language alongside Pali and Sanskrit. In the fifth century Buddhist nuns carried their ordination lineage from Sri Lanka to China. Between 400 and 700 a stream of Chinese pilgrims traveled to India via Central Asia and Southeast Asia in order to visit sacred sites and monasteries and to collect additional scriptures and commentaries. Some of these, such as Fa-hsien, Hsüan-tsang, and I-ching, wrote travel accounts that provide information concerning Buddhist civilization in its fullest development. In the sixth century Buddhism was formally introduced into Japan; in the following century Buddhists from Central Asia, India, and China made their way into Tibet. Beginning in the eighth and ninth centuries monks from Japan visited China in order to receive Buddhist training and acquire Buddhist texts. These are only a few illustrations of the kind of travel and interaction that characterized this period. [*See the biographies of Fa-hsien; Hsüan-tsang; and I-ching.*]

While Buddhism was reaching its apogee as a civilizational religion, the teachings of the Hīnayāna tradition were further extended and refined. New commentaries were produced in both Sanskrit and in Pali. During the fifth century these commentaries were supplemented by the appearance of two very important manuals, Vasubandhu's *Abhidharmakośa,* composed in the Sarvāstivāda-Sautrāntika context in Northwest India, and Buddhaghosa's *Visuddhimagga* (Path of Purification), written in the Theravādin context in Sri Lanka. [*See the biographies of Vasubandhu and Buddhaghosa.*] Moreover, many Hīnayāna themes remained basic to the other Buddhist traditions with which it coexisted. Most Buddhists continued to recognize the Buddha Gautama as an important figure, and to focus attention on the single-world cosmology that posited the existence of three realms—the realm beyond form associated with the most exalted gods and the highest meditational states, the realm of form associated with slightly less exalted gods and meditational states, and the realm of desire constituted by the six *gati*s previously mentioned. This latter realm was especially prominent as the context presumed by pan-Buddhist teachings concerning karmic retribution and the value of giving, particularly to the members of the monastic community.

Within the Mahāyāna tradition this period of Buddhist efflorescence as a civilizational religion was characterized by a high level of creativity and by a variety of efforts toward systematization. In the earlier centuries the Mahāyānists produced a rich and extensive collection of new *sūtra*s, including the *Saddharmapuṇḍarīka Sūtra* (Lotus of the True Law), the *Mahāparinirvāṇa Sūtra,* the *Laṅkāvatāra Sūtra*, and the *Avataṃsaka Sūtra.* With the passage of time, voluminous commentaries were written on many of these *sūtra*s in India, Central Asia, and China. These *sūtra*s and commentaries developed new teachings concerning the emptiness of the phenomenal world, the storehouse consciousness *(ālaya-vijñāna),* and the "embryo of the Tathāgata" *(tathāgata-garbha).* [*See* Ālaya-vijñāna *and* Tathāgata-garbha.] These teachings were given scholastic forms in various Mahāyāna groups such as the Mādhyamika and Yogācāra schools, which originated in India, and the T'ien-t'ai and Hua-yen schools, which originated in China. [*See* Yogācāra; T'ien-t'ai; *and* Hua-yen.]

In addition, these *sūtras* and commentaries recognized a vast pantheon of Buddhas and *bodhisattvas* (future Buddhas) and acknowledged the existence of a plurality, even an infinity, of worlds. Some went on to affirm the reality of an eternal, cosmic Buddha whom they took to be the ultimate source of these innumerable Buddhas, *bodhisattvas*, and worlds (and of all else as well). Some of these texts highlighted various kinds of soteriological help that particular Buddhas and *bodhisattvas* could provide to those who sought their aid. In addition to Maitreya and Amitābha, mentioned above, other Buddhas and *bodhisattvas* who became particularly important include Bhaiṣajyaguru (the Buddha of healing), Avalokiteśvara (the *bodhisattva* exemplar of compassion), Mañjuśrī (the *bodhisattva* patron of the wise), and Kṣitigarbha (the *bodhisattva* who specialized in assisting those who suffer in hell). [*See* Bhaiṣajyaguru; Avalokiteśvara; Mañjuśrī; Kṣitigarbha; *and* Celestial Buddhas and Bodhisattvas.]

By the second half of the first millennium CE a new strand of Buddhist tradition, the Vajrayāna, or Esoteric Vehicle, began to come into the foreground in India. This new vehicle accepted the basic orientation of the Mahāyāna, but supplemented Mahāyāna insights with "new and dramatic forms of practice, many of them esoteric in character. The appearance of this new Buddhist vehicle was closely associated with the composition of new texts, including new *sūtras* (e.g., the *Mahāvairocana Sūtra*), and the new ritual manuals known as *tantras*. By the eighth and ninth centuries this new vehicle had spread through virtually the entire Buddhist world and was preserved especially in Japan and in Tibet. But before the process of systematization of the Vajrayāna could proceed very far the infrastructure that constituted Buddhist civilization began to break down, thus at least partially accounting for the very different form that this tradition took in Tibet and in Japan, where it became known as Shingon. [*See* Buddhism, Schools of, *article on* Esoteric Buddhism *and* Mahāsiddhas.]

During the period of its hegemony as a pan-Asian civilization, Buddhism retained a considerable degree of unity across both the regional and text-oriented boundaries that delimited particular Buddhist traditions. In each cultural area and in each of the three *yānas* there were ascetics and contemplatives who practiced Buddhist meditation; there were ecclesiastics and moralists whose primary concern was Buddhist discipline; there were monks and laypersons who were involved in Buddhist devotion; and there were those who took a special interest in Buddhist magic and exorcism. These diverse groups and individuals shared—and many realized that they shared—beliefs, attitudes, and practices with like-minded Buddhists in distant areas and other *yānas*.

Moreover, during the period of its ascendancy as a civilizational religion, Buddhism provided a successful standard of cultural unification such that other religious traditions, including the Hindu in India, the Manichaean in Central Asia, the Taoist in China, the Shintō in Japan, and the Bon in Tibet, responded to it with their own innovations shaped by Buddhist ideas and values. [*See the articles on these traditions.*] During this period, in other words, Buddhism set the standards, religious, philosophical, artistic, and so on, to which a whole range of other Asian traditions were forced to respond. Buddhism also served as a civilizational religion by encompassing other elements—logic, medicine, grammar, and technology, to name but a few—that made it attractive to individuals and groups, including many rulers and members of various Asian aristocracies who had little or no interest in the spiritual aspect of religion.

Buddhism as Cultural Religion

For more than a thousand years, from the time of King Aśoka to about the ninth century, Buddhism exhibited a civilizational form that began as pan-Indian and ultimately became pan-Asian in character. Like the sectarian pattern that preceded it, this civilizational pattern left an indelible mark on all subsequent Buddhist developments. Buddhism never completely lost either its concern for inclusiveness or its distinctively international flavor. But beginning in about the fifth century the civilizational structure suffered increasingly severe disruptions, and a new pattern began to emerge. All across Asia, Buddhism was gradually transformed, through a variety of historical processes, into what we have chosen to call "cultural religion."

THE PERIOD OF TRANSITION

Buddhist civilization, which characteristically strove for both comprehensiveness and systematic order, was dependent on the security and material prosperity of a relatively small number of great monasteries and monastic universities that maintained contact with one another and shared common interests and values. This institutional base was, in fact, quite fragile, as was demonstrated when historical events threatened the well-being of these monasteries and their residents. New developments arose within the Buddhist community as a result of these vicissitudes, developments that eventually transformed Buddhism into a series of discrete cultural traditions.

Some indication of these developments can be seen quite early, even as Buddhist civilization was at the peak of its brilliance. Events in Central Asia during the fifth and sixth centuries were not favorable to the Buddhist kingdoms along the Silk Route that connected Northwest India and northern China. These kingdoms were invaded and in some cases conquered by different nomadic peoples such as the Huns, who also invaded India and the Roman empire. The Chinese pilgrim Hsüan-tsang, who visited Sogdiana in 630, saw only ruins of Buddhist temples and former Buddhist monasteries that had been given over to the Zoroastrians.

The instability in the crucial linking area between India and China during the fifth and sixth centuries seems to have been sufficient to weaken Buddhism's civilizational structure. For the first time we see the emergence of new Buddhist schools in China that are distinctively Chinese. The appearance of synthetic Chinese schools like T'ien-t'ai and Hua-yen suggests a continuation of the civilizational orientation. These schools sought to reconcile the divergent views found in Buddhist literature through an extended elaboration of different levels of teaching. This is, of course, characteristic of Buddhism as a civilizational religion, but the manner of reconciliation reflects a style of harmonization that is distinctively Chinese.

The increasing importance of Tantra in late Indian Buddhism and the success of the Pure Land (Ching-t'u) and Ch'an (Zen) schools in China during the Sui and T'ang period (598–907) are further indications that the Buddhist tradition was becoming more local in self-definition. [*See* Ching-t'u *and* Ch'an.] Chinese Buddhism had a new independent spirit in contrast to the earlier India-centered Buddhism. Moreover, the new movements that emerged at that time seem to be the result of a long development that took place apart from the major cosmopolitan centers. Far more than in the past, expressions of Buddhism were being made at all levels of particular societies, and there was a new concern for the interrelation of those levels within each society.

During the last centuries of the first millennium CE, Buddhist civilization developed a new, somewhat independent center in China that reached its peak during the Sui and T'ang dynasties. Thus, when Buddhist texts and images were introduced into Japan during the sixth century they were presented and appropriated as part and parcel of Chinese culture. The new religion gained support from the prince regent, Shōtoku Taishi, who wanted to model his rule after that of the Buddhist-oriented Sui dynasty. Chinese Buddhist schools such as Hua-yen (Jpn., Kegon) also prospered in the Nara period in Japan (710–784) as Chinese cultural influence continued to flourish. [*See the biography of Shōtoku Taishi.*]

The two centers of Buddhist civilization, China and India, also competed with each other, as can be seen in a situation that developed in Tibet. Buddhism had been brought to Tibet by King Sroṅ-btsan-sgam-po (d. 650), who established the first stable state in the area. Buddhist texts were translated into Tibetan from both Sanskrit and Chinese. A later king, Khri-sroṅ-lde-btsan (755–797), officially adopted Buddhism as the state religion and determined to resolve the tension between Indian and Chinese influence. He sponsored the famous Council of Lhasa, in which a Chinese party representing a Ch'an "sudden enlightenment" point of view debated an Indian group that advocated a more gradualist understanding of the Buddhist path. Both sides claimed victory, but the Indian tradition gained predominance and eventually translations were permitted only from Sanskrit. [*See the biography of Kamalaśīla.*]

During the ninth and tenth centuries the two Buddhist civilizational centers in India and China were themselves subject to attack, both internally and externally. The combination of Hindu resurgence and Muslim invasions led to the effective disappearance of the Buddhist community in India by the thirteenth century. [*See* Islam, *article on* Islam in South Asia.] Repeated invasions by Uighurs and Turkic peoples, as well as official persecutions and the revival of the Confucian tradition, resulted in a decisive weaking of institutional Buddhism in China. [*See* Turkic Religions *and* Confucianism, *article on* Neo-Confucianism.]

The processes of acculturation that had first become evident in the sixth century in India and China repeated themselves beginning in the tenth century in Japan, Korea, Tibet, Sri Lanka, and Southeast Asia. In each of these areas distinct cultural forms of Buddhism evolved. There was a reorganization of the Buddhist community with an increased emphasis on the bonds between elite and ordinary Buddhists in each particular area. There was a renewed interest in efficacious forms of Buddhist practice and the Buddhist schools that preserved and encouraged such practice. Within each area there was a development of Buddhist symbols and rituals that became representative of distinct Buddhist cultures, particularly at the popular level.

In Central Asia the Buddhist community had no success in surviving the Muslim expansion. [*See* Islam, *article on* Islam in Central Asia.] Buddhism had some limited success in India during the last centuries of the first millennium. It benefited from extensive royal and popular support in northeastern India under the Pāla dynasty from the eighth to the twelfth century, but Hindu philosophy and theistic *(bhakti)* movements were aggressive critics of Buddhism. Hardly any distinct Buddhist presence continued in India after the last of the great monasteries were destroyed by the Muslims. In China there was more success, although the Confucian and Taoist traditions were powerful rivals. As a result of persecutions in the ninth century,

Buddhism lost its distinctively civilizational role, but it continued as a major component of Chinese religion, becoming increasingly synthesized with other native traditions. In Sri Lanka, Southeast Asia (except for Indonesia and the Malay Peninsula, where Buddhism suffered the same fate that it suffered in India), Japan, Korea, and Tibet (from whence it eventually spread to Mongolia), areas where Buddhism did not have to compete with strongly organized indigenous traditions, it was successful in establishing itself as the dominant religious tradition. The religious creativity of these areas, once the periphery of the Buddhist world, resulted in a Buddhist "axial age" that dramatically transformed the tradition as a whole.

MONASTIC ORDER, ROYAL ORDER, AND POPULAR BUDDHISM

The transformation of Buddhism from a civilizational religion to a cultural religion depended on a fundamental realignment in the structure of the Buddhist community. As a civilizational religion, Buddhist community life had come to include a largely monastic elite that traveled extensively, was multilingual, and operated at the civilizational level; an imperial elite made up of monks and laypersons associated more closely with royal courts and related aristocracies; and a less exalted company of ordinary monks and laypersons living not only in urban areas but in the countryside as well. In Buddhism's zenith as a civilizational religion the central organizing relationship was that between the largely monastic civilizational elite and the imperial elites, consisting of kings, queens, and other high-placed members of the laity on the one hand, and the monks whom they supported on the other. The ordinary members of the laity and the less exalted monks played a role, of course, but in most areas at most periods of time they seem to have been somewhat distanced from the mainstream of Buddhist community life. With the transformation of Buddhism into a cultural religion, however, this situation was drastically altered.

One aspect of this transformation was major changes that took place at three different levels: monastic, imperial, and popular. The demise of the monastic network through which the civilizational aspect of Buddhism had been supported and maintained was decisive. To be sure, there were elements of the monastic community that never lost their international vision, and travel and exchanges between specific cultural areas was never totally absent, particularly between China and Japan, China and Tibet, and Sri Lanka and mainland Southeast Asia. Nevertheless, it would be difficult to speak of a pan-Asian Buddhist elite after the ninth or tenth century.

The pattern at the imperial level was altered by the loss of monastic power and influence coupled with increased state control in monastic affairs. During the period that Buddhism was an effective civilizational religion its great monasteries functioned practically as "states within the state." Monasteries commanded extensive resources of land and labor and were often actively involved in commercial enterprises. This public splendor made the monasteries inviting targets, especially after their usefulness as civilizational centers had declined. If the monasteries were not simply destroyed, as they were in India and Central Asia, they were often deprived of their resources, as occurred at one time or another in virtually every Buddhist area. With the decline of monastic influence at the imperial level, the control of the state over monastic affairs inevitably increased. In China and Japan, and to a lesser extent in Korea and Vietnam, state control became thoroughly bureaucratized. In Sri Lanka and the Theravāda areas of Southeast Asia, state control was implemented more indirectly and with considerably less efficiency by royal "purifications" of the *sangha.* Specific local conditions in Tibet led to a unique situation in which monastic and royal functions became so tightly interlocked that they were often completely fused.

The demise of the international Buddhist elite and the weakening of the large and powerful establishments were counterbalanced by a strengthening of Buddhist life at the grass-roots level. Smaller, local institutions that for a long time had coexisted with the great monasteries took on new importance as focal points in Buddhist community life. For example, smaller so-called merit cloisters *(kung-te yüan)* supported by wealthy laymen were significant components in the development and life of Chinese Buddhism. In Sri Lanka and Southeast Asia the emergence of cultural Buddhism was closely associated with monks who were called *gāmavāsins* (village dwellers) and who strengthened Buddhist influence among the people in the major cities and in the more distant provinces as well. In contrast to civilizational Buddhism, in which the crucial structural alignment was that between the civilizational elite and the monks and laity at the imperial level, the crucial structural alignment in cultural Buddhism was between the monks and laity of the imperial or state elites, who were located primarily in the capital cities, and the ordinary people who inhabited local monasteries and villages.

THE PREEMINENCE OF PRACTICE

The era of comprehensive Buddhist philosophizing and the formulation of original systems of thought came to an end, for the most part, with the demise of Buddhism as a civilizational religion. There continued to be philosophical innovations, and some of the great systems that were already formulated were adjusted to meet new circumstances. However, the real creativity of Buddhism as a cultural religion came to the fore in schools and movements that emphasized efficacious modes of Buddhist practice.

A major component in the development of various Buddhist cultures is the ascendancy of schools or movements that combined a strong emphasis on the importance of discipline (particularly although not exclusively the monastic discipline) with an accompanying emphasis on meditation. [*See* Meditation, *article on* Buddhist Meditation.] In China and Japan, Ch'an and Zen, with their emphasis on firm discipline and meditative practices such as "just sitting" and the contemplation of *kung-an* (Jpn., *kōan;* enigmatic verses), are representative of this kind of Buddhist tradition. [*See* Zen.] These were the schools that became more prominent as Mahāyāna Buddhism emerged as a cultural religion in East Asia, and they continued to exert influence on the various East Asian political and aesthetic elites from that time forward. The Āraññikas, or "forestdwelling monks," represented an analogous orientation and played a similar role in Sri Lanka and subsequently in Southeast Asia. The Āraññikas appeared on the Sri Lankan scene in the ninth and tenth centuries as a group of monks who had chosen to withdraw from the wealthy monasteries of the capital, to adopt a strictly disciplined mode of life, and to devote themselves to study and/or meditation. In the twelfth century the Āraññikas led a major reform in Sri Lanka and in subsequent centuries they extended their reform movement throughout the Theravāda world, which included not only Sri Lanka but also Burma, Thailand, Cambodia, and Laos. The Āraññikas in the Theravāda world, like the Ch'an and Zen practitioners in East Asia, were closely affiliated with the elite segments of the various societies in which they were active. A similar kind of emphasis was placed on discipline, study, and meditation in Tibet, where the Vajrayāna tradition was established by Atīśa, the monk who in the eleventh century inaugurated the "second introduction" of Buddhism into the country. In the fifteenth century another infusion of discipline-oriented reform was provided by reformers who established the Dge-lugs-pa, the so-called Yellow Hats, which became the preeminent Tibetan (and Mongolian) school subsequently headed by the well-known line of Dalai Lamas. [*See* Dge-lugs-pa; Dalai Lama; *and the biography of Atīśa.*]

Each expression of Buddhism as a cultural religion generated, as a kind of counterpoint to its more elitist, discipline-oriented schools and movements, other schools and movements that focused on more populist forms of devotional or Esoteric (Tantric) practice. In the East Asian Mahāyāna areas the most important development was the increasing prominence of the Pure Land schools in the early centuries of the second millennium CE. The Chinese Pure Land schools remained in close symbiosis with the practitioners of Ch'an and retained a relatively traditional mode of monastic practice. Their Japanese counterparts, however, became more differentiated and considerably more innovative. During the Kamakura period (1185–1333) a number of new, distinctively Japanese Pure Land and related schools were founded by charismatic leaders such as Hōnen, Shinran, and Nichiren; these schools took on a distinctively Japanese cast. For Nichiren, the Pure Land was Japan itself. [*See* Jōdoshū; Jōdo Shinshū; Nichirenshū; *and the biographies of Hōnen, Shinran, and Nichiren.*]

Although less important than Pure Land and related kinds of devotion, Esoteric or Tantric modes of religion also were a significant part of cultural Buddhism in East Asia. In China the Esoteric elements were closely related to influences from the Vajrayāna tradition in Tibet as well as interactions with forms of indigenous Taoism. [*See* Chen-yen.] In Japan more sophisticated Esoteric elements persisted in the Tendai (Chin., T'ien-t'ai) and Shingon schools, while more rustic and indigenous elements were prominent in groups that were integrated into these schools, for example, the Shugendō community that was made up of mountain ascetics known as *yamabushi.* [*See* Shūgendō; Tendaishū; *and* Shingonshū.]

In Sri Lanka in the twelfth and thirteenth centuries (the period of Hōnen, Shinran, and Nichiren in Japan) devotional religion also seems to have been influential in the Buddhist community, generating new genres of Buddhist literature that were written primarily in Sinhala rather than Pali. Although no specifically devotional "schools" were formed, a whole new devotional component was incorporated into the Theravāda tradition and subsequently diffused to the Theravāda cultures in Southeast Asia. Similarly, there were, as far as we know, no "schools" that were specifically Esoteric or Tantric in character. However, there is some evidence that indicates that Esoteric elements played a very significant role in each of the premodern Theravāda cultures. This kind of influence seems to have been particularly strong in northern Burma, northern Thailand, Laos, and Cambodia.

In Tibet and Mongolia, as one would expect given their Vajrayāna ethos, the primary counterpoints to the more discipline-oriented traditions were the schools, such as the Rñiṅ-ma-pa and Bka'-brgyud-pa, that emphasized the performance of Esoteric and Tantric rituals in order to achieve worldly benefits and to proceed along a "fast path" to salvation. However, just as in the other Buddhist cultures devotion was supplemented by recourse to Esoteric and Tantric techniques, so in Tibet and Mongolia Esoteric and Tantric techniques were supplemented by the practice of devotion.

Another important component of Buddhism as a cultural religion was the mitigation, in some circles at least, of traditional distinctions between monks and laity. This trend was least evident in the more discipline-oriented contexts, but even here there was some movement in this direction. For example, in the Ch'an and Zen monasteries, monks, rather than being prohibited from engaging in productive work as the Vinaya had stipulated, were actually required to work. In the Pure Land schools in Japan, and in some of the Esoteric schools in Japan and Tibet, it became permissible and common for clergy to marry and have families. Also, certain kinds of monastic/lay and purely lay associations played important roles in China and Japan. These included both straightforward religious associations devoted to the various Buddhist causes, and, particularly in China, a number of secret societies and messianically oriented groups. [*See* Millenarianism, *article on* Chinese Millenarian Movements.] Even in Sri Lanka and Southeast Asia tendencies toward the laicization of the monastic order can from time to time be observed, but in these strongly Theravāda areas the process was always thwarted by royal intervention before the innovations could take root.

THE PERVASIVENESS OF RITUAL

Alongside the particular schools and movements that characterized Buddhism as a cultural religion there were also modes of Buddhist practice that, although influenced by those schools and movements, were more pervasively involved in Buddhist cultures as such. Pilgrimage was in the forefront of these practices.

Virtually every instance of Buddhism as a cultural religion had its own particular patterns of Buddhist pilgrimage. [*See* Pilgrimage, *articles on Buddhist pilgrimage.*] In many cases these pilgrimage patterns were a major factor in maintaining the specificity of particular, often overlapping, religious and cultural complexes. In some contexts these pilgrimage patterns delimited Buddhist cultural complexes that supported and were supported by particular political kingdoms. An example of this situation was the Sinhala pattern, in which there were sixteen major sites systematically distributed throughout all of Sri Lanka. In other situations, for example in Southeastern Asia, these patterns often delimited Buddhist cultural complexes that cut across political divisions.

Many of the sites that were the goals of major Buddhist pilgrimages were mountain peaks or other places that had been sacred from before the introduction of Buddhism and continued to have sacred associations in other traditions that coexisted with Buddhism. [*See also* Mountains.] Through pilgrimage practices at these sites Buddhism assimilated various deities and practices associated with local religious traditions. At the same time, of course, the Buddhist presence imbued those deities and practices with Buddhist connotations. In Japan, Buddhas and *bodhisattva*s became virtually identified in many situations with indigenous *kami* (divine spirits). In China great *bodhisattva*s such as Kṣitigarbha, Mañjuśrī, and Avalokiteśvara became denizens of sacred mountains that were popular pilgrimage sites, and in those pilgrimage contexts underwent a thoroughgoing process of sinicization. Stupas, footprints, and other Buddhist objects of pilgrimage in Southeast Asia became, for many who venerated them, representations in which the Buddha was closely associated with indigenous spirits (e.g., *nats* in Burma, *phī* in Thailand, etc.) who served as the local guardians or protectors of Buddhist institutions. [*See* Nats.]

Wherever Buddhism developed as a cultural religion it penetrated not only the sacred topography of the area but also the cycle of calendric rites. In China, for example, the annual cycle of Buddhist ritual activities included festivals honoring various Buddhas and *bodhisattvas*, festivals dedicated to significant figures from Chinese Buddhist history, a great vegetarian feast, and a very important "All Soul's" festival in which the Chinese virtue of filial piety was expressed through offerings intended to aid one's ancestors. While these rituals themselves involved much that was distinctively Chinese, they were interspersed with other festivals, both Confucian and Taoist, and were supplemented by other, lesser rituals associated with daily life that involved an even greater integration with non-Buddhist elements. In Sri Lanka the Buddhist ritual calendar included festivals honoring events of the Buddha's life; a festival that celebrated the coming of Mahinda, Aśoka's missionary son, to establish Buddhism in Sri Lanka; a festival in the capital honoring the Buddha relic that served as the palladium of the kingdom; and the monastic-centered *kathin* (Pali, *kaṭhina;* giving of robes) ceremony that marked the end of the rainy season. These Buddhist rituals were interspersed with non-Buddhist celebrations that were, in this case, largely Hindu. These large-scale rituals were supplemented by more episodic and specialized rites that involved an even wider variety of indigenous elements such as offerings to local spirits. In the Tibetan cultural area the Buddhist calendar encompassed great festivals sponsored by monasteries in which the introduction of Buddhism to Tibet was celebrated as the Buddhist defeat of indigenous demons, as well as festivals honoring Buddhist deities (e.g., Tārā) and Tibetan Buddhist heroes (e.g., Padmasambhava). [*See* Tārā *and the biography of Padmasambhava.*] The Tibetan Buddhist calendar also included other large- and small-scale rituals in which Buddhist and indigenous shamanistic elements were combined. [*See* Buddhist Religious Year.]

Buddhism in its various cultural expressions also became associated with life cycle rites, especially those of the male initiation into adulthood and those associated with death. The Buddhist involvement in male initiation rites was limited primarily to Southeast Asia. In many Buddhist countries children and young men were educated in the monasteries, but only in Southeast Asia did temporary initiation into the order, either as a novice (as in Burma) or at a later age as a full-fledged monk (as in central Thailand), become a culturally accepted necessity for the attainment of male adulthood. Buddhist involvement in funerary rituals was, on the other hand, a phenomenon that appeared again and again all across Asia. For example, in the Theravāda countries where Buddhism has been the dominant cultural religion elaborate cremations patterned after the ceremony reportedly performed for the Buddha himself have become the rule for members of the royal and monastic elites. Simpler ceremonies, based on the same basic model, were the norm for those of lesser accomplishment or status. Even in cultures where Buddhism coexisted with other major religions on a more or less equal basis, Buddhists have been the preferred officiants in the funerary context. [*See* Priesthood, *article on* Buddhist Priesthood.]

The prime example is China, where Buddhists developed elaborate masses for the dead that were widely used throughout the whole of society. Originally introduced into China by the now defunct Chen-yen (Vajrayāna) school, these masses for the dead were adapted to their new Chinese environment and became an integral component of Chinese Buddhist culture.

All across Asia Buddhism expressed itself as a cultural religion through different kinds of ritual at different levels of society. It was through these ritual forms, more than in any other way, that it became an integral component in the life of different Asian peoples, molding cultures in accordance with its values and being itself molded in the process. Once Buddhism became established as a cultural religion, it was these rituals that enabled it to maintain its position and influence, and to do so century after century on into the modern era. [*See* Pūjā, *article on* Buddhist Pūjā, *and* Worship and Cultic Life, *articles on Buddhist cultic life.*]

Buddhism in the Modern World

The beginnings of European mercantilism and imperialism in the sixteenth century initiated a chain of events that continue to stimulate and to threaten the Buddhist community in its parts and as a whole. Traditional social and economic patterns on which the various Buddhist cultures depended were disrupted and eventually displaced by new patterns. These new patterns inextricably linked individual Buddhist societies to a global community and especially to the West. As a result, all of the profound transformations that have occurred in European civilization in the last three centuries, the advent of rationalism, scientific materialism, nationalism, relativism, technology, democracy, and communism, have challenged Buddhists in Asia just as they have challenged religious men and women in Europe and the Americas.

The modern encounter of cultures and civilizations has not been monolithic. Three stages can be identified in Buddhist Asia. The first was the arrival of missionaries with traders in various parts of Asia. These missionaries came to convert and instruct, and they brought printing presses and schools as well as Bibles and catechisms. There was a missionary onslaught on Asian religious traditions, including Buddhism, in Sri Lanka, Southeast Asia, China, and Japan. This onslaught was sometimes physically violent, as in the Portuguese destruction of Buddhist temples and relics in Sri Lanka, but for the most part it was an ideological assault. A second stage was more strictly colonial, as some European powers gained control over many different areas of the Buddhist world. Some Buddhist countries, such as Sri Lanka, Burma, and the Indochinese states, were fully colonized while others, such as Thailand, China, and Japan, were subjected to strong colonial influences. In virtually every situation (Tibet was a notable exception), the symbiotic relationship between the political order and the monastic order was disrupted, with adverse effects for Buddhist institutions.

The twentieth-century acceptance of Western political and economic ideologies, whether democratic capitalism or communism, represents a third stage. Buddhists in China, Mongolia, Tibet, and parts of Korea and Southeast Asia now live in communist societies, and the future of Buddhist communities in these areas looks bleak. Capitalism has been dominant in Japan, South Korea, Sri Lanka, and parts of Southeast Asia (Thailand being the prime example), and greater possibilities for the

Buddhist tradition are presumed to exist in these areas. But capitalism, as well as communism, has undercut the claim that Buddhist thought and values are of central significance for contemporary life. Buddhist monuments and institutions are in many cases treated as museum pieces, while Buddhist beliefs are often banished to the sphere of individual opinion. In many situations Buddhism is deplored as backward and superstitious, and is for that reason criticized or ignored. As Edward Conze noted in his *A Short History of Buddhism* (London, 1980), "One may well doubt whether capitalism has been any more kind to Buddhism than communism" (p. 129).

Despite the difficulties that Buddhists have faced, they have responded creatively to the turmoil of recent history. They have engaged in many efforts to adapt to their changing environment, just as they have done repeatedly in the past. Thus far, however, they have drawn on their traditional heritage for suitable models, and their varied responses can thus be grouped as cultural, civilizational, and sectarian.

CULTURAL RESPONSES

The initial responses to European civilization were cultural in character, and often reactionary. Some Buddhist kingdoms, after an initial exposure to elements of European civilization, attempted to isolate themselves as a way of preserving their cultural identity. This was done in Japan, Korea, and Tibet, and was attempted in China. In other cases, Buddhist revivals were inspired by the missionary challenges. In Sri Lanka and China, Buddhist intellectuals responded to the efforts of Christian missionaries to criticize Buddhism with their own spirited apologetics. These intellectuals readily adopted the methods and instruments of the Christian missionary, the printing press and the school, as well as his militancy, to promote the Buddhist cause. Some processes that began in the period of Buddhist culture, especially the mitigation of distinctions between monks and laity, were also stimulated by these innovations. Modern technology, such as improved modes of transportation, also made it easier for more people to engage in traditional practices like pilgrimage.

The Buddhist revivals often were inspired by cultural loyalism. To choose Buddhism as one's religious identity in the face of the Christian challenge also meant that one was choosing to be Sinhala, Thai, or Chinese. It was an emphatic denial that things Chinese, for example, were inferior, even if this was suggested by the power and prestige of Christianity and European civilization.

The association between Buddhism and cultural loyalism has been strongest in Sri Lanka and Southeast Asia. Buddhists, both laity and monks, were actively involved in the local independence movements. In these contexts Buddhism has been given a sharply defined nationalistic character by drawing on both the heritage of indigenous Buddhist culture and the example of Aśoka's imperial religion. Buddhism has been used as an instrument for national integration in postcolonial politics and elements of Buddhism have been appropriated by emerging civic religions in Sri Lanka, Burma, and Thailand.

The colonial disestablishment of Buddhism in Sri Lanka and Southeast Asia, and its analogues in Ch'ing-dynasty China and Meiji Japan, altered again the lay-monk relationship and encouraged the emergence of an active lay leadership. Monasteries, deprived of government maintenance and generally without sufficient resources of their own, found it necessary to cultivate the support of local patrons. A larger number of people from various economic and social levels thus became actively involved in religious affairs focusing on the monasteries. This, of course, often led to controversy, with further segmentation of the monastic communities resulting. It also created an environment in which laity and monks could come together in new kinds of associations, much as had happened in the development of Buddhist cultures. Some of the strikingly successful "new religions" of Japan and Korea, such as Reiyūkai (Association of the Friends of the Spirit) and Won Buddhism, are products of this environment. [*See* New Religions, *article on* New Religions in Japan, *and* Reiyūkai Kyōdan.]

The disestablishment of Buddhism also encouraged the development of an active lay leadership among the new urban elites who were most influenced by European civilization. These elites introduced "reformed" interpretations of elements of the Buddhist tradition in order to bring those elements into harmony with the expectations of European civilization. Modern reformers' interpretations of the Buddha's biography have emphasized his humanity and his rational approach to the problem of human suffering. Some modernists have sought to relate Buddhist thought to Western philosophical perspectives and also to scientific patterns. Many Buddhist reformers have stressed the relevance of Buddhist teachings to social and ethical issues.

CIVILIZATIONAL RESPONSES

The encounter between European civilization and Buddhist cultures encouraged a new awareness among Buddhists of their common heritage. New contacts among Buddhists began on a significant scale, and, as a result, there was also a renewed sense of Buddhism as a civilizational religion.

This sense that Buddhism could again be a civilizational standard that could encompass the conflicting ideologies present in modern Asia and the world had great appeal to the new urban elites. In many countries Buddhist apologists maintained that Buddhism could be the basis for a truly democratic or socialist society and, as a nontheistic religion, could be the basis for world peace and unity. Sōka Gakkai (Value Creation Society), a Japanese "new religion" stemming from the Nichiren tradition, for example, presents an understanding of Buddhism as the "Third Civilization," which can overcome the opposition of idealism and materialism in thought and, when applied to the economy, can bring about a synthesis of capitalism and socialism. [*See* Sōka Gakkai.]

New missionary efforts to Asian countries such as India, Indonesia, and Nepal, where Buddhist influence had waned, and to the West have been encouraged by this view of Buddhism as "the supreme civilization" and the antidote to the spiritual malaise generated by European civilization.

SECTARIAN DEVELOPMENTS

New sectarian developments in the modern period have resulted from the expansion of Buddhism, through missionary work, and from Buddhist losses that have occurred through the encounter with European civilization. These developments are evidence that the idea of a new Buddhist civilization remains, as yet, more an aspiration than a reality.

Sectarian developments resulting from expansion can be seen in the establishment of Buddhism in the West, which has been accomplished at a certain distance from the mainstream communities, whether among immigrant groups or among intellectuals and spiritual seekers disaffected by Western cultures and religious traditions. Another sectarian development resulting from expansion is the neo-Buddhist movement among *harijans*, or scheduled castes, in India, led by B. R. Ambedkar. [*See the biography of Ambedkar.*]

A resurgence of sectarian patterns, resulting from Buddhist losses, can be seen in totalitarian communist areas. These developments tend to be pragmatic and defensive in character. Buddhists have attempted to isolate their community from the mainstream of communist society and thus avoid criticism and attack, but these efforts have rarely been successful. Sectarian isolation, however, has often been enforced by new communist governments as a way of weakening and discrediting Buddhist influence. Through a combination of criticism of Buddhist teaching by communist ideology and the radical disestablishment of Buddhist monasteries, communist governments have been able to divest Buddhist leaders and institutions of their cultural power and influence very quickly. This has occurred in the Soviet Union, Mongolia, North Korea, Vietnam, and with special ferocity in Cambodia (Kampuchea) and Tibet.

The Tibetan experience provides a tragic example of a new sectarian development in Buddhism. Buddhist institutions and leaders have been subject to a brutal attack as part of the effort to incorporate Tibet into the People's Republic of China. This has often taken the form of sinicization, with Buddhism being attacked because of its central place in traditional Tibetan culture. Following the Chinese invasion of 1959, thousands of Tibetans, including the Dalai Lama, fled the country. They have established refugee communities in North America, Europe, and India, where they are trying to preserve the heritage of Tibetan Buddhist culture.

Finally, the growth of millenarian movements among Buddhists in the modern period, especially in Burma, Thailand, and Vietnam, may be described as sectarian developments resulting from Buddhist losses. Like so much else of Buddhism in the modern period, Buddhist millenarian movements were transitory responses to crises of power and interpretation within the Buddhist community.

Conclusion

Buddhism as a whole has not yet developed a distinctive character in the modern period. On the contrary, there is a great deal of continuity between the historical development of Buddhism and the current responses and innovations. Thus the sectarian, civilizational, and cultural patterns continue to exert a predominant influence in the evolution of Buddhist tradition.

At the same time, we can see that Buddhism, like other world religions, participates in a modern religious situation that is, in many respects, radically new. Buddhism has thus come to share certain modern elements with other contemporary religions. We can see such elements in the search for new modes of religious symbolism, as is found in the writings of the Thai monk Buddhadasa and the Japanese Kyoto school of Buddhist philosophy. We can also see these common elements in the preoccupation with the human world and this-worldly soteriology that is emerging in many Buddhist contexts. A modern Sinhala Buddhist, D. Wijewardena, expressed this attitude in a polemical tract, *The Revolt in the Temple* (Colombo, 1953), by saying that Buddhists must pursue "not a will-o'-the-wisp Nirvana secluded in the cells of their monasteries, but a Nirvana attained here and now by a life of self-forgetful activity . . . [so that] they would live in closer touch with humanity, would better understand and sympathize with human difficulties" (p. 586).

This diversity, representing both tradition and present situation, reminds those of us who would study and understand Buddhism and Buddhists that, in the end, the decisive meaning of our concept of Buddhism must be that of cumulative tradition. Our concept must remain open-ended to allow for future transformations of the Buddhist tradition for as long as men and women associate their lives with the name of Buddha.

[*For further discussion of the doctrinal and practical stance(s) of the tradition, see* Buddhist Philosophy; Soteriology, *article on* Buddhist Soteriology; Language, *article on* Buddhist Views of Language; Nirvāṇa; *and* Buddhist Ethics. *For an overview of some of the means by which Buddhism and local cultures become syncretized, see* Folk Religion, *article on* Folk Buddhism. *Various regional surveys treat Buddhism as a component of local and regional cultures. See in particular* Indian Religions, *overview article;* Southeast Asian Religions, *article on* Mainland Cultures; Tibetan Religions, *overview article;* Chinese Religion, *overview article;* Mongol Religions; Korean Religions; *and* Japanese Religion, *overview article. Each of these articles provides further cross-references to Buddhist-inspired elements in local art, architecture, literature, dance, and drama.*]

BIBLIOGRAPHY

"A Brief History of Buddhist Studies in Europe and America" is provided by J. W. de Jong in two successive issues of *Eastern Buddhist,* n.s. 7 (May and October 1974): 55–106 and 49–82, which he has brought up to date in his "Recent Buddhist Studies in Europe and America 1973–1983," which appeared in the same journal, vol. 17 (Spring 1984): 79–107. One of the few books that treats a significant theme within this fascinating scholarly tradition is G. R. Welbon's *The Buddhist Nirvāṇa and its Western Interpreters* (Chicago, 1968).

Among the book-length introductory surveys of Buddhism, the second edition of Richard H. Robinson and Willard L. Johnson's *The Buddhist Religion* (Encino, Calif., 1977) is, overall, the most satisfactory. The only modern attempt to present a full-scale historical survey by a single author is to be found in the Buddhism sections of Charles Eliot's three-volume work *Hinduism and Buddhism,* 3d ed. (London, 1957), taken together with his *Japanese Buddhism* (1935; reprint, New York, 1959). Although these books are seriously dated (they were first published in 1921 and 1935, respectively), they still provide a valuable resource. Five other important works that attempt cross-cultural presentations of a particular aspect of Buddhism are Junjirō Takakusu's *The Essentials of Buddhist Philosophy,* 3d ed., edited by Wing-tsit Chan and Charles A. Moore (Honolulu, 1956); Paul Mus's wide-ranging *Barabuḍur: Esquisse d'une histoire du bouddhisme fondée sur la critique archéologique des textes,* 2 vols. (Hanoi, 1935); Robert Bleichsteiner's *Die gelbe Kirche* (Vienna, 1937), which was translated into French and published as *L'église jaune* (Paris, 1937); W. Randolph Kloetzli's *Buddhist Cosmology* (Delhi, 1983); and David L. Snellgrove's edited collection *The Image of the Buddha* (London, 1978).

Many of the most important studies of the early, sectarian phase of Buddhism in India extend their discussions to the later phases of Indian Buddhism as well. This is true, for example, of Sukumar Dutt's *Buddhist Monks and Monasteries of India* (London, 1962) and of Edward Conze's *Buddhist Thought in India* (Ann Arbor, 1967). For those interested in Buddhist doctrines, Conze's book may be supplemented by David J. Kalupahana's *Causality: The Central Philosophy of Buddhism* (Honolulu, 1975), which focuses on sectarian Buddhism, and Fredrick J. Streng's *Emptiness: A Study in Religious Meaning* (New York, 1967), which examines the work of the famous early Mahāyāna philosopher Nāgārjuna.

A historical account that is focused more exclusively on the sectarian period and the transition to civilizational Buddhism is provided by Étienne Lamotte in his authoritative *Histoire du bouddhisme indien: Des origines á l'ère Śaka* (Louvain, 1958). A somewhat different perspective on the same process of development is accessible in three closely related works that can profitably be read in series: Frank E. Reynolds's title essay in *The Two Wheels of Dhamma,* edited by Frank E. Reynolds and Bardwell L. Smith, "AAR Studies in Religion," no. 3 (Chambersburg, Pa., 1972); John C. Holt's *Discipline: The Canonical Buddhism of the Vinayapiṭaka* (Delhi, 1981); and John Strong's *The Legend of King Aśoka: A Study and Translation of the Aśokāvadāna* (Princeton, 1983).

Good books that treat Buddhism as an international civilization are hard to come by. Three that provide some assistance to those interested in the topic are Trevor O. Ling's *The Buddha: Buddhist Civilization in India and Ceylon* (London, 1973); Erik Zürcher's *The Buddhist Conquest of China: The Spread and Adaptation of Buddhism in Early Medieval China,* 2 vols. (Leiden; 1959); and René Grousset's *In the Footsteps of the Buddha,* translated by J. A. Underwood (New York, 1971). Works that focus on the process of acculturation of Buddhism in various contexts include Hajime Nakamura's *Ways of Thinking of Eastern Peoples,* the revised English translation of which was edited by Philip P. Wiener (Honolulu, 1964); Alicia Matsunaga's *The Buddhist Philosophy of Assimilation* (Tokyo and Rutland, Vt., 1969); and Kenneth Ch'en's *The Chinese Transformation of Buddhism* (Princeton, 1973).

Studies of particular Buddhist cultures are legion. Some valuable studies focus on Buddhism in the context of the whole range of religions that were present in a particular area. Good examples are Giuseppe Tucci's *The Religions of Tibet,* translated by Geoffrey Samuel (Berkeley, 1980), and Joseph M. Kitagawa's *Religion in Japanese History* (New York, 1966). Other treatments of particular Buddhist cultures trace the Buddhist tradition in question from its introduction into the area through the period of acculturation and, in some cases, on into modern times. Two examples are *Religion and Legitimation of Power in Sri Lanka,* edited by Bardwell L. Smith (Chambersburg, Pa., 1978), and Kenneth Ch'en's comprehensive *Buddhism in China* (Princeton, 1964). Finally, some interpretations of particular Buddhist cultures focus more narrowly on a specific period or theme. See, for example, Lal Mani Joshi's *Studies in the Buddhistic Culture of India* (Delhi, 1967), which deals primarily with Buddhist culture in Northeast India during the seventh and eighth centuries; Daniel Overmyer's *Folk Buddhist Religion: Dissenting Sects in Late Traditional China* (Cambridge, Mass., 1976); and William R. La Fleur's *The Karma of Words: Buddhism and the Literary Arts in Medieval Japan* (Berkeley, 1983).

There is also a myriad of books and articles that consider the development of Buddhism in the modern period. The most adequate overview of developments through the early 1970s is provided in *Buddhism in the Modern World,* edited by Heinrich Dumoulin and John Maraldo (New York, 1976). In addition, there are two excellent trilogies on particular traditions. The first, by Holmes Welch, includes *The Practice of Chinese Buddhism, 1900–1950* (1967), *The Buddhist Revival in China* (1968), and *Buddhism under Mao* (1972), all published by the Harvard University Press. The second, by Stanley J. Tambiah, includes *Buddhism and the Spirit Cults in North-East Thailand* (1970), *World Conqueror and World Renouncer: A Study of Buddhism and Polity in Thailand against a Historical Background* (1976), and *The Buddhist*

Saints of the Forest and the Cult of Amulets (1984), all published by the Cambridge University Press.

For those interested in pursuing the study of Buddhism in a cross-cultural, thematic manner, Frank E. Reynolds's *Guide to the Buddhist Religion* (Boston, 1981), done with the assistance of John Holt and John Strong, is a useful resource. It provides 350 pages of annotated bibliography of English, French, and German materials (plus a preface and 65 pages of index) organized in terms of eleven themes, including "Historical Development," "Religious Thought," "Authoritative Texts," "Popular Beliefs and Literature," "Social, Political and Economic Aspects," "The Arts," "Religious Practices and Rituals," and "Soteriological Experience and Processes: Path and Goal."

2 THE BUDDHA

Frank E. Reynolds and Charles Hallisey

Etymologically, the Sanskrit/Pali word *buddha* means "one who has awakened"; in the context of Indian religions it is used as an honorific title for an individual who is enlightened. This metaphor indicates the change in consciousness that, according to Buddhism, is always characteristic of enlightenment. It suggests the otherness and splendor associated with those named by this epithet in various Buddhist traditions. *Buddha* is also related etymologically to the Sanskrit/Pali term *buddhi,* which signifies "intelligence" and "understanding." A person who has awakened can thus be said to be "one who knows."

Within the traditional Buddhist context *buddha* is an appellative term or title—that is, a term or title that is inclusive in character. As with all titles of office (e.g., king), the term *buddha* denotes not merely the individual incumbent but also a larger conceptual framework. As an appellative, *buddha* describes a person by placing him or her within a class, instead of isolating and analyzing individual attributes. It emphasizes the paradigm that is exhibited, rather than distinctive qualities or characteristics.

The designation *buddha* has had wide circulation among various religious traditions of India. It has been applied, for example, by Jains to their founder, Mahāvīra. [*See* Mahāvīra.] The definition of the inclusive category has varied, however, and *buddha* has been used to describe a broad spectrum of persons, from those who are simply learned to those rare individuals who have had transforming and liberating insight into the nature of reality. Buddhists have, in general, employed the term in this second, stronger sense.

Buddhists adopted the term *buddha* from the religious discourse of ancient India and gave it a special imprint, just as they have done with much of their vocabulary. It seems, however, that the early Buddhists may not have immediately applied the term to the person—the historical Gautama—whom they recognized as the founder of their community. In the accounts of the first two Buddhist councils (one held just after Gautama's death, the other several decades later) Gautama is spoken of as *bhagavan* ("lord," a common title of respect) and *śāstṛ* ("teacher"), not as *buddha.* However, once the term *buddha* was adopted, it not only became the primary designation for Gautama but also assumed a central role within the basic structure of Buddhist thought and practice.

We will begin our discussion by focusing on the question of the historical Buddha and what—if anything—we know about him and his ministry. This issue has not been of particular importance for traditional Buddhists—at least not in the way that it is formulated here. But it has been of major significance for modern scholars of Buddhism, and it has become of great interest to many contemporary Buddhists and others who have been influenced by modern Western notions of history.

We will then turn to the term *buddha* as it has been employed within the various traditions that constitute classical Buddhism. As an appellative term utilized in classical Buddhist contexts, *buddha* has had three distinct, yet interwoven, levels of meaning. It has referred, first of all, to what we will call "the Buddha"—otherwise known as the Gautama Buddha or the Buddha Śākyamuni ("sage of the Śākyas"). Most Buddhists recognize Gautama as the *buddha* of our own cosmic era and/or cosmic space, and they honor him as the founder of the existing Buddhist community. As a perfectly enlightened being, Gautama is understood to have perfected various virtues (*pāramitās*) over the course of numerous lives. [*See* Pāramitās.] These prodigious efforts prepared Gautama to awake fully to the true nature of reality just as other Buddhas had awakened before him. The preparation also gave him—as it did other Buddhas—the inclination and ability to share with others what he had discovered for himself. Following his Enlightenment, Gautama became a teacher who "set in motion the wheel of Dharma" and oversaw the founding of the Buddhist comunity of monks, nuns, laymen, and laywomen.

The second level of meaning associated with *buddha* as an appellative term has to do with "other Buddhas." Many Buddhas of different times and places are named in Buddhist literature. Moreover, anyone who attains release *(mokṣa, nirvāṇa)* from this world of recurring rebirths *(saṃsāra)* can be called—in some contexts at least—a Buddha. Buddhas, then, are potentially as "innumerable as the sands of the River Ganges." But all Buddhas are not equal: they possess different capabilities according to their aspirations and accomplishments. The enlightened insight of some is greater than that of others. Some attain enlightenment only for themselves (e.g., *pratyekabuddha*), others for the benefit and welfare of many (e.g., *samyaksaṃbuddha*). Some accomplish their mission through their earthly careers, others through the creation of celestial Buddha fields into which their devotees seek rebirth.

Finally, the term *buddha* as an appellative has a third level of meaning that we will designate as Buddhahood—a level that provides its widest conceptual context. This level is constituted by the recognition that the Buddha and other Buddhas are, in a very profound sense, identical with ultimate reality itself. Consequently, Buddhists have given the more personal and active connotations associated with the Buddha and other Buddhas to their characterizations of absolute reality as *dharma* (salvific truth), *śūnyatā* ("emptiness"), *tathatā* ("suchness"), and the like. At the same time, the term *Buddhahood* has on occasion given a somewhat depersonalized cast to the notions of the Buddha and other Buddhas. For example, early Buddhists, who were closest to the historical Buddha, were reluctant to depict Gautama in anthropomorphic forms and seem to have intentionally avoided biographical structures and iconic imagery. They used impersonal and symbolic representation to express their perception that the Buddha whose teachings they had preserved was fully homologous with reality itself. In some later traditions the pervading significance of this third level of meaning was expressed through the affirmation that the Buddha's impersonal and ineffable *dharmakāya* ("*dharma* body") was the source and truth of the other, more personalized manifestations of Buddhahood.

The Historical Buddha

The scholars who inaugurated the critical study of Buddhism in the late nineteenth and early twentieth centuries were deeply concerned with the question of the "historical Buddha." But their views on the subject differed radically. The field was largely divided between a group of myth-oriented scholars, such as Émile Senart, Heinrich Kern, and Ananda Coomaraswamy, and a group of more historically oriented philologists, such as Hermann Oldenberg and T. W. and C. A. F. Rhys Davids. The myth-oriented interpreters placed emphasis on the study of Sanskrit sources and on the importance of those elements in the sacred biography that pointed in the direction of solar mythology; for these scholars, the historical Buddha was, at most, a reformer who provided an occasion for historicizing a classic solar myth. In contrast, the historically oriented philologists emphasized the texts written in Pali, as well as those elements in these texts that they could use to create (or reconstruct, in their view) an acceptable "historical" life of the Buddha. From the perspective of these scholars, the mythic elements—and other supposedly irrational elements as well—were later additions to a true historical memory, additions that brought about the demise of the original Buddhism of the Buddha. Such pious frauds were to be identified and discounted by critical scholarship.

More recently, scholars have recognized the inadequacy of the older mythic and historical approaches. Most scholars working in the field at present are convinced of the existence of the historical Gautama. The general consensus was well expressed by the great Belgian Buddhologist Étienne Lamotte, who noted that "Buddhism would remain inexplicable if one did not place at its beginning a strong personality who was its founder" (Lamotte, 1958, p. 707). But at the same time scholars are aware that the available tests provide little information about the details of Gautama's life.

The difficulties involved in saying anything significant about the historical Buddha are illustrated by the lack of certainty concerning the dates of his birth and death. Since different Buddhist traditions recognize different dates, and since external evidence is slight and inconclusive, scholars have ventured diverging opinions.

Two chronologies found in Buddhist texts are important for any attempt to calculate the date of the historical Buddha. A "long chronology," presented in the Sri Lankan chronicles, the *Dīpavaṃsa* and the *Mahāvaṃsa,* places the birth of the historical Buddha 298 years before the coronation of King Aśoka, his death 218 years before that event. If we accept the date given in the chronicles for the coronation of Aśoka (326 BCE), that would locate the Buddha's birth date in 624 BCE and his death in 544. These dates have been traditionally accepted in Sri Lanka and Southeast Asia and were the basis for the celebration of the 2500th anniversary of the Buddha's death, or *parinirvāṇa,* in 1956. However, most modern scholars who accept the long chronology believe, on the basis of Greek evidence, that Aśoka's coronation took place around 268 or 267 BCE and that the Buddha's birth and death should therefore be dated circa 566 and circa 486, respectively. These later dates are favored by the majority of Buddhologists in Europe, America, and India.

A "short chronology" is attested to by Indian sources and their Chinese and Tibetan translations. These sources place the birth of the Buddha 180 years before the coronation of Aśoka and his death 100 years before that event. If the presumably reliable Greek testimony concerning Aśoka's coronation is applied, the birth date of the Buddha is 448 and the date of his death, or *parinirvāṇa,* is 368. This short chronology is accepted by many Japanese Buddhologists and was spiritedly defended by the German scholar Heinz Bechert in 1982.

Although there seems to be little chance of resolving the long chronology/short chronology question in any kind of definitive manner, we can say with some certainty that the historical Buddha lived sometime during the period from the sixth through the fourth centuries BCE. This was a time of radical thought and speculation, as manifested in the pre-Socratic philosophical tradition and the mystery cults in Greece, the prophets and prophetic schools of the Near East, Confucius and Lao-tzu in China, the Upaniṣadic sages and the communities of ascetic wanderers (*śramaṇas*) in India, and the emergence of "founded" religions such as Jainism and Buddhism. These intellectual and religious movements were fostered by the formation of cosmopolitan empires, such as those associated with Alexander in the Hellenistic world, with the Ch'in and Han dynasties in China, with Darius and Cyrus in Persia, and with the Maurya dynasty in India. Urban centers were established and soon became the focal points around which a new kind of life was organized. A significant number of people, cut off from the old sources of order and meaning, were open to different ways of expressing their religious concerns and were quite ready to support those engaged in new forms of religious and intellectual endeavor.

The historical Buddha responded to this kind of situation in northeastern India. He was a renouncer and an ascetic, although the style of renunciation and asceticism he practiced and recommended was, it seems, mild by Indian standards. He shared with other renunciants an ultimately somber view of the world and its pleasures, and he practiced and recommended a mode of religious life in which individual participation in a specifically religious community was of primary importance. He experimented with the practices of renunciants—begging, wandering, celibacy, techniques of self-restraint *(yoga),* and the like—and he organized a community in which discipline played a central role. Judging from the movement he inspired, he was not only an innovator but also a charismatic personality. Through the course of his ministry he gathered around him a group of wandering mendicants and nuns, as well as men and women who continued to live the life of householders.

Can we go beyond this very generalized portrait of the historical Buddha toward a fuller biography? Lamotte has advised caution, observing in his *Histoire* that writing the life of the historical Gautama is "a hopeless enterprise" (p. 16). There are, however, a few details that, though they do not add up to a biography, do suggest that there is a historical core to the later biographical traditions. These details are presented in almost identical form in the literature of diverse Buddhist schools, a reasonable indication that they date from before the fourth to third centuries BCE, when independent and separate traditions first began to develop.

Some of these details are so specific and arbitrary or unexpected that it seems unlikely that they were fabricated. These include the details that Gautama was of the *kṣatriya* caste, that he was born in the Śākya clan (a more distinguished pedigree could have been created), that he was marrried and had a child, that he entered the ascetic life without the permission of his father, that his first attempts to share the insights that he had gained through his Enlightenment met with failure, that his leadership of the community he had established was seriously challenged by his more ascetically inclined cousin, and that he died in a remote place after eating a tainted meal. But these details are so few and disconnected that our knowlege of the historical Buddha remains shadowy and unsatisfying. In order to identify a more meaningful image of Gautama and his career we must turn to the Buddha who is explicitly affirmed in the memory and practice of the Buddhist community.

The Buddha

The general history of religions strongly suggests that the death of a founder results in the loss of a charismatic focus. This loss must be dealt with if the founded group is to survive. In his classic article "Master and Disciple: Two Religio-Sociological Studies," Joachim Wach suggests that "the image" of the beloved founder could produce a unity sufficient for the group to continue (*Journal of Religion* 42, 1962, p. 5).

Each founded religion has developed original ways of preserving the image of their master: Christians with the Gospels and later artistic expressions, Muslims with *ḥadīth* and Miʿrāj stories of Muḥammad's journeys to heaven, and so on. Buddhists, it seems, have addressed this crisis with the assumption—explicitly stated in the words of a fifth-century CE Mahāyāna text known as the *Saptaśatikā-prajñāpāramitā*—that "a Buddha is not easily made known by words" (Rome, 1923, p. 126). This recognition has not proved to be a restraint but has instead inspired Buddhists to preserve the image of Gautama through the creation and explication of epithets, through a variety of "biographical" accounts, and through a tradition of visual representation in monumental architecture and art. The image of the founder became, in Joachim Wach's phrase, "an objective center of crystalization" for a variety of opinions concerning the nature and significance of his person.

The creative preservation of the image of the Buddha was closely related to evolving patterns of worship—including pilgrimage, contemplation, and ritual—in the Buddhist community. This reminds us that the various ways of portraying the Buddha are the result of innumerable personal efforts to discern him with immediacy, as well as the product of the desire to preserve and share that image.

EPITHETS

Certainly one of the earliest and most ubiquitous forms in which Buddhists have expressed and generated their image of Gautama Buddha was through the medium of epithets. For example, in the *Majjhima Nikāya* (London, 1948, vol. 1, p. 386), a householder named Upāli, after becoming the Buddha's follower, acclaims him with one hundred epithets. The Sanskrit version of this text adds that Upāli spoke these epithets spontaneously, as an expression of his faith and respect. Over the centuries the enumerations of these and other epithets focused on the extraordinary aspects of the Buddha's person, on his marvelous nature. In so doing they became a foundation for Buddhist devotional literature, their enunciation a support of devotional and contemplative practice.

Countless epithets have been applied to the Buddha over the centuries, but *buddha* itself has been a particular favorite for explanation. Even hearing the word *buddha* can cause people to rejoice because, as the Theravāda commentary on the *Saṃyutta Nikāya* says, "It is very rare indeed to hear the word *buddha* in this world" (London, 1929, vol. 1, p. 312). The *Paṭisambhidā,* a late addition to the Theravāda canon, explored the significance of the word *buddha* by saying that "it is a name derived from the final liberation of the Enlightened Ones, the Blessed Ones, together with the omniscient knowledge at the root of the Enlightenment Tree; this name "buddha" is a designation based on realization" (*The Path of Purification,* translated by Ñyāṇamoli, Colombo, 1964, p. 213). Sun Ch'o, a fourth-century Chinese writer, explicated the *buddha* epithet in a rather different mode, reminiscent of a Taoist sage: " 'Buddha' means 'one who embodies the Way'. . . . It is the one who reacts to the stimuli (of the world) in all pervading accordance (with the needs of all beings); the one who abstains from activity and who is yet universally active" (quoted in Erik Zürcher's *The Buddhist Conquest of China,* Leiden, 1959, p. 133).

Particular epithets accentuate specific qualities of the Buddha that might otherwise remain unemphasized or ambiguous. Thus the epithet "teacher of gods and men" *(satthar devamanussānāṃ)* is used in the *Mahāniddesa,* another late canonical text in the Theravāda tradition, to display the Buddha as one who helps others escape from suffering. The techniques used—exploiting ordinary polysemy and puns and deriving elaborate etymologies—are favorites of Buddhist commentators for exposing the significance of an epithet.

> *He teaches by means of the here and now, of the life to come, and of the ultimate goal, according as befits the case, thus he is Teacher* (satthar).
>
> *"Teacher* (satthar)*": the Blessed One is a caravan leader* (satthar) *since he brings home caravans. Just as one who brings a caravan home gets caravans across a wilderness. . . gets them to reach a land of safety, so too the Blessed One is a caravan leader, one who brings home the caravans; he gets them across. . . the wilderness of birth.*
>
> *(Ñyāṇamoli, p. 223)*

Some of the epithets of the Buddha refer to his lineage and name: for example, Śākyamuni, "sage of the Śākya tribe," and his personal name, Siddhārtha, "he whose aims are fulfilled." Some refer to religio-mythic paradigms with which he was identified: *mahāpuruṣa* means "great cosmic person"; *cakravartin* refers to the "universal monarch." the possessor of the seven jewels of sovereignty who sets in motion the wheel of righteous rule. Some—such as *bhagavan*—convey a sense of beneficent lordship. Others—such as *tathāgata* ("thus come," or "thus gone")—retain, at least in retrospect, an aura of august ambiguity and mystery.

Various epithets define the Buddha as having attained perfection in all domains. His wisdom is perfect, as are his physical form and manner. In some cases the epithets indicate that the Buddha is without equal, that he has attained "the summit of the world." André Bareau concluded his study "The Superhuman Personality of the Buddha and its Symbolism in the *Mahāparinirvāṇasūtra,*" which is largely an examination of the epithets in this important text, by stating that through these epithets the authors "began to conceive the transcendence of the Buddha. . . . Perfect in all points, superior through distance from all beings, unique, the Beatific had evidently taken, in the thought of his followers, the place which the devotees of the great religions attributed to the great God whom they adored" (*Myths and Symbols,* edited by Charles H. Long and Joseph M. Kitagawa, Chicago, 1969, pp. 19–20).

The epithets of the Buddha, in addition to having a central place in Buddhist devotion, are featured in the *buddhānusmṛti* meditation—the "recollection of the Buddha." This form of meditation, like all Buddhist meditational practices, had as its aim the discipline and purification of the mind; but, in addition, it was a technique of visualization, a way of recovering the image of the founder. [*See* Nien-fo.] This practice of visualization by contemplation on the epithets is important in the Theravāda tradition, both monastic and lay, and it was also very popular in the Sarvāstivāda communities in northwestern India and influential in various Mahāyāna traditions in China. It was instrumental in the development of the Mahāyāna notion of the "three bodies" *(trikāya)* of the Buddha, particularly the second, or visualized, body that was known as his *saṃbhogakāya* ("body of enjoyment").

BIOGRAPHIES

Like the tradition of uttering and interpreting epithets that extolled the exalted nature and virtues of the Buddha, the tradition of recounting biographical episodes is an integral part of early Buddhism. Episodic fragments, preserved in the Pali and Chinese versions of the early Buddhist literature, are embedded in sermons attributed to the Buddha himself and illustrate points of practice or doctrine. Such episodes are also used as narrative frames to provide a context indicating when and where a particular discourse was taught. It appears certain that other episodic fragments were recounted and generated at the four great pilgrimage centers of early Buddhism—the sites that were identified as the locations of the Buddha's birth, of his Enlightenment, of the preaching of his first sermon, and of his death, or *parinirvāṇa.* Some of the scattered narratives do seem to presuppose a developed biographical tradition, but others suggest a fluidity in the biographical structure. Thus, a crucial problem that is posed for our understanding of the biographical process in the Buddhist tradition is when and how a more or less fixed biography of the Buddha actually took shape.

The most convincing argument for the very early development of a comprehensive biography of the Buddha has been made by Erich Frauwallner (1956). Frauwallner argues, on the basis of a brilliant text-critical analysis, that a no longer extant biography of the Buddha, complete up to the conversion of the two great disciples, Śāriputra and Maudgalyāyana, was written approximately one hundred years after the Buddha's death and well prior to the reign of King Aśoka. This biography, he maintains, was composed as an introduction to the *Skandhaka,* a text of monastic discipline (Vinaya) that was reportedly confirmed at the Second Buddhist Council held at Vaiśālī. Appended to the *Skandhaka,* according to Frauwallner, was an account of the Buddha's death, or *parinirvāṇa,* and of the first years of the fledgling monastic community. Frauwallner contends that all subsequent Buddha biographies have been derived from this basic ur-text. The fragmentary biographies found in the extant Vinaya literature of the various Buddhist schools indicate a crumbling away of this original biography; later autonomous biographies are versions cut from the original Vinaya context and subsequently elaborated.

A different argument has been made, also on the basis of close text-critical study, by scholars such as Alfred Foucher, Étienne Lamotte, and André Bareau. They have argued that there was a gradual development of biographical cycles, with only a later synthesis of this material into a series of more complete biographies. According to this thesis, the earliest stages of the development of the Buddha biography are the fragments in the Sūtra and Vinaya texts, which show no concern for chronology or continuity. The Sūtra literature emphasizes stories of the Buddha's previous births *(jātaka),* episodes leading up to the Enlightenment, the Enlightenment itself, and an account of his last journey, death, and funeral. André Bareau states that the biographical material in the Sūtras was "composed for the most part of episodes taken from separate traditions, from which the authors chose with complete freedom, guided only by their desire to illustrate a particular point of doctrine" (Bareau, 1963, p. 364). The Vinaya texts, on the other hand, focus on the Buddha as teacher and incorporate—in addition to accounts of the events associated with his Enlightenment—narratives that describe the early days of his ministry, including an account of the conversion of his first disciples. The air of these Vinaya fragments seems to be to confer authenticity on the monastic rules and practices set forth in the rest of the text.

The oldest of the surviving autonomous biographies is the *Mahāvastu,* an unwieldly anthology written in Buddhist Hybrid Sanskrit about the beginning of the common era. Other more tightly constructed biographies were produced soon after the *Mahāvastu*—notably, the *Lalitavistara,* which played an important role in various Mahāyāna traditions; the *Abhiniṣkramaṇa Sūtra,* which was especially popular in China, where at least five Chinese works were, nominally at least, translations of it; and the very famous and popular *Buddhacarita,* attributed to Aśvaghoṣa. Much later, between the fourth and fifth centuries, still another autonomous biography, known as the Vinaya of the Mūlasarvāstivādins, was given its final form. This voluminous compendium of biographical traditions provided later Mahāyāna schools with a major source for stories about the Buddha and his career.

These new autonomous biographies continued to incorporate stories that had developed at the pilgrimage sites associated with the Buddha's birth and great renunciation, his Enlightenment, and his first sermon. For example, in the *Lalitavistara* an episode is recounted that is clearly related to a specific shrine at the Buddhist pilgrimage site at Kapilavastu—namely, the story in which the Buddha's charioteer leaves him and returns to the palace in Kapilavastu. What is more, these new autonomous biographies also continued to exhibit structural elements that had been characteristic of the biographical segments of the older Vinaya literature. For example, all of the early autonomous biographies (with the exception of the "completed" Chinese and Tibetan versions of the *Buddhacarita*) follow the Vinaya tradition, which ends the story at a point soon after the Buddha had begun his ministry.

These new autonomous biographies testify to three important changes that affected the traditions of Buddha biography during the centuries immediately following the death of King Aśoka. The first is the inclusion of new biographical elements drawn from non-Buddhist and even non-Indian sources. The autonomous biographies were the products of the cosmopolitan civilizations associated with the Śātavāhana and Kushan (Kuṣāṇa) empires, and therefore it is not surprising that new episodes were adapted from Greek and West Asian sources. Somewhat later, as the autonomous Buddha biographies were introduced into other areas, changes were introduced to accentuate the Buddha's exemplification of new cultural values. Thus, in a fourth-century Chinese "translation" of the *Abhiniṣkramaṇa,* great emphasis was placed on the Buddha's exemplification of filial piety through the conversion of his father, King Śuddhodana.

The second important change exhibited by these new autonomous biographies was the ubiquitous inclusion of stories about the Buddha's previous lives *(jātaka)* as a device for explicating details of his final life as Gautama. This is particularly evident in the *Mahāvastu* and in certain versions of the *Abhiniṣkramaṇa Sūtra,* in which, according to Lamotte, "the Jātakas become the prime mover of the narration: each episode in the life of the Buddha is given as the result and reproduction of an event from previous lives" (Lamotte, 1958, p. 725).

The third discernible change is the increasing placement of emphasis on the superhuman and transcendent dimensions of the Buddha's nature. Earlier narratives refer to the Buddha's fatigue and to his susceptibility to illness, but in the autonomous biographies he is said to be above human frailties. There is a tendency to emphasize the Buddha's superhuman qualities, not only of mind, but also of body: "It is true that the Buddhas bathe, but no dirt is found on them; their bodies are radiant like golden amaranth. Their bathing is mere conformity with the world" (*Mahāvastu,* translated by J. J. Jones, London, 1949, vol. 1, p. 133). As a function of this same emphasis on transcendence, the Buddha's activities are increasingly portrayed in the modes of miracle and magic. With the emergence and development of Mahāyāna, new narratives began to appear that portrayed the Buddha preaching a more exalted doctrine, sometimes on a mountain peak, sometimes in a celestial realm, sometimes to his most receptive disciples, sometimes to a great assembly of *bodhisattva*s (future Buddhas) and gods.

Whereas the Mahāyāna accepted the early autonomous biographies and supplemented them with additional episodes of their own, the Theravāda community displayed a continuing resistance to developments in the biographical tradition. For almost nine centuries after the death of Gautama, the various elements of the Buddha biography were kept separate in Theravāda literature. But in the fifth century CE, about half a millennium after the composition of the first autonomous biographies, the Theravādins began to create their own biographical genres. These brought together and synthesized, in their own, more restrained style, many of the previously fragmented narratives.

Two types of Buddha biographies have had an important impact and role in the later history of the Theravāda tradition. The model for the classical type is the *Nidānakathā,* a text that serves as an introduction to the fifth-century *Jātaka Commentary* and thus continues the pattern of using biography to provide a narrative context that authenticates the teaching. It traces the Buddha's career from the time of his previous birth as Sumedha (when he made his original vow to become a Buddha) to the year following Gautama's Enlightenment, when he took up residence in the Jetavana Monastery. Subsequent Theravāda biographies, based on the *Nidānakathā,* continued the narration through the rest of Gautama's ministry and beyond.

The second type of Theravāda biography—the chronicle *(vaṃsa)* biography—illustrates a distinctive Theravāda understanding of the Buddha. From very early in their history the Theravādins had distinguished between two bodies of the Buddha, his physical body *(rūpakāya)* and his body of truth *(dharmakāya).* After the Buddha's death, or *parinirvāṇa,* the *rūpakāya* continued to be present to the community in his relics, and his *dharmakāya* continued to be present in his teachings. In the fourth to fifth centuries CE the Theravādins began to compose biographical chronicles that focused on these continuing legacies. These begin with previous lives of the Buddha, then provide an abbreviated account of his "final" life as Gautama. They go on to narrate the history of the tradition by interweaving accounts of kings who maintain the physical legacy (in the form of relics, stupas, and the like) with accounts of the monastic order, which maintains his *dharma* legacy (in the form of proper teaching and discipline). Examples of this type of biographical chronicle are numerous, beginning with the *Dīpavaṃsa* and *Mahāvaṃsa* and continuing through many other *vaṃsa* texts written in Sri Lanka and Southeast Asia.

Throughout the premodern history of Buddhism, all of the major Buddhist schools preserved biographies of the Buddha. And in each situation, they were continually reinterpreted in relation to contemporary attitudes and experiences. But in the modern period, a new genre of Buddha biographies has been introduced. This new type of biography has been influenced by Western scholarship on Buddhism and by Western attempts to recover the historical Buddha, who had—from the modernist perspective—been hidden from view by the accretions of tradition. New, largely urbanized elites throughout the Buddhist world have sought to "demythologize" the Buddha biography, deleting miraculous elements of the Buddha's life and replacing them with an image of the founder as a teacher of a rationalistic ethical system or a "scientific" system of meditation or as a social reformer committed to the cause of democracy, socialism, or egalitarianism. This new genre of Buddha biography has appeared in many Buddhist contexts and has made an impact that has cut across all the traditional lines of geographical and sectarian division.

VISUAL REPRESENTATIONS

The images of the founder that Buddhists have generated and expressed visually are more enigmatic than the images presented in epithets and biographies. The history of Buddhist monumental architecture, art, and sculpture does not neatly fit such accustomed categories as "mythologization" or "divinization." Furthermore, the association of various kinds of visual representation with veneration and worship challenges many stereotypes about the secondary place of cult activity in the Buddhist tradition. The situation is further complicated by the fact that the function and significance of visual representations of the Buddha are only explained in relatively late Buddhist literature, after both doctrine and practice had become extremely complex.

The most important of the very early visual representations of the Buddha was the burial mound, or stupa (Skt., *stūpa*). The interment of the remains of kings and heroes in burial mounds was a well-established practice in pre-Buddhist India. Buddhists and Jains adopted these mounds as models for their first religious monuments and honored them with traditional practices. In the Pali *Mahāparinibbāna Suttanta* and its parallels in Sanskrit, Tibetan, and Chinese, the Buddha gives instructions that his funeral rites should be performed in the manner customary for a "universal monarch" *(cakravartin),* an epithet that was applied to the Buddha. [*See* Cakravartin.] After his cremation his bones were to be deposited in a golden urn and placed in a mound built at the crossing of four main roads. Offerings of flowers and garlands, banners, incense, and music characterized both the funeral rites themselves and the continuing worship at a stupa.

As Buddhism developed, the stupa continued to serve as a central visual representation of the founder. Seeing a stupa called to memory the greatness of the Buddha and—for some at least—became equivalent to actually seeing the Buddha when he was alive. Since the Buddha's physical remains could be divided, replicated, and distributed, new stupas containing relics could be constructed. They became a focal point for worship wherever Buddhism spread, first within India and then beyond. What is more, the stupa had symbolic connotations that exerted a significant influence on the way in which the Buddha was perceived. For example, stupas had a locative significance through which the Buddha was associated with specific territorial units. They also came increasingly to represent a cosmology and cosmography ordered by Buddhist principles, thus symbolically embodying the notion of the Buddha as a cosmic person.

The later literature explains that a stupa is worthy of worship and reverence not only because it contains a relic or relics but also because its form symbolizes the enlightened state of a Buddha, or Buddhahood itself. In some texts the stupa is described as the *dharmakāya,* or transcendent body, of the Buddha, and each of its layers and components is correlated with a set of spiritual qualities cultivated to perfection by a Buddha. Such symbolic correlations made evident what, in some circles at least, had been long accepted, namely, the notion that the stupa represents the Buddha's spiritual, as well as his physical, legacy.

The beginnings of Buddhist art are found on post-Aśokan stupas, such as those found at Bhārhut, Sāñcī, and Amarāvatī. These great stupas and their gates are decorated with narrative reliefs of events from the Buddha's life and with scenes of gods and men "rendering homage to the Lord." The Buddha is always depicted symbolically in these reliefs, with emblems appropriate to the story. For example, in friezes depicting scenes associated with his birth he is often represented by a footprint with the characteristic marks of the *mahāpuruṣa* (the cosmic man destined to be either a *cakravartin* or a Buddha). In scenes associated with his Enlightenment he is often represented by the Bodhi Tree under which he attained Enlightenment, or the throne on which he was seated when that event occurred. When the subject is the preaching of his first sermon he is often represented by an eight-spoked wheel that is identified with the wheel of *dharma.* When the subject is his death, or *parinirvāṇa,* the preferred symbol is, of course, the stupa. [*See also* Stupa Worship.]

The motivation for this aniconic imagery is not clear, especially since the friezes abound with other human figures. However, it is probable that abstract art was more adaptable to contemplative uses that we have already seen emphasized in connection with the epithets of the Buddha and with the symbolic interpretation of the stupa. It may also be that these aniconic images imply a conception of the Buddha as a supramundane being similar to that of the docetic portrayals found in the autonomous biographies that appear somewhat later. This suggests that at this time Buddhism may have been richer in its concrete reality, in its practice, than in its doctrine, as it took centuries for a doctrinal understanding of the significance of these first representations to be formulated in the literature.

The stupa and other aniconic symbols emblematic of the Buddha have remained an integral component of Buddhist life in all Buddhist areas and eras. Toward the end of the first century BCE, however, another form of visual representation began to appear, namely, the anthropomorphic image that subsequently assumed paramount importance in all Buddhist countries and sects. The first of these images are contemporary with the autonomous biographies of the Buddha, and like these texts, they appropriate previously non-Buddhist and non-Indian motifs to express Buddhist conceptions and experiences. At Mathurā, in North-Central India, where the first statues seem to have originated, sculptors employed a style and iconography associated with *yakṣa*s, the popular life-cult deities of ancient India, to create bulky and powerful figures of the Buddha. At Gandhāra in northwestern India, another major center of early Buddhist image-making, the artists sculpted the Buddha images quite differently, appropriating Hellenistic conventions introduced into Asia by the Greeks, who ruled the area in the centuries following the invasions of Alexander the Great.

A great many styles have developed for the Buddha image; and just as at Mathurā and Gandhāra, local conventions have been fully exploited. There has been a continuity, however, to all these creations: the Buddha image has consistently served a dual function as both an object of worship and a support for contemplation. It seems clear that the basic form of the image was shaped by conceptions of the Buddha as *lokottara* (supramundane), *mahāpuruṣa, cakravartin,* omniscient, and so on, and standardized iconography was used to convey these various dimensions. The sculpted (and later painted) image was both an expression of, and an aid for, the visualization of the master and the realization of his presence.

If aniconic symbols lend themselves especially well to contemplative uses, anthropomorphic images seem more appropriate to emotion and prayer, as well as to worship as such. In fact, the patterns of veneration and worship that developed in connection with Buddha images show a strong continuity with the ancient devotional and petitionary practices associated with the *yakṣa*s and other folk deities. Throughout Buddhist history the veneration and worship of Buddha images have involved sensuous offerings of flowers, incense, music, food, and drink, and have often been closely tied to very immediate worldly concerns.

Later Buddhist literature explains that the Buddha image is worthy of honor and worship because it is a likeness of the Buddha. Popular practice often ascribes a living presence to the statue, whether by placing a relic within it or by a ritual of consecration that infuses it with "life." Thus the image of the Buddha, like the stupa, is both a reminder that can inspire and guide and a locus of power. [*See also* Iconography, *article on* Buddhist Iconography.]

Other Buddhas

The representations of the Buddha in epithet, biography, and image have been shared in their main outlines by the great majority of Buddhist schools. However, the recognition of other Buddhas, the roles other Buddhas have played, and the evaluation of their significance (and hence the role and significance of Gautama himself) have varied greatly from one tradition to another.

BUDDHAS OF THE PAST AND FUTURE

Quite early, Gautama is perceived as one of several Buddhas in a series that began in the distant past. In the early canonical literature, the series of previous Buddhas sometimes appears as a practically anonymous group, deriving probably from the recognition that Gautama could not have been alone in achieving enlightenment. It is thus not surprising that in texts such as the Saṃyutta Nikāya the interest in these previous Buddhas focuses on their thoughts at the time of enlightenment, thoughts that are identical with those attributed to Gautama when he achieved the same experience.

The most important early text on previous Buddhas is the *Mahāvadāna Sutta,* which refers to six Buddhas who had appeared prior to Gautama. This text implicitly contains the earliest coordinated biography of the Buddha, for it describes the pattern to which the lives of all Buddhas conform. Thus, describing the life of a Buddha named Vipaśyin, Gautama narrates that he was born into a royal family, that he was raised in luxury, that he was later confronted with the realities of sickness, aging, and death while visiting a park, and that he subsequently took up the life of a wandering mendicant. After Vipaśyin realized the truth for himself, he established a monastic order and taught what he had discovered to others. In the narratives of the other Buddhas, some details vary; but in every instance they are said to have discovered and taught the same eternal truth.

There is clear evidence that Buddhas who were thought to have lived prior to Gautama were worshiped in India at least from the time of Aśoka through the period of Buddhist decline. In the inscription, Aśoka states that he had doubled the size of the stupa associated with the Buddha Konākamana, who had lived earlier than Gautama and was his immediate predecessor. During the first millennium of the common era, successive Chinese pilgrims recorded visits to Indian monuments dedicated to former Buddhas, many of them attributed to the pious construction activities of Aśoka.

The *Buddhavaṃsa* (Lineage of the Buddhas), which is a late text within the Pali canon, narrates the lives of twenty-four previous Buddhas in almost identical terms. It may be that the number twenty-four was borrowed from Jainism, which has a lineage of twenty-four *tīrthaṃkara*s that culminates in the figure of the founder, Mahāvīra. The *Buddhavaṃsa* also embellished the idea of a connection between Gautama Buddha and the lineage of previous Buddhas. It contains the story that later came to provide the starting point for the classic Theravāda biography of Gautama—the story in which the future Gautama Buddha, in his earlier birth as Sumedha, meets the previous Buddha Dīpaṃkara and vows to undertake the great exertions necessary to attain Buddhahood for himself.

According to conceptions that are closely interwoven with notions concerning previous Buddhas, the appearance of a Buddha in this world is determined not only by his own spiritual efforts but also by other circumstances. There can only be one Buddha in a particular world at a given time, and no Buddha can arise until the teachings of the previous Buddha have completely disappeared. There are also cosmological considerations. A Buddha is not born in the beginning of a cosmic aeon *(kalpa)* when human beings are so well off and live so long that they do not fear sickness, aging, and death; such people, like the gods and other superhuman beings, would be incapable of insight into the pervasiveness of suffering and the impermanence of all things and therefore would not be prepared to receive a Buddha's message. Furthermore, Buddhas are born only in the continent of Jambudvīpa (roughly equivalent to India) and only to priestly *(brāhmaṇa)* or noble *(kṣatriya)* families.

The idea of a chronological series of previous Buddhas, which was prominent primarily in the Hīnayāna traditions, accentuates the significance of Gautama by designating him as the teacher for our age and by providing him with a spiritual lineage that authenticates his message. This idea also provides a basis for hope because it suggests that even if the force of Gautama's person and message has begun to fade, there remains the possibility that other Buddhas are yet to come.

The belief in a future Buddha also originated in the Hīnayāna tradition and has played an important role in various Hīnayāna schools, including the Theravāda. The name of this next Buddha is Maitreya ("the friendly one"), and he seems to have come into prominence in the period after the reign of King Aśoka. (Technically, of course, Maitreya is a *bodhisattva*—one who is on the path to Buddhahood—rather than a Buddha in the full sense. However, the degree to which the attention of Buddhists has been focused on the role that he will play when he becomes a Buddha justifies consideration of him in the present context.) [*See* Maitreya *and* Kingship, *article on* Kingship in Southeast Asia.]

According to the Maitreyan mythology that has been diffused throughout the entire Buddhist world, the future Buddha, who was one of Gautama Buddha's disciples, now dwells in Tuṣita Heaven, awaiting the appropriate moment to be reborn on earth, where he will inaugurate an era of peace, prosperity, and salvation. As the Buddha of the future, Maitreya assumed many diverse roles. Among other things he became an object of worship, a focus of aspiration, and a center of religio-political interest both as a legitimator of royalty and as a rallying point for rebellion. [*See especially* Millenarianism, *article on* Chinese Millenarian Movements.]

The wish to be reborn in the presence of Maitreya, whether in Tuṣita Heaven or when he is reborn among humans, has been a sustaining hope of many Buddhists in the past, and it persists among Theravādins even today. The contemplation and recitation of the name of Maitreya inspired devotional cults in northwestern India, Central Asia, and China, especially between the fourth and seventh centuries CE. But in East Asia his devotional cult was superseded by that dedicated to Amitābha, a Buddha now existing in another cosmic world.

CELESTIAL AND COSMIC BUDDHAS

The recognition that there could be other Buddhas in other world systems described in Buddhist cosmology builds on implications already present in the idea of past and future Buddhas. Like the first Buddhas of the past, the first Buddhas associated with other worlds are largely anonymous, appearing in groups to celebrate the teaching of the Buddha Gautama. The many epithets of the Buddha were sometimes pressed into service as personal names for individual Buddhas who needed to be identified.

The idea of Buddhas existing in other worlds comes to the fore in the early Mahāyāna literature. It was first employed, as in the *Saddharmapuṇḍarīka Sūtra* (Lotus of the True Law), to authenticate new teachings, just as the tradition of former Buddhas had done for the teachings of the early community. In the course of time, some of these Buddhas came to be recognized individually as very powerful, their worlds as indescribably splendid and blissful. They were Buddhas in superhuman form, and their careers, which were dedicated to the saving of others, lasted for aeons. Their influence was effective beyond their own worlds, and they could provide assistance—through the infinite merit they had accumulated—to the inhabitants of other world systems, including our own. The traditions that have focused attention on these Buddhas have inevitably deemphasized the importance of Gautama Buddha by removing his singularity in human experience and by contrasting him with more powerful Buddhas who could make their assistance and influence immediately and directly available. [*See also* Pure and Impure Lands; Merit, *article on* Buddhist Concepts; *and* Cosmology, *article on* Buddhist Cosmology.]

While the number of such coexisting celestial Buddhas is, in principle, infinite, and a great number are named in Buddhist literature, distinct mythological, iconic, and devotional traditions have only developed in a few cases. Amitābha ("boundless light") is one of the most important of the Buddhas who did become the focus of a distinctive tradition. Originating in northwest India or Central Asia, his appeal subsequently spread to China, Tibet, and Japan. Amitābha rules over a paradise that contains all the excellences of other Buddha lands. He offers universal accessibility to this Pure Land (called Sukhāvatī), granting rebirth to those who practice the Buddha's determination to be reborn in it, and even to those who merely recite his name or think of him briefly but with faith. In the Amitābha/Pure Land traditions, which have had continuing success in China and Japan, we see a concentration on patterns of contemplation, visualization, and recitation first developed in connection with the epithets of the Buddha. [*See* Amitābha.]

Another celestial Buddha who came to hold a position of importance in the Buddhist tradition is Bhaiṣajyaguru, the Master of Medicine. Bhaiṣajyaguru rules over his own paradisiacal realm, which, in contrast to Amitābha's western paradise, is traditionally located in the east. Unlike Amitābha, he does not assist human beings in reaching final liberation, nor does he even offer rebirth in his land. Rather, the repetition or rememberance of his name relieves various kinds of suffering, such as sickness, hunger, and fear. The ritual worship of his statue brings all things that are desired. In the cult dedicated to Bhaiṣajyaguru—popular in China and Japan, where it was often influenced by Amitābha traditions—we see a magnification of the patterns of worship that had originally coalesced around the stupa and the Buddha image. [*See* Bhaiṣajyaguru.]

In other contexts, conceptions of integrated pantheons of Buddhas were developed and exerted widespread influence. For example, in the traditions of Esoteric Buddhism a strong emphasis was placed on a primordial, central Buddha. He was taken to be the essence or source of a set of Buddhas who were positioned in the form of a cosmic *maṇḍala* ("circle") that was vividly depicted in iconography and ritual, for example, in the *tanka* paintings of Tibet. In certain Indo-Tibetan traditions the central Buddha was Vajradhara ("diamond holder") or sometimes, when the emphasis was more theistic, the Ādi ("primordial") Buddha. In other Indo-Tibetan traditions the central Buddha was Vairocana ("resplendent"), who also served as the preeminent Buddha in the Esoteric (Shingon) tradition of Japan, where he was identified with the all-important solar deity in the indigenous pantheon of *kami.* [*See* Mahāvairocana.] In both cases—the one associated with Vajradhara and the Ādi Buddha and the one associated with Vairocana—the pantheon encompassed other Buddhas (and sometimes their "families"), who were identified with subsidiary cosmic positions. These included the east, a position often occupied by Akṣobhya ("imperturbable"); the south, often occupied by Ratnasambhava ("jewel-born"); the west, often occupied by Amitābha; and the north, often occupied by Amoghasiddhi ("infallible success"). In both cases the pantheon had a macrocosmic reference to the universe as a whole and a microcosmic reference in which the Buddhas of the pantheon were homoligized with the mystic physiology of the human body. [*See also* Buddhism, Schools of, *article on* Esoteric Buddhism.]

LIVING BUDDHAS

In addition to the Buddha, *pratyekabuddhas*, previous Buddhas, the future Buddha, celestial Buddhas, and cosmic Buddhas, still another kind of Buddha was recognized by some Buddhists—what we shall call a "living Buddha." Living Buddhas are persons in this world who have, in one way or another, achieved the status of a fully enlightened and compassionate being. In some cases these living Buddhas have attained Buddhahood through various, usually Esoteric, forms of practice; in others they are incarnations of a Buddha, ordinarily a celestial Buddha, already included in the established pantheon. The presence of living Buddhas tends, of course, to diminish to a new degree the significance of Gautama Buddha (except in rare cases where it is he who reappears). However, their presence also reiterates with new force two characteristic Mahāyāna-Vajrayāna emphases: that the message of the Buddhas continues to be efficaciously available in the world and that the community still has direct access to the kind of assistance that only a Buddha can provide.

Like the notions of previous Buddhas and the Buddhas of other worlds, the concept of living Buddhas began to be elaborated in a context in which a new kind of teaching and practice was being introduced. In this case the new teaching and practice was Esoteric in character and was focused on ritual activities that promised to provide a "fast path" to Buddhahood. Thus the new kind of Buddha—the living Buddha—was both a product of the new movement and a mode of authenticating it. The analogy between the earlier development of the notion of celestial Buddhas and the later development of the notion of living Buddhas can be carried further. Just as only a few celestial Buddhas received their own individual mythology, iconography, and devotional attention, so too a limited number of living Buddhas were similarly singled out. It is not surprising that many of these especially recognized and venerated living Buddhas were figures who initiated new strands of tradition by introducing practices, revealing hidden texts, converting new peoples, and the like. A classic example of a living Buddha in the Tibetan tradition is Padmasambhava, the famous missionary from India who is credited with subduing the demons in Tibet, converting the people to the Buddhist cause, and founding the Rñiṅ-ma-pa order. [*See the biography of Padmasambhava.*] An example of the same type of figure in Japan is Kūkai, the founder of the Esoteric Shingon tradition, who has traditionally been venerated both as master and as savior. [*See the biography of Kūkai.*]

The notion of living Buddhas as incarnations of celestial Buddhas also came to the fore with the rise of Esoteric Buddhism. In this case there seems to have been an especially close connection with Buddhist conceptions of kingship and rule. In both the Hīnayāna and Mahāyāna contexts, the notion of the king as a *bodhisattva,* or future Buddha, was ancient; in the case of the rather common royal identifications with Maitreya, the distinction between the king as an incarnation of the celestial *bodhisattva* and the king as a living Buddha had been very fluid. With the rise of the Esoteric Buddhist traditions a further step was taken. Thus, after the Esoteric tradition had been firmly established in the Khmer (Cambodian) capital of Angkor, the king came to be explicitly recognized and venerated as Bhaiṣajyaguru, Master of

Medicine. Somewhat later in Tibet, the Panchen Lamas, who have traditionally had both royal and monastic functions, were identified as successive incarnations of the Buddha Amitābha.

Buddhahood

The epithets, biographies, and images of Śākyamuni and other Buddhas weigh the distinctiveness of each Buddha against his inclusion within a series or assembly of similar beings. However, as the appellative character of the term *buddha* suggests, at the level of Buddhahood each tradition has affirmed the ultimate identity of all those they have recognized as Buddhas. Even the Theravādins, who have consistently given pride of place to Gautama, have acknowledged this final level at which differentiations are not relevant. The same is true for those movements that focus primary attention on Amitābha or Mahāvairocana. The consensus of Buddhists in this respect is voiced by the *Milindapañha* (The Questions of King Milinda), a Hīnayāna text dating from the beginning of the common era: "There is no distinction in form, morality, concentration, wisdom, freedom...among all the Buddhas because all Buddhas are the same in respect to their nature" (London, 1880, p. 285).

This initial consensus concerning the ultimate identity of all Buddhas notwithstanding, the actual delineation of Buddhahood has varied significantly from one Buddhist tradition to another. This third level of meaning of the term *buddha* has always been discussed in connection with questions concerning the nature and analysis of reality. Early Buddhists believed that a Buddha awoke to and displayed the causal process (*pratītya-samutpāda,* co-dependent origination) that perpetuates this world, allowing himself and others to use those processes to end further rebirth. [*See* Pratītya-samutpāda.] The early Mahāyāna, especially in the Prajñāpāramitā literature, saw Buddhahood as awakening to the absence of self-nature in all things *(śūnyatā)* and proclaimed this absence as the ultimate reality *(tathatā)*. [*See* Śūnyam and Śūnyatā *and* Tathatā.] Later Mahāyāna schools, such as the Yogācārins, held a more idealistic worldview; for them Buddhahood was the recovery of an originally pure and undefiled mind. The Hua-yen (Jpn., Kegon) school, an East Asian tradition based on the *Avataṃsaka Sūtra,* posited the infinite mutual interaction of all things and developed a striking conception of a universal, cosmic Buddha who is allpervasive. In such contexts Buddhahood itself became an alternative way of describing reality. [*See* Yogācāra *and* Hua-yen.]

Between the consensus about the identity of all Buddhas and the diversity of interpretations, there are at least two different languages in which Buddhahood has traditionally been conceived and described. The first is the identification of Buddhahood in terms of the special characteristics associated with a Buddha. The second is the discussion of the Buddha bodies that make up Buddhahood. These two clusters of concepts allow us to see patterns of continuity in the midst of the very different ways in which Buddhahood has been understood.

Buddhist scholasticism developed subtle catalogs of the unique powers and qualities of a Buddha, culminating in lists of *āveṇika dharmas* (special characteristics). These special characteristics vary in number from 6 to 140, depending on the text and context. What interests us here is not the multitude of qualities and powers that are mentioned but, rather, the fact that these qualities and powers are often grouped under four major headings. These four headings are conduct and realization, which apply to the attainment of Buddhahood, and wisdom and activity, which apply to the expression of Buddhahood.

Throughout Buddhist history these four dimensions of Buddhahood have been interpreted in different ways. For example, Hīnayānists have tended to emphasize motivated conduct as a means to the realization of Buddhahood, whereas Mahāyānists and Vajrayānists have tended to stress that Buddhahood (often in the form of Buddha nature) is in important respects a necessary prerequisite for such conduct. [*See* Buddhist Ethics.] Similarly, Hīnayānists have often recognized a certain distance between the attainment of wisdom and a commitment to compassionate activity, whereas in the Mahāyāna and Vajrayāna traditions the stress has been placed on the inseparable fusion of wisdom on the one hand and the expression of compassion on the other. [*See* Prajñā, Karuṇā, *and* Upāya.] These differences notwithstanding, the four basic dimensions are present in virtually all Buddhist conceptions of Buddhahood.

When we turn to the way Buddhahood has been expressed through the language of Buddha bodies, we discern the same sort of continuity in the midst of difference. In the early Buddhist literature (e.g., *Dīgha Nikāya,* vol. 3, p. 84) the Buddha is described as having a body "born of *dharma,*" that is, a *dharmakāya.* In this early period, and in the subsequent Theravāda development, the notion that Gautama possessed a *dharmakāya* seems to have served primarily as a metaphor that affirmed a continuity between the personal realizations that he had achieved and truth or reality itself. In some later Hināyāna traditions such as the Sarvāstivāda, and in the Mahāyāna, the notion of *dharmakāya* took on a stronger meaning. It served as a primary means through which an increasingly transcendent vision of Buddhahood could subsume the inescapable fact of Gautama's death. According to such texts as the *Saddharmapuṇḍarīka,* the *dharmakāya* is the true meaning of Buddhahood; Buddhas such as Gautama who appear, teach, and die among human beings are mere manifestations. In this early Mahāyāna context, however, the correlated notions of Buddhahood and *dharmakāya* are still conditioned by their close association with philosophical conceptions such as *śūnyatā* ("emptiness") and *tathatā* ("suchness").

The *dharmakāya* is given a more ontological cast in other Mahāyāna and Vajrayāna traditions. In these cases, *dharmakāya* denotes a "ground" or "source" that is the reality that gives rise to all other realities; this provides the basis for a new understanding of the whole range of Buddha bodies. Buddhahood comes to be explicated in terms of a theory of three bodies. The *trikāya* ("three bodies") are the *dharmakāya,* the primal body that is the source of the other two; the emanated *saṃbhogakāya* ("enjoyment body"), a glorious body seen in visions in which Buddhas of other worlds become manifest to devotees in this world; and the "magical" and ephemeral *nirmāṇakāya,* the physical body in which Gautama, for example, appeared among his disciples.

In some Mahāyāna and Vajrayāna contexts, this more ontological conception of the Buddhahood and *dharmakāya* was also connected with the important soteriological notion of a Buddha nature, or *tathāgata-garbha* (*tathāgata* is an epithet for a Buddha, *garbha* means "womb"), which is the source and cause of enlightenment as well as its fruit. In these traditions, Buddha nature, or *tathāgata-garbha,* is taken to be the *dharmakāya* covered with defilements. Enlightenment, and therefore Buddhahood, is the recovery of this pure, original state of being that is identical with ultimate reality itself. In other Mahāyāna and Vajrayāna contexts, even the dichotomy between purity and defilement is transcended at the level of Buddhahood. [*See Tathāgata-garbha.*]

Conclusion

In the course of our discussion of *buddha* as an appellative term we have distinguished three basic levels of meaning—those associated with Gautama Buddha, with other Buddhas, and with Buddhahood as such. However, it is important to note that Buddhist usage has always held the three levels of meaning closely together, with the result that each level has had a continuing influence on the others. Thus, even though a distinction between the different denotations of *buddha* is helpful for purposes of interpretation and understanding, it cannot be drawn too sharply.

In fact, these three meanings represent three different modes of reference that, according to some Indian theories of denotation, are common to all names. The word *cow,* for example, refers to individual cows ("a cow"), the aggregation of cows, and the quality of "cowness" common to all cows. There are obvious parallels to the uses of *buddha.* It might be helpful for those unfamiliar with such theories to think of *buddha* in terms of set theory: individual Buddhas are members of subsets of the set of Buddhahood. Just as mathematical sets exist without members, so Buddhahood exists, according to the affirmation of Buddhists, even when it is not embodied by individual Buddhas.

[*For further discussion of the nature of Buddhas and Buddhahood see* Celestial Buddhas and Bodhisattvas *and* Tathāgata. *The religious career culminating in Buddhahood is treated in* Bodhisattva Path. *"Enlightenment" is discussed in* Buddhist Philosophy *and* Nirvāṇa.]

BIBLIOGRAPHY

Scholarship that is available in European languages generally treats the different levels of meaning of the appellative *buddha* in isolation. The interrelations among the different levels of meaning still remain largely unexplored.

Two books by Edward J. Thomas, if read in conjunction, can serve as a suitable introduction to the subject. *The Life of Buddha as Legend and History* (1927; 3d rev. ed., London, 1949) remains the standard work on the biography of the Buddha in English. *The History of Buddhist Thought* (1933; 2d ed., New York, 1951) surveys the development of ideas of other Buddhas and Buddhahood against the backdrop of the Indian Buddhist tradition. Thomas, however, does not include any of the developments in Tibet or East Asia, and his work has a definite bias in favor of the Pali tradition. A useful supplement for Tibet is David L. Snellgrove's *Buddhist Himālaya* (Oxford, 1957), which provides an introduction to the Vajrayāna interpretations. East Asian innovations were largely in connection with the meaning of Buddhahood. They may be approached through Junjirō Takakusu's *The Essentials of Buddhist Philosophy,* edited by Wing-Tsit Chan and Charles A. Moore (Honolulu, 1947), although, as the title suggests, Takakusu is not primarily concerned with Buddhological patterns as such.

Heinz Bechert's important article "The Date of the Buddha Reconsidered," *Indologica Taurinensia* 10 (1982): 29–36, provides helpful summaries of the arguments favoring the long and short chronologies for calculating the date of the Buddha, although his conclusion in favor of the short chronology is by no means definitive. The cultural context of the historical Buddha is outlined by Padmanabh S. Jaini in his "*Śramaṇas:* Their Conflict with Brāhmaṇical Society," in *Chapters in Indian Civilization,* rev. ed., edited by Joseph W. Elder (Dubuque, 1970) vol. 1, pp. 39–81. This article should be read together with J. A. B. van Buitenen's "Vedic and Upaniṣadic Bases of Indian Civilization," which immediately preceeds it in the same volume (pp. 1–38).

A helpful starting point for the study of the Buddha biography is Frank E. Reynolds's "The Many Lives of Buddha: A Study of Sacred Biography and Theravada Tradition" in *The Biographical Process,* edited by Reynolds and Donald Capps ("Religion and Reason Series," vol. 11, The Hague, 1976). It provides a survey of the patterns of interpretation that have developed in connection with the Buddha biography in Western scholarship, as well as an overview of the relevant Hīnayāna and later Theravāda texts.

The most important recent research on the biographies of the Buddha is written in French. An argument for successive stages in the development of the Buddha biography is found in Étienne Lamotte's *Histoire du bouddhisme indien* (Louvain, 1958), pp. 707–759, in which Lamotte responds to Erich Frauwallner's thesis that there was a very early, complete biography. Frauwallner presented this thesis in *The Earliest Vinaya and the Beginnings of Buddhist Literature* (Rome, 1956). An indispensable aid to serious work on the Buddha biography is André Bareau's *Recherches sur la biographie du Buddha dans les Sūtrapitaka et les Vinayapiṭaka anciens,* 2 vols. (Paris; 1963–1971). In these volumes Bareau documents and improves upon Lamotte's arguments in favor of a gradual development of the biographical cycles.

Alfred Foucher presents a composite biography of the Buddha from the beginning of the common era in *The Life of the Buddha according to the Ancient Texts and Monuments of India,* abridged translation by Simone B. Boas (Middletown, Conn., 1963). Foucher also includes an introduction that is of particular importance because it highlights the significance of early Buddhist pilgrimages in the development of the biographical tradition.

Several of the autonomous biographies, as well as some later biographies from Tibet, China, and Southeast Asia, have been translated into European languages. The most readable is Aśvaghoṣa's *Buddhacarita, or, Acts of the Buddha,* 2 vols. in 1, edited and translated by Edward H. Johnston (Calcutta, 1935–1936; 2d ed., New Delhi, 1972). This translation should be supplemented by Samuel Beal's translation of the Chinese version of the same text, *The Fo-Sho-hing-tsan-king: A Life of Buddha by Asvaghosha Bodhisattva* (Oxford, 1883; reprint, Delhi, 1966).

The role of the stupa as a preeminent Buddha symbol in Buddhist thought and practice is introduced in the collection *The Stūpa: Its Religious, Historical and Architectural Significance,* edited by Anna Libera Dallapiccola in collaboration with Stephanie Zingel-Ave Lallemant (Wiesbaden, 1980). Gustav Roth's article in this collection, "Symbolism of the Buddhist Stupa," is especially significant for its investigation of the symbolic interpretation of the stupa in Buddhist literature. A convenient and beautiful survey and appraisal of the visual representations of the Buddha throughout the Buddhist world is *The Image of the Buddha,* edited by David L. Snellgrove (London, 1978).

Modern research on "other Buddhas" is much less extensive than the research focused on the biographies and symbols associated with Gautama. Those interested in short, well-done introductions to Akṣobhya, Amitābha (Amita), and Bhaiṣajyaguru should consult the *Encyclopaedia of Buddhism,* edited by G. P. Malalasekera (Colombo, 1968). Vairocana is discussed by Ryūjun Tajima in his *Étude sur le Mahāvairocana sūtra (Dainichikyō),* (Paris, 1936). Material on "living Buddhas" can be gleaned from various sections of Giuseppe Tucci's *The Religions of Tibet,* translated from the Italian and German by Geoffrey Samuel (Berkeley, 1980).

A work of monumental importance for the study of the concept of the Buddha and of Buddhism in general, is Paul Mus's *Barabaḍur,* 2 vols. (1935; reprint, New York, 1978). It is perhaps the only academic work that exploits the full potential of the appellative character of the term *buddha.* It contains seminal discussions of Buddhology in early, Hīnayāna, and Mahāyāna traditions; of the symbolism of the stupa and the relics; of celestial and cosmic Buddhas; and of the origin of Pure Land symbolism and thought. Unfortunately, this ponderously long work has not been translated, and the French is extremely difficult.

Readers seeking more specialized references (e.g., available translations of biographical texts or studies of particular developments) should consult the annotated entries in Frank E. Reynolds's *Guide to Buddhist Religion* (Boston, 1981), especially section 8, "Ideal Beings, Hagiography and Biography," and section 9, "Mythology (including Sacred History), Cosmology and Basic Symbols."

3 BUDDHISM IN INDIA

Luis O. Gómez

A contemporary visitor to the South Asian subcontinent would find Buddhism flourishing only outside the mainland, on the island of Sri Lanka. This visitor would meet small pockets of Buddhists in Bengal and in the Himalayan regions, especially in Ladakh and Nepal, and as the dominant group in Bhutan and Sikkim. Most of the latter Buddhists belong to the Mahāyāna and Vajrayāna forms of Buddhism and represent denominations and orders of Tibetan and Nepalese origin. Buddhists may also be found in the subcontinent among Tibetan refugees (mostly in Himachal Pradesh and Bangalore), among the Ambedkar Buddhists of Maharashtra, and among pilgrims and missionaries flocking to the sacred sites of India. The diversity of manifestations is not new, but the specific forms are not representative of what Indian Buddhism was in the past.

Origins

Approximately twenty-five hundred years ago the founder of the Buddhist religion was born into the Śākya tribe in a small aristocratic republic in the Himalayan foothills, in what is today the kingdom of Nepal. In his youth he descended to the Ganges River valley in search of spiritual realization. After several years of study at the feet of spiritual masters he underwent a profound religious experience that changed his life; he became a teacher himself, and lived for the rest of his adult life as a mendicant peripatetic. His worldview and personal preoccupations were shaped in the cultural milieu of India of the sixth century BCE; the religious communities that trace their origin to him developed their most distinctive doctrines and practices in Indian soil.

SOURCES AND SETTING

Unfortunately, we do not possess reliable sources for most of the history of Buddhism in its homeland; in particular, we have precious little to rely on for its early history. Textual sources are late, dating at the very least five hundred years after the death of the Buddha. The archaeological evidence, abundant as it is, is limited in the information it can give us. A few facts are nevertheless well established. The roots of Indian Buddhism are to be found in the "shramanic" movement of the sixth century BCE, which owes the name to its model of religious perfection, the *śramaṇa,* or wandering ascetic. The *śramaṇa*s set religious goals that stood outside, and in direct opposition to, the religious and social order of the *brāhmaṇa*s (brahmans), who represented the Indo-Aryan establishment. Most of the values that would become characteristic of Indian, and therefore Hindu, religion in general were shaped by the interaction of these two groups, especially by a process of assimilation that transformed the Brahmanic order into Hindu culture. [*See* Vedism and Brahmanism.]

The appearance of two major shramanic religions, Buddhism and Jainism, marked the end of the Vedic-Brahmanic period and the beginning of an era of cross-fertilization between diverse strata of Indian culture. This new age, sometimes called the Indic period, was characterized by the dominant role of "heterodox" or non-Hindu religious systems, the flourishing of their ascetic and monastic orders, and the use of the vernaculars in preference to Sanskrit.

We can surmise that this new age was a time of social upheaval and political instability. The use of iron had changed radically the character of warfare and the nature of farming. The jungle was cleared, farmland could support a court bureaucracy, and palaces and city walls could be built. A surplus economy was created that made possible large state societies, with concentrated populations and resources, and consequently with heightened political ambition.

The Buddha must have been touched directly by these changes: shortly before his death the republic of the Śākyas was sacked by the powerful kingdom of Kośala, which in turn would shortly thereafter fall under the power of Magadha. At the time of the Buddha sixteen independent states existed in North Central India, a century later only one empire would rule in the region, and in another hundred years this empire, Magadha, would control all of northern India and most of the South. The unity of the empire was won at a price: political and social systems based on family or tribal order crumbled; the old gods lost their power.

As the old order crumbled, the brahmans claimed special privileges that other groups were not always willing to concede. Those who would not accept their leadership sought spiritual and moral guidance among the *śramaṇa*s. Although recent research has shown that the interaction between these two groups was more complex than we had previously imagined, it is still accepted that the shramanic movement represented some of the groups displaced by the economic and political changes of the day, and by the expansion of Brahmanic power. The *śramaṇas,* therefore, were rebels of sorts. They challenged the values of lay life in general, but especially the caste system as it existed at the time. Thus, what appeared as a lifestyle designed to lead to religious realization may have been at the same time the expression of social protest, or at least of social malaise.

The shramanic movement was fragmented: among the shramanic groups, Buddhism's main rival was Jainism, representing an ancient teaching whose origin dated to at least one or two generations before the Buddha. A community of mendicants reformed by Vardhamāṇa Mahāvīra (d. around 468 BCE) shortly before the beginning of Buddha's career, Jainism represented the extremes of world denial and asceticism that Buddhism sought to moderate with its doctrine of the Middle Way. Buddhists also criticized in Jainism what they saw as a mechanistic conception of moral responsibility and liberation. Another school criticized by early Buddhists was that of Makkhali Gosāla, founder of the Ājīvikas, who also taught an extreme form of asce-

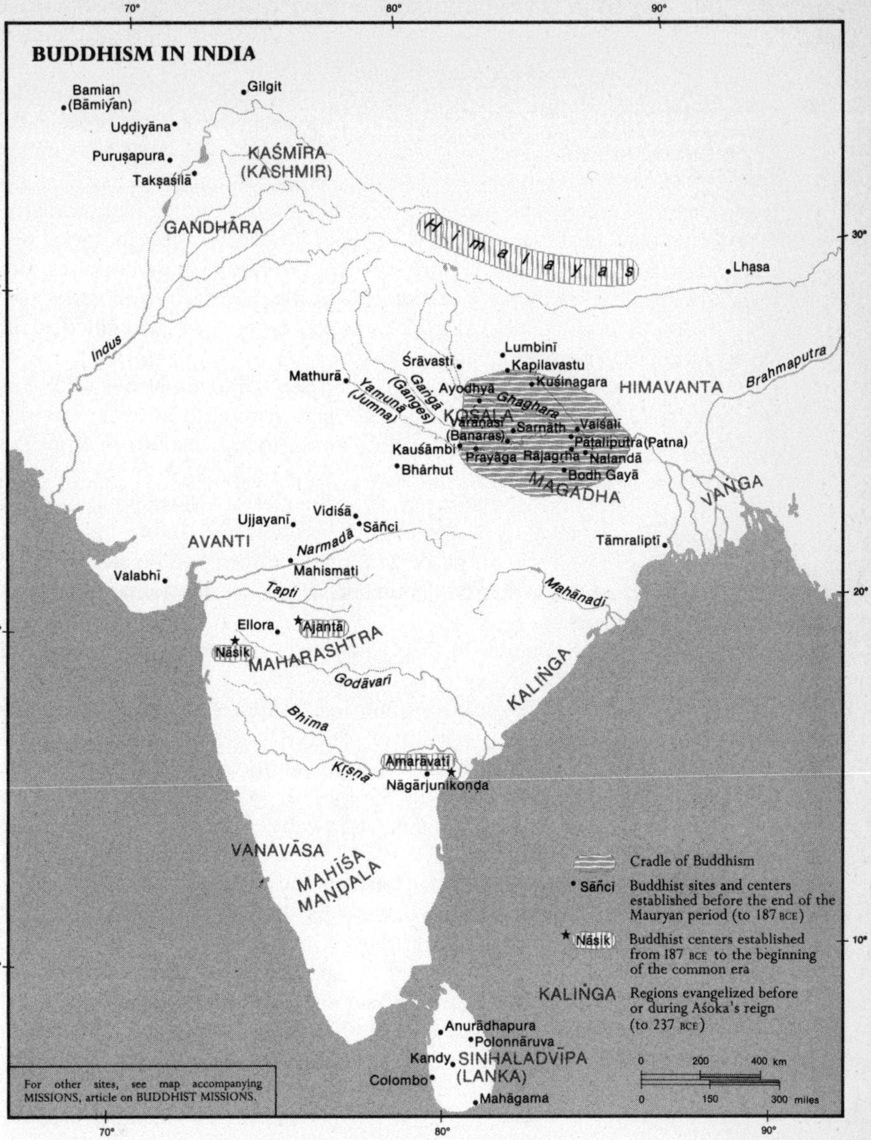

ticism that was based, strangely, on a fatalistic doctrine. [*See* Jainism; Mahāvīra; Ājīvikas; *and the biography of Gośāla.*]

We have to understand the shramanic movements as independent systems and not as simple derivations or reforms of Brahmanic doctrine and practice. One can find, nevertheless, certain elements common to all the movements of the age: the *śramaṇa*s, called "wanderers" (*parivrājaka*s), like the forest dwellers of Brahmanism, retired from society. Some sought an enstatic experience; some believed that particular forms of conduct led to purity and liberation from suffering; others sought power through knowledge (ritual or magical) or insight (contemplative or gnostic); but most systems contained elements of all of these tendencies.

Among the religious values formed during the earlier part of the Indic age, that is, during the shramanic period, we must include, above all, the concept of the cycle and bondage of rebirth *(saṃsāra)* and the belief in the possibility of liberation *(mokṣa)* from the cycle through ascetic discipline, world renunciation, and a moral or ritual code that gave a prominent place to abstaining from doing harm to living beings *(ahiṃsā)*. This ideal, like the quest for altered states of consciousness, was not always separable from ancient notions of ritual purity and spiritual power. But among the shramanic movements it sometimes took the form of a moral virtue. Then it appeared as opposition to organized violence—political, as embodied in war, and religious, as expressed in animal sacrifice.

The primary evil force was no longer envisioned as a spiritual personality, but as an impersonal moral law of cause and effect *(karman)* whereby human actions created a state of bondage and suffering. In their quest for a state of rest from the activities of *karman,* whether the goal was defined as enstasy or knowledge, the new religious specialists practiced a variety of techniques of self-cultivation usually known as *yoga*s. The sustained practice of this discipline was known as a "path" *(mārga),* and the goal was a state of peace and freedom from passion and suffering called *nirvāṇa*. [*See* Karman, *article on* Hindu and Jain Concepts; Mokṣa; Yoga; Saṃsāra; Ahiṃsā; *and* Saṃnyāsa.]

As a shramanic religion, Buddhism displayed similar traits but gave to each of these its unique imprint. The conception of rebirth and its evils were not questioned, but suffering was universalized: all human conditions lead to suffering, suffering has a cause, and that cause is craving, or "thirst" *(tṛṣṇā)*. To achieve liberation from the cycle of rebirth one must follow the spiritual discipline prescribed by the Buddha, summarized in the Eightfold Path. The follower of Buddhism was expected to renounce the lay life and become a wandering ascetic, an ideal epitomized by the spiritual career of the founder.

Most shramanic groups made provisions for their lay supporters, essentially members of the community who by circumstance or choice could not follow the wanderer's path. Buddhist laymen could begin moving in the right direction—with the hope of being able to renounce the world in a future birth—by "taking refuge" *(śaraṇa-gamana),* that is, by making a confession of faith in the Buddha, his teachings, and his monastic order, and by adopting five fundamental moral precepts *(pañcaśīla):* not to deprive a living thing of life, not to take what is not given to you, not to engage in illicit sexual conduct, not to lie, and not to take intoxicating drinks.

THE THREE JEWELS

Perhaps all we can say with certainty about the roots of Buddhist doctrine and doctrinal continuity in Buddhism is that the figure of the Buddha and his experience dominate most of Buddhist teachings. If we wish to understand Buddhism as a doctrinal system, we can look at its oral and written ideology—including its scriptures—as the effort of diverse Buddhist communities to explore and define the general issues raised by the Buddha's career. These include questions such as the following:

Does the Buddha "exist" after liberation? Is the experience of awakening ineffable? Which of the two experiences, awakening or liberation, is the fundamental one?

On the other hand, if we wish to understand Buddhism as a religion rather than as a system of doctrines, its focus or fulcrum must be found in the religious communities and their objects of veneration. The early community was represented primarily by the gathering of mendicants or monks called the *saṃgha,* held together by ascetic or monastic codes *(prātimokṣa)* attributed to the Buddha himself, and by the objects of worship represented by (1) the founder himself as the "Awakened One" *(buddha);* (2) his exemplary and holy life, his teachings and his experience *(dharma);* and (3) the community *(saṃgha)* itself, sustained by the memory of his personality and teaching. These objects of veneration are known as the "Three Treasures" *(triratna),* and the believer's trust in these ideals is expressed, doctrinally and ritually, in the "Three Refuges" (to rely on the Buddha, the Dharma, and the Sangha). To this day, this formula serves at once as an indication of the meaning of monastic ordination and a lay confession of faith.

Buddha. No Western scholar today would claim to know the exact details of the founder's biography, or for that matter the exact content of his teachings. The above is merely an educated guess based on formulations from a time removed by several centuries from their origins. Scholars agree, nevertheless, on the historicity of the founder. That is to say, though they may doubt the accuracy of the information transmitted in traditional "biographies" (beginning with his personal name, Siddhārtha Gautama) or in legends about the Buddha's sermons, Western scholars accept the existence of an influential religious figure, called Śākyamuni ("the sage of the Śākya tribe") by his disciples, who at some point in the sixth century BCE founded in the Ganges River valley the community of wandering mendicants that would eventually grow into the world religion we now call Buddhism.

Scholars generally tend to accept the years 563 to 483 BCE as the least problematic, if not the most plausible, dating for the life of Gautama Buddha. (Other dating systems exist, however, that place his life as much as a century later.) Assuming, moreover, that the legend is reliable in some of its details, we can say that the history of the religion begins when Śākyamuni was thirty-five (therefore, in about 528), with his first sermon at Sārnāth (northeast of the city of Vārāṇasī).

Before and after his enlightenment, Śākyamuni followed the typical career of a wanderer. At twenty-nine he abandoned the household and sought a spiritual guide. An early legend claims that Śākyamuni actually studied under two teachers of the age, Āḷāra Kālāma and Udraka Rāmaputra. From such teachers the young ascetic learned techniques of meditation that he later rejected, but the imprints of which remain in Buddhist theories of meditation. Dissatisfied with what he had learned, he tried the life of the hermit. Finally, after six years of struggle, he "awakened" under a pipal tree *(Ficus religiosa)* near the border town of Uruvilvā (Bodh Gayā).

His first sermon was followed by forty-five years of wandering through the Ganges River valley, spreading his teachings. Although tradition preserves many narratives of isolated episodes of this half century of teaching, no one has been able to piece together a convincing account of this period. For the tradition this was also a time for the performance of great miracles, and historical accuracy was never an important consideration.

At the age of eighty (c. 483), Siddhārtha Gautama, the Buddha Śākyamuni, died near the city of Kuśināgara. To his immediate disciples perhaps this fading away of the Master confirmed his teachings on impermanence, but the Buddha's death would soon come to be regarded as a symbol of his perfect peace and renunciation: with death he had reached his *parinirvāṇa,* that point in his career after which he would be reborn no more. His ashes, encased in a reliquary buried in a cairn, came to stand for the highest achievement of an awakened being, confirming his status as the one who had attained to truth, the Tathāgata—an epithet that would come to denote ultimate truth itself. [*See* Buddha *and* Tathāgata.]

Dharma. The first preaching, known as the "First Turning of the Wheel of Dharma" (or, in the West, the "Sermon at Banaras" or the "Deer Park Sermon"), symbolizes the appearance in history of the Buddhist teaching, whereas Śākyamuni's enlightenment experience, or "Great Awakening" *(mahābodhi),* which occurred in the same year, represents the human experience around which the religion would develop its practices and ideals. This was the experience whereby Śākyamuni became an "Awakened One" *(buddha).* His disciples came to believe that all aspects of Buddhist doctrine and practice flow from this experience of awakening *(bodhi)* and from the resultant state of freedom from passion, suffering, and rebirth called *nirvāṇa.* The teachings found in the Buddha's sermons can be interpreted as definitions of these two experiences, the spiritual practices that lead to or flow from them, and the institutions that arose inspired by the experience and the human beings who laid claim to it. [*See* Nirvāṇa.]

However, it is difficult, if not impossible, to surmise which, if any, among the many doctrines attributed by tradition to the founder are veritably his. Different Buddhists, even when they can agree on the words, will interpret the message differently. Although most would find the nucleus of Śākyamuni's teachings in the "First Sermon," especially in the doctrine of the Four Noble Truths allegedly preached therein, a host of other doctrinal statements compete for the central position throughout the history of Buddhism in India and beyond. Moreover, a number of texts that can claim great antiquity are not only silent about the Four Noble Truths but actually do not seem to presuppose them in any way. The same can be said about other doctrines that would become central to the development of Buddhist doctrinal speculation, for instance, the principle of conditioned arising *(pratītya-samutpāda)* and the analysis of the human personality into its constituent parts (*skandha*s, etc.).

It is difficult to determine to what extent early Buddhism had an accompanying metaphysics. Some of the earliest strata of Buddhist literature suggest that the early community may have emphasized the joys of renunciation and the peace of abstention from conflict—political, social, and religious—more than a philosophical doctrine of liberation. Such are the ascetic ideals of one of the earliest texts of the tradition, the *Aṭṭhakavagga (Suttanipāta).* The mendicant abstains from participating in the religious and metaphysical debates of brahmans, *śramaṇa*s, and sages. He is detached from all views, for

> Purity is not [attained] by views, or learning,
> by knowledge, or by moral rules, and rites.
> Nor is it [attained] by the absence of views,
> learning, knowledge, rules or rites.

Abandoning all these, not grasping at them,
he is at peace; not relying, he would not
hanker for becoming. (*Suttanipāta* 839)

There is in this text a rejection of doctrine, rule, and rite that is a critique of the exaggerated claims of those who believed they could become pure and free through ritual, knowledge, or religious status. The lonely ascetic seeks not to become one thing or the other and avoids doctrinal disputes.

If such statements represent some of the earliest moments in the development of the doctrine, then the next stage must have brought a growing awareness of the need for ritual and creed if the community was to survive. This awareness would have been followed in a short time by the formation of a metaphysic, a theory of liberation, and a conscious system of meditation. In the next strata of early Buddhist literature these themes are only surpassed in importance by discussions of ascetic morality. The ascetic ideals of the early community were then expanded and defined by doctrine—as confession of faith, as ideology, and as a plan for religious and moral practice. The earliest formulations of this type are perhaps those of the Eightfold Path, with its triple division into wisdom, moral practice, and mental concentration. The theoretical or metaphysical underpinnings are contained in the Four Noble Truths and in the Three Marks (impermanence, sorrow, and no-self), both traditionally regarded as the subject matter of the Buddha's first sermons. [*See* Four Noble Truths; Eightfold Path; Karman, *article on* Buddhist Concepts; Soul, *article on* Buddhist Concepts; *and* Dharma, *article on* Buddhist Dharma and Dharmas.]

Saṃgha. With the first sermon the Buddha began a ministry that would last forty-five years. During this period he established a religious order—perhaps only a mendicant order in its beginnings—and trained a number of distinguished disciples who would carry on the teaching after the founder's death. Tradition preserves the names of many of his disciples and immediate heirs to his teaching: Kauṇḍinya, the first convert to be admitted into the Buddha's religious order *(saṃgha);* Yasa, the first householder to receive full lay initiation with the Three Refuges; Śāriputra, the master of wisdom; Maudgalyāyana, the great thaumaturge; Upāli, the expert in the monastic code; Ānanda, the Buddha's cousin and beloved disciple; Mahāprajāpati, the first woman admitted into the monastic order; and Mahākāśyapa, who undertook to preserve the Buddha's teaching and organized the First Council. The Buddha's disciples represented a wide spectrum of social classes. Yasa was the son of a wealthy gild master; Upāli, a humble barber; Śāriputra, a brahman; Ānanda, a member of the nobility *(kṣatriya).* Among the early followers we find not only world renouncers but believers from a variety of walks of life; King Bimbisāra, the wealthy banker Anāthapiṇḍika, the respectable housewife Viśākhā, and the courtesan Amrapālī, for instance.

Although the Buddhist monastic community was an integral part of Indian society, serving as an instrument of legitimation and cohesion, it also served on occasions as a critic of society. Especially in its early development, and in particular during the period of the wandering mendicants, the *saṃgha* was a nonconformist subgroup. The variety of social classes represented by the roster of early disciples in part reflects the fluid state of Indian society at the time; but it also reflects the Buddha's open opposition to the caste system as it existed then. Although the challenge was religious and political as well as social, the Buddha's critique of Brahmanism made his order of mendicants an alternative community, where those who did not fit in the new social order could find a sense of belonging, acceptance, and achievement. Buddhist reforms and institutions would waver in their function as rebels and supporters of social order until Buddhism ultimately became absorbed into Hinduism during the centuries following the first millennium of the common era.

We can surmise that the earliest community did not have a fixed abode. During the dry season the Buddhist *śramaṇa*s would sleep in the open and wander from village to village "begging" for their sustenance—hence their title *bhikṣu,* "mendicant" (fem., *bhikṣuṇī*). They were persons who had set forth *(pravrajyā)* from the household to lead the life of the wanderer *(parivrājaka).* Only during the rainy season would they gather in certain spots in the forest or in special groves provided by lay supporters. There they would build temporary huts that would be dismantled at the end of the rainy season, when they would set out again in their constant wandering to spread the Buddha's Dharma.

The main ideals of the mendicant life of the "wanderers" is expressed in a passage that is presented as the creed or code (the Prātimokṣa) recited by the followers of the "former Buddha" Vipaśyin when they interrupted the wandering to meet and renew their common ideals:

> Enduring patience is the highest austerity,
> *nirvāṇa* is the highest condition—say the Buddhas.
> For he who injures another is not a true renouncer,
> He who causes harm to others is not a true ascetic.
> Not to do any evil, to practice the good,
> to purify one's own mind:
> This is the teaching of the Buddhas.
>
> Not to speak against others, not to harm others,
> and restraint according to the rule *(prātimokṣa),*
> Moderation in eating, secluded dwelling,
> and the practice of mental cultivation *(adhicitta):*
> This is the teaching of the Buddhas.
>
> *(Mahāpadāna Suttanta)*

These verses outline important aspects of the early teaching: the centrality of *ahiṃsā,* the two aspects of morality—abstention and cultivation—and the practice of meditation, all in the context of a community of ascetics for whom a life of solitude, poverty, and moderation was more important than the development of subtle metaphysics. [*For a discussion of ascetic practices, see* Soteriology, *article on* Buddhist Soteriology.]

Probably—and the earliest scriptures suggest this—the first aspect of Buddhist teachings to be systematized was the rule, first as a confession of faith for dispersed communities of mendicants, soon as a monastic rule for sedentary ascetics. Also at an early stage, the community sought to systematize its traditions of meditation, some of which must have been pre-Buddhistic (the Buddha himself having learned some of these from his teachers). Thus, Buddhist techniques of meditation represent a continuation of earlier processes of *yoga,* though we cannot be certain as to the exact connection, or the exact content of the early practices.

The first of these developments brought the community closer together by establishing a common ritual, the recitation of the rule *(prātimokṣa)* at a meeting held on the full and new moon and the quarter moons *(uposatha).* The second development confirmed an important but divisive trait of the early community: the primary source of authority remained with the individual monk and his experience in solitude. Thus, competing systems of meditation and doctrine probably developed more rapidly than differences in the code. [*See* Saṃgha, *especially the overview article.*]

The Cenobium

As India moved into an age of imperial unity under the Maurya (322–185) and Śuṅga dynasties (185–73), the Buddhist community reached its point of greatest unity. Although the *saṃgha* split into schools or sects perhaps as early as the fourth century BCE, differences among Buddhists were relatively minor. Transformed into a monastic brotherhood, Buddhism served a society that shared common values and customs. Unity, however, was shortlived, and Buddhism, like India, would have to adapt rapidly to new circumstances as the first invasions from Central Asia would put an end to the Śuṅga dynasty in 175. Until then, however, during the approximately three hundred years from the death of the founder to the beginning of the age of foreign invasions, Buddhist monks and laymen began the process of systematization that defined the common ground of Indian Buddhism in practice, scripture, and doctrine.

The primary element of continuity became the Prātimokṣa, the rules for the maintenance of the community and the liturgical recitation thereof; differences in this regard would be more serious than differences of doctrine. Thus the Second Council, which is supposed to have caused the most serious split in the history of the community, is said to have been called to resolve differences in the interpretation and formulation of minor details in the monastic regulations. In order to justify and clarify the rules that held the community together a detailed commentary of the Prātimokṣa rules had to be developed. The commentary, attributed to the Buddha himself, eventually grew into the Vinaya, an extensive section of the canon.

But the full development of the monastic code presupposes a sedentary *saṃgha.* We can surmise that not long after the Buddha's death the retreat for the rainy season began to extend into the dry season, perhaps at the invitation of the lay community, perhaps owing to dwindling popular support for the mendicant wanderers. Soon the temporary huts were replaced by more or less permanent structures built of wood, and the community of wanderers became a cenobium. The stone and gravel foundation of one of the earliest monasteries remains in the vicinity of Rājagṛha (Bihar). These are the ruins of the famous "Jivaka's Mango Grove" (Jivakāmravaṇa) Monastery, built on a plot of land donated to the order at the time of the Buddha. In its early history it may have been used only during the rainy season, but it already shows the basic structure of the earliest monasteries: living quarters for the monks and a large assembly hall (perhaps for the celebration of the Uposatha).

As the community settled down, rules and rituals for regulating monastic life became a necessity. At least some of the items in the *Prātimokṣa* section of the Vinaya and some of the procedural rules discussed in the *Karmavācanā* may go back to the time of the Buddha. The rule and the procedures for governing the *Saṃgha* are clearly based on republican models, like the constitution of the Licchavis of Vaiśālī, which is praised in the canonical texts. If this admiration goes back to the founder, then we can say that the Buddha ordered his community of wandering mendicants on the political model provided by the disappearing republics of North India. Such a rule would encourage order and harmony on the one hand, and peaceful disagreement and individual effort on the other. It provided for mutual care and concern in matters of morals, but lacked a provision for a central authority in political or doctrinal matters. [*See* Vinaya *and* Monasticism, *article on* Buddhist Monasticism.]

THE COMMON DOCTRINAL GROUND

The Buddha realized the true nature of things, their "suchness" *(tathatā),* and therefore is one of those rare beings called *tathāgata*s. Yet, whether there is a *tathāgata* to preach it or not, the Dharma is always present, because it is the nature of all things *(dharmatā).* Four terms summarize this truth known by the *tathāgata*s: impermanence, sorrow, no-self, *nirvāṇa.* The first implies the second, for attachment to what must change brings sorrow. Our incapacity to control change, however, reveals the reality of no-self—nothing is "I" or "mine." The experience of no-self, on the other hand, is liberating; it releases one from craving and the causes of sorrow; it leads to peace, *nirvāṇa.*

These principles are summarized also in a doctrine recognized by all schools, that of the Four Noble Truths: sorrow, its cause, its cessation, and the path leading to cessation. Buddhist tradition, therefore, will spend much of its energy in understanding the causes of suffering and the means to put an end to it, or, in doctrinal shorthand, "arising" and "cessation." Since cessation is in fact the obverse of arising, a proper understanding of arising, or causation, becomes central to Buddhist speculation in India. The most important doctrine for this aspect of the religion is the principle of dependent arising *(pratītya-samutpāda):* everything we regard as "the self" is conditioned or compounded; everything conditioned depends on causes and conditions; by understanding the causes of our idea of the self and of the sorrow that this idea brings to us we can become free of suffering. [*See* Pratītya-samutpāda.] This doctrine is summarized in a stanza that has become one of the best known Buddhist creeds throughout Asia:

> The Tathāgata has proclaimed the cause,
> as well as the cessation,
> of all things *(dharma)* arising from a cause.
> This is the Great *Śramaṇa's* teaching.
> (*Mahāvastu* 2.62; Pali *Vinaya* 1.40)

Abstract theories of causation were perceived as having an ultimately soteriological meaning or function, for they clarified both the process of bondage (rebirth forced upon us as a consequence of our actions) and the process of liberation (freedom from rebirth by overcoming our ignorance and gaining control over the causes of bondage). Liberation was possible because the analysis of causation revealed that there was no reincarnating or suffering self to begin with.

Impermanence and causation were explained by primitive theories of the composition of material reality (the four elements) and mental reality (the six senses, the six types of sense objects, etc.) and, what is more important, by the theory of the constituents *(skandhas)* of human personality. These notions would become the main focus of Buddhist philosophy, and by the beginning of the common era they were being integrated into systematic treatments of the nature of ultimately real entities *(dharma).* [*See* Dharma, *article on* Buddhist Dharma and Dharmas.]

Although the themes of impermanence and causation will remain at the heart of Buddhist philosophical speculation for several centuries, from the religious point of view the question of no-self plays a more important role. At first seen as an insightful formulation of the meaning of awakening and liberation, the doctrine of no-self raised several difficulties for Buddhist dogma. First, it was not at all obvious how moral (or karmic) responsibility could be possible if there was no continuous self. Second, some Buddhists wondered what was the meaning of liberation in the absence of a self.

Closely related to these issues was the question of the nature and status of the liberated being. In other words, what sort of living being is a *tathāgata?* Some Buddhists considered the *tathāgata* as a transcendent or eternal being, while others saw him as someone who by becoming extinct was nonexistent; still others began to redefine the concept of liberation and no-self in an attempt to solve these questions and in response to changes in the mythological or hagiographic sphere. These issues are an essential part of the changes in doctrine and practice that would take place during the age of invasions, culminating in the emergence of Mahāyāna Buddhism.

WORSHIP AND RITUAL

The most important ritual of the monastic community continued to be Upavasatha or Uposatha, a gathering of the *saṃgha* of a given locality or "parish" *(sīmā)* to recite the rules of the Prātimokṣa. These meetings were held at every change in the moon's phase. A similar ceremony, but with greater emphasis on the public confession of individual faults, was held at the end of the rainy season. At this time too was held the *kaṭhina* ceremony, in which the monks received new robes from the lay community. Other rituals, such as the ordination ceremony, had a more limited impact on the community at large, but were nevertheless important symbols of the status of the religious specialist in society at large.

Above all other rituals, one of Shramanic origin offered continued reinforcement of the ties that bound the religious order with the laity. The *bhikṣu,* as his title indicates, was expected to receive his sustenance from the charity *(dāna)* of pious laymen and laywomen. Accordingly, the monks would walk the villages every morning to collect alms. By giving the unsolicited gift the layperson was assured of the merit *(puṇya)* necessary to be reborn in a state of being more favorable for spiritual or material progress. According to some traditions, the monk received the benefits of helping others gain merit; but some believed the monk could not gain merit except by his own virtue.

In the early stages lay followers were identified by their adherence to the fivefold moral precept *(pañcaśīla)* and the formal adoption of the Three Refuges. These practices continued throughout the history of Indian Buddhism. It is also likely that participation of lay members in Upavasatha meetings with the *saṃgha* was also an early and persistent practice.

At first the cenobitic life of the monks probably had no room for explicit acts of devotion, and the monk's religion was limited to a life of solitude and meditation. The early monastic ruins do not show evidence of any shrine room. It was essential to have the cells open onto a closed courtyard, to keep out the noise of the world; it was essential to have an assembly hall for teaching and the recitation of the Prātimokṣa; a promenade *(caṅkrama)* for walking meditation was also necessary. But there were no shrine rooms.

With the institutionalization of Buddhism, however, came new forms of lay and monastic practice. The monastic brotherhood gradually began to play a priestly role; in tandem with the lay community, they participated in nonmonastic rituals, many of which must have been of pre-Buddhist origin. [*See* Priesthood, *article on* Buddhist Priesthood.] One practice that clearly was an important, nonascetic ritual, yet characteristic of Buddhism, was the worship of the relics of the Buddha and his immediate disciples. The relics were placed in a casket, which was then deposited in a cairn or tumulus *(stūpa, caitya),* to which the faithful would come to present their offerings. Already by the time of Aśoka (mid-third century BCE) we find evidence of a flourishing cult of the relics, often accompanied by the practice of pilgrimage to the sacred sites consecrated by their role in the life of Śākyamuni—especially the birth place, the site of the Great Awakening, the site of the First Sermon, and the spot where the Buddha was believed to have died. [*See also* Pilgrimage, *article on* Buddhist Pilgrimage in South and Southeast Asia.] Following an ancient custom, tumuli were built on these spots—perhaps at first as reliquaries, later as commemorative monuments. Monasteries near such sites assumed the role of shrine caretakers. Eventually, most monasteries became associated with stupas.

Aśoka erected columns and stupas (as many as eighty thousand, according to one tradition) marking the localities associated with the life of the Buddha as well as other ancient sacred sites, some associated with "former Buddhas," that is, mythical beings believed to have achieved Buddhahood thousands or millions of lives before the Buddha Śākyamuni. The latter practice and belief indicates the development of a new form of Buddhism, firmly based on the mythology of each locality, that expanded the concept of the Three Treasures to include a host of mythical beings who would share in the sanctity of Śākyamuni's experience and virtue and who were therefore deserving of the same veneration as he had received in the past.

The cairn or tumulus eventually became sacred in itself, whether there was a relic in it or not. Chapels were built to contain the *caitya.* The earliest surviving examples of these structures are built in stone and date from the first or second century BCE, but we can surmise that they existed in wood from an earlier date. These "*caitya* halls" became the standard shrine room of the monastery: a stylized memorial tumulus built in stone or brick, housed in an apsidal hall with a processional for the ritual circumambulation of the tumulus. [*See* Temple, *article on* Buddhist Temple Compounds.]

Reliefs at the *caitya* hall at Bhājā in Western India (late Śuṅga, c. end of the second century BCE) suggest various aspects of the cult: the main form of worship was the ritual of circumambulation *(pradakṣiṇa),* which could be carried out individually or in groups. The stupa represented the sacred or cosmic mountain, at whose center was found the *axis mundi* (now represented by the Buddha's royal parasol); thus the rite of circumambulation expressed veneration for the Buddha and his teaching, while at the same time it served as a symbolic walking of the sun's path around the cosmic mountain.

Stupas were often erected at ancient sacred sites, hills, trees, the confluence of streams, which in many cases were sacred by virtue of non-Buddhist belief. Thus, pre-Buddhist practice, if not belief, survived side by side, and even within, Buddhist liturgy and belief. There is ample evidence of a coexisting cult of the tree (identified with the "Tree of Awakening"), of forest spirits *(yakṣas)* and goddesses *(devatā),* and the persistence of Vedic deities, albeit in a subordinate role, beside a more austere, and presumably monastically inspired, cult of aniconic symbolizations of Buddhahood: the tree and the throne of enlightenment standing for the Great Awakening, the stupa representing the *nirvāṇa,* the wheel representing the doctrine of the Buddha. But one must not assume that the implied categories of "high tradition" and popular cult were mutually exclusive. [*See* Stupa Worship *and* Nāgas and Yakṣas. *For a discussion of Buddhist/local syncretism, see* Folk Religion, *article on* Folk Buddhism. *See also* Worship and Cultic Life, *article on* Buddhist Cultic Life in Southeast Asia.]

THE COUNCILS AND THE BEGINNING OF SCRIPTURAL TRADITION

The First Council, or Council of Rājagṛha, if a historical fact, must have served to establish the Buddhist *saṃgha* and its doctrine for the community of the Magadhan capital. In all probability the decisions of the Council were not accepted by all Buddhists. Further evidence of disagreement, and geographical fragmentation is found in the legend of the Second Council, one hundred years after the Buddha's death.

Since the early community of wanderers, there had been ample room for disagreement and dissension. But certain forces contributed to maintaining unity: the secular powers, for instance, had much at stake in preserving harmony within the *saṃgha,* especially if they could maintain some kind of control over it. Thus, as the legends have it, each of the three major councils were sponsored by a king: Ajātaśatru, Kālāśoka, and Aśoka, respectively. Within the *saṃgha,* there must have been interests groups, mainly conservative, seeking to preserve the religion by avoiding change—two goals that are not always conciliable. There must have been, therefore, a strong pressure to recover the ideal unity of the early community (as we have seen, probably a fantasy), by legislation. These efforts took two forms: in the first place, there was the drive to establish a common monastic code, in the second place, there was the drive to fix a canon of scriptures. Both tendencies probably became stronger toward the beginning of the common era, when a number of political factors recreated a sense of urgency and a yearning for harmony and peace similar to the one that had given rise to the religion. [*See* Councils, *article on* Buddhist Councils.]

The most important result of the new quest for harmony was the compilation and redaction of scriptures. Transmitted and edited through the oral tradition, the words of the Buddha and his immediate disciples had suffered many transformations before they came to be compiled, to say nothing of their state when they were eventually written down. We have no way of determining which, if any, of the words contained in the Buddhist scriptures are the words of the founder: in fact we have no hard evidence for the language used by the Buddha in his ministry. Scholars have suggested an early form of Māgadhī, since this was probably the lingua franca of the kingdom of Magadha, but this is at best an educated guess. If it is correct, then none of the words of the Buddha have come to us in the original language.

Although the Theravādin tradition claims that the language of its canon, Pali, is the language spoken by the Buddha, Western scholars disagree. Evidently, the Pali canon, like other Buddhist scriptures, is the creation, or at least the compilation and composition, of another age and a different linguistic milieu. As they are preserved today, the Buddhist scriptures must be a collective creation, the fruit of the effort of several generations of memorizers, redactors, and compilers. Some of the earliest Buddhist scriptures may have been translations from logia or sayings of the Buddha that were transmitted for some time in his own language. But even if this is the case, the extant versions represent at the very least redactions and reworkings, if not creations, of a later age.

Since the *saṃgha* was from the beginning a decentralized church, one can presume that the word of the Buddha took many forms. Adding to this the problem of geographical isolation and linguistic diversity, one would expect that the oral transmission would have produced a variegated textual tradition. Perhaps it is this expectation of total chaos that makes it all the more surprising that there is agreement on so many points in the scriptures preserved to this day. This is especially true of the scriptures of the Theravāda school (preserved in Pali), and fragments of the canon of the Sarvāstivāda school (in the original Sanskrit or in Chinese translation). Some scholars have been led to believe, therefore, that these two traditions represent the earliest stratum of the transmission, preserving a complex of pericopes and logia that must go back to a stage when the community was not divided: that is, before the split of the Second Council. Most scholars tend to accept this view; a significant minority, however, sees the uniformity of the texts as reflecting a late, not an early stage, in the redaction of the canon.

The early canon, transmitted orally, must have had only two major sections, Dharma and Vinaya. The first of these contained the discourses of the Buddha and his immediate disciples. The Vinaya contained the monastic rules. Most Western scholars agree that a third section, Abhidharma, found in all of the surviving canons, could not have been included in early definitions of canonicity, though eventually most schools would incorporate it in their canon with varying degrees of authority.

Each early school possessed its own set of scriptural "collections" (called metaphorically "baskets," *piṭaka*). Although eventually the preferred organization seems to have been a tripartite collection of "Three Baskets," the Tripiṭaka, divided into monastic rules, sermons, and scholastic treatises (Vinaya, Sūtra, Abhidharma), some schools adopted different orderings. Among the collections that are now lost there were fourfold and fivefold subdivisions of the scriptures. Of the main surviving scriptural collections, only one is strictly speaking a Tripiṭaka, the Pali corpus of the Theravādins. (The much later Chinese and Tibetan collections have much more complex subdivisions and can be called Tripiṭakas only metaphorically.) [*See* Buddhist Literature, *article on* Canonization.]

The Age of Foreign Invasions

The decline and fall of the Maurya dynasty (324–187) brought an end to an age of assured support for Buddhist monastic institutions. Political circumstances unfavorable to Buddhism began with persecution under Puṣyamitra Śuṅga (r. about 187–151). The Śuṅga dynasty would see the construction of some of the most important Buddhist sites of India: Bhārhut, Sāñcī, and Amarāvatī. But it also foreshadowed the beginning of Hindu dominance. The rising cult of Viṣṇu seemed better equipped to assimilate the religion of the people and win the support of the ruling classes. Although Buddhism served better as a universal religion that could unite Indians and foreign invaders, the latter did not always choose to become Buddhists. A series of non-Indian rulers—Greek, Parthian, Scythian (Saka), Kushan—would hesitate in their religious allegiances.

Among the Greek kings, the Buddhist tradition claims Menander (Milinda, c. 150 BCE) as one of its converts. The Scythian tribe of the Sakas, who invaded Bactriana around 130 BCE, roughly contemporaneous with the Yüeh-chih conquest of the Tokharians, would become stable supporters of Buddhism in the subcontinent. [*See* Inner Asian Religions.] Their rivals in South India, the Tamil dynasty of the Sātavāhana (220 BCE–236 CE), sponsored in Andhra the construction of major centers of worship at Amarāvatī and Nāgārjunīkoṇḍa. The Yüeh-chih (Kushans) also supported Buddhism, though perhaps less consistently. The most famous of their rulers, Kaniṣka, is represented by the literature as a pious patron of Buddhism (his dates are uncertain; proposed accession in 78 or 125 CE). During the Kushan period (c. 50–320 CE) the great schools of Gandhāra and Mathurā revolutionized Indian, especially Buddhist, art. Both the northern styles of Gandhāra and Mathurā and the southern school of Andhra combined iconic and ani-conic symbolization of the Buddha: the first Buddha images appeared around the third century of the common era, apparently independently and simultaneously in all three schools.

THE APPEARANCE OF SCHOOLS AND DENOMINATIONS

Any understanding of the history of composition of the canons, or of their significance in the history of the religion, is dependent on our knowledge of the geographic distribution, history, and doctrine of the various sects. Unfortunately, our knowledge in this regard is also very limited. [*See* Buddhism, Schools of, *overview article*.]

Developments in Doctrine and in Scholastic Speculation. As the original community of wandering mendicants settled in monasteries, a new type of religion arose, concerned with the preservation of a tradition and the justification of its institutions. Although the "forest dweller" continued as an ideal and a practice—some were still dedicated primarily to a life of solitude and meditation—the dominant figure became that of the monk-scholar. This new type of religious specialist pursued the study of the early tradition and moved its doctrinal systems in new directions. On the one hand, the old doctrines were classified, defined, and expanded. On the other hand, there was a growing awareness of the gap that separated the new developments from the transmitted creeds and codes. A set of basic or "original" teachings had to be defined, and the practice of exegesis had to be formalized. In fact, the fluidity and uncertainty of the earlier scriptural tradition may be one of the causes for the development of Buddhist scholasticism. By the time the canons were closed the degree of diversity and conflict among the schools was such, and the tradition was overall so fluid, that it was difficult to establish orthodoxy even when there was agreement on the basic content of the canons. In response to these problems Buddhists soon developed complicated scholastic studies.

At least some of the techniques and problems of this early scholasticism must go back to the early redactions of the Sūtra section of the canon, if not to a precanonical stage. The genre of the *mātṛkā*, or doctrinal "matrices," is not an uncommon form of Sūtra literature. It is suggested in the redaction of certain sections of the Pali and Sarvāstivādin canons, is found in early Chinese translations (e.g., the *Dharmaśarīraka Sūtra* and the *Daśottara Sūtra*), and continues in Mahāyāna Sūtra literature. It is a literary form tht probably represents not only an exegetic device but an early technique of doctrinal redaction—a hermeneutic that also served as the basis for the redaction of earlier strata of the oral transmission.

The Early Sects. Given the geographical and linguistic diversity of India and the lack of a central authority in the Buddhist community one can safely speculate that Buddhist sects arose early in the history of the religion. Tradition speaks of a first, but major, schism occurring at (or shortly after) the Second Council in Vaiśālī, one hundred years after the death of the founder. Whether the details are true or not, it is suggestive that this first split was between the Sthaviras and the Mahāsāṃghikas, the prototypes of the two major divisions of Buddhism: "Hīnayāna" and Mahāyāna.

After this schism new subdivisions arose, reaching by the beginning of the common era a total of approximately thirty different denominations or schools and subschools. Tradition refers to this state of sectarian division as the period of the "Eighteen Schools," since some of the early sources count eighteen groups. It is not clear when these arose. *Faut de mieux*, most Western scholars go along with classical Indian sources albeit with a mild skepticism, and try to sort out a consistent narrative from contradictory sources. Thus, we can only say that if we are to believe the Pali tradition, the Eighteen Schools must have been in existence already in the third century BCE, when a legendary Moggaliputtatissa compiled the *Kathāvatthu*. But such an early dating raises many problems. [*See the biography of Moggaliputtatissa.*]

In the same vein, we tend to accept the account of the Second Council that sees it as the beginning of a major split. In this version the main points of contention were monastic issues—the exact content and interpretation of the code. But doctrinal, ritual, and scholastic issues must have played a major role in the formation of separate schools. Many of the main points of controversy, for instance, centered on the question of the nature of the state of liberation and the status of the liberated person. Is the liberated human *(arhat)* free from all moral and karmic taint? Is the state of liberation *(nirvāṇa)* a condition of being or nonbeing? Can there be at the same time more than one fully awakened person *(samyaksaṃbuddha)* in one world system? Are persons already on their way to full awakening, the *bodhisattvas* or future Buddhas, deserving of worship? Do they have the ability to descend to the hells to help other sentient beings?

Among these doctrinal disputes one emerges as emblematic of the most important fissure in the Buddhist community. This was the polemic surrounding the exalted state of the *arhat* (Pali, *arahant*). Most of the Buddhist schools believed that only a few human beings could aspire to become fully awakened beings *(samyaksaṃbuddha),* others had to content themselves with the hope of becoming free from the burden of past *karman* and attaining liberation in *nirvāṇa,* without the extraordinary wisdom and virtue of Buddhahood. But the attainment of liberation was in itself a great achievement, and a person who was assured of an end to rebirth at the end of the present life was considered the most saintly, deserving of the highest respect, a "worthy" *(arhat).* Some of the schools even attributed to the *arhat* omniscience and total freedom from moral taint. Objections were raised against those who believed in the faultless wisdom of the *arhat,* including obvious limitations in their knowledge of everyday, worldly affairs. Some of these objections were formalized in the "Five Points" of Mahādeva, after its purported proponent. These criticisms can be interpreted either as a challenge to the belief in the superhuman perfection of the *arhat* or as a plea for the acceptance of their humanity. Traditionally, Western scholars have opted for the first of these interpretations. [*See* Arhat.]

The controversies among the Eighteen Schools identified each group doctrinally, but it seems unlikely that in the early stages these differences lead to major rifts in the community, with the exception of the schism between the two trunk schools of the Sthavira and the Mahāsāṃghika; and even then, there is evidence that monks of both schools often lived together in a single monastic community. Among the doctrinal differences, however, we can find the seeds of future dissension, especially in the controversies relating to ritual. The Mahīśāsakas, for instance, claimed that there is more merit in worshiping and making offerings to the *saṃgha* than in worshiping a stupa, as the latter merely contains the remains of a member of the *saṃgha* who is no more. The Dharmaguptakas replied that there is more merit in worshiping a stupa, because the Buddha's path and his present state (in *nirvāṇa*) are far superior to that of any living monk. Here we have a fundamental difference with both social and religious consequences, for the choice is between two types of communal hierarchies as well as between two types of spiritual orders. [*For further discussion of sectarian splits in early Buddhism, see* Buddhism, Schools of, *article on* Hīnayāna Buddhism. *For specific* nikāyas, *see* Sarvāstivāda; Sautrāntika; Mahāsāṃghika; *and* Theravāda.]

DEVELOPMENTS IN THE SCRIPTURAL TRADITION

Apart from the Theravāda recension of the Pali canon and some fragments of the Sarvāstivādin Sanskrit canon nothing survives of what must have been a vast and diverse body of literature. For most of the collections we only have the memory preserved in inscriptions referring to *piṭaka*s and *nikāya*s and an occasional reference in the extant literature.

According to the Pali tradition of Sri Lanka, the three parts of the Tripiṭaka were compiled in the language of the Buddha at the First Council. The Second Council introduced minor revisions in the Vinaya, and the Third Council added Moggaliputtatissa's *Kathāvatthu*. A few years later the canon resulting from this council, and a number of extracanonical commentaries, were transmitted to Sri Lanka by Mahinda. The texts were transmitted orally *(mukhapāṭhena)* for the next two centuries, but after difficult years of civil war and famine, King Vaṭṭagāmaṇī of Sri Lanka ordered the texts written down. This task was carried out between 35 and 32 BCE. In this way, it is said, the canon was preserved in the original language. Although the commentaries were by that time extant only in Sinhala, they continued to be transmitted in written form until they were retranslated into Pali in the fifth century CE.

Modern scholarship, however, questions the accuracy of several points in this account. Pali appears to be a literary language originating in Avantī, western India; it seems unlikely that it could be the vernacular of a man who had lived in eastern India all his life or, for that matter, the lingua franca of the early Magadhan kingdom. The Pali texts as they are preserved today show clear signs of the work of editors and redactors. Although much in them still has the ring of oral transmission, it is a formalized or ritualized oral tradition, far from the spontaneous preaching of a living teacher. Different strata of language, history, and doctrine can be recognized easily in these texts. There is abundant evidence that already at the stage of oral transmission the tradition was fragmented, different schools of "reciters" *(bhāṇaka)* preserving not only different corpuses (the eventual main categories of the canons) but also different recensions of the same corpus of literature. Finally, we have no way of knowing if the canon written down at the time of Vaṭṭagāmaṇī was the Tripiṭaka as we know it today. There is evidence to the contrary, for we are told that the great South Indian scholar Buddhaghosa revised the canon in the fifth century when he also edited the commentaries preserved in Sinhala and translated them into Pali, which suggests that Pali literature in general had gone through a period of deterioration before his time.

Most scholars, however, accept the tradition that would have the Pali canon belong to a date earlier than the fifth century; even the commentaries must represent an earlier stratum. However late may be its final recension, the Pali canon preserves much from earlier stages in the development of the religion.

Of the Sanskrit canon of the Sarvāstivāda school we only possess a few isolated texts and fragments in the original, mostly from Central Asia. However, extensive sections survive in Chinese translation. This canon is supposed to have been written down at a "Fourth Council" held in Jālandhara, Kashmir, about 100 CE, close to the time when the same school systematized its Abhidharma in a voluminous commentary called the *Mahāvibhāṣa*. If this legend is true, two details are of historical interest. We must note first the proximity in time of this compilation to the date of the writing down of the Pali canon. This would set the parameters for the closing of the "Hīnayāna" canons between the first century BCE and the first century CE. Second, the close connection between the closing of a canon and the final formulation of a scholastic system confirms the similar socioreligious function of both activities: the establishing of orthodoxy.

DEVELOPMENTS IN PRACTICE

The cult at this stage was still dominated by the practice of pilgrimage and by the cult of the *caitya*, as described above. However, we can imagine an intensification of the devotional aspect of ritual and a greater degree of systematization as folk belief and "high tradition" continued to interact. Sectarian differences probably began to affect the nature of the liturgies, as a body of liturgical texts became part of

But side by side with the tradition of ineffability, there was a need to define at the very least the process of liberation. For the gradual realization of selflessness was understood as personal growth. Accordingly, a set of standard definitions of liberation was accompanied by accepted descriptions of the stages on the path to liberation, or of degrees of spiritual achievement. The canonical collections already list, for instance, four types of saints *(āryapudgala):* the one who will be reborn no more *(arhat);* the one who will not come back to this world, the "non-returner" *(anāgamin);* the one who will return only once more *(sakṛdāgamin);* and the one who has entered the path to sainthood, the "stream-enterer" *(srotāpanna).*

Canonical notions of levels or hierarchies in the path to liberation became the focus of much scholastic speculation—in fact, the presence of these categories in the canons may be a sign of scholastic influence on the redaction of the scriptures. The construction of complex systems of soteriology, conceived as maps or detailed descriptions of the path, that integrated the description and analysis of ethical and contemplative practices with philosophical argumentation, characterized the Abhidharmic schools. This activity contributed to the definition of the doctrinal parameters of the sects; but it also set the tone for much of future Buddhist dogmatics. The concerns of the Abhidharmists, ranging from the analysis of enstasy and the contemplative stages to the rational critique of philosophical views of reality, had a number of significant doctrinal consequences: (1) scholars began devising "maps of the path," or theoretical blueprints of the stages from the condition of a common human being *(pṛthag-jana)* to the exalted state of a fully awakened being *(samyaksaṃbuddha);* (2) Buddhist scholars engaged other Indian intellectuals in the discussion of broad philosophical issues; (3) various orthodox apologetics were developed, with the consequent freezing of a technical terminology common to most Buddhists; (4) the rigidity of their systems set the stage for a reaction that would lead to the creation of new forms of Buddhism.

The Sects and the Appearance of Mahāyāna

Most of the developments mentioned above overlap with the growth of a new spirit that changed the religion and eventually created a distinct form of Buddhist belief and practice. The new movement referred to itself as the "Great Vehicle" (Mahāyāna) to distinguish itself from other styles of Buddhism that the followers of the movement considered forms of a "Lesser Vehicle" (Hīnayāna). [*See* Buddhism, Schools of, *article on* Mahāyāna Buddhism.]

THE EARLY SCHOOLS OUTSIDE INDIA

If we accept the general custom of using the reign of Aśoka as the landmark for the beginning of the missionary spread of Buddhism, we may say that Buddhism reached the frontiers of India by the middle of the second century BCE. By the beginning of the common era it had spread beyond. In the early centuries of the era Mahāyāna and Hīnayāna spread in every direction; eventually certain areas would become predominantly Mahāyāna, others, predominantly Hīnayāna. [*See* Missions, *article on* Buddhist Missions, *and the biography of Aśoka.*]

Mahāyāna came to dominate in East and Central Asia—with the exception of Turkistan, where Sarvāstivādin monasteries flourished until the Muslim invasion and conversion of the region. Hīnayāna was slower to spread, and in some foreign lands had to displace Mahāyāna. It lives on in a school that refers to itself as the Theravāda, a Sinhala derivative of the Sthavira school. It spread throughout Southeast Asia where it continues to this day.

THE GREAT VEHICLE

The encounter of Buddhism with extra-Indian ethnic groups and the increasing influence of the laity gradually transformed the monastic child of shramanic Buddhism into a universal religion. This occurred in two ways. On the one hand, monasticism adapted to the changing circumstances, strengthened its ties to the laity and secular authorities, established a satisfactory mode of coexistence with nonliterary, regional forms of worship. Both Mahāyāna and Hīnayāna schools participated in this aspect of the process of adaptation. But Buddhism also redefined its goals and renovated its symbols to create a new synthesis that in some ways may be considered a new religion. The new style, the Mahāyāna, claimed to be a path for the many, the vehicle for the salvation of all sentient beings (hence its name, "The Great Vehicle"). Its distinctive features are: a tilt toward world affirmation, a laicized conception of the human ideal, a new ritual of devotion, and new definitions of the metaphysical and contemplative ideals.

The Origins of Mahāyāna. The followers of Mahāyāna claim the highest antiquity for its teachings. Their own myths of origin, however, belie this claim. Mahāyāna recognizes the fact that its teachings were not known in the early days of Buddhism by asserting that Śākyamuni revealed the Mahāyāna only to select *bodhisattvas* or heavenly beings who kept the texts hidden for centuries. One legend recounts that the philosopher Nāgārjuna had to descend to the underworld to obtain the Mahāyāna texts known as the "Perfection of Wisdom" (Prajñāpāramitā).

Western scholars are divided on the question of the dates and location of the origins of Mahāyāna. Some favor an early (beginning of the common era) origin among Mahāsāṃghika communities in the southeastern region of Andhra. Others propose a northwestern origin, among the Sarvāstivādins, close to the second and third centuries CE. It may be, however, that Mahāyāna arose by a gradual and complex process involving more than one region of India. It is clear that Mahāyāna was partly a reform movement, partly the natural development of pre-Mahāyāna Buddhism; still in another sense, it was the result of new social forces shaping the Indian subcontinent.

The theory of a southern origin assumes that the Mahāsāṃghika monastic centers of Andhra continued to develop some of the more radical ideals of the school, until some of these communities saw themselves as a movement completely distinct from other, so-called Hīnayāna schools. This theory also recognizes external influences: the Iranian invaders as well as the non-Aryan substratum of southern India, the first affecting the mythology of the celestial *bodhisattvas*, the second incorporating non-Aryan concepts of the role of women into the mainstream of Buddhist religious ideals.

For the sake of clarity one could distinguish two types of causes in the development of Mahāyāna: social or external, and doctrinal or internal. Among the first one must include the Central Asian and Iranian influences mentioned above, the growing importance of the role of women and the laity, especially as this affected the development of the cultus, and the impact of the pilgrimage cycles. The foreign element is supposed to have introduced elements of light symbolism and solar cults, as well as a less ascetic bent.

Doctrinal factors were primarily the development of the myth of the former lives of Śākyamuni and the cult of former Buddhas, both of which contributed to a critique of the *arhat* ideal. The mythology of the Buddha's former lives as a *bodhisattva* led to the exaltation of the *bodhisattva* ideal over that of the *arhat*. The vows of the *bodhisattva* began to take the central role, especially as they were seen as an integral part of a developing liturgy at the center of which the dedication of merit was transformed as part of the exalted *bodhisattva* ideal.

It seems likely, furthermore, that visionaries and inspired believers had continued to compose *sūtras*. Some of these, through a gradual process we can no longer retrace, began to move away from the general direction of the older scholastic traditions and canonical redactors. Thus it happened that approximately at the time when the older schools were closing their canons, the Mahāyāna was composing a set of texts that would place it in a position of disagreement with, if not frank opposition to, the older schools. At the same time, the High Tradition began to accept Mahāyāna and therefore argue for its superiority; thus, a Mahāyāna *śāstra* tradition began to develop almost at the same time as the great Sarvāstivādin synthesis was completed.

In the West, the gap between Mahāyāna and Hīnayāna is sometimes exaggerated. It is customary to envision Mahāyāna as a revolutionary movement through which the aspirations of a restless laity managed to overcome an oppressive, conservative monastic establishment. Recent research suggests that the opposition between the laity and the religious specialists was not as sharp as had hitherto been proposed. Furthermore, it has become apparent that the monastic establishment continued to be a powerful force in Indian Mahāyāna. It seems more likely that Mahāyāna arose gradually and in different forms in various points of the subcontinent. A single name and a more or less unified ideology may have arisen after certain common aspirations were recognized. Be that as it may, it seems evident that the immediate causes for the arising of this new form of Buddhism were the appearance of new cultic forms and widespread dissatisfaction with the scholastic tradition.

Merit, Bodhisattvas, and the Pure Land. Inscriptional evidence shows that the doctrine of merit transference had an important role in the cultus even before the appearance of Mahāyāna. Although all Buddhists believe that virtuous thoughts and actions generate merit, which leads to a good rebirth, it appears that early Buddhists believed that individuals could generate merit only for themselves, and that merit could only lead to a better rebirth, not to liberation from the cycle of rebirth. By the beginning of the common era, however, some Buddhists had adopted a different conception of merit. They believed that merit could be shared or transferred, and that it was a factor in the attainment of liberation—so much so that they were offering their own merit for the salvation of their dead relatives.

Dedication of merit appears as one of the pivotal doctrines of the new Buddhism. Evidently, it served a social function: it made participation in Buddhist ritual a social encounter rather than a private experience. It also contributed to the development of a Buddhist high liturgy, an important factor in the survival of Buddhism and its assimilation of foreign elements, both in and outside India. [*See* Merit, *article on* Buddhist Concepts.]

This practice and belief interacted with the cult of former Buddhas and the mythology of the former lives to create a Buddhist system of beliefs in which the primary goal was to imitate the virtue of Śākyamuni's former lives, when he was a *bodhisattva* dedicated to the liberation of others rather than himself. To achieve this goal the believer sought to imitate Śākyamuni not as he appeared in his last life or after his enlightenment, when he sought and attained *nirvāṇa,* but by adopting a vow similar to Śākyamuni's former vow to seek awakening *(bodhi)* for the sake of all sentient beings. On the one hand, this shift put the emphasis on insight into the world, rather than escape from it. On the other hand, it also created a new form of ideal being and object of worship, the *bodhisattva*. [*See* Bodhisattva Path.]

Contemporary developments in Hindu devotionalism *(bhakti)* probably played an important role in the development of Buddhist liturgies of worship *(pūjā)*, but it would be a mistake to assume that the beginnings of Mahāyāna faith and ritual can be explained adequately by attributing them merely to external theistic influences. [*See* Bhakti.] For instance, the growth of a faith in rebirth in "purified Buddha fields," realms of the cosmos in which the merit and power of Buddhas and *bodhisattva*s create an environment where birth without suffering is possible, can be seen as primarily a Buddhist development. The new faith, generalized in India through the concept of the "Land of Bliss" (the "Pure Land" of East Asian Buddhism), hinged on faith in the vows of former *bodhisattva*s who chose to transfer or dedicate their merit to the purification of a special "field" or "realm." The influence of Iranian religious conceptions seems likely, however, and one may have to seek some of the roots of this belief among Central Asian converts. [*See* Pure and Impure Lands *and* Amitābha.]

Formation of a New Scriptural Tradition. With the new cult and the new ideology came a new body of scriptures. Mahāyāna *sūtra*s began to be composed probably around the beginning of the Christian era, and continued to be composed and redacted until at least the fifth or sixth century CE. Unlike the canons of the earlier schools, the Mahāyāna scriptures do not seem to have been collected into formal, closed canons in the land of their origin—even the collections edited in China and Tibet were never closed canons.

In its inception Mahāyāna literature is indistinguishable from the literature of some of the earlier schools. The *Prajñāpāramitā* text attributed to the Pūrvaśailas is probably an earlier version of one of the Mahāyāna texts of the same title; the *Ratnakūṭa* probably began as part of a Mahāsāṃghika canon; and the now lost *Dhāraṇī Piṭaka* of the Dharmaguptaka school probably contained prototypes of the *dhāraṇī-sūtra*s of the Mahāyāna tradition. The Mahāyānist monks never gave up the pre-Mahāyāna Vinaya. Many followed the Dharmaguptaka version, some the Mahāsāṃghika. Even the Vinaya of a school that fell squarely into the Hīnayāna camp, the Sarvāstivāda, was used as the basis for Mahāyāna monastic rule.

Still, the focus of much Mahāyāna rhetoric, especially in the earlier strata of the literature, is the critique of non-Mahāyāna forms of Buddhism, especially the ideal of the *arhat*. This is one of the leading themes of a work now believed to represent an early stage in the development of Mahāyāna, the *Raṣṭrapālaparipṛcchā,* a text of the *Ratnakūṭa* class. In this text, the monastic life is still exalted above all other forms of spiritual life, but the *bodhisattva* vows are presented for the first time as superior to the mere monastic vows.

It is difficult, if not impossible, to establish with any degree of certainty the early history of Mahāyāna literature. It seems, however, that the earliest extant Mahāyāna *sūtra* is the *Aṣṭasāhasrikāprajñāpāramitā,* or its verse rendering, the *Ratnaguṇa-saṃcayagāthā*. Both reflect a polemic within Buddhism, centering on a critique of the "low aspirations" of those Buddhists who chose not to take the vows of the *bodhisattvas*. The *Ratnaguṇa* defines the virtues of the *bodhisattva,* emphasizing the transcendental insight or "perfect wisdom" *(prajñāpāramitā)* that frees him from all forms of attachment and preconceived notions—including notions of purity and world renunciation. An important aspect or complement of this wisdom is skill in means *(upāya-kauśalya)*—defined here as the capacity to adapt thought, speech, and action to circumstances and to the ultimate purpose of Buddhist practice, freedom from attachment. This virtue allows the *bodhisattva* to remain in the world while being perfectly free from the world.

The *Aṣṭasāhasrikā* treats these same concepts, but also expands the concept of merit in at least two directions: (1) dedication of merit to awakening means here seeing through the illusion of merit as well as applying merit to the path of liberation; and (2) dedication of merit is an act of devotion to insight (wisdom, *prajñā*). As the goal and ground of all perfections *(pāramitā)*, Perfection of Wisdom is personified as the Mother of All Buddhas. She gives birth to the mind of awakening, but she is present in concrete form in the Sacred Book itself. Thus, the *Aṣṭasāhasrikāprajñāpāramitā Sūtra* is at the same time the medium expressing a sophisticated doctrine of salvation by insight and skill in means, the rationalization of a ritual system, and the object of worship. [*See* Pāramitās; Prajñā; *and* Upāya.]

Another early Mahāyāna text, the *Saddharmapuṇḍarīka* (Lotus Sutra), also attacks the *arhat* ideal. This *sūtra* is considered the paradigmatic text on the developed Buddhology of the Mahāyāna: the Buddha is presented as a supernatural being, eternal, unchanging; at the same time he is Buddha by virtue of the fact that he has become free from all conceptions of being and nonbeing. The Buddha never *attained* awakening or *nirvāṇa*—because he *is* Buddhahood, and has been in awakening and *nirvāṇa* since eternity, but also because there is no Buddhahood or *nirvāṇa* to be attained.

The widespread, but clearly not exclusively popular, belief in the Land of Bliss (Sukhāvatī) finds expression in two texts of the latter part of the early period (c. first to second century CE). The two *Sukhāvatī sūtras* express a faith in the saving grace of the *bodhisattva* Dharmākara, who under a former Buddha made the vow to purify his own Buddha field. The vows of this *bodhisattva* guarantee rebirth in his Land of Bliss to all those who think on him with faith. Rebirth in his land, furthermore, guarantees eventual enlightenment and liberation. The Indian history of these two texts, however, remains for the most part obscure.

The attitude of early Mahāyāna *sūtras* to laity and to women is relatively inconsistent. Thus, the *Ugradattaparipṛcchā* and the *Upāsakaśīla,* while pretending to preach a lay morality, use monastic models for the householder's life. But compared to the earlier tradition, the Mahāyāna represents a significant move in the direction of a religion that is less ascetic and monastic in tone and intent. Some Mahāyāna *sūtras* of the early period place laypersons in a central role. The main character in the *Gaṇḍavyūha,* for instance, is a young lay pilgrim who visits a number of *bodhi-*

sattvas in search of the teaching. Among his teachers we find laymen and laywomen, as well as female night spirits and celestial *bodhisattvas*. The *Vimalakīrtinirdeśa* is more down-to-earth in its exaltation of the lay ideal. It represents the demythologizing tendencies of Mahāyāna, which are often carried out to the extreme of affirming that the metaphoric meaning of one doctrine is exactly its opposite.

The Development of Mahāyāna

Although Buddhism flourished during the classical age of the Guptas, the cultural splendor in which it grew was also the harbinger of Hindu dominance. Sanskrit returned as the lingua franca of the subcontinent, and Hindu devotionalism began to displace the ideals of the Indic period. Mahāyāna must have been a divided movement even in its inception. Some of the divisions found in the Hīnayāna or pre-Mahāyāna schools from which Mahāyāna originated must have carried through into Mahāyāna itself. Unfortunately, we know much less of the early sectarian divisions in the movement than we know of the Eighteen Schools. It is clear, for instance, that the conception of the *bodhisattva* found among the Mahāsāṃghikas is different from that of the Sarvāstivādins. It appears also that the Prajñaptivādins conceived of the unconditioned *dharmas* in a manner different from other early schools. However, though we may speculate that some of these differences influenced the development of Mahāyāna, we have no solid evidence.

As pre-Mahāyāna Buddhism had developed a scholastic system to bolster its ideological position, Mahāyāna developed special forms of scholarly investigation. A new synthesis, in many ways far removed from the visionary faith underlying the religious aspects of Mahāyāna, grew in the established monasteries partly as a critique of earlier scholastic formulations, partly due to the need to explain and justify the new faith. Through this intellectual function the monastery reasserted its institutional position. Both monk and layman participated in giving birth to Mahāyāna and maintaining its social and liturgical life, but the intellectual leadership remained monastic and conservative. Therefore, Mahāyāna reform brought with it an element of continuity—monastic institutions and codes—that could be at the same time a cause for fossilization and stagnation. The monasteries would eventually grow to the point where they became a burden on society, at the same time that, as institutions of conservatism, they failed to adapt to a changing society.

Still, from the beginning of the Gupta dynasty to the earlier part of the Pāla dynasty the monasteries were centers of intellectual creativity. They continued to be supported under the Guptas, especially Kumāra Gupta I (414–455), who endowed a major monastery in a site in Bihar originally consecrated to Śāriputra. This monastic establishment, called Nālandā after the name of a local genie, probably had been active as a center of learning for several decades before Kumāra Gupta decided to give it special recognition. It would become the leading institution of higher learning in the Buddhist world for almost a thousand years. Together with the university of Valabhī in western India, Nālandā represents the scholastic side of Mahāyāna, which coexisted with a nonintellectual (not necessarily "popular") dimension, the outlines of which appear through archaeological remains, certain aspects of the Sūtra literature, and the accounts of Chinese pilgrims.

Some texts suggest a conflict between forest and city dwellers that may in fact reflect the expected tension between the ascetic and the intellectual, or the meditator and the religious politician. But, lest this simple schema obliterate important aspects of Buddhist religious life, one must note that there is plentiful evidence of intense and constant interaction between the philosopher, the meditator, and the devotee—often all three functions coinciding in one person. Furthermore, the writings of great philosophical minds like Asaṅga, Śāntideva, and Āryadeva suggest an active involvement of the monk-*bodhisattva* in the social life of the community. The nonintellectual dimensions of the religion, therefore, must be seen as one aspect of a dialectic that resolved itself in synthesis as much as rivalry, tension, or dissonance.

Mahāyāna faith and devotion, moreover, was in itself a complex phenomenon, incorporating a liturgy of the High Tradition (e.g., the *Hymn to the Three Bodies of the Buddha,* attributed to Aśvaghoṣa) with elements of the nonliterary and non-Buddhist religion (e.g., pilgrimage cycles and the cult of local spirits, respectively), as well as generalized beliefs such as the dedication of merit and the hope of rebirth in a purified Buddha Land.

DEVELOPMENTS IN DOCTRINE

In explaining the appearance of Mahāyāna, two extremes should be avoided carefully. On the one hand, one can exaggerate the points of continuity that link Mahāyāna with pre-Mahāyāna Buddhism; on the other, one can make a distinction so sharp that Mahāyāna appears as a radical break with the past, rather than a gradual process of growth. The truth lies somewhere between these two extremes: although Mahāyāna can be understood as a logical expansion of earlier Buddhist doctrine and practice, it is difficult to see how the phenomenon could be explained without assuming major changes in the social fabric of the Indian communities that provided the base for the religion. These changes, furthermore, are suggested by historical evidence.

The key innovations in doctrine can be divided into those that are primarily critiques of early scholastic constructs and those that reflect new developments in practice. In both types, of course, one should not ignore the influence of visionary or contemplative experience; but this aspect of the religion, unfortunately, cannot always be documented adequately. The most important doctrine of practical consequence was the *bodhisattva* doctrine; the most important theoretical development was the doctrine of emptiness *(śūnyatā).* The first can be understood also as the result of a certain vision of the concrete manifestation of the sacred; the second, as the expression of a new type of mystical or contemplative experience.

The Bodhisattva. In pre-Mahāyāna Buddhism the term *bodhisattva* referred primarily to the figure of a Buddha from the time of his adoption of the vow to attain enlightenment to the point at which he attained Buddhahood. Even when used as an abstract designation of an ideal of perfection, the value of the ideal was determined by the goal: liberation from suffering. In the teachings of some of the Hīnayāna schools, however, the *bodhisattva* became an ideal with intrinsic value: to be a *bodhisattva* meant to adopt the vow *(praṇidhāna)* of seeking perfect awakening *for the sake of living beings;* that is, to follow the example set by the altruistic dedication of the Buddha in his former lives, when he was a *bodhisattva,* and not to aspire merely to individual liberation, as the *arhat*s were supposed to have done. The Mahāyāna made this critique its own, and the *bodhisattva* ideal its central religious goal.

This doctrinal stance accompanied a shift in mythology that has been outlined above: the belief in multiple *bodhisattvas* and the development of a complex legend of the former lives of the Buddha. There was likewise a change in ritual centered around the cult of the *bodhisattva,* especially of mythical *bodhisattvas* who were believed to be engaged in the pursuit of awakening primarily, if not exclusively, for the sake of assisting beings in need or distress. Closely allied with this was the increasing popularity of the recitation of *bodhisattva* vows.

Whereas the *bodhisattva* of early Buddhism stood for a human being on his way to become a liberated being, the *bodhisattva* that appears in the Mahāyāna reflects the culmination of a process of change that began when some of the Hīnayāna schools extended the apotheosis of the Buddha Śākyamuni to the *bodhisattva*—that is, when they idealized both the Buddha and the spiritual career outlined by the myth of his previous lives. Mahāyāna then extended the same religious revaluation to numerous mythical beings believed to be far advanced in the path of awakening. Accordingly, in its mythology Mahāyāna has more than one object of veneration. Especially in contrast to the more conservative Hīnayāna schools (the Sarvāstivāda and the Theravāda, for instance), Mahāyāna is the Buddhism of multiple Buddhas and *bodhisattvas*, residing in multiple realms, where they assist numberless beings on their way to awakening. [*See* Celestial Buddhas and Bodhisattvas.]

Accordingly, the early ideal of the *bodhisattva* as future Buddha is not discarded; rather it is redefined and expanded. As a theory of liberation, the characteristic position of Mahāyāna can be summarized by saying that it emphasizes *bodhi* and relegates *nirvāṇa* to a secondary position. Strictly speaking, this may represent an early split within the community rather than a shift in doctrine. One could speculate that it goes back to conflicting notions of means to liberation found among the shramanic religions: the conflict between enstasy and insight as means of liberation. But this analysis must be qualified by noting that the revaluation of *bodhi* must be seen in the context of the *bodhisattva* vow. The unique aspiration of the *bodhisattva* defines awakening as "awakening for the sake of all sentient beings." This is a concept that cannot be understood properly in the context of disputes regarding the relative importance of insight.

Furthermore, one should note that the displacement of *nirvāṇa* is usually effected through its redefinition, not by means of a rejection of the basic concept of "freedom from all attachment." Although the formalized texts of the vows often speak of the *bodhisattva* "postponing" his entrance into *nirvāṇa* until all living beings are saved, and the Buddha is asked in prayer to remain in the world without entering *nirvāṇa,* the central doctrine implies that a *bodhisattva* would not even consider a *nirvāṇa* of the type sought by the *arhat*. The *bodhisattva* is defined more by his aspiration for a different type of *nirvāṇa* than by a rejection or postponement of *nirvāṇa* as such. The gist of this new doctrine of *nirvāṇa* can be summarized in a definition of liberation as a state of peace in which the liberated person is neither attached to peace not attached to the turmoil of the cycle of rebirth. It is variously named and defined: either by an identity of *saṃsāra* and *nirvāṇa* or by proposing a *nirvāṇa* in which one can find no support *(apratiṣṭhita-nirvāṇa)*. [*See* Soteriology, *article on* Buddhist Soteriology.]

As noted above, in the early conception a *bodhisattva* is a real human being. This aspect of the doctrine is not lost in Mahāyāna, but preserved in the belief that the aspiration to perfect awakening (the *bodhicitta*) and the *bodhisattva* vow should be adopted by all believers. By taking up the vow—by conversion or by ritual repetition—the Mahāyāna Buddhist, monk or layperson, actualizes the *bodhicitta* and progresses toward the goal of becoming a *bodhisattva*. Also uniquely Mahāyāna is the belief that these human aspirants to awakening are not alone—they are accompanied and protected by "celestial *bodhisattvas*," powerful beings far advanced in the path, so perfect that they are free from both rebirth and liberation, and can now choose freely if, when, and where they are to be reborn. They engage freely in the process of rebirth only to save living beings.

What transforms the human and ethical ideal into a religious ideal, and into the object of religious awe, is the scale in which the *bodhisattva* path is conceived. From the first aspiration to awakening *(bodhicitta)* and the affirmation of the vow to the attainment of final enlightenment and liberation, countless lives intervene. The *bodhisattva* has to traverse ten stages *(bhūmi)*, beginning with the intense practice of the virtue of generosity (primarily a lay virtue), passing through morality in the second stage, patience in the third, then fortitude, meditation, insight, skill in means, vows, powers, and the highest knowledge of a Buddha. The stages, therefore, correspond with the ten perfections *(pāramitā)*. Although all perfections are practiced in every stage, they are mastered in the order in which they are listed in the scheme of the stages, suggesting at one end of the spectrum a simple and accessible practice for the majority of believers, the human *bodhisattva*, and at the other end a stage clearly unattainable in the realm of normal human circumstances, reserved for semidivine Buddhas and *bodhisattvas*, the object of worship. Although some exceptional human beings may qualify for the status of advanced *bodhisattvas*, most of these ideal beings are the mythic objects of religious fervor and imagination.

Among the mythic or celestial *bodhisattvas* the figure of Maitreya—destined to be the next Buddha of this world system after Śākyamuni—clearly represents the earliest stage of the myth. His cult is especially important in East Asian Buddhism. Other celestial *bodhisattvas* include Mañjuśrī, the *bodhisattva* of wisdom, the patron of scripture, obviously less important in the general cultus but an important *bodhisattva* in monastic devotion. The most important liturgical role is reserved for Avalokiteśvara, the *bodhisattva* of compassion, whose central role in worship is attested by archaeology. [*See also* Maitreya; Mañjuśrī; *and* Avalokiteśvara.]

Emptiness. The doctrine of emptiness *(śūnyatā)* represents a refinement of the ancient doctrine of no-self. In some ways it is merely an extension of the earlier doctrine: the denial of the substantial reality of the self and what belongs to the self, as a means to effect a breaking of the bonds of attachment. The notion of emptiness, however, expresses a critique of our common notions of reality that is much more radical than the critique implicit in the doctrine of no-self. The Mahāyāna critique is in fact unacceptable to other Buddhists, for it is in a manner of speaking a critique of Buddhism. Emptiness of all things implies the groundlessness of all ideas and conceptions, including, ultimately, Buddhist doctrines themselves.

The doctrine of emptiness was developed by the philosophical schools, but clearly inspired by the tradition of the Mahāyāna *sūtras*. Thus we read: "Even *nirvāṇa* is like a magical creation, like a dream, how much more any other object or idea *(dharma)*. . . ? Even a Perfect Buddha is like a magical creation, like a dream. . ." (*Aṣṭasāhasrikā*, p. 40). The practical correlate of the doctrine of emptiness is the concept of "skill in means" *(upāya)*: Buddhist teachings are not absolute statements about reality, they are means to a higher goal beyond all views. In their cultural context these two doctrines probably served as a way of making Buddhist doctrine malleable to diverse populations. By placing the truth of Buddhism beyond the specific content of its religious practices, these two doctrines justified adaptation to changing circumstances and the adoption of new religious customs.

But emptiness, like the *bodhisattva* vows, also reflects the Mahāyāna understanding of the ultimate experience of Buddhism—understood both as a dialectic and a meditational process. This experience can be described as an awareness that nothing is self-existent. Dialectically, this means that there is no way that the mind can consistently think of any thing as having an existence of its own. All concepts of substance and existence vanish when they are examined closely and rationally. As a religious experience the term *emptiness* refers to a direct perception of this absence of self-existence, a perception that is only possible through mental cultivation, and which is a liberating experience. Liberation, in fact, has been redefined in a way reminiscent of early texts such as the *Suttanipāta*. Liberation is now the freedom resulting from the negation of all assumptions about reality, even Buddhist assumptions.

> The cessation of grasping and reifying,
> calming the plural mind—this is bliss.
> The Buddha never taught any thing/doctrine [*dharma*]
> to anyone anywhere. (*Madhyamakakārikā* 25.24)

Finally, emptiness is also an affirmation of the immanence of the sacred. Applied to the turmoil of the sphere of rebirth *(saṃsāra)*, it points to the relative value and reality of the world and at the same time transforms it into the sacred, the experience of awakening. Applied to the sphere of liberation *(nirvāṇa)*, emptiness is a critique of the conception of liberation as a religious goal outside the world of impermanence and suffering. [*See* Śūnyam and Śūnyatā.]

Other Views of the Absolute. Mahāyāna developed early notions of the supernatural and the sacred that guaranteed an exalted status to the symbols of its mystical and ethical ideals. Its notion of extraordinary beings populating supernal Buddha fields and coming to the aid of suffering sentient beings necessitated a metaphysic and cosmology that could offer concrete images of a transcendent sacred. Accordingly, the abstract, apophatic concept of emptiness was often qualified by, or even rejected in favor of, positive statements and concrete images.

Pre-Mahāyāna traditions had emphasized impermanence and no-self: to imagine that there is permanence in the impermanent is the most noxious error. Mahāyāna introduced the notion of emptiness, urging us to give up the notion of permanence, but to give up the notion of impermanence as well. Within the Mahāyāna camp others proposed that there was something permanent within the impermanent. Texts like the [*Mahāyāna*] *Mahāparinirvāṇa Sūtra* asserted that the Buddha himself had taught a doctrine of permanence: the seed of Buddhahood, innate enlightenment, is permanent, blissful, pure—indeed, it is the true self, present in the impermanent mind and body of sentient beings.

The *Tathāgata* as object of worship was associated with "suchness" *(tathatā)*, his saving actions were seen as taking effect in a world formed in the image of the

Dharma and its ultimate truth *(dharmadhātu)*, and his form as repository of all goodness and virtue represented his highest form. [*See* Tathatā.]

A doctrine common to all Mahāyānists sought to establish a link between the absolute and common human beings. The Tathāgata was conceived of as having several aspects to his person: the human Buddha or "Body of Magical Apparition" *(nirmāṇakāya)*, that is, the historical persons of Buddhas; the transcendent sacred, the Buddha of the paradises and Buddha fields, who is also the form that is the object of worship *(saṃbhogakāya)*; and the Buddha as Suchness, as nonduality, the *tathāgata* as embodiment of the *dharmadhātu*, called the "Dharma Body" *(dharmakāya)*.

DEVELOPMENTS IN PRACTICE

The practice of meditation was for the Mahāyānist part of a ritual process beginning with the first feelings of compassion for other sentient beings, formulating the vow, including the expression of a strong desire to save all sentient beings and share one's merit with them, followed by the cultivation of the analysis of all existents, reaching a pinnacle in the experience of emptiness but culminating in the dedication of these efforts to the salvation of others.

Worship and Ritual. The uniquely Mahāyāna aspect of the ritual is the threefold service *(triskandhaka)*. Variously defined, this bare outline of the essential Mahāyāna ritual is explained by the seventh-century poet Śāntideva as consisting of a confession of sins, formal rejoicing at the merit of others, and a request to all Buddhas that they remain in the world for the sake of suffering sentient beings. A pious Buddhist was expected to perform this threefold ritual three times in the day and three times in the night.

A text known as the *Triskandhaka*, forming part of the *Upālipariprcchā*, proves the central role of confession and dedication of merit. The act of confession is clearly a continuation of the ancient Prātimokṣa ritual. Other elements of continuity include a link with early nonliterary tradition (now integrated into scripture) in the role of the dedication of merit, and a link with the general Buddhist tradition of the Three Refuges.

More complicated liturgies were in use. Several versions remain in the extant literature. Although many of them are said to be "the sevenfold service" *(saptavidhānuttarapūjā)*, the number seven is to be taken as an abstract number. The most important elements of the longer liturgies are the salutation to the Buddhas and *bodhisattvas*, the act of worship, the act of contrition, delight in the merit of others, and the dedication of merit. Hsüan-tsang, the seventh-century Chinese pilgrim to India, describes, albeit cursorily, some of the liturgies in use in the Indian monasteries of his time.

Most common forms of ritual, however, must have been less formalized and less monkish. The common rite is best represented by the litany of Avalokiteśvara, preserved in the literature and the monuments. In its literary form it is a solemn statement of the *bodhisattva*'s capacity to save from peril those who call on his name. But in actual practice, one can surmise, the cult of Avalokiteśvara included then, as it does today in East Asia, prayers of petition and apotropaic invocations.

The basic liturgical order of the literary tradition was embellished with elements from general Indian religious custom, especially from the styles of worship called *pūjā*. These included practices such as bathing the sacred image, carrying it in procession, offering cloth, perfume, and music to the icon, and so forth. [*See* Pūjā, *especially the article on* Buddhist Pūjā.]

Ritual practices were also expanded in the monastic tradition. For instance, another text also going by the title *Triskandhaka* (but preserved only in Tibetan translation) shows an intimate connection between ritual and meditation, as it integrates—like many monastic manuals of meditation—the typical daily ritual cycle with a meditation session.

Meditation. The practice of meditation was as important in the Mahāyāna tradition as it had been before. The maps of the path and the meditation manuals of Mahāyāna Buddhists give us accounts, if somewhat idealized ones, of the process of meditation. Although no systematic history of Mahāyāna meditation has been attempted yet, it is obvious that there are important synchronic and diachronic differences among Mahāyāna Buddhists in India. Considering, nevertheless, only those elements that are common to the various systems, one must note first an element of continuity with the past in the use of a terminology very similar to that of the Mahīśāsakas and the Sarvāstivāda, and in the acceptance, with little change, of traditional lists of objects and states of contemplation. [*See* Meditation, *article on* Buddhist Meditation.]

The interpretation of the process, however, and the definition of the higher stages of contemplation differed radically from that of the Hīnayāna schools. The principal shift is in the definition of the goal as a state in which the object of contemplation *(ālambana)* is no longer present to the mind *(nirālambana)*. All the mental images (or "marks," *nimitta, saṃjñā*) that form the basis for conceptual thought and attachment must be abandoned through a process of mental calm and analysis, until the contemplative reaches a state of peaceful concentration free of mental marks *(ānimitta)*, free of conceptualizations *(nirvikalpa-samādhi)*.

These changes in contemplative theory are closely connected to the abandonment of the *dharma* theory and the doctrine of no-self as the theoretical focus of speculative mysticism. One may say that the leading theme of Mahāyāna contemplative life is the meditation on emptiness. But one must add that the scholastic traditions are very careful to define the goal as constituted by both emptiness and compassion *(karuṇā)*. The higher state of freedom from conceptions (the "supramundane knowledge") must be followed by return to the world to fulfill the vows of the *bodhisattva*—the highest contemplative stage is, at least in theory, a preparation for the practice of compassion. [*See* Karuṇā.]

The New Ethics. The *bodhisattva* ideal also implied new ethical notions. Two themes prevail in Mahāyāna ethical speculation: the altruistic vow and life in the world. Both themes reflect changes in the social context of Buddhism: a greater concern, if not a stronger role for, lay life and its needs and aspirations and a cultural context requiring universal social values. The altruistic ideal is embodied in the *bodhisattva* vows and in the creation of a new set of ethical rules, commonly known as the "Bodhisattva Vinaya." A number of Mahāyāna texts are said to represent this new "Vinaya." Among these, the *Bodhisattvaprātimokṣa* was especially important in India. It prescribes a liturgy for the ritual adoption of the *bodhisattva* vows, which is clearly based on the earlier rites of ordination *(upasaṃpadā)*. Although the Mahāyāna Vinaya Sūtras never replaced in India the earlier monastic codes, they preserved and transmitted important, and at times obligatory, rites of monastic and lay initiation, and were considered essential supplements to traditional monastic Vinaya. [*See also* Buddhist Ethics.]

The High Tradition and the Universities

The most important element in the institutionalization of Mahāyāna was perhaps the establishment of Buddhist universities. In these centers of learning the elaboration of Buddhist doctrine became the most important goal of Buddhist monastic life. First at Nālandā and Valabhī, then, as the Pāla dynasty took control of East Central India (c. 650), at the universities of Vikramaśīla and Odantapurī, Mahāyāna scholars trained disciples from different parts of the Buddhist world and elaborated subtle systems of textual interpretation and philosophical speculation.

THE MAHĀYĀNA SYNTHESIS

Although eventually they would not be able to compete with more resilient forms of Buddhism and Hinduism, the Mahāyāna scholars played a leading role in the creation of a Mahāyāna synthesis that would satisfy both the intelligentsia and the common believers for at least five hundred years. Devotion, ritual, ethics, metaphysics, and logic formed part of this monument to Indian philosophical acumen. Even as the ruthless Mihirakula, the Ephthalite ("White") Hun, was invading India from the northwest (c. 500–528) and the Chalukya dynasty was contributing to a Hindu renaissance in the southwest (c. 550–753), India allowed for the development of great minds—such distinguished philosophical figures as Dignāga and Sthiramati, who investigated subtle philosophical issues. Persecution by Mihirakula (c. 550) was followed by the reign of one of the great patrons of Buddhism, Harṣa Vardhana (c. 605–647). Once more Buddhism was managing to survive on the seesaw of Indian politics.

SCHOOLS

The scholastic tradition of Mahāyāna can be divided into three schools: Mādhyamika (Madhyamaka), Yogācāra, and the school of Sāramati. The first two dominated the intellectual life of Mahāyāna in India. The third had a short-lived but important influence on Tibet, and indirectly may be considered an important element in the development of East Asian Buddhism.

Mādhyamika. The founder of this school can also be regarded as the father of Mahāyāna scholasticism and philosophy. Nāgārjuna (fl. c. 150 CE) came from South India, possibly from the Amarāvatī region. Said to have been the advisor to one of the Śātavāhana monarchs, he became the first major philosopher of Mahāyāna and a figure whose ideas influenced all its schools. The central theme of his philosophy is emptiness *(śūnyatā)* understood as a corollary of the pre-Mahāyāna theory of dependent origination. Emptiness is the Middle Way between affirmations of being and nonbeing. The extremes of existence and nonexistence are avoided by recognizing certain causal relations (e.g., the path and liberation) without predicating a self-existence or immutable essence *(svabhāva)* to either cause or effect. To defend his views without establishing a metaphysical thesis, Nāgārjuna argues by reducing to the absurd all the alternative philosophical doctrines recognized in his day. For his own "system," Nāgārjuna claims to have no thesis to affirm beyond his rejection of the affirmations and negations of all metaphysical systems. Therefore, Nāgārjuna's system is "the school of the Middle" *(madhyamaka)* both as an ontology (neither being nor nonbeing) and as a logic (neither affirmation nor negation). In religious terms, Nāgārjuna's Middle Way is summarized in his famous statement that *saṃsāra* and *nirvāṇa* are the same. [*See the biography of Nāgārjuna.*]

Three to four centuries after Nāgārjuna the Mādhyamika school split into two main branches, called Prāsaṅgika and Svātantrika. The first of these, represented by Buddhapālita (c. 500) and Candrakīrti (c. 550–600), claimed that in order to be faithful to the teachings of Nāgārjuna, philosophers had to confine themselves to the critique of opposing views by *reductio ad absurdum*. The Svātantrikas, on the other hand, claimed that the Mādhyamika philosopher had to formulate his own thesis; in particular, he needed his own epistemology. The main exponent of this view was Buddhapālita's great critic Bhāvaviveka (c. 500–550). The debate continued for some time but was eclipsed by other philosophical issues; for the Mādhyamika school eventually assimilated elements of other Mahāyāna traditions, especially those of the logicians and the Yogācārins. [*See the biographies of Buddhapālita, Bhāvaviveka, and Candrakīrti.*]

Mādhyamika scholars also contributed to the development of religious literature. Several hymns *(stava)* are attributed to Nāgārjuna. His disciple Āryadeva discusses the *bodhisattva*'s career in his *Bodhisattva-yogācāra-catuḥśataka*, although the work deals mostly with philosophical issues. Two anthological works, one attributed to Nāgārjuna, the *Sūtrasamuccaya,* and the other to the seventh-century Śāntideva, the *Śikṣāsamuccaya,* became guides to the ritual and ethical practices of Mahāyāna. Śāntideva also wrote a "guide" to the *bodhisattva*'s career, the *Bodhicaryāvatāra,* a work that gives us a sampling of the ritual and contemplative practices of Mādhyamika monks, as well as a classical survey of the philosophical issues that engaged their attention. [*See also* Mādhyamika *and the biographies of Āryadeva and Śāntideva.*]

Yogācāra. Approximately two centuries after Nāgārjuna, during the transition period from Kushan to Gupta power, a new school of Mahāyāna philosophy arose in the northwest. The founders of this school, the brothers Asaṅga (c. 310–390) and Vasubandhu (c. 320–400), had begun as scholars in the Hīnayāna schools. Asaṅga, the elder brother, was trained in the Mahīśāsaka school. Many important features of the Abhidharma theories of this school remained in Asaṅga's Mahāyāna system. Vasubandhu, who converted to Mahāyāna after his brother had become an established scholar of the school, began as a Sautrāntika with an extraordinary command of Sarvāstivādin theories. Therefore, when he did become a Mahāyānist he too brought with him a Hīnayāna scholastic grid on which to organize and rationalize Mahāyāna teachings.

The school founded by the two brothers is known as the Yogācāra, perhaps following the title of Asaṅga's major work, the *Yogācārabhūmi* (sometimes attributed to Maitreya), but clearly expressing the centrality of the practice of self-cultivation, especially through meditation. In explaining the experiences arising during the practice of yoga, the school proposes the two doctrines that characterize it: (1) the experience of enstasy leads to the conviction that there is nothing but mind *(cittamā-*

tratā), or the world is nothing but a perceptual construct *(vijñaptimātratā)*; (2) the analysis of mind carried out during meditation reveals different levels of perception or awareness, and, in the depths of consciousness, the basis for rebirth and karmic determination, a storehouse consciousness *(ālaya-vijñāna)* containing the seeds of former actions. Varying emphasis on these two principles characterize different modes of the doctrine. The doctrine of mind-only dominates Vasubandhu's *Viṃśatikā* and *Triṃśikā*; the analysis of the *ālaya-vijñāna* is more central to Asaṅga's doctrine. Since both aspects of the doctrine can be understood as theories of consciousness *(vijñāna),* the school is sometimes called Vijñānavāda.

One of the first important divisions within the Yogācāra camp reflected geographical as well as doctrinal differences. The school of Valabhī, following Sthiramati (c. 500–560), opposed the Yogācārins of Nālandā, led by Dharmapāla (c. 530–561). The point at issue, whether the pure mind is the same as the storehouse consciousness, illustrates the subtleties of Indian philosophical polemics but also reflects the influence of another school, the school of Sāramati, as well as the soteriological concerns underlying the psychological theories of Yogācāra. The debate on this point would continue in the Mādhyamika school, involving issues of the theory of perception as well as problems in the theory of the liberated mind. [*See also* Yogācāra; Vijñāna; Ālaya-vijñāna; *and the biographies of Asaṅga, Vasubandhu, Sthiramati, Dharmapāla, and Śīlabhadra.*]

Tathāgata-garbha Theory. Another influential school followed the tendency—already expressed in some Mahāyāna *sūtras*—toward a positive definition or description of ultimate reality. The emphasis in this school was on the ontological basis for the experience and virtues of Buddhahood. This basis was found in the underlying or innate Buddhahood of all beings. The school is known under two names; one describes its fundamental doctrine, the theory of *tathāgata-garbha* (the presence of the Tathāgata in all beings), the other refers to its purported systematizer, Sāramati (c. 350–450). The school's emphasis on a positive foundation of being associates it closely with the thought of Maitreyanātha, the teacher of Asaṅga, to whom is often attributed one of the fundamental texts of the school, the *Ratnagotravibhāga*. It may be that Maitreya's thought gave rise to two lines of interpretation—*tathāgata-garbha* and *cittamātratā*.

Sāramati wrote a commentary on the *Ratnagotravibhāga* in which he explains the process whereby innate Buddhahood becomes manifest Buddhahood. The work is critical of the theory of emptiness and describes the positive attributes of Buddhahood. The *bodhisattva*'s involvement in the world is seen not so much as the abandonment of the bliss of liberation as it is the manifestation of the Absolute *(dharmadhātu)* in the sphere of sentient beings, a concept that can be traced to Mahāsāṃghika doctrines. The *dharmadhātu* is a positive, metaphysical absolute, not only eternal, but pure, the locus of ethical, soteric, and epistemological value. This absolute is also the basis for the *gotra,* or spiritual lineage, which is a metaphor for the relative potential for enlightenment in living beings. [*See also* Tathāgatagarbha.]

The Logicians. An important development in Buddhist scholarship came about as a result of the concern of scholastics with the rules of debate and their engagement in philosophical controversies with Hindu logicians of the Nyāya school. Nāgārjuna and Vasubandhu wrote short treatises on logic, but a creative and uniquely Buddhist logic and epistemology did not arise until the time of Dignāga (c. 480–540), a scholar who claimed allegiance to Yogācāra but adopted a number of Sautrāntika doctrines. The crowning achievement of Buddhist logic was the work of Dharmakīrti (c. 600–650), whose *Pramāṇavārttika* and its *Vṛtti* revised critically the whole field. Although his work seems on the surface not relevant for the history of religion, it is emblematic of the direction of much of the intellectual effort of Mahāyāna scholars after the fifth century. [*See the biographies of Dignāga and Dharmakīrti.*]

Yogācāra-Mādhyamika Philosophers. As India moved away from the security of the Gupta period, Mahāyāna Buddhist philosophy gradually moved in the direction of eclecticism. By the time the university at Vikramaśīla was founded in the eighth century the dominant philosophy at Nālandā was a combination of Mādhyamika and Yogācāra, with the latter as the qualifying term and Mādhyamika as the core of the philosophy. This movement had roots in the earlier Svātantrika Mādhyamika and like its predecessor favored the formulation of ontological and epistemological theses in defense of Nāgārjuna's fundamental doctrine of emptiness. The most distinguished exponent of this school was Śāntirakṣita (c. 680–740); but some of his theories were challenged from within the movement by his contemporary Jñānagarbha (c. 700–760). The greatest contribution to religious thought, however, came from their successors. Kamalaśīla (c. 740–790), a disciple of Śāntirakṣita who continued the latter's mission in Tibet, wrote a number of brilliant works on diverse aspects of philosophy. He traveled to Tibet, where he wrote three treatises on meditation and the *bodhisattva* path, each called *Bhāvanākrama,* which must be counted among the jewels of Indian religious thought. [*See the biographies of Śāntirakṣita and Kamalaśīla.*]

NEW SCRIPTURES

The philosophers found their main source of inspiration in the Mahāyāna *sūtras,* most of which did not advocate clearly defined philosophical theories. Some *sūtras,* however, do express positions that can be associated with the doctrines of particular schools. Although scholars agree that these compositons are later than texts without a clear doctrinal affiliation, the connection between the *sūtras* and the schools they represent is not always clear.

For instance, some of the characteristic elements of the school of Sāramati are clearly pre-Mahāyānic, and can also be found in a number of *sūtras* from the *Avataṃsaka* and *Ratnakūṭa* collections. However, Sāramati appealed to a select number of Mahāyāna *sūtras* that clustered around the basic themes of the school. Perhaps the most famous is the *Śrīmālādevīsiṃhanāda*, but equally important are the [*Mahāyāna*] *Mahāparinirvāṇa Sūtra*, the *Anūnatvāpūrṇatvanirdeśa*, and the *Dhāraṇīrāja*.

A number of Mahāyāna *sūtras* of late composition were closely associated with the Yogācāra school. Although they were known already at the time of Asaṅga and Vasubandhu, in their present form they reflect a polemic than presupposes some form of proto-Yogācāra theory. Among these the *Laṅkāvatāra* and the *Saṃdhinirmocana* are the most important from a philosophical point of view. The first contains an early form of the theory of levels of *vijñāna.*

DECLINE OF MAHĀYĀNA

It is difficult to assess the nature and causes of the decay of Mahāyāna in India. Although it is possible to argue that the early success of Mahāyāna led to a tendency to look inward, that philosophers spent their time debating subtle metaphysical, logical, or even grammatical points, the truth is that even during the period of technical scholasticism, constructive religious thought was not dormant. But it may be that as Mahāyāna became more established and conventional, the natural need for religious revival found expression in other vehicles. Most likely Mahāyāna thinkers participated in the search for new forms of expression, appealing once more to visionary, revolutionary and charismatic leaders. But the new life gradually would adopt an identity of its own, first as Tantric Buddhism, eventually as Hinduism. For, in adopting Tantric practices and symbols, Mahāyāna Buddhists appealed to a symbolic and ritual world that fit naturally with a religious substratum that was about to become the province of Hinduism. [*For Hindu Tantrism, see* Tantrism *and* Hindu Tantric Literature.]

The gradual shift from Mahāyāna to Tantra seems to have gained momentum precisely at the time when Mahāyāna philosophy was beginning to lose its creative energy. We know of Tantric practices at Nālandā in the seventh century. These practices were criticized by the Nālandā scholar Dharmakīrti but apparently were accepted by most distinguished scholars of the same institution during the following century. As Tantra gained respectability, the Pāla monarchs established new centers of learning, rivaling Nālandā. We may say that the death of its great patron, King Harṣa, in 657 signals the decline of Mahāyāna, whereas the construction of the University of Vikramaśīla under Dharmapāla about the year 800 marks the beginning of the Tantric period. [*For Buddhist Tantrism, see* Buddhism, Schools of, *article on* Esoteric Buddhism.]

Tantric Innovations

As with Mahāyāna, we must assume that Tantra reflects social as well as religious changes. Because of the uncertainties of the date of its origin, however, few scholars have ventured any explanation for the arising of Tantra. Some advocate an early origin for Tantra, suggesting that the literature existed as an esoteric practice for many centuries before it ever came to the surface. If this were the case, then Tantra must have existed as some kind of underground movement long before the sixth century. But this theory must still explain the sudden appearance of Tantrism as a mainstream religion.

In its beginnings, Buddhist Tantra may have been a minority religion, essentially a private cult incorporating elements from the substratum frowned upon by the Buddhist establishment. It echoed ancient practices such as the critical rites of the *Atharvaveda* tradition, and the initiatory ceremonies, Aryan and non-Aryan, known to us from other Brahmanic sources. Starting as a marginal phenomenon, it eventually gained momentum, assuming the same role Mahāyāna had assumed earlier; a force of innovation and a vehicle for the expression of dissatisfaction with organized religion. The followers of Tantra became the new critics of the establishment. Some asserted the superiority of techniques of ritual and meditation that would lead to a direct, spontaneous realization of Buddhahood in this life. As wandering saints called *siddhas* ("possessed of *siddhi*," i.e., realization or magical power), they assumed the demeanor of madmen, and abandoned the rules of the monastic code. [*See* Mahāsiddhas.] Others saw Tantra as the culmination of Mahāyāna and chose to integrate it with earlier teachings, following established monastic practices even as they adopted beliefs that challenged the traditional assumptions of Buddhist monasticism.

The documented history of Tantra, naturally, reveals more about the second group. It is now impossible to establish with all certainty how the substratum affected Buddhist Tantra—whether, for instance, the metaphoric use of sexual practices preceded their explicit use, or vice versa. But is seems clear that the new wandering ascetics and their ideology submitted to the religious establishment even as they changed it. Tantra followed the pattern of cooperation with established religious institutions set by Mahāyāna in its relationship to the early scholastic establishment. Tantric monks would take the *bodhisattva* vows and receive monastic ordination under the pre-Mahāyāna code. Practitioners of Tantra would live in the same monastery with non-Tantric Mahāyāna monks. Thus Tantric Buddhism became integrated into the Buddhist high tradition even as the *siddhas* continued to challenge the values of Buddhist monasticism.

Although it seems likely that Tantric Buddhism existed as a minority, esoteric practice among Mahāyāna Buddhists before it made its appearance on the center stage of Indian religion, it is now impossible to know for how long and in what form it existed before the seventh century. The latter date alone is certain because the transmission of Tantra to China is marked by the arrival in the Chinese capitals of Tantric masters like Śubhākarasiṃha (arrives in Ch'ang-an 716) and Vajrabodhi (arrives in Lo-yang 720), and we can safely assume that the exportation of Tantra beyond the Indian border could not have been possible without a flourishing activity in India. [*See the biographies of Vajrabodhi, Śubhākarasiṃha, and Amoghavajra.*] Evidence for an earlier origin is found in the occasional reference, critical or laudatory, to *mantras* and *dhāraṇīs* in the literature of the seventh century (Dharmakīrti, Śāntideva) and the presence of proto-Tantric elements in Mahāyāna *sūtras* that must date from at least the fourth century *(Gaṇḍavyūha, Vimalakīrtinirdeśa, Saddharmapuṇḍarīka).*

Tantra in general makes use of ritual, symbolic, and doctrinal elements of earlier form of Buddhism. Especially the apotropaic and mystical formulas called *mantras* and *dhāraṇis* gain a central role in Tantrayāna. [*See* Mantra.] The *Mahāmāyūrī,* a proto-Tantric text of the third or fourth century, collects apotropaic formulas associated with local deities in different parts of India. Some of these formulas seem to go back to *parittas* similar to those in the Pali canonical text *Āṭānātiya Suttanta* (*Dīgha Nikāya* no. 32). Although one should not identify the relatively early, and pan-Buddhist, genre of the *dhāraṇī* and *paritta* with the Tantrayāna, the increased use of these formulas in most existing forms of Buddhism, and the appearance of *dhāraṇī-sūtras* in late Mahāyāṇa literature perhaps marks a shift towards greater emphasis on the magical dimension of Buddhist faith. The Mahāyāna *sūtras* also foreshadow Tantra with their doctrine of the identity of the awakened and the afflicted minds *(Dharmasaṅgīti, Vimalakīrtinirdeśa)*, and innate Buddhahood (Tathāgata-garbha *sūtras*).

VARIETIES OF TANTRA

Whatever may have been its prehistory, as esoteric or exoteric practice, the new movement—sometimes called the third *yāna*, Tantrayāna—was as complex and fragmented as earlier forms of Buddhism. A somewhat artificial, but useful classification distinguishes three main types of Tantra: Vajrayāna, Sahajayāna, and Kālacakra Tantra. The first established the symbolic terminology and the liturgy that would characterize all forms of the tradition. Many of these iconographic and ritual forms are described in the *Mañjuśrīmūlakalpa* (finished in its extant form c. 750), the *Mahāvairocana Sūtra,* and the *Vajraśekhara* (or *Tattvasaṃgraha*) *Sūtra*, which some would, following East Asian traditions, classify under a different, more primitive branch of Tantra called "Mantrayāna." The Sahajayāna was dominated by long-haired, wandering *siddhas*, who openly challenged and ridiculed the Buddhist establishment. They referred to the object of their religious experience as "the whore," both as a reference to the sexual symbolism of ritual Tantra and as a challenge to monastic conceptions of spiritual purity, buth also as a metaphor for the universal accessibility of enlightenment. The Kālacakra tradition is the farthest removed from earlier Buddhist traditions, and shows a stronger influence from the substratum. It incorporates concepts of messianism and astrology not attested elsewhere in Buddhist literature.

Unfortunately, the history of all three of these movements is clouded in legend. Tibetan traditions considers the Mantrayāna a third "turning of the wheel [of the Dharma]" (with Mahāyāna as the second), taking place in Dhānyakaṭaka (Andhra) sixteen years after the enlightenment. But this is patently absurd. As a working hypothesis, we can propose that there was an early stage of Mantrayāna beginning in the fourth century. The term *Vajrayāna* could be used then to describe the early documented manifestations of Tantric practice, especially in the high tradition of the Ganges River valley after the seventh century.

Sahajayāna is supposed to have originated with the Kashmirian yogin Lūi-pa (c. 750–800). The earliest documented Sahajayānists are from Bengal, but probably from the beginning of the ninth century. Regarding the Kālacakra, Western scholarship would not accept traditional views of its ancient origins in the mythic land of Shambhala. It must be dated not earlier than the tenth century, probably to the beginning of the reign of King Mahīpāla (c. 974–1026). Its roots have been sought in the North as well as in the South.

The Vajrayāna. The Vajrayāna derives its name from the centrality of the concept of *vajra* in its symbolism. The word *vajra* means both "diamond" and "cudgel." It is therefore a metaphor for hardness and destructiveness. Spiritually, it represents the eternal, innate state of Buddhahood possessed by all beings, as well as the cutting edge of wisdom. The personification of this condition and power is Vajrasattva, a deity and an abstract principle, which is defined as follows:

> By *vajra* is meant emptiness;
> *sattva* means pure cognition.
> The identity of these two is known
> as the essence of Vajrasattva.
> (*Advayavajra Saṃgraha*, p. 24)

Behind this definition is clearly the metaphysics of Yogācāra-Mādhyamika thought. Vajrasattva stands for the nondual experience that transcends both emptiness and pure mind. In religious terms this principle represents a homology between the human person and the essence of *vajra*: in the human body, in this life, relative and absolute meet.

The innate quality of the nondual is also represented by the concept of the "thought of awakening" *(bodhicitta)*. But innate awakening in Vajrayāna becomes the goal: enlightenment is present in its totality and perfection in this human body; the thought of awakening *is* awakening:

> The Thought of Awakening is known to be
> Without beginning or end, quiescent,
> Free from being and nonbeing, powerful,
> Undivided in emptiness and compassion.
> (*Guhyasamāja* 18.37)

This identity is established symbolically and ritually by a series of homologies. For instance, the six elements of the human body are identified with different aspects of the body of Mahāvairocana, the five constituents of the human personality *(skandhas)* are identified with the five forms of Buddha knowledge.

But the most characteristic aspect of Tantric Buddhism generally is the extension of these homologies to sexual symbolism. The "thought of awakening" is identified with semen, dormant wisdom with a woman waiting to be inseminated. Therefore, wisdom *(prajñā)* is conceived as a female deity. She is a mother *(jananī)*, as in the Prajñāpāramitā literature; she is the female yogi *(yoginī)*; but she is also a low-caste whore *(ḍombī caṇḍālī)*. Skillful means *(upāya)* are visualized as her male consort. The perfect union of these two *(prajñopāya-yuganaddha)* is the union of the nondual. Behind the Buddhist interpretation, of course, one discovers the non-Aryan substrantum, with its emphasis on fertility and the symbolism of the mother goddess. [*See* Goddess Worship, *article on* The Hindu Goddess.] But one may also see this radical departure from Buddhist monkish prudery as an attempt to shock the establishment out of self-righteous complacency.

Because the sexual symbolism can be understood metaphorically, most forms of Buddhist Tantra were antinomian only in principle. Thus, Vajrayāna was not without its vows and rules. As *upāya,* the symbols of ritual had as their goal the integration of the Absolute and the relative, not the abrogation of the latter. Tantric vows included traditional monastic rules, the *bodhisattva* vows, and special Tantric rules—some of which are contained in texts such as the *Vinayasūtra* and the *Bodhicittaśīlādānakalpa.*

The practice of the higher mysteries was reserved for those who had mastered the more elementary Mahāyāna and Tantra practices. The hierarchy of practice was established in systems such as the "five steps" of the *Pañcakrama* (by the Tantric Nāgārjuna). Generally, the order of study protected the higher mysteries, establishing the dividing line between esoteric and exoteric. Another common classification of the types of Tantra distinguished external daily rituals (Kriyā Tantra), special rituals serving as preparation for meditation, (Caryā Tantra), basic meditation practices (Yoga Tantra), and the highest, or advanced meditation Tantras (Anuttarayoga Tantra). This hermeneutic of sorts served both as an apologetic and a doctrinal classification of Tantric practice by distinguishing the audience for which each type of Tantra was best suited: respectively *śrāvakas, pratyekabuddhas,* Yogācārins, and Mādhyamikas.

Elements of Tathāgata-garbha theory seem to have been combined with early totemic beliefs to establish a system to Tathāgata families or clans that also served to define the proper audience for a variety of teachings. Persons afflicted by delusion, for instance, belonged to Mahāvairocana's clan, and should cultivate the homologies and visualizations associated with this Buddha—who, not coincidentally, represents the highest awakening. This system extends the homologies of *skandhas*, levels of knowledge, and so forth, to personality types. This can be understood as a practical psychology that forms part of the Tantric quest for the immanence of the sacred.

The Sahaja (or Sahajiyā) Movement. Although traditional Sahaja master-to-disciple lineages present it as a movement of great antiquity, the languages used in extant Sahaja literature belong to an advanced stage in the development of New Indic. These works were written mostly in Apabhrāṃśa (the *Dohākośa*) and early Bengali (the *Caryāgīti*). Thus, although their dates are uncertain, they cannot go as far back as suggested by tradition. Scholars generally agree on a conjectural dating of perhaps eighth to tenth century.

Works attributed to Sahaja masters are preserved not only in New Indian languages (Saraha, c. 750–800, Kaṇha, c. 800–850, Ti-lo-pa, c. 950–1000); a few commentaries exist in Sanskrit. The latter attest to the influence of the early wandering *siddhas* on the Buddhist establishment.

The basic doctrinal stance of the Sahaja movement is no different from that of Vajrayāna: *sahaja* is the innate principle of enlightenment, the *bodhicitta,* to be realized in the union of wisdom and skillful means. The main difference between the two types of Tantra is in the life-style of the adept. The Sahajiyā was a movement that represented a clear challenge to the Buddhist establishment: the ideal person was a homeless madman wandering about with his female consort, or a householder-sorcerer—either of which would claim to practice union with his consort as the actualization of what the high tradition practiced only in symbolic or mystical form. The Vajrayāna soon became integrated into the curriculum of the universities, controlled by the Vinaya and philosophical analysis. It was incorporated into the ordered program of spiritual cultivation accepted in the monasteries, which corresponded to the desired social and political stability of the academic institutions and their sponsors. The iconoclastic staints of the Sahaja, on the other hand, sought spontaneity, and saw monastic life as an obstacle to true realization. The force of their challenge is seen in quasi-mythic form in the legend that tells of the bizarre tests to which the *siddha* Ti-lo-pa submitted the great scholar Nā-ro-pa when the latter left his post at Vikramaśīla to follow the half-naked madman Ti-lo-pa.

This particular Tantric tradition, therefore, best embodied the iconoclastic tendencies found in all of Tantra. It challenged the establishment in the social as well as the religious sphere, for it incorporated freely practices from the substratum and placed women and sexuality on the level of the sacred. In opposition to the bland and ascetic paradises of Mahāyāna—where there were no women or sexual intercourse—Tantrism identifies the bliss of enlightment with the great bliss *(mahāsukha)* of sexual union.

The Kālacakra Tantra. This text has several features that separate it from other works of the Buddhist tradition: an obvious political message, suggesting an alliance to stop the Muslim advance in India, and astrological symbolism and teachings, among the others. In this work also we meet the concept of "Ādibuddha," the primordial Buddha, whence arises everything in the universe.

The high tradition, however, sees the text as remaining within the main line of Buddhist Tantrism. Its main argument is that all phenomena, including the rituals of Tantra, are contained within the initiate's body, and all aspects of time are also contained in this body. The concept of time *(kāla)* is introduced and discussed and its symbolism explained as a means to give the devotee control over time and therefore over the impermanent world. The *Sekoddeśaṭīkā,* a commentary on part of the *Kākacakra* attributed to Nā-ro-pa (Nāḍapāda, tenth century), explains that the time *(kāla)* of the *Kālacakra* is the same as the unchanging *dharmadhātu,* whereas the wheel *(cakra)* means the manifestations of time. In *Kālacakra* the two, absolute and relative, *prajñā* and *upāya,* are united. In this sense, therefore, in spite of its concessions to the substratum and to the rising tide of Hinduism, the *Kālacakra* was also integrated with mainline Buddhism.

TANTRIC LITERATURE

The word *tantra* means "thread" or "weft" and, by extension, "text." The sacred texts produced as the new dispensation, esoteric or exoteric, were called Tantras, and formed indeed a literary thread interwoven with the secret transmission from master to disciple. Some of the most difficult and profound Tantras were produced in the early period (before the eighth century); the *Mahāvairocana, Guhyasamāja,* the earlier parts of the *Mañjuśrīmūlakalpa,* and the *Hevajra.* By the time Tantra became the dominant system and, therefore, part of the establishment, a series of commentaries and authored works had appeared. Nāgārjuna's *Pañcakrama* is among the earliest. The Tantric Candrakīrti (ninth century) wrote a commentary on the *Guhyasamāja,* and Buddhaguhya (eighth century) discussed the *Mahāvairocana.* Sanskrit commentaries eventually were written to fossilize even the spontaneous poems of Sahaja saints.

TANTRA AND THE HIGH TRADITION

Thus, Tantra too, like its predecessors, eventually become institutionalized. What arose as an esoteric, intensely private, visionary and iconoclastic movement, became a literary tradition, ritualized, often exoteric and speculative.

We have abundant evidence of a flourishing Tantric circle at Nālandā, for instance, at least since the late seventh century. Tantric masters were by that time established members of the faculty. Especially during the Pāla dynasty, Tantric practices and speculation played a central role in Buddhist universities. This was clearly the period of institutionalization, a period when Tantra became part of the mainstream of Buddhism.

With this transformation the magical origins of Tantra were partly disguised by a high Tantric liturgy and a theory of Tantric meditation paralleling earlier, Mahāyāna theories of the path. Still, Tantric ritual and meditation retained an identity of their own. Magic formulas, gestures, and circles appeared transformed, respectively, into the mystical words of the Buddhas, the secret gestures of the Buddhas, and charts *maṇḍalas)* of the human psyche and the path.

The mystical diagram *(maṇḍala)* illustrates the complexity of this symbolism. It is at the same time a chart of the human person as it is now, a plan for liberation, and a representation of the transfigured body, the structure of Buddhahood itself. As a magic circle it is the sphere in which spiritual forces are evoked and controlled, as religious symbol it is the sphere of religious progress, experience, and action. The primitive functions remain: the *maṇḍala* is still a circle of power, with apotropaic functions. For each divinity there is an assigned meaning, a sacred syllable, a color, and a position within the *maṇḍala*. Spiritual forces can thus be evoked without danger. The sacred syllable is still a charm. The visualization of Buddhas is often inseparable from the evocation of demos and spirits. New beings populated the Buddhist pantheon. The Buddhas and *bodhisattvas* are accompanied by female consorts—these spiritual sexual partners can be found in explicit carnal iconographic representations. [*See* Maṇḍala, *article on* Buddhist Maṇḍalas.]

Worship and Ritual. Whereas the esoteric ritual incorporated elements of the substratum into a Buddhist doctrinal base, the exoteric liturgies of the Tantric high tradition followed ritual models from the Mahāyāna tradition as well as elements that evince Brahmanic ritual and Hindu worship. The daily ritual of the Tantric Buddhist presents a number of analogies of Brahmanic *pūjā* that cannot be accidental. But the complete liturgical cycle is still Buddhist. Many examples are preserved, for instance, in the Sanskrit text *Ādikarmapradīpa*. The ritual incorporates Tantric rites (offering to a *maṇḍala*, recitation of *mantras*) into a structure composed of elements from pre-Mahāyāna Buddhism (e.g., the Refuges), and Mahāyāna ritual (confession, vows, dedication of merit).

More complex liturgies include rites of initiation or consecration *(abhiṣeka)* and empowerment *(adhiṣṭhāna)*, rites that may have roots going as far back as the *Atharvaveda*. The burnt-offering rites *(homa)* also have Vedic and Brahmanic counterparts. Elements of the substratum are also evident in the frequent invocation of *yakṣas* and *devatās*, the propitiation of spirits, and the underlying sexual and alchemical symbolism.

Meditation. The practice of Tantric visualization *(sādhana)* was even more a part of ritual than the Mahāyāna meditation session. It was always set in a purely ritual frame similar to the structure of the daily ritual summarized above. A complete *sādhana* would integrate pre-Mahāyāna and Mahāyāna liturgical and contemplative processes with Tantric visualization. The meditator would first go through a gradual process of purification (sometimes including ablutions) usually constructed on the model of the Mahāyāna "sevenfold service." He would then visualize the mystical syllable corresponding to his chosen deity. The syllable would be transformed into a series of images that would lead finally to clear visualization of the deity. Once the deity was visualized clearly, the adept would become one with it. But this oneness was interpreted as the realization of the nondual; therefore, the deity became the adept as much as the adept was turned into a deity. Thus, the transcendent could be actualized in the adept's life beyond meditation in the fulfillment of the *bodhisattva* vows.

Tantric Doctrine. Tantric symbolism was interpreted in the context of Mahāyāna orthodoxy. It is therefore possible to explain Tantric theoretical conceptions as a natural development from Mahāyāna. The immanence of Buddhahood is explicitly connected with the Mahāyāna doctrine of the identity of *saṃsāra* and *nirvāṇa* and the teachings of those Yogācārins who believed that consciousness is inherently pure. The magical symbolism of Tantra can be traced—again through explicit references—to the doctrine of the *bodhisattva* as magician: since the world is like a dream, like a magical apparition, one can be free of it by knowing the dream as dream—knowing and controlling the magical illusion as a magician would control it. The *bodhisattva* (and therefore the *siddha*) is able to play the magical trick of the world without deceiving himself into believing it real.

One should not forget, however, that what is distinctively Tantric is not limited to the externals of ritual and symbolism. The special symbolism transforms its Mahāyāna context because of the specifically Tantric understanding of immanence. The Buddha is present in the human body innately, but the Buddha nature is manifested only when one realizes the "three mysteries," or "three secrets." It is not enough to be free from the illusion of the world; one becomes free by living *in* illusion in such a way that illusion becomes the manifestation of Buddhahood. Tantra seeks to construct an alternative reality, such that a mentally constructed world reveals the fundamental illusion of the world and manifests the mysterious power of the Buddha through illusion. The human body, the realm of the senses, is to be transformed into the body of a Buddha, the senses of a Buddha.

The body, mind, and speech of the Buddha (the Three Mysteries) have specific characteristics that must be recognized and reproduced. In ritual terms this means that the adept actualizes Buddhahood when he performs prostrations and ritual gestures (*mudrās*); he speaks with the voice of the Buddha when he utters *mantras*; his mind is the mind of the Buddha when he visualizes the deity. The magical dimension is evident: the power of the Buddha lives in the formalized "demeanor of a Buddha." But the doctrine also implies transforming the body by a mystical alchemy (rooted in substratum sexual alchemy) from which is derived the soteriological meaning of the doctrine: the ritual changes the human person into a Buddha, all his human functions become sacred. Then this person's mind is the mind of an awakened being, it knows all things; the body assumes the appearance appropriate to save any living being; the voice is able to speak in the language of any living being needing to be saved. [*See also* Soteriology, *article on* Buddhist Soteriology.]

The Decline of Buddhism in India

With Harṣa's death Indian Buddhism could depend only on the royal patronage of the Pāla dynasty of Bihar and Bengal (c. 650–950), who soon favored the institutions they had founded—Vikramaśīla (c. 800), Odantapurī (c. 760). The last shining lights of Nālandā were the Mādhyamika masters Śāntirakṣita and Kamalaśīla, both of whom participated actively in the conversion of Tibet. Then the ancient university was eclipsed by its rival Vikramaśīla, which saw its final glory in the eleventh century.

Traditionally, the end of Indian Buddhism has been identified with the sack of the two great universities by the troops of the Turk Muḥammad Ghūrī: Nālandā in 1197 and Vikramaśīla in 1203. But, although the destruction of Nālandā put an end to its former glory, Nālandā lingered on. When the Tibetan pilgrim Dharmasvāmin (1197–1264) visited the site of the ancient university in 1235 he found a few monks teaching in two monasteries remaining among the ruins of eighty-two others. In this way

Buddhism would stay on in India for a brief time, but under circumstances well illustrated by the decay witnessed by Dharmasvāmin—even as he was there, the Turks mounted another raid to further ransack what was left of Nālandā.

For a long time scholars have debated the causes for the decline of Buddhism in India. Although there is little chance of agreement on a problem so complex—and on which we have precious little evidence—some of the reasons adduced early are no longer widely accepted. For instance, the notion that Tantric Buddhism was a "degenerate form" of Buddhism that contributed to or brought about the disappearance of Buddhism is no longer entertained by the scholarly community. The image of a defenseless, pacifist Buddhist community annihilated by invading hordes of Muslim warriors is perhaps also a simplification. Though the Turkish conquerors of India were far from benevolent, the Arabs who occupied Sindh in 711 seem to have accepted a state of peaceful coexistence with the local population. Furthermore, one must still understand why Jainism and Hinduism survived the Muslim invasion while Buddhism did not.

Buddhist relations with Hindu and Jain monarchs were not always peaceful—witness the conquest of Bihar by the Bengali Śaiva king Śaśīṅka (c. 618). Even without the intervention of intolerance, the growth of Hinduism, with its firm roots in Indian society and freedom from the costly institution of the monastery, offered a colossal challenge to Buddhism. The eventual triumph of Hinduism can be followed by a number of landmarks often associated with opposition to Buddhism: the spread of Vaiṣṇavism (in which the Buddha appears as a deceptive *avatāra* of Viṣṇu); the great Vaiṣṇava and Śaiva saints of the South, the Āḻvārs and Nāyaṉārs, respectively, whose Hindu patrons were openly hostile to Buddhism and Jainism; the ministry of Śaṅkara in Mysore (788–850), a critic of Buddhism who was himself accused of being a "crypto-Buddhist"; and the triumph of Śaivism in Kashmir (c. 800). [*See* Vaiṣṇavism, *overview article;* Āḻvars; Śaivism, *overview article and article on* Nāyaṉārs; Kṛṣṇaism; Avatāra; *and the biography of Śaṅkara.*]

But the causes for the disappearance of Buddhism were subtle: the assimilation of Buddhist ideas and practices into Hinduism and the inverse process of the Hinduization of Buddhism, with the advantage of Hinduism as a religion of the land and the locality. More important than these were perhaps the internal causes for the decline: dependence on monastic institutions that did not have broad popular support but relied exclusively on royal patronage; and isolation of monasteries from the life of the village community, owing to the tendency of the monasteries to look inward and to lose interest in proselytizing and serving the surrounding communities.

The disappearance of Buddhism in India may have been precipitated by the Muslim invasion, but it was caused primarily by internal factors, the most important of which seems to have been the gradual assimilation of Buddhism into Hinduism. The Muslim invasion, especially the Turkish conquest of the Ganges Valley, was the *coup de grace;* we may consider it the dividing line between two eras, but it was not the primary cause for the disappearance of Buddhism from India. [*See* Islam, *articles on* Islam in Central Asia *and* Islam in South Asia.]

Buddhist Remnants and Revivals in the Subcontinent

After the last days of the great monastic institutions (twelfth and thirteenth centuries) Indian Buddhism lingered on in isolated pockets in the subcontinent. During the

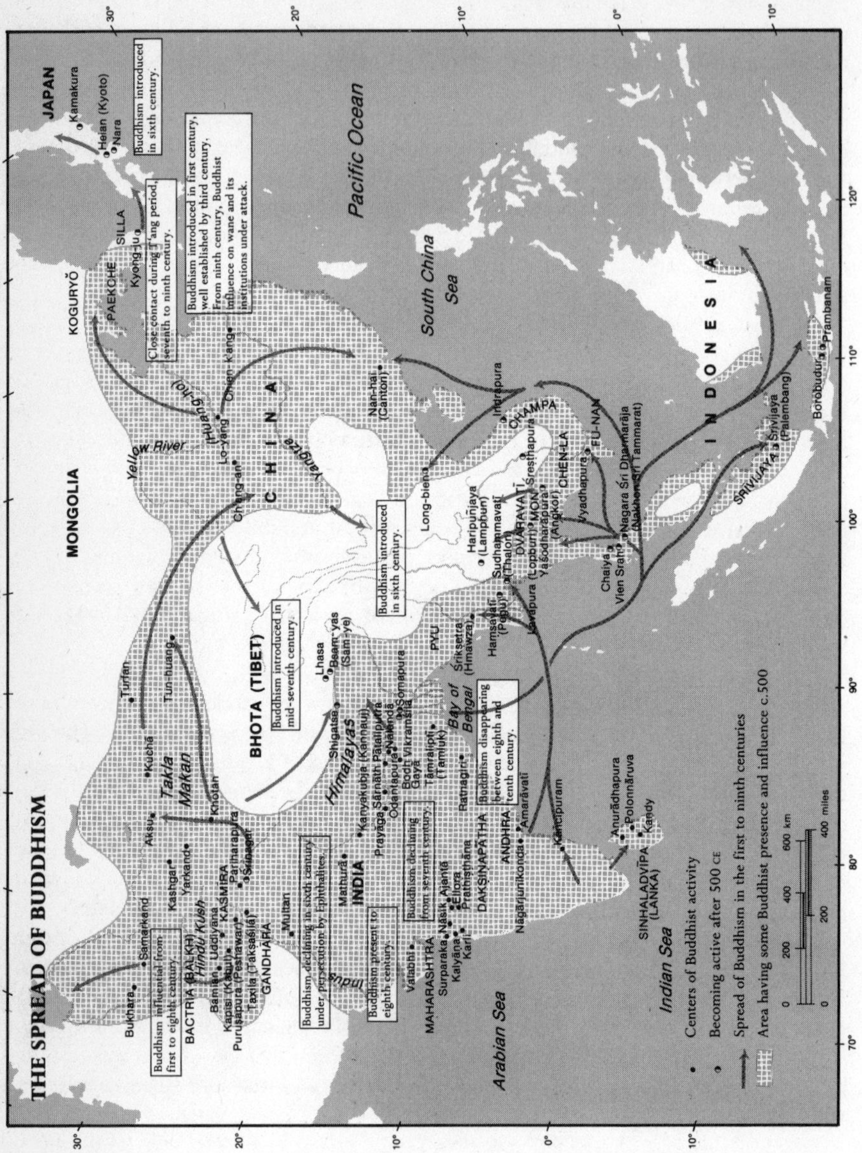
THE SPREAD OF BUDDHISM
MONGOLIA
JAPAN
Kamakura
Heian (Kyoto)
Nara
Buddhism introduced in sixth century.
KOGURYŌ
PAEKCHE
SILLA
Kyong-ju
Close contact during T'ang period, seventh to ninth century.
Buddhism introduced in first century, well established by third century. From ninth century, Buddhist influence on wane and its institutions under attack.
Pacific Ocean
South China Sea
Yellow River
Lo-yang
Ch'ang-an
Chien-kang
CHINA
Yangtze
Nan-hai (Canton)
Buddhism introduced in sixth century.
BHOTA (TIBET)
Buddhism introduced in mid-seventh century.
Lhasa
Bsam-yas (Sam-ye)
Shigatse
Himalayas
Turfan
Tun-huang
Kucha
Aksu
Takla Makan
Khotan
Kashgar
Yarkand
Bukhara
Samarkand
Buddhism influential from first to eighth century.
BACTRIA (BALKH)
Hindu Kush
Bamian
Uddiyana
KASMIRA
Kapisi (Kabul)
Purusapura (Peshawar)
Taxila (Taksasila)
GANDHARA
Parihasapura
Srinagar
Multan
Indus
Buddhism declining in sixth century under persecution by Ephthalites.
Buddhism present to eighth century.
Mathura
INDIA
Kanyakubja (Kannauj)
Prayaga
Sarnath
Pataliputra
Nalanda
Odantapuri
Somapura
Vikramasila
Bodh Gaya
Buddhism declining from seventh century.
Tamralipti (Tamluk)
Bay of Bengal
Buddhism disappearing between eighth and tenth century.
Valabhi
MAHARASHTRA
Surparaka
Nasik
Ajanta
Ellora
Kalyana
Karli
Pratishthana
DAKSINAPATHA
Ratnagiri
ANDHRA
Amaravati
Nagarjunikonda
Kancipuram
Arabian Sea
Indian Sea
SINHALADVIPA (LANKA)
Anuradhapura
Polonnaruva
Kandy
PYU
Sriksetra (Hmawza)
Hamsavati (Pegu)
Sudhammavati (Thaton)
Haripunjaya (Lamphun)
DVARAVATI
MON
Lavapura (Lopburi)
Yasodharapura (Angkor)
Srestapura
CHEN-LA
CHAMPA
Indrapura
Long-bien
Vyadhapura
FU-NAN
Chaiya
Vien Srah
Nagara Sri Dharmaraja (Nakhon Sri Tammarat)
SRIVIJAYA
Srivijaya (Palembang)
Borobudur
Prambanam
INDONESIA
Centers of Buddhist activity
Becoming active after 500 CE
Spread of Buddhism in the first to ninth centuries
Area having some Buddhist presence and influence c.500
0 200 400 600 km
0 200 400 miles

period of Muslim and British conquest (thirteenth to nineteenth century) it was almost completely absorbed by Hinduism and Islam, and gave no sign of creative life until modern attempts at restoration (nineteenth and twentieth centuries). Therefore, a hiatus of roughly six hundred years separates the creative period of Indian Buddhism from its modern manifestations.

BUDDHISM OF THE FRONTIER

As the Turk occupation of India advanced, the last great scholars of India escaped from Kashmir and Bihar to Tibet and Nepal. But the flight of Buddhist talent also responded to the attraction of royal patronage and popular support in other lands. The career of Atīśa (Dīpaṃkara Śrījñāna, 982–1054), who emigrated to Tibet in 1042, is emblematic of the great loss incurred by Indian Buddhism in losing its monk-scholars. He combined extensive studies in Mahāyāna philosophy and Tantra in India with a sojourn in Sumatra under the tutorship of Dharmakīrti. He had studied with Bodhibhadra (the successor of Nā-ro-pa when the latter left Vikramaśīla to become a wandering ascetic), and was head master *(upādhyāya)* of Vikramaśīla and Odantapurī at the time of King Bheyapāla. He left for Tibet at the invitation of Byaṅ-chub-'od, apparently attracted by a large monetary offer. [*See the biography of Atīśa.*]

The migration of the Indian scholars, and a steady stream of Tibetan students, made possible the exportation of Buddhist academic institutions and traditions to Tibet, where they were preserved until the Chinese suppression of 1959. The most learned monks were pushed out to the Himalayan and Bengali frontiers in part because the Indian communities were no longer willing to support the monasteries. Certain forms of Tantra, dependent only on householder priests, could survive, mostly in Bengal and in the Himalayan foothills. But some Theravādin Buddhists also survived in East Bengal—most of them taking refuge in India after the partition, some remaining in Bangladesh and Assam. [*See* Bengali Religions.]

Himalayan Buddhism of direct Indian ancestry remains only in Nepal, where it can be observed even today in suspended animation, partly fused with local Hinduism, as it must have been in the Gangetic plain during the twelfth century. Nepalese Buddhists produced what may very well be considered the last major Buddhist scripture composed in the subcontinent, the *Svayaṃbhū Purāṇa* (c. fifteenth century). This text is an open window into the last days of Indian Buddhism. It reveals the close connection between Buddhist piety and non-Buddhist sacred localities, the formation of a Buddhist cosmogonic ontology (the Ādibuddha), and the role of Tantric ritual in the incorporation of religious elements from the substratum. Nepalese Buddhism survives under the tutelage of married Tantric priests, called *vajrācārya*s. It is therefore sometimes referred to as "Vajrācārya Buddhism."

Buddhism of Tibetan origin survives in the subcontinent mostly in Ladakh, Sikkim, and Bhutan, but also in Nepal. [*See* Himalayan Religions.] Perhaps the most significant presence in modern India, however, is that of the Tibetan refugee communities. The Tibetan diaspora includes about eighty thousand persons, among which are several thousand monks. Some have retained their monastic robes and have reconstructed in India their ancient Buddhist academic curricula, returning to the land of origin the disciplines of the classical universities. So far their impact on Indian society at large has been insignificant and their hope of returning to Tibet dwindles with the passing of time. But the preservation, on Indian soil, of the classical traditions of Nālandā and Vikramaśīla is hardly a trivial accomplishment.

ATTEMPTED REVIVAL: THE MAHĀBODHI SOCIETY

Attempts to revive Buddhism in the land of its origin began with the Theosophical Society, popularized in Sri Lanka in the early 1880s by the American Henry S. Olcott. Although the society eventually became the vehicle for broader and less defined speculative goals, it inspired new pride in Buddhists after years of colonial oppression. [*See* Theosophical Society.] The Sinhala monk Anagārika Dharmapāla (1864–1933; born David Hewavitarane) set out to modernize Buddhist education. He also worked untiringly to restore the main pilgrimage sites of India, especially the temple of Bodh Gayā, which had fallen in disrepair and had been under Hindu administration for several centuries. To this end he founded in 1891 the Mahābodhi Society, still a major presence in Indian Buddhism.

AMBEDKAR AND "NEO-BUDDHISM"

The most significant Buddhist mass revival of the new age was led by Dr. Bhimrao Ramji Ambedkar (1891–1956). He saw Buddhism as the gospel for India's oppressed and read in the Buddhist scriptures ideals of equality and justice. After many years of spiritual search, he became convinced that Buddhism was the only ideology that could effect the eventual liberation of Indian outcastes. On 14 October 1956 he performed a mass "consecration" of Buddhists in Nagpur, Maharashtra. The new converts were mostly from the "scheduled caste" of the *mahārs*. Although his gospel is in some way on the fringes of Buddhist orthodoxy, Buddhist monks from other parts of Asia have ministered to the spiritual needs of his converts, and inspired Indian Buddhists refer to him as "Bodhisattva Ambedkar." [*See* Marathi Religions *and the biography of Ambedkar.*]

OTHER ASPECTS OF MODERN BUDDHISM

The most fruitful and persistent effort in the rediscovery of Indian Buddhism has been in the West, primarily among Western scholars. The achievements of European scholars include a modern critical edition of the complete Pali canon, published by the Pāli Text Society (founded in London in 1881), and the recovery of original texts of parts of the canon of the Sarvāstivāda. The combined effort of Indian, North American and European historians, archaeologists, and art historians has placed Indian Buddhism in a historical and social context, which, though still only understood in its rough outlines, allows us to see Buddhism in its historical evolution.

Japanese scholarship has also made great strides since the beginning of the twentieth century. The publication in Japan of three different editions of the Chinese canon between 1880 and 1929 may be seen as the symbolic beginning of a century of productive critical scholarship that has placed Japan at the head of modern research into Indian Buddhism. [*See* Buddhist Studies.]

Another interesting phenomenon of the contemporary world is the appearance of "neo-Buddhists" in Europe and North America. Although most of these groups have adopted extra-Indian forms of Buddhism, their interest in the scriptural traditions of India has created an audience and a demand for research into India's Buddhist past. The Buddhist Society, founded in London in 1926, and the Amis du Bouddhisme, founded in Paris in 1928, both supported scholarship and encouraged the Buddhist revival in India.

In spite of the revived interest in India of the last century, the prospects of an effective Buddhist revival in the land of Śākyamuni seem remote. It is difficult to imagine a successful living Buddhism in India today or in the near future. The possibility of the religion coming back to life may depend on the reimportation of the Dharma into India from another land. It remains to be seen if Ambedkar and Anagārika Dharmapāla had good reasons for hope in a Buddhist revival, or if in fact the necessary social conditions for the existence of Indian Buddhism disappeared with the last monarchs of the Pāla dynasty.

[*See also* Indian Religions.]

BIBLIOGRAPHY

Bareau, André. "Le bouddhisme indien." In *Les religions de l'Inde,* vol. 3, pp. 1–246. Paris, 1966. In addition to this useful survey, see Bareau's "Le bouddhisme indien," in *Histoire des religions,* edited by Henri-Charles Puech vol. 1, (Paris, 1970), pp. 1146–1215. Bareau has written the classical work on the question of the dating of the Buddha's life, "La date du Nirvāṇa," *Journal asiatique* 241 (1953): 27–62. He surveys and interprets classical documents on the Hīnayāna schools in "Les sectes bouddhiques du Petit Véhicule et leurs Abhidharmapiṭaka." *Bulletin de l'École Française d'Extrême-Orient* 50 (1952): 1–11; "Trois traités sur les sectes bouddhiques dus à Vasumitra, Bhavya et Vinitadeva," *Journal asiatique* 242–244 (1954–1956); *Les premiers conciles bouddhiques* (Paris, 1955); *Les sectes bouddhiques de Petit Véhicule* (Saigon, 1955); "Les controverses rélatives à la nature de l'arhant dans le bouddhisme ancien," *Indo-Iranian Journal* 1 (1957): 241–250. Bareau has also worked extensively on the "biography" of the Buddha: *Recherches sur la biographie duBouddha,* 3 vols. (Paris, 1970–1983); "Le parinirvāṇa du Bouddha et la naissance de la religion bouddhique," *Bulletin de l'École Française d'Extrême-Orient* 61 (1974): 275–300; and, on a more popular but still scholarly bent, *Le Bouddha* (Paris, 1962).

Basham, A. L. *The Wonder That Was India.* London, 1954. This is the most accessible and readable cultural history of pre-Muslim India. A more technical study on the religious movements at the time of the Buddha is Basham's *History and Doctrine of the Ājīvikas* (London, 1951).

Beal, Samuel. *Travels of Fa-hian and Sung-Yun, Buddhist Pilgrims from China to India (400 A.D. and 518 A.D.).* London, 1869. The travel records of two early pilgrims. See also Beal's *Si-yu-ki: Buddhist Records of the Western World,* 2 vols. (London, 1884). Translation of Hsüan-tsang's accounts of his travels to India.

Bechert, Heinz. "Zur Frühgeschichte des Mahāyāna-Buddhismus." *Zeitschrift der Deutschen Morgenländischen Gesellschaft* 113 (1963): 530–535. Summary discussion of the Hīnayāna roots of Mahāyāna. On the same topic, see also "Notes on the Formation of Buddhist Sects and the Origins of Mahāyāna," in *German Scholars on India,* vol. 1 (Varanasi, 1973), pp. 6–18; "The Date of the Buddha Reconsidered," *Indologica Taurinensia* 10 (1982): 29–36; "The Importance of Aśoka's So-called Schism Edict," in *Indological and Buddhist Studies in Honour of Prof. J. W. de Jong* (Canberra, 1982), pp. 61–68; and "The Beginnings of Buddhist Historiography," in *Religion and Legitimation of Power in Sri Lanka,* edited by Bardwell L. Smith (Chambersburg, Pa., 1978), pp. 1–12. Bechert is also the editor of the most recent contribution to the question of the language of Buddha and early Buddhism, *Die Sprache der ältesten buddhistischen Überlieferung / The Language of the Earliest Buddhist Tradition* (Göttingen, 1980).

Bechert, Heinz, and Georg von Simson, eds. *Einführung in die Indologie: Stand, Methoden, Aufgaben.* Darmstadt, 1979. A general introduction to Indology, containing abundant materials on Indian history and religion, including Buddhism.

Bechert, Heinz, and Richard Gombrich, eds. *The World of Buddhism*. London, 1984. This is by far the most scholarly and comprehensive survey of Buddhism for the general reader. Indian Buddhism is treated on pages 15–132 and 277–278.

Demiéville, Paul. "L'origine des sectes bouddhiques d'après Paramārtha." In *Mélanges chinois et bouddhiques,* vol. 1, pp. 14–64. Brussels, 1931–1932.

Demiéville, Paul. "A propos du Concile de Vaiśālī." *T'oung pao* 40 (1951): 239–296.

Dutt, Nalinaksha. *Aspects of Mahāyāna Buddhism and Its Relation to Hīnayāna.* London, 1930. Although Dutt's work on the development of the Buddhist sects is now largely superseded, there are no comprehensive expositions to replace his surveys. His *Mahāyāna Buddhism* (Calcutta, 1973) is sometimes presented as a revision of *Aspects,* but the earlier work is quite different and far superior. Most of Dutt's earlier work on the sects, found hidden in various journals, was compiled in *Buddhist Sects in India* (Calcutta, 1970). See also his *Early Monastic Buddhism*, rev. ed. (Calcutta, 1960).

Dutt, Sukumar. *The Buddha and Five After-Centuries*. London, 1957. Other useful, although dated, surveys include *Early Buddhist Monachism* (1924; new ed., Delhi, 1960) and *Buddhist Monks and Monasteries in India* (London, 1962).

Fick, R. *The Social Organization in Northeast India in the Buddha's Time*. Calcutta, 1920.

Frauwallner, Erich. "Die buddhistische Konzile." *Zeitschrift der Deutschen Morgenländischen Gesellschaft* 102 (1952): 240–261.

Frauwallner, Erich. *The Earliest Vinaya and the Beginnings of Buddhist Literature*. Rome, 1956.

Frauwallner, Erich. "The Historical Data We Possess on the Person and Doctrine of the Buddha." *East and West* 7 (1956): 309–312.

Fujita Kotatsu. *Genshi jōdoshisō no kenkyū*. Tokyo, 1970. The standard book on early Sukhāvatī beliefs.

Glasenapp, Helmuth von. "Zur Geschichte der buddhistischen Dharma Theorie." *Zeitschrift der Deutschen Morgenländischen Gesellschaft* 92 (1938): 383–420.

Glasenapp, Helmuth von. "Der Ursprung der buddhistischen Dharma-Theorie." *Wiener Zeitschrift für die Kunde des Morgenlandes* 46 (1939): 242–266.

Glasenapp, Helmuth von. *Buddhistische Mysterien*. Stuttgart, 1940. Discusses most of the theories on early Brahmanic influence on Buddhist doctrine.

Glasenapp, Helmuth von. *Buddhismus und Gottesidee*. Mainz, 1954.

Gokhale, Balkrishna Govind. *Buddhism and Aśoka*. Baroda, 1948. Other of this author's extensive writings on the social and political contexts of early Buddhism include "The Early Buddhist Elite," *Journal of Indian History* 43 (1965): 391–402; "Early Buddhist View of the State," *Journal of the American Oriental Society* 89 (1969): 731–738; "Theravāda Buddhism in Western India," *Journal of the American Oriental Society* 92 (1972): 230–236; and "Early Buddhism and the Brāhmaṇas," in *Studies in History of Buddhism,* edited by A. K. Narain (Delhi, 1980).

Gómez, Luis O. "Proto-Mādhyamika in the Pāli Canon." *Philosophy East and West* 26 (1976): 137–165. This paper argues that the older portions of *Suttanipāta* preserve a stratum of the tradition that differs radically from the dominant themes expressed in the rest of the Pali canon, especially in its Theravāda interpretation. The question of dedication of merit in the Mahāyāna is discussed in "Paradigm Shift and Paradigm Translation: The Case of Merit and Grace in Buddhism," in *Buddhist-Christian Dialogue* (Honolulu, forthcoming). On Mahāyāna doctrine and myth, see also my "Buddhism as a Religion of Hope: Polarities in the Myth of Dharmākara," *Journal of the Institute for Integral Shin Studies* (Kyoto, in press).

Grousset, René. *The Civilizations of the East,* vol. 2, *India*. London, 1931. One of the best surveys of Indian history. See also his *Sur les traces du Bouddha* (Paris, 1957) for a modern expansion and retelling of Hsüan-tsang's travels.

Hirakawa Akira. *Indo bukkyōshi*. 2 vols. Tokyo, 1974–1979. A valuable survey of Indian Buddhism from the perspective of Japanese scholarship (English translation forthcoming from the University Press of Hawaii). The development of the earliest Vinaya is discussed in *Ritsuzō no kenkyū* (Tokyo, 1960) and in *Shoki daijō bukkyō no kenkyū* (Tokyo, 1969). The author's "The Rise of Mahāyāna Buddhism and Its Relationship to the Worship of Stupas," *Memoirs of the Research Department of the Tōyō Bunko* 22 (1963): 57–106, is better known in the West and summarizes some of the conclusions of his Japanese writings.

Horner, I. B. *Early Buddhist Theory of Man Perfected*. London, 1936. A study of the *arhat* ideal in the Pali canon. See also Horner's translation of the dialogues between King Menander and Nāgasena, *Milinda's Questions* (London, 1964), and *Women under Primitive Buddhism* (1930; reprint, Delhi, 1975).

Horsch, P. "Der Hinduismus und die Religionen der primitivstämme Indiens." *Asiatische Studien / Études asiatiques* 22 (1968): 115–136.

Horsch, P. "Vorstufen der Indischen Seelenwanderungslehre." *Asiatische Studien / Études asiatiques* 25 (1971): 98–157.

Jayatilleke, K. N. *Early Buddhist Theory of Knowledge*. London, 1963. Discusses the relationship between early Buddhist ideas and śramaṇic and Upaniṣadic doctrines.

Jong, J. W. de. "A Brief History of Buddhist Studies in Europe and America." *Eastern Buddhist* 7 (May 1974): 55–106, (October 1974): 49–82. For the most part these bibliographic surveys, along with the author's "Recent Buddhist Studies in Europe and America: 1973–1983," *Eastern Buddhist* 17 (1984): 79–107, treat only the philological study of Indian Buddhism. The author also tends to omit certain major figures who are not in his own school of Buddhology. These articles are nonetheless the most scholarly surveys available on the field, and put forth truly excellent models of scholarly rigor.

Joshi, Lal Mani. *Studies in the Buddhistic Culture of India*. Delhi, 1967. Indian Buddhism during the middle and late Mahāyāna periods.

Kajiyama Yūichi. "Women in Buddhism." *Eastern Buddhist* 15 (1982): 53–70.

Kajiyama Yūichi. "Stūpas, the Mother of Buddhas, and Dharma-body." In *New Paths in Buddhist Research,* edited by A. K. Warder, pp. 9–16. Delhi, 1985.

Kimura Taiken. *Abidammaron no kenkyū*. Tokyo, 1937. A survey of Sarvāstivāda Abhidharma, especially valuable for its analysis of the *Mahāvibhāṣā*.

Lamotte, Étienne. "Buddhist Controversy over the Five Propositions." *Indian Historical Quarterly* 32 (1956). The material collected in this article is also found, slightly augmented, in Lamotte's *magnum opus*, *Histoire du bouddhisme indien des origines à l'ère Śaka* (Louvain, 1958), pp. 300–319, 542–543, 575–606, 690–695. This erudite work is still the standard reference tool on the history of early Indian Buddhism (to circa 200 CE). Unfortunately, Lamotte did not attempt a history of Indian Buddhism for the middle and late periods. He did, however, write an article on the origins of Mahāyāna titled "Sur la formation du Mahāyāna," in *Asiatica: Festschrift Friedrich Weller* (Leipzig, 1954), pp. 381–386; this is the definitive statement on the northern origin of Mahāyāna. See also *Der Verfasser des Upadeśa und seine Quellen* (Göttingen, 1973). On early Buddhism, see "La légende du Buddha," *Revue de l'histoire des religions* 134 (1947–1948): 37–71; *Le bouddhisme de Śākyamuni* (Göttingen, 1983); and *The Spirit of Ancient Buddhism* (Venice, 1961). Lamotte also translated a vast amount of Mahāyāna literature, including *Le traité de la grande vertu de sagesse,* 5 vols. (Louvain, 1944–1980); *La somme du Grand Véhicule d'Asaṅga,* 2 vols. (Louvain, 1938); and *L'enseignement de Vimalakīrti* (Louvain, 1962), containing a long note on the concept of Buddha field (pp. 395–404).

La Vallée Poussin, Louis de. *Bouddhisme: Études et matériaux*. London, 1898. One of the most productive and seminal Western scholars of Buddhism, La Vallée Poussin contributed to historical studies in this and other works, as *Bouddhisme: Opinions sur l'histoire de la dogmatique* (Paris, 1909), *L'Inde aux temps des Mauryas* (Paris, 1930), and *Dynasties et histoire de l'Inde depuis Kanishka jusqu'aux invasions musulmanes* (Paris, 1935). Contributions on doctrine include *The Way to Nirvāṇa* (London, 1917); *Nirvāṇa* (Paris, 1925); "La controverse du temps et du pudgala dans la *Vijñānakāya*," in *Études asiatiques, publiées à l'occasion du vingt-cinquième anniversaire de l'École Française d'Extrême-Orient*, vol. 1 (Paris, 1925), pp. 358–376; *La morale bouddhique* (Paris, 1927); and *Le dogme et la philosophie du bouddhism* (Paris, 1930). On Abhidharma, see "Documents d'Abhidharma," in *Mélanges chinois et bouddhiques,* vol. 1 (Brussels, 1931–1932), pp. 65–109. The Belgian scholar also translated the most influential work of Abhidharma, *L'Abhidharmakośa de Vasubandhu*, 6 vols. (1923–1931; reprint, Brussels, 1971). His articles in the *Encyclopaedia of Religion and Ethics,* edited by James Hastings, are still of value. Especially useful are "Bodhisattva (In Sanskrit Literature)," vol. 2 (Edinburgh, 1909), pp. 739–753; "Mahāyāna," vol. 8 (1915), pp. 330–336; and "Councils and Synods (Buddhist)," vol. 7 (1914), pp. 179–185.

Law, B. C. *Historical Gleanings*. Calcutta, 1922. Other of his numerous contributions to the early history of Buddhism include *Some Kṣatriya Tribes of Ancient India* (Calcutta, 1924), *Tribes in Ancient India* (Poona, 1943), and *The Magadhas in Ancient India* (London, 1946).

Law, B. C., ed. *Buddhistic Studies*. Calcutta, 1931. A collection of seminal essays on the history and doctrines of Indian Buddhism.

Legge, James. *A Record of Buddhist Kingdoms*. Oxford, 1886. English translation of Fa-hsien's accounts.

Majumdar, R. C., ed. *History and Culture of the Indian People,* vols. 2–5. London, 1951. A major survey of the periods of Indian history when Buddhism flourished.

Masson, Joseph. *La religion populaire dans le canon bouddhique Pāli*. Louvain, 1942. The standard study on the interactions of high tradition Buddhism with the substratum, not superseded yet.

Masuda Jiryō. "Origins and Doctrines of Early Indian Buddhist Schools." *Asia Major* 2 (1925): 1–78. English translation of Vasumitra's classical account of the Eighteen Schools.

May, Jacques. "La philosophie bouddhique de la vacuité." *Studia Philosophica* 18 (1958): 123–137. Discusses philosophical issues; for historical survey, see "Chūgan," in *Hōbōgirin,* vol. 5 (Paris and Tokyo, 1979), pp. 470–493, and the article coauthored with Mimaki (below). May's treatment of the Yogācāra schools (including the school of Sāramati), on the other hand, is both historical and doctrinal; see "La philosophie bouddhique idéaliste," *Asiatische Studien / Études asiatiques* 25 (1971): 265–323.

Mimaki Katsumi and Jacques May. "Chūdō." In *Hōbōgirin*, vol. 5, pp. 456–470. Paris and Tokyo, 1979.

Mitra, Debala. *Buddhist Monuments*. Calcutta, 1971. A handy survey of the Buddhist archaeological sites of India.

Mitra, R. C. *The Decline of Buddhism in India*. Calcutta, 1954.

Nagao Gadjin. "The Architectural Tradition in Buddhist Monasticism." In *Studies in History of Buddhism*, edited by A. K. Narain, pp. 189–208. Delhi, 1980.

Nakamura Hajime. *Indian Buddhism: A Survey with Bibliographical Notes*. Tokyo, 1980. Disorganized and poorly edited, but contains useful information on Japanese scholarship on the development of Indian Buddhism.

Nilakanta Sastri, K. A. *Age of the Nandas and Mauryas*. Varanasi, 1952. See also his *A History of South India from Prehistoric Times to the Fall of Vijayanagar* (Madras, 1955) and *Development of Religion in South India* (Bombay, 1963).

Oldenberg, Hermann. *Buddha, sein Leben, seine Lehre, seine Gemeinde* (1881). Revised and edited by Helmuth von Glasenapp. Stuttgart, 1959. The first German edition was translated by W. Hoey as *Buddha, His Life, His Doctrine, His Order* (London, 1882).

Paul, Diana. *The Buddhist Feminine Ideal: Queen Śrīmālā and the Tathāgatagarbha*. Missoula, Mont., 1980. See also her *Women in Buddhism* (Berkeley, 1980).

Prebish, Charles S. "A Review of Scholarship on the Buddhist Councils." *Journal of Asian Studies* 33 (February 1974): 239–254. Treats the problem of the early schools and the history and significance of their Vinaya. Other works on this topic include Prebish's "The Prātimokṣa Puzzle: Facts Versus Fantasy," *Journal of the American Oriental Society* 94 (April–June 1974): 168–176; and *Buddhist Monastic Discipline: The Sanskrit Prātimokṣa Sūtras of the Mahāsāṅghikas and the Mūlasarvāstivādins* (University Park, Pa., 1975).

Prebish, Charles S., and Janice J. Nattier. "Mahāsāṅghika Origins: The Beginning of Buddhist Sectarianism." *History of Religions* 16 (1977): 237–272. An original and convincing argument against the conception of the Mahāsāṃghika as "liberals."

Rhys Davids, T. W. *Buddhist India*. London, 1903. A classic, although its methodology is questionable. Also of some use, in spite of its date, is his "Sects (Buddhist)," in the *Encyclopaedia of Religion and Ethics,* edited by James Hastings, vol. 11 (Edinburgh, 1920), pp. 307–309.

Robinson, Richard H. "Classical Indian Philosophy." In *Chapters in Indian Civilization,* edited by Joseph Elder, vol. 1, pp. 127–227. Dubuque, 1970. A bit idiosyncratic, but valuable in its attempt to understand Buddhist philosophy as part of general Indian currents and patterns of speculative thought. Robinson's "The Religion of the Householder Bodhisattva," *Bharati* (1966): 31–55, challenges the notion of Mahāyāna as a lay movement.

Robinson, Richard H., and Willard L. Johnson. *The Buddhist Religion: A Historical Introduction*. 3d rev. ed. Belmont, Calif., 1982. A great improvement over earlier editions, this book is now a useful manual, with a good bibliography for the English reader.

Ruegg, David S. *The Study of Indian and Tibetan Thought*. Leiden, 1967. The most valuable survey of the main issues of modern scholarship on Indian Buddhism, especially on the early period. The author has also written the definitive study of the Tathāgata-garbha doctrines in *La théorie du tathāgatagarbha et du gotra* (Paris, 1969). See also on the Mādhyamika school his "Towards a Chronology of the Madhyamaka School," in *Indological and Buddhist Studies in Honour of J. W. de Jong* (Canberra, 1982), pp. 505–530, and *The Literature of the Madhyamaka School of Philosophy in India* (Wiesbaden, 1981).

Schayer, Stanislaus. "Precanonical Buddhism." *Acta Orientalia* 7 (1935): 121–132. Posits an early Buddhism not found explicitly in the canon; attempts to reconstruct the doctrines of Buddhism antedating the canon.

Schopen, Gregory. "The Phrase '*sa pṛthivīpradeśaś caityabhūto bhavet*' in the *Vajracchedikā*: Notes on the Cult of the Book in Mahāyāna." *Indo-Iranian Journal* 17 (1975): 147–181. Schopen's work has opened new perspectives on the early history of Mahāyāna, emphasizing its religious rather than philosophical character and revealing generalized beliefs and practices rather than the speculations of the elite. See also "Sukhāvatī as a Generalized Religious Goal in Sanskrit Mahāyāna Sūtra Literature," *Indo-Iranian Journal* 19 (1977): 177–210; "Mahāyāna in Indian Inscriptions," *Indo-Iranian Journal* 21 (1979): 1–19; and "Two Problems in the History of Indian Buddhism: The Layman/Monk Distinction and the Doctrines of the Transference of Merit," *Studien zur Indologie und Iranistik* 10 (1985): 9–47.

Schlingloff, Dieter. *Die Religion des Buddhismus*. 2 vols. Berlin, 1963. An insightful exposition of Buddhism, mostly from the perspective of canonical Indian documents.

Snellgrove, David L., ed. *Buddhist Himālaya*. Oxford, 1957. Although the context of this study is modern Himalayan Buddhism, it contains useful information on Buddhist Tantra in general. Snellgrove's two-volume *The Hevajra Tantra: A Critical Study* (London, 1959) includes an English translation and study of this major Tantric work. In *The Image of the Buddha* (Tokyo and London, 1978) Snellgrove, in collaboration with other scholars, surveys the history of the iconography of the Buddha image.

Stcherbatsky, Theodore. *The Central Conception of Buddhism and the Meaning of the Word "Dharma"* (1923). Reprint, Delhi, 1970. A classic introduction to Sarvāstivādin doctrine. On the Mādhyamika, Stcherbatsky wrote *The Conception of Buddhist Nirvana* (Leningrad, 1927). On early Buddhism, see his "The Doctrine of the Buddha," *Bulletin of the School of Oriental Studies* 6 (1932): 867–896, and "The 'Dharmas' of the Buddhists and the 'Guṇas' of the Sāṃkhyas," *Indian Historical Quarterly* 10 (1934): 737–760. Stcherbatsky categorized the history of Buddhist thought in "Die drei Richtungen in der Philosophie des Buddhismus," *Rocznik Orjentalistyczny* 10 (1934): 1–37.

Takasaki Jikidō. *Nyoraizō shisō no keisei—Indo daijō bukkyō shisō kenkyū.* Tokyo, 1974. A major study of Tathāgata-garbha thought in India.

Thapar, Romila. *Asoka and the Decline of the Mauryas.* London, 1961. Controversial study of Aśoka's reign. Her conclusions are summarized in her *History of India*, vol. 1 (Baltimore, 1965). Also relevant for the study of Indian Buddhism are her *Ancient Indian Social History: Some Interpretations* (New Delhi, 1978), *Dissent in the Early Indian Tradition* (Dehradun, 1979), and *From Lineage of State* (Bombay, 1984).

Thomas, Edward J. *The Life of the Buddha as Legend and History* (1927). New York, 1960. Still the only book-length, critical study of the life of Buddha. Less current, but still useful, is the author's 1933 work *The History of Buddhist Thought* (New York, 1975).

Varma, V. P. *Early Buddhism and Its Origins.* New Delhi, 1973.

Vetter, Tilmann. "The Most Ancient Form of Buddhism." In his *Buddhism and Its Relation to Other Religions.* Kyoto, 1985.

Warder, A. K. *Indian Buddhism.* 2d rev. ed. Delhi, 1980. One of the few modern surveys of the field, this work includes a bibliography of classical sources (pp. 523–574). Unfortunately, the author does not make use of materials available in Chinese and Tibetan translation.

Watanabe Fumimaro. *Philosophy and Its Development in the Nikāyas and Abhidhamma.* Delhi, 1983. The beginnings of Buddhist scholasticism, especially as seen in the transition from Sūtra to Abhidharma literature.

Watters, Thomas. *On Yuan Chwang's Travels in India.* 2 vols. London, 1904–1905. Extensive study of Hsüan-tsang's travels.

Wayman, Alex. *The Buddhist Tantras: Light on Indo-Tibetan Esotericism.* New York, 1973. Not a survery or introduction to the study of Indian Tantra, but a collection of essays on specific issues and problems. Chapter 1.2 deals with the problem of the early history of Tantra. See also Wayman's *Yoga of the Guhyasamājatantra: The Arcane Lore of Forty Verses; A Buddhist Tantra Commentary* (Delhi, 1977). In his "The Mahāsāṅghika and the Tathāgatagarbha (Buddhist Doctrinal History, Study 1)," *Journal of the International Association of Buddhist Studies* 1 (1978): 35–50, Wayman discusses possible connections between the Mahāsāṃghika subsects of Andhra and the development of Mahāyāna. His "Meditation in Theravāda and Mahīśāsaka," *Studia Missionalia* 25 (1976): 1–28, is a study of the doctrine of meditation in two of the leading schools of Hīnayāna.

Winternitz, Moriz. *Geschichte der indischen Literature*, vol. 2. Leipzig, 1920. Translated as *A History of Indian Literature* (Delhi, 1983). Largely dated but not superseded.

Zelliot, Eleanor. *Dr. Ambedkar and the Mahar Movement.* Philadelphia, 1969.

TWO

THE PAN-ASIAN BUDDHIST WORLD

4

BUDDHISM IN SOUTHEAST ASIA

DONALD K. SWEARER

Conventional wisdom labels the Buddhism of Southeast Asia as Theravāda. Indeed, customarily a general distinction pertains between the "southern," Theravāda, Buddhism of Southeast Asia, whose scriptures are written in Pali, and the "northern," Sanskrit Mahāyāna (including Tantrayāna), Buddhism of Central and East Asia. A Thai or a Burmese most likely thinks of the Buddhism of his country as a continuation of the Theravāda tradition, which was allegedly brought to the Golden Peninsula (Suvaṇṇabhūmi) by Aśoka's missionaries Soṇa and Uttara in the third century BCE. But modern scholarship has demonstrated that prior to the development of the classical Southeast Asian states, which occurred from the tenth or eleventh century to the fifteenth century CE, Buddhism in Southeast Asia—the area covered by present-day Burma, Thailand, Vietnam, Cambodia (Kampuchea), and Laos—defies rigid classification. Both archaeological and chronicle evidence suggest that the religious situation in the area was fluid and informal, with Buddhism characterized more by miraculous relics and charismatic, magical monks than by organized sectarian traditions. In short, the early period of Buddhism in Southeast Asia was diverse and eclectic, infused with elements of Hindu Dharmśāstra and Brahmanic deities, Mahāyāna Buddhas such as Lokeśvara, Tantric practices, Sanskrit Sarvāstivādin texts, as well as Pali Theravāda traditions.

The classical period of Southeast Asian Buddhism, which lasted from the eleventh to the fifteenth century, began with the development of the monarchical states of Śrīvijaya in Java, Angkor in Cambodia, Pagan in Burma, Sukhōthai in Thailand, and Luang Prabang in Laos, and culminated in the establishment of a normative Pali Theravāda tradition of the Sinhala Mahāvihāra monastic line. Hence, by the fourteenth and fifteenth centuries the primary, although by no means exclusive, form of Buddhism in Burma, Thailand, Laos, and Cambodia was a Sinhala orthodoxy that was dominated doctrinally by "the commentator" (Buddhaghosa) but enriched by various local traditions of thought and practice. By this time, what is now Malaysia and Indonesia, with the exception of Bali, had been overrun by Islam, and the popular religion there was an amalgamation of animism, Brahmanic deities, and the religion of the Prophet. The colonial interregnum, which infused Western and Christian elements into the religious and cultural milieu of Southeast Asia, gradually challenged the dominance of the Indian Buddhist worldview and its symbiotically related institutional realms of kingship *(dhammacakka)* and monastic order *(sāsanacakka)*. From the nineteenth century onward Buddhism in Southeast Asia has faced the challenges of Western science; provided cultural and ideological support for modern nationalist movements; offered idiosyncratic, sometimes messianically flavored, solutions to the stresses and strains of political, economic, and social change; and formulated doctrinal innovations challenging the Abhidammic orthodoxy of Buddhaghosa that characterizes the Sinhala Theravāda.

The following essay will examine Buddhism in Southeast Asia in terms of its early development, the establishment of a normative Theravāda orthodoxy, and the diverse responses of this tradition to the challenges of the modern period. The future of Buddhism in Southeast Asia may not hang in the balance; nevertheless, it does appear to be problematic. Political events in Cambodia (Kampuchea) and Laos have threatened the very foundations of institutional Buddhism in those countries. Thailand's rapid and widespread modernization and secularization have undermined many traditional aspects of the religion *(sāsana)*, and internal political strife in Burma has had severe, detrimental effects on the *sangha* (Skt., *saṃgha*). Our attention to Southeast Asian Buddhism should not ignore its fragility or its potential contribution to the continuing self-definition and self-determination of these civilizations.

EARLY DEVELOPMENT

From its earliest beginnings to the establishment of the major monarchical states, Buddhism in Southeast Asia can only be characterized as diverse and eclectic. Its presence was felt as part of the Indian cultural influence that flourished throughout the area. During these early centuries Buddhism competed successfully with indigenous forms of magical animism and Brahmanism, undoubtably becoming transformed in the process. Its propagation probably followed the same pattern that was seen in Central and East Asia, with which we are more familiar: Padmasambhava-type monks subjugating territorial guardian spirits; monks accompanying traders and bringing in objects of power and protection, such as relics and images, as well as a literary tradition in the forms of magical chants in sacred languages and also written texts. We glean something of this pattern from Buddhist chronicles in Pali and in Southeast Asian vernacular languages of a later time. When the *Sāsanavaṃsa* of Burma or the *Mūlasāsana* of Thailand relates the story of the Buddha's visit to these countries to establish the religion, we interpret myth in historical terms, reading "the Buddha" to mean "unnamed Buddhist monks" who were bearers of a more advanced cultural tradition. While the chronicles, more so than the early inscriptions, paint a picture of dubious historical accuracy, they correctly associate Buddhism with a high continental way of life in contrast to the less sophisticated life of tribal peoples. Buddhism, then, abets the development of a town or urban culture, provides symbols of translocal value, and articulates a worldview in which diverse communities can participate and find a new identity, a language in which they can communicate, and institutions in which an organized religious life can be pursued and systematically taught.

Such a general description of the early centuries of Buddhism in Southeast Asia does not preclude the establishment of identifiable Buddhist traditions in the area.

These include not only strong Pali Theravāda tradition but also other Buddhist sects and schools representing Mahāyāna and Tantric traditions. Pali inscriptions found in Hmawza, the ancient Pyu capital of Śrīkṣetra in lower Burma, indicate the existence of Theravāda Buddhism by the fifth or sixth century CE. Their Andhra-Kadamba script points to connections with Kāñcīpuram, Negapatam, and Kāverīpaṭṭanam in South India. The Chinese traveler I-ching, who visited Shih-li-cha-to-lo (Śrīkṣetra, or Prome) in the seventh century, mentions the presence of not only Theravādins (Āryasthaviras) but also the Āryamahāsāṃghika, Āryamūlasarvāstivāda, and Āryasammatīya schools. We know of the Mahāsāṃghikas as among the forerunners of the Mahāyāna tradition. While their original home was in Magadha, their tradition established itself in parts of northern, western, eastern, and southern India. The Amarāvatī and Nāgārjunikoṇḍa inscriptions, for instance, mention the Mahāsāṃghikas and state that their canon was written in Prakrit. The three other sects are Hīnayāna schools. The Mūlasarvāstivāda, according to one tradition, was one of the seven branches of the Sarvāstivādin tradition and was widespread in India, although it was especially strong in the north, whence it was propagated under the aegis of King Kaniṣka during the late first century CE. Its canon was written in a Buddhist Hybrid Sanskrit. The Sammatīya sect, also known as the Vātsīputrīya or Vajjipattaka, came from Avanti, but inscriptions point to its presence in Sārnāth during the fourth century and in Mathurā during the fifth century. The great early seventh-century ruler Harṣavardhana is thought to have supported the Sammatīyas in the early part of his reign. Hence, the four sects whose presence in the Prome area was attested to by I-ching are all associated with important Indian Buddhist centers and with the reigns of powerful monarchs reputed to have been supporters of various Buddhist sectarian traditions.

Evidence of the diverse nature of sectarian Buddhism during the formative period of Southeast Asian history comes from Burmese and other sources in both mainland and insular Southeast Asia. The T'ang dynastic chronicles (seventh to tenth century CE) state that Buddhism flourished in the P'iao (Pyu) capital of Shih-li-cha-to-lo (Śrīkṣetra) in the eighth and ninth centuries. Archaeological and sculptural evidence of the same period from Prome and Hmawza portray the Buddha in scenes from the Jātakas and from popular commentarial stories. Terra-cotta votive tablets depicting scenes from the life of the Buddha and of the Mahāyāna *bodhisattvas* have also been found, as well as inscriptions written in Sanskrit, Pali, mixed Pali and Sanskrit, and Pyu written in South Indian alphabets. Evidence from ruined stupas in Hmawza, which date from the fifth to the eighth centuries, reinforce the claim to a strong but diverse Buddhist presence.

The Mon, or Talaing, lived south of the Pyu, occupying the coastal area of lower Burma, with flourishing centers at Pegu (Haṃsavatī) and Thaton (Sudhammavatī). This region, known as Rāmaññadesa in Burmese and Thai chronicles, extended over much of present-day Thailand; one major Mon center was as far north as Haripuñjaya (present-day Lamphun). In Nakorn Prathom, thirty miles southwest of Bangkok, archaeological evidence points to a flourishing Mon Buddhist culture in the region known as Dvāravatī, in which forms of both Hīnayāna and Mahāyāna Buddhism were present. Amarāvatī-style Buddha images in the vicinity of Nakorn Prathom and Pong Tuk date from the fourth to fifth century CE, and images of both early and late Gupta are also found there. While Mon-Dvāravatī Buddhism in Thailand and lower Burma lacked the homogeneity attributed to it by later chroniclers, both archaeological and textual evidence suggest a strong Pali Theravāda presence, especially in comparison to that found in Pagan.

Pagan, near the sacred Mount Popa on the Irrawaddy Plains of upper Burma, had become the locus of power of the Mrammas, a Tibeto-Dravidian tribe who eventually dominated and consequently named the entire region. During the tenth and eleventh centuries, the Buddhism present among people of the Pagan-Irrawaddy River basin seems to have been dominated by an eclectic form of Mahāyāna Tantrism similar to that found in esoteric Śaivism or in animistic *nāga* cults. According to the Burmese chronicles, the monks of this sect, who are referred to as Ari, rejected the teachings of the Lord Buddha. They believed in the efficacy of magical *mantra*s over the power of *karman* and propagated the custom of sending virgins to priests before marriage. In addition to numerous figures of Mahāyāna *bodhisattva*s, such as Avalokiteśvara and Mañjuśrī, findings include remnants of murals that depict deities embracing their consorts.

According to the *Hmannān mạha yazạwintawkyī* (Glass Palace Chronicle, begun 1829) of Burma, the country's political and religious history was changed by the effect of Shin Arahan, a charismatic Mon Theravāda monk from Thaton, on the Burmese ruler Aniruddha (Anawratha), who ascended to power in Pagan in 1044 CE. According to this account, Shin Arahan converted Aniruddha to a Theravāda persuasion, advising him to secure relics, *bhikkhu*s (monks), and Pali texts from Manuha (Manohari), the king of Thaton. Manuha's refusal became the excuse for Aniruddha's invasion of Thaton, the eventual subjugation of the Mons in lower Burma, and the establishment of Theravāda under Kyanzittha (fl. 1084–1113) as the dominant, although by no means exclusive, Buddhist sect.

As part of the Indian cultural expansion into "greater India," Mahāyāna, Tantric, and Hīnayāna forms of Buddhism were established in other parts of mainland and insular Southeast Asia from the fifth century onward. Guṇavarman is reputed to have taken the Dharmaguptaka tradition from northern India to Java in the fifth century, and by the seventh century Buddhism was apparently flourishing in the Sumatra of Śrīvijaya. An inscription from 684 CE, for instance, refers to a Buddhist monarch named Jayanāśā. I-ching, who spent several months in Java on his return to China in order to copy and translate Buddhist texts, indicates that both Hīnayāna and Mahāyāna forms of Buddhism were present at that time. Indonesia was also visited by Dharmapāla of Nālandā University and by two prominent South Indian monks, Vajrabodhi and Amoghavajra, both adherents of a Tantric form of Buddhism. Two inscriptions from the late eighth century refer to the construction, under the aegis of Śailendra rulers, of a Tārā temple at Kalasan and an image of Mañjuśrī at Kelunak. The Śailendras were great patrons of the North Indian Pāla form of Mahāyāna Buddhism. [*See the biographies of Dharmapāla, Vajrabodhi, and Amoghavajra. Evidence for the flourishing of Tantric forms of Buddhism in Southeast Asia is treated in* Buddhism, Schools of, *article on* Esoteric Buddhism.]

The rulers of Champa, in southern Annam (Vietnam), also patronized Buddhism. According to I-ching, the dominant tradition in Champa was that of the Āryasammatīya *nikāya,* but the Sarvāstivādins were also present. Amarāvatī-style Buddha images and monastery foundations from the ninth century have been discovered in Quang Nam Province, and an inscription of the same period from An-Thai records the erection of a statue of Lokanātha and refers to such Mahāyāna deities as Amitābha and Vairocana.

Although Hinduism was initially the dominant religion in Cambodia, there is some evidence of Buddhism from the fifth century CE. Jayavarman of Fu-nan sent representatives to China in 503 CE, who took as gifts a Buddha image; and an inscription by Jayavarman's son, Rudravarman, invokes the Buddha. In the eleventh century Sūryavarman was given the posthumous Buddhist title of Nirvāṇapada, and Jayavarman VII, the Khmer empire's greatest monarch and builder of Angkor Thom, patronized Buddhism of the Mahāyāna variety. A Pali inscription from 1308, during the reign of Śrīndravarmadeva, refers to a Hīnayāna form of Buddhism, and a Chinese source from about the same time refers to Hīnayāna Buddhism as flourishing in Cambodia at that time.

The evidence cited supports the contention that throughout much of Southeast Asia Buddhism was present as part of the larger Indian cultural influence. Various sources, ranging from testimony of Chinese and indigenous chronicles, diaries of Chinese monk-travelers, as well as a large amount of archaeological and inscriptional evidence, support the contention that both Mahāyāna and Hīnayāna forms of Buddhism existed side by side, dependent on such factors as the particular regional Indian source and the predilection of a given ruler. Clearly, before the emergence of the major classical Southeast Asian states, no standard form of Buddhism existed.

It is also true that various types of Buddhism in this period competed with autochthonous forms of animism as well as Brahmanic cults. Were the early states in Burma, Cambodia, Thailand, and Indonesia—such as Fu-nan, Champa, Śrīkṣetra, Dvāravatī, and so on—Buddhist or Hindu? Or were these great traditions themselves so accommodated and transformed by the Southeast Asian cultures that they qualified the labels "Buddhist" and "Hindu" almost beyond recognition? Although rulers in these preclassical states may be characterized as Hindu or Buddhist and their brand of Buddhism defined by a given sect or school, in all probability they supported a variety of priests, monks, and religious institutions and worshiped various gods and spirits ranging from territorial guardians to Viṣṇu, Śiva, and Vairocana. In some cases we are prone to assign labels when, in reality, the diversity of the situation makes labeling a problematic enterprise at best. Such a qualification does not mean that we are unable to make certain claims about the nature of Buddhism in Southeast Asia in the formative period; however, evidence supporting the presence of particular Buddhist schools and sects should be understood within the general framework of the varied and eclectic nature of Buddhism in this era.

CLASSICAL PERIOD

While diversity and eclecticism continue to mark the character of Buddhism during the period of the foundation of the classical Southeast Asian monarchical states, homogeneity of form and institutional orthodoxy began to emerge during this period. On the one hand, Buddhism and Hinduism contributed to the development of the nature and form of Southeast Asian kingship. On the other hand, the symbiotic relationship that developed between the monarchy and the Buddhist *sangha* tended to support a loose religious orthodoxy. Historically, this orthodoxy follows the Sinhala Theravāda tradition and accompanies the ascendancy of the Burmese and the Tai in mainland Southeast Asia. Vietnam, Malaysia, and Indonesia, however, depart from this pattern: Vietnamese culture was strongly influenced by China, and Malaysia and Indonesia were affected by the advent and spread of Islam during the thirteenth century. We shall first examine Buddhism at the level of the nature and form of classical Southeast Asian kingship and then trace the emergence of Sinhala Theravāda Buddhism as the normative tradition in Burma, Thailand, Cambodia, and Laos after the thirteenth century.

Buddhism and Monarchy. The relationship between Buddhism and the rise of the monarchical states in the classical period of Southeast Asian history is customarily referred to as symbiotic, that is, one of mutual benefit. Rulers supported Buddhism because it provided a cosmology in which the king was accorded the central place and a view of society in which the human community was dependent on the role of the king. Ideologically, Buddhism legitimated kingship, providing a metaphysical rationale and moral basis for its existence. The Buddhist *sangha,* in turn, supported Southeast Asian monarchs because the material well-being, success, and popularity of institutional Buddhism depended to a significant degree on the approval, support, and largess of the ruling classes.

The Theravāda picture of the cosmos, set forth classically in the *Aggañña Suttanta* of the *Dīgha Nikāya,* depicts the world as devolving from a more perfect, luminous, undifferentiated state to a condition of greater opacity and differentiation. Imperfection results because differences in sex, comeliness, size of rice fields, and so on engender desire, greed, lust, and hatred, which, in turn, lead to actions that destroy the harmony and well-being of the inhabitants of the world. Recognizing the need to correct the situation, the people select a person whose comeliness, wisdom, virtue, and power enable him to bring order to this disharmonious, chaotic situation. That person, the ruler or king, is referred to in the text as *mahāsammata* because he is chosen by the people. He is *rāja* (king) because he rules by the Dhamma, and he is also *khattiya,* or lord of the fields, responsible for maintaining the economic and political order. Social order is dependent upon the righteous ruler, who creates and maintains the fourfold social structure (the traditional Indian *varṇa* hierarchy). Such a peaceful and harmonious situation also allows for the sustenance of *bhikkhus*, who seek a higher, nonmundane end, that is, *nibbāna* (Skt., *nirvāṇa*). The ruler, then, is responsible for the peace, harmony, and total well-being of the people, which includes the opportunity to pursue a religious or spiritual life.

Buddhism's contribution to the classical conception of Southeast Asian kingship is particularly noteworthy in its emphasis on Dhamma and on the role of the ruler as a moral exemplar. The king is a *cakkavattin,* one whose rule depends upon the universal Dhamma of cosmic, natural, and moral law. His authority stems from the place he assumes in the total cosmic scheme of things. But his power and, hence, his effectiveness rest on his virtue. While the king rules by strength of arms, wealth, intellect, able ministers, and the prestige of his own status, his embodiment of the Dhamma and, hence, his ability to rule depend on his maintenance of the ten *rājadhammas*: liberality, good conduct, nonattachment, straightforwardness, mildness, austerity, suppression of anger, noninjury, patience, and forbearance. The ideal king should cleanse his mind of all traces of avarice, ill will, and intellectual confusion and eschew the use of force and weapons of destruction. These moral virtues represent the highest ideals of Theravāda Buddhism, an overlapping of two "wheels" *(cakka),* or realms: the mundane *(ānācakka, lokiya)* and the transmundane *(sāsanacakka, lokuttara),* or the ideals of the political leader *(cakkavattin)* and the religious exemplar (Buddha).

This symbiotic relationship between political and religious leadership roles takes a particular mythic pattern in many of the classical Southeast Asian chronicles, such as the *Jinakālamālipakaraṇaṃ,* (The Sheaf of Garlands of the Epochs of the Conqueror), a pattern also present in the Pali chronicles of Sri Lanka (e.g., the *Mahāvaṃsa*). Essentially, the chroniclers hold that the Budda sacralizes a region by visiting it. He frequently converts the indigenous populations and teaches them the Dhamma. To be sure, the monastic authors had a vested interest in establishing the precedence of Buddhism in the land, but the Buddha's visits to such places as the Tagaung kingdom of Burma and Haripuñjaya in northern Thailand serve the additional purpose of grounding a later interrelationship between Buddhism and kingship. In the northern Thai chronicles, for example, when the Buddha visits the Mon-Lava state of Haripuñjaya in the Chiangmai Valley, he predicts that his bone relic will be discovered by King Ādicca (Āditarāja), one of the principal twelfth-century monarchs of this state. This tale not only points to royal support of the *sāsana,* it makes the king the symbolic actualizer of the tradition, which he celebrates by building a *cetiya* for the relic. Furthermore, the Buddha in effect engenders the monarch with the power necessary to rule, a magical potency inherent in the relic. The *cetiya* reliquary mound thus functions as a magical center, or *axis mundi,* for the kingdom. In Haripuñjaya, alliances between the northern Tai kingdom of Lānnā and other states were sealed in front of the magical center. The Emerald Buddha image has played a similar role in Lao and Tai religious history, with various princes of the kingdom swearing fealty to the reigning monarch who possessed it.

The nature of the interrelationship between Buddhism and classical monarchical rule in Southeast Asia manifests itself architecturally in the great *cetiya* or stupa (Skt., *stūpa*) monuments of Borobudur, Angkor, Pagan, and other ancient capitals. The earliest of these, Borobudur, was constructed on the Kedu Plain outside of present-day Jogjakarta on the island of Java in the mid-eighth century CE under a dynasty known as the Śailendras, or "kings of the mountain." The monument's strong Mahāyāna influence is reflected in bas-reliefs that depict stories from the *Lalitavistara*, *Divyāvadāna*, *Jātakamālā*, and *Gaṇḍavyūha.* The seventy-two perforated, hollow stupas on the top of three circular platforms cover seated images of the Buddha Vairocana. Scholars have argued that the monument, as a cosmic mountain, connects royal power with the Dharma, the basis of all reality; it may also synthesize an autochthonous cult of "kings of the mountain" with the Ādibuddha, or universal Buddha nature. In support of this connection it is speculated that Śailendra inscriptions use the Sanskrit term *gotra* to signify both "line of the ancestors" as well as "family of the Buddha," thereby identifying the Śailendra ancestral line with that of the Tathāgata.

Angkor, in Cambodia, has been even more widely studied as a source for understanding the interrelationships between Southeast Asian kingship and religion, especially regarding the *devarāja* (god-king) concept. It may be that this concept originated in Fu-nan, a Chinese term derived from the Mon-Khmer *bnam*, meaning "mountain" and possibly referring to a cult of a national guardian spirit established by the founder of the state. In the early ninth century the Khmer ruler Jayavarman II built on this background, adopting Śaivism as the state religion and thus requiring that the king be worshiped as a manifestation of Śiva. This identification was symbolized by a *liṅga* that was set upon the central altar of a pyramidal temple as an imitation of Mount Meru and the center of the realm. The *devarāja* cult took on Mahāyāna Buddhist forms under Sūryavarman I in the early eleventh century and under Jayavarman VII (1181–1218), who constructed the great Bayon Temple, in which Jayavarman and Lokeśvara appear to be identified, at Angkor Thom at the end of the twelfth century. It can be inferred that in the tradition of the *devarāja*, Sūryavarman and Jayavarman became *buddharājas*, or incarnate Buddhas.

Other classical Southeast Asian capitals and major royal and religious monuments exhibit the influence of both Hindu and Buddhist worldviews. The remains of over five thousand stupas can be seen at the site of ancient Pagan, an area covering sixteen square miles. It was unified by Aniruddha (1040–1077) and the commander of his forces and successor, Kyanzittha (fl. 1084–1113). The Schwezigon Pagoda, possibly begun by Aniruddha but certainly completed by Kyanzittha, enshrines three sacred Buddha relics, symbolizing the power of the *cakkavattin* as the defender of the sacred order of things *(dhamma)*. Other stupas, such as the Mingalazedi, which was completed in the late thirteenth century, reflect the basic macro-micro cosmological symbolism of Borobudur; it has truncated pyramidal and terraced bases and a central stairway on each side. The Ānanda Temple, the stupa that dominated Pagan, was constructed by Kyanzittha in the late eleventh century and combines both cosmic mountain and cave symbolism: an ascetic's cave in which the Buddha meditates and a magical *axis mundi* that empowers the entire cosmos. A small kneeling image facing the large Buddha image in the temple is thought to represent Kyanzittha, corroborating inscriptional claims that he saw himself as a *bodhitsatta* and *cakkavattin*.

The mythic ideal of the *cakkavattin* is embodied in the moral example of Aśoka Maurya. Similarly, the *cakkavattin* of the Suttas provides the legendary charter for the idealized kingly exemplar of the Southeast Asian Theravāda chronicles. Aśoka was the moral exemplar *par excellence*, in whose footsteps, so say the chronicles and inscriptions, the monarchs of Burma, Thailand, and Laos follow. Aśoka's conversion divides his biography into two halves—the first tells of warring, wicked Aśoka (Pali, Caṇḍāsoka) and the second of the just, righteous Aśoka (Pali, Dhammāsoka). Similarly Aniruddha kills his brother to become the ruler of Pagan but then becomes a patron of Buddhism, and Tilokarāja (1441–1487) of Chiangmai revolts against his father but then devotes much of his attention to the prosperity of the Buddhist *sangha*. Southeast Asian rulers are also reputed to have called councils, as did Aśoka, in order to purify the *sangha* and regularize the Tipiṭaka. These activities, which supported Buddhism, represented ways the monarch could uphold his reputation for righteousness in ruling the state and in his dealings with the people. In his famous 1292 inscription, Rāma Khamhaeng (Ramkhamhaeng) of Sukhōthai says that the king adjudicates cases of inheritance with complete impartiality, does not kill or beat captured enemy soldiers, and listens to the grievances of his subjects. This paternalistic model of the dhammically righteous king is obviously indebted to the Aśoka model. [*See* Kingship, *article on* Kingship in Southeast Asia; Cakravartin; *and the biography of Aśoka.*]

Dominance of Sinhala Theravāda Buddhism. The shift to a Sinhala Theravāda orthodoxy in what became, in the true sense, Buddhist Southeast Asia (Burma, Thailand, Laos, and Cambodia) took place gradually from the late eleventh to the early thirteenth century and onward. This development reflected several factors: the decline of Buddhism in parts of Asia that had influenced the Southeast Asian mainland; the rising influence of Sri Lanka under Vijayabāhu I (1055–1110) and Parākramabāhu

I; the consolidation of power by the Burmese and Tai; an increasing interrelationship among Sri Lanka, Burma, and Thailand; and the spread of popular Theravāda practice among the general population of mainland Southeast Asia. The general outline of the story of the establishment of Sinhala Theravāda Buddhism in Southeast Asia is reasonably clear, although disparities between epigraphic and chronicle sources make historical precision difficult. Consequently, scholars disagree on dates, and historical reconstructions keep on changing.

Pali Theravāda and Sanskrit Hīnayāna forms of Buddhism were present at a relatively early time. Pali inscriptions found in central Thailand and lower Burma and associated with Mon culture support this claim, as does chronicle testimony, such as the story of Aniruddha's excursion into Rāmaññadesa to secure Pali scriptures. Inscriptional evidence makes it reasonable to assume that the roots of Mon Theravāda lay in the Kāñcīpuram area along the east coast of India. Even the popular Burmese tradition that holds that Buddhaghosa, who has been associated with Kāñcī, either came from Thaton or went there after visiting Sri Lanka may contain a kernel of historical truth, namely, the spread of Kāñcī Theravāda Buddhism into the Mon area. The presence of Pali Theravāda Buddhism among the Mon, who strongly influenced both the Burmese and Tai, provides the religio-cultural backdrop to the eventual consolidation of Sri Lankan forms of Theravāda Buddhism. As we shall see, both the Burmese and the Tai assimilated elements of Mon culture: its religion, legal traditions, artistic forms, and written script. Mon Theravāda, in effect, mediated Sinhala Theravāda. On the one hand, Theravāda Buddhism from Sri Lanka provided continuity with Mon religio-cultural traditions; on the other, it enabled the Burmese and Tai to break away from a Mon religio-cultural dominance. We must now explore some of the details of this story of cultural transformation and religious consolidation.

Burma. Contact between Burma and Sri Lanka dates from the establishment of the Pagan era by Aniruddha. Because of the disruption of Sri Lanka caused by wars with the Cōḻas in the mid-eleventh century, Vijayabāhu I, knowing of the strength of the Mon Theravāda traditions, sought help from Aniruddha to restore valid ordination. Aniruddha responded by sending a group of monks and Pali scriptures to Sri Lanka. In turn, Aniruddha requested, and was sent, a replica of the Buddha's tooth relic and a copy of the Tipiṭaka with which to check the copies of the Pali scriptures acquired at Thaton. The tooth relic was enshrined in Pagan's Schwezigon Pagoda, which became Burma's national palladium. Although archaeological evidence calls into question the chronicler's claim regarding the acquisition of the entire Pali Tipiṭaka, the tale might well be interpreted to indicate the growing importance of Sinhala Buddhism, not simply because the texts were more authoritative, but because the alliance between the king and the new sectarian tradition legitimated his authority over the Mon religio-cultural tradition.

Sinhala Buddhism flourished during the reign of Narapatisithu (1173–1210), and the Mahāvihāra tradition became normative at this time. Sinhala Buddhism, in particular the Mahāvihāra tradition, gained position partly through visits of distinguished Burmese monks to Sri Lanka. Panthagu, successor to Shin Arahan as the nominal head of the Pagan Buddhist *sangha*, visited the island in 1167. The Mon monk Uttarajīva Mahāthera followed in his predecessor's footsteps by journeying to Sri Lanka in 1180 with a group of monks that included a Mon novice named Chapaṭa, who was to figure most prominently in establishing the precedent authority of the Mahāvihāra. Chapaṭa and four others remained in Sri Lanka for ten years and were reordained as Mahātheras in the Mahāvihāra lineage. Their return to Burma marked the permanent establishment of Sinhala Buddhism in mainland Southeast Asia and brought about a schism in the Burmese Buddhist *sangha* between the Theravāda school of Thaton and Kāñcī, characterized by Shin Arahan's orthodoxy; and the Sinhala Theravāda tradition. When Chapaṭa returned to Pagan, Narapatisithu requested that he and the other four Mahātheras reordain Burmese monks of the Shin Arahan tradition, thereby establishing the superior legitimacy of the Sinhala orthodoxy over the Mon form of Theravāda. The chronicles refer to the Shin Arahan tradition as the "early school" *(purimagaṇa)* and to Chapaṭa's Sīhaḷa Sangha simply as the "late school" *(pacchāgaṇa)*. Owing to disciplinary and personal reasons, the *pacchāgaṇa* was to divide into several branches each loyal to one or another of the Mahātheras who had returned from Sri Lanka. One point of dispute among the branches was whether gifts could be given to particular monks or to the *sangha* at large.

The Sīhaḷa order was introduced to lower Burma at Dala, near Rangoon, by Sāriputta, who bore the title Dhammavīlasa, meaning a scholar of great repute. This tradition is referred to as the Sīhaḷapakkhabhikkhu Sangha, in contrast with the Ariyārahantapakkhabhikkhu Sangha, which represents the Mon Theravāda tradition. The chronicles also call this school the Kambojasanghapakka on the grounds that it was headquartered near a settlement of Kambojans (Cambodians). This title may reflect historical fact or refer to the earlier Theravāda of the Mon-Khmer areas to the east (i.e., Dvāravatī), which found its way into lower Burma. The Sīhaḷa Sangha was also introduced to Martaban by two Mon monks, Buddhavaṃsa Mahāthera and Mahāsāmi Mahāthera, who had been reordained in Sri Lanka. According to the Kalyāṇī inscriptions of Pegu, by the thirteenth century six Buddhist schools—the Mon Ariyārahanta and five Sīhaḷa sects—existed in Martaban. Sectarianism in Burmese Theravāda has continued into the modern period and contrasts with the relative homogeneity of Theravāda Buddhism in Thailand.

Buddhism prospered during the reign of Narapatisithu (1173–1210). Many beautiful temples were built under his sponsorship (e.g., Sulamani, Gawdawpalin), and Pali scholarship flourished. For example, Chapaṭa (also known as Saddhammajotipāla) wrote a series of famous works dealing with Pali grammar, discipline (Vinaya), and higher philosophy (e.g., *Suttaniddesa, Sankhepavaṇṇanā, Abhidhammatthasangha)*, and Sāriputta wrote the first collection of laws composed in Rāmaññadesa, known as the *Dhammavīlasa* or *Dhammathāt.* The shift away from a dominant Mon influence that occurred during Narapatisithu's reign is also reflected in the architectural style and the use of Burmese in inscriptions.

Thailand. The development of Buddhism among the Tai followed roughly the same pattern as in Burma. As the Tai migrated from southwestern China into the hills east of the Irrawaddy (home of the Shans), the upper Menam Plain (the Siamese), and farther east to the Nam U (the Lao), and as they gradually moved into the lowland area dominated by the Mons and the Khmers, they came into contact with Theravāda and Mahāyāna forms of Buddhism as well as with Brahmanism. After Khubilai Khan's conquest of Nan-chao in 1254 caused ever greater numbers of Tai to push south, they began to establish domination over the Mon and Khmer and to absorb elements of these more advanced cultures. As was the case in Burma, Mon Buddhism in particular became a major influence on the Tai as they extended their sway over much of what we now know as modern Thailand. This influence is seen in the establishment of two major Tai states in the late thirteenth and fourteenth centuries, Sukhōthai and Chiangmai.

Both Sukhōthai and Chiangmai became powerful centers of Tai settlement under the leadership of the able rulers Rāma Khamhaeng (r. c. 1279–1299) and Mengrai respectively. Sukhōthai, which had been a Khmer outpost from at least the time of Jayavarman VII, became an independent Tai state in the middle of the thirteenth century. Two Tai chieftains, Phe Mu'ang and Bang Klang Hao, seized Śrī Sajanalāya and drove the Khmer governor from Sukhōthai. Bang Klang Hao, was installed as ruler of Sukhōthai with the title Indrāditya. Indrāditya's third son, Rāma Khamhaeng, was to become Sukhōthai's greatest monarch and one of the exemplary Buddhist kings of Tai history. During his reign, which extended over the last two decades of the century, Rāma Khamhaeng asserted his sway over a large area extending from Haṃsavatī (Pegu) to the west, Phrae to the north, Luang Prabang to the east, and Nakorn Sri Dhammaraja (Nagara Śrī Dharmarāja; Ligor or Tambraliṅga) to the south. Nakorn Sri Dhammaraja, although dominated by Śrīvijaya from the eighth to the twelfth century and later by the Khmer, was an important center of Theravāda Buddhism by the eleventh century. Prior to Rāma Khamhaeng's ascendance to power in Sukhōthai, Chandrabhānu of Nagara Śrī Dharmarāja had sent a mission to Sri Lanka, and the *Cūlavaṃsa* reports that Parākramabāhu II invited Dhammakitti Mahāthera, a monk from Nagara Śrī Dharmarāja, to visit Sri Lanka. Rāma Khamhaeng, who was well aware of the strength of Theravāda Buddhism at Nagara Śrī Dharmarāja, invited a Mahāthera from the forest-dwelling tradition *(araññaka)* there to reside in Sukhōthai. Rāma Khamhaeng's famous 1292 stela inscription refers to various religious sanctuaries in Sukhōthai, including the *araññaka* monastery (Wat Taphan Hin), a Khmer temple (Wat Phra Phai Luang), and a shrine to the guardian spirit of the city, Phra Khaphung. In short, while we have definitive evidence that Rāma Khamhaeng supported Theravāda Buddhism, religion in thirteenth-century Sukhōthai was varied and eclectic.

During the reigns of Rāma Khamhaeng's successors—his son Lö Tai (1298–1347), and his grandson Lü Thai (1347–1368/74?)—Sinhala Buddhism became normative. According to the *Jīnakālamāli,* a Sukhōthai monk named Sumana studied under, and received ordination from, a Sinhala Mahāthera, Udumbara Mahāsāmi, who was resident in Martaban. Sumana returned to Sukhōthai to establish the Sīhaḷa Sangha there, and, along with his colleague Anōmadassī, he proceeded to spread the Sīhaḷa order throughout much of Thailand (Ayuthayā, Pitsanulōk, Nān, Chiangmai, and Luang Prabang). King Lü Thai, in particular, was noted for his piety and his support of Buddhism. He brought Buddha relics and images and established Buddha "footprints" *(buddhapada)* in an effort to popularize Buddhist practice throughout his realm. A Buddhist scholar of note, he was particularly known as the author of the *Traibhūmikathā* (Verses on the Three Worlds), thought to be the first systematic Theravāda cosmological treatise.

About the same time that Sinhala Buddhism was coming into its own in Sukhōthai, it was also being spread to Tai states to the north and northeast, namely, Chiangmai and Luang Prabang. Chiangmai was established as the major Tai state in northern Thailand by Mengrai, who expanded his authority from Chiangsaen to encompass Chiangrai, Chiangkhong, and Fāng. He subjugated the Mon-Lava center of Haripuñjaya in 1291 before founding Chiangmai in 1296. According to both inscriptional and chronicle evidence, Sumana Mahāthera brought the Sinhala Buddhism he had learned from his preceptor in Martaban to Chiangmai in 1369 at the invitation of King Küna (1355–1385). Küna built Wat Suan Dọk to house the Buddha relic brought by Sumana, and Sinhala Buddhism gained favored status over the Mon Theravāda traditions of Haripuñjaya. As in the case of Sukhōthai and Pagan, Sinhala Buddhism functioned not only as a means to build continuity with the Mon Theravāda tradition over which the Tai and the Burmese established their authority but also as a means to assert their unique religio-cultural traditions.

The apogee of the development of the Sīhaḷa order in Chiangmai was reached during the reigns of Tilokarāja, one of the greatest of the Tai monarchs, and Phra Mu'ang Kaew (1495–1526). Tilokarāja legitimated the overthrow of his father, Sam Fang Kaen, through the support of the Mahāvihāra order, which had been brought to Chiangmai in 1430. According to the Mūlasāsana of Wat Pa Daeng in Chiangmai, the center of this sect, this tradition was brought to Thailand by a group of thirty-nine monks from Chiangmai, Lopburi, and lower Burma who had visited Sri Lanka in 1423 during the reign of Parākramabāhu VI of Kotte. They returned to Ayutthayā, a Tai state that subjugated Sukhōthai under the Indrarāja in 1412, and dominated central Thailand until they were conquered by the Burmese at the end of the eighteenth century. According to the northern Tai chronicles, members of this mission spread throughout central and northern Thailand, reordaining monks into the new Sīhaḷa order. Tilokarāja made this Wat Pa Daeng-Mahāvihāra group the normative monastic tradition in Chiangmai at a general council in 1477. The Pa Daeng chronicles depict Tilokarāja as a great supporter of the *sangha* and as a righteous and exemplary monarch in the Aśokan mode. During the reign of Tilokarāja's successor, Phra Mu'ang Kaew, Pali Buddhist scholarship in Chiangmai flourished. The *Māṅgaladīpaṇi,* a Pali commentary on the *Māṅgala Sutta,* was written at this time and is still used as the basis of higher-level Pali studies, and the most important northern Tai chronicle, the *Jīnakālamālipakaraṇa,* also dates from this period.

Contemporaneous with the apogee of Buddhism in Chiangmai was the reign of Dhammaceti (1472–1492), who ruled Burma from Pegu, in the lower part of the country. According to the northern Tai and Burmese chronicles as well as the Kālyaṇī inscriptions, during Dhammaceti's reign there were several religious missions to Sri Lanka from Pegu and Ava, and Sīhaḷa monks, in turn, visited Burma. Burmese monks were reordained and visited sacred shrines on the island. Like Tilokarāja, Dhammaceti wanted to unify the *sangha* and used the new ordination to unite Buddhists in the Pegu kingdom. Monks from all over lower Burma, Ava, Tougoo, from the Shan kingdoms, Thailand, and Cambodia came to Pegu to be ordained during what the chronicles portray as the "golden age" of lower Burma.

Cambodia and Laos. Theravāda Buddhism was introduced to Cambodia by the Mon of the lower Menam Chaophraya River valley. In the eleventh and twelfth centuries, Theravāda also existed alongside Mahāyāna forms of Buddhism as well as Brahmanism. Mahāyāna Buddhism certainly received royal patronages in the eleventh century, and Jayavarman VII, the builder of the Bayon Temple at Angkor Thom, was identified with the Buddha Lokeśvara in the divine-royal symbiosis of the Khmer *devarāja/buddharāja* cult. Yet, typical of the classical Southeast Asian monarchs, Jayavarman's patronage of Mahāyāna Buddhism was not exclusive. According to the

Kālyaṇī inscriptions and *The Glass Palace Chronicle,* a Cambodian monk, possibly Jayavarman's son, was part of the Burmese mission to Sri Lanka in the twelfth century. There was certainly an influx of Mon Buddhists from the Lopburi region in the face of Tai pressure in the thirteenth and early fourteenth centuries. Testimony of Chau Ta Kuan, a member of a late thirteenth century mission to Angkor, indicates that Theravāda monks were present in the Khmer capital during that period. The *Jīnakālamāli* account of the Chiangmai mission to Sri Lanka in 1423 CE includes reference to eight Khmer monks who brought the Sīhaḷa order of the Mahāvihāra to Cambodia.

The development of Buddhism in Laos was influenced by both Cambodia and Thailand. According to the Lao chronicles, Jayavarman Parmesvara (1327–1353) helped Phi Fa and Fa Ngum establish the independent kingdom of Lān Chāng, which earlier had been under the political hegemony of Sukhōthai. An inscription at Wat Keo in Luang Prabang refers to three Sinhala Mahātheras—including Mahāpasaman, Fa Ngum's teacher at Angkor—who went from Cambodia to Lān Chāng as part of a religious mission. Certainly, from the late fourteenth century onward, Buddhism in Laos and Cambodia was primarily influenced by the Tai as a consequence of their political dominance in the area. Even in the modern period, Theravāda sectarian developments in Thailand were reflected in Cambodia and Laos, and prior to the Communist revolution, monks from Cambodia and Laos studied in the Buddhist universities in Bangkok.

Summary. During the period that marks the rise of the classical Southeast Asian states, Buddhism existed in many guises. Pali Theravāda was introduced principally through the Mon of Dvāravatī and lower Burma and was considered a "higher" culture appropriated by the Burmese and the Tai. A strong Mahāyāna Buddhist presence is apparent not only in Śrīvijaya and Angkor but also in Pagan and the early Tai states. Furthermore, these forms of Buddhism competed with, and were complemented by, autochthonous animistic cults and Brahmanism. Buddhism made a decisive contribution to the conception of Southeast Asian kingship and monarchical rule through its ideal of the *dhammarāja,* who was not only represented by King Aśoka in India but by such Southeast Asian monarchs as Kyanzittha, Rāma Khamhaeng, and Tilokarāja.

Sri Lanka played the decisive role in the increasing dominance of Theravāda Buddhism in mainland Southeast Asia. Several factors contributed to this development, but I have singled out two: the rise to power of the Burmese and the Tai, who appropriated the Theravāda Buddhism of the Mon; and their subsequent adoption of Sinhala Buddhism as a way of establishing their own distinctive cultural and religious identity. While Sinhala influence can be traced to the eleventh century, the Sīhaḷa order only became dominant with the rise and development of the classical states from the mid-twelfth to the end of the fifteenth century. Sinhala Buddhism contributed to the legitimation of the ruling monarchies through its worldview, interpretation of history, monastic institution, education, and language; however, just as important, it became the religion of the masses through the worship of relics and sacred images and through the development of popular syncretic cults.

Vietnam has been largely excluded from the story of the development of the classical Buddhist Southeast Asian states because of the predominance of Hinduism among the Chams during early Vietnamese history and the overwhelming cultural influence of China on the country. Until the eleventh century the Vietnamese were effectively a group within the Chinese empire, and they looked to China for cultural inspiration even after they achieved independence under the Ly dynasty (1009–1224). Mahāyāna Buddhism was certainly part of the Chinese cultural influence, and the Ch'an (Viet., Thien) school, allegedly first established in 580 CE by Ti-ni-da-lu'u-chi, was the major Buddhist tradition in Vietnam. The elite eventually came to prefer Confucianism, but Buddhism continued to be important among the masses.

SOUTHEAST ASIAN BUDDHISM IN THE MODERN PERIOD

The classical Southeast Asian religio-cultural synthesis, of which Theravāda Buddhism has been a major component, has given the cultures of Burma, Thailand, Cambodia, Laos, and Vietnam a unique sense of identity and has sustained them to the present. Faced with Western imperialistic expansion from the seventeenth century onward and the challenge of modernity, the classical religious worldview, institutional structures, and cultural ethos have been changed, modified, and reasserted in a variety of ways. We shall examine how Buddhism has adapted to this challenge, its role in the development of the modern nation-state, and what the most recent trends suggest for the future of Buddhism in the region.

The condition of Southeast Asian Buddhism in the modern period reflects, to a large degree, the forces unleashed during the colonial period, especially during the nineteenth and twentieth centuries. Although modern religious histories of Burma, Thailand, and Indochina differ because of internal factors as well as the uniqueness of their colonial experiences—just as the Enlightenment fundamentally challenged the medieval synthesis of Christian Europe—the last century and a half has called into question the traditional Buddhist-Brahmanic-animistic synthesis of Southeast Asia and, consequently, the institutions and values associated with that worldview. The challenge to the classical worldview, and to the traditional moral community that was based on it, occurred on many fronts. Throughout the region the educational role of the *sangha* has been undermined by Western education. The status of the monk as one who was educated and as an educator and the significance of what was traditionally taught have also suffered. In Burma, the destruction of the institution of Buddhist kingship in 1885, as well as the relatively open posture of the British toward Buddhism, left the *sangha* in disarray, without the authority and direction the king traditionally provided. Thailand's rapid urbanization over the past fifty years has dramatically changed the village or town milieu that has historically informed and supported Buddhist religious practice. The communist revolutions in Laos, Cambodia, and Vietnam have displaced Buddhism as the fundamental mediator of cultural values. These are but a few of the challenges that Southeast Asian Buddhism has faced in the modern and contemporary periods.

Modernization and Reform. The eve of the assertion of colonial power in the Buddhist countries of Southeast Asia found them in differing states and conditions. The Burmese destruction of Ayutthayā in 1767 provided the Thai (the designation applied to Tai living in the modern nation-state) the opportunity to establish a new capital on the lower Chaophraya River at present-day Bangkok. Because of its accessibility to international commerce the new site was much better situated for the new era about to dawn; the new dynastic line was better able to cope with the increasing impact of Western influence and was also committed to building a new sense of national unity. The Burmese, on the other hand, tired of wars under Alaungpaya and his son, were beset by religious and ethnic fractionalism. They were disadvantaged by the more isolated location of their capital (Ava, Amarapura, and then Mandalay), and governed by politically less astute rulers such as King Bagyidaw, who lost the Arakan and lower Burma to the British in the Anglo-Burmese Wars. Cambodia, in the eighteenth and early nineteenth centuries, basically fell victim to either the Thai or the Vietnamese until the French protectorate was established over the country in the 1860s. The Lao kingdoms of Luang Prabang and Vientiane were subject to Thai dominance in the nineteenth century until King Norodom was forced to accept French protection in 1863. Only in the 1890s were the French able to pacify Cochin China, Annam, and Tongkin, which, together with Cambodia, were formed into the Union Indochinoise in 1887. With the rest of Buddhist Southeast Asia disrupted by the colonial policies of France and Great Britain, Thailand's independence and able leadership under Mongkut (Rama IV, 1851–1868) and Chulalongkorn (1868–1910) abetted religious modernization and reform, making Thailand the appropriate focus for this topic.

The classical Thai Buddhist worldview had been set forth in the *Traibhūmikathā* of King Lü Thai of Sukhōthai. In one sense this text must be seen as part of Lü Thai's program to reconstruct an administrative and political framework and to salvage the alliance structure that had collapsed under the policies of his predecessor. In laying out the traditional Buddhist stages of the deterioration of history, Lü Thai meant to affirm the meaningfulness of a karmically calculated human life within a given multitiered universe. As a Buddhist sermon it urges its listeners to lead a moral life and by so doing to reap the appropriate heavenly rewards. Within its great chain of being framework of various human, heavenly, and demonic realms, the text focuses on a central figure, the universal monarch, or *cakkavattin,* exemplified by the legendary king Dharmaśokarāja. Lü Thai's traditional picture of the world, the role of the king, the nature of karmic action, and the hope of a heavenly reward provide a rationale for Sukhōthai political, social, and religious order. That King Rama I (1782–1809), who reestablished the fortunes of the Thai monarchy, commissioned a new recension of the *Traibhūmi* testifies to its longevity and also to its utility as a charter for order and stability during yet another time of political and social disruption.

The worldview of the *Traibhūmi* was soon to be challenged by the West, however. European and American missionaries, merchants, and travelers came to Bangkok in the 1830s and 1840s, and by 1850 Thailand, or Siam, had signed commercial treaties with several Western nations. Led by Mongkut, who was crowned king in 1851, and by Chao Phraya Thiphakorawong, his able minister of foreign affairs, the Siamese noble elite proved to be interested in and open to Western technology and culture. A pragmatic type of scientific empiricism began to develop among them, leading even the devout Mongkut to articulate a demythologized Buddhism somewhat at odds with the traditional *Traibhūmi* worldview. This critique was formally set forth in 1867 in Chao Phraya Thiphakorawong's *Kitchanukit* (A Book Explaining Various Things), which explains events not in terms of traditional cosmological and mythological sources but using astronomy, geology, and medicine. For example, he argues that rain falls not because the rainmaking deities venture forth or because a great serpent thrashes its tail but because the winds suck water out of clouds; illness, he says, is caused not by a god punishing evil deeds but by air currents. Although the explanations were inaccurate, they were naturalistic rather than mythological or religious. The *Kitchanukit* presents Buddhism as primarily a system of social ethics; heaven and hell are not places but have a moral or pedagogical utility; *kamma* (Skt., *karman*) is not an actual causal force but a genetic principle that accounts for human diversity. Mongkut's successor, his son Chulalongkorn, moved even further from the mythic cosmology of the traditional Southeast Asian Buddhist worldview, declaring the *Traibhūmi* simply an act of imagination.

Modernization of the Thai Buddhist worldview was accompanied by a reform of the Buddhist *sangha,* led initially by Mongkut and continued during the reign of Chulalongkorn. Before his coronation in 1851 Mongkut had been a monk for twenty-five years. During that time his study of the Pali scriptures and his association with Mon monks of a stricter discipline convinced him that Thai Buddhism had departed from the authentic Buddhist tradition. He advocated a more serious study of Pali and Buddhist scripture as well as the attainment of proficiency in meditation. His efforts at religious reform resulted in an upgrading of monastic discipline in an effort to make it more orthodox. The group of monks who gathered around Mongkut at Wat Bovornives called themselves the Thammayut ("those adhering to the doctrine") and formed the nucleus of a new, stricter sect of Thai Buddhism. With its royal origins and connections, the Thammayut, or Dhammayuttika, sect has played a very influential role in the development of modern Thai Buddhism. In 1864 the Khmer royal family imported it to Cambodia, where it played a similar role. Its impact in Laos, however, was less significant. [*See the biography of Mongkut.*]

The development of a reformist Buddhist tradition that embodied Mongkut's ideals brought about further changes in the monastic order, especially as the *sangha* became part of the policies and programs of Mongkut's son Chulalongkorn. At the same time that he implemented reforms designed to politically integrate outlying areas into the emergent nation-state of Thailand, Chulalongkorn also initiated policies aimed at the incorporation of all Buddhists within the kingdom into a single national organization. As a consequence, monastic discipline, as well as the quality of monastic education, improved throughout the country. A standard monastic curriculum, which included three levels of study in Buddhist history, doctrine, and liturgy, and nine levels of Pali study, was established throughout the country. In addition, two Buddhist academies for higher studies were established in Bangkok.

The modernization and reform of Buddhism in Thailand in the late nineteenth and early twentieth centuries stand out, but the Thai case must be seen as part of a general trend in all the Southeast Asian Buddhist countries. In the area of text and doctrine a new scripturalism, epitomized by the new redaction of the Tipiṭaka in conjunction with the general Buddhist council held in Burma in 1956 and 1957, has emerged. Doctrinal reinterpretation has followed three major lines: an emphasis on the ethical dimensions of the tradition at the expense of the supernatural and mythical; a rejection of magical elements of popular thought and practice as incompatible with the authentic tradition; and a rationalization of Buddhist thought in terms of Western categories, along with an apologetic interest in depicting Buddhism as scientific. Some apologists, such as U Chan Htoon of Burma, have claimed that all modern scientific concepts preexisted in Buddhism. Others make less sweeping claims but cite specific correlations between such Buddhist doctrines as interdependent co-arising *(paṭicca samuppāda;* Skt., *pratītya-samutpāda)* and Einstein's relativity theory. Generally speaking, Buddhist apologists have attempted to prove that Buddhism is more scientific than other religions, particularly Christianity; that the empirical approach or methodology of Buddhism is consistent with modern science; and that science proves or validates particular Buddhist teachings.

Institutional modernization and reform have also taken place along the lines that we have examined in some detail in regard to Thailand. Cambodia, for example, not only adopted the Dhammayuttika sect from Thailand but also reorganized the *sangha* along national lines. In Laos and Burma various Buddhist organizations and associations with reformist intent emerged, often under lay leadership.

Buddhism and the Modern Nation-state. Buddhism proved to be a crucial factor during the end of the colonial and the postcolonial periods, as Burma, Thailand, Cambodia, Laos, and Vietnam became modern nation-states. On the one hand, Buddhism contributed decisively to the development of the new nationhood; on the other, it resisted in various ways to changes forced upon traditional Buddhist thought and practice. We shall first examine the Buddhist contributions to the national independence movements and to the maintenance of national identity and unity; second, we shall explore Buddhist resistance to pressures put on the tradition by the organization of the modern nation-state.

Historically, Buddhism played an important role in the definition of the classical Southeast Asian states. It was inevitable, therefore, that it would be a crucial factor in the redefinition of these states. In those cases, for example, in which a country was dominated by a colonial power, nationalist movements grew out of, or were identified with, a religious base or context. Take Burma as a case in point. Buddhism provided the impetus for the independence movement that arose there during the first decades of the twentieth century. The YMBAs (Young Men's Buddhist Association) of Rangoon and elsewhere in Burma quickly assumed a political role. The first issue of major consequence was the "no footwear" controversy of 1918. The YMBAs argued that Europeans, in keeping with Burmese custom, should be prohibited from wearing shoes in all pagodas; accordingly, the British government allowed the head monk of each pagoda to decide the regulations applying to footwear. During the next decade the nationalist cause was led primarily by the General Council of Burmese Associations and by such politically active monks as U Ottama, who was imprisoned for urging a boycott of government-sponsored elections, and U Wisara, who became a martyr to the independence movement when he died during a hunger strike in a British jail.

When U Nu became prime minister in January 1948, following Aung San's assassination, he put Buddhism at the heart of his political program. Although he rejected Marxism, he espoused a Buddhist socialism. In essence, he believed that a national community could be constructed only if individuals are able to overcome their own self-acquisitive interests. Sufficient material needs should be provided for everyone, class and property distinctions should be minimized, and all should strive for moral and mental perfection. The state was to meet the material needs of the people and Buddhism their spiritual needs. To this end he created a Buddhist Sasana Council in 1950 to propagate Buddhism and to supervise monks, appointed a minister of religious affairs, and ordered government departments to dismiss civil servants thirty minutes early if they wished to meditate. In 1960 U Nu committed himself and his party to making Buddhism the state religion of Burma, an unpopular move with such minorities as the Christian Karens. This attempt was one of the reasons given for General Ne Win's coup in March 1962, which deposed U Nu as prime minister.

While in many ways naive and politically unrealistic, U Nu's vision of Buddhist socialism harked back to an earlier vision of the political leader as one who ruled by *dhamma* and who would engender peace and prosperity by the power of his own virtue. But such a vision proved incompatible with the political realities of the 1960s.

Buddhism figured prominently in other Southeast Asian countries, both as a basis of protest against ruling regimes and as an important symbolic component of political leadership. In the 1960s politically active Vietnamese monks contributed to the downfall of the Diem regime, and afterward the United Buddhist Association, under the leadership of Thich Tri Quang and Thich Thien Minh, remained politically active. In Cambodia, Prince Sihanouk espoused a political philosophy based on Buddhist socialism and was the last Cambodian ruler to represent, although in an attenuated way, the tradition of classical Southeast Asian Buddhist rule.

In addition to providing the inspiration for political independence movements, contributing to a political ideology with uniquely Buddhist features, and being the motivating force challenging political power structures, Southeast Asian Buddhism has been used to promote political unity within the boundaries of the nation-state. U Nu's hope that making Buddhism the state religion would promote national unity was naive; it did not take into account the contending factions within the Buddhist *sangha* and the presence of sizable non-Buddhist minorities who feared they might be threatened by covert, if not overt, pressure from the Buddhist majority.

In Thailand the centralization of the Thai *sangha* under King Chulalongkorn and his able *sangharāja,* Vajirañāṇa, not only improved monastic discipline and education but also integrated the monastic order more fully into the nation-state. Chulalongkorn's successor, Vajiravudh (1910–1925), made loyalty to the nation synonymous with loyalty to Buddhism; in effect, he utilized Buddhism as an instrument to promote a spirit of nationalism. In particular, he glorified military virtues and identified nationalism with the support of Thai Buddhism. He founded the Wild Tigers Corps, resembling the British Territorial Army; the Tiger Cubs, a branch of the corps, was later assimilated into the Boy Scout movement. Both encouraged loyalty to nation, religion (i.e., Buddhism), and the king.

Buddhism has continued to be an important tool in the government's policy to promote national unity. In 1962 the Buddhist Sangha Act further centralized the organization of the monastic order under the power of the secular state. In the same year the government organized the Dhammadhuta program, and in 1965 the Dhammacarikạ program. The former supported Buddhist monks abroad and those working in sensitive border areas, especially the northeastern region of the country, while the latter has focused on Buddhist missions among northern hill tribes.

Buddhism, however, has not only functioned as a kind of "civil religion," contributing to the definition and support of the new Southeast Asian nation-states in the postcolonial period. It has also resisted the kind of accommodation and change brought on by the new nationalism. In some cases this resistance has been generated by the desire to maintain traditional religious practices and more local autonomy; in others, it has come in the form of armed rebellion and messianic, millenarian movements. As an example of the former we cite Khrūbā Sīwichai, a northern Thai monk of the early twentieth century, and of the latter we cite the Saya San rebellion (1930–1931) in Burma.

While the vast majority of the Buddhist *sangha* in Thailand cooperated with the central government's attempts in the early twentieth century to standardize monastic organization, discipline, and education, there were a few notable exceptions. Khrūbā Sīwichai of the Chiangmai region of northern Thailand was one of them. He ran into problems with the *sangha* hierarchy because he ordained monks and novices according to northern Thai custom although he had not been recognized as a preceptor by the national order. He also singlehandedly raised vast sums of money to rebuild monasteries that had fallen into disrepair and to construct a road, using manual labor, to the famous Mahādhātu Temple on Doi Sutēp Mountain, overlooking Chiangmai. Because of his success in these enterprises, miraculous powers were attributed to him. In 1919, however, he was ordered to report to Bangkok to answer charges of clerical disobedience and sedition, but high Thai officials, fearing the repercussions that punishment of Khrūbā Sīwichai might have, intervened on his behalf. Although eventually Sīwichai submitted to the laws of the Thai national monastic order, *sangha* officials tacitly agreed to permit the northern clergy to follow some of its traditional customs.

Other, more radical Buddhist responses to the emerging nation-state developed in various parts of Southeast Asia and usually centered on a charismatic leader who was sometimes identified as an incarnation of the *bodhisattva* Maitreya. In Burma several rebellions in the early twentieth century aimed to overthrow British rule and to restore the fortunes of both Burmese kingship and Burmese Buddhism. One of these was led by Saya San, who had been a monk in the Tharrawaddy district in lower Burma but disrobed to work in a more directly political way to overthrow the British. Saya San's movement had a strongly traditional religious and royal aura, and much of his support came from political monks associated with nationalistic associations *(wunthanu athin*s) that had formed in the 1920s. Saya San was "crowned" as "king" in a thoroughly traditional Burmese manner in a jungle capital on 28 October 1930. An armed group was trained and the rebellion launched toward the end of December. As the conflict spread throughout lower Burma and into the Shan States, the British army was called in to help the police forces repress the rebellion. Only after eight months of fighting did the warfare end.

Recent Trends. The chapter on Southeast Asian Buddhism's future within the context of the modern nation-state has yet to be closed. The disestablishment of the *sangha* in Cambodia and Laos has shaken, but by no means rooted out, the tradition, even though Pol Pot's genocidal regime attempted such wholesale destruction in the aftermath of American withdrawal from the war in Indochina. Laos and Cambodia, however, have experienced a breakdown of the traditional religio-cultural synthesis. This is taking place more slowly in Thailand and even in Burma, which has been much more isolated from Western influences since the early 1960s. The political and economic contexts of Southeast Asian Buddhism, in short, have obviously affected the state of Buddhism in Southeast Asia. The trends that have emerged seem paradoxical, if not contradictory. We shall examine three sets or pairs: increasingly active lay leadership and the veneration of monks to whom supernatural powers are ascribed; a revival of meditation practice and an emphasis on active political and social involvement; rampant magical, syncretic ritual practice and insistence on the purity of the authentic teaching.

The modern period has seen increased lay leadership at various levels of religious life. The YMBAs of Burma and the Buddhist "Sunday schools" that have arisen in Thailand have obviously been influenced by Western Christian models. Lay associations have developed for various purposes. For example, prior to the revolution Cambodia had the Buddhist Association of the Republic of Cambodia (1952), the Association of Friends of the Buddhist Lycée (1949), the Association of Friends of Religious Welfare Aid Centers, the Association of Religious Students of the Republic of Cambodia (1970), the Association of the Buddhist Youth of Cambodia (1971), and so on. Buddhist laity have also been actively involved in the worldwide Buddhist movement. Most notable of the laity groups are the World Fellowship of Buddhists, which has headquarters in Bangkok, and the World Council of Churches, which holds interreligious dialogue consultations.

The increasingly significant role of the laity in a religious tradition noted for the centrality of the monk reflects many developments in modern Southeast Asian countries, not the least of which is the spread of secular, Western education among the elites. Coupled with this phenomenon, however, we find a polar opposition—a persistent cult of the holy man to whom supernatural powers are attributed. In some instances the holy monk becomes a charismatic leader of a messianic cult (e.g., the Mahagandare Weikzado Apwegyoke in Burma), while in others the form of veneration is more informal and generalized (e.g., Phra Acharn Mun in Thailand). In many cases the holy monk makes few, if any, miraculous or supernatural claims, but these will be ascribed to him by his followers. Hagiographic literature, describing cosmic portents of the monk's birth, extraordinary events during his childhood, and other characteristics of this genre, will often emerge. While the monk as miracle worker is not a new phenomenon in Theravāda Buddhism, it has persisted to the present time and, some observers claim, has been on the upswing in the contemporary period.

Meditation has always been the *sine qua non* of Buddhist practice, but traditionally it was the preserve of the forest-dwelling *(araññavāsī)* or meditating *(vipassana dhura)* monk. In the modern period, meditation has been more widely practiced as part of the routines of ordinary Buddhist temples and, more particularly, in meditation centers that either include or are specifically for lay practice. The lay meditation movement was especially strong in Burma under the leadership of such meditation masters as U Ba Khin and Ledi Sayadaw (1856–1923). Westerners have been particularly attracted to some of Southeast Asia's renowned meditation teachers, such as Acharn Cha of Wat Pa Pong in Ubon Ratchathani. Some meditating monks have also gained reputations not only for their method of meditation or for holiness but for the attainment of extraordinary powers as well.

While meditation has become a lay as well as monastic practice in contemporary Southeast Asian Buddhism, this development has not precluded a movement to formulate a strong, activist social ethic. The Vietnamese Zen monk Thich Nhat Hahn attempted to work out a Buddhist solution to the military conflict in his country during the 1960s, and there has been a widespread interest in formulating a Buddhist theory of economic development that is critical of Western capitalism but not necessarily indebted to Marxism. Buddhists have also acted to solve particular social problems, such as drug addiction, and have spoken out strongly against the proliferation of nuclear arms. Southeast Asian Buddhists have also joined with members of other religious groups, both within their own countries as well as in international organizations, to work for such causes as world peace and basic civil rights for all peoples. Buddhist interpreters, such as the Thai monk Bhikkhu Buddhadāsa, have referred to Buddhism as a practical system of personal and social morality.

Buddhadāsa has also been strongly critical of conventional Thai Buddhist religious practice, which has stressed merit-making rituals. These are aimed at obtaining personal benefit and propitiating various supernatural powers for protection or good luck. In his writings and at his center in Chaiya, southern Thailand, he emphasizes the importance of overcoming greed and attachment. *Nibbāna,* for Buddhadāsa, is the state that is achieved when egoism is overcome. This is the goal of all Buddhists, not just monks. Indeed, he argues, this is the purpose of all religions. Buddhadāsa's critique reflects the magical nature of popular Buddhist ritual practice not only in Thailand but, more generally, in Southeast Asian Buddhism, the goal of which is to improve one's life materially through the mechanism of gaining merit or improving one's karmic status. Buddhadāsa's proposal that such teachings as *nibbāna* and *anatta* (not-self), which represent the essence of the Buddha's teachings, must be part of every Buddhist's religious practice exemplifies an interest on the part of many contemporary Buddhist thinkers to restore the kernel of the authentic tradition, which has often been hidden beneath layers of cultural accretions. Thus, while the popular religious ethos is syncretic and emphasizes the attainment of worldly goals, various apologists in Burma and Thailand are attempting to make the core of the tradition a part of the understanding and practice of the Buddhist populace at large. Some critical observers have referred to this trend as a "protestantizing" of Southeast Asian Buddhism.

The contemporary ethos of Buddhism in Southeast Asia reflects an ancient heritage but also points in new directions. It is difficult to predict how the *sangha* will fare under the Marxist regimes in Laos and Cambodia or, for that matter, in the urban and increasingly materialistic environment of Bangkok and Chiangmai. Can the Theravāda monk maintain his place in society when his education cannot compare with that of the elite? Can Buddhism effectively address problems of overpopulation, prostitution, malnourishment, and economic exploitation? To what extent can the tradition change with the times and retain its identity? These and other questions face a religion that has not only been fundamental in the identity of the Burmese, Thai, Laotians, Cambodians, and Vietnamese but has also contributed much to world culture.

[*For a discussion of the institutional history of the Buddhist order in Southeast Asia, see* Theravāda. *An examination of the relationship between the* saṃgha *and the larger societies of which it is a part can be found in* Saṃgha, *article on* Saṃgha and Society. Southeast Asian Religions, *article on* Mainland Cultures *treats local Buddhist traditions in Southeast Asia. See also* Buddhism, *article on* Folk Buddhism; Pilgrimage, *article on* Buddhist Pilgrimage in South and Southeast Asia; Worship and Cultic Life, *article on* Buddhist Cultic Life in Southeast Asia; Burmese Religion; Khmer Religion; Lao Religion; Thai Religion; *and* Vietnamese Religion.]

BIBLIOGRAPHY

Works on Buddhism in Southeast Asia include text translations and doctrinal studies, histories of the development of Buddhism in various Southeast Asian countries, anthropological treatments of popular, village Buddhism, and studies of Buddhism and political change. Georges Coedès's studies, *The Indianized States of Southeast Asia,* edited by Walter F. Vella and translated by Susan Brown Cowing (Canberra, 1968), and *The Making of South-East Asia,* translated by H. M. Wright (Berkeley, 1966), are standard treatments of the region, as is Reginald Le May's *The Culture of South-East Asia* (London, 1954). The classic study of Southeast

Asian religion and kingship is Robert Heine-Geldern's *Conceptions of State and Kingship in Southeast Asia* (Ithaca, N.Y., 1956). A readable, general study of the history of Theravāda Buddhism in Southeast Asia and its present teachings and practices is Robert C. Lester's *Theravada Buddhism in Southeast Asia* (Ann Arbor, 1973). My *Buddhism and Society in Southeast Asia* (Chambersburg, Pa., 1981) is an analysis of Theravāda Buddhism in terms of the themes of syncretism, political legitimation, and modernization. The theme of Buddhism and political legitimation is discussed in several seminal articles in *Buddhism and Legitimation of Power in Thailand, Laos, and Burma,* edited by Bardwell L. Smith (Chambersburg, Pa., 1978).

The monumental work on the early Pagan period is Gordon H. Luce's *Old Burma—Early Pagán,* 3 vols. (Locust Valley, N.Y., 1969–1970). Two of the important Burmese chronicles have been translated: *Hmannān mạha yazạwintawkyī: The Glass Palace Chronicle of the Kings of Burma,* translated by Pe Maung Tin and G. H. Luce (London, 1923); and Pannasami's *The History of the Buddha's Religion (Sāsanavaṁsa),* translated by B. C. Law (London, 1952). Standard treatments of both Pali and Sanskritic Buddhism in Burma are Nihar-Ranjan Ray's *An Introduction to the Study of Theravāda Buddhism in Burma* (Calcutta, 1946), and his *Sanskrit Buddhism in Burma* (Calcutta, 1936). A more recent study is Winston L. King's *A Thousand Lives Away* (Cambridge, Mass., 1964). Two standard anthropological studies are Melford E. Spiro's *Buddhism and Society: A Great Tradition and its Burmese Vicissitudes,* 2d. ed. (Berkeley, 1982), and Manning Nash's *The Golden Road to Modernity* (New York, 1965). Nash was also the general editor of *Anthropological Studies in Theravada Buddhism* (New Haven, 1966), which contains valuable articles on Burmese and Thai Buddhism by Nash, David E. Pfanner, and Jasper Ingersoll. E. Michael Mendelson's *Sangha and State in Burma,* edited by John P. Ferguson (Ithaca, N.Y., 1965), although difficult going is a mine of information. Buddhism and the early nationalist period are studied in Emanuel Sarkisyanz's *Buddhist Backgrounds of the Burmese Revolution* (The Hague, 1965), and Donald E. Smith's *Religion and Politics in Burma* (Princeton, 1965).

The standard Thai history with much information about Thai Buddhism is David K. Wyatt's *Thailand: A Short History* (New Haven, 1984); Kenneth E. Wells's *Thai Buddhism: Its Rites and Activities* (Bangkok, 1939), while somewhat dated and rather dry is still very useful. One of the major northern Thai chronicles, Ratanapanya's *Jinakālamālīpakaranam,* has been translated by N. A. Jayawickrama as *The Sheaf of Garlands of the Epochs of the Conqueror* (London, 1968). Frank E. Reynolds and Mani B. Reynolds have translated the major Thai cosmological treatise, *Trai Phūmi Phra Rūang,* as *Three Worlds according to King Ruang* (Berkeley, 1982). Prince Dhani-Nivat's *A History of Buddhism in Siam,* 2d ed. (Bangkok, 1965), provides a brief historical overview of the development of Buddhism in Thailand. Much recent, significant work on Thai Buddhism has been done by anthropologists; see especially Stanley J. Tambiah's *World Conqueror and World Renouncer* (Cambridge, 1976) and several articles by Charles F. Keyes, for example, "Buddhism and National Integration in Thailand," *Journal of Asian Studies* 30 (May 1971): 551–567. Historians of religion have also contributed to our knowledge of Thai Buddhism. Frank E. Reynolds has written several articles including, "The Holy Emerald Jewel: Some Aspects of Buddhist Symbolism and Political Legitimation in Thailand and Laos," in *Religion and Legitimation of Power in Thailand, Laos, and Burma,* edited by Bardwell L. Smith (Chambersburg, Pa., 1978), pp. 175–193. I have analyzed a major northern Thai monastery in *Wat Haripuñjaya: A Study of the Royal Temple of the Buddha's Relic, Lamphun, Thailand* (Missoula, Mont., 1976).

French scholars have made the major contribution to the study of Buddhism in Laos, Cambodia, and Vietnam. Louis Finot's "Research sur la littérature laotienne," *Bulletin de l'École Française d'Extrême-Orient* 17 (1917) is an indispensable tool in the study of Lao Buddhist literature. Marcel Zago's *Rites et cérémonies en milieu bouddhiste lao* (Rome, 1972) provides a comprehensive treatment of Lao religion, although Charles Archaimbault's "Religious Structures in Laos," *Journal of the Siam Society* 52 (1964): 57–74, while more limited in scope is very useful. Lawrence Palmer Brigg's "The Syncretism of Religions in Southeast Asia, especially in the Khmer Empire," *Journal of the American Oriental Society* 71 (October–December 1951): 230–249, provides a survey of the development of religion in Cambodia. Adhémard Leclère's classic study, *Le bouddhisme au Cambodge* (Paris, 1899) remains the standard work. The classic study of Vietnamese religion is Leopold Michel Cadière's *Croyances et pratiques religieuses des Viêtnamiens,* 3 vols. (Saigon, 1955–1958), but more accessible is the brief sketch in the trilingual volume by Chanh-tri Mai-tho-Truyen, *Le bouddhisme au Vietnam, Buddhism in Vietnam, Phat-giao Viet-nam* (Saigon, 1962). Thich Thien-An's *Buddhism and Zen in Vietnam in Relation to the Development of Buddhism in Asia,* edited by Carol Smith (Los Angeles, 1975), studies the development of Buddhist schools from the sixth to the seventeenth century. Thich Nhat-Hanh's *Vietnam: Lotus in a Sea of Fire* (New York, 1967) puts the Buddhist situation in the 1960s into historical perspective.

Interested readers may also wish to consult the following works: Heinz Bechert's three-volume study, *Buddhismus, Staat und Gesellschaft in den Ländern Theravāda-Buddhismus* (Frankfurt, 1966–1973); *Religion in South Asia,* edited by Edward B. Harper (Seattle, 1964), especially the articles by Michael Ames and Nur Yalman; and *Religion and Progress in Modern Asia,* edited by Robert N. Bellah (New York, 1965).

5 BUDDHISM IN CENTRAL ASIA

Ronald Eric Emmerick

It is not known exactly how or when Buddhism first spread northward into Bactria, but there is strong evidence that it was actively promoted in the Indo-Iranian border region as a result of the missionary activity encouraged by the Indian emperor Aśoka in the third century BCE. Aśoka set up inscriptions in widely distant parts of his kingdom. The most famous are the so-called Rock Edicts and Pillar Edicts, which are of varied content but consistently promulgate the ethical standards of Buddhist teaching that he wished to inculcate. Two Aśokan inscriptions have been found as far north as Qandahar in Afghanistan. Aśoka was renowned also for his building activity and he is credited by popular legend with the erection of eighty-four thousand stupas. The stupas of the time of Aśoka and his immediate successors were markedly distinct in style from those built later under the Kushans. This difference had already been noticed by the famous seventh-century Chinese pilgrim Hsüan-tsang, who observed a large number of stupas in the Aśokan style in the northwest, for example, three at Taxila, two in Uḍḍiyāna, five in Gandhāra, three near Nagarahāra (Jelalabad), dozens in Jāguḍa (near Qandahar), and even one at Kāpiśī (Begram). [*See the biography of Aśoka.*]

The first centuries of the common era saw the consolidation and expansion of the Kushan empire founded by Kujula Kadphises. The Kushans were a people of uncertain extraction who in Gandhāra adopted as their official language an East Iranian language nowadays called Bactrian. They controlled the famous caravan route that proceeded from Taxila via Bamian to Balkh and thence to Termez on the Afghan border. Archaeological remains of Kushan Buddhist occupation have been found along the entire route and to the east of it.

A new era in Indian history is associated with the most renowned Kushan ruler, Kaniṣka I (first to second century CE). Kaniṣka is celebrated in Buddhist sources as a second Aśoka and similar legends arose concerning him, but it is likely that his patronage of Buddhism proceeded from his tolerance rather than from his conversion. Although the figure of a Buddha is depicted on one of his coins, they portray a varied pantheon. Archaeological evidence indicates that the Kushans mainly worshiped Śiva and the Iranian goddess Ardoxšo, but that Buddhism was gaining ground. Kaniṣka is traditionally associated with the famous Buddhist authors Aśvaghoṣa, Mātṛceṭa, and Vasubandhu, as well as with the well-known physician Caraka.

Such traditions have little value beyond confirming what we know otherwise, namely, that under Kaniṣka Buddhism flourished and spread as never before.

The Kushan empire embraced various peoples living side by side. In particular, several Iranian tribes were represented as well as Greeks and Indians. Greeks had been living in Bactria and Gandhāra since the time of Alexander in the fourth century BCE; Saka tribes penetrated the area in the second century BCE. It is generally agreed that it was due to Greek influence in communities where religious tolerance was observed that the style of Buddhist art known as Gandharan developed. The most noticeable feature of this style was the depiction in human form of the Buddha, whose person had previously been considered beyond the reach of artists and who had accordingly been represented in art only symbolically, for example by a wheel. Also noteworthy is the common portrayal of the Buddhist laity in this art. One episode often depicted is the giving of food to the Buddha by the two merchant brothers Trapusa and Bhallika, who were shown in a second-century relief at Shotorak as bearded and dressed in an Indo-Scythian manner. Bhallika has traditionally been associated with Balkh.

It is also significant that the cult of the *bodhisattva* is reflected early in Gandharan art. Best known are the representations of the *bodhisattva* Maitreya, the future Buddha. As recently as 1977 there came to light in Mathurā a fragmentary sculpture of the Buddha Amitābha. It is identified by an accompanying inscription that dates the sculpture to 106 CE.

Much controversy surrounds the question of the date and place of origin of Mahāyāna Buddhism. There are, however, many indications that it arose during the first century CE in a cosmopolitan environment such as Gandhāra. The depiction of the Buddha in human form certainly betrays Greek influence, but at the same time it conforms with Mahāyāna Buddhist teaching that the historical Buddha Śākyamuni should be regarded merely as one of many Buddhas.

Kushan influence is known to have spread northwards into Khorezm and Sogdiana, but it seems clear that those regions were never actually under Kushan rule, and there is not much evidence of Buddhism there in the time of the Kushans. The sites excavated at Varakhsha near Bukhara, and at Afrāsiyāb and Panjikent near Samarkand, are conspicuously non-Buddhist, while the Buddhist sites further east at Ajina Tepe near Kurgan-Tyube, at Kuva in Ferghana, and at Ak-Beshim near Frunze all belong to the seventh or eighth century. Even at this date Buddhism cannot have been well established around the capital, as the sites near Bukhara and Samarkand show clearly enough. Hsüan-tsang found little Buddhist adherence in Samarkand in the seventh century, and despite Hsüan-tsang's claim to conversions there, the Korean pilgrim known by his Chinese name Hui-ch'ao found only a solitary Buddhist monastery with a single monk when he visited Samarkand in the eighth century. [*See the biography of Hsüan-tsang.*]

Although the Kushans adopted Bactrian as the official language for their coins and for the inscription at the dynastic temple at Surkh Kotal, the language of their administration was Indian, the so-called Gāndhārī Prakrit written in Kharoṣṭhī script. Kushan influence extended well into China during the first centuries CE and administrative documents dating from the period between 200 and 320 written in Gāndhārī have been found in the kingdom of Shan-shan (Kroraina), which stretched from the Niya River a short distance east of Khotan as far as Lob Nor. A Kharoṣṭhī well inscription probably dating from the second half of the second century was found at Lo-yang in China. Gāndhārī was the language used by a Hīnayāna Buddhist sect, the Dharmaguptakas, whose *Dīrghāgama* and Vinaya were translated into Chinese by Buddhayaśas between 410 and 413. One of the Niya documents contains the final verses of the Dharmaguptaka recension of the *Prātimokṣa Sūtra,* and we know from the Chinese traveler Fa-hsien that in 400 there were more than four thousand Hīnayāna monks in Shan-shan.

One of the oldest manuscripts of any Indian text is the Gāndhārī recension of the *Dharmapada,* which also is the only extant literary text written in the Kharoṣṭhī script. It came to light in the vicinity of Khotan, but although it is said to have come from Kohmari Mazar it has not been possible to establish any connection with an archaeological site. It is written in essentially the same dialect as that used for the Niya documents from the nearby kingdom of Shan-shan and it may in fact have been written in one of the monasteries there. The Gāndhārī *Dharmapada* may date to the second century, and its discovery in the vicinity of Khotan lends support to the thesis that the first Buddhist mission to eastern Central Asia was led by the Dharmaguptakas. Whether the Dharmaguptakas came to Khotan or not, speakers of Gāndhārī certainly did, as the Khotanese language is in its oldest strata already permeated by loanwords from Gāndhārī.

By the Kushan period monks of another Buddhist Hīnayāna sect, the Sarvāstivāda, were spreading throughout Central Asia, taking with them palm-leaf manuscripts written in Buddhist Sanskrit. The earliest manuscripts have been found mainly in the cave monasteries of the Kuchā oasis and near Qarashahr. During the Kushan period works on Abhidharma and poetic literature predominated. Recent paleographic research has established a close connection between the monasteries in Bamian and Gilgit on the one hand and those in Eastern Turkistan on the other. There is thus good reason for assuming that missionary activity on the part of the Sarvāstivādins had its point of departure in Afghanistan and Kashmir.

The precise date of Buddhism's initial establishment in Khotan is unknown. A late tradition would indicate about 84 BCE, which is not unlikely. According to Chinese sources, there was a Buddhist community in Khotan by the second century CE, and, as mentioned above, the Gāndhārī *Dharmapada* found near Khotan probably dates to the second century. Chu Shih-hsing, who studied Prajñāpāramitā literature at Lo-yang in the third century, went west in search of the *Pañcaviṃśatisāhasrikā-prajñāpāramitā Sūtra,* which he found in Khotan. Mokṣala, who translated this work into Chinese in 291, was a Khotanese, and another Khotanese, Gītamitra, took a copy of the same text with him to Ch'ang-an (modern Sian) in 296. Thus, Khotan was already a well-established center of Mahāyāna studies in the third century.

Many fragments of Sanskrit manuscripts of Prajñāpāramitā literature have been found in Khotan but most of them await publication. Already published is an incomplete text of the *Vajracchedikā,* of which fourteen out of nineteen folios are extant. A complete manuscript of a Khotanese translation of this popular Mahāyāna work is also extant. It dates from a much later period and incorporates some interesting commentatorial additions. The fact that so many fragments of Mahāyāna manuscripts have been found in Khotan testifies to the reliability of Chinese reports concerning the dominance of the Mahāyāna in Khotan. Much of this material still awaits publication. One large manuscript of the *Saddharmapuṇḍarīka Sūtra,* which must originally have come from Khotan, has been the object of much study in recent years. It contains several colophons written in Late Khotanese.

The Central Asian recensions of Buddhist Sanskrit texts are of particular interest because they shed light on the way in which these texts were transmitted to Tibet and China. It was only at a relatively late date that the Sanskrit texts were translated into Central Asian languages. The Buddhist scriptures were first translated into Chinese from Gāndhārī and thereafter from Sanskrit. Many of the early translators of Indian works into Chinese spoke Central Asian languages themselves. Typical is the complaint of a Khotanese poet: "The Khotanese do not value the [Buddhist] Law at all in Khotanese. They understand it badly in Indian. In Khotanese it does not seem to them to be the Law. For the Chinese the Law is in Chinese." It must have been particularly frustrating for the poet to find so little appreciation in view of the efforts of Khotanese missionaries such as Devaprajña, Śikṣānanda, and Śīladharma in translating Buddhist texts into Chinese at Lo-yang and Ch'ang-an.

The king of Khotan is said to have converted Kashgar to Buddhism in about 100 CE. At this date the Mahāyāna had probably not yet fully emerged and Khotan would have followed Hīnayāna teaching. Hīnayāna was mainly followed in Kashgar and its subsequent links were rather with the cities of the northern route across the Takla Makan. The same is true of Tumshuq, whose Buddhist monastery is thought to date from the fourth or fifth century. Nothing is known of its history but the style of its artistic remains shows connections with Qizil in the Kuchā region. That it was inhabited by Saka monks is shown by the discovery of a manuscript fragment containing the ceremonial formulas for the ordination of Buddhist laywomen. It is written in a Middle Iranian dialect closely related to Khotanese but in the same kind of Brāhmī script used for writing Tocharian. The many archaic features of Tumshuqese reveal that it separated very early from Khotanese, which developed along different lines. Archaeological evidence indicates that the monastery complex was destroyed by fire about the tenth century, which would be the time when the Karakhanids imposed Islam on the area.

Although there is not much evidence of Buddhism in the heart of Sogdiana, the Sogdians were one of the main peoples responsible for the diffusion of Buddhism throughout Central Asia and China. They were merchants who established trading colonies all along the northern Silk Route as far as the Chinese capital at Lo-yang. The Sogdians took with them not only Buddhism but also Manichaeism and Christianity, and we have translations into the Middle Iranian Sogdian languageof the scriptures of all three religions. The Sogdians acquired a knowledge of Chinese for trading purposes, but they put it to use by translating Chinese Buddhist literature into Sogdian. Moreover, some of the early translators of Buddhist Sanskrit literature into Chinese were of Sogdian extraction such as K'ang (i.e., Samarkand) Meng-hsiang, who worked at Lo-yang from 194 to 199.

Still extant are four letters written in Tun-huang in the Sogdian language. They can be dated with considerable certainty to the year 313. Thus, there was a Sogdian colony in Tun-huang before building began in 366 at the famous site of Ch'ien-fo-tung ("caves of the thousand Buddhas"), nine miles southwest of the city. It was among the hundreds of cave-temples there that a famous medieval library of Central Asian manuscripts was discovered at the beginning of the present century. Among other things, this library included the largest proportion of extant Khotanese literature and most of the surviving Buddhist Sogdian manuscripts.

Buddhism must have come to Tun-huang by the beginning of the common era, but it is first attested in literature in the third century. The greatest translator of

Buddhist texts before Kumārajīva was the Indo-Scythian Dharmarakṣa (Chin., Fa-hu), who was born in Tun-huang around 230 CE. He is known to have traveled extensively throughout Central Asia in search of Buddhist scriptures and to have acquired knowledge of many Central Asian languages. He collaborated with Indians and Kucheans, with a Yüeh-chih, a Khotanese, and probably also a Sogdian. It was one of his Chinese disciples, Fa-ch'eng, who in about 280 founded a large monastery in Tun-huang.

The earliest inscription in a Turkic language is a funeral stela discovered near Bugut about 170 kilometers from the site of the eighth-century royal Turkic inscriptions at Orkhon in Mongolia. It is the epitaph of a prince of the Eastern Turks who became kaghan in 571. The inscription, which dates to approximately 581, is written in Sogdian and in the kind of Sogdian writing found in the later Buddhist Sogdian manuscripts. From this kind of Sogdian writing the Uighur script used by the Eastern Turks for their translations of Buddhist works later developed. The inscription mentions the establishment of a Buddhist community, and there is evidence that two of the rulers of the Eastern Turks mentioned in it were Buddhists. It is known that a Buddhist monk from Kāpiśī (Begram) called Jinagupta (528–605), who had spent some time in the kingdom of Khotan, taught Buddhism at the court of the Eastern Turks.

Kocho, modern Karakocho, a few miles east of Turfan, was the principal city of the Turfan region until the end of the fourteenth century. The name of the city in Chinese sources is usually Kao-ch'ang or Ho-chou. It began as a Chinese military colony in the first century BCE. In about 790 it was conquered by the Tibetans and after the fall of the Uighur empire in the Orkhon Basin in 840–843 the Uighurs made Kocho their southern capital. The Uighurs who came from the Orkhon regionwere Manichaeans, not Buddhists, but Kocho had long been inhabited by Sogdians and Chinese professing Buddhism. Most of the Buddhist texts in the Uighur language were found in the Turfan region and derive from the Sarvāstivāda and Mahāyāna canons. The language of these texts has been profoundly influenced by Sogdian, and it may be assumed accordingly that the Sogdians played an important role in instructing the Uighurs in Buddhism. However, most of the texts seem to have been translated from Chinese, perhaps with the help of Sogdian translators. The Sogdians themselves usually translated Buddhist literature from Chinese into Sogdian. The Buddhist communities in the Turfan area and elsewhere remained in contact with Tibetan Buddhists; from the eleventh to the fourteenth century a number of Tantric texts were translated from Tibetan into Uighur.

The most famous Buddhist text in Uighur is the *Maitrisimit* (Skt., *Maitreya-samiti*). It was evidently quite popular, as indicated by the number of copies found in different places. It bears a colophon according to which a Sarvāstivādin called Prajñārakṣita translated it from Tocharian. A substantial amount of the Tocharian version is extant but most of it awaits publication. The Tocharians were a non-Turkic people speaking an Indo-European language, of which two dialects are attested. East Tocharian, or Tocharian A, is the dialect spoken mainly in Qarashahr; West Tocharian, or Tocharian B, is the dialect spoken mainly in Kuchā. East Tocharian is the better known dialect and it is in this that the *Maitrisimit* and the well-known *Puṇyavanta Jātaka* were written. However, much material written in West Tocharian remains unpublished. Most of the Tocharian Buddhist texts were translated from Sanskrit works of the Sarvāstivādins and date from the sixth to eighth century.

There are indications that Buddhism probably was present in Kuchā before the beginning of the common era. It was certainly well established by the time of the famous translator Kumārajīva (344–413). Kumārajīva was the son of an Indian father and a Kuchean mother. His mother, a younger sister of the king of Kuchā, became a Buddhist nun. Before the age of twenty, Kumārajīva turned from Hīnayāna to Mahāyāna. During his lifetime he translated numerous works, both Hīnayāna and Mahāyāna, into Chinese, but he is chiefly remembered in China for having introduced the Chinese to Mahāyāna was held in high esteem in Kuchā for some time. [*See the biography of Kumārajīva.*] However, an Indian monk called Dharmakṣema reported that at the beginning of the fifth century most of the population of Kuchā followed the Hīnayāna. Around 583 the king of Kuchā was an adherent of Mahāyāna, but in 630 Hsüan-tsang reported that most Kucheans followed the Hīnayāna teaching. According to the eighth-century Korean pilgrim Hui-ch'ao, the local population followed the Hīnayāna whereas the Chinese inhabitants were devotees of Mahāyāna. At the beginning of the fourth century a prince of Kuchā called Po Śrīmitra introduced to southern China the Kuchean art of melodic recitation of Buddhist texts.

From the brief review above it is clear that throughout the first millennium CE the whole of Central Asia was under strong Buddhist influence. Several centers of Buddhist learning emerged in Eastern Turkistan: Khotan, Turfan, Kocho, Tun-huang. Various peoples were converted to Buddhism: Iranian peoples, especially the Tumshuqese, Khotanese, and Sogdians; the Tocharians; Turkic peoples such as the Eastern Turks and the Uighurs; and the Chinese. Expatriate Indians took their religion with them, but it was the Sogdians and the Chinese who were especially active as missionaries. It is difficult to assess the contribution made by Central Asian Buddhists to the development of Buddhism. The Sogdians and the Tocharians appear to have confined themselves to translation of the scriptures and propagation of the religion. There is some evidence that the Khotanese and the Uighurs, like the Chinese, brought original ideas to bear upon the traditions they had adopted. Khotan may have played a role in the development of the Mahāyāna and of the later kinds of Tantric Buddhism, for the Tibetans came in contact with Khotanese Buddhism during their occupation of Khotan and Tun-huang.

[*See the maps accompanying* Missions, *article on* Buddhist Missions, *and* Chinese Religion, *overview article. See also* Inner Asian Religions.]

BIBLIOGRAPHY

The most detailed survey of Buddhism in Central Asia is provided by Lore Sander's article "Buddhist Literature in Central Asia," in the *Encyclopaedia of Buddhism,* edited by G. P. Malalasekera, vol. 4, fasc. 1 (Colombo, 1979). This article, however, contains many inaccuracies of detail and must be used with caution. The article by B. A. Litvinskii in the same volume, although entitled "Central Asia," deals with Buddhism in Soviet Central Asia and Afghanistan only. The same applies to his book *Outline History of Buddhism in Central Asia,* edited by G. M. Bongard-Levin (Moscow, 1968). *Buddhism in Afghanistan and Central Asia,* 2 vols., by Simone Gaulier, Robert JeraBezard, and Monique Maillard (Leiden, 1976), is a brief commentary on the artistic treasures as exemplified by 124 illustrations. Annemarie von Gabain's well-known article "Buddhistische Türkenmission," in *Asiatica: Festschrift Friedrich Weller* (Leipzig, 1954), pp. 160–173, is confined to the part played by the Turks. Her undocumented article "Der Buddhismus in Zentralasien," in *Religionsgeschichte des Orients in der Zeit der Weltreligionen* (Leiden, 1961), pp. 496–514, neglects the role played by the Iranian peoples. For this, see my chapter "Buddhism among Iranian Peoples," in *The Cambridge History of Iran,* edited by Ehsan Yarshater (Cambridge, 1983), pp. 949–964. Useful surveys of Buddhist literature in Central Asia are my *A Guide to the Literature of Khotan* (Tokyo, 1979); David A. Utz's *A Survey of Buddhist Sogdian Studies* (Tokyo, 1978); Wolfgang Scharlipp's "Kurzer Überblick über die buddhistische Literatur der Türken," *Materialia turcica* 6 (1980): 37–53; and Werner Thomas's "Die tocharische Literatur," in *Die Literaturen der Welt in ihrer mündlichen und schriftlichen Überlieferung,* edited by Wolfgang von Einsiedel (Zurich, 1964), pp. 967–973.

6 BUDDHISM IN CHINA

Erik Zürcher

Both literary and archaeological evidence indicate that Buddhism reached China in the first century of the common era and that it entered the country from the northwest, after having spread through the oasis kingdoms that had sprung up along the Silk Road, the transcontinental caravan route that at that time linked two powerful empires. At its western extremity, Buddhism flourished in the Kushan, or Indo-Scythian, empire that from its base in northwestern India dominated the Indo-Iranian border lands from present-day Bu khara to Afghanistan. In the east, it had its terminal at the frontier town of Tun-huang, on the border of the Han empire that ruled over most of present-day China and at times also extended its military dominance far into Central Asia. Thus, the oasis kingdoms were exposed to cultural influences from both sides. They became the main stations in the developing commercial and diplomatic relations between Han China and the Middle East, and, at the same time, flourishing centers of Buddhism. There are some indications that Buddhism also reached China along the sea route as early as the second century CE, but those contacts cannot be compared to the constant influx of Buddhist missionaries, scriptures, and artistic impulses from what the Chinese vaguely called the Western Region: present-day Sinkiang and Soviet Central Asia, and the even more distant lands of Parthia, Kashmir, and northwestern India.

CONSEQUENCES OF THE GEOGRAPHICAL SETTING

The geographical configuration has in various ways been a conditioning factor in the development of Chinese Buddhism, particularly in its formative phase. In the first place, it has led to a certain regionalization in Chinese Buddhism. In general, the centers in the north and northwest remained in direct contact with the Western Region. For many centuries, the most prominent foreign missionaries were active mainly in the north, and it was also there that most Chinese versions of Buddhist scriptures were produced. The greater awareness of the foreign origin of Buddhism no doubt enhanced its popularity among the non-Chinese conquerors who ruled the northern half of China from the early fourth century until 589 CE. In the southern parts of China, which in those centuries were ruled by a succession of indigenous Chinese dynasties and had no direct overland communications with the Western Region, a much more sinicized type of Buddhism developed, less concerned with translation and scriptural studies, and much more focused upon the interpretation of Buddhist ideas in terms of traditional Chinese philosophy and religion. After the reunification of the empire under the Sui (589 CE), these two main streams of Chinese Buddhism amalgamated; their mixture and integration heralded the golden age of Buddhism under the Sui and T'ang dynasties (589–906).

Another important consequence was that China for centuries absorbed Buddhism from many different centers representing various types of Buddhism. This diversity was due not only to regional differences, but also to the fact that Buddhism in India steadily evolved new schools and movements that spread over the continent and eventually reached China. Thus, right from the beginning, the Chinese were confronted with Buddhism not as one homogeneous and fairly consistent religious system, but rather as a bewildering mass of diverse teachings that occasionally contradicted each other on essential points: thousands of scriptures of both Theravāda and Mahāyāna origin; a great variety of scholastic treatises; monastic rules of many different schools; sectarian texts and tantric rituals—all of which claimed to be part of the Buddha's original message, and hence to be of impeccable orthodoxy. This ever-growing diversity stimulated the Chinese religious leaders to explore new ways in order to eliminate the contradictions and to reduce the Buddhist message to one basic truth, transcending all difference of expression. The Chinese reaction was twofold. On the one hand, attempts were made to integrate all Buddhist teachings into vast structures of "graded revelation," differentiated according to periods of preaching and the varying spiritual levels of the audience. On the other hand, we find the most radical rejection of diversity by the propagation of a "direct," intuitive way to enlightenment and the abandonment of all scriptural study. The first tendency eventually produced the great scholastic systems of medieval Chinese Buddhism; the second one is most clearly (though not exclusively) represented by Ch'an (Jpn., Zen) Buddhism.

Finally, the factor of sheer distance between China and India, and consequently the infrequency of direct contact between the monastic communities in China and religious centers in the homeland of Buddhism, had important consequences for the way in which Buddhism developed in China. Apart from the few pilgrims who were able to undertake the journey to India and to stay there for study, Chinese masters had no firsthand knowledge of Indian Buddhism; throughout the history of Chinese Buddhism, only a handful of Chinese are known to have mastered Sanskrit. On the other hand, the foreign missionaries who came to China (some from India, but as often from Buddhist centers in Central and Southeast Asia) seldom were fluent in Chinese. The production of Chinese versions of Buddhist texts typically was done by a translation team, the foreign master reciting the text and making, mostly with the help of a bilingual interpreter, a very crude translation, that was written down and afterward revised and polished by Chinese assistants. It is easy to see the hazards of misunderstanding inherent in such a procedure. Buddhist concepts lost much of their original flavor once they were expressed in Chinese terms; the linguistic barrier remained a formidable obstacle to a direct understanding of Buddhism as it had developed outside China, and direct communication with Indian centers of learning—or, indeed, with any Buddhist center outside China—was too incidental to change the overall picture. But it is also clear that these same factors contributed to the profound sinicization of Buddhism in China and to its absorption into Chinese culture. Once translated into a peculiar kind of semiliterary Chinese (that became standardized as a Chinese scriptural language around the fifth century CE), any scripture, because of the special nature of the Chinese ideographic script, could be read all over China, and be interpreted in a great variety of ways, without any external guidance. It is a pattern of independent diffusion that led to countless forms of hybridization with indigenous non-Buddhist forms of religious thought and practice. By the sixth century, Buddhism had already become fully "interiorized": when around that time the most influential schools of Chinese Buddhism took form, they owed their existence to the creative and independent thought of Chinese masters working in a purely Chinese environment, in which the foreign missionaries played only a marginal role.

BUDDHISM AND CHINESE CULTURE

Once it had entered China, Buddhism was confronted with formidable obstacles: a colossal empire and a civilization dominated by political and social ideas and norms that had crystallized in the course of centuries. Especially at the level of the cultural elite, these dominant ideas ran counter to some of the most fundamental notions of Buddhism, both as a doctrine and as an institution. As representatives of the orthodox Confucian tradition, the Chinese literati maintained a worldview that was essentially pragmatic and secular, despite their assent to certain religious ideas belonging to the sphere of "political theology." The Confucian worldview was based on the idea that the world of man forms a single organic whole with Heaven and earth, and that the ruler, sanctified by the mandate of Heaven, maintains the cosmic balance by the perfect administration of government. His sphere of activity is therefore, in principle, unlimited: the emperor, and, by extension, the scholar-official class through which he rules, form the single focus of power, prestige, and authority in all matters, secular as well as religious. The basic values are those of stability, hierarchical order, harmony in human relations, and painstaking observance of the ritual rules of behavior, notably those pertaining to the mutual obligations within the family, and in the relation between ruler and subject. The ideal state is an agrarian society with a productive, hard-working population that is subjected to the paternalistic but all-embracing rule of a bureaucratic elite of ideologically trained managers. This characteristic and deeply rooted combination of political, moralistic, and cosmological ideas formed the central tradition of Chinese thought; in spite of periodic ups and downs, it had maintained its primacy from the second century BCE to the beginning of the modern era. Thus, even at the time of its highest flowering, Buddhism always was subordinated to the claims of the secular order. It had to grow up in the shadow of the all-powerful central tradition.

As a doctrine, Buddhism was bound to meet with the disapproval of the Confucian elite, who maintained that the basic ideals of human existence are to be realized in this life, and that doctrines must be appreciated according to their practical applicability and sociopolitical effectiveness rather than for their metaphysical qualities. In general, the quest for purely individual salvation was rejected as narrow-minded and selfish: man can perfect himself only within society. To a large extent, these attitudes also characterize the major non-Confucian indigenous tradition of religious and philosophical thought in China, that of Taoism: there, too, the goals are concrete and tangible—harmony with the forces of nature and the prolongation of bodily existence. In view of these concepts and attitudes, it goes without saying that Buddhism, once it was transplanted into Chinese soil, was subjected to heavy pressures.

Its rejection of all existence as illusory and its belief in ideas like rebirth, the retribution of all acts *(karman),* and the pursuit of metaphysical aims, such as enlightenment and *nirvāṇa,* that in India had been universally accepted both within and outside Buddhist circles, in China became outlandish novelties that ran counter to the teachings of China's most revered sages. And the non-Chinese origin of the doctrine was in itself sufficient to condemn Buddhism as "barbarian," and therefore unfit to be propagated in the Middle Kingdom, the only region of true order and civilization.

At the institutional level, the tensions were even more evident. The monastic ideal, implying, among other things, the total rejection and abandonment of family life, was bound to come into conflict with the very basis of Confucian morality, according to which man's primary duty lies in fulfilling his obligations toward his family: the cult of his ancestors, the observance of filial piety toward his parents, and marriage and the engendering of male offspring in order to ensure the continuity of the family. If the monks' life was branded as immoral, it was also condemned as parasitical. Since every subject was supposed to be a useful, that is, productive, member of society, the Buddhist clergy easily became stigmatized as an antisocial body within the state—in the Confucian perspective, a natural reaction to the fact that monks were not allowed to perform manual labor, normally spent part of their lives wandering, and were supposed to beg for their food. And, finally, much ill will and suspicion was created by the traditional claim of the Buddhist clergy to be regarded as an unworldly body, not subject to any temporal obligations (including corvée labor, military service, and the payment of taxes), and exempt from any form of government supervision. The idea that "the monk does not bow before the king" was an ancient conception in Buddhism that had always been accepted as selfevident in its land of origin. In China, the very thought of such an alien body within the state was considered both subversive and sacrilegious; it became the subject of heated controversies and conflicts for centuries, until, in late imperial times, the Buddhist clergy had to abandon its claims, and lost even the semblance of independence.

In spite of all these inhibiting factors, Buddhism was able to take root in China and to become an important factor in Chinese civilization, both spiritually and materially. To some extent, this was owing to the fact that its formative phase largely coincided with a period of political disintegration, coupled with a temporary decline of Confucianism as a powerful ideology. It is no coincidence that when in 220 CE the Han empire fell, Buddhism had existed in China for more than one and a half centuries in almost complete obscurity, and thereafter rapidly developed into a prominent religious movement in the period of disunity (311–589 CE) when the empire had fallen asunder, and large parts of China were under the sway of "barbarian" dynasties. In those dark ages, Confucianism, the ideology of imperial unity and universal power, had lost much of its prestige, and Buddhism could profit from this, as it did from the general state of political chaos and polycentrism. When the empire was reunified, Buddhism had gained a position from which it could no longer be removed, in spite of all opposition from Confucian quarters.

However, Buddhism obviously never could have gained any foothold in China if the environment had been totally hostile. There also were positive factors stimulating its spread and assimilation. In the first place, the Confucian opposition in medieval times was limited to an extremely small elite. The mass of the population had not yet been confucianized, as it eventually came to be in late imperial times, and was therefore open to the influence of new and heterodox movements. In many fields there were points of convergence, where elements of Buddhist origin could be grafted onto traditional ideas and practices with which they had (or seemed to have) a certain affinity. Thus the monastic ideal became associated with the indigenous tradition of "retired scholarship"; Buddhist meditation with certain forms of Taoist mental techniques; the Mahāyāna concept of salvation of all beings with the cult of the ancestors; Buddhist lay congregations with traditional peasant associations, and so forth. In this way, through an extremely complicated process of convergence and hybridization, Buddhist ideas and practices were woven into the fabric of Chinese civilization. Another reason why Buddhism, in spite of all opposition from conservative quarters, was able to maintain its influence even among a part of the educated elite, lies in the fact that it could present itself not as a rival of Confucianism, but as an enrichment of it: precisely because Confucianism was almost exclusively directed toward the ordering of state and society, it could be argued that Buddhism would serve as a kind of metaphysical complement to the social and political teachings of the Sage, just as it could provide the Taoist Way with the higher (but complementary) goals of Enlightenment and *nirvāṇa.* Finally, in certain periods official patronage played an important role, not only for reasons of imperial piety, but also—or even primarily—because the Buddhist clergy by its prayers and rituals could provide a magical protection for the dynasty, the state, and society. In spite of these positive factors, however, it remains true that even when Buddhism reached its zenith in Sui and T'ang times, China never became a "Bud dhist country" in the true sense of the word.

MAIN PERIODS

For the purpose of a short survey, a division into five main periods seems appropriate, though it must be kept in mind that this periodization scheme is primarily based on social and institutional developments, and that the dividing lines would be drawn somewhat differently if it were exclusively based on doctrinal criteria.

1. *The embryonic phase* (from the first appearance of Buddhism in China in the mid-first century CE to c. 300 CE). This was a phase in which Buddhism played only a marginal role in religious and intellectual life. In Chinese dynastic terms it covers the Later Han (25–220 CE), the era of the Three Kingdoms (220–265), and the Western Chin (265–326).
2. *The formative phase* (c. 300–589 CE). Politically, the formative phase covers the period of division, during which northern China was occupied by a great number of "barbarian" dynasties of conquest, while the Yangtze basin and southern China were governed by a series of feeble Chinese dynasties. Intellectually, it marks the penetration of Buddhism into the educated minority, and within the clergy itself, the formation of an elite group of scholarly monks. During this period Buddhism spread to all regions of China and to all social levels, including the Chinese and "barbarian" courts. By the end of this period the stage was set for the rise of indigenous Chinese Buddhist schools.
3. *The phase of independent growth* (coinciding with the second era of imperial unification during the Sui and T'ang dynasties, 589–906 CE). The phase of independent growth was the "High Middle Ages" of Chinese history. On the one

hand, indigenous Chinese sects or schools formed; on the other hand, some Indian forms of Buddhism were transplanted to China. During this period there was unprecedented material prosperity and economic activity in the large monasteries. In 845 a severe repression occurred that is commonly regarded as the beginning of the gradual decline of Buddhism in China.

4. *Buddhism in premodern China* (from the tenth to the nineteenth century). In the urbanized and bureaucratized "gentry" society, and under the pressure of a revived and expanded Confucianism, Buddhism gradually lost the support of the cultured elite and was more and more reduced to a despised popular religion. Ch'an (meditation) Buddhism alone continued to exert a limited appeal in intellectual circles.
5. *Buddhism in modern and contemporary China* (c. 1880–present). The attempt to revive Buddhism remains a small and rather elitist movement. In the twentieth century, and especially since the 1920s, Buddhism has been increasingly exposed to the combined pressure of nationalism, modernization, and Marxism-Leninism.

The Embryonic Phase. According to a famous story, the Han emperor Ming (reigned 58–75 CE) once had a dream in which he saw a "golden man." When one of his counselors informed him that this was a foreign god called Buddha, he sent envoys to northwestern India who returned three years later, accompanied by two Indian missionaries. For them the emperor founded the first monastery in China, the Pai-ma Ssu, or White Horse Monastery, in the capital, Loyang. The story is no more than a propagandistic tale that is probably not older than the late second century. It may, however, contain a memory of the existence of Buddhism in court circles at the time of the emperor Ming, as an early and reliable historical source refers to the presence of Buddhist monks and laymen in the entourage of an imperial prince in 65 CE. This is the first authentic—but, unfortunately, quite isolated—sign of the existence of Buddhism in China. It actually is not known precisely when Buddhism entered China. In the course of the first century CE, under the circumstances previously mentioned, it must have infiltrated from the northwest via the Kansu corridor to the Yellow River basin and the North China Plain. For a considerable time its devotees may have largely consisted of foreigners on Chinese soil.

The scene becomes clearer from the middle of the second century onward, when the first known foreign missionaries (Parthians, Kushans, Sogdians, and only a few Indians) started their translation activities in the Lo-yang area. Together they produced a considerable number of Chinese versions of Buddhist texts, about thirty of which have been preserved. This activity— proof that Buddhism had started to spread among the Chinese—marks the beginnings of an immense translation effort that was to remain one of the most impressive achievements of Buddhist culture in China. To judge from the works selected for translation, the scope of Buddhism in the last decades of the Han was rather limited. Much attention was given to short texts dealing with meditation or trance *(dhyāna),* probably because of its resemblance to certain Taoist mental and physical techniques. After the fall of the Han (220 CE), the scope widened. Hundreds of texts were translated, including the first crude versions of some of the classics of Mahā yāna Buddhism such as the *Lotus Sutra* and the *Teachings of Vimalakīrti.* Apart from the activity of translation, not much is known about the spread and organization of Buddhism in China in the embryonic phase. Its role still was very modest—that of a new, "exotic" way of salvation that gained its adherents from the lower social ranks, as is proven by the fact that up to the end of the third century Buddhism is hardly mentioned in secular Chinese literature, the domain of the cultured upper class.

The Formative Phase. Early in the fourth century a political and cultural landslide took place, the effects of which were to last for almost four centuries. Making use of China's internal weakness, various non-Chinese tribes invaded the ancient homeland of Chinese culture from the northern frontier regions; in 311 the capital was sacked by the invaders, and the Chinese court had to flee in disgrace to the area south of the Yangtze. From 311 onward, China was divided into two halves: northern China, ruled by a great variety of non-Chinese in very unstable regimes, and southern China, governed by a series of equally short-lived Chinese dynasties. However, especially in southern China, political weakness was combined with cultural brilliance and an intense and many-sided activity in the field of thought. The decline of Confucianism had led to a new intellectual atmosphere, one more inclined to accept alternative ways of escape from the horrors of incessant warfare, chaos, and misery. Taoism, in both its religious and philosophical varieties, gained many adherents among the cultured elite, and there was a vivid interest in metaphysical problems based on the cryptic musings of the classical Taoist thinkers (notably Lao-tzu and Chuang-tzu), and on the even more mysterious *I ching* (Book of Changes). In this atmosphere, Buddhism was able to catch the attention of the cultured upper class; at the same time we see the formation of a clerical elite of scholarly monks—often themselves belonging to the educated class by birth—who were able to propagate the new creed in that milieu. Thus, in southern China we see the development of a particular type of "high-class Buddhism" characterized by extensive hybridization and a clear emphasis on Buddhism's more philosophical aspects, notably the Mahāyāna doctrine of universal emptiness *(śūnyatā)*. Scholar-monks like Chih Tun (314–366) and Hui-yüan (334–416) explained the doctrine to the cultured public in terms of traditional Chinese thought and thereby laid the foundation of Chinese Buddhist philosophy.

The influence of Buddhism and the material prosperity of the larger monasteries reached their zenith under the emperor Wu of the Liang dynasty (r. 502–549), who took the Buddhist vows of the layman, personally explained Buddhist scriptures in the palace, forbade the use of animals in sacrifice, and officially prohibited the Taoist religion. It was under his reign that Bodhidharma, the reputed founder of Ch'an (Zen) Buddhism, is said to have come to China. However, the spread of Buddhism was by no means restricted to the upper classes. To the masses of exploited peasants Buddhism was attractive for various reasons. On the one hand, they could find solace in the more elementary teachings and rituals of devotional Mahāyāna Buddhism: the invocation of saving Buddhas and *bodhisattvas*, the magic spells, and the colorful temple festivals. But in those difficult times the Buddhist monastery also offered a refuge from the burdens of military service, taxes, and forced labor. By 400 CE the southern territory counted already more than 1,700 monasteries and 80,000 monks and nuns—a sudden expansion that for the first time aroused the opposition of anti-Buddhist circles, who urged measures to restrict the growth of the "antisocial" clergy. In "barbarian"-occupied northern China, Buddhism was, for various reasons, generally patronized by the foreign rulers. At first they welcomed monks as a new type of shaman, able to ensure prosperity and military victory by magical means.

Later they tended to employ monks at their courts, since Buddhism, as an alien doctrine, could be used to counterbalance Confucianism, and also because the monastic life prevented monks from having dangerous family connections.

Throughout this period, northern Buddhism was characterized by a close connection between church and state, with all its positive and negative side effects. The grandiose government patronage (of which the Yün-kang cave temples, founded by the proto-Mongolian Toba Wei rulers in the fifth century, represent the most impressive testimony) was reflected in the enormous growth of monastic institutions: in the early fifth century the Wei empire counted some thirty thousand monasteries and two million monks and nuns. On the other hand, there was close supervision of the church by stateappointed clerical officials, a government-sponsored system of temple serfdom that enabled large monasteries to expand their economic activities, and also, partly due to Buddhist-Taoist rivalry, occasional outbursts of anticlericalism culminating in ruthless persecutions (452–466 and 574–578). Doctrinally, the most important event was the arrival, in 402 CE, of the great missionary and translator Kumārajīva at Ch'ang-an (present-day Sian), then the capital of a fervently Buddhist proto-Tibetan ruler. Kumārajīva, who had already become a famous scholar in his native Kuchā in Central Asia, introduced to China the Mahāyāna philosophy of the Middle Path (Mādhyamika), in which the ultimate truth of nonreality transcends both being and nonbeing. He produced an enormous number of superior translations of Buddhist scripture with the help of the largest translation team known in history. At the end of this period, Buddhism had come to permeate Chinese society at all levels. The clergy had become a distinct social group with considerable spiritual and material influence. The most important texts had been translated, and Chinese masters had begun their own doctrinal systems on the basis of these works.

The Phase of Independent Growth. Under the Sui and T'ang dynasties, Chinese Buddhism reached its apogee. There was great and creative activity in every field. Under various emperors Buddhism was patronized on a lavish scale, though not always for purely religious reasons. Under the notorious empress Wu (reigned 690–705), both state sponsorship and the political use of Buddhism reached excessive proportions. Official patronage was, however, always combined with attempts to place the clergy under bureaucratic control and to check its growth. Once more under Chinese control, Central Asia retained its function as a diffusion area and as a transit zone between China and India until the late seventh century. There was an upsurge of pilgrimage, the most famous pilgrim being Hsüan-tsang (c. 559–664), an exceptional figure in Chinese Buddhism not only for his remarkable journey (629–645) and the quality of his observations, but also for his mastery (then rare among Chinese) of Sanskrit and his work as a great scholar and translator. In the late seventh century, the Arab conquests obstructed the overland route to India. The last wave of pilgrimage took place by the sea route, from the southern coast of China to Tāmra liptī (near modern Calcutta) and Sri Lanka.

In the early T'ang, Buddhism was by far the most creative movement in the religious and intellectual life of the era. Some of the schools or sects that flourished from the late sixth to the ninth century were directly inspired by India: Hsüan-tsang founded the Chinese counterpart of Indian "idealistic" (Yogācāra) Buddhism, and somewhat later various types of esoteric (Tantric) Buddhism were introduced by Indian masters. The most prominent schools, however, were basically Chinese, and they independently developed theories of great originality. Some schools, such as the Ching-t'u (Pure Land) sect, were devotional, advocating faith, repentance of sins, and surrender to the saving grace of the Buddha Amitābha and the *bodhisattva* Kuan-yin (the Indian Avalokiteśvara, who in China assumed a female form) as a simple way to salvation. Other schools were scholastic in nature. Partly in reaction to the doctrinal diversity of Buddhism as it was presented to the Chinese, such schools of "graded revelation" concentrated upon one particular scripture held to contain the final and highest revelation; all other teachings were not rejected, but were regarded as preliminary instruments that served to prepare the minds of less advanced hearers. Thus, the prestigious T'ien-t'ai school (so called after a mountain in Chekiang) classified, in a stupendous scholastic structure, all known teachings according to a scheme of five phases of teaching, the whole culminating in the doctrine of the *Lotus Sutra* as the expression of ultimate Truth.

The Meditation School, known in China as Ch'an (a transcription of the Sanskrit term *dhyāna,* "meditation, trance") and in Japan as Zen, appeared in the seventh century as a unique blend of Chinese (notably Taoist) and Mahāyāna notions and practices. Starting from the basic idea that the highest Truth is inaccessible to speech and rational thought, it propagated a direct, intuitional approach to enlightenment without recourse to canonical texts or rational reflection. It held that all reasoning must be broken down, by means of exhausting meditation sessions, the use of bizarre themes for concentration, including paradoxes, and even deliberate forcible blows from the master. When the ultimate state of "no-mind" has been realized, not gradually but as a sudden explosion, all distinction between holy and profane is obliterated, so that "the Highest Truth is contained in carrying water and chopping firewood." Ch'an Buddhism exerted an enormous influence, especially in intellectual circles. It has had a great impact on art and literature in China and Korea, where it persisted after the disappearance of most other schools, and even more in Japan, where it has flourished up to the present time.

As long as the T'ang state prospered, it was able to tolerate the growing privileges of the innumerable monastic institutions and clerical domains. But when, in the second half of the T'ang, the state was undermined by political turmoil and economic crisis, anticlericalism gained force. Buddhism was also losing ground intellectually, for the ninth century witnesses the beginning of a revival of Confucianism and, consequently, an increasing aversion to Buddhism as a basically un-Chinese creed. In 845, the combined forces of economic considerations, Confucian anticlericalism, and the influence of Taoist masters at the court led to persecution of Buddhism on an unprecedented scale. More than 40,000 temples were destroyed, and 260,500 monks and nuns were forced to return to lay life. Later, the clergy was allowed to grow again, but its economic power had suffered a blow from which it never recovered.

The Premodern Period (c. 900–c. 1880). The beginning of the premodern period is marked by the great political, social, and economic processes of change that in the tenth and eleventh centuries transformed the agrarian-based, aristocratic society of the Chinese Middle Ages into that of late imperial China: an urbanized and bureaucratized society with a sophisticated urban civilization that was shared by an elite of gentry and rich merchants. Confucian values increasingly predominated. The eleventh and twelfth centuries witnessed a powerful "Neo-Confucian" revival, in which earlier Confucianism was expanded into a vast scholastic system including a metaphysical superstructure that incorporated certain Buddhist ideas. In the fourteenth century, one of these Neo-Confucian systems became the official orthodoxy, and the orthodox interpretation of the Confucian classics became the only one valid for the state examinations that opened the way to a career in public office. The family and clan system, with its typically Confucian code of behavior, was propagated throughout the population.

In late imperial times (Sung, 960–1279; Ming, 1368–1644; Ch'ing, 1644–1912) Chinese society had become thoroughly confucianized. Under such circumstances, Buddhism declined steadily, though not in quantitative terms. At the grass-roots level, the religion flourished in countless forms of popular devotion, and the size of the clergy remained impressive. The decline was mainly intellectual: the interest of the cultured minority shifted from Buddhism to Neo-Confucianism. This shift ultimately reduced Buddhism to a despised creed of the lower classes, with the exception of Ch'an, which in a much petrified form maintained its popularity in some intellectual circles. The doctrinal impoverishment of Chinese Buddhism is also shown by the disappearance of most of the schools of T'ang Buddhism. There was a general tendency toward syncretism and mutual borrowing, by which the earlier schools gradually lost their identity; in Ming times, only Ch'an and popular Pure Land devotionalism remained as recognizable trends of Buddhist thought and practice. Syncretism became the prevailing trend: the idea of the "basic unity of the Three Teachings" (Confucianism, Taoism, and Buddhism) gained great popularity. Another characteristic feature of this late Buddhism was the ever more important part played by the laity, whose role in religious life became more prominent as the status of the clergy declined. Between 1280 and 1368 China was part of the Mongol empire, a curious intermezzo in later Chinese history. The Mongol rulers of the Yüan dynasty were mainly interested in Tantric Buddhism in its Tibetan form, and the influence of Lamaism in China dates from that period. Under the last two dynasties, Tibetan and, somewhat later, Mongolian Lamaism were sponsored by the court, largely for political reasons. But at the same time religious life was more than ever subjected to dirigistic government control.

Buddhism in Modern and Contemporary China. The late nineteenth century witnessed the first attempts, undertaken by some cultured laymen, to revive Buddhism. It was part of a general tendency to overcome China's backwardness in the face of Western and Japanese dominance, and also, more specifically, a reaction to the impact of the Christian missions in China. After the revolution and the establishment of the republic (1912), various attempts were made to organize the Buddhist clergy on a national scale, to raise its cultural level through the founding of Buddhist seminars, and to establish contacts with Japan, India, and the Buddhist countries in South and Southeast Asia. From the late 1920s, the movement, or at least its more progressive wing, was led by the venerable abbot T'ai-hsü (1899–1947), who devoted his whole adult life to the regeneration of Chinese Buddhism. Not much came of it. The general intellectual climate left little room for a religious renaissance. Both a large part of the new educated elite and the Nationalist government itself tended to reject all religion as "feudal superstition," and even within the Buddhist community only a tiny minority was touched by the movement at all. The revivalist movement also suffered from the fact that in the years preceding World War II the Japanese government consciously used it to foster pro-Japanese sentiments.

Following the establishment in 1949 of the People's Republic, official Chinese policy toward the Buddhist clergy oscillated between political supervision (exercised through a completely politicized Buddhist Association) and violent suppression, notably during mass campaigns such as the Cultural Revolution (1966–1969). Where Buddhism is tolerated, it is clearly a truncated Buddhism, limited to devotional activities and divested of all the social and economic functions that the monasteries once had. The clergy itself, on which no reliable quantitative data are available, has no doubt been dec imated by laicization and the lack of new ordinations. In general, prospects for Buddhism on the Chinese mainland are gloomy. Even if in the most recent years (since 1976) there are signs of a somewhat more liberal policy, the pressure of a hostile ideology, this time combined with an excessive emphasis on modernization, science, and technology, is not favorable to the existence, let alone the flourishing, of Buddhism as an organized religion.

[*See also* Buddhism, Schools of, *Article on* Chinese Buddhism, *and the biographies of the principal figures mentioned above. For a general discussion of Buddhism's role in Chinese religion, see* Chinese Religion, *overview article; for an overview of religious practice, see* Worship and Cultic Life, *article on* Buddhist Cultic Life in East Asia.]

BIBLIOGRAPHY

The best and most up-to-date monographic works dealing with the history of Chinese Buddhism as a whole are Kenneth Ch'en's *Buddhism in China* (Princeton, 1964) and *The Chinese Transformation of Buddhism* (Princeton, 1973). The best short presentation of the subject is to be found in Paul Demiéville's masterly survey *Le bouddhisme chinois* (Paris, 1970). A. F. Wright's *Buddhism in Chinese History* (1959; reprint, Stanford, Calif., 1965) is readable but somewhat superficial. The history of Indo-Chinese relations as illustrated by Chinese Buddhism is treated by Probodh C. Bagchi in *India and China: A Thousand Years of Cultural Relations,* 2d ed. (Bombay, 1950). The early period (until the early fifth century CE) is extensively covered in my book *The Buddhist Conquest of China,* 2 vols. (1959; reprint, Leiden, 1979). The social and economic aspects of the Buddhist clergy in the medieval period (fifth to ninth centuries) have been excellently treated by Jacques Gernet in *Les aspects économiques du bouddhisme* (Saigon, 1956). There is a voluminous Western-language literature on Ch'an (Zen) Buddhism, most of which is of mediocre quality. Positive exceptions are *The Secrets of Chinese Meditation* (London, 1964) by Charles Luk (K'uan Yü Lu) and *The Platform Sūtra of the Sixth Patriarch,* edited and translated by Philip B. Yampolsky (New York, 1967). On the tensions between state and church in premodern China the only overall study still is the now outmoded and rather partisan *Sectarianism and Religious Persecution in China,* 2 vols. (Amsterdam, 1903–1904), by J. J. M. de Groot. The best surveys of Chinese Buddhism in modern times can be found in the relevant parts of Wing-tsit Chan's *Religious Trends in Modern China* (New York, 1953) and of Yang Ch'ing-k'un's *Religion in Chinese Society* (Berkeley, 1961); for a more detailed treatment of Chinese Buddhism in the twentieth century, see Holmes Welch's *The Practice of Chinese Buddhism, 1900–1950* (Cambridge, Mass., 1967) and *The Buddhist Revival in China* (Cambridge, Mass., 1968). Welch has also described the fate of Buddhism in the People's Republic of China up to the late 1960s in *Buddhism under Mao* (Cambridge, Mass., 1972).

7 BUDDHISM IN KOREA

Robert Evans Buswell, Jr.

In any examination of the Korean Buddhist tradition, it is essential to recall that in no way was Korea isolated from neighboring regions of Northeast Asia. During its prehistory, Korean culture was most closely akin to that of the seminomadic tribes of the Central and North Asian steppes. From the Warring States period (403–221 BCE) on, however, when refugees from the northern Chinese states of Yen, Ch'i, and Chao immigrated to the peninsula to escape the ravages of the mainland wars, Han civilization began to eclipse that indigenous culture at an ever-increasing pace. It is for this reason that Korean Buddhism must be treated as part and parcel of a larger East Asian Buddhist tradition. Indeed, Korea's later appellation as the "hermit kingdom" notwithstanding, there was in fact an almost organic relationship between the Korean, Chinese, and, during its incipient period, the Japanese Buddhist traditions. Admittedly, the Silk Route afforded China closer ties with the Buddhism of India and Central Asia, and China's overwhelming size, both in territory and population, inevitably led to its domination of the doctrinal trends within East Asian Buddhism. This does not deny, however, that Korean exegetes working on both the peninsula and the Chinese mainland made seminal contributions to the development of what are commonly considered to be distinctively "Chinese" schools of Buddhism, such as T'ien-t'ai, Hua-yen, and Ch'an. At the same time, many Chinese Buddhist theological insights were molded into new forms in Korea, innovations comparable to the Chinese syntheses of Indian and Central Asian Buddhist teachings. Hence, any appraisal of characteristically East Asian developments in the Buddhist tradition cannot neglect to take into account the contributions made by Koreans.

THREE KINGDOMS BUDDHISM (C. LATE FOURTH CENTURY– 668 CE)

According to such traditional Korean historical sources as *Samguk sagi* (Historical Record of the Three Kingdoms), *Haedong kosŭng chŏn* (Biographies of Eminent Korean Monks), and *Samguk yusa* (Memorabilia and Mirabilia of the Three Kingdoms), Buddhism was transmitted to Korea from the Chinese mainland during the (Korean) Three Kingdoms period. The introduction of Buddhism into Korea is presumed to have occurred in 372 CE, when King Fu Chien (r. 357–384) of the Former Ch'in dynasty (351–394) sent a monk-envoy, Shun-tao (Kor., Sundo), to the Koguryŏ court with scriptures and images. Former Ch'in hegemony over the remarkably cosmopolitan region of eastern Turkistan had brought Chinese culture into intimate contact with Indian, Iranian, and Hellenistic civilizations, ultimately engendering a new, sinified form of Buddhism. Fu Chien's defeat, in 370, of the Former Yen state, which had for decades laid siege to Koguryŏ, initiated close ties between Fu Chien and his Koguryŏ contemporary, King Sosurim (r. 371–383). These contacts allowed this vibrant northern Chinese culture, which included the Buddhist religion, to be introduced into Korea. While a paucity of information remains by which we can evaluate the characteristics of the Buddhism of this early period, it is probable that it was characterized by thaumaturgic practices, a symbiotic relationship between the ecclesia and the state, Maitreya worship, and the study of scriptures affiliated with the Mahāyāna branch of Buddhism. A monastery is said to have been erected for Sundo in 376, the first reference to a formal Buddhist institution on Korean soil.

Sundo was followed in 384 by the Serindian monk Maranant'a (*Mālānanda; *Kumārānandin), who is reputed to have come via sea to Paekche from the Chinese state of Eastern Chin (317–420). His enthusiastic reception by the royal court initiated the rapid diffusion of Buddhism throughout the Paekche kingdom. Less than a year after his arrival a monastery had been founded on Mount Han for Maranant'a and the first Korean natives ordained as Buddhist monks. Studies on Buddhist monastic discipline (Vinaya) appear particularly to have flourished in Paekche. In both Koguryŏ and Paekche, there is evidence that such schools as Samnon (Mādhyamika), Sarvāstivādin Abhidharma, Nirvāṇa, Satyasiddhi, and Ch'ŏnt'ae (Chin., T'ien-t'ai) flourished, though few works from this period are now extant. [*These Chinese traditions are reviewed in* Buddhism, Schools of, *article on* Chinese Buddhism.] Of vital importance for the dissemination of Buddhism throughout East Asia, however, was Paekche's nautical skill, which made the kingdom the Phoenicia of medieval East Asia. Over its well-developed sea lanes, Paekche began in 554 to dispatch Buddhist doctrinal specialists, psalmodists, iconographers, and architects to Japan, thus transmitting to the Japanese the rudiments of sinified Buddhist culture and laying the foundation for the rich Buddhist culture of the Asuka and Nara periods. Silla expansion throughout southern Korea also prompted massive emigration of Koreans to Japan (where they were known as *kikajin*), and many of the cultural and technical achievements of early Japan—such as the development of paddy fields, the construction of palaces and temples, and town planning—were direct results of the expertise introduced by these successive waves of emigrants. These advancements ultimately paved the way for Japan's first constitution, purportedly written by Prince Shōtoku in 604, and led to the Taika reform of 646, which initiated a sinified bureaucracy in Japan. [*See also* Buddhism, *article on* Buddhism in Japan.]

It was not until 529, following the martyrdom of Ich'adon (Pak Yŏmch'ok), that Silla, the last of the three kingdoms to consolidate its power, officially embraced Buddhism. Political exigencies were probably the catalyst for the acceptance of Buddhism in Silla. The Silla nobility, who continued their drive for peninsular unification, found strong incentive to embrace Buddhism in an effort to accommodate the newly conquered Koguryŏ and Paekche aristocracy, which had embraced Buddhism long before. The vital role played by the Buddhist religion as a conduit through which Chinese civilization was introduced into Silla closely parallels the sinification of non-Chinese tribes that occurred throughout Chinese history.

Three Kingdoms Buddhism seems to have been a thoroughgoing amalgamation of the foreign religion and indigenous local cults. Autochthonous snake and dragon cults, for example, merged with the Mahāyāna belief in dragons as protectors of the Dharma, forming the unique variety of *hoguk pulgyo* ("state-protection Buddhism") that was thereafter to characterize Korean Buddhism. One of the earliest examples of this amalgamation was the vow of the Silla king Munmu (r. 661– 681) to be reborn as a sea dragon after his death in order to guard his country and its new faith from foreign invasion. Buddhism and the state subsequently evolved a symbiotic relationship in which the monks entreated the Buddhas and *bodhisattvas* to protect the state and the state provided munificent support for the dissemination of the religion throughout the empire. Many of the most visible achievements of the Korean church throughout its history, such as the xylographic carvings of the Buddhist canon undertaken during the succeeding Koryŏ dynasty, were products of this concern with national protection. Buddhist monks also sought to demonstrate correspondences between Korean ancestral heroes and the new religion, thereby accelerating the assimilation of the religion among Koreans. Attempts were made, for example, to prove that Hwanin, the Celestial Emperor, was identical to Śakro Devāṇām Indra (Chesŏk-ch'ŏn), the Indian and Buddhist king of the gods, and that Tan'gun, the progenitor of the Korean race, was the theophany of Śrī Mahādevī (Kilsang-ch'ŏn). Vestiges of the dispensations of previous Buddhas were alleged to have been uncovered in Korea, and the advent of the future Buddha, Maitreya, was prophesied to occur in the south of the peninsula. Modern-day visitors to a Korean monastery will notice on the perimeter of the campus shrines devoted to the mountain god or to the seven stars of the Big Dipper, the presence of which is indicative of the synthesis of common sinified culture with Buddhism. [*For an overview of indigenous Korean religion, see* Korean Religion.]

One of the most prominent institutions of Three Kingdoms Buddhism that is commonly assumed to have been indicative of this interaction between Buddhism and indigenous Korean culture was the Hwarang (Flower Boy) movement. According to the *Samguk sagi,* this movement was instituted around 576 by the Silla king Chinhŭng (r. 540–575), and was patterned upon a more primitive association of shamanesses. The formation of the Hwarang movement is considered to have been part of the expansionist policies of the Silla court, and was intended to instill in the sons of nobility a regard for ethical virtues and an appreciation of refined culture. A later Silla writer relates that they were trained in Confucian filial piety and national loyalty, Taoist quietism, and Buddhist morality. The prominent religious orientation of the Hwarang as related in this and other accounts militates against the popular notion that it was a paramilitary organization. The group aesthetic celebrations—such as singing and dancing out in the open—that are commonly associated with the Hwarang has suggested to a number of scholars the shamanistic activities of initiation journeys and pilgrimages. While the Hwarang's Buddhist affinities are far from certain, their eventual identification with Maitreya assured that tradition would regard the movement as one intended to disseminate the Buddhist faith among Koreans.

UNIFIED SILLA BUDDHISM (668–935)

After the unification of the peninsula under the Silla banner in 668, the fortunes of the new religion expanded on an unprecedented scale. It was during this period that the major schools of scholastic Buddhism that had developed in China were introduced into Korea. The doctrinal teachings that had begun to be imported during the Three Kingdoms period were consolidated during the Unified Silla into five major ideological schools: the Kyeyul-chong, which stressed the study and training in Buddhist monastic discipline (Vinaya); the Yŏlban-chong, which promulgated the teachings of the *Mahāparinirvāṇa Sūtra;* the Pŏpsŏng-chong (Dharma Nature), a uniquely Korean school of Buddhism that stressed a syncretic outlook toward Buddhist doctrine; the Wŏnyung-chong, which was the early Korean branch of the Flower Garland (Kor., Hwaŏm; Chin., Hua-yen) school; and the Pŏpsang-chong, based on the "consciousness-only" *(vijñāptimātratā)* teachings of Yogācāra. Some of the greatest achievements of early Korean philosophy occurred during this period, and such important scholiasts as Wŏnhyo (617–686) and Ŭisang (625–702) forged approaches to Buddhist philosophy that would become the hallmarks of the Korean church from that time onward. Korean exegetes working in China also played major roles in the development of Chinese schools of Buddhism. Both Wŏnhyo and Ŭisang were important vaunt-couriers in the Hua-yen school, as reflected in their influence on the systematizer of the Chinese Hua-yen school, Fa-tsang (643–712). Wŏnch'ŭk (613–696), a close disciple of Hsüan-tsang (d. 664), was a prominent exegete in the Chinese Fa-hsiang school, whose commentaries on such texts as the *Saṃdhinirmocana Sūtra* exerted profound influence on early Tibetan Buddhism. [*See* Hua-yen *and the biographies of* Wŏnhyo, Ŭisang, Fa-tsang, and Hsüan-tsang.]

It was during this era of ardent scholarly activity that one of the most characteristic features of the mature Korean Buddhist tradition developed: that of syncretism. From the inception of Buddhism in East Asia, the religion had formed around a number of disparate scriptural and commentarial traditions that had developed first in India and later in Central Asia. For this reason, the Chinese church became characterized by a loosely-structured sectarianism. The various extremes each of these factional divisions took led to an attempt, begun first in China and considerably refined later in Korea, to see these various approaches, each ostensibly Buddhist yet each so different, in some common light, so as to find some means by which their discordant elements could be reconciled. Certain features of the Korean tradition contributed to the syncretic tendency of the religion. Owing to the smaller size of Korea and its monastic population, there was little hope that Buddhism could continue as a stable and influential force within the religious arena if it was divided into contentious factions. In addition, the constant threat of foreign invasion created the need for a unified, centrally organized ecclesiastical institution. The quest to discover the common denominators in all of these sectarian interpretations—and subsequently to use those unifying elements in order to establish an interdenominational approach *(t'ong pulgyo)* to the religion that could incorporate all elements of Buddhist philosophy and practice—was to inspire the efforts of all major Korean Buddhist philosophers. This attitude prompted the Koreans to evolve what remains one of the most ecumenical traditions of Buddhism to be found anywhere is Asia.

One of the most momentous developments in the history of Korean Buddhism occurred during the Unified Silla period: the introduction of the Ch'an teachings, known in Korea as Sŏn. The earliest transmission of Sŏn to the peninsula is attributed to the monk Pŏmnang (fl. 632–646), a Korean who is said to have trained with the fourth patriarch of the Chinese Ch'an school, Tao-hsin (580–646). While little is known of Pŏmnang's life or thought, there are indications that he attempted to combine the teachings of two distinct Chinese Ch'an lineages—that of Bodhidharma (c. fifth century), Hui-k'o (487–592), and Seng-ts'an (d. 606) and that of Tao-hsin and

Hung-jen (688–761)—with the syncretic *tathāgata-garbha* theory of the *Ta-sheng ch'i-hsin lun* (Awakening of Faith). [*See* Tathāgata-garbha.] A successor in Pŏmnang's lineage eventually founded the Hŭiyang-san school, the oldest of the Korean Sŏn schools. During the eighth and ninth centuries, other Korean adepts returning from the mainland established eight other mountain Sŏn sites, forming what came to be known as the Nine Mountains school of Sŏn (Kusan Sŏnmun). Of these eight, seven were affiliated with the Hung-chou lineage of the Middle Ch'an period, which eventually evolved into the Lin-chi school of the mature Ch'an tradition; one, the Sumi-san school, was derived from the lineage of Ch'ing-yüan Hsing-ssu (d. 740), from which developed the Ts'ao-tung school. Korean masters on the mainland, however, also played major roles in the development of Chinese Ch'an. Perhaps the most prominent of these Koreans was the monk Musang, also known as Kim Ho-shang (694?–762), who was regarded as a patriarch of the Pao-t'ang school of the Szechwan region, and was the first Ch'an master known to the Tibetans. Despite the continued traffic of Sŏn adepts between China and Korea, the entrenched position of the scholastic schools within the Korean ecclesia thwarted the propagation of Nine Mountains Sŏn. Continued frustration at their inability to disseminate their message led such Sŏn adherents as Toŭi (d. 825) and Muyŏm (799–888) to attack the scholastic schools directly, leading ultimately to a bifurcation of the Korean Buddhist church into two vociferous factions. [*See also* Ch'an.]

KORYŎ BUDDHISM (937–1392)

The principal contribution of Koryŏ Buddhists to the evolution of the Korean church was the reconciliation they effected between the Sŏn and scholastic schools. It was Ŭich'ŏn (1055–1101) who made the first such attempt, by seeking to combine both the Nine Mountains and scholastic schools into a revived Ch'ŏnt'ae school. [*See the biography of Ŭich'ŏn.*] Ch'ŏnt'ae teachings are known to have been present on the peninsula prior to Ŭich'ŏn's time. A century before, for example, Ch'egwan (d. 971), a renowned Korean Ch'ŏnt'ae adept, had been invited to T'ang China to reintroduce long-lost T'ien-t'ai manuals; during his expatriation Ch'egwan systematized the school's philosophies in his *T'ien-t'ai ssu-chiao i,* one of the most important of Chinese T'ien-t'ai exegetical writings. [*See* T'ien-t'ai.] Ŭich'ŏn's efforts to revitalize the school, however, have led to his being considered the effective founder of its Korean branch. It appears that Ŭich'ŏn regarded the meditative exphasis of the Ch'ŏnt'ae teachings as the ideal vehicle for accommodating the varying concerns of the Sŏn and scholastic schools. Unfortunately, his premature death at the age of forty-six brought a sudden end to his endeavor and left the sectarian scene still more unsettled.

Ŭich'ŏn's efforts were followed some three generations later by those of Chinul (1158–1210), a charismatic Sŏn master who was similarly motivated by a syncretic vision of the unity of Sŏn and the scholastic teachings. Unlike Ŭich'ŏn's scholastic orientation, however, Chinul sought to merge the various Buddhist schools of his time into a new Sŏn school that would synthesize a disparate variety of Buddhist soteriological approaches. Chinul introduced into Korean Sŏn practice the investigation of the "critical phrase" (Kor., *hwadu;* Chin., *hua-t'ou),* better known by the closely synonymous term *kongan* (Chin., *kung-an;* Jpn., *kōan*), as it had been developed in China by Ta-hui Tsung-kao (1089–1163). Chinul then sought to incorporate this investigation into the soteriological scheme of sudden awakening/gradual cultivation taught by Tsung-mi (780–841), and finally to amalgamate this approach to Sŏn with the interpretation of Hwaŏm thought given by Li T'ung-hsüan (635–730). Chinul's synthesis of Sŏn and the scholastic teachings came to be regarded as a distinctively Korean school of Sŏn, called the Chogye-chong. His efforts revitalized the enervated Koryŏ church, and marked the ascendancy of Sŏn thought in the Korean Buddhist tradition. [*See the biographies of Chinul and Tsung-mi.*]

It was Chinul's disciple, Chin'gak Hyesim (1178–1234), who assured the acceptance of *hwadu* practice as the principal meditative technique in Korean Sŏn Buddhism. Following the model of Chinese thinkers of the Sung dynasty (960–1279), Hyesim examined the points of convergence between the three religions of Buddhism, Confucianism, and Taoism. This attempt to extend the embrace of Chinul's syncretic outlook so as to accommodate still other religions was to inspire a series of such investigations by later Korean authors. A Sŏn master of the later Koryŏ period, T'aego Pou (1301–1382), worked prodigiously to merge the remnants of the Nine Mountains Sŏn schools with the new Chogye-chong, and sought to graft onto this ecumenical school the Chinese Lin-chi (Kor., Imje; Jpn., Rinzai) lineage, into which he had received transmission in Yüan-dynasty China. The efforts of these and other teachers assured that the Chogye-chong would remain the predominant school of Korean Buddhism, a position it has retained down to the present.

YI BUDDHISM (1392–1910)

With the advent of the Yi dynasty in 1392 the fortunes of Buddhism began to wane. While the official policies of the Yi dynasty are commonly considered to have been Confucian in orientation, many of the kings continued to give munificent personal support to Buddhism. For example, the founder of the dynasty, Yi T'aejo (r. 1392–1398), appointed the renowned monk, Muhak Chajo (1327–1398), to the official post of preceptor to the royal family *(wangsa),* and the account of T'aejo's reign in the *Yijo sillok* (Veritable Record of the Yi Dynasty) teems with references to his sponsorship of temple construction projects, maigre offerings to monks, and various Buddhist rites. Confucian bureaucrats, however, continued to pressure the throne for stricter selection procedures for Buddhist monks, limits on the number of temples and hermitages, reduction in the number of officially sanctioned sects, and reorganization of the ecclesiastical system, all in order to effect more centralized supervision of the religion. Such policies were formally adopted by T'aejong (r. 1400–1418), the third Yi sovereign, and carried out on a massive scale by his successor, King Sejong (r. 1418–1450). In Sejong's proclamation of 1424, the Chogye, Ch'ŏnt'ae, and Vinaya schools were amalgamated into a single Sŏn (Meditative) school, and the remaining scholastic schools were merged into the Kyo (Doctrinal) school. New regulations were adopted for obtaining monk's certificates, making ordination much more difficult, and many monks already ordained were defrocked. The official ranks of national master *(kuksa)* and royal master *(wangsa)* were abolished. Temple paddy lands and forest properties were confiscated by the state and the legions of serfs retained by the monasteries were drafted into the army. Buddhist temples were no longer permitted within the capital or major cities. It is not surprising that during this dire period, Buddhist activities were as much concerned with the very survival of the tradition as with novel scholarly and meditative endeavors.

During this extremely difficult period in Korean Buddhist history, it is Sŏsan Hyujŏng (1520–1604) who epitomizes the continued Sŏn orientation of the church.

Drawing his inspiration from Chinul's earlier vision of the unity of the Sŏn and scholastic schools, Hyujŏng produced a succinct manual of practice, titled the *Sŏn'ga kugam* (Guide to the Sŏn School). His other guides to Confucianism and Taoism were intended to sustain the reconciliation between Buddhism and its rival religions that was begun during the mid-Koryŏ and to outline their many similarities of purpose. Despite all the attempts of Hyujŏng's lineage, however, Buddhism's creative drive continued to wane. [*See also* Confucianism in Korea *and the biography of Hyujŏng.*]

BUDDHISM DURING THE MODERN ERA

Japanese inroads on the peninsula from the late nineteenth century onward presented both new opportunities and new pressures for the Korean Buddhist tradition. Following the ratification of the Korea-Japan treaty of 1876, Japanese Buddhist sects, beginning with the Higashi Honganji sect of Pure Land, began to proselytize among the increasing number of Japanese immigrants resident in Korea, an activity that soon spread to the native Korean populace as well. Remonstrations by Japanese Nichiren missionaries compelled the impotent Yi court in 1895 to lift the centuries-old prohibition against the presence of Buddhist monks in the capital of Seoul. During the same period, a resurgence of Sŏn practice was catalyzed by the Korean Sŏn master Kyŏnghŏ (1857–1912) and his disciples, and successors in his lineage continue to teach today.

After the annexation of Korea in 1910, some Korean monks felt that the fortunes of the religion were dependent upon arranging a merger with a major Japanese sect. Yi Hoe-gwang went so far as to negotiate a combination of the Korean church with the Japanese Sōtō sect, but most Korean Sŏn monks regarded the gradualistic teachings of the Sōtō sect as anathema to the subitist orientation of their own tradition, and managed to block the merger. Another movement threatened to further divide the Buddhist church. As early as 1913, Han Yong-un (1879–1944), the only Buddhist signatory to the 1919 Korean independence declaration and a major literary figure, had shocked his contemporaries by advocating that monks be allowed to marry, a move he felt was necessary if Buddhism were to maintain any viable role in modern secular society. While this position was diametrically opposed to the traditional celibate orientation of the Korean ecclesia, the Japanese colonial government ultimately sustained it in 1926 with its promulgation of new monastic regulations that legalized matrimony for monks. Within a decade, virtually all temple abbots were married, thereby producing a dramatic change in the traditional moral discipline of the Korean church. Other reform movements designed to present Buddhism in a way that would be more relevant to modern concerns arose with increasing frequency. Among the most prominent of these was Wŏn Buddhism, founded in 1916 by Pak Chung-bin (1891–1943), which combined Buddhist teachings with a disparate variety of elements drawn from Confucianism, Taoism, Tonghak, and even Christianity.

After independence in 1945, Korean Buddhism was badly split between two irreconcilable sects. The T'aego-chong, a liberal sect of married monks, had flourished under Japanese patronage and was based principally in the cities where it catered to the lay Buddhist population. The Chogye-chong was a smaller, religiously conservative faction of monks who had managed to maintain their celibacy during the long years of Japanese occupation; their concern was to restore the meditative, scholastic, and disciplinary orientations of traditional Korean Buddhism. Only after years of intense conflict did the Chogye-chong finally win government support for its position in 1954. While litigation continues between the two sects, all of the major monasteries have reverted to its control. Now the predominant sect of Buddhism in Korea, the Chogye-chong has had considerable success in attracting a new generation of lay believers and monastic postulants to the teachings and practices of Buddhism. [*See also* Worship and Cultic Life, *article on* Buddhist Cultic Life in East Asia.]

BIBLIOGRAPHY

It remains difficult for the nonspecialist to find reliable books on Korean Buddhism in Western languages. Some summaries of research by Korean and Japanese scholars have appeared in *Buddhist Culture in Korea,* "Korean Culture Series," vol. 3, edited by Chun Shin-yong (Seoul, 1974). J. H. Kamstra's *Encounter or Syncretism: The Initial Growth of Japanese Buddhism* (Leiden, 1967), part 3, includes a useful survey of Three Kingdoms Buddhism and its influence on early Japan. The biographies of several prominent monks of the early Three Kingdoms period are translated in Peter H. Lee's *Lives of Eminent Korean Monks: The Haedong Kosŭng Chŏn* (Cambridge, Mass., 1969). A liberal rendering of a major Korean hagiographical and doxographical collection dealing with Three Kingdoms Buddhism appears in *Samguk Yusa: Legends and History of the Three Kingdoms of Ancient Korea,* translated by Tae-hung Ha and Grafton K. Mintz (Seoul, 1972). The travelogue of a Korean monk's pilgrimage to India and central Asia has been newly translated by Han Sung Yang, Yün-hua Jan, and Shotarō Iida in *The Hye Ch'o Diary* (Berkeley, 1984). Korean Hwaŏm thought receives some coverage in Steve Odin's *Process Metaphysics and Hua-yen Buddhism: A Critical Study of Cumulative Penetration vs. Interpenetration* (Albany, N.Y., 1982); the appendix includes a translation of Ŭisang's outline of Hwaŏm philosophy. Ch'egwan's survey of Ch'ŏnt'ae philosophy has been translated in David W. Chappell and Masao Ichishima's *T'ien-t'ai Buddhism: An Outline of the Fourfold Teachings* (Honolulu, 1984).

Korean Sŏn Buddhism is covered in my own book *The Korean Approach to Zen: The Collected Works of Chinul* (Honolulu, 1983). My introduction there includes a rather extensive survey of the early history of Korean Buddhism, and particularly the Sŏn tradition, in order to trace the contexts of Chinul's life and thought; specialists may also consult the bibliography of works in Asian languages on Korean Buddhism that appears there. Chinul's contributions to Korean Buddhism have also been examined in Hee-sung Keel's *Chinul: Founder of the Korean Sŏn Tradition* (Berkeley, 1984). A provocative exposition of Korean Sŏn practice appears in Sung Bae Park's *Buddhist Faith and Sudden Enlightenment* (Albany, N.Y., 1983). The principal works of Wŏn Buddhism are translated in Chon Pal-khn's *The Canonical Textbook of Won Buddhism* (Seoul, 1971). A number of seminal literary compositions by Korean Buddhists from all periods are translated in Peter H. Lee's *Anthology of Korean Literature: From Early Times to the Nineteenth Century* (Honolulu, 1981). A representative selection of philosophical and hagiographical writings by Korean Buddhist authors will appear in *Sources of Korean Tradition,* edited by Peter H. Lee (New York, forthcoming). The few Western-language works on Korean Buddhism written up to 1979 are listed in *Studies on Korea: A Scholar's Guide,* edited by Han-Kyo Kim (Honolulu, 1980); see chapter 4, "Philosophy and Religion."

8

BUDDHISM IN JAPAN

TAMARU NORIYOSHI

Buddhism, originating in India and journeying a long distance through Central Asia and China, reached the islands of Japan in the middle of the sixth century CE. At the time of inception, it was an essentially alien religion quite dissimilar in outlook to the unorganized complex of indigenous beliefs and cults that later came to be known by the name of Shintō. In the ensuing fifteen hundred years, however, it not only took firm root among the Japanese, but also played an important part in their social, cultural, and religious life. Indeed, its impact has been and remains so powerful that any attempt to comprehend these dimensions of Japanese life would be insufficient if it did not pay due attention to Buddhism. This is not to say, however, that Japan became a completely Buddhist country. At no point in Japanese history did Buddhism exercise a religious monopoly; rather, it coexisted with other religious and intellectual traditions such as Shintō, Confucianism, and, in modern times, Christianity. Furthermore, in the course of development on Japanese soil, Buddhism has itself been significantly modified under the influence of indigenous culture so as to exhibit peculiarly Japanese traits. Thus, the phenomenon of Japanese Buddhism may be viewed in two contrasting perspectives: how far and in what manner Buddhism has contributed to the formation of Japanese culture and, conversely, how the alien religion of Buddhism was transformed in the process of adaptation to the social and intellectual milieu of the nation.

HISTORICAL SETTING AND GENERAL FEATURES

Before describing this twofold process of impact and modification through the ages, a few circumstances that determined Buddhism's general character may be pointed out. In the first place, it must be noted that the Buddhism brought to Japan was by no means uniform but comprised diverse elements derived from successive stages of its history. According to the *Nihonshoki* (720 CE), Japan's first official chronicle, Buddhism was introduced to Japan from Paekche, a kingdom in Korea, in 552 CE. (Another source gives the date as 538 CE.) Intermittently from the sixth to the seventeenth century, knowledge of Buddhism was acquired directly from China by official envoys and missionary monks. Inasmuch as Buddhism was transmitted to Japan by this northern route, Japanese Buddhism is usually classified as a branch of Mahāyāna, as opposed to Theravāda, which is found in several Southeast Asian countries. Such a characterization is not incorrect, for Japanese Buddhism, especially in its present form, is obviously quite different from Theravāda and other of the so-called Hīnayāna schools, of which the core is the monastic orders of the *saṃgha*. Yet it must be remembered that in Japan elements not only of Mahāyāna but also of Hīnayāna can be found. More concretely, the scriptures, teachings, disciplines, and rituals belonging to nearly every phase of Buddhist development have been transmitted, preserved, and studied here.

In a sense, Japanese Buddhism may be thought of as a kind of summary of the whole of Buddhist history from its Indian beginning to the manifestations of later days. Consideration of the location of Japan may render this fact readily intelligible. Since the Japanese archipelago is located near the eastern border of the Chinese mainland, it naturally formed a terminus of the Buddhist pilgrimage. The further transplantation of Buddhism from Japan to other parts of the world, notably to the American continents and Europe, is only of recent date. [*See also* Missions, *article on* Buddhist Missions.]

Second, Buddhism was accepted in Japan in close association with other elements of Chinese culture. This, again, can be accounted for by the historical circumstances in which the Japanese found themselves. Broadly speaking, Japan was one of the satellite societies surrounding the powerful center of highly developed civilization that was China. These societies, with China as their center, formed a sort of semiautonomous circle that may be dubbed "the East Asian world" and shared some common elements: the Chinese system of writing; political and legal organization based upon the Chinese model; broadly Confucian teachings; and Buddhism, which, although Indian in origin, took on Chinese attributes. Since China was by far superior, both politically and culturally, to these neighboring societies, it was only natural that for them China served as a source of new information and cultural skills. When, beginning in the fifth century, the Japanese came into contact with imperial China, they were politically in the process of building a new social order by uniting the previously autonomous clans under the centralized leadership of the imperial clan. Culturally, Japan was in a rather primitive stage of development and remained as yet preliterate. It is no wonder that in such a situation Buddhism was welcomed as an element of a highly refined culture. This applies especially to the initial period after its introduction, but this situation prevailed more or less until the advent of Western civilization in the modern age.

What attracts one's attention at this juncture is the fact that in Japanese history there seems to be a peculiar pattern of alternating periods: periods in which contact with the external world is eagerly sought and elements of foreign culture are diligently absorbed, and periods in which people are more intent upon digesting what they received and creating something of their own. These may be called periods of "outward orientation" and "inward orientation," respectively. In this respect, too, the insular position of Japan was of decisive importance, because it enabled the Japanese to be selective in importation and then to concentrate on naturalizing and refining the alien elements without being disturbed. Thus, the centuries following Buddhism's introduction were characterized by an enormous zeal to appropriate it as an integral part of continental culture, while the period after about the end of the eighth century was spent mostly in elaborating it to produce distinctively indigenized expressions. When, after a rather long period of internal maturation, Japan experienced another large-scale encounter with the external world, that is, during the sixteenth century and again more markedly after the middle of the nineteenth, it was no longer Buddhism but Christianity that figured as the chief agent of a new era.

The fact that Buddhism was first introduced as part and parcel of the superior culture of China was not unrelated to the patterns of development it experienced in Japan. In earlier times, in particular, those who readily accepted and aligned themselves with the newly arrived faith were recruited from the members of the imperial family and influential court nobles. This does not mean, to be sure, that Buddhism did not affect the lives of the common people at all. On the contrary, as early as during the Nara period (710–784) there are some signs of Buddhist influence on the lives of people of humble birth. Taken as a whole, however, it was not until the medieval age of the Kamakura (1185–1333) and the Muromachi (1338–1573) periods that Buddhism began to genuinely influence wider circles of population. Therefore, Buddhism spread geographically from the center to the periphery and sociologically from the upper strata of society to the lower. For this reason, Japanese Buddhism in its early stage is frequently called "aristocratic," while the later forms are regarded as mass movements.

The above statement of the overall characteristics should not be taken to mean that Japanese Buddhism has been uniform in terms of doctrine and/or practice. On the contrary, it has always encompassed a wide variety of positions that resulted partly from the complexity of the tradition prior to its entry into Japan and partly from the changes it underwent during the process of appropriation. On the organizational level, too, Japanese Buddhism has been and is classified into a number of "sects" *(shū).* Since in Japan there has never been a semblance of a Buddhist church with a universal claim, the term *sect* is a bit misleading; a more appropriate term is *school.* It is clear that this internal variety is an outcome of the historical development of Buddhism in Japanese history, of which a brief survey may be in order. In this attempt the conventional historiographical distinction of periods will be employed as the general framework, for the status of Buddhism in Japan has been affected, if not completely determined, by the events in the political, social, and cultural lives of the people.

FROM THE INTRODUCTION TO THE END OF THE NARA PERIOD

One of the most crucial periods in the history of Japanese Buddhism is no doubt that which started with its official introduction in the middle of the sixth century and came to its culmination in the Nara period. It is, as suggested earlier, the formative era of the unified Japanese state. During these centuries Buddhism was first accepted by influential clans and court nobles in central Japan and thence gradually gained ground in Japanese society, laying the foundation for all later developments.

Upon closer examination, however, one sees that acceptance of the new faith did not proceed without obstruction. For one thing, the position of the emperor was based on the Shintō-derived notion of theocracy that united religious and political functions in one person. For emperors to embrace an alien religion would have meant a threat to the very basis of their power. In addition, there was internal strife between two camps among the influential clans, one advocating and the other rejecting the new religion until, finally, the more liberal Soga clan succeeded in securing imperial permission to practice Buddhism in the form of a private cult. What seems remarkable about this conflict is that, to all appearances, neither the supporters nor the opponents possessed a proper understanding of the Buddhist teaching. For them, the Buddha was merely a kind of *kami* (numinous force, divinity) from abroad; they admired Buddha statues mainly for their exquisite beauty and accepted Buddhism only as superior magical means to achieve practical benefits such as healing from illness or prosperity.

Shōtoku Taishi. In this early stage, Prince Shōtoku (574–622) played a decisive role in furthering the cause of Buddhism and at the same time prepared the way for a deeper understanding of its ideas. As a statesman and thinker he pursued two complementary objectives: he sought, on the one hand, to establish a centralized state under the authority of the emperor and based on the model of Chinese bureaucracy and, on the other, to enrich the spiritual life of the nation by officially endorsing Buddhism. For this purpose, he sent a governmental envoy to the Chinese court in 607 that brought back valuable information about Chinese institutions and Buddhist *sūtra*s and teachings. This contact he opened with China proved to be of utmost importance to the development of Japanese Buddhism for the next several centuries. At the same time, he initiated the construction of a number of great temples in the capital or its vicinity, of which Horyūji, the oldest Buddhist structure in Japan, may be mentioned. Considering these achievements, Shōtoku has been rightly admired as the father of Japanese Buddhism.

Shōtoku was influential not only in these activities, but also in his intellectual grasp of the essence of Buddhist teaching. The phrase attributed to him, "the world is illusory, the Buddha alone is true," reveals a knowledge of Buddhism far more deep than that of his contemporaries. The phrase is noteworthy as the first testimony to the idea of world negation, hitherto unknown in Japan. In addition, there are several documents traditionally accredited to his authorship: the so-called Seventeen-Article Constitution and the commentaries on three important Mahāyāna *sūtra*s (the *Saddharmapuṇḍarīka Sūtra*, the *Vimalakīrtinirdeśa Sūtra*, and the *Śrīmālāsiṃhanāda Sūtra*). The Constitution consists of a set of moral and administrative injunctions, of which the contents are largely Confucian mingled with some Legalist elements, but it gives Buddhism a predominant role as the source of ultimate value. As for the commentaries, they show not only a surprisingly correct understanding of Buddhist principles but a singularly Japanese tendency to adapt Buddhist ideas to the needs of practical life. [*See the biography of Shōtoku Taishi.*]

The Nara Schools. Generally speaking, the developments after the death of Shōtoku took place along the course envisioned by him. Measures like the Taika Reforms of 645 and the promulgation of the Taihō Code in 701 had as their aim the establishment of a centralized administration, the Ritsuryō system, coupled with the promotion of religion, most notably of Buddhism. After the completion of the first permanent capital of Heijōkyō (modern Nara), this policy of government support for Buddhism reached its climax. Of particular importance in this respect was the official decree issued by Emperor Shōmu in 741 to build a network of state-subsidized temples (*kokubunji*) in each province. Further, he had a gigantic bronze statue of Vairocana Buddha cast and erected at the main temple in Nara, Tōdaiji, in 749. Completed and consecrated with ceremonial pomp three years later, this Vairocana Buddha was at once a symbol of the magnificent universe and of the centralized state. Shōmu, in addition, was the first emperor to declare himself a servant of

Buddhism, thus confessing his personal commitment to the faith and elevating it almost to the status of a national religion. [*See also* Mahāvairocana.]

Another feature of Nara Buddhism was that it comprehended diverse viewpoints within Buddhism. Each of the so-called six Nara schools represented a tradition of study of a particular text or textual cycle of Indian Buddhism that flourished in the T'ang capital, Ch'ang-an, during the eighth century:

1. Ritsu, named after the Chinese Lü, or Vinaya tradition, concerned itself with exegesis of the Vinaya (the Buddhist code of monastic discipline). Based principally on Tao-hsüan's Nan-shan branch of the tradition, this sect was also responsible in Japan for the ordination of the clergy. [*See the biography of Ganjin.*]
2. Jōjitsu refers to an exegetical tradition that takes its name from the *Satyasiddhi* (Chin., *Ch'eng-shih lun*; Jpn., *Jōjitsuron*), a text attributed to the Indian monk Harivarman.
3. Kusha is named for Vasubandhu's *Abhidharmakośa* (Chin., *Chü-she lun*; Jpn., *Kusharon*), a systematic treatise on the Abhidharma thought of the Sarvāstivāda-Sautrāntika tradition of Hīnayāna Buddhism.
4. Sanron (Mādhyamika) derives from the "three treatises" (*sanron*) that form the basis of the Mādhyamika tradition in East Asia: the *Madhyamakakārikā* (Chin., *Chung-lun*) and the *Dvādaśadvāra* (Chin., *Shih-erh-men lun*) of Nāgārjuna, and Āryadeva's *Śataśāstra* (Chin., *Po-lun*). [*See* Mādhyamika.]
5. Hossō (Yogācāra) is based on the Yogācāra tradition introduced into China by the famous pilgrim-monk Hsüan-tsang (596?–664) and called there Fa-hsiang (Jpn., Hossō; "*dharma* characteristic"). [*See* Yogācāra.]
6. Kegon is devoted to the study of the *Avataṃsaka Sūtra* (Chin., *Hua-yen ching*; Jpn., *Kegongyō*), a major Mahāyanā scripture. [*See* Hua-yen.]

Although commonly referred to as sects, these traditions were schools of thought rather than concrete sectarian institutions, and it was not unusual for a monk of those days to receive instruction in more than one of these "schools." The first three traditions shared a pronounced Hīnayāna orientation, the latter three were devoted to the study of Mahāyāna texts; together, they covered nearly the entire range of Buddhist thought as transmitted to China by the eighth century. It must be emphasized, however, that these distinctions obtained primarily in the academic study of Buddhist dogmatics. In the actual life of the nation the major function of Buddhists and Buddhist institutions was to conduct certain rites and services believed to be efficacious in securing the welfare of the state and to offer prayers for the achievement of mundane requests on behalf of their patrons. [*For further discussion of the antecedents of the Nara sects, see* Buddhism, Schools of, *article on* Chinese Buddhism.]

While geared mostly to the political objectives of the government and the ruling aristocracy, Nara Buddhism did not lack its popular aspect. This popular side was best exemplified by the semilegendary figure of Gyōgi (c. 670–749), a recluse monk living in the vicinity of the capital who allegedly was in possession of miraculous powers. Tradition maintains that he traveled through the countryside performing many beneficial deeds for the populace, and that Emperor Shōmu had to ask his cooperation for the successful accomplishment of the building of the great Buddha statue. These accounts seem to indicate that Buddhism had already begun to penetrate into wider circles of the population, associating itself with the native shamanistic beliefs. Here we notice the beginning of the undercurrent of folk Buddhism that increased in influence with the passage of time. [*See also* Hijiri *and the biography of Gyōgi.*]

Of the so-called six Nara schools, three have survived until this day: the Hossō school represented by Kōfukuji (Kōfuku Temple) and Yakushiji, the Kegon school with Tōdaiji as its center, and the Ritsu school based at Tōshōdaiji. To this group, the Shōtoku school with Hōryūji as its center may be added. Confined to the district of Nara and having few lay adherents, the social impact of these schools is rather limited compared with other later and more powerful organizations. However, they possess a certain symbolic value, as evocative of the heyday of Buddhism in ancient times and as the fountainhead from which all the later schools have sprung.

THE BUDDHIST SYNTHESIS OF THE HEIAN PERIOD

With the move of the capital from Nara to Heiankyō (modern Kyoto) in 794, Japanese history entered the second half of its antiquity. During this period, known as the Heian era (794–1185), the centralized bureaucratic system partly realized in the preceding era slowly declined and eventually gave rise to the feudalism of the next age. Although nominal power continued to rest with the imperial court, actual political initiative gradually passed into the hands of a few aristocrats, the Fujiwara clan in particular, whose basis of power was in privately owned estates. In this general trend toward disintegration, Buddhist institutions gained a certain amount of autonomy in relation to the state but, on the other hand, had to associate themselves in some way or other with the interests of the ruling aristocrats. In addition, official contact with China was suspended at the end of the ninth century and the constant flow of religious influences from the continent came to a halt, a circumstance that favored indigenization.

In the earliest part of this period the two new schools of Tendai and Shingon were founded separately by two distinguished leaders: Saichō (767–822, generally known by his posthumous title of Dengyō Daishi) and Kūkai (774–835, commonly referred to as Kōbō Daishi). Although quite different in character and temperament, these monks nevertheless were similar in a number of respects. They both had as their aim the establishment of a new center for Japanese Buddhism, one free from the control of the orthodox Nara schools. For this purpose they both went to China to acquaint themselves with the latest forms of Buddhist doctrine and practice and upon returning erected their headquarters on sacred mountains outside the turmoil of the city. What is more important, however, is that their schools were quite comprehensive and synthetic in orientation: both sought to work out an all-encompassing framework in which different points of view, Buddhist and non-Buddhist alike, could be assigned a place. Because of this emphasis, Tendai and Shingon teachings offered an excellent theoretical basis for the fusion of indigenous beliefs and Buddhism that gradually took place.

Tendai. Tendai is a Japanese form of the Chinese T'ien-t'ai, the name of a mountain in China, the temple located on that mountain, and a school established there by the monk Chih-i (fl. sixth century). [*See* T'ien-t'ai.] Having studied in his youth at Tōdaiji in Nara and become somehow disillusioned by the formalism of the traditional schools, Saichō sought a new form of teaching capable of uniting different viewpoints into one, an orientation he was to find in T'ien-t'ai. Meanwhile, Saichō had managed to gain the personal favor of Emperor Kammu and was chosen as a student to be sent to China. The Chinese T'ien-t'ai attached particular value to the *Saddharmapuṇḍarīka* (Lotus) *Sūtra* and developed an elaborate philosophical system concerning the realization of the ultimate truth coupled with the practice of meditation. Saichō faithfully learned these teachings but, in contrast to the Chinese model, assigned equal importance to such other elements as moral discipline, Zen meditation, and Tantric (Esoteric) ritualism. In brief, Saichō's Tendai was more eclectic in nature than Chinese T'ien-t'ai. In addition, we can recognize a certain ethnocentric tendency in his thought, for he considered the pursuit of Buddhist teaching as part of the service for the protection of the nation.

Saichō returned home to Enryakuji, a monastery he had built a short distance northeast of the capital on Mount Hiei, and devoted the latter half of his life to establishing Tendai as an independent school. During his lifetime, however, this goal remained unrealized. In order for any Buddhist group to be officially acknowledged, it was necessary for it to have the right to ordain monks, which in those days was the sole prerogative of the Ritsu school. In spite of Saichō's eager requests the government withheld permission for some time, but finally granted it a few days after his death. Since that day, the Mount Hiei monastery has grown to become one of the most important centers in Japan for the study of and training in Buddhism. Its historical significance may be inferred from the fact that all the major schools emerging in the subsequent Kamakura period, that is, Pure Land, Zen, and Nichiren, were connected in one way or another with Mount Hiei. [*See also* Tendaishū *and the biography of Saichō.*]

Shingon. The term Shingon, derived from the Chinese term for *mantra*, *chen-yen*, means the word embodying a mysterious power that can bring about unusual effects, both spiritual and material. This form of Buddhism, introduced to Japan by Kūkai, stems from Tantrism, which arose during the last phase of Buddhist development in India. [*See* Buddhism, Schools of, *article on* Esoteric Buddhism.] It may be characterized as a mixture of highly sophisticated metaphysical ideas and elaborate rituals deeply imbued with magic. Kūkai, trained for a career in government service, at the age of eighteen suddenly abandoned his studies of Confucianism and Taoism to turn to Buddhism. Fortunate enough to be selected as a member of the mission sailing for China, he visited the Chinese capital of Ch'ang-an and devoted himself to the study of Esoteric Buddhism then in vogue. Over the next three years he successfully mastered the teaching and was appointed the eighth patriarch of the Esoteric transmission. [*See* Chen-yen.] On returning to Japan he established Kongōbuji on Mount Kōya, south of Nara, and Tōji in Kyoto in order to propagate his teaching.

As Kūkai was a versatile genius talented in the fields of art and literature as well, his influence was far-reaching. His most important achievement, however, was the systematic account of the teaching of Esoteric Buddhism. This he accomplished in his *Jūjūshinron* (Treatise on the Ten Stages of Spiritual Development) in which he classified Buddhist and non-Buddhist points of view on an ascending scale of stages that starts with the natural state of consciousness and culminates in the perfect state of being realized in Esoteric Buddhism. According to Esoteric Buddhism, ultimate truth is symbolically present in all phenomena, but above all exists in three forms: *mantras*, mysterious formulas; *maṇḍalas*, the graphic representations of the orders of the universe; and *mudrās*, ritual gestures symbolic of religious truth. Because of this symbolism, Esoteric Buddhism has exerted a remarkable influence on Buddhist iconography and fine arts. At the same time, there is no denying the fact that in subsequent eras Esoteric Buddhism was not infrequently exposed to the danger of degenerating into mere ritualism. [*See also* Shingonshū *and the biography of Kūkai.*]

Other Trends. During this period, a series of trends that were to determine the future course of Buddhist history became increasingly conspicuous. One was a strong tendency toward syncretism with the native religion of Shintō. On the practical level, it led to the construction of many *jingūji* (shrine-temples) where Buddhist rituals were performed within the precincts of a Shintō shrine. On the ideological level the fusion was comprehended by the *honjisuijaku* theory, according to which the Shintō *kami* were secondary manifestations in Japan of certain Buddhas or *bodhisattvas*. This syncretism, which was primarily based on the synthetic Tendai and Shingon teachings, was a dominant feature of Japanese Buddhism until the beginning of the Meiji period (1868), when by governmental decree the fusion was somewhat violently broken. [*See* Honjisuijaku.] Another factor that came to the fore, especially in the late Heian period, was a keen sense of historical crisis and the accompanying search for new forms of teaching. The sense of crisis, no doubt exacerbated by the general instability of the contemporary social order, expressed itself in the theory of *mappō*. This theory held that the Buddhist religion was destined to decline in three successive stages, and, more ominously, that the last stage had already begun. [*See* Mappō.] In fact, one can observe in these centuries a gradual rise of belief in various savior figures, Amida (Skt., Amitābha) in particular, among both the aristocrats and the common people, thus preparing the way for the next age. [*See the biography of Kōya.*]

NEW MOVEMENTS OF THE KAMAKURA PERIOD

The establishment of the Kamakura shogunate (1185–1333) opened a new period in Japanese history. Political power passed from the hands of aristocrats living at the imperial court in Kyoto to the newly arisen military class, initiating an age of feudalism that would last until 1868. Almost parallel to this shift in the political sphere was the appearance of a series of new movements in Buddhism, of which three are especially worth mentioning: the Pure Land, Zen, and Nichiren schools.

Sometimes at variance with each other, these schools nevertheless shared a few common characteristics. To begin with, the three each derived from the Tendai tradition. Each chose from among the synthetic teachings of the previous era one particular teaching or practice and made it the focus of exclusive attention. Thus, Pure Land Buddhism selected the way of salvation through faith in Amida Buddha, Zen employed the way of meditation, and the Nichiren school concentrated on the path of devotion to the truth as revealed in the *Lotus Sutra*. In a word, all three, in marked contrast to the comprehensive approach of the Tendai and Shingon schools, were selective and sectarian in orientation. As a consequence of this one-sidedness, they often had to face conflicts with the long-established schools.

Historically, each of them had a different background. Among the three, Zen is somewhat exceptional in that it owed much to the direct influence of Sung China. The practice of meditation (Skt., *dhyāna;* Chin., *ch'an*; Jpn., *zen*) was of course, an essential element of Buddhism from its inception. In the hands of the practical-minded Chinese, however, an independent "meditation" tradition (the Ch'an school) arose, which claimed to eschew metaphysical speculation in favor of direct insight gained through meditation. Pure Land Buddhism, whose origins date almost from the beginning of the Mahāyāna era, had both Indian and Chinese prototypes, although its increasing popularity during the late Heian and early Kamakura periods must be interpreted in the context of the historical situation at that time. The Nichiren school, finally, had no foreign antecedent. In this respect it differs from Zen and Pure Land Buddhism and may be regarded as most typically Japanese.

The Pure Land Schools. As mentioned earlier, faith in the saving mercy of Amida and the idea of birth into his Pure Land *(jōdo)* named Sukhāvatī ("land of bliss") was not unfamiliar during the Heian period. [*See* Amitābha *and* Pure and Impure Lands.] However, it was Hōnen (1133–1212, also known as Genkū) who gave the trend the decisive turn that made it one of the most powerful streams in Japanese Buddhism. Hōnen studied at the Mount Hiei Tendai monastery but became dissatisfied with the prevailing scholasticism; he thus left to seek out a sort of Buddhism that would be more appropriate to the needs of the people. In 1175, after a long period of spiritual quest, Hōnen found this Buddhist practice in the teaching of the Nembutsu, the simple calling of the Buddha's name. [*See* Nien-fo.] In order to defend his view, he later composed his principal work *Senchaku hongan nembutsu shū* (Treatise on the Selection of Nembutsu of the Original Vow). In it, he divided all Buddhism into two types: one in which the goal of enlightenment is sought by means of disciplined self-endeavor, and one in which the goal is to be reborn into the Pure Land through a wholehearted reliance on the mercy of Amida, there to hear Amida preach and thus to gain enlightenment. Of the two, he favored the latter and declared all traditional exercises other than the Nembutsu merely auxiliary.

In this way, Hōnen introduced reliance on a single, easy practice, an idea that was completely new in the history of Japanese Buddhism. The choice of reliance on Amida was supported not only by confidence in his mercy but also by the conviction that people were so deeply enmeshed in sinfulness that they could not even attempt to make an effort to become enlightened. In a degenerate age such as his, Hōnen thought, it was simply not possible for men to achieve enlightenment by their own power *(jiriki)*; instead, they had to rely on the "power of another" *(tariki)*. No doubt such a pessimistic view of human nature and of history was related to the political and social instability of the age. What is most important about his teaching, however, is that by denouncing lofty speculation and elaborate, costly rituals and by replacing them with a simple act of faith, Hōnen opened a way of salvation to the common people. [*See* Jōdoshū *and the biography of Hōnen*.]

Hōnen had many an able disciple, but it was Shinran (1173–1262) who gave his master's teaching its most radical interpretation. He emphasized an idea in Hōnen's system that, while basic, remained for Hōnen only one among others, namely, the idea of the all-encompassing and absolute mercy of Amida. Firmly believing in the compassion and saving power of the Buddha, Shinran came to the conclusion that Amida Buddha had *already* completed his salvific scheme. Each person, regardless of his or her status and quality, was already saved, although he or she might not realize it. Accordingly, the Nembutsu was regarded by Shinran as an expression of gratitude to Amida rather than a practice leading to birth in his Pure Land. Out of this conviction, Shinran also dared to take an extraordinary step: calling himself "neither monk nor layman" *(hizō hizoku),* he deliberately ignored the rules of monastic life by marrying and raising children. Through this act he established a new model for the integration of secular life and the religious quest. His Jōdo Shinshū (the True Pure Land school, as distinct from Hōnen's Jōdoshū or Pure Land school) grew in size and influence in the following centuries and remains one of the most powerful Buddhist institutions in Japan. [*See* Jōdo Shinshū *and the biography of Shinran.*]

Zen Buddhism. The establishment of Zen, which was the second of the major schools to appear during the Kamakura period, marked a departure from traditional Buddhism insofar as Zen put aside abstruse metaphysics and complicated rituals and tried instead to concentrate on the personal experience of enlightenment in the midst of daily life. This stance is best expressed in the famous Zen motto *kyōge betsuden* ("a special transmission outside the formal teaching"). In this search for simplicity Zen was in basic agreement with the Pure Land school; however, in contrast with members of this school, who in a pietistic manner taught salvation from without, Zen's proponents firmly retained the more traditional notion that enlightenment is gained through one's own endeavors.

Having enjoyed wide popularity in Sung China, Zen was transmitted to Japan by several figures. [*See* Ch'an.] One of the first was Eisai (1141–1214), originally a Tendai monk, who visited China twice. In 1191, after his second sojourn, Eisai introduced the Rinzai (Chin., Lin-chi) version of Zen, one of the so-called five houses then prevailing in China. With the aid of the Kamakura shogunate he was able to found two bases for his activities, Jufukuji in Kamakura and Kenninji in Kyoto. The fact that he turned to the rising warrior class for support is noteworthy, for in Kyoto he was liable to be exposed to severe criticisms from the Tendai establishment on Mount Hiei, and because the aristocrats living in Kyoto generally had a natural predilection for the traditional schools of Buddhism. Even though he thus made the first step in transplanting Zen, his was not a pure Zen inasmuch as it was still mingled with some elements of earlier schools, Esoteric ritualism in particular. In this respect, Eisai stood with one foot in the tradition of Heian Buddhism and one in the newer tradition of Zen. [*See the biography of Eisai.*]

Some thirty-six years later, Dōgen (1200–1253) introduced from China the Sōtō (Ts'ao-tung) school of Zen. The main difference between Rinzai and Sōtō consists in the approach to achieving enlightenment: while Rinzai employs a question-and-answer technique between master and disciple focusing on *kōan,* riddle-like topics taken mostly from the anecdotes of past masters, Sōtō concentrates almost exclusively on the practice of sitting meditation. This Dōgen called *shikantaza,* sitting straight without entertaining vain thoughts, for according to him enlightenment is not separate from practice and practice equals enlightenment. In contrast to Eisai, Dōgen held a stricter attitude toward other schools: he did not engage himself in ritualism and rejected Nembutsu practice as utterly useless. Such an austere spirit also led him to stay aloof from worldly affairs; during the latter half of his life he withdrew to a remote province in northern Japan and sequestered himself in Eiheiji, dedicating all his energy to the training of a few elect disciples. [*See the biography of Dōgen.*]

In their subsequent development, Rinzai and Sōtō, the two major schools of Zen in Japan, took markedly different courses. As is clear from the examples of Eisai and many of his successors, the Rinzai school flourished chiefly by the patronage of high-ranking samurai who were now in positions of power. Its headquarters, the so-called five temples *(gozan)*, were located in either Kyoto or Kamakura and served as centers of both Zen education and the study of newly introduced Chinese learning, including Neo-Confucianism. Thus Rinzai came to play an important role in the dissemination of refined culture. [*See* Gozan Zen.] The Sōtō school, on the contrary, sought its adherents mostly among provincial samurai and the peasantry. In order to win these people's support, the rigid and elitist stance of Dōgen had to be abandoned in favor of a more conciliatory attitude in relation to their religious needs. As a means of gaining their allegiance Sōtō assimilated a certain amount of popular beliefs and rituals but devised, above all, funeral and memorial services for the dead, a trait that was to become one of the characteristic features of almost all Buddhist schools in Japan. [*See also* Zen.]

Nichirenshū. The thirteenth century also witnessed the emergence of a unique movement that bears the name and the imprint of its founder, Nichiren (1222–1282). One of the most charismatic personalities in the religious history of Japan, Nichiren was deeply concerned with the material and spiritual state of the country and fought incessantly for its improvement. His aim was *risshō ankoku* ("restore the right teaching [and thereby] achieve the security of the nation"). In a sense, his was a sort of reform movement from within the Tendai school, but in its exclusive pursuit of its goal it went far beyond the traditional forms to become a new, independent school.

Troubled from his youth by doubts concerning the cause of natural and social calamities that plagued his day, Nichiren reached the conclusion that they were due to the disappearance of the "true (Buddhist) teaching" and that the country would never be safe before true Buddhism was restored. This "right teaching" he believed to have found in the *Lotus Sutra* as interpreted in the Tendai tradition. Accordingly, he urged people to praise the *Lotus Sutra* as the only true text, and harshly condemned all schools that depended on other scriptural sources (particularly Ritsu, Shingon, Zen, and above all Pure Land) as being false doctrines. Nichiren was not content with criticizing other schools, however; he made remonstrances to the Kamakura shogunate, demanding a reform of Buddhism and of the government in keeping with the spirit of the *sūtra*. Such drastic behavior naturally aroused the enmity of his opponents and met with repeated opposition on the part of the shogunate until finally he was exiled to the island of Sado in northern Japan. Although his efforts did not have any actual results during his lifetime, he attracted a dedicated following and inspired many an influential movement in later centuries.

Nichiren's teaching came to be embraced by members of the merchant class in Kyoto and other cities. During the fifteenth century, in the general collapse of political order, the adherents of the Nichiren school even equipped themselves with arms, and their uprising, called Hokke-ikki, had formidable effects. It is interesting to notice that the Nichiren school exhibits a strong propensity toward active political and social involvement; this prophetic vein is what distinguishes it from other branches of Buddhism in Japan and elsewhere. Nichiren's legacy is still very much alive, as may be readily seen in the contemporary new religious movements of Buddhist origin. The fact that many powerful organizations, such as Reiyūkai, Risshō

Kōseikai, and Sōka Gakkai, are all related in a substantial way to his teaching testifies to the lasting influence of this school. [*See* Nichirenshū; Reiyūkai; Risshō Kōseikai; Sōka Gakkai; *and the biography of Nichiren.*]

INSTITUTIONAL CONSOLIDATION OF THE TOKUGAWA PERIOD

In many expositions, the history of Japanese Buddhism is related as if Buddhism reached its apex during the Kamakura period. In a sense this holds true, for by the close of the period all the major schools in Japan had made their appearance, and what occurred thereafter constituted, by and large, merely internal developments within each group. For this reason it is possible to divide Japanese Buddhism roughly into Nara Buddhism, and the Tendai, Shingon, Pure Land, Zen, and Nichiren schools, a scheme that is adopted in contemporary official statistics as well. This does not imply, to be sure, that there were no developments of importance in subsequent eras. On the contrary, although no new doctrines or practices emerged during the Tokugawa period (1600–1867), Buddhism underwent a process of institutional consolidation hitherto unknown in its history. The changes that took place during this time bear directly upon the nature of Buddhism in the modern age.

On the whole, Buddhist schools enjoyed official recognition during this period, while at the same time they were made subservient to the political and administrative objectives of the Tokugawa regime. In the early part of the seventeenth century Buddhist temples, along with Shintō shrines, were brought under the control of commissioners (*jisha bugyō*) appointed both at the national and local level. In each school temples were organized to form a hierarchical system of head and branch temples. Furthermore, concurrent with the banishment of Christianity, then commonly known as Kirishitan, the shogunate ordered every Japanese to be affiliated with a particular temple, which issued certificates *(tera-uke)* attesting that the person in question was not a member of the forbidden religion. These measures resulted in the formation of a network of parish-like organizations in which every household was at least nominally affiliated with a Buddhist temple. This system, called *danka seido*, although legally abolished since the early years of the Meiji period (1868–1912), still continues to provide an important social basis for many Buddhist organizations.

It is clear that this policy of the Tokugawa regime contributed much to the stability of the various Buddhist schools. Since it demanded the presence of a temple in each locality the number of temples actually increased. However, it is equally clear that this stability was obtained at a high cost. The material well-being of many temples often led to the moral corruption of the clergy. Harsh criticisms resulted: inside Buddhist organizations, the distrust of priests sometimes gave rise to a kind of underground religious activity by devout members of the laity; critical voices from without also increased as time went on. In this context, too, there was a remarkable decline of intellectual creativity on the part of Buddhists, despite the seeming prosperity of scholarship in the many academies established by various groups. Since new teachings were not allowed to be propounded, effort was concentrated on elaborating and refining the details of traditional dogmatics. While Buddhists were previously among the foremost thinkers of each period, now it was Confucian and, to some extent, Shintō scholars who addressed themselves to the real social and religious problems of the time. [*See also* Confucianism in Japan.]

BUDDHISM IN MODERN JAPAN

The modern period in Japanese history began with the Meiji restoration in 1868 and brought a series of radical changes in all spheres of life, including religion. Buddhism was deeply affected both in a positive and negative sense by the rapid process of modernization. One of the most pronounced changes took place on the institutional level, particularly in the relation of Buddhism to the state. In its attempt to mobilize the nation under the authority of the emperor, the Meiji government gave a definite priority to Shintō and thereby put an end to the age-old Shintō-Buddhist syncretism. Certainly, in the beliefs and practices of the common people the two traditions are still regarded as harmoniously united. Even today, many Japanese pay homage to Shintō shrines at the same time that they are associated with Buddhist temples. Yet it is clear that, at least legally, Buddhism is no longer in possession of the privileged status it formerly enjoyed and has become one tradition among others in a religiously pluralistic society.

These changes in the social milieu, combined with the influences from the Christian West that began to enter the country beginning in the latter half of the nineteenth century, elicited a number of responses from traditional Buddhist organizations on different levels and in various forms. One was a new and active engagement in educational and social work projects. Previously, many Buddhist temples had served as centers of education and of social welfare. Now they made it their task to promote these activities in conformity with modern institutional regulations. Parallel to this trend, one can also observe a renewal of missionary efforts, which in some cases even led to the establishment of overseas missions. These and similar efforts may be summarized under the rubric of organizational reform.

Side by side with these reforms, many Buddhist leaders felt the need to cope with the challenge of modernity. Thus, new academic studies of Buddhism, both philosophical and philological in nature, were initiated. When Buddhism first encountered Christianity during the sixteenth century, theoretical reflection on the basic premises of each religion had already begun in the form of disputations. In the modern period, however, Buddhism was confronted not only with Christianity but also with the modern scientific worldview. Out of this encounter emerged various attempts at reinterpreting the Buddhist teaching; these have continued until the present. On the other hand, the introduction of modern research techniques after the 1880s, coupled with the availability in Japan of materials from nearly all stages of Buddhist history, has led to the flowering of Buddhist studies in accordance with rigorous standards of modern scholarship. [*See* Buddhist Studies.]

Finally, a number of new movements appeared on the fringes of or outside the established groups. Insofar as they do not conform to the traditional clerical framework, they may be loosely characterized as lay Buddhist movements. Some of them remain rather small, consisting of only a handful of people dedicated to spiritual quest and the study of Buddhist ideas. The *seishinshugi* ("spiritualism") movement, initiated in 1900 by Kiyozawa Manshi (1863–1903) and, in the post–World War II period, Zaike Bukkyō Kyōkai (Buddhist Laymen's Association), founded by Katō Benzaburō (1899–1983), may be cited as examples. Others, such as Reiyūkai, Risshō Kōseikai, and Sōka Gakkai, have grown to nationwide organizations with membership in the tens of thousands. These latter occupy an important section of the so-called new religious movements *(shinkō shūkyō* or *shin shūkyō)* that have appeared in the course of the twentieth century. [*See* New Religions, *article on* New Religions in Japan.] Their presence, as well as various reform measures and intensive academic activities, seem to indicate the lasting relevance of Buddhism to Japanese life.

[*For an overview of the role of Buddhism in Japanese culture, see* Japanese Religion. *For further discussion of the history and development of the Japanese Buddhist schools, see* Buddhism, Schools of, *article on* Japanese Buddhism. *Buddhist syncretism with indigenous Japanese traditions is treated in* Shugendō *and* Shintō. *For Buddhist cultic life, see* Worship and Cultic Life, *article on* Buddhist Cultic Life in East Asia; Domestic Observances, *article on* Japanese Practices; *and* Pilgrimage, *article on* Buddhist Pilgrimage in East Asia.]

BIBLIOGRAPHY

Works in English. The number of Western-language materials dealing with this subject belies its importance. Among the few works now available, some treat Buddhism within the larger context of Japanese religion. A standard reference of this category remains Masaharu Anesaki's *History of Japanese Religion with Special Reference to the Social and Moral Life of the Nation* (1930; reprint, Rutland, Vt., and Tokyo, 1963), although some of its data and interpretations are naturally outdated. Fortunately we have an excellent successor to it in Joseph M. Kitagawa's *Religion in Japanese History* (New York, 1966). Intending to treat Japanese religion as a whole, the book traces the intricate relationship between various religious systems of Japan roughly from the third century to the post–World War II period. It also contains an extensive bibliography and glossary.

For the study of the position and role of Buddhism in Japan, the pertinent sections of H. Byron Earhart's *Japanese Religion: Unity and Diversity*, 3d rev. ed. (Belmont, Calif., 1982) as well as of *Japanese Religion* (Tokyo and Palo Alto, Calif., 1972), issued by the Agency for Cultural Affairs of the Japanese Government, may be consulted with profit. As for books addressing themselves specifically to Buddhism in Japan, Charles Eliot's *Japanese Buddhism* (1935; reprint, New York, 1959) deserves attention. While not exhaustive, it nevertheless gives important insights into some aspects of Buddhism in Japan. Very useful is Daigan Matsunaga and Alicia Matsunaga's *Foundation of Japanese Buddhism*, 2 vols. (Los Angeles and Tokyo, 1974–1976). These volumes contain detailed information about the historical transmission and the basic tenets of major schools together with a brief description of the social background, but their coverage is limited roughly to the end of the medieval period.

Generally, Buddhism after the medieval period is a subject that has so far been relatively neglected and publications in this area are scarce even in Japanese. In this sense, *Japanese Religion in the Meiji Era*, compiled and edited by Hideo Kishimoto and translated by John F. Howes (Tokyo, 1956), is noteworthy as it gives a succinct account of the situation of Buddhism from the Tokugawa through the Meiji era.

Specialized studies. In addition to works of a more general nature, there are materials dealing either with a particular period, a particular school, or personalities, of which the following represents only a tentative selection. About the ancient period, we have Marinus Willem de Visser's *Ancient Buddhism in Japan*, 2 vols. (Paris, 1928–1935). There have been relatively few titles on Esoteric Buddhism despite its popularity. Minoru Kiyota's *Shingon Buddhism: Theory and Practice* (Los Angeles, 1978) is one of the recent books to fill in this gap, together with E. Dale Saunders's *Mudrā: A Study of Symbolic Gestures in Japanese Buddhist Sculpture* (New York, 1960). Of the works on the life and thought of Hōnen, the founder of the Jōdoshū, Harper Coates and Ryūgaku Ishizuka's *Hōnen, the Buddhist Saint*, 5 vols. (1925; reprint, Kyoto, 1949) is most basic, being the translation of the authorized biography with a careful introduction. Nichiren, the founder of another influential school, is vividly portrayed in Masaharu Anesaki's *Nichiren the Buddhist Prophet* (1916; reprint, Gloucester, Mass., 1966). Heinrich Dumoulin's *A History of Zen Buddhism*, translated by Paul Peachey (New York, 1963), gives a good survey both of the historical background and of the development of Zen in Japan. The influence of Zen on Japanese culture is a topic that has enjoyed some popularity, for which D. T. Suzuki's *Zen and Japanese Culture,* 2d ed., rev. & enl. (1959; reprint, Princeton, 1970), may be regarded as classic, although the author tends to stress somewhat one-sidedly the impact of Zen. As for the new religious movements derived from Buddhism, basic information can be found in Clark B. Offner and Henry van Straelen's *Modern Japanese Religions* (Leiden, 1963) as well as in Harry Thomsen's *The New Religions of Japan* (Tokyo and Rutland, Vt., 1963).

Further references. Because of the nature of the subject, the bulk of source materials as well as of research results are published in Japanese. In order to supplement the perhaps uneven selection listed above, a few descriptive bibliographies in English on Japanese publications may be cited. These are *A Bibliography on Japanese Buddhism*, edited by Shōjun Bandō, Shōyū Hanayama, Ryōjun Satō, Shinkō Sayeki, and Keiryū Shima (Tokyo, 1958), and *K. B. S. Bibliography of Standard Reference Books for Japanese Studies, with Descriptive Notes*, vol. 4, *Religion*, edited by the Kokusai Bunka Shinkōkai (Tokyo, 1963). The former has about 1,660 entries and the latter, under the heading of Buddhism, 92 basic works. A successor to the latter is *An Introductory Bibliography for Japanese Studies* (Tokyo, 1975–), published by the Japan Foundation in two- to three-year intervals. It gives a brief report on the research works done in the area of Japanese Buddhism during the years under review.

Works in Japanese. Each of the major schools of Japanese Buddhism has collected its own textual corpus. See *Tendaishū zensho*, 25 vols., edited by the Tendai Shūten Kankōkai (Tokyo, 1935–1937); *Shingonshū zensho*, 42 vols., edited by the Shingonshū Zensho Kankōkai (Wakayama, 1933–1939); *Jōdoshū zensho*, 21 vols., edited by the Jōdoshū Shūten Kankōkai (Tokyo, 1929–1931), and its sequel, *Zoku Jōdoshū zensho*, 20 vols., edited by the Shūsho Hozonkai (Tokyo, 1940–1942); *Shinshū zensho*, 74 vols., edited by Tsumaki Naoyoshi (Tokyo, 1913–1916); *Kokuyaku Zengaku taisei*, 25 vols., edited by Miyauchi Sotai and Satō Kōyō (Tokyo, 1930–1931); and *Nichirenshū zensho*, 30 vols., edited by the Nichirenshū Zensho Shuppankai (Tokyo, 1910–1916). These sources provide fuller documentation for the sectarian traditions than is available in such standard canonical collections as the *Taishō shinshū daizōkyō*, 100 vols. (Tokyo, 1924–1932) or the *Dainihon zokuzōkyō*, 150 boxes (Kyoto, 1905–1912).

While Buddhist studies in the premodern period had been pursued mostly in the form of dogmatic exegesis, historical scholarship has flourished in this century. Among its many achievements, by far the most basic reference is Tsuji Zennosuke's *Nihon bukkyōshi*, 11 vols. (Tokyo, 1944–1953). Covering the whole of Buddhist history from its inception down to the dawn of the Meiji era, it gives a vivid picture of Buddhism in the context of the social, political, and intellectual situation of each period. While not as voluminous, Tamamuro Taijō's *Nihon bukkyōshi gaisetsu* (Tokyo, 1940) is very instructive. Written from the perspective of socioeconomic history, it successfully clarifies the position of Buddhist organizations throughout Japanese history. Representative of a different, intellectual history, approach are Ienaga Saburō's *Jōdai bukkyō shisōshi kenkyū* (Tokyo, 1948) and *Chūsei bukkyō shisōshi kenkyū* (Kyoto, 1947). In many essays collected in these two books, Ienaga tries to decipher the peculiarity of the Buddhist outlook and its impact on the Japanese mentality. On the history of Buddhism in modern Japan, a hitherto unexplored field, Yoshida Kyūichi's *Nihon kindai bukkyōshi kenkyū* (Tokyo, 1959) gives a succinct overview. Finally, *Bukkyōgaku kankei zasshi rombun bunrui mokuroku*, 2 vols., edited by the Ryūkoku Daigaku Toshokan (Kyoto, 1931–1961), serves as a useful guide to the research works undertaken from the beginning of the Meiji era to the late 1950s.

9 BUDDHISM IN TIBET

Herbert Guenther

Buddhism in Tibet constitutes an immensely complex phenomenon. Its rich and subtle philosophy is combined with a highly developed depth psychology that involves advanced techniques such as visualization coupled with other transformative operations. It has developed a cosmology that in a certain sense is a joint enterprise of philosophy, psychology, and the arts and sciences, as well as religion. "Religion" in this context may be defined as a blend of a deeply moving inner experience and an evocative theory that attempts to communicate rationally and discursively what is experienced and felt holistically. As such, religion enters into an intimate relationship with society by catering to the aspirations and anxieties of individuals, and by regulating their relationships to each other. Indeed, Buddhism never lost sight of living man, who is held to construct within his mind, from all the information he receives, the various "worlds" with their welter of gods and other, primarily human, beings.

Tibetan Buddhism developed in the wake of Mahāyāna Buddhism, which was marked by a growing social awareness expressed by the guiding image of the *bodhisattva,* who stands in the service of mankind, as contrasted with the Hīnayāna guiding image of the *arhat,* who allegedly stands aloof from the rest of society. Since a *bodhisattva* is not necessarily a monk, but may come from any walk of life, the emphasis on his social character introduced a tension between this newer guiding image and that of the *arhat,* who could come only from the ranks of the monks, who had a privileged status in the early phase of Buddhism, and who tried to maintain that status even when social and economic conditions had changed. In Tibet this tension led to a proliferation of monastic establishments that struggled for political power. [*See also* Bodhisattva Path.]

From an intellectual and spiritual point of view, Mahāyāna Buddhism is represented by an epistemology-oriented approach to the human situation, codified in the Sūtras, and an experiential approach, codified in the Tantras. The Indian word *tantra* means, literally, "loom." In its expanded sense, the term may also refer to "living one's possibilities." These possibilities constitute the individual's indestructible core and value: the individual presents a value by virtue of his being, not because of some hypothetical *ātman* or "self." The indigenous Indian term for this indestructible core and value is *vajra.* This term, rich in connotations, is better left untranslated in order to avoid perpetuating the many past misconceptions about its meaning.

INITIAL TRANSMISSION

In addition to being its own "way," Buddhism has had a tendency to gather within it, if not take credit for, disparate folk customs and religious rituals by reinterpreting whatever it has absorbed. At the time that Buddhism arrived in Tibet (beginning in the eighth century CE) it found itself in a highly developed intellectual climate, one that later followers, once Buddhism had become firmly established, tended to belittle. Our picture of this early climate is obscured by two major factors. One is the fact that before Buddhism was officially recognized the dominant intellectual force was Bon, itself still a subject of considerable uncertainty due to lack of early sources. Besides adherents of Bon, called Bon-pos, there were storytellers *(sgruṅ)* and riddlemasters *(lde'u),* who represented the "religion of men" *(mi chos).* Buddhism claimed to have superseded both *mi chos* and Bon, the "religion of gods" *(lha'i chos).* That it could make this claim was due to the fact that the ground for its reception had already been prepared by Buddhist ideas that had come from Central Asia and China. The other factor that contributed to confusion was the notion that whatever had preceded the predominantly Indian version of Buddhism that reached Tibet was something uncivilized, primitive, and barbarous. In fact, the religious situation in Tibet at the time of the arrival of Buddhism was already far from primitive.

It is important to note that Buddhism was well received by the highly sophisticated world of governmental and educated people, but in order to become firmly established, it needed official patronage as well. Thus, almost from its very beginning in Tibet, Buddhism was involved in activities that today would be termed "political," including rivalries of families and clans as well as feuding between pro-China and pro-India factions. It was this involvement in politics that eventually led to Tibet's status as an ecclesiastical state operating on two levels, that of the central government and that of the more or less independent local states. Every lay official had his monastic counterpart. Underlying this division is the age-old problem of the One and the Many, which in the Tibetan context has been solved through the concept of incarnate beings. Through the symbol of Avalokiteśvara, mankind is seen as One (i.e., mankind's spiritual unity); through the symbol of incarnate beings, mankind is seen as the Many (i.e., mankind's physical plurality). Each Dalai Lama is considered to be the reincarnation of his historical, physical predecessor; similarly, the hierarchs of the various schools of Tibetan Buddhism are held to be reincarnations of their predecessors.

The whole history of Buddhism in Tibet reflects the complementarity of two structural movements, one of which takes precedence over, but does not exclude, the other. These two movements are a prereflective-nonthematic, nonobjectifying (and hence also nonsubjectifying), "mystical" thinking and a reflective-thematic, objectifying (and hence also subjectifying), representational, "rational" thinking. Mystical thinking attempts to keep the immediacy of experience alive and perhaps to recapture it by reaching out and merging with the universe (a movement that—if it happens—happens all at once); rational thinking stands outside of experience, as it were, analyzes it, makes distinctions, catalogs what has taken place, and argues about it endlessly.

Historical events related to the official recognition of Buddhism bear out this underlying complementarity. Mes-ag-tshom, the father of King Khri-sroṅ-lde-btsan (756–797?), showed an interest in Buddhism even at this early date and sent emissaries to India to invite some monks who were engaged in mystical contemplation inthe Źaṅ-źuṅ area. They, however, merely sent him some texts in reply. Because of the anti-Buddhist feeling in court circles the king surreptitiously sent a certain Saṅ-śi of the Sba (alt., Rba) clan to China to procure additional Buddhist texts. On his return Saṅ-śi had to go into hiding, because the old king had died while his son and heir was still a minor, and the various calamities that subsequently befell the court were ascribed to the interest in Buddhism. When on attaining majority, Khri-sroṅ-lde-btsan took charge, he renewed, with due caution, his father's interest in Buddhism. The young king sent Gsal-snaṅ of Sba, who later was ordained as a monk under the name Ye-śes-dbaṅ-po, to India and Nepal with an invitation for the Indian *paṇḍita* Śāntirakṣita. However, the *paṇḍita* had to leave Tibet almost as soon as he arrived because of internal turmoil. It was only after the anti-Buddhist party was ousted by exiling its followers and assassinating its leader, Ma-źaṅ Khrom-pa-skyes, that Śāntirakṣita was able to return to Tibet.

Śāntarakṣita had no success in Tibet. As a follower of the Yogācāra-Svātantrika-Mādhyamika school, he emphasized rational thought and its accompanying tendency to argue for argumentation's sake. [*See the biography of Śāntirakṣita.*] Realizing his limitations, the *paṇḍita* advised the king to invite the monk Padmasambhava, about whose life no available sources agree (except about the fact that he had to leave Tibet under threat) and whose birthplace, Uḍḍiyāna, has not yet been satisfactorily located. Padmasambhava seems to have been capable of thinking both mystically and rationally by starting from a common experiential source and thereby avoiding the "nothing-but" fallacy that dictates a choice between mysticism and rationality. Relating his teaching to praxis-oriented experience, Padmasambhava was not content with mere abstractions or purely perceptual analysis. To label this figure an exorcist, as some scholars have done, is to misunderstand what mysticism means and to confuse it with occultism. In fact, it was through Padmasambhava that a link could be forged with those "mystical"—but non-Buddhist—elements in Tibetan civilization that have given Tibetan Buddhism its distinct flavor. [*See also the biography of Padmasambhava.*] This holds true especially for the Rdzogs-chen teaching to which both Bon and Buddhism lay claim. This school regards as one of its patrons Myaṅ Tiṅ-ne-'dzin, who led the revolt against Ye-śes-dbaṅ-po and replaced him by Dpal-dyaṅs, a prominent member of the mystical tradition with links to Ch'an Buddhism. Myaṅ Tiṅ-ne'dzin was also chosen by the then ruling king as the guardian of the throne's heir, Khri-lde-sroṅ-btsan. Nevertheless, Ye-śes-dbaṅ-po fought back by inviting Kamalaśīla, another representative of the "rationalist" (Yogācāra-Svātantrika) trend in Buddism. [*See the biography of Kamalaśīla.*] The outcome of the alleged debate of Bsam-yas, according to late and hence not very trustworthy Tibetan sources, marked the ascendence of the purely Indian rationalist and monastic trend. In the political bickering between rationalism-only and/or mysticism-only, their complementarity was overlooked, and the rift grew ever wider. Furthermore, while mysticism emphasized the immediacy of experience as being copresent with and pervading all particular experiences, rationalism insisted on a gradual passage from one spiritual state to another, which requires for its success that the person or community involved in this process be supported by donations.

PERSECUTION AND REVIVAL

The ensuing establishment of monastic centers soon gave rise to self-governing economic units active in business transactions and even in trade. The monasteries, having gradually acquired large estates that had been bequeathed to them by wealthy families, became powerful landowners themselves, and smaller landowners, unable to hold out against them, eventually became their tenants. Since the monasteries were tax-exempt, the state was deprived of considerable resources in both manpower and revenue. As the monastic centers grew in economic power, they became increasingly arrogant and demanded more and more privileges. These were the main reasons for the persecution of Buddhism by Glaṅ-dar-ma (838–842).

The persecution deprived Buddhism not only of its court patronage, but also of all its property. However, on the political front, the assassination in 842 or 846 of Glaṅ-dar-ma by a monk, Dpal-gyi-rdo-rje of Lha-luṅ, did not save Tibet from political fragmentation. (After this deed Dpal-gyi-rdo-rje fled to the area of Hsünhwa, in Amdo, where he is said to have been indirectly instrumental in reviving monastic ordination.) Chinese frontier towns such as Tun-huang and Sha-chou, which had been occupied for some time by the Tibetans, were lost; the minister in command was beheaded (866) and his army scattered into splinter groups along the borderlands, where they formed the nucleus of evolving communities. Shortly thereafter the Tibetans were expelled from Turkistan by the Uighurs and Karluk Türk. On the spiritual-intellectual side the sobering influence of the monasteries and religious communities was no longer felt.

After Glaṅ-dar-ma's assassination his two sons, Yum-brtan (by his first wife, or at least brought up by her, as he is said to have been kidnapped from another woman) and 'Od-sruṅ (by his second wife), ruled separately over parts of Tibet. 'Od-sruṅ's son, Dpal-'khor-btsan, is said to have been a pious Buddhist who was slain by his subjects. Dpal-'khor-btsan's two sons took western Gtsaṅ, which once had been part of the central kingdom, and the three lands of Mṅa'-ris: Mar-yul (which lasted as a Buddhist kingdom until about 1100), Spu-hraṅ(s), and Źaṅ-źuṅ or Gu-ge, respectively. The son and grandson of Dpal-'khor-btsan's first son founded local principalities at Guṅ-thaṅ, as well as in Ñaṅ/Myaṅ, at Tsoṅ-kha in Amdo, and in Yar-kluṅ. Thus, in these areas Buddhism continued and was eventually revitalized, at first in the eastern part of what had been Tibet. (Accounts found in Tibetan chronicles are open to doubt, since their authors had a vested interest in validating their claims to the continuity of the lineage to which they belonged.)

What is of interest in the process of this revival of Buddhism in the east is the fact that the connection with Chinese or non-Indian Buddhism was retained. The story goes that during the period of persecution three Buddhist monks, Rab-gsal of Gtsaṅ, G.yo-dge'byuṅ of Bo-doṅ, and Dmar Śākyamuni of Stod-luṅ, set out via Ladakh and the region held by the Karluk Türk to the west, passed through the region held by the Uighurs, and ended up in Amdo. An ex-Bon-po who lived there, Dge-rab-gsal of the Mu-zi (Mu-zu) clan (822–915? or 892–975?) from Tsoṅ-kha, had been converted toBuddhism, which in its Rdzogs-chen form seems to have flourished in this area due to the presence of Vairocana, a follower of Padmasambhava, who had been banished during the reign of Khri-sroṅ-lde-btsan. Impressed by the conduct of the three monks, Dge-rab-gsal wanted to be ordained as a monk also. Since ordination requires the presence of five ordained monks, two Hwa-shaṅ monks were added to make up the quorum. In this connection it should be noted that the pro-India Tibetan Buddhists, in their hostility against anything non-Indian, have consistently failed to distinguish between Hwa-śaṅ, probably a Chinese Taoist, and Hwa-śaṅ Mahāyāna, a Chinese Buddhist.

The account of the arrival of Buddhism in the central part of Tibet is modeled after the events that had taken place in the eastern part and, for this reason alone, is highly suspicious. During the ninth and tenth centuries, events of tremendous importance for the subsequent history of Buddhism in Tibet took place in the western part of the land through the efforts of the kings of Mṅa'-ris. King 'Khor-re abdicated in favor of his younger brother Sroṅ-ṅe, and took the robe under the name (Lha Bla-ma) Ye-śes-'od. He sent several young men to study the monastic tradition in Kashmir. Kashmir at that time retained the last splendors of Buddhism (which had practically disappeared from India). Here both the mystical and the rational approaches to the Buddhist teaching were still flourishing. "Rational" here refers to the Sarvāstivāda, Sautrāntika, Mādhyamika, and Yogācāra schools of Buddhism, all of which were classified by the Tibetans as *rgyu-mtshan,* that is, epistemology-oriented, or what may be typified as "causality." "Mystical," on the other hand, refers to the *rgyud* (Skt., *tantra*) or experience-oriented "existential" approach.

When the young men returned to their homeland at the end of their studies, they brought with them a number of teachers and artists. This rekindled interest in Buddhism quickly spread to the central parts of Tibet, and soon a continual stream of pilgrims passed between Tibet and India.

Two figures dominated the western Tibetan scene during this time, the Tibetan Rin-chen-bzaṅ-po (958-1055), one of the young men sent to India by Ye-śes-'od, and Atīśa Dīpaṃkara Śrījñāna (982–1054), described as the son of the king of Zahor and said to be well versed in all aspects of Buddhism. Atīśa Dīpaṃkara Śrījñāna was invited to Gu-ge by Byaṅ-chub-'od, nephew or grandnephew of Ye-śes-'od, and he arrived there in 1042. [*See also the biography of Atīśa.*]

Rin-chen-bzaṅ-po was active in the erection of numerous chapels. (Tradition puts the number at 108, but it must be noted that 108 recurs frequently as one of the sacred numbers in Indian religious thought.) The largest temple founded by him in western Tibet is Mtho-liṅ, famous for its frescoes. It is likely that he founded Tabo and Nako in Spiti. He also was active in the translation of Buddhist texts from India. (These translations included original texts as well as revisions of already translated texts.) A total of 158 of these texts were included in the large collections of the Bka'-'gyur (Kanjur; the texts claimed to have been "spoken" by the Buddha) and the Bstan-'gyur (Tanjur; treatises by Indian scholars analyzing and commenting on the "Buddha word"). Rin-chen bzaṅ-po marks the dividing line between the "new" tradition and the "old" tradition, a division relating to the texts of a mystical nature. This division, applicable only to Tibet, has distinctly political (i.e., pro-Indian) overtones, and seems to have been made arbitrarily on the basis of whether or not "older" texts were available in an Indian (either Sanskrit or Prakrit) version. Texts that were said to have been translated from an extinct Indian source were simply excluded and branded as "spurious" or "incorrect."

Atīśa found Buddhism in the process of renewal as he traveled to the heartland of Tibet. At Sñe-thaṅ, a few kilometers from Lhasa, he came into contact with a group of monks from Khams who became his disciples. One of its leading members was 'Brom-ston Rgyal-ba'i 'byuṅ-gnas (1008–1064), a native of Dbus, who had brought back the monastic discipline from Khams; there the spiritual lineage of Padmasambhava had been kept alive through Vairocana, among whose disciples was the daughter of the king of that region. Vairocana's specific Rdzogs-chen teaching was transmitted to a former Bon-po Ya-zi Bon-ston, who also had been taught by an ascetic (A-ro Ye-śes-'byuṅ-gnas), who continued both the Indian and Chinese traditions. This ascetic was established at Ldan Gloṅ (Kloṅ-thaṅ), where a monk from Nepal, Smṛti by name, had founded a school for the study of the *Abhidharmakośa*. Smṛti had been a teacher of 'Brom-ston before he moved to Liangchow. A-ro Ye-śes-'byuṅ-gnas taught Roṅ-zom Chos-kyi-bzaṅ-po the Rdzogs-chen teaching according to the Khams tradition. One of Roṅ-zom Chos-kyi-bzaṅ-po's works is *Theg pa chen po'i tshul la 'jug pa'i sgo* (The Gate to enter the Practice of Mahāyāna), a profound Rdzogs-chen treatise that was highly praised by Atīśa, who had met Roṅ-zom during his travels.

THE BKA'-GDAMS-PA ORDER

Atīśa himself wrote a small work, *Bodhipathapradīpa* (The Lamp on the Road to Enlightenment), which became very influential. It is related that when 'Brom-ston asked Atīśa whether the texts (*bka'*, "Buddha word," and *bstan bcos,* exegetic works by Indian scholars) or one's teacher's instruction were of greater importance, Atīśa replied that the teacher's instructions were more important, since such directness would guarantee a correct understanding of the concealed intention to which the disciple was committed or had an obiligation *(gdams).* In fact, the importance of the teacher or lama (Tib., *bla ma*) in his direct contact with the disciple gave Tibetan Buddhism its often used epithet Lamaism. In this personal relationship the function of the teacher was to become increasingly indispensable and unquestionable; in a certain sense, the teacher was considered to be the living presence of Buddhahood. The mediator of Buddhahood was known as a "spiritual friend," and many of Atīśa's followers, who formed the first indigenous school of Buddhism in Tibet, the Bka'-gdams-pa, were considered to belong to this category. Addressing the laity, they aimed at cleansing their listeners' minds of preconceived notions by the use of illustrative stories. The whole approach, however, remained predominantly rational; even the mystical aspect, although not totally rejected, was given an intellectualist twist. This may be the reason why Atīśa's teaching had no wide appeal. His favorite disciple, 'Brom-ston, avoided every kind of publicity, even refusing to give instruction, and after founding the monastery of Rwa-sgreṅ in 1059 lived in his cell in utter seclusion until his death.

While the teacher-disciple relationship was strictly personal, on the communal level there was a close reciprocal connection between the lay world and the religious community within it. The religious community provided the laity with spiritual sustenance and was, in turn, materially supported by the laity; this led not only to rivalries among orders but also to their political and economic expansion. Furthermore, the resultant reestablishment of monasteries began to serve a double function. First, they became centers of learning, and thus contributed to the general high standard of cultural life; second, they also became receiving centers for surplus population, and thus contributed to a fairly high level of economic existence by avoiding parcellation of arable land into unproductive lots. Nevertheless, the monks' rational approach to the problems of human existence, together with such injunctions as those imposed upon members of the Bka'-gdams-pa order—abstention from marriage, intoxicants, travel, and the possession of money—had little impact, above all because this approach left out a vital component of man's complex nature: the mystical, emotionally moving, and spiritually satisfying side. Most prominent among those who sought to fill the vacuum were 'Brog-mi (992–1072) and Mar-pa (Marpa, 1012–1096).

THE SA-SKYA-PA ORDER

'Brog-mi, with financial assistance from the local rulers of western Tibet, had set out for India and Nepal. Having studied Sanskrit extensively in Nepal, he then pursued his studies at Vikramaśīla under the guidance of the *mahāsiddha* ("accomplished master") Śānti-pa, who had written a commentary on the *Hevajra Tantra.* This text explains the experiential character of spiritual growth, expressed in the symbols and images of femininity. However, 'Brog-mi received most of his teaching in Tibet from an Indian master after paying him a considerable sum of money. 'Brog-mi later translated the *Hevajra Tantra* into Tibetan, and it became one of the basic texts of the Sa-skya-pa order. This order is named after the place where one of 'Brog-mi's disciples, Dkon-mchog Rgyal-po of the 'Khon family, founded a monastery in 1073. The monastery lies on the trade route linking the Nepal valley with the rich agricultural area around Shigatse, with further extensions into the nomad lands that supply the order with butter and wool. Thus trade and natural resources contributed to the growing wealth of the areas dominated by the Sa-skya-pa. Dkon-mchog Rgyal-po's son and successor, the great Sa-skya Kun-dga'-sñiṅ-po (1092–1158), formulated the tenets of this school, which became known as Lam-'bras ("the path and its fruition"), and ultimately can be traced back to another Indian *mahāsiddha,* Virūpa.

Supported by wealthy landowners and using his own organizational capacity Kun-dga'-sñiṅ-po laid the foundation for the greatness of the Sa-skya-pas. Eventually they were granted sovereignty over Tibet by Khubilai Khan of the Yüan dynasty (the Mongol rulers of China), through the good office of 'Phags-pa (1235–1280?). Apart from their involvement in political struggles, the scholars of the Sa-skya-pa order were most active in the fields of philosophy and linguistics. Thus Bsod-nams-rtse-mo (1142–1182) worked on the systematization of Tantric literature; Grags-pa-rgyal-mtshan (1147–1216) was the author of the first history of the early development of Buddhism in Tibet, but also wrote on medicine. Sa-skya *paṇḍita* Kun-dga'-rgyal-mtshan (1182–1251) wrote on grammar, poetics, and logic. His monumental work, the famous *Tshad ma rigs pa'i gter,* is a distinct development of Buddhist logic beyond Dharmakīrti's *Pramāṇavārttika,* from which it starts. Finally, 'Phags-pa, a prolific writer on every conceivable topic in Buddhism, not only wrote stylistically elegant letters to the Mongol princes, but also devised for the Mongolian language a script that goes by his name. A truly independent thinker in this order was Roṅ-ston Smra-ba'iseṅ-ge (1367–1449), author of sixty-four exegetic and instructional works. He came from a Bon-po family.

The scholar and artist Bu-ston (1290–1364) was not strictly a Sa-skya-pa but a follower of the Źwa-lu-pas (so named after the monastery of Źwa-lu in Gtsaṅ which had been founded in 1040 by Lce). Bu-ston (1290–1364), who hardly differed in outlook from the Sa-skya-pas, undertook the immense task of revising and arranging the vast literature contained in the Bka'-'gyur and Bstan-'gyur. His prejudice against the works of the "older" order (Rñiṅ-ma-pa)—only out of deference to one of his teachers did he include a few such works—is at the root of the growing hostility in later times against the Rñiṅ-ma-pas, particularly on the part of the Dge-lugs-pas. [*See also the biography of Bu-ston.*]

THE BKA'-BRGYUD AND KARMA-PA ORDERS

Mar-pa, whose real name was Chos-kyi-blo-gros of Mar, was born in the fertile district of Lha-brag in southern Tibet of very wealthy parents. Since he had a violent temper, his parents sent him to 'Brog-mi. For twelve years he studied under the guidance of Nā-ro-pa (Naḍapāda) whose "Six Principles" he brought back to Tibet. Mar-pa's most important student was Mi-la-ras-pa (Milarepa, 1040–1123), who continued the ascetic tradition of India, which by that time had succumbed to physically oriented techniques. He is mostly known for his beautiful and moving songs (*mgur*) modeled after the *dohās* in which Indian *mahāsiddhas* expressed their peak experiences. The order thus initiated became known as the *Bka'-brgyud* ("continuity of the Buddha word"); its teaching centers on the *mahāmudrā* ("great seal") experience. It highlights the principle of complementarity, whose realization is aimed at by the synthesis of the multiple "phenomenal" *(snaṅ-ba)* and the unitary "nothing" *(stoṅ pa)*. As contrasted with the pure, mystical teaching of the Rdzogs-chen tradition, the *mahāmudrā* teaching has slightly rational overtones. [*See the biographies of Mar-pa, Nā-ro-pa, and Mi-la-ras-pa.*]

Mi-la-ras-pa's most important disciple was Sgam-po-pa (1079–1153), whose influence was far-reaching. He was born of a noble family and first studied medicine, but was drawn more and more to the contemplative arts. At Dwags-po he founded a monastery, where he actively guided the most learned men of his time. He is the first to have written a guide to the "stages on the path" *(lam rim),* which found countless imitations. One of his three greatest immediate disciples and successors, Phag-mo-gru (1110–1170), spent his life in a simple grass hut that was enshrined in the great and wealthy monastery of Gdan-sa-mthil that developed after his death due to the support of the noble family of Klaṅs, which then provided the religious head of the monastery and the chief lay administrative officer. The monastery remained a family affair, however, and despite its influence failed to establish a definite line of thought. A disciple of Phag-mo-gru, Mi-ñag Sgom-rin (fl. c. twelfth century), set up 'Bri-guṅ monastery, but its real foundation was the work of 'Jig-rten-mgon-po, also known as 'Bri-guṅ Rin-po-che (1143–1212), a monk from 'Dan, in 1179. It soon rose to fame and power and came into conflict with the Sa-skya-pas. Dus-gsum-mkhyen-pa (1110–1193), a native of Khams and second of Sgam-po-pa's three most important disciples, founded in 1147 the Karma Gdan-sa Monastery and (among other monasteries) in 1185 the monastery of Mtshur-phu, the modern seat of the Karma-pas. These lamas spent most of their time traveling from one monastery to another; having no wealthy patrons, they were supported by landed and nomad families. They derive their name from a black hat symbolizing the totality of all Buddha activities *(phrin-las;* Skt., *karman).* The representatives of this order reign to this day as the "Black Hat" lineage.

A related line, known as the "Red Hats," originated with Grags-pa-seṅ-ge (1283–1345). Sgom-pa (1116– 1169), the third eminent disciple of Sgam-po-pa, established another school through his disciple Lama Źaṅ (1123–1193) at Guṅ-thaṅ, near Lhasa, in the district of Mtshal. The name *Mtshal* was applied to the school as well as to the family supporting the school. The family became active in politics, and one of its members negotiated the Tibetan submission to Chinggis Khan. Among the many other "sub-orders" the 'Brug-pa and the Śaṅs-pa must be mentioned. The former order, founded by Gliṅ-ras-pa Padma-rdo-rje (1128–1188), derived its name from the monastery at 'Brug in Dbus. This order became most active in Bhutan and the western Himalayas. Pad-ma Dkar-po (1526–1592) was one of its outstanding scholars; his *Phyag chen gan mdzod* is a mine of information. The Śaṅs-pa order traces its origin to Khyuṅ-po-rnal-'byor, a Bon-po who converted to Buddhism; he received his teaching from many Indian scholars, but particularly from Ni-gu-ma, the wife (sister?) of Nā-ro-pa. Its main instructions passed through the Jo-naṅ-pa order, which was made famous by Śes-rab-rgyal-mtshan (1296–1361) and counted among its followers and sympathizers such illustrious figures as 'Ba-ra-ba Rgyal-mtshan-dpal-bzaṅ (1310–1391); Thaṅ-stoṅ-rgyal-po (1385–1464), noted for his construction of iron chain bridges and who became the patron saint of the theater under the nickname "the Madman of the Empty Valley"; and the historian Tāranātha (b. 1575). Its distinctive philosophical position, partly based on the syncretistic *Kālacakra Tantra,* became the target of Dge-lugs-pa intolerance. The Dge-lugs-pa ruthlessly destroyed or converted the Jo-naṅ-pa monasteries into Dge-lugs-pa monasteries and even burned the books of the Jo-naṅ-pa school.

Two other ascetic orders that originated in the philosophical and religious ferment of the eleventh and twelfth centuries were the Źi-byed ("pacifiers of suffering"), founded by a South Indian ascetic, and the Gcod ("cutting through the affective processes"), founded by Ma-gcig Lab-kyi-sgron-ma (1055–1145), a remarkable woman disciple of Pha-dam-pa. The order, which later divided into two lines, the "male" Gcod and "female" Gcod, still has followers in the western Himalayas.

THE DGE-LUGS-PA ORDER

This intellectual activity, which emphasized its Indian source of inspiration, lost its spiritual force and died away in the face of political power struggles between monasteries, feuds between noble houses, and growing Mongol and Chinese expansionism. Thus, the Karma-pas were eclipsed by the Sa-skya-pas, and these, in turn, by the Dge-lugs-pas who, through the intervention of Gu-śri Khan were given, in the person of the Fifth Dalai Lama, Ṅag-dbaṅ-blo-bzaṅ-rgya-mtsho (1617–1682), the authority to reign over all Tibet, although he had to accept a "governor" imposed upon him by his Mongol patron.

The Dge-lugs-pas consider Tsoṅ-kha-pa Blo-bzaṅ-grags-pa (1357–1419) to be the founder of their movement, which gained prominence through the determination of his ambitious and power-hungry disciples. Tsoṅ-kha-pa was the son of an official in the Kokonor region and in his youth studied under the most famous lamas of his time, but a lasting influence was exerted on him by the Sa-skya lama Red-mda'-pa, who had been a disciple of Roṅ-ston Smra-ba'i-seṅ-ge, and the Bka'-gdams-pa lama Dbu-ma-pa, who made him familiar with the teaching of Atīśa. At the age of forty he joined the Bka'-gdams-pa monastery of Rwa-sgreṅ, where he is said to have had a vision of Atīśa.

Tsoṅ-kha-pa earned his fame because of personal integrity. He was not an independent thinker; his noted *Lam rim chen mo* (The Great Exposition of the Stages on the Path), expatiating on Atīśa's *Bodhipathapradīpa,* is basically a voluminous collection of quotations from Indian texts that are either still extant in their original Sanskrit or long lost. Similarly, his *Sṅags rim chen mo,* purporting to deal with the mystical aspect of Buddhism, emphasizes a meticulous enumeration and description of ritualistic implements. Passed on to his followers, his doctrine was transformed into dogmatism with strong political overtones. A remarkable exception is the fifth Dalai Lam, whose wide-ranging interest included a personal concern for Rñiṅ-ma-pa forms of meditation; for this reason the Rñiṅ-ma-pas escaped persecution during his time. In 1408 Tsoṅ-kha-pa instituted the Smon-lam Chen-mo (the annual New Year ceremony of the Great Prayer), at the Jo-khaṅ temple in Lhasa, thought to have been built by Sroṅ-btsan-sgam-po. One year later he founded his own monastery of Ribo Dga'-ldan where he taught and wrote and supervised the fledgling community according to strict monastic rules. His two chief disciples founded two other monasteries that were to become famous, 'Bras-spuṅs in 1416 and Se-ra in 1419. However, it was Tsoṅ-kha-pa's own circumscribed interests that set the tone and the politcal direction of the Dge-lugs-pa movement, which from the outset came into conflict with the orders already stablished, in many cases themselves torn by inner strife. The political preoccupation of the Dge-lugs-pas climaxed in the succession of the various Dalai Lamas by means of reincarnation, an idea first developed by the 'Bri-guṅ-pas and Sa-skya-pas. Despite the mystique that surrounds this notion, as a device for preventing the wealth and power of the family or monastery from passing into the hands of others it was essentially too lucrative to be passed up by any one order—even by the Rñiṅ-ma-pas, who had no political pretensions. Another aspect of this notion was that the declaration that the most gifted were "reincarnations" naturally enhanced the intellectual standard of the establishment to which they were attached. On the whole, this ingenious device worked very well. [*See also the biography of Tsoṅ-kha-pa*]

THE RÑIṄ-MA-PA ORDER

As already noted, the most remarkable figure in the Rñiṅ-ma tradition is Padmasambhava, who is credited with having written the first *lam rim* text, the *Gsaṅ sṅags lam gyi rim pa rin po che gsal ba'i sgron me,* an explanation of the experiential character of Buddhism. This little work belongs to the group of works that Padmasambhava is said to have hidden in order that they might be rediscovered at propitious times. This kind of literature is known as *gter ma* ("hidden treasures"). Many of these works are certainly apocryphal, but many others are adaptations of genuine documents; examples of this latter category are the *Bka' thaṅ lde lṅa* and the *Padma thaṅ-yig,* which, though it was constantly rewritten, contains the testament of Khri-sroṅ-lde-btsan. It should be noted that the term *gter ma* does not merely refer to texts concealed in caves or under rocks, but also to what a person might bring out of the hidden recesses of his mind and thus to what can be described as contributing to the development of thought and innovative ideas. Such "discoveries" began at a very early stage, with Saṅs-rgyas-bla-ma (c. 1000–1080), the first 'discoverer' *(gter ston).* Other notable "discoverers" were Ñaṅ-ral Ñi-ma-'od-zer (1124–1192), ruler of Ñaṅ; Guru Chos-kyi-dbaṅ-phyug (1212–1270 or 1273) and his wife Jo-mo Sman-mo (1248–1283); Orgyan Gliṅ-pa (1323–c. 1360), and Ratna Gliṅ-pa (1403–1479), collector and compiler of the *Rñiṅ ma rgyud 'bum,* which Bu-ston had excluded from his codification of the Bka'-'gyur and Bstan-'gyur. In this connection, Dṅos-grub-rgyal-mtshan, also known as Rig-'dzin Rgodkyi-ldem-'phru-can (1337–1408), a representative of the northern *gter ma* tradition, must be mentioned; the southern tradition is linked with Lo-chen Dharma-śrī (1654–1717), younger brother of Gter-bdag Gliṅ-pa (1646–1714) of the monastery of Smin-grol-gliṅ, which was supported by the fifth Dalai Lama. This monastery and the monastery of Rdo-rje-brag, the seat of the northern tradition, were both destroyed during the Dzungar revolt of 1717–1718 in which Lo-chen Dharma-śrī was murdered.

As I have mentioned above, Roṅ-zom Chos-kyi-bzaṅ-po represents the Rdzogs-chen line of thought. But the most outstanding representative is Kloṅ-chen Rab-'byams-pa (1308–1363/64). To this day Kloṅ-chen has remained a lone figure, unmatched in the lucidity of his presentation, a poet in his own right, who for all his erudition is never pedantic but always thought-provoking. His *Mdzod bdun* (Seven Treasures) and *Skor gsum gsum* (Three Sets with Three Members Each) are indispensable for the understanding of Rdzogs-chen thought and practice, and his *Sñiṅ thig ya bzhi,* a summary of Vimalamitra's teaching, is the very quintessence of Rdzogs-chen experience. It is not too much to say that Kloṅ-chen Rab-'byams-pa *is* Rñiṅ-ma and Rdzogs-chen philosophy. Since Rñiṅ-ma thought is essentially a process philosophy and religion in which experience is of utmost importance, it frequently came under attack by the various structure-oriented schools with their reductionist tendencies of accepting as authentic only that which came from India. Among those who countered these attacks, at least three authors stand out prominently. The first, 'Gos Lo-tsā-ba Gźon-nu-dpal (1392– 1481), wrote the *Deb ther sṅoṅ po* (Blue Annals), a masterpiece of historical writing and a critique of Bu-ston (who, as I have noted, was responsible for the exclusion of the Rñiṅ-ma *tantra*s from the canonical collection of Buddhist writings). Also important is Mṅa'-ris Paṇ-chen Padma-dbaṅ-rgyal (1487–1542), whose *Sdom gsum rnam ṅes* (The Definitive Gradation of the Three Statuses) is in its psychological insight far superior to Sa-skya Paṇ ḍita's *Sdom gsum rab dbye,* an attack on the *Dgoṅs gcig* theory propounded by Dbon-po Śes-rab-'byuṅ-gnas (1187–1241), a nephew of the 'Bri-guṅ-pa master 'Jigrten-mgon-po. The third major defendant of Rñiṅ-ma thought is Sog-zlog-pa Blo-gros-rgyal-mtshan ("repeller of the Mongols"; 1552–1624), who is supposed to have defended his area at one time against a Mongol invasion force (hence the epithet Sog-zlog-pa). He was most famous as a physician and for having written a history of Buddhism. The seventeenth century witnessed the foundation of five of the six greatest Rñiṅ-ma monasteries, Rdo-rje-brag (1610), Ka'-thog (1656), Dpal-yul (1665), Smin-grol-gliṅ (1676), and Rdzogs-chen (1685). Each played a significant role in the development of Rñiṅ-ma thought.

THE MODERN ERA

Among the intellectual giants of the eighteenth century, Ka'-thog Rig-'dzin Tshe-dbaṅ-nor-bu (1698–1755) must be mentioned. He was not content with merely repeating what secondary sources claimed to be authoritative, but attempted to go back to the original sources, often reaching startling conclusions. His main interests were history and geography. No less important is 'Jigs-med-gliṅ-pa (1730–1798) whose major contributions are the *Kloṅ chen sñiṅ thig* practices, which he developed after having had a vision of Kloṅ-chen Rab-'byams-pa. Despite his wide interests, profoundness of thought, and remarkable scholarship, 'Jigs-med-gliṅ-pa never attained the brilliant organization and beauty of style that mark the writings of his model, Kloṅ-chen Rab-'byams-pa. Another important figure of this period was Gźan-phan-mtha'-yas (b. 1740), who stressed the importance of monastic rules (which he considered indispensable for education) and held that monks had an obligation to society. In this sense he was the first social reformer in Tibet.

The sense of a newly awakened social conscience in the spirit of Gźan-phan-mtha'-yas, together with the essence of *Kloṅ chen sñiṅ thig* teachings and practices, define the character of Rdza-sprul O-rgyan 'Jigs-med-chos-kyi-dbaṅ-po (b. 1808), better known to Tibetan tradition as Rdza Dpal-sprul or, as he liked to call himself, A-bu-hral-po ("the tattered old man"), who spent most of his life among the nomads. He specialized in the *Bodhicaryāvatāra,* a text that had always been a favorite with the Rñiṅ-ma-pas; their interpretation of the ninth chapter had aroused the ire of the Dge-lugs-pas, who in turn lost no opportunity to attack and vilify the Rñiṅ-ma scholars. Rdza Dpal-sprul's most significant contribution is his *Kun bzaṅ bla ma'i zhal luṅ,* a unique rational-mystical blend designed to introduce the profound *Rdzogs chen* teachings to a simple audience. Here one sees the new trend in education, whereby the teacher selected a number of Indian texts in their Tibetan translation and then helped the student to fully comprehend the texts in all their implications. This reorientation, as well as the inherent attempt to rise above sectarianism, became known as the Ris-med movement. It originated in eastern Tibet at Sde-dge, perhaps brought about in part by events surrounding the tragedy that befell the royal house of Sde-dge.

The fame of 'Jigs-med-gliṅ-pa had reached the ears of the young queen of Sde-dge. When she met him, a deep faith in him was born in her. 'Jigs-med-gliṅ-pa and his disciple Rdo-ba-grub-chen rapidly became the most influential teachers at Sde-dge. The honors bestowed on these Rñiṅ-ma-pa followers aroused the jealousy of the Ngor-pa lamas and their patrons among the aristocracy. When in 1790 the young king of Sde-dge, Sa-dbang-bzaṅ-po (alias Kun-'grub Bde-dge'-bzaṅ-po) died at the age of twenty-two while on a pilgrimage, he left a son and daughter behind. Their mother, Tshe-dbaṅ lha-mo of the Sga-rje family, became regent for her infant son. This princess was regarded as a reincarnation of Ngaṅ-tshul-byang-chub, the queen of Khri-sroṅ-lde'u-btsan and disciple of Padmasambhava. Her patronage of 'Jigs-med-gliṅ-pa and Rdo-ba-grub-chen led in 1798 to a rebellion in which the Rñiṅ-ma-pa faction was defeated. The queen and Rdo-ba-grub-chen, accused of having been the queen's lover, were first imprisoned and later exiled. A number of Rñiṅ-ma-pa partisans were executed or forced to flee. The twelve-year-old prince became the nominal ruler of Sde-dge and was placed under the tutelage of lamas who were hostile to the Rñiṅ-ma-pas. When he had secured his succession to the throne, he renounced the world to become a monk. While he restated the time-honored special relationship that existed between the ruling house of Sde-dge and the Sa-skya-pa school, he insisted that a commitment to tolerance and patronage of all schools should be the basis of the religious policy at Sde-dge.

The Ris-med movement counted among its members such illustrious persons as 'Jam-mgon Koṅ-sprul Blo-gros-mtha'-yas (1813–1899), a competent physician and the author of the encyclopedia *Śes bya kun khyab* and a unique nonsectarian collection of texts pertaining to spiritual training, the *Gdams ṅag mdzod;* 'Jam-dbyaṅs Mkhyen-brtse'i-dbaṅ-po (1820–1892), a master of Buddhist poetry; and, last but not least, 'Ju Mi-pham 'Jam-dbyaṅs-rnam-rgyal-rgya-mtsho (1841–1912), who wrote on every imaginable topic. There were, and still are, other figures of significance.

When the Chinese occupied Tibet in 1959, a move that probably was a preemptive strike against other aspirants, the initial policy was one of destruction. This policy has changed from time to time, however, and reports coming from Tibet are conflicting. What may be stated with assurance is that the political power that the monasteries once wielded is a matter of the past. In those monasteries where the lamas are permitted to continue to perform religious ceremonies, no other activities are allowed, which means that no intellectual support is forthcoming. While ceremonies play an important role in the life of a community, they are not the whole of religion; there is thus an intellectual vacuum. With the annexation of Tibet by China, a chapter in the history of Buddhism—although certainly not Buddhism itself—came to a close.

[*For further discussion of Tibetan Buddhist doctrine, see* Buddhism, schools of, *articles on* Tibetan Buddhism *and* Esoteric Buddhism. *The interactions between Buddhism and indigenous Tibetan religions are discussed in* Bon *and in* Himalayan Religions. *For an overview of the* siddha *ideal in Tibetan Buddhism, see* Mahāsiddhas. *The quests for "hidden treasures" are further discussed in* Pilgrimage, *article on* Tibetan Pilgrimage. *See also* Dge-lugs-pa *and* Dalai Lama.]

BIBLIOGRAPHY

The best readily available book on Buddhism in Tibet is Giuseppe Tucci's *The Religions of Tibet* (Berkeley, 1980), translated from the German and Italian by Geoffrey Samuel. This book also contains an exhaustive bibliography, although the Tibetan titles listed may be difficult to locate. Valuable material is also found in R. A. Stein's *Tibetan Civilization* (Stanford, Calif. 1972), translated by J. E. Stapleton Driver. In this book the Tibetan source material has been listed so as to be identifiable. Stein has also used Chinese sources. David Snellgrove and Hugh Richardson's *A Cultural History of Tibet* (New York, 1968) is very readable but is sketchy and politically oriented.

10 BUDDHISM IN MONGOLIA

Walther Heissig

Early Mongolian contacts with Buddhism are dated to the fourth century CE, when the activities of Chinese monks among the population of this border area are reported in contemporary Chinese sources. Buddhist influences spread as far as the Yenisei region by the seventh century, as evidenced by Buddhist temple bells with Chinese inscriptions found there. Another factor in the spread of Buddhism into Mongolia was the flourishing of Buddhist communities in the predominantly Uighur oasis-states along the Silk Route. Furthermore, the palace that was built by Ögedei Khan (r. 1229–1241) in Karakorum, the Mongol capital, was constructed on the foundations of a former Buddhist temple; some of the murals from this temple have been preserved. Sources for this early Buddhist activity are rather scarce.

Reports in Mongolian sources on the early spread of Buddhism shroud these missionary activities in a cloak of mysterious events that testify to the superiority of Tantric Buddhism over other religions during the reign of Khubilai Khan (r. 1260–1294). Contacts with the Sa-skya *paṇḍita* Kun-dga'-rgyal-mtshan (1182–1251) were established during Ögedei's reign, but Buddhism only gained influence with the Mongols after their expeditions into Tibet, which resulted in the sojourn of Tibetan monks as hostages at the Mongol court. The activities there of the lama (Tib., *bla ma*) 'Phags-pa (1235–1280) resulted in an increase in conversions to Buddhism; his invention, in 1269, of a block script led to the translation into Mongolian of great numbers of Buddhist religious literature, the translations often based on already existing Uighur translations. The legend that Chinggis Khan had previously invited the Sa-skya abbot Kun-dga'-sñiṅ-po (1092–1158) lacks proof.

In spite of the extensive translation and printing of Buddhist tracts, conversion seems to have been limited to the nobility and the ruling families. Judging from the Mongols' history of religious tolerance, it is rather doubtful that Buddhism spread among the general population on a large scale. Syncretic influences resulted in the transformation of popular gods into Buddhist deities and the acceptance of notions from other religions during this period.

After Mongol rule over China ended in 1368 the practice of Buddhism diminished among the Mongols, deteriorating into mere superstition or giving way once again to the indigenous religious conceptions of the Mongols and to shamanism. It was not until the sixteenth century that a second wave of Buddhist conversion began, brought about by the military expeditions of Altan Khan of the Tümet (1507–1583) into the eastern border districts of Tibet, which resulted in contacts with lamaist clerics. Within the short period of fifty years, beginning with the visit of the third Dalai Lama to Altan Khan's newly built residence, Köke Khota, in 1578, practically all of the Mongolian nobility was converted to Buddhism by the missionary work of many devoted lamaist priests. The most famous of these were Neyiči Toyin (1557–1653), who converted the eastern Mongols, and Zaya Paṇḍita, who converted the western and northern Mongols. Sustained by princes and overlords who acted according to the maxim "huius regio, eius religio," inducing the adoption of the new faith by donations of horses, dairy animals, and money, the population willingly or forcedly took to Lamaism. Shamanism was outlawed, its idols sought out and burned. The establishment of many new monasteries opened to a greater part of the population the opportunity to become monks, resulting in a drain on Mongolian manpower. The monasteries, however, became similar to those of early medieval Europe; they were the cradles of literature and science, particularly of Buddhist philosophy. By 1629 many other lamaist works were translated into Mongolian, including the 1,161 volumes of the lamaist canon, the Bka'-'gyur (Kanjur). Tibetan became the lingua franca of the clerics, as Latin was in medieval Europe, with hundreds of religious works written in this language.

During the Ch'ing dynasty in China, particularly during the K'ang-hsi, Yung-cheng, and Ch'ien-lung reign periods, the printing of Buddhist works in Mongolian was furthered by the Manchu emperors as well as by the Mongolian nobility. Donating money for copying scripture, cutting printing blocks, and printing Buddhist works were thought of as meritorious deeds. Works on medicine, philosophy, and history were also published and distributed. The spiritual life of Mongolia became strongly influenced by religious and semireligious thoughts and ethics. Sponsored by the K'ang-hsi emperor, a revised edition of the Mongolian Bka'-'gyur was printed from 1718 to 1720; translation of the Bstan-'gyur (Tanjur) was begun under the Ch'ien-lung emperor in 1741 and was completed in 1749. Copies of the completed edition (in 108 and 223 volumes, respectively, for the Bka'-'gyur and Bstan-'gyur) were given as imperial gifts to many monasteries throughout Mongolia.

In the eighteenth century elements of indigenous Mongolian mythology were incorporated into a national liturgy composed entirely in Mongolian. A century later there were about twelve hundred lamaist temples and monasteries in Inner Mongolia and more than seven hundred in the territory of the present-day Mongolian People's Republic. More than a third of the entire male population of Mongolia belonged to the clergy. The monasteries, possessing their own economic system and property, formed a separate administrative and political organization. In the twentieth century the decline of monasteries and Lamaism was brought about by inner strife and a changing moral climate as well as by political movements and new ideologies. Only recently have some monasteries been reopened in the Mongolian parts of China, in the Mongolian People's Republic, and in Buriat-Mongolia in the U.S.S.R., but the question of whether the younger members of the population will embrace the faith again remains open.

[*See also* Mongol Religions.]

BIBILIOGRAPHY

Heissig, Walther. *Die Pekinger lamaistischen Blockdrucke in mongolischer Sprache.* Wiesbaden, 1954.

Heissig, Walther. "Zur geistigen Leistung der neubekehrten Mongolen des späten 16. und frühen 17. Jahrhunderts." *Ural-Altaische Jahrbücher* 26 (1954): 101–116.

Heissig, Walther. *The Religions of Mongolia.* Translated by Geoffrey Samuel. Berkeley, 1980.

Ligeti, Lajos. *Catalogue du Kanjur mongol imprimé.* Budapest, 1942–1944.

Tucci, Giuseppe. *Tibetan Painted Scrolls.* 2 vols. Translated by Virginia Vacca. Rome, 1949.

Tucci, Giuseppe. *The Religions of Tibet.* Translated by Geoffrey Samuel. Berkeley, 1980.

THREE

BUDDHIST SCHOOLS AND SECTS

11 HINAYANA BUDDHISM

André Bareau

Translated from French by David M. Weeks

The term *Hīnayāna* refers to the group of Buddhist schools or sects that appeared before the beginning of the common era and those directly derived from them. The word *Hīnayāna*, which means "small vehicle," that is, "lesser means of progress" toward liberation, is pejorative. It was applied disdainfully to these early forms of Buddhism by the followers of the great reformist movement that arose just at the beginning of the common era, which referred to itself as the Mahāyāna, or "large vehicle," that is, "greater means of progress" toward liberation. Indeed, the adherents of the Mahāyāna charged those of the Hīnayāna with selfishly pursuing only their own personal salvation, whereas they themselves claimed an interest in the liberation of all beings and vowed to postpone their own deliverance until the end of time. In other words, the ideal of the practitioners of the Hīnayāna was the *arhat* (Pali, *arahant*), the saint who has attained *nirvāṇa*, while that of the Mahāyāna was the *bodhisattva*, the all-compassionate hero who, resolving to become a Buddha in some far-distant future, dedicated the course of his innumerable lives to saving beings of all kinds. It would be more correct to give the name "early Buddhism" to what is called Hīnayāna, for the term denotes the whole collection of the most ancient forms of Buddhism: those earlier than the rise of the Mahāyāna and those that share the same inspiration as these and have the same ideal, namely the *arhat*. [*See* Arhat.]

Although it is directly descended from the earliest Buddhism—that originally preached by the Buddha himself—this early Buddhism is distinguished from it by the continual additions and reformulations of its adherents and teachers in their desire to deepen and perfect the interpretation of the ancient teaching. This constant, and quite legitimate, effort gave rise to many debates, controversies, and divisions that resulted in the appearance of a score of sects or schools. The actual, original teaching of the Buddha is accessible to us only through the canonic texts of these schools, texts that were set down in writing only about the beginning of the common era and reflect the divergences that already existed among these sects. Moreover, only a very small part of this vast canonic literature has survived, either in its original Indian language or in Chinese or Tibetan translation, and for this reason our knowledge of the doctrine taught by the Buddha himself still remains rather vague and conjectural. We do not possess all the documents necessary to recover it with certainty: even by compiling all the doctrinal and other elements common to the canonic texts we do have, we can reach, at best, only a stage of Buddhist doctrine immediately prior to the divergence of these schools. Their texts have been preserved for us by the mere chances of history.

The Indic word, both Sanskrit and Pali, that we translate here as "school" or "sect" is *nikāya*, meaning, properly, "group." In our context, it refers to a group of initiates, most likely monks *(bhikṣus)* rather than laymen, who sincerely profess to be faithful disciples of the Buddha but are distinguishable from other similar groups in that they base their beliefs on a body of canonic texts that differs from others to a greater or lesser extent. These differences between canonic texts involve not only their wording or written form but also a certain number of doctrinal elements and rules of monastic discipline. Despite the disaggregative pressures to which they were exposed (the same pressures, indeed, that created them), despite their geographical expansion and sometimes considerable dispersion, and notwithstanding the vicissitudes of history, which often posed new problems for them, most of these groups preserved a remarkable internal cohesiveness throughout several centuries. Still, schisms did occur within many of them, leading to the formation of new schools. Moreover, to judge from the documents we have—though these are unfortunately very scarce—it seems that relations among these various groups were generally good. Their disputes remained at the level of more or less lively discussion and degenerated into more serious conflicts only when involving questions of economics or politics.

Several factors account for these divisions and for the formation of these sects or schools. First of all, the Buddhist monastic community *(saṃgha)* never knew a supreme authority, imposing its unity by powerful and diverse methods, as was long the case in Christianity with its papacy. If we believe some canonic texts that seem to faithfully reflect reality, the Buddha himself was probably faced with several instances of insubordination on the part of certain groups of his monks and was not always able to overcome them. The oldest traditions, furthermore, agree that he did not designate a successor to head the community but only counseled his followers to remain faithful to his Doctrine (Dharma). This was a fragile defense against the forces that tried to break up the community once it was "orphaned" by the death of its founder.

For at least five centuries, the Buddha's teaching was actually preserved by oral transmission alone, very probably in different, though related, dialects. This, and the absence of an authoritative ecclesiastical hierarchy in the *saṃgha*, constitute two obvious sources of progressive distortion and alteration of the message left by the Blessed One to his immediate disciples. Furthermore, this message was not entirely clear or convincing to everyone it addressed, leading Buddhist preachers to furnish explanations and interpretations of the teaching. Finally, the teaching given by the Buddha was far from a complete system containing solutions to all the problems that might occur to the minds of people as diverse as those it was destined to reach. Thus, monks and lay disciples, as well as people outside Buddhism but curious and interested in its doctrine—brahman opponents, Jains, and others—easily found numerous flaws, errors, and contradictions in the teaching. These troubled the *saṃgha* but pleased those who were determined to refute or discredit it. Although the Buddhist preachers who improvised answers to these varied questions and objections were guided by what they knew and understood of the Buddha's teaching, their attempts expanded upon the original teaching and at the same time inevitably created new causes for differences and disputes within the heart of the community itself.

According to some eminent scholars, we must distinguish Buddhist "sects" from "schools." Sects, under this interpretation, were invariably born from serious dissent over issues of monastic discipline. Such dissent resulted in a fracturing of the community, a *saṃghabheda*, or schism, the participants in which ceased to live together or carry on a common religious life. By contrast, schools were differentiated by divergences of opinion on doctrinal points, but their dissension in these matters never gave rise to actual schisms or open hostility. This interpretation is certainly attractive, but it must be mitigated somewhat by the recognition that the actual situation prevailing between the various communities of the early church was somewhat more complex and variable than that indicated by the theory advanced here.

ORIGIN AND RELATIONSHIP OF THE SECTS AND SCHOOLS

All the documents from which we can draw information about the origin of the early Buddhist groups were written after the beginning of the common era and are therefore unreliable. Nevertheless, since the oldest of these texts generally agree on the main points, we can attempt to restore with a certain amount of confidence the common tradition from which they derive. This should provide a fairly accurate reflection of the true interrelationships among the sects and schools.

The first division of the community probably occurred toward the middle of the fourth century BCE, some time after the council of Vaiśālī but having no direct connection with this event, the claims of the Sinhala (Theravāda) tradition notwithstanding. The schism was probably caused by a number of disagreements on the nature of the *arhat*s, who, according to some authorities, retained imperfections even though they had attained *nirvāṇa* in this world. Because they were more numerous, the supporters of these ideas formed a group called the Mahāsāṃghikas, "those of the larger community"; their opponents, who claimed to remain faithful to the teaching of the Buddha's first disciples and denied that the *arhat* could retain any imperfections, took the name Sthaviravādins, "those who speak as the elders" or "those who teach the doctrine of the old ones."

Each of these two groups were then, in turn, divided progressively into several sects or schools. Although we are in little doubt about their origins as Mahāsāṃghikas or Sthaviravādins, we often do not know precisely how these subsequent sects were linked with the first two groups, nor do we know the circumstances or time in which they appeared. We are particularly bereft of information about the sects and schools that arose directly or indirectly from the Mahāsāṃghika.

Among the groups that developed from the Mahāsāṃghika were the Ekavyāvahārika, then the Gokulika, and finally the Caitika schools. The Ekavyāvahārikas probably gave rise, in turn, to the Lokottaravādins, but it may be that the Lokottaravādins were simply a form taken by the Ekavyāvahārikas at a particular time because of the evolution of their doctrine. From the Gokulikas came the Bahuśrutīyas and the Prajñaptivādins. At least a part of the Caitika school settled in southern India, on the lower Krishna River, shortly before the beginning of the common era. From them two important sects soon arose: the Pūrvaśailas and the Aparaśailas, then a little later the Rājagirikas and the Siddhārthikas. Together, the four sects formed Andhraka group, which took its name from the area (Andhra) where they thrived during the first few centuries CE.

The Sthaviravāda group seems to have remained united until about the beginning of the third century BCE, when the Vātsīputrīyas, who maintained the existence of a quasi-autonomous "person" *(pudgala),* split off. A half century later, probably during the reign of Aśoka (consecrated c. 268 BCE), the Sarvāstivādins also separated from the non-Vātsīputrīya Sthaviravādins and settled in northwest India. This time the dispute was over the Sarvāstivādin notion that "everything exists" *(sarvam asti).* In the beginning of the second century, the remaining Sthaviravādins, who appear to have taken at this time the name Vibhajyavādins, "those who teach discrimination," to distinguish themselves from the Sarvāstivādins, found themselves divided once again. Out of this dispute were born the Mahīśāsakas and the Dharmaguptakas, who opposed each other over whether the Buddha, properly speaking, belonged to the monastic community and over the relative value of offerings made to the Blessed One and those made to the community. At an unknown date about the beginning of the common era four new groups sprang from the Vātsīputrīyas: the Dharmottarīyas, the Bhadrayānīyas, the Ṣaṇṇagarikas, and the Sammatīyas. The Sammatīyas, who were very important in Indian Buddhism, later gave rise to the Avantaka and the Kurukulla schools. One group broke from the Sarvāstivādins: the Sautrāntikas, who can be identified with the Dārṣṭāntikas and the Saṃkrāntivādins.

Some of the Vibhajyavādins settled in southern India and Lanka in the mid-third century BCE and seem to have maintained fairly close relations for some time with the Mahīśāsakas, whose presence is attested in the same area. Adopting Pali as a canonical language and energetically claiming their teaching to be the strict orthodoxy, they took the name Theravādins, a Pali form of the Sanskrit Sthaviravādins. Like the Sthaviravādins, they suffered from internal squabbles and divisions: some years before the common era, the Abhayagirivāsins split from the Mahāvihāras, founded at the time of the arrival of Buddhism in Lanka; later, in the fourth century, the Jetavanīyas appeared.

Finally, three sects derived from the Sthaviravādins present some problems regarding their precise relationship and identity. The Kāśyapīyas, whose basic position was a compromise between those of the Sarvāstivādins and the Vibhajyavādins, apparently broke from the latter shortly after the split that created the Sarvāstivāda and Vibhajyavāda *nikāyas*. More mysterious are the Haimavatas, about whom the facts are both scarce and contradictory. As for the Mūlasarvāstivādins, or "radical Sarvāstivādins," they appeared suddenly at the end of the seventh century with a huge "basket of discipline" (Vinaya Piṭaka) in Sanskrit, much different in many respects from that of the earlier Sarvāstivādins. It is impossible to determine exactly what connection the Mūlasarvāstivādins had with the Sarvāstivādins.

Except for a few of the more important of these sects and schools—such as the Theravādins, who left us the treasure of their celebrated Sinhala chronicles—we know nothing of the history of these different groups. Their existence is nevertheless assured, thanks to the testimony of a fair number of inscriptions and other substantial documents. To judge from the information given by Hsüan-tsang and I-ching, by the time they made their long visits to India in the seventh century, most of the sects had already disappeared. Of all the many groups descended from the original Mahāsāṃghikas, only the Lokottaravādins were still numerous and thriving, but

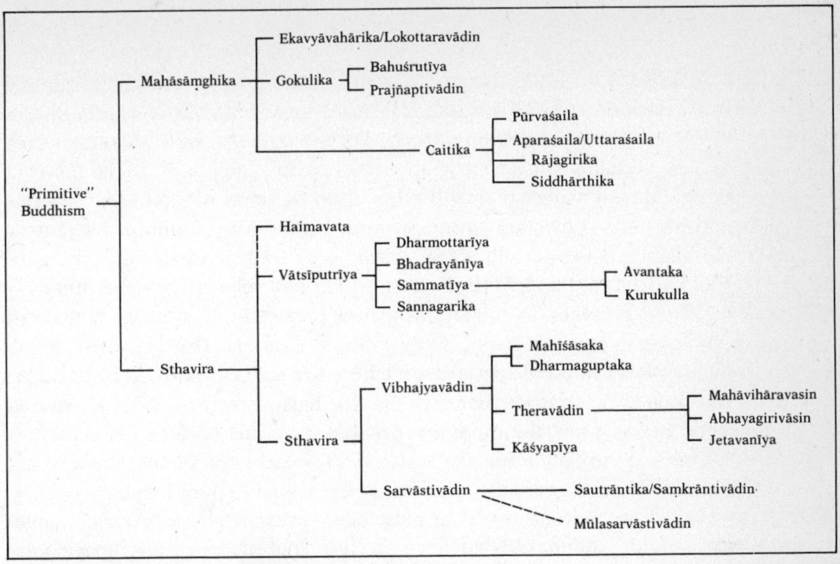

FIGURE 1: Filiation of the Hīnayāna Sects

only in a very specific location, Bamian (Bāmiyān, in present-day Afghanistan). (See figure 1.)

Here arises an important question, one whose answer is still uncertain: what connections existed between these early Buddhist sects and schools, known as Hīnayāna, and the groups formed by the followers of the Mahāyāna? Were any of them—in particular those of Mahāsāṃghika origin—converted in large numbers to the Mahāyāna, or did they perhaps give birth to it through the natural evolution of their doctrine? Should we interpret in this sense the expression Mahāyāna-Sthaviravādin, which Hsüan-tsang used to refer to numerous Buddhist communities he encountered throughout India, and deduce from it that their followers were Sthaviravādins converted to the Mahāyāna? Or did believers of both groups live together, without mingling, in the areas where they were found? This second interpretation strikes one as more satisfactory; nevertheless, the first cannot be rejected definitively.

GEOGRAPHICAL DISTRIBUTION

Two types of records inform us about the geographical distribution of the sects and schools: inscriptions and the reports of a number of Chinese pilgrims who came to India. Numbering only a few tens and ranging in time between the second century BCE and the sixth century CE, the inscriptions that mention early sects give us only spotty and very insufficient data. Although they may actually attest to the presence of a given group in a specific place at a particular date, they leave us completely ignorant about the presence or absence of this sect in other places and at other times. The information supplied by the Chinese travelers, principally Hsüan-tsang and to a lesser extent I-ching, is incomparably more complete, but it is valid only for the seventh century, when their journeys took place.

The study of these two kinds of sources—like that of the Sinhala chronicles, which are concerned mostly with Sri Lankan Buddhism—reveals some important general features about the early Buddhist schools. None of the groups was present everywhere throughout India and its neighboring countries; on the other hand, no area was the exclusive domain of any one group. For reasons that unfortunately nearly always escape us, certain groups were in the majority in some places, in the minority in others, and completely absent in still others but, as far as we can tell, coexisted in varying proportions with other groups wherever they were found. For example, in a number of places—especially those that history or legend made holy in the eyes of Buddhist devotees and were important places of pilgrimage—the monks of various sects lived together in neighboring monasteries and often venerated the same sacred objects—topes (*stūpa*s), Bodhi trees, and others. This was the case not only in the holy places in the Ganges Basin, where the major events in the Buddha's life occurred, but also far from there, in Sāñchī, Karlī, Amarāvatī,Nāgārjunikoṇḍa, and elsewhere. In Sri Lanka, the three great monasteries that became the centers of the three subsects of the Theravāda, the Mahāvihāra, the Abhayagiri, and the Jetavana, were located on the outskirts of the island's ancient capital, Anurādhapura.

All of the sects and schools seem to have been present in the middle Ganges Basin, which is easily understandable since the principal places of pilgrimage were located there. The more important ones, which originatedin both the Mahāsāṃghika and Sthaviravāda groups, also appear to have coexisted in eastern India, Bengal, and nearby areas, at least in the seventh century, as reported by both Hsüan-tsang and I-ching.

The Theravādins always dominated most of Sri Lanka and still do today. In the eleventh century, they also largely converted the Burmese, followed a little later by the people of Thailand, Cambodia, and Laos, where they continue to exercise religious dominion today. In the seventh century, the Vibhajyavāda Sthaviravādins, who were very close, if not identical, to the Theravādins, likewise controlled all the Tamil country, the part of India nearest to Sri Lanka, and were also extremely numerous in the coastal region north of Bombay and near Buddhist holy places on the Ganges from which people embarked on journeys to Lanka and southern India.

Very little is known about the location of the sects most closely related to these. The presence of the Mahīśāsakas is recorded both in the Indian northwest, on the banks of the Krishna, and in Sri Lanka; that of the Dharmaguptakas in the Indian northwest only; and that of the Kāśyapīyas mostly in the Indian northwest but also around Bombay. The Sarvāstivādins were clearly in a majority over all of northwest India, from the upper Ganges Basin to Kashmir, from the mid-third century BCE to at least the seventh century CE.

In the seventh century, the Sammatīyas formed the sect comprising the largest number of monks and generally controlled all of western India, from the middle Indus Valley to southeast of Bombay. They were also very numerous throughout the Ganges Basin and in eastern India. Several inscriptions testify to the presence, at the beginning of the common era, of Dharmottarīyas and Bhadrayānīyas in the area of Bombay.

Data concerning the Mahāsāṃghika proper, and most of the sects that developed from it, are rare and widely scattered. We know for certain that the Mahāsāṃghika existed in northwestern India, around Bombay and on the banks of the lower Krishna. Caitikas also inhabited these last two areas but primarily the second, where

Bahuśrutīyas also resided. By the seventh century, the Lokottaravādins had made Bamian, in the heart of present-day Afghanistan, one of the main centers of Buddhism in the Indo-Iranian realms and were still very numerous there, as Hsüan-tsang reports. The Pūrvaśailas, Aparaśailas, Rājagirikas, and Siddhārtikas prospered during the first centuries of the common era in the lower Krishna Valley, which they covered with magnificent monuments, but by the beginning of the seventh century they had almost disappeared.

MAJOR DOCTRINAL DIFFERENCES

We are well acquainted with the principal doctrinal differences that gave rise to many of these schools, the basic ideas that distinguish them, and the reactions and rebuttals the various sects offered each other. In most cases, though, and particularly with regard to the apparently less important sects, our information is unfortunately too vague, and sometimes even contradictory or nonexistent, to tell us anything about the specifics of their doctrine.

Although many questions divided all or some of the schools, they did not provoke the formation of new sects. These debates were sometimes very important for the evolution of Buddhism as a whole. Often, various of the early sects that we might expect to hold similar views given their genesis in fact adopted doctrinal opinions at great variance with one another. Thus, there often came about, among schools with similar opinions on specific questions, entirely different regroupings from those one would expect in light of their traditional relationships. Let us first examine the fundamental ideas that appear to have brought about the formation of the principal sects.

The Mahāsāṃghikas probably separated from the Sthaviravādins over the belief that certain *arhats*, although they had attained *nirvāṇa* in this world, could be subject to nocturnal defilements as a result of erotic dreams; that they still harbored vestiges of ignorance; that they had areas of doubt on matters outside Buddhist doctrine; that they could be informed, indeed saved, by other people; and, finally, that they utter certain words when they meditated on the Path of Liberation. The Sthaviravādins denied these five possibilities, arguing that the *arhat* is completely free of all imperfections.

The Vātsīputrīyas and the schools that later developed from them, the Sammatīyas and others, believed in the existence of a "person" *(pudgala)* who is neither identical to the five aggregates (*skandhas*) that make up the living being nor different from them; neither within these five aggregates nor outside them. Although differing from the Brahmanic "soul" *(ātman),* denied unanimously by Buddhist doctrine, this "person" lives on from one existence to the next, thus ensuring the continuing identities of the agent of an act and of the being who suffers its effects in this life or the next. All the other schools rejected this hypothesis, maintaining the logical impossibility of conceptualizing this "person" and seeing in it simply a disguised form of the *ātman*.

The Sarvāstivādins claimed that "everything exists" *(sarvam asti),* that is, that the past and the future have real and material existence. This belief enabled them to explain several phenomena that were very important to Buddhists: the act of consciousness, which is made up of several successive, individual mental actions; memory or consciousness of the past; foresight or consciousness of the future; and the "ripening" *(vipāka)* of "actions" *(karman),* which takes place over a longer or shorter span of time, often exceeding the length of a single life. For the other sects, however, it was perfectly clear that what is past exists no longer and that what is to come does not yet exist.

The Kāśyapīyas, also called Suvarṣakas, maintained a position between these two, namely, that a past action that has not yet borne fruit exists, but the rest of the past does not. This approach, however, satisfied neither the Sarvāstivādins nor their critics.

The Sautrāntikas distinguished themselves from the Sarvāstivādins insofar as they considered the canonic "basket of sermons" (Sūtra Piṭaka) to be the only one to contain the authentic words of the Buddha, whereas the "basket of higher teaching" (Abhidharma Piṭaka) is the work of the Blessed One's disciples. According to some of our sources, the Sautrāntikas were also called Saṃkrāntivādins because they held that the five aggregates (*skandhas*) constituting the living being "transmigrate" *(saṃkrānti)* from one existence to the next; probably this should be understood to mean that, in their view, four of these aggregates were absorbed at the moment of death into the fifth, a subtle consciousness. It also seems that the Sautrāntikas can be identified with the Dārṣṭāntikas, who were often criticized in the Sarvāstivāda writings and apparently gained their name because of their frequent use of comparisons or parables (*dṛṣṭāntas*) in their discussions.

An important disagreement separated the Mahīśāsakas from the Dharmaguptakas. For the former, the Buddha is part of the monastic community *(saṃgha);* hence a gift given to the community produces a "greatfruit" *(mahāphalam),* but one directed specifically to the Buddha does not. The Dharmaguptakas, on the other hand, held that the Buddha is separate from the community, and as he is far superior to it—since it is composed only of his followers—only the gift given to the Buddha produces a great fruit. These two opposing views had considerable influence on the religious practices of early Buddhism.

The Lokottaravādins differed from other Mahāsāṃghika schools in holding that the Buddhas are "otherworldly" *(lokottara),* a word having several very different senses but which they employed loosely to attribute an extraordinary nature to the Buddhas. According to them, the Buddhas are otherworldly not only because their thought is always perfectly pure but also because they remain outside and above the world. Thus it would seem to be among the Lokottaravādins that we should seek the origin of Buddhist docetism, that is, the distinction between the real, transcendent, and infinite Buddha, the "body of doctrine" *(dharmakaya),* and the apparent Buddha, the "body of magical creation" *(nirmāṇakāya)*—a kind of phantom emanating from the real one. To rescue beings, the *nirmāṇakāya* becomes incarnate, taking on their form and thus seeming to be born, to grow up, to discover and preach the doctrine of enlightenment, and to finally die and become completely extinguished. The Lokottaravādins must have also extolled the extraordinary character of the *bodhisattva,* undoubtedly on account of their supernatural conception of the Buddhas. These singular notions lead one to believe that this sect played an important part in the formation of the Mahāyāna, whose teaching adopted and developed similar ideas.

As their name seems to indicate, the Prajñaptivādins were probably distinguished from the other schools that arose from the Mahāsāṃghika group because they taught that all things are mere products of linguistic convention *(prajñapti)* and, hence, are devoid of actual existence. One might see here the origin of the famous theory of the universal "void" *(śūnyatā),* which is one of the basic elements of the Mahāyāna doctrine and is the main theme, reiterated with the greatest insistence, of its oldest works, the first Prajñāpāramitā Sūtras.

Unfortunately, we do not know the basic premises of the other schools, whether they arose from the Sthaviravāda group or the Mahāsāṃghika. The data that have come down to us concerning a few of them, such as the Gokulikas (also called Kukkuṭikas), the Bahuśrutīyas, the Sammatīyas, and some others, are very doubtful, vague, or extremely obscure, even contradictory. For others, we possess no information at all.

As noted above, hundreds of controversies also set the various schools apart from one another without provoking new divisions of the community. Most of these debates apparently concerned only two or three sects and lasted for a short time—unless this impression is due solely to our lack of information. On the other hand, certain of these arguments affected, and even impassioned, a large number of schools for long periods, sometimes for centuries, as evidenced by the treatises and commentaries on canonic texts that have come down to us. In these more important controversies the distribution of the sects between the two opposing camps is often independent of their derivational connections. It may be that relations of good neighborliness and, hence, ties based on geographical distribution favored such doctrinal alliances. In any case, I will point out the most significant of these divergences of opinion, which are important features in the history of early Buddhist thought.

The Sarvāstivādins, the Sammatīyas, and the Pūrvaśailas firmly believed in an "intermediate existence" *(antarābhava)* that linked death and rebirth. This concept was rejected by the Theravādins and the Mahāsāṃghikas. The latter, along with the Andhakas and the Sarvāstivādins, maintained that the *bodhisattva* may be born in the so-called "evil existences" *(durgati),* even in the various hells, to lighten the sufferings of the beings who live in them. The Theravādins denied that this was possible because, in their view, of the automatic retribution consequent upon all actions, a retribution that completely determines the circumstances of rebirths. According to the Vātsīputrīyas, the Sammatīyas, the Sarvāstivādins, and the Pūrvaśailas, the *arhat*s could backslide in varying degrees and even lose *nirvāṇa,* but the Theravādins, Mahāsāṃghikas, and Sautrāntikas refused to accept this idea. The Theravādins, the Sarvāstivādins, and the Dharmaguptakas agreed that it was possible for the gods to practice the sexual abstinence *(brahmacarya)* of ascetics, whereas the Sammatīyas and the Mahīśāsakas judged this impossible. For the Theravādins and the Sarvāstivādins, there were only five fates (*gati*s), namely, those of gods, men, animals, starving ghosts (*preta*s), and the damned, but the Andhakas and the Vātsīputrīyas added another, that of the *asura*s, the superhuman beings who were adversaries of the gods (*deva*s) yet were not devils in the Christian sense.

The Mahāsāṃghikas, the Theravādins, and the Mahīśāsakas taught that the clear understanding *(abhisamaya)* of the Four Noble Truths *(catvāry āryasatyāni)* was instantaneous, whereas the Andhakas, the Sarvāstivādins, and the Sammatīyas believed that it happened gradually. So important was this dispute that it was still the central theme of the council of Lhasa (held in the eighth century), where Chinese and Tibetan Buddhist teachers opposed each other in doctrinal debate. The Sarvāstivādins seem to have been alone in denying that "thought" *(citta)* is inherently pure and contaminated only by accidental impurities, a belief held by the Mahāsāṃghikas, the Theravādins, and the neighboring schools.

The Theravādins, the Vātsīputrīyas, and the Sammatīyas recognized only one absolute, or "unconditioned" *(asaṃskṛta) dharma,* namely, *nirvāṇa,* but the majority of schools also considered empty space *(ākāśa)* an unconditioned *dharma.* Several of them taught that "dependent origination" *(pratītya-samutpāda),* the path *(mārga)* of enlightenment, and sometimes other entities as well, in particular the "suchness" *(tathatā)* or "permanence" *(sthitatā)* of things, were equally absolute and unconditioned. Thus, the ideas of these schools were quite close to those of the Mahāyāna.

Several important debates centered on the nature of the passions, more specifically, latent passions or tendencies *(anuśaya)* and active passions or obsessions *(paryavasthāna).* The Mahāsāṃghikas, the Andhakas, and the Mahīśāsakas set up a very precise distinction between them, while the Theravādins and Sarvāstivādins chose to see in them only two aspects of the same passions. For the Theravādins and the Sarvāstivādins, tendencies and obsessions alike were connected, or cofunctioned, with thought (*cittasaṃprayukta*), whereas for the Mahāsāṃghikas, the Vātsīputrīyas, the Sammatīyas, and the Mahīśāsakas, tendencies were unconnected, did not cofunction, with thought *(cittaviprayukta),* while obsessions were connected with it. As for the Andhakas, they held that obsessions and tendencies were equally separate from thought.

According to the Sarvāstivādins and the Vātsīputrīyas, ascetics of other, non-Buddhist beliefs *(tīrthika)* could, through their efforts, obtain the five lesser supernatural faculties *(abhijñā)* and thus work various miracles—perceiving the thoughts of others, recollecting their past lives, seeing the rebirths of creatures as conditioned by their past actions, and so forth. The Mahīśāsakas and the Dharmaguptakas, however, declared that the five supernatural faculties—like the sixth, the cleansing of impurities, that is, the attainment of *nirvāṇa*—could be acquired only by Buddhist ascetics treading the Path of Enlightenment.

The relation between "matter" *(rūpa)* and the mechanism of the ripening *(vipāka)* of actions *(karman)* also gave rise to disagreements. For the Theravādins, matter is independent of the ripening of actions, and it is not the fruit of this ripening. It is morally neither good nor bad but inherently neutral. In contrast, the Sarvāstivādins, Sammatīyas, and Mahīśāsakas taught that matter can be good or bad when it participates, through the body of man, in a good or bad act. Matter is also the fruit of ripening when it becomes the body—be it handsome or ugly, robust or sickly—received by a person at birth as a consequence of past deeds.

According to the Sarvāstivādins, the five forms of sensory perception are always associated with passionate desires (*rāgas*). The Mahāsāṃghikas and the Mahīśāsakas thought that they were sometimes associated and sometimes unassociated with them, while the Vātsīputrīyas rejected both these possibilities, declaring that the five forms of sensory perception are morally neutral by nature and thus can never be either good or bad.

LITERATURE

The literature of early Buddhism must have been very important in extent and interest because what has been preserved for us, even though it represents only a small part of the whole, is considerable. The great majority of this literature vanished with the sects that produced it; let us recall that only one, the Theravāda, still flourishes today in Sri Lanka and Southeast Asia. Most of the schools have left us nothing, save perhaps a few fragments, isolated *sūtras*, and other brief works in the original Indian language or more often in Chinese translation. Which sects they belonged to nearly always remains undetermined.

Roughly half of what has been handed down to us is in the original Indian language, in a more or less "hybrid" Sanskrit, in various Middle Indic dialects, and above all in Pali. It is in Pali that the body of Theravāda literature, which we possess practically in its entirety, was written. The remainder, of approximately the same size, has come down to us only in Chinese or Tibetan translations. The scope of what was preserved in the Tibetan version, as far as the Hīnayāna in particular is concerned, is much more limited than that of the Chinese translation and, moreover, is confined almost solely to works of the Sarvāstivādins and Mūlasarvāstivādins. In Mahāyāna literature, in contrast, the enormous amount of material translated into Tibetan is virtually equal to what was translated into Chinese.

Thus, it seems that a greater proportion of the canonical literature—properly speaking, that which belonged to the Tripiṭaka ("three baskets")—than of the postcanonical literature has been passed on to us. It comprises, primarily, the complete Pali Tipiṭaka, made up of its Sutta Piṭaka ("basket of sermons"), its Vinaya Piṭaka ("basket of discipline"), and its Abhidhamma Piṭaka ("basket of higher teaching").

The Sutta Piṭaka, in turn, is composed of five Nikāyas, or "groupings," bringing together the "long" *(dīgha),* "medium" *(majjhima),* and "grouped" *(saṃyutta)* sermons; those arranged according to number of categories *(aṅguttara);* and, lastly, the "minor" *(khuddaka)* sermons, the longest and most varied section of all. The *Khuddaka Nikāya* assembles the legends of the former "births" *(jātaka)* of the Buddha, legends recounting the "deeds" *(apadāna*; Skt., *avadāna)* of the great disciples, didactic stanzas *(gāthā)* attributed to them, a famous but anonymous collection of other instructional stanzas called the *Dhammapada*, and ten or so other equally varied works.

Like the other Baskets of Discipline that have survived, the Pali Vinaya Piṭaka essentially contains three parts. These provide detailed definitions and explanations of the numerous rules of discipline imposed on monks (*bhikku*s), those to be observed by nuns (*bhikkunī*s), and specific rules concerning the material life of both: the correct use of objects they were allowed to own, ceremony, sentencing of offenders, settling of disputes, and so on.

The Pali Abhidhamma Piṭaka consists of seven different works, in which the doctrine set forth in no particular order in the sermons (*sutta*s) is reorganized, classified systematically, and fleshed out at numerous points. One of these seven books, the *Kathāvatthu* (Points of Controversy), refutes more than two hundred opinions held by other Buddhist schools and in the process reveals the doctrines peculiar to the Theravāda.

Sadly, we do not possess a complete Tripiṭaka from any other early sect, but more or less significant parts of several of them have been preserved. Thus, five Vinaya Piṭakas have come to us intact: those of the Mahāsāṃghikas, Mahīśāsakas, Dharmaguptakas, Sarvāstivādins, and Mūlasarvāstivādins, all in Chinese translation, plus more or less extensive fragments of the last two in the original Sanskrit. We have an entire Tibetan translation of the Mūlasarvāstivādin Vinaya Piṭaka, which is much more voluminous and written later than the others. In addition, we have a detached portion of the Lokottaravāda Vinaya Piṭaka under the name *Mahāvastu* (Great Tale) in Hybrid Sanskrit. This is actually a traditional and partial biography of the Buddha, heavily encrusted with legendry.

The non-Theravāda sects used the term *āgama* ("tradition") for the four or five parts that made up their Sūtra Piṭakas, which correspond to the Pali Nikāyas. Five of these Āgamas, evidently complete, have survived in Chinese translation: the *Dīrghāgama* of the Dharmaguptakas; the *Madhyamāgama* of the Sarvāstivādins; the *Saṃyuktāgamas* of the Sarvāstivādins and the Kāśyapīyas; and, finally, an *Ekottarāgama* that most probably belongs to a sect derived from the Mahāsāṃghikas but different from the Lokottaravādins. There are also more than 150 isolated *sūtras*, nearly all preserved in Chinese and a few in their original Indian language, but it is generally impossible to determine what school they come from. No collection corresponding to the Pali *Khuddaka Nikāya* survives, but we do have the Chinese translations of some seventy works similar to those that make up the Theravāda collection, as well as the Indian originals of a number of others.

Two complete Abhidharma Piṭakas have survived in Chinese translation: that of the Sarvāstivādins (one part of this also exists in Tibetan) and one entitled *Śāriputraabhidharma,* which seems to have belonged to the Dharmaguptakas but was perhaps also influenced by the Mahāsāṃghika. Like the Abhidharma Piṭaka of the Theravādins, that of the Sarvāstivādins comprises seven works, but its overall structure is very different, as is its doctrine, although there are notable similarities between some parts of the two works. The *Śāriputraabhidharma,* which is made up of four main sections, differs even more from the Theravādin text. For the most part these three collections definitely postdate the first appearance of the sects that composed them and defended their own positions in them. The teaching given by the sermons in the various Nikāyas or Āgamas of the Sūtra Piṭakas, in contrast, presents a truly remarkable consistency, whatever their school of origin, and, thus, a great fidelity to the common early Buddhist base, predating the community's division into sects. The same is true for most of the monastic rules contained in the various Vinaya Piṭakas, which are distinguished mainly by details of secondary or minor aspects of the ascetic life.

The postcanonical literature was undoubtedly very important, but even less of it remains than of the canonic material, and it is more unevenly distributed. Luckily, we possess in Pali the greater part of what was written by the Theravādins—commentaries on the canonic texts, treatises on doctrine, collections of legends, and devotional poems. We have also the principal Sarvāstivāda treatises, several commentaries on these works and on the major portion of their Abhidharma Piṭaka, as well as a few other late works. Unfortunately, the postcanonic literature available to us from all the other schools is limited to a half-dozen works.

The whole series of commentaries in Pali on the Theravāda canonic texts was composed in the fourth and fifth centuries CE by Buddhadatta, Buddhaghosa, and Dhammapāla, who made use of ancient commentaries, now lost, in Old Sinhala. We also owe to Buddhaghosa, the wisest and most renowned of all the Theravāda masters, a substantial treatise entitled *Visuddhimagga* (The Path of Purity), in which the Mahāvihāra school's entire doctrine is set forth. Anotherfamous treatise is the *Abhidhammatthasaṅgaha* (Collection of Interpretations of the Higher Doctrine), written by the Sinhala monk Anuruddha about the eleventh century. Other, less important treatises of the Mahāvihāra school were composed by various authors between the fourth and fifteenth centuries. Each of these works was the subject of one or more commentaries, most of which have not survived. Only one non-Mahāvihāra Theravāda work—strangely, in Chinese translation—is extant: a large treatise called *Vimuttimagga* (The Path of Liberation), attributed to Upatissa, who must have lived some time before Buddhaghosa and was probably a master of the Abhayagiri school.

To the treatises may be added the *Lokapaññatti* (Description of the World), a fourteenth-century adaptation by the Burmese monk Saddhammaghosa of a lost Sanskrit work, and especially the well-known *Milindapañha* (Questions of King Milinda), likewise inspired by a lost work. This seems to have been a little Buddhist propaganda manual aimed at the Greeks and Eurasians, such as King Menander (Milinda), who lived in northwestern India in the second century BCE. Besides the Pali version, there are two Chinese translations of the *Milindapañha* that rather differ from each other and even more so from the Theravāda text.

The postcanonic Theravāda literature also includes instructional poems and collections of legends in verse or prose. Among the instructional poems are the *Anāgatavaṃsa* (History of the Future), in which the monk Kassapa recounts the life of the next Buddha, named Metteyya, and the *Jinacarita* (Story of the Conqueror), Medhaṃkara's account of the miraculous life of the historical Buddha. The *Rasavāhinī* (Transportress of Flavors), translated into Pali by Vedeha from an Old Sinhala poem, is a collection of some one hundred legends meant to encourage a life of piety.

However, it is its famous chronicles, a genre almost entirely abandoned in ancient India, that make Theravāda literature stand apart from that of the other sects. The series of the *Dīpavaṃsa* (History of the Island), *Mahāvaṃsa* (Great History), and *Cūḷavaṃsa* (Lesser History) records in verse the whole history of Sri Lanka, from its beginning to the end of the eighteenth century, from the very specific point of view of the "elders" (*theras*) of the Mahāvihāra, the principal Sinhala Theravāda school. Other chronicles recount, in grandiose verse style, the stories of sacred relics: the *Bodhivaṃsa* tells the story of the Bodhi tree, the *Thūpavaṃsa* that of the principal mound of Anurādhapura, and the *Dāṭhāvaṃsa* that of the Buddha's tooth.

The main works of the Sarvāstivādin postcanonic literature have generally survived in Chinese or Tibetan translation. Complete or partial Sanskrit originals of several of them have also been found.

Only two commentaries on the postcanonic literature of the Sarvāstivādins have come down to us. One concerns the rules of monastic discipline and is entitled *Sarvāstivāda-vinaya-vibhāṣā*; the other, called *Abhidharma-mahāvibhāṣā*, comments on the *Jñānaprasthāna*, the principal work of the Abhidharma Piṭaka of this sect. This *Mahāvibhāṣā* (Great Commentary) is an immense summation of the doctrine of the Sarvāstivādins or, more precisely, of their most important school, known as the Vaibhāṣika, "supporter of the *(Mahā-) Vibhāṣā*." It is one of the most voluminous works in all Buddhist literature.

The Sarvāstivādins left several treatises written in Sanskrit during the first few centuries of the common era. The principal and best known is the *Abhidharmakośa* (Treasury of Higher Doctrine), written by Vasubandhu in the fifth century and the subject of numerous commentaries, many of which are extant in the Sanskrit original or in Chinese or Tibetan translation. Vasubandhu was accused of holding Sautrāntika views by his contemporary Saṃghabhadra, a strictly orthodox Sarvāstivādin. Saṃghabhadra refuted these views in a large treatise entitled *Abhidharma-nyāyānusāra*

(Consistent with the Logic of the Further Doctrine) and in a long commentary on the didactic stanzas (*kārikās*) ofthe *Abhidharmakośa*. The Sarvāstivādins also composed a *Lokaprajñapti* (Description of the World) according to Buddhist ideas, which has survived in Chinese and Tibetan translations.

The other schools have left only Chinese translations of a few treatises and commentaries, often very short and of unknown origin. Among the commentaries, which all correspond to complete or partial Vinaya Piṭakas, we may mention the *Vinayasaṃgraha* (Collection of Discipline) by the Mūlasarvāstivādin Viśeṣamitra and the *Vinayamātṛkā* (Summary of Discipline), the sectarian affinity of which is uncertain.

All that remains of the literature of the Vātsīputrīyas and related schools, which must have been considerable, are the Chinese translations, sadly inferior and obscure, of two small treatises summarizing their teaching. The most important of these is entitled *Sammatīya-nikāya-śāstra* (Treatise of the Sammatīya Sect).

Two other works of the same type have also survived in Chinese translation, but although they are better translated and are much longer, their sectarian origin presents some difficulty. One, called *Satyasiddhi* (Realization of the Truths), written by Harivarman around the third century CE, teaches and defends the doctrine of a Mahāsāṃghika-derived school, probably the Bahuśrutīyas. The other is the *Vimuttimagga*, mentioned above, whose author, Upatissa, probably belonged to the Sinhala Abhayagiri school; its Pali original was recently rediscovered.

The literary genre of devotional legends in verse or prose was also a great inspiration to authors of all sects, most of whom remained as anonymous as those of the canonic texts. Some of these works recounted the life of the historical Buddha, embellishing it with numerous miracles for the sake of greater glory. Two of the three most famous were preserved by chance in their Indian originals. These were composed in Hybrid Sanskrit, which is to say greatly influenced by the Prakrit dialects: the *Mahāvastu* (Great Tale) and the *Lalitavistara* (Account of the Sport), both important sources for the development of the Buddha legend. The first is a detached portion of the Lokottaravāda Vinaya Piṭaka, but in scope, as well as in specific subject matter, it can be considered a distinct and, moreover, rather late work. The *Lalitavistara* was first compiled by the Sarvāstivādins but later revised by followers of the Mahāyāna. In contrast with these two, the *Buddhacarita* (Story of the Buddha) was written in classical Sanskrit by one of the greatest Indian poets, Aśvaghoṣa, who lived around the second century CE; only half of the Sanskrit text has been recovered, but the Chinese translation is complete.

The collections of legendary material recounting the edifying deeds of Buddhist saints, or the previous incarnations of these or the future Buddha, are numerous, whether in Hybrid Sanskrit originals or in Chinese versions. We shall mention here only the best known, the *Avadānaśataka* (Hundred Exploits) and the *Divyāvadana* (Divine Exploits).

NOTABLE PERSONALITIES

Be they Buddhists, brahmans, or otherwise, the Indians of ancient times had practically no interest in history as we understand it, with its concern for the exact recording of events, dates, names, and biographies of important figures in order to preserve a precise record of them. This is especially true for the history of Indian Buddhism and the lives of its great masters. With very rare exceptions, to us the masters are only names attached to one or more literary works or, much less often, to an important item or event in the history of Buddhism—such as an idea that was declared heretical, a dispute, or a council. Nearly always, we know nothing whatever of the lives of these people, including the regions where they were born or lived and the centuries in which they were active. Moreover, the scant information that tradition has preserved about them is either vague, contradictory, or obviously distorted by legend, obliging us to make use of it with great skepticism. Even the biographies of the principal Sinhala elders (*theras*) of the Theravāda sect, whose history is told at length and in detail by the chronicles of Sri Lanka, are hardly better known to us than those of the masters of other groups and schools of early Indian Buddhism. In any case, we possess infinitely less detail about the lives of these *theras* than about those of the kings, princes, and generals who studded the history of Sri Lanka and protected the island's monastic community for two thousand years. Nonetheless, these chronicles permit us to know the names of a much larger number of these Sinhala Theravāda elders than of the masters of other sects, and thanks to them we are generally informed with some precision about the time and place in which many of them lived.

Among the most noteworthy figures of the Theravāda, we must first point out the three great scholars to whom all of the commentaries on the Pali canon and several important treatises on doctrine are attributed. The most famous is certainly Buddhaghosa, author of the *Visuddhimagga*. [*See the biography of Buddhaghosa.*] According to tradition, Buddhaghosa was an Indian brahman from Bihar who converted to Buddhism, then probably came to live in the Tamil country and afterward in the Sri Lankan capital, Anurādhapura, during the reign of Mahānāma (409–431). Buddhadatta, who was, it seems, a little older than Buddhaghosa, was probably born in the Tamil country, on the banks of the Kāverī, and spent most of his life there, but he probably sojourned in Anurādhapura as well. Finally, Dhammapāla was probably also a Tamil, born in Kāñcīpuram in the late fourth century, and most likely lived mainly in his native land but also journeyed to Lanka. Thus, it would seem that in the early fifth century, Tamil India was an important seat of Buddhist—or, more precisely, Theravāda—culture, on a par with Sri Lanka and perhaps even more active.

The reign of Parakkamabāhu (Parākramabāhu) I (1153–1186), an especially prosperous epoch for the Sinhala Theravādins, was made illustrious by a number of scholar-monks. The most famous was Sāriputta, a pupil of Kassapa of Udumbaragiri, who had played a pivotal role in the reform of the community ordered by the king and was himself a great scholar. Sāriputta turned his residence, the new monastery of Jetavana at Polonnaruwa, into the major center of knowledge and Buddhist learning of his time. Author of several authoritative subcommentaries on canonic texts, highly esteemed grammarian and poet, he was as well versed in Sanskrit as in Pali and composed his works in both languages. Several of his many students became learned monks and authors of valued literary works, notably Dhammakitti, Saṅgharakkhita, Sumaṅgala, Buddhanāga, Medaṅkara, and Vācissara.

In modern times, mention must be made of one first-rank figure whose influence on the evolution of Theravāda Buddhism was both decisive and extensive. Prince Mongkut, the youngest son of the Siamese king Rama II, became a monk and, during the quarter-century that he spent in yellow robes, undertook a great reform of the community in his country. In particular, he founded a new monastic order, the

Thammayut, which observed the rules of discipline more strictly than did its contemporaries, but he also kept abreast of the social realities of Siam and enthusiastically studied the culture and religions of the West. Becoming king on the death of his elder brother, he ruled under the name Rama IV (1851–1868), completing his work and transforming his country into a modern state largely open to trade and external influence. He is one of the principal architects of the great reform of Theravāda Buddhism that took place after the mid-nineteenth century not only in Siam but also in the neighboring kingdoms and in Sri Lanka. This movement was characterized by a return to the sources of the religion, namely the Pali Tipiṭaka, and also by a necessary and rational adaptation to modern circumstances. [*See the biography of Mongkut.*]

The best-known figure of the Sarvāstivādins is certainly Vasubandhu, the author of the *Abhidharmakośa*. Unfortunately, our information about this great master is suspect and seemingly contradictory, so that his life remains a subject of debate. Is Vasubandhu the Sarvāstivādin identical with Vasubandhu the Yogācāra, the brother of Asaṅga? Did he live in the fourth or the fifth century of our era? Was he born at Puruṣapura (present-day Peshawar) into a brahman family? Did he live in Kashmir, and then Ayodhyā (present-day Fyzabad), where he probably died? No agreement has been reached on these or other, lesser points of his biography. [*See the biography of Vasubandhu.*]

We know even less about his principal adversary, Saṃghabhadra, except that he was Vasubandhu's contemporary, a Kashmiri, and a staunch defender of Vaibhāṣika Sarvāstivāda orthodoxy. As for other great teachers of this sect, to whom are attributed various interpretations of the notion of *sarvam asti* or the treatises that have come down to us in Chinese translation, they are hardly more than names to us: Vasumitra (one or several?), Kātyāyanīputra, Dharmaśrī, Ghoṣaka, Upaśānta, Dharmatrāta. . . . Indeed, the Sarvāstivāda's founder, Madhyāntika, who probably settled with his disciples in Kashmir during the reign of Aśoka, seems himself to belong more to legend than to history.

The founders of other schools are also nothing but names to us, and even these have been handed down: Mahādeva for the Mahāsāṃghikas, Vātsīputra for the Vātsīputrīyas, Uttara for the Sautrāntikas, and so on. We only know two or three other masters, whose names have been preserved by chance, such as Śrīlāta of the Sautrāntika and Harivarman, the author of the *Satyasiddhi*. Of Śrīlāta we know nothing more than his opinions, as these were criticized in Sarvāstivādin tracts. Harivarman was probably a brahman from the middle Ganges basin, who most likely lived around the third century CE and was converted to Buddhism as a follower of one of the Mahāsāṃghika sects, probably the Bahuśrutīya, to judge from the study of his long treatise.

EXPANSION OF THE SCHOOLS OUTSIDE OF INDIA

Owing to the pious zeal of the emperor Aśoka, from the mid-third century BCE Buddhism began to expand outside of India proper, southeastward into Sri Lanka and northwestward into what is now Afghanistan. Numerous important epigraphic and archaeological monuments show that it soon prospered in both these areas. From this evidence and from the Sinhala chronicles we know that the Theravādins very quickly became, and remained, the dominant group in Sri Lanka, but we do not know exactly which sects flourished at the same time—during the last three centuries BCE—in the mountainous areas of the northwest, then called Gandhāra and Kapiśa. It seems, however, that the Sarvāstivādins, traditionally believed to have originated in nearby Kashmir during the reign of Aśoka, began the conversion of these lands to Buddhism and were joined somewhat later by schools of the Mahāsāṃghika group.

A few very scarce inscriptions, but especially the reports of the famous Chinese pilgrims Hsüan-tsang and I-ching, as well as the numerous discoveries of Buddhist manuscripts in Central Asia, provide information on the presence of various early sects outside India. Sects were found in Southeast Asia, Indonesia, Central Asia, and China in the first few centuries of the common era, especially in the seventh century.

At this same time, the Theravādins had found their way into Indonesia, where the Sarvāstivādins or Mūlasarvāstivādins were a strong majority. These two groups were extremely numerous and nearly alone in all of Central Asia, and they also flourished in southern China, where the Mahīśāsakas, Dharmaguptakas, and Kāśyapīyas prospered as well. These last three sects thrived in Indonesia, and Dharmaguptakas were also found in eastern China as well as in Shensi Province. As for the Sammatīyas, they were in the majority in Champa, in the center of present-day Vietnam. Such is the information provided by I-ching.

The Chinese translations of three different works of early Indian Buddhist sects formed the basis of an equal number of distinctively Chinese schools, which were introduced shortly afterward into Japan. The oldest is known by the name Ch'eng-shih, which is the title of Kumārajīva's Chinese translation (411–412) of Harivarman's *Satyasiddhi*. The main doctrine of this treatise, which attracted and held the attention of its Chinese followers, distinguishes two truths: a mundane or relative truth and a supreme or absolute truth. It teaches that all things are empty of substance, not only the individual person made up of the five aggregates of phenomena, but also the whole of the external world. Thus, the teaching of this work would seem to lie between those of the Hīnayāna and the Mahāyāna or, more precisely, the Mādhyamika. The Ch'eng-shih school was in fact founded by two direct disciples of Kumārajīva, Seng-tao and Seng-sung, who each headed a different branch, one centered in An-hui and the other in Kiangsu. These two masters and some of their disciples composed many commentaries on the *Satyasiddhi* or, more exactly, on its Chinese translation, which helped make it widely known throughout southern China. The leaders of the Chinese Mahāyānist San-lun sect, who were faithful followers of the Mādhyamikas, vigorously combatted this teaching, insisting that its concept of the void was mistaken. Their attacks resulted in the decline of the Ch'eng-shih school in the mid-seventh century and in its disappearance shortly afterward. Still, in 625, a Korean monk introduced the Chinese translation of the *Satyasiddhi* and its teaching to Japan, but the sect, which received the name Jōjitsu (after the Japanese pronunciation of Ch'eng-shih), found less success there than in China and was quickly absorbed by the rival school of Sanron, the Japanese form of San-lun.

The second sect was called Chü-she, a transliteration of the Sanskrit *kośa*, because it was based on the famous *Abhidharmakośa* of Vasubandhu, translated into Chinese by Paramārtha in 563–567 and by Hsüan-tsang in 651–654. The Sarvāstivāda realism expounded in this treatise was not very successful in China, where Mahāyāna doctrines were then dominant; consequently, the Chü-she school died out in the late eighth century, when it was absorbed by the Chinese form of Yogācāra known as Fa-hsiang. Previously, as early as 658, two Japanese monks, Chitsu and Chitatsu, had introduced the sect to Japan, where it bacame known as the Kusha. There it had less success and longevity as an independent school than in China, for Chitsu and Chitatsu themselves were followers of Fa-hsiang, called Hossō in Japan. Hossō had already attained considerable importance, and it soon absorbed the Kusha school.

The third and final Chinese school derived from early Buddhism was quite different from the other two. Called Lü ("discipline"), it was established in the mid-seventh century by the eminent monk Tao-hsüan as a reaction against the doctrinal disputes that preoccupied Chinese Buddhists of the time. He maintained that moral uprightness and strict monastic discipline were much more necessary for the religious life than empty intellectual speculations. Consequently, he imposed on his followers the well-defined rules in the *Ssu-fen-lü*, a Chinese translation of the Vinaya Piṭaka of the Dharmaguptakas made by Buddhayaśas and Chu Fo-nien in 412. Although his school never had many adherents of its own, it had a clear and lasting influence on Chinese Buddhism. Thanks to the school's activities, the *Ssu-fen-lü* became, and remains, the sole collection of disciplinary rules to be followed by all Chinese Buddhist monks regardless of their school, including followers of the Mahāyāna. The school was introduced to Japan in 753 by the Chinese monk Chien-chen (Jpn., Ganjin), who was welcomed with open arms at the court of Nara. [*See the biography of Ganjin.*] Known by the name of Ritsu (not to be confused with a homophonous branch of the Shingon sect), it is still active in Japan today (it also existed in China early in this century) but no longer has many adherents.

However, the only early Buddhist sect to thrive after spreading outside of India is the Theravāda. Its lasting success (it still flourishes today) can be explained by the fact that it was established well before the common era in Sri Lanka, a relatively isolated region, and that it has almost always maintained a strongly preferential relationship with the island's political authorities and has known how best to profit from it. Much less certain was the extension of this phenomenon to a compact group of countries of mainland Southeast Asia from the eleventh century, a time when Buddhism, especially the early, so-called Hīnayāna Buddhism, was dying out throughout India itself. At that time, Hīnayāna Buddhism could claim only a very few followers, scattered among small and failing communities, in the whole vast territory of India. We can understand how the effect of such a happy chance could have seemed miraculous to Buddhist devotees.

This process began in Burma, in the mid-eleventh century, when Anorātha, who ruled the central and northern parts of the country, conquered the southern, maritime region, where Theravāda monks had recently converted the ruler. Anorātha, too, soon adopted the Buddhist faith of the Theravādins. Driven by religious zeal, he compelled all of his subjects to follow his example. From that time on, Theravāda has remained the religion of the majority of the Burmese people.

Two centuries later, when the Thai descended from the mountains to the north and took control of the entire country known today as Thailand, the same process took place. Their king converted to the Theravāda and exercised all his authority to promote its extension to the whole of the population.

In the following century, under circumstances that are still poorly known, neighboring Cambodia, where Mahāyāna Buddhism and Hinduism had flourished until then, became completely Theravādin in a short space of time and has remained so to the present day. The petty kingdoms of Laos, stretched out along the middle Mekong, were not long in following suit.

In contrast to what had happened in India, this distribution of Theravāda Buddhism among a number of different countries, which were (except for Sri Lanka) in close proximity to each other, helped ensure the sect's lasting prosperity. Indeed, when a monastic community in one of these countries found itself in difficulty or in decline, which happened a number of times here and there, the pious Buddhist king would ask for and receive help from another country's ruler, who would then send him a group of knowledgeable, respected monks to resolve the problems in question and restore the Theravāda to its full value and strength. Similarly, whatever reforms and progress were made in one country quickly spread to the Theravāda communities in others. Such was the case in the last century, when the prince-monk Mongkut, who became King Rama IV of Siam, instituted great transformations that allowed the Theravāda to adapt to the modern world at the same time that he carried out a return to its distant canonic sources.

[*For treatment of particular Hīnayāna schools, see* Mahāsāṃghika; Sarvāstivāda; Sautrāntika; *and* Theravāda. *Hīnayāna thought is treated in greater detail in* Four Noble Truths; Eightfold Path; Karman, *article on* Buddhist Concepts; Dharma, *article on* Buddhist Dharma and Dharmas; Pratītya-samutpāda; Nirvāṇa; Soteriology, *article on* Buddhist Soteriology; *and* Buddhist Philosophy. *For further discussion of Hīnayāna sectarianism, see* Councils, *article on* Buddhist Councils, *and* Saṃgha, *overview article. For the geographical distribution of Hīnayāna, see* Missions, *article on* Buddhist Missions; Buddhism, *articles on* Buddhism in India *and* Buddhism in Southeast Asia; Sinhala Religion; *and* Southeast Asian Religions, *overview article. For an overview of Hīnayāna literature, see* Buddhist Literature, *article on* Survey of Texts.]

BIBLIOGRAPHY

Aung, Schwe Zan, and C. A. F. Rhys Davids, trans. *Points of Controversy* (1915). London, 1969. A translation of the Pali *Kathāvatthu*, a text treating the doctrinal controversies between the various Hīnayāna sects from the Theravāda point of view.

Bareau, André. *Les sectes bouddhiques du Petit Véhicule*. Publications de l'École Français d'Extrême-Orient, vol. 38. Saigon, 1955. An exhaustive survey based on all available documents.

Bechert, Heinz, and Richard Gombrich. *The World of Buddhism*. London, 1984. This excellent work includes a discussion of schisms on page 82.

Ch'en, Kenneth. *Buddhism in China; a Historical Survey*. Princeton, 1964. See pages 129–131 and 301–303 for information on the Hīnayāna-derived Chinese sects.

Demiéville, Paul. "L'origine des sectes bouddhiques d'après Paramārtha." In *Mélanges chinois et bouddhiques*, vol. 1, pp. 15–64. Brussels, 1932. A masterfully annotated French translation of one of the principal documents on the subject.

Dube, S. N. *Cross Currents in Early Buddhism*. New Delhi, 1980. Interesting study of doctrinal disputes among early sects, but based primarily on the *Kathāvatthu*.

Dutt, Nalinaksha. *Buddhist Sects in India*. 2d ed. Calcutta, 1978. Good general description of the history and, especially, the doctrines of the Hīnayāna sects.

Fujishima Ryauon. *Les bouddhisme japonais: Doctrines et histoire de douze sectes bouddhiques du Japon* (1889). Reprint, Paris, 1983. This old book is the most complete description in a

Western language of Japanese Buddhist sects, particularly the three derived from the Hīnayāna.

Hajime, Nakamura. *Indian Buddhism: A Survey with Bibliographical Notes*. Hirakata, 1980. This large work brings into focus our knowledge of the whole of Indian Buddhism and contains an extremely rich and up-to-date bibliography. A long chapter concerns the Hīnayāna sects (pp. 90–140).

Lamotte, Étienne. *Histoire du bouddhisme indien: Des origines à l'ère Śaka*. Louvain, 1958. A large part (pp. 571–705) of this excellent work discusses early sects, their origins and distribution, Buddhist languages, and the sects' doctrinal evolution.

La Vallée Poussin, Louis de, trans. *L'Abhidharmakośa de Vasubandhu* (1923–1931). 6 vols. Reprint, Brussels, 1971. This French translation of the famous treatise includes copious notes and a very long introduction by the great Belgian scholar. It is rich in information on the doctrinal controversies that concerned the Sarvāstivādins.

Law, Bimala Churn. *A History of Pāli Literature*. London, 1933. Complete, very detailed description of Theravāda literature.

Masuda Jiryō. "Origins and Doctrines of Early Indian Buddhist Schools." *Asia Major* 2 (1925); 1–78. English translation, with notes, of the *Samayabhedoparacanacakra*, an account of the Hīnayāna sects and their main tenets.

Renou, Louis, and Jean Filliozat. *L'Inde classique*. Paris, 1953. Volume 2, pages 315–608, deals especially with the Hīnayāna sects, their literature, and doctrines. The collaboration of the Sinologist Paul Demiéville and the Tibetologist Marcelle Lalou is invaluable.

Shizutani Masao. *Shōjō bukkyōshi no kenkyū; Buha bukkyō no seiritsu to hensen*. Kyoto, 1978. The most recent work on the origin and evolution of the Hīnayāna sects. Detailed and complete study of literary and epigraphic sources.

Takakusu Junjirō, trans. *A Record of the Buddhist Religion as Practiced in India and the Malay Archipelago (A.D. 671–695)* (1896). Reprint, Dehli, 1966. English translation of I-ching's account of his pilgrimage to South and Southeast Asia.

Warder, A. K. *Indian Buddhism*. 2d rev. ed. Dehli, 1980. Treats Hīnayāna sects at length, offering interesting solutions to the problems they pose.

Watters, Thomas, trans. *On Yuan Chwang's Travels in India, 629–645 A.D.* 2 vols. London, 1904–1905. English translation of numerous extracts from the accounts of Hsüan-tsang's journey, with excellent commentary correcting most of the many errors of earlier translations (those of Stanislas Julien, Samuel Beal, etc.), which are today unusable.

12 MAHAYANA BUDDHISM

Nakamura Hajime

The Sanskrit term *mahāyāna* literally means "the great vehicle [to enlightenment]." It refers to a form of Buddhism that developed in northern India and Central Asia from about the first century before the advent of the common era, and that is prevalent today in Nepal, Sikkhim, Tibet, China, Mongolia, Vietnam, Korea, and Japan. Mahāyāna Buddhism was also transmitted to Sri Lanka and the Indo-Chinese peninsula, but it eventually vanished from South Asia.

The name *Mahāyāna* is rendered *theg pa chen po* in Tibetan, *ta-sheng* in Chinese, and *daijō* in Japanese. The meanings "greater, numerous," and "superior" are all reflected in the *ta* or *dai* of the Chinese and Japanese translations, for, according to Mahāyāna, its teachings are greater than those of the Hīnayāna tradition, and those delivered from suffering by Mahāyāna more numerous than those saved by the other, more conservative wing of the tradition. According to its devotees, the Mahāyāna is therefore superior to Hīnayāna. More objectively, it can be observed that when compared with Theravāda and other Hīnayāna forms, Mahāyāna is more speculatively ambitious, embraces a broader range of practices, some specifically intended to address the needs of lay practitioners, and is more frankly mythological in its conception of Buddhahood and the religious career that leads to it. Mahāyāna Buddhism also stresses altruistic attitudes and proclaims as its goal the universal enlightenment of all beings. Its scriptures were originally written in Sanskrit, but most of these have been lost; many, however, have been preserved in Tibetan and Chinese. (Works for which no attested Sanskrit title is available are identified here by the title of the translation.)

Origins

The origins of Mahāyāna are not yet entirely understood. Its first propounders seem to have been homeless ascetics who did not belong to orthodox *saṃghas* (Buddhist orders). Early Mahāyāna *sūtras* address among their audiences *kulaputras* and *kuladuhitṛs* ("good sons and daughters"), suggesting that lay men and women were also of some importance in the first Mahāyāna orders, which were probably entirely separate from the Hīnayāna orders. These Mahāyāna orders appeared in the second century CE in northwestern India, and the movement later spread to other areas. One such order, the Śiṣyagaṇa ("congregation of disciples"), seems to have devoted itself to altruistic activities.

The Mahāyāna movement probably began with groups of religious individuals whose activities centered around certain stupas. [*See* Stupa Worship.] These groups later became orders whose members, consisting of both clergy and laity, called themselves *bodhisattvas*, by which they designated as the goal of their practice nothing less than Buddhahood itself. They were led by preachers and reciters of scripture (called *dharmabhāṇakas*) and by practitioners of meditation. Thus, in time the early Mahāyāna orders moved away from the worship of stupas and the building of temples—activities stressed in the Hīnayāna *nikāyas* (what I have chosen to refer to here as Conservative Buddhism)—toward recitation of the *sūtras* (the sermons of the Buddha), an approach that had more appeal to (and was more practical for) the ordinary laity. The glorification of Buddhas and the magical character with which Mahāyāna endowed itself were also effective in the competition with the emerging *bhatki* movements of the contemporary Hindu tradition. [*See* Bhatki; Vaiṣṇavism; Kṛṣṇaism; Avatāra; *and* Śaivism.]

Epigraphic evidence and the dates of Chinese translations of Mahāyāna texts have been used by Shizutani Masao to distinguish between "Proto-Mahāyāna," a movement that did not use the appellation *Mahāyāna,* and the more self-conscious "Early Mahāyāna." (The first scripture to use the term *Mahāyāna* is the *Aṣṭasāhasrikā Sūtra,* dating in its earliest verses to perhaps the first century BCE but containing sections from later periods.) Shizutani designates the period 100 to 1 BCE as the incipient stage of Proto-Mahāyāna, 1 to 100 CE as its developed stage, 50 to 100 as the incipient stage of Early Mahāyāna, and 100 to 250 as the developed stage of Early Mahāyāna.

The development of the Mahāyāna *sūtras* began with the incipient Proto-Mahāyāna stage and culminated in about the seventh or eighth century. These *sūtras* as a group are often given the epithet *vaipulya* ("extensive, glorious"). Many are literary masterpieces, artfully created to produce their effects. They contain no information about when and where they were created, but they were probably produced not only in India and the northern part of what is now Pakistan but also in Central Asia, where the Buddhist orders were also sizable. Some *sūtra* manuscripts discovered in Central Asia are very early; those written on birch bark may date to the first century BCE or the following century. Some *sūtras* appeared first in Prakrit or in the languages of Central Asia (e.g., Tocharian and Uighur), but by the sixth century, when the *sūtras* were studied at the university at Nālandā, they had been rewritten in Sanskrit (with some lingering traces of Prakrit colloquialism). It was the adoption of Sanksrit as the official language of the Gupta dynasty in 320 CE that caused the shift from Prakrit. Nearly all the inscriptions on pre-Gupta monuments and tablets are in Prakrit, but almost all similar inscriptions made after the founding of the Gupta dynasty are in Sanskrit. Large numbers of Buddhist Sanskrit manuscripts have been discovered within the last hundred years at Gilgit (in Kashmir) and elsewhere in Central Asia. These, and others in Central Asian languages, are the basic material for modern study; their Chinese translations can be used for cross-reference. Significantly, the Sanskrit *sūtra* copies produced in Central Asia also differ from those discovered in Nepal.

Doctrinally, Mahāyāna Buddhism was not at first completely distinct from Conservative Buddhism. The *bodhisattva* doctrine, to which Mahāyāna owes its existence, can in fact be traced to pre-Mahāyāna Buddhist literature. The concept of the *bodhisattva* apparently emerged between the beginning of the first century BCE and the middle of the first century CE, after the carving of the Bhārhut sculptures and before the appearance of the early Mahāyāna scriptures. In fact, archaeological evidence from this period indicates that the *bodhisattva* idea preceded that of Mahāyāna itself: *bodhisattva* images have been found only in shrines of Conservative Buddhism that date from this time; none have been found at the sites of Mahāyāna structures. The various virtues emphasized in Hīnayāna (e.g., the *pāramitās*) were also appropriated by the Mahāyāna, but in their hands the virtues of benevolence *(maitrī)* and compassion *(karuṇā)* became central. [*See* Karuṇā.] Another, related notion that emerged as a major feature of Mahāyāna is the belief in multiple Buddhas; this too has its antecedents in pre-Mahāyāna belief.

Major Features

Mahāyāna Buddhism is characterized by a variety of doctrines, practices, and orientations that at once distinguish it from the Hīnayāna tradition.

WORSHIP OF MULTIPLE BUDDHAS AND BODHISATTVAS

In early Buddhism the term *bodhisattva* referred to the Buddha (or, later, to *a* Buddha) prior to the time of his enlightenment, including all previous existences during which he had aspired to become a Buddha. In keeping with the soteriology and cosmology of these early teachings, it was assumed that there was only one *bodhisattva* in any one world cycle. Later, this idea was elaborated and integrated into the Jātaka stories, tales of Śākyamuni Buddha's previous lives. A few Conservative Buddhists embraced the belief that there were many Buddhas at any one time, but this belief was most highly developed in Mahāyāna, where myriads of Buddhas are said to inhabit myriads of world systems simultaneously. [*See* Buddha.]

Some Mahāyāna *sūtras* enjoin adoration of all Buddhas in an equal manner (e.g., *The Sutra Enumerating Buddha's Names*) and some twenty-one *sūtras* extol recitation of the names of many Buddhas. Repeated utterance of the names of Buddhas and *bodhisattvas* is also encouraged in the *Nāmasaṃgīti.* Another *sūtra* (T.D. no. 427) describes invocations of eight specific Buddhas; in the *Ratnacandraparipṛcchā Sūtra* Śākyamuni calls for worship of ten Buddhas who dwell in Pure Lands in each of the ten directions, while the *Bhadrakalpasamādhi Sūtra* (one of twelve similar *sūtras*) extols the thousand Buddhas that are said to live in the present age and calls for the practice of eighty-four thousand "perfections" (*pāramitās*). This text seems to have been composed between 200 and 250 CE.

But it is not simply in their profusion that the Buddhas of the Mahāyāna differ from their Hīnayāna counterparts. Mahāyāna Buddhas enjoy many more superhuman and divine traits than does the single Buddha of the Conservative tradition. Nonetheless, they retain many of the same physical and spiritual characteristics. Glorification of and speculation on the nature of Buddhas led Mahāyāna practitioners to develop the theory of the "triple body" *(trikāya)* of the Buddha, in which the Buddha is conceived as having three aspects or "bodies": a cosmic body *(dharmakāya),* the ineffable Absolute itself; an "enjoyment" body *(saṃbhogakāya),* a body of magical transformation that the Buddha "enjoys" as the fruit of the merit generated through aeons of religious practice (often conceived as surrounded by a supernal region, a Pure Land, similarly generated); and the body that appears in living form to save people from suffering *(nirmāṇakāya).* Śākyamuni, of course, is such a Buddha (i.e., *nirmāṇakāya*) for our age. [*See* Celestial Buddhas and Bodhisattvas.]

In Mahāyāna Buddhism, the common hope for rebirth in a heaven often took the form of yearning for the Pure Lands of various Buddhas, where, it was believed, the Law was preached for the benefit of the beings born there. [*See* Pure and Impure Lands.] Akṣobhya Buddha's Pure Land in the east and that of Amitābha in the west appear in contrast throughout Mahāyāna scripture. The *Karuṇāpuṇḍarīka* (Lotus of Mercy) *Sūtra* describes the Padma wonderland of the Buddha Padmottara, whose life lasted for thirty ages of the world, but the text also responds to those *sūtra*s that praise Akṣobhya and Amitābha by praising the compassion that Śākyamuni exercises within this world. An important figure in this *sutra* is Mahākāruṇika Mahāśramaṇa, who saves living beings from suffering. A similar figure is the *bodhisattva* Vāyuviṣṇu, *avatāra* of the deity Viṣṇu.

The *bodhisattva* Mañjuśrī plays an important role in many *sūtra*s. One *sūtra* (T.D. no. 463) describes the efficacy of worship of Mañjuśrī at the moment of death. In another (T.D. no. 464), Mañjuśrī explains enlightenment; and elsewhere (T.D. no. 843) he demonstrates *ānimitta* ("formlessness") through magical power. In the *Acintyabuddhaviṣayanirdeśa* he explains *bodhisattva* practices. Mañjuśrī often appears with a counterpart *bodhisattva,* Samantabhadra. The association of Mañjuśrī with Wu-t'ai Shan, a mountain in China, was established by the seventh century and was widely known even in India. The *bodhisattva* Samantabhadra is often mentioned in conjunction with Mañjuśrī. [*See* Mañjuśrī.]

As in Hīnayāna Buddhism, the *bodhisattva* Maitreya was worshiped as a Buddha of the future, one who, at some time to come, will leave his present abode in the Tuṣita Heaven and be born on earth for the benefit of sentient beings. Devotees of Maitreya thus focused their aspirations on rebirth in Tuṣita and eventual descent to earth in his company. Three Maitreya *sūtra*s were especially esteemed in China and Korea: the *Mi-le ta-ch'eng-fo ching,* composed in the third century CE; the *Mi-le hsia-sheng ch'eng-fo ching (Maitreyavyākaraṇa* or *Maitreyasamiti),* also composed in the third century; and the *Kuan-mi-le shang-tou-shuai-t'ien ching,* composed at the end of the fourth century. In the *Maitreyaparipṛcchā* the Buddha Śākyamuni explains *bodhisattva* practices to Maitreya. The *Adhyāśayasaṃcodana Sūtra* tells how sixty *bodhisattva*s who had fallen into distraction and laziness are led into the presence of the Buddha by Maitreya, who seeks advice on their behalf. This *sūtra* is well known for the phrase, "whatever is well spoken is spoken by the Buddha." [*See* Maitreya.]

But the *bodhisattva* most adored throughout Asia is Avalokiteśvara, the "Lord Who Looks Down [with infinite pity on all beings]." His name appears as Avalokitasvara in early manuscripts. Some of his features are those of the Vedic deity Aśvin. Avalokiteśvara is regarded as a savior of suffering beings and his response to petitions for aid is immediate. The best-known scripture concerning his virtues is the twenty-fourth chapter of the *Saddharmapuṇḍarīka* (Lotus Sutra), which emphasizes the rewards in this world that he grants to believers and the virtue of helpfulness to others that he represents. In the *Gaṇḍavyūha,* his homeland is called Potalaka. In Pure Land Buddhism, he is Amitābha's companion and attendant. [*See* Avalokiteśvara.]

Chapters 22 and 23 of the Chinese version of the *Lotus Sutra* shows how another *bodhisattva,* Bhaiṣajyarāja ("king of the art of healing"), protects his worshipers and grants wishes. This idea was further developed in the figure of Bhaiṣajyaguru, who also became the object of intense adoration, and independent scriptures consecrated to him extolled his powers. One of these, the *Bhaiṣajyaguru-vaiḍūryaprabhāsa-pūrvapraṇidhānaviśeṣavistara Sūtra,* is concerned with benefits in this world as well as the future and describes paradises in both east and west. [*See* Bhaiṣajyaguru.]

But if there is one feature of the Mahāyāna *bodhisattva* doctrine that truly separates it from that of other forms of Buddhism, it is the Mahāyāna insistence that the goal of all religious practice is Buddhahood itself, making all those whose conceive of the aspiration to be liberated *bodhisattvas*, or future Buddhas. Mahāyāna practice thus begins with the formulation of this aspiration (*bodhicitta,* the "mind set upon enlightenment") in a vow *(praṇidhāna)* to become a fully enlightened Buddha and is articulated in a series of "stages" (*bhūmis*) leading to the goal. The conspicuous feature of this vow and practice, however, is the resolve of the practitioner to delay final liberation, to remain "in the world," as it were, until all beings have been saved. The Mahāyāna *bodhisattva* is committed to work ceaselessly for the benefit of other beings and to transmit to them the merit generated by his or her own religious practice. While a few *bodhisattvas*, some mentioned above, are frankly mythological in their conception, they represent, ideally, spiritual attainments accessible to all practitioners. In the words of one Mahāyāna scripture, the Buddha nature (i.e., enlightenment) is the endowment of all beings without exception. [*See* Bodhisattva Path.]

DISCIPLINES

There is no unanimously agreed upon code of discipline in Mahāyāna, reflecting the fact that it is institutionally less coherent than is Conservative Buddhism. But Mahāyāna distinguishes two ways of practice: the *śrāvakamārga* ("way of the disciples") for those who follow the Hīnayāna practices and the *bodhisattvamārga* ("way of *bodhisattvas*") for those who adhere to Mahāyāna values, particularly the intention to save other suffering beings. Those who practice the latter way are deemed worthy of worship and are relied upon because they have refrained from entering Buddhahood, preferring instead to dwell among the living in order to save them from their sufferings. The *bodhisattvamārga* was first described in pre-Mahāyāna works collectively called Avadānas. At first, these described *bodhisattvas* who resembled the person and character of the historical Buddha Śākyamuni, but later other qualifications for the *bodhisattva* were appended, namely, vows *(praṇidhāna)* and practice *(bhāvanā).* All *bodhisattvas* make the same basic vows, but some (e.g., Amitābha) add certain others that are unique to them. The privilege of becoming a *bodhisattva* is open to all who seek enlightenment; hence the *bodhisattva* ideal is accessible to every human being.

The basic institutional structure of the Conservative Buddhist order (specifically, the Vinaya, or monastic rules) continued to be observed in Mahāyāna, but Mahāyāna ethics set its orders apart from its Hīnayāna counterparts. [*See* Vinaya.] When the Chinese pilgrim Hsüan-tsang visited India in the first half of the seventh century, he found that some monks were specifically called Mahāyāna-Sthaviras. Some Mahāyāna *sūtras* prescribe ethical practices for both monks and nuns, lay-men and lay women.

In particular, practice of the "ten virtues" *(daśakuśala-śīlāni)* was encouraged. Compared to the ethics of Conservative Buddhism, Mahāyāna ethics were more flexible, and were altered in various environments. The ideal virtues were codified as six "perfections" (*pāramitās*) incorporated within the *bo-dhisattva* ideal: liberality *(dāna),* morality *(śīla),* effort *(vīrya),* forbearance *(kṣānti),* meditation *(dhyāna),* and transcendental insight *(prajñā).* A seventh perfection, "expedient means" *(upāya),* was added in some texts, and others expanded the concept to ten perfections. In general, *dāna,* or selfless giving (the rendering of help to others) was stressed. The *Āryasaṃgītigāthāśataka* is a collection of one hundred verses in praise of this perfection. The Buddha's great compassion was interpreted as his gift to sentient beings. The transference of merit to others *(pariṇāmanā)* was also encouraged as a form of giving. [*See* Pāramitās *and* Merit, *article on* Buddhist Concepts.]

Mahāyāna ethics were most explicitly set forth in the "Discipline Sūtras," the essence of which is altruism. Among the *sūtra*s that provided the theoretical basis for the Mahāyāna orders is the *Sarvadharmapravṛttinirdeśa,* which was highly esteemed by the Japanese monk Saichō (767–822). Others that explicated Mahāyāna discipline are the "Buddha Treasure Sutra" (T.D. no. 653), the "Enlightenment-mind Sutra" (T.D. no. 837), and the *Dharmavinayasamādhi Sūtra.* Some texts reflect the Mahāyāna idea that discipline is to be practiced by both clergy and laity; one, the *Bodhisattvaprātimokṣa Sūtra,* sets forth the "Vinaya" of *bodhisattva*s, here referring to both clerics and lay practitioners. The precepts in the *Śrīmālādevī Sūtra* were well known in China and Japan.

The most famous and controversial of these texts is the *Brahmajāla Sūtra.* Greatly esteemed in China, it became the fundamental discipline text for Japanese monks. Scholars now believe that this text was produced in China, where there is evidence that it was in use in some form as early as the year 350. Another text bearing on the conduct of the *bodhisattva,* the *Bodhisattvabhūmi,* calls upon all aspirants to the Way of *Bodhisattva*s—both monks and laymen—to observe three kinds of *bodhisattva* practice: adherence to all the precepts *(saṃvaraśīla; prātimokṣa),* practice of all virtuous deeds *(kuśaladharma-saṃgrāhakaṃ śīlam),* and the granting of mercy to all sentient beings *(sattvārtha-kriyāśīlam).* The first element in this code represents a retention of the traditional Vinayas of Conservative Buddhism, while the second and third are expressions of Mahāyāna ideals.

The *Śikṣāsamuccaya,* Śāntideva's eighth-century compendium of Mahāyāna literature, explains that the principle of compassion can even sanction physical love; according to Śāntideva, carnal desire is not nearly so sinful as anger. Eventually, married monks appeared among the Mahāyāna orders. In the fifth century, King Meghavāhana's consort built a monastery in Kashmir, half of which was occupied by *bhikṣu*s (mendicants) whose conduct conformed to the precepts, and half of which was reserved for those who had wives, children, cattle, and property. Some later *sūtras* (e.g., the *Mahāsaṃnipāta Sūtra*), however, refer to the marriage of monks as evidence of decadence in the orders. Today, Nepalese monks are free to marry, and marriage is to some extent common among Tibetan and Buriat Mongolian monks as well. The Jōdo Shin sect was the first in Japan to sanction the marriage of monks; since the introduction of Western civilization, marriage of Japanese monks has become more common.

Repentance is the theme and object of several Mahāyāna *sūtra*s. One of these *sūtra*s (T.D. no. 1493) shows that repentance leads to delight in the deeds of others, moral admonition, and transference of merit. Another text teaches that a reaffirmation of the insight that all things are originally pure can dissolve the obstacles created by *karman* (T.D. no. 1491). Bondage in *karman (karmāvaraṇa)* can be destroyed by repentance, meditation, or by repeated application of magical formulas.

While some *sūtras* describe and promote various meritorious deeds (T.D. no. 683, for example), others focus on specific practices such as circumambulation of stupas (T.D. no. 700) and the offering of votive lights at stupas and *caityas* (T.D. no. 702). Worship of both stupas and Buddhas was combined in others (T.D. no. 688). The merit attributed to the manufacture of images of Buddhas and *bodhisattvas* (T.D. nos. 692–694) suggests the fervor of image-making activity in Gandhāra and Mathurā. Another *sūtra* gives details of the rite of anointing Buddha images (T.D. no. 697). The use of rosaries, a practice adopted from the brahman priests, is extolled in yet another *sūtra* (T.D. no. 788). Originally, brahmans, not Buddhist monks, were officiants at South Asian funerals, but eventually Mahāyāna monks took their place. One *sūtra* encourages the observance of funeral rites as an affirmation of impermanence (T.D. no. 801). Later, officiating at funerals was to become a major duty of Japanese monks.

LAY BUDDHISM

The position of the layman was recognized and exalted by most Mahāyāna texts, although a few display a tendency to place the ascetic life of the monk above the lay life. However, the notion of emptiness *(śūnyatā)* that is the foundation of most Mahāyāna thought provides for the identity of liberation and mundane existence, *nirvāṇa* and *saṃsāra,* thus providing a rationale for the sanctity of lay life. This led many to the conclusion that the essence of religion should be sought in the life of householders rather than in the life of renunciants; hence, lay Buddhism came to be advocated in the Mahāyāna as a religious ideal. The grace of *bodhisattvas* was believed to extend to laymen; Mañjuśrī, for example, is said to save ordinary laymen and even nonbelievers.

To be sure, many Mahāyāna practitioners were *bhikṣus*, and some were termed *bodhisattva bhikṣus* (in the *Mahāyānasūtrālaṃkāra,* the *Śikṣāsamuccaya,* etc.). But the tendency toward lay Buddhism remained conspicuous. The *Ugradattaparipṛcchā,* an early Discipline Sūtra composed before Nāgārjuna (fl. 150–250), prescribes five conditions for the lay practice of the Mahāyāna. Later, codes of discipline intended specifically for laymen were composed. Among the disciplines required of laymen was observance of the regulations for *upoṣadha* days (when the fortnightly confessions were made).

The *Vimalakīrtinirdeśa Sūtra,* in which the pious layman Vimalakīrti gives a sermon to monks and denounces the homeless ascetic life they lead, is perhaps the best expression of the lay Buddhist ideal. This *sūtra* was composed no later than 150 or 200, and was studied and lectured upon frequently in China and Japan. Other *sūtras* represent extensions of its teaching, and in some the central figures are laywomen. In the *Candrottarādārikā-vyākaraṇa Sūtra,* the central figure, Vimalakīrti's daughter, expresses views that meet with the Buddha's approval. The central figure of another *sūtra* (T.D. no. 818) is a prostitute who teaches Buddhist doctrine to her lover during a rendezvous in a forest. The *Śrīmālādevīsiṃhanāda Sūtra* (which became quite important in China and Japan) is delivered by a queen, with the Buddha's sanction. An eight-year-old girl, Sumati, delivers a sermon in the *Sumatidārikā-paripṛcchā.* These *sūtra*s defy the stereotypical view (otherwise common to most Mahāyāna texts) that women are mentally and physiologically inferior to men—assumptions that reflected the inequality of the sexes in Indian society.

The presence of the notion of filial piety, another lay ideal, in Buddhism represents an accommodation and syncretization of values that occurred under the stimulus of Chinese culture. Filial piety was the most important virtue in Confucian ethics, which required one-sided obedience from children toward their parents. [*See* Hsiao.] This idea was never more than a minor one in Indian Buddhism. There is no single term in the original Sanskrit and Prakrit texts that corresponds to the Chinese *hsiao* (filial piety), but the character is found frequently in Chinese versions of scripture. To reconcile the two traditions, Chinese Buddhists created such spurious *sūtras* as the *Fu-mu-en-chung ching* and the *Tai-pao-fu-mu-chung ching,* which teach filial piety in the guise of Buddhist morality. A Buddhist concept of filial piety also took shape in the *Ullambana Sūtra,* which extols a rite that centers on offerings to one's dead parents. The *sūtra* appears to have originated in part in India and was later expanded upon in China. The Ullambana rite itself became a very important one in China, Vietnam, Korea, and Japan (where it is called Obon). [*See* Worship and Cultic Life, *article on* Buddhist Cultic Life in East Asia.]

Major Scriptures

Unlike the various recensions of the Hīnayāna canon, which were virtually closed by the early centuries of the common era and which shared, at least ideally, a common structure (Vinaya, Sūtra, Abhidharma; i.e., the Tripiṭaka), the Mahāyāna scriptures were composed in a variety of disparate social and religious environments over the course of several centuries, diverge widely from each other in content and outlook, and were in many cases meant to stand as individual works representing (it has been conjectured) rivals to the entire Hīnayāna corpus. Thus, when treating this literature it is perhaps most fruitful to consider the various textual *classes* that constitute Mahāyāna Sūtra literature.

THE WISDOM SŪTRAS

The earliest Mahāyāna *sūtras* are those that deal with *prajñāpāramitā* ("perfection of wisdom"); they constitute the philosophical basis of much of later Buddhist thought as well. The earliest Prajñāpāramitā text is almost surely a version in eight-thousand *ślokas*, the *Aṣṭasāhasrikā-prajñāpāramitā Sūtra,* dating in the earliest of its verse portions to perhaps 100 BCE and probably completed in the first century CE. The Pūrvaśailas, a Hīnayāna sect, are said to have possessed the Prajñāpāramitā Sūtras in a Prakrit edition, but most Japanese scholars claim that these *sūtra*s first came into existence in South India, perhaps in Andhra, among the Mahāsāṃghikas. Others maintain that the Prajñāpāramitā Sūtras were initially composed in Northwest India. The origins of the *Vajracchedikā-prajñāpāramitā Sūtra* (The Diamond Cutter Sutra) and the *Prajñāpāramitāhṛdaya Sūtra* (The Heart Sutra) should be placed between 150 and 200 CE. The *Diamond Cutter* is actually the ninth section of an extremely long text, the *Mahāprajñāpāramitā Sūtra;* the *Heart Sutra* is an even more condensed version. The *Mahāprajñāpāramitā Sūtra* is very early and was very enthusiastically transmitted, recited, explained, and commented upon in Central Asia, Tibet, China, Korea, and Japan, where interest in it is far greater than in India, the land of its origination. Other Prajñāpāramitā Sūtras, for instance, the *Pañcaviṃśatisāhasrikā, Daśasāhasrikā, Saptaśatikā, Śatasāhasrikā,* and *Adhyardhaśatikā,* followed the *Aṣṭasāhasrikā.* These generally represent either inflations or conflations of the basic text.

Most of the technical terms used in the Wisdom Sutras were inherited from Conservative Buddhism, but the ideas presented here are very new indeed. The central theme of these texts is that the "perfection of wisdom"—recognition of the truth of human existence—can be attained only through the realization that nothing exists in and of itself, that all things are like dreams or are the creations of magical power *(māyā).* [*See* Māyā.] The ultimate truth of existence is comprehended by the term "emptiness" *(śūnyatā),* one of the subtlest and most sophisticated concepts in the philosophical armory of Mahāyāna Buddhism. Understanding of *śūnyatā* entails the awareness that all things rely for their existence on causal factors and as such are devoid of any permanent "own-being" *(svabhāva).* The purely relative existence of all *dharma*s taught by this doctrine entails the realization that the things of this world, the self *(ātman)* included, are merely the reifications of conceptual and linguistic distinctions formed under the productive influence of fundamental ignorance *(avidyā).* Insofar as the things of this world derive their reality solely from a nexus of causal conditions *(pratītya-samutpāda),* their nature, what they all share, is precisely a "lack" of self-nature. [*See* Śūnyam and Śūnyatā; Dharma, *article on* Buddhist Dharma and Dharmas; Avidyā; *and* Pratītya-samutpāda.]

In practical terms, the perfection of wisdom involves the cultivation of a nondual insight into this fundamental (non)nature, characterized in the Mahāyāna as *dharmatā* ("dharmaness") or *tathatā* ("suchness"), that is, things just as they are without the duality imposed by conceptual categories. Other synonyms for emptiness are *dharmadhātu, dharmakāya,* and *buddhadhātu.* The Wisdom Sutras reinterpreted the traditional concepts of *nirvāṇa* and transmigration in this light: the goal of salvation is no longer *nirvāṇa* but an understanding of the reality of transmigration as emptiness. Ultimately, emptiness itself is eneffable, but the idea of emptiness can be taught in accordance with the mental ability of those who would learn about it. Thus, "expedient means" *(upāya)* are established in the Wisdom Sutras as the link between emptiness and compassion. In order to be effective guides to the liberation of beings, the *sūtra*s teach, the Buddhas must make concessions to the understanding of their audience. While it may be that the self and all *dharma*s lack real existence, to baldly assert such without any preliminary preparation would engender lack of confidence in the Dharma and a nihilism that is far from what is meant by *śūnyatā.* Thus the Buddhas have recourse to a variety of "expedient" teachings by which they prepare the practitioner for the revelation of final truth. In literary terms, such devices are often couched as metaphors and parables (this is especially true of texts such as the *Lotus,* a *sūtra* from another Mahāyāna tradition) that offer the devotee a more simple (if imperfect) grasp of the teachings of the Buddhas. [*See* Prajñā; Tathatā; Upāya; *and* Nirvāṇa.]

All of the Wisdom Sutras encourage an attitude of nonattachment. Devotees of Wisdom Sutras held that the theory of emptiness is not nihilism but rather a basis for practice, and the wisdom literature does offer practical assistance: those who desire to diminish their personal cares may use these *sūtra*s as a guide to the practice of the disciplined contemplation of spiritual truths and the cultivation of the Six

Perfections. Nor do the scriptures overlook the necessity for the gradual development of the mind of the aspirant to enlightenment: the texts proclaim a series of ten stages *(bhūmi)* through which the practitioner may approach enlightenment. Another important contribution of the Wisdom Sutras is the concept of the "original purity of mind" *(cittasya prakṛtiprabhāsvaratā),* a concept fundamental to Mahāyāna soteriology.

MEDITATION SŪTRAS

The Meditation Sutras of Mahāyāna may have originated among the Yogācāras, a Buddhist tradition that emphasized the practice of meditation. Of course, esteem for meditation characterized the Buddhist tradition from its inception and both early Buddhism and the Hīnayāna *nikāya*s had their own characteristic meditative disciplines. [*See* Meditation, *article on* Buddhist Meditation.] In Mahāyāna, meditation on various Buddhas and their "Pure Lands" became a means for calming the mind, eliminating mental defilements, and attaining awareness of emptiness. Meditation was also held to confer miraculous powers on the practitioner.

The *Yogācārabhūmi Sūtra* (for which the Sanskrit has been lost) sets forth a systematic scheme of the stages of meditation. It is, in essence, an anthology of passages relevant to meditation by Saṃgharakṣa. The *Dharmataradhyāna Sūtra* gives a systematic explanation of meditations as understood by Dharmatara and Buddhasena. It was important in the development of Ch'an (Zen) Buddhism and the meditation on *maṇḍala*s of Vajrayāna Buddhism. The *Pratyutpanna-buddha-saṃmukhāvasthitasamādhi Sūtra* teaches a *samādhi* that makes all the Buddhas in the ten directions visible to and present with the practitioner. Other *sūtra*s (e.g., the *Kuan-fo san-mei-hai ching*) teach a meditation on just one Buddha, Amitābha. The *Samādhirāja* or *Samādhirājacandrapradīpa Sūtra* explains how a *bodhisattva* can attain the highest knowledge by means of a series of meditations that culminate in the "king of meditations" *(samādhirāja).*

TRANSMIGRATION SŪTRAS

Another group of *sūtra*s describes aspects of the transmigration of living beings. Some depict sufferings in five spheres *(gati)* of transmigratory existence: the spheres of gods, men, beasts, ghosts *(preta),* and denizens of the Buddhist hells. In the *Saḍgatikārikā,* a sixth sphere, that of the *asura*s (warlike demons), is also depicted. Other *sūtra*s analyze the patterns of karmic retribution that lead to rebirth in one sphere or another. In one, Maudgalyāyana responds to a *preta*'s questions about these causal patterns. The *Saddharmasmṛtyupasthāna Sūtra* and the *Dharmaśarīla Sūtra* place this analysis in the larger context of Buddhist cosmology, then turn to meditations upon the human body. The *Chan-cha-shan-e-pao ching,* which enumerates the forms of retribution for specific good and bad deeds, was probably composed in China.

Some of these *sūtra*s treat in detail the theory of *pratītya-samutpāda,* or "dependent origination," the classic Buddhist explanation for the conditions that account for the genesis of sentient beings and their involvement in the cycles of samsaric existence. Some devote particular attention to the concept of ignorance *(avidyā)* as the first of the series of causal links *(aṅga)* that make up sentient existence. In the

Śālistamba Sūtra, the theory of dependent origination in twelve links is metaphorically likened to the growth of a rice plant.

THE LOTUS SŪTRA AND RELATED WORKS

Probably the single most influential Mahāyāna *sūtra* is the *Saddharmapuṇḍarīka Sūtra* (The Lotus of the Superb Religion). Its central part was probably composed by the end of the first century CE, and the whole *sūtra* was most likely completed around the end of the second century in Gandhāra or perhaps in the area of Kapiśa. The *sūtra* as a whole is a narrative drama in which scenes change often and suddenly; Buddhas, *bodhisattvas*, and mortals interact in lively discourse. Some scholars believe that the character of the *sūtra* was influenced by Indian theatrical forms that may have been themselves influenced by the conventions of Greek drama.

The *Lotus* refers to all living beings as "children of Buddha," and its teachings are esteemed for their insistence that all those who have faith in the Buddha and his Dharma will become Buddhas. In the first half of the *sūtra* the traditional division of soteriological paths into those of the *śrāvaka* (the Hīnayāna devotee), the *pratyekabuddha* (those who are enlightened without having heard the Dharma preached), and the *bodhisattva* (the Mahāyāna practitioner) is declared a mere "expedient device" *(upāya)* conceived by the Buddha to lure to the Dharma beings of differing levels of spiritual attainment. In reality, the *sūtra* declares, the "three vehicles" are but one vehicle *(ekayāna):* the Buddha vehicle itself. Under this dispensation, the spiritual destiny of all beings is nothing less than Buddhahood.

The second half of the *sūtra* reveals that the Buddha's existence among beings in this world—his birth, renunciation, enlightenment, and death—are mere elements in a cosmic drama of salvation. In reality, theBuddha is eternal, and his apparent enlightenment at Bodh Gayā a mere device to provoke faith in his teachings. The Buddha has always (or so the text implies) been enlightened. These teachings, and the dramatic and moving way in which the text presents them, have made the *sūtra* enormously influential, especially in East Asia. In particular, the T'ien-t'ai tradition and its derivatives have looked to this text as the revelation of the Buddha's true message and the very justification for his appearance on earth. [*See* T'ien-t'ai *and* Tendaishū.]

Several *sūtras* present ideas related to those expounded in the *Lotus.* The "Sutra on the Immeasurable Meanings" (T.D. no. 276) presents the concept of emptiness as the theoretical basis of "one vehicle" thought and teaches the way to attain sudden enlightenment. Some scholars think that this *sūtra* was composed in China; the *Samantabhadra-bodhisattva-dhyānacaryādharma Sūtra* claims that it was taught by the Buddha at the end of his life. The *Mahāsatya-nirgranthaputra-vyākaraṇa Sūtra* and its prototype (T.D. no. 173) are scriptures that expand upon the conciliatory character of the *Lotus.* Here, the spirit of tolerance is personified in the figure of a Jain ascetic who preaches Buddhist teachings. The *Suvarṇaprabhāsa Sūtra* also has traits that are comparable to the *Lotus.* It elucidates the infinity of the life of the Buddha, addresses political ideas, and reflects Esoteric trends; it also describes worship of the (originally Hindu) goddess Sarasvatī. [*See* Sarasvatī.] Its magical qualities and the ritual for repentance appended to this text made it very popular in China and Japan.

THE BUDDHĀVATAṂSAKA SŪTRA

The *Buddhāvataṃsaka Sūtra* has been influential in many Buddhist cultures. The work is a composite of various smaller, independent texts and textual cycles that by about 350 CE had been redacted into a single work comprising in its first complete Chinese recension some sixty fascicles. References to China and Kashgar in the *Buddhāvataṃsaka Sūtra* suggest that its compilation took place somewhere in Central Asia. Some scholars believe that portions of the *sūtra* were extant prior to the second century CE. Its major components, the Sanskrit texts entitled the *Gaṇḍavyūha Sūtra* and the *Daśabhūmika Sūtra,* were both known to Nāgārjuna. The *Daśabhūmika Sūtra* was compiled between 50 and 150 CE, and linguistic evidence indicates that the *Gaṇḍavyūha* probably belongs to the same period; it may have been composed early in the Kuṣāṇa dynasty. Scenes and characters from it are represented in the eighth- and ninth-century reliefs at Borobudur. The influence of the text was felt most strongly in China, Korea, and Japan, where, in the Hua-yen, Hwaŏm, and Kegon traditions, respectively, its teachings were made the basis of perhaps the most subtle and doctrinally sophisticated systems of the tradition. The great Buddha image at the Tōdaiji in Nara, the Daibutsu, is a representation of the Buddha Vairocana, the cosmic figure who is the central focus of the text. [*See* Mahāvairocana *and* Hua-yen.]

Unlike most *sūtra*s, in which it is Śākyamuni who preaches, this sermon is delivered by *bodhisattva*s and other divine beings as well as by mortals, who preach in eight assemblies in a variety of locales, including the Buddhist heavens. Their teachings are given religious sanction and authority insofar as the beings who preach them live in the period immediately following the Buddha's enlightenment. This text undertakes to sets forth the content of the Buddha's enlightenment exactly as it was, without concession to the spiritual capacities of its audience. This ultimate state of the Enlightened One is here characterized as the "ocean seal meditation" *(sāgaramudrā samādhiḥ),* symbolizing in its images of depth and boundlessness the ineffable and profound character of enlightenment itself.

In the *Daśabhūmika* portion of the text the doctrine of the ten *bodhisattva bhūmi*s is systematically outlined, while the *Gaṇḍavyūha* relates the spiritual quest of the youth Sudhana, who seeks instruction from some fifty-two teachers in his search for enlightenment. His quest, a metaphor for our own, is itself a depiction of the *bodhisattva* career. The *sūtra* also stresses the interconnection between each individual being and the whole universe; it asserts that the altruistic spirit of benevolence or compassion is the fundamental principle of Mahāyāna. The Buddha's own great compassion toward living beings *(tathāgatagotra-saṃbhava)* is seen as the force that causes all manner of Buddha activities to arise from his cosmic body. The *Avataṃsaka* also holds that the essence of the Tathāgata exists "in embryo form" in all living beings, even though they are unaware of it.

PURE LAND TEXTS

Pure Land Buddhism probably appeared first among early lay orders. It focuses on a Buddha who is known by two names: Amitāyus ("limitless life") and Amitābha ("limitless light"). The latter name appeared earlier, and later was associated with the Jātaka-like story of the monk Dharmākara, who is said to have made a series of vows (forty-eight in one recension of the text that recounts the story) to save living beings from suffering. The vows express Dharmākara's intention to establish a "Pure

Land" where sentient beings, free from all manner of affliction, could hear the Dharma preached by a Buddha and hence win enlightenment. The text of each vow includes Dharmākara's resolution to refuse final enlightenment until the terms of the vow shall have been fulfilled. The *sūtra* goes on to relate that Dharmākara is now, aeons later, the Buddha Amitābha, and that he resides in a splendid land in the western quarter of our universe known as Sukhāvatī ("land of ease"). Beings who have faith in this Buddha, the *sūtra* relates, and who focus their mind upon him for up to ten successive moments can be reborn in this Pure Land, and can attain enlightenment easily from there. [*See* Amitābha.]

Because in the fully elaborated Buddhology of Mahāyāna Buddhism other Buddhas, residing in their own Pure Lands, were also acknowledged, it is not surprising that these figures should also become the focus of cultic activity. (Akṣobhya is conspicuous in this respect.) But the special quality of compassionate concern for suffering beings that pervades the Amitābha mythic cycle made this Buddha a figure of great popular appeal, especially in East Asia, where the various Pure Land traditions, Ching-t'u, Jōdoshū, Jōdo Shinshū, and others enjoy wide followings. [*See* Ching-t'u; Jōdoshū; *and* Jōdo Shinshū.]

Amitābha Buddha figures in many *sūtras*, but the teaching of the Pure Land as the Buddha land of Amitābha is based chiefly on three scriptures: the "smaller" *Sukhāvatīvyūha Sūtra,* the "larger" *Sukhāvatīvyūha Sūtra,* and the *Kuan wu-liang-shou-fo ching (Amitāyurbuddhadhyāna Sūtra).* The *Larger Sukhāvatīvyūha Sūtra* was compiled before 200 CE, during the Kuṣāṇa dynasty, by an order of the Mahīśāsaka *bhikṣus* of Gandhara. The*Amitāyurbuddhadhyāna Sūtra* is more advanced than the *Sukhāvatīvyūha Sūtra* in that it deals less with elaborate descriptions of the blessed land than with the practice of meditations *(dhyāna)* on Amitāyus and the Pure Land by means of which the meditator may reach it. Cultivation of the *bodhi* (enlightenment) mind, hearing the name of Amitābha, directing one's thoughts toward him, and planting roots of goodness are all described by this text as causes for birth in the Pure Land.

But meditation on Amitābha *(buddhānusmṛti)* is the essential practice espoused by all the Pure Land scriptures of India. These emphasize the attainment of a pure and tranquil state of mind *(prasāda).* The original concept of faith in the Pure Land *sūtras* was not *bhakti,* devotional faith in the Buddha who preached them, but *śraddhā,* or faith in their teachings, a much different conception than that advocated by later Chinese and Japanese Pure Land Buddhists. The magical character of Amitābha worship was especially appreciated in China, where the inescapable resonances between worship of a divinity of "limitless life" and Taoist conceptions of immortality went far toward guaranteeing the popularity of Pure Land practices. In a reflection of this trend, the Chinese monk Shan-tao reinterpreted *buddhānusmṛti* (Chin., *nien-fo;* Jpn., *nembutsu*) as the oral recitation of the *name* of Amitābha. This remained the normative interpretation of *nien-fo* among subsequent Pure Land thinkers, especially in Japan. [*See* Nien-fo.] Later, in a more intellectual and sophisticated view of Amitābha as "principle" (Chin., *li*) rather than person, his essential body was interpreted as *dharma,* the universal law.

THE RATNAKŪṬA SŪTRA

The *Mahāratnakūṭa-dharmaparyāya-śatasāhasrikā-grantha* took its present form sometime after the fifth century. Its core, now its forty-third part, is the *Kāśyapapa-*

rivarta. The whole text consists of a long series of "questions" (*paripṛcchās*), the contents of many of which have not yet been fully analyzed.

THE MAHĀPARINIRVĀṆA SŪTRA

The Sanskrit original of the Mahāyāna version of the *Mahāparinirvāṇa Sūtra* (Sutra of the Great Decease [of the Buddha]) must have been compiled between 200 and 400 CE. (A text of Hīnayāna province of the same name is much earlier; both purport to record the final sermon of the Buddha.) One passage quotes Śākyamuni's prediction that "seven hundred years after my *nirvāṇa* Māra will gradually destroy the *saddharma*" ("true Dharma"). This and other passages seem to reflect the the deterioration and persecution of the order that was taking place at the time of the *sūtra*'s composition. [*See* Mappō.]

As the text claims to be the last sermon preached by Śākyamuni before his death, it allegedly reveals secret teachings that had not been preached before (i.e., that had not appeared in other *sūtras*). Basic Buddhist doctrine denies the existence of a permanent underlying element, an *ātman,* or "soul," in sentient beings; here, however, the Buddha teaches a theory of a "great *ātman*" and a view of *nirvāṇa* as "permanent, joyous, personal, and pure," assertions that were characteristically denied in other Buddhist texts. The *sūtra* emphatically maintains that the cosmic body of the Buddha is permanent and eternal, and that every human being is endowed with Buddhahood. The Buddhist order represented in the first part of the *sūtra* consists of homeless monks and nuns, like those of Conservative Buddhism, but in the latter half of the text the Buddhist order clearly is taken to include laymen, and faith is emphasized as the force that binds the order together. Harsh punishment, even execution, is prescribed for those who slander Mahāyāna teachings—an attitude that is rarely expressed in Buddhist literature.

YOGĀCĀRA SŪTRAS

The *sūtras* instrumental to the development of the Yogācāra tradition, that branch of Mahāyāna that sees consciousness as constituitive of all phenomena, include especially the *Mahāyāna-abhidharma Sūtra* (now lost but quoted in other works), the *Saṃdhinirmocana Sūtra,* and the *Laṅkāvatāra Sūtra.* The *Avataṃsaka,* another text with a pronounced idealistic orientation, is often mentioned as having influenced the tradition. The *Saṃdhinirmocana Sūtra* brings together for the first time the variety of terms and doctrines commonly associated with Yogācāra thought: "storehouse consciousness" *(ālaya-vijñāna),* the "three natures" and "triple unreality" of phenomena, and a detailed accounting of meditative practices *(śamatha* and *vipaśyanā)* enabling the practitioner to gain insight into the fundamental role of consciousness in constructing phenomenal existence. The *Laṅkāvatāra Sūtra,* a less than completely systematic work, also emphasizes that phenomena are the products of mind, lacking all independent reality *(svacitta-dṛśya bāhyabhāvābhāva);* it also asserts the identity of the *ālaya-vijñāna* with the *tathāgata-garbha* ("matrix [womb] of the Tathāgatas"), a concept expressive of the fundamental enlightenment present in all beings.

THE MAHĀSAṂNIPĀTA AND OTHER SŪTRAS

The various chapters of the *Mahāvaipulya-mahāsaṃnipāta Sūtra* seem to have been composed at different times. Some claim that the completed text dates from between

200 and 300 CE, but it probably did not achieve its present form until much later. This *sūtra* expresses the pessimistic belief that the Buddha's "True Religion" would last for a mere thousand years, after which the order would suffer gradual decay until its complete disappearance from the world. This notion may reflect the social tumult contemporary with the composition of the text caused by the invasion of India by the Ephthalites in the sixth century.

The *Lien-hsu-mien-ching* was probably produced in Kashmir in the first half of the sixth century. Its content appears to be influenced by the invasion of India by the Ephthalites and the destructive conquests of Mihirakula, which occurred between 502 and 542; the work wastranslated into Chinese in 584, so it must have been written between 542 and 584.

Worship of the *bodhisattva* Kṣitigarbha (Chin., Ti-tsang; Jpn., Jizō) may have originated in the belief in the Vedic earth goddess, Pṛthivī. Some scholars believe that when Iranian peoples immigrated to the southern region of the Tarim Basin in the fourth century, they introduced the idea of angels from Zoroastrianism; this may have led to worship of Kṣitigarbha as an independent *bodhisattva.* Ti-tsang was also worshiped in Chinese Manichaeism. In the many *sūtra*s extolling him—the *Daśacakra-Kṣitigarbha Sūtra* and the *Kṣitigarbha-praṇidhāna Sūtra* are our principal scriptural sources—he is always represented as a monk. Passages of *Sūtra*s extolling him are also cited in Mahāyāna treatises. [*See* Kṣitigarbha.]

The *Ākāśagarbha Sūtra* describes the virtues of the *bodhisattva* Ākāśagarbha and the benefits he bestows on those who believe in him. The *sūtra* seems to have been written by Iranian Buddhists in Kashgar, and shows the influence of conceptions of Amitābha.

The Philosophical Schools

To what extent the rise of Mahāyāna *sūtra* literature represents the growth of philosophical "schools" is not at all clear. Like much of Indian social history, the institutional history of the *saṃgha* presents a puzzle that perhaps will never be entirely understood. Certainly, we can infer from the contents of specific works a group of practices or doctrines that characterized a given religious community; but beyond this bare inference, the origins of the texts and the life of the communities that produced them remains obscure. We know of course that the Mahāyāna first conceived of itself as an alternate soteriological path centered around the figure and career of the *bodhisattva.* At a certain point in the history of the movement nameable figures appear to whom doctrinal treatises (*śāstra*s)—often commentaries on scripture—can be attributed. These figures produced works on a variety of subjects: meditation, logic, epistemology, liturgy, and so forth. Around such works clusters of commentaries, subcommentaries, rebuttals, and refinements developed, enabling us to speak in textual terms at least of various philosophical and practical traditions. But little information is available to us concerning the institutional profile of such traditions.

One of the earliest, and certainly the greatest, of the Mahāyāna *ācārya*s was Nāgārjuna (fl. 150–250), the *de facto* founder of the first doctrinal "school" of Mahāyāna, the Mādhyamika (Madhyamaka). Nāgārjuna was the first Mahāyāna thinker whose works survive to address the topics raised by the Mahāyāna *sūtra*s, particularly the Prajñāpāramitā *corpus,* in a philosophically self-conscious and critical way.

EARLY MĀDHYAMIKA AND NĀGĀRJUNA

The origins of the Mādhyamika school are obscure. Some scholars assert that it was influenced by the Mahāsāṃghika school. [*See* Mahāsāṃghika.] Its central philosophy of emptiness *(śūnyatā)* was propounded by Nāgārjuna, whose influence in the Buddhist tradition is so great that he is regarded as a patriarchal figure of eight Mahāyāna schools by the Japanese. A great number of works are attributed to him, including the *Mūlamadhyamakakārikā,* the *Dvādaśadvāra Śāstra* (extant only in Chinese), the *Vigrahavyāvartanī* (a refutation of Nyāya thought), the *Vaidalyasūtra* and its autocommentary, the *Vaidalyaprakaraṇa* (both refutations of Nyāya thought), the *Yuktiṣaṣṭikā,* the *Śūnyatāsaptati* (extant only in Tibetan), the *Ratnāvalī* and the *Suhṛllekha* (both discourses on statecraft), the *Pratītyasamutpādahṛdaya,* the *Daśabhūmikavibhāṣā Śāstra,* and the *Mahāprajñāpāramitopadeśa* (extant only in Chinese). The authenticity of some of these works, however, is highly questionable.

Nāgārjuna strove not to establish a fixed dogma but to prove the fallacies of other doctrines; he sought to refute all dogmatic views *(dṛṣṭi)* by showing how their initial propositions lead to unwarranted conclusions. This method of refutation is called *prasaṅga (reductio ad absurdum),* and Nāgārjuna's works were dominated by it. With it he eschews discussion of metaphysical problems, reduces the verbiage of speculative philosophy, and dismisses meaningless propositions. No substance can abide forever, he holds; all things are dependent upon causal conditions; nothing has independent existence.

The notion of *śūnyatā,* the core of Mādhyamika thought, is explained in many ways in Nāgārjuna's writings. In the *Madhyamakakārikā,* for example, it is identified with dependent origination *(pratītya-samutpāda):* since things arise dependently, he argues, they are without essence of their own; as they are without essence, they are void (i.e., devoid of the thing itself), and hence empty of "own-being." The "Middle Way" is a synonym in Nāgārjuna's writings for "voidness" and dependent origination; enlightenment, according to Mādhyamika thought, is the realization of the Middle Way. The term *nonself* was also here equated with voidness, explained here as substancelessness *(niḥsvabhāvatā),* which was declared the true nature of reality itself. The Mādhyamika adoption of these ideas led to its theory of two kinds of truth, *saṃvṛti-satya* and *paramārtha-satya.* The former is our everyday, mundane, linguistically constructed truth; the latter is the ultimate, inexpressible truth, the truth of the lack of own-being of all *dharma*s. Under this doctrine, however, the two truths depend upon each other. Mundane and ultimate truths do not constitute separate "essences," for the distinction between mundane and ultimate, *saṃsāra* and *nirvāṇa,* is itself empty of reality. [*See* Mādhyamika *and the biography of* Nāgārjuna.]

Nāgārjuna's most famous disciple was Āryadeva (c. 170–270), whose harsh attacks on other schools made him an object of hatred and led to his assassination. His works include the *Śataśāstra, Catuḥśataka,* and *Akṣaraśataka;* others attributed to him are spurious but philosophically important. A set of twenty-one verses in praise of the *Prajñāpāramitā* by his follower Rāhula (or Rāhulabhadra, c. 200–300) is preserved in both Sanskrit and Chinese. Nāgārjuna's *Madhyamakakārikā* and *Dvādaśadvāra Śāstra* and Āryadeva's *Śataśāstra,* all translated into Chinese by Kumārajīva (d. 413), were highly esteemed in China and Japan, and formed the basis of the teachings of the San-lun (Jpn., Sanron), or Three Treatises, school there. [*See the biographies of Āryadeva and Kumārajīva.*]

EARLY VIJÑĀNAVĀDA

Mādhyamika thought, in its refusal to posit any "view" (proposition) whatsoever, was content to employ its critical philosophy against the views of others, views, the Mādhyamika thinkers contended, that were themselves the source of karmic suffering. Not content with this purely critical spirit, the Vijñānavādins (or Yogācāras, as they are also known) sought to systematically account for the origin of sentient existence and the relationship between mundane existence and enlightenment. As the name *Yogācāra* indicates, they advocated the practice of meditation as the means for attaining release from *saṃsāra*.

Mādhyamika analysis had gone beyond the assertions of early Buddhism, which declared the "self" *(ātman)* a poisonous fiction that was the source of suffering, to declare that the *dharmas* (elements of existence) themselves were empty of independent existence. Like the Mādhyamika, Yogācāra thought denies the reality of the phenomenal world, but it accepts the reality of the consciousness that produces it. It is from this doctrine that the school derives its alternate name, Vijñānavāda, the doctrine that all existences are the creation of consciousness.

For the Yogācāras, all phenomena are mere manifestations of "seeds" *(bīja)* deposited by past actions. These seeds are held in a "receptacle" or "storehouse" consciousness *(ālaya-vijñāna),* by which is designated, however, no substantial entity but merely the collectivity of the seeds themselves. The aggregation of the *bīja*s is itself the *ālaya-vijñāna.* Under the appropriate conditions, these seeds manifest themselves as our psychophysical selves and as the contents of our everyday consciousnesses—the various sensory events that present themselves to us as an objective world. Thus, no object exists apart from the function of cognition by the subject; objects appear only on the basis of this cognitive function of the subject. Vijñānavāda incorporation of the concept of the Middle Way led to a description of all things as neither "decidedly existing" nor "decidedly nonexisting," and the claim that realization of the Middle Way is achieved through active insight into the fact that phenomenal existences are none other than "mere representations" *(vijñaptimātratā)* appearing in our consciousness. The *ālaya-vijñāna* was identified as the basis of the twelve links of dependent origination. [*See* Ālaya-vijñāna.]

The founder of this school of thought was Maitreya (Maitreyanātha, c. 270–350), sometimes identified with the *bodhisattva* of the same name. Maitreya's works include:

1. *Yogācārabhūmi,* the fundamental text of the Yogācāras. One of its sections, the *Bodhisattvabhūmi,* sets forth the *bodhisattva*'s discipline and describes his ideal life. The work is attributed to Maitreya's disciple Asaṅga (c. 310–390) by the Tibetans.
2. *Mahāyānasūtrālaṃkāra,* a systematic exposition of the stages of the *bodhisattva* that shares the same structure as the *Bodhisattvabhūmi* section of the aforementioned *Yogācārabhūmi.* The work is attributed to Asaṅga by the Chinese.
3. *Madhyāntavibhāga,* a discussion of the theories of *vijñaptimātratā,* the triple body of the Buddha, the three natures of reality, and other Yogācāra topics. The

prose section is often attributed to Vasubandhu (c. 320–400), allegedly Asaṅga's younger brother.

4. *Abhisamayālaṃkāra,* a synopsis of the contents of the *Aṣṭasāhasrikā,* thus not specifically a Yogācāra work. The work was commented upon in the eighth century by Haribhadra.
5. *Dharmadharmatāvibhaṅga,* a short treatise on the function of "unreal imagination" *(abhūta-parikalpa)* in the production of phenomenal existence.
6. *Vajracchedikavyākhya,* a treatise on the *Diamond Cutter Sutra.*

The *tathāgata-garbha* theory is discussed in several of Maitreya's works and in the *Ratnagotravibhāga-mahāyānauttaratantra Śāstra,* attributed in the Tibetan tradition to Maitreya but probably composed by Sāramati (c. 350–450). All of the works of Maitreya and his followers hold that the Buddha nature underlies the existence of all living things.

Maitreya's disciple Asaṅga inherited and systematized Maitreya's teachings. In the *Mahāyānasaṃgraha* he presents a three-part classification of phenomena conceived by the human consciousness. Under this analysis, all phenomena have three "natures":

1. *Parikalpita-svabhāva:* as fictive creations of mind, things are in this sense devoid of original substance and are thus not real.
2. *Paratantra-svabhāva:* to the extent that things are the products of dependent origination they have a provisional or temporary existence, one dependent upon causes.
3. *Parinispanna-svabhāva:* the nature of reality in and of itself as perfect suchness *(tathatā),* divested of all false imaginings that go toward the construction of images in our consciousness.

Paratantra-svabhāva is a mixture of pure and defiled aspects; it makes possible the turn from defilement toward purity. Realization of *parinispanna-svabhāva* is tantamount to attainment of "representation only" awareness.

Other of Asaṅga's works include the *Abhidharmasamuccaya* and the *Hsien-yang-sheng-chiao lun (*Āryadeśanāvikhyāpana).* This latter work is an abridgement of the *Yogācārabhūmi.* [*See the biography of Asaṅga.*]

In his many works, Vasubandhu carried on the systematization of *vijñaptimātratā* philosophy and in the process became the tradition's greatest systematic thinker. His *Viṃśatikā* (Twenty Verses) refutes the belief in the objective world; the work betrays the influence of Sautrāntika thought. Vasubandhu is alleged to have been an exponent of the philosophy of Conservative Buddhism prior to his conversion to Mahāyāna by his brother, Asaṅga. His *Triṃśikā* (Thirty Verses) explains how *vijñānapariṇāma* ("modification of consciousness"), the process by which the various consciousnesses (the six sense consciousnesses of early Buddhism and an "I consciousness" called *manas*) arise from the *bījas*, takes place. This, perhaps the fundamental text of the Yogācāra tradition, was widely commented on by later thinkers. Other of Vasubandhu's works include a treatise on the Buddha nature known in China as the *Fo-hsing lun;* the *Karmasiddhiprakaraṇa,* treating the notion of *karman* from a Vijñānavāda standpoint; the *Trisvabhāvanirdeśa;* and the *Pañcaskandhaprakaraṇa,* a Hīnayāna-oriented work on the *skandhas*.

In Vasubandhu's works, the philosophical system of Vijñānavāda, which rests on the theory of *ālaya-vijñāna,* contains an idealistic or spiritualistic individualism: its description of *manas* and *ādāna* ("seizing") consciousnesses suggests Buddhist counterparts to the Western concept of "I" or "ego." This school also considered the problem of subjectivity, a fundamental element in Buddhist philosophy. The strict idealism espoused by Vasubandhu—his denial of the existence of objects in the external world—provoked severe criticism from other schools. [*See* Yogācāra *and the biography of Vasubandhu.*]

LATER DEVELOPMENTS IN VIJÑĀNAVĀDA AND MĀDHYAMIKA

After Vasubandhu, a number of philosophers made further developments in the ideas of their predecessors. Both Mādhyamika and Yogācāra developed as independent schools, side by side with the Sarvāstivāda, Sautrāntika, and other philosophical schools of Conservative Buddhism, and they exchanged ideas with one another. These schools conflated, diversified, and separated into distinct branches.

The Vijñānavādins. One branch, the Nirākāra-vijñānavāda, which held that consciousness is pure and possesses no forms, that is, that the forms of both object and subject are of fictive nature and hence unreal, was expounded by Sthiramati (c. 510–570) and others and introduced into China by Paramārtha (499–590). The Yogācāra teachings introduced to China by Paramārtha were called there the She-lun teachings, after Asaṅga's *Mahāyānasaṃgraha* (Chin., *She-lun*), the basic text of the school. Another branch of Yogācāra thought, the Sākāra-vijñānavāda, which maintained that consciousness is necessarily endowed with the forms of the subject and the object, originated with Dignāga (c. 400–480), was transmitted by Asvabhāva, and systematized by Dharmapāla (530–561). Dharmapāla's system was conveyed to China by Hsüan-tsang, where, as the Fa-hsiang ("dharma characteristic") school, it enjoyed a brief vogue. Thereafter, it was transmitted to Japan (where it was known as the Hossō school) and became one of the major scholastic traditions of the Nara period (710–785). Other exponents of the Sākāra-vijñānavāda tradition include Śīlabhadra and Śubhagupta (c. 650–750). [*See the biographies of Sthiramati, Paramārtha, Dignāga, Dharmapāla, Hsüan-tsang, and Śīlabhadra.*]

Dignāga's philosophical works led to innovations in Vijñānavāda thought. In his *Prajñāpāramitā-piṇḍārtha-saṃgraha* he discusses eighteen "emptinesses" and ten types of discriminative knowledge *(vikalpa).* The subject *(vijñāna)* is held to exist, but objects *(vijñeya),* as mere *parikalpita,* do not. However, in the undifferentiated, perfect form of knowledge *(prajñāpāramitā)* there is no confrontation of subject and object. Other of his works include the *Ālambanaparīkṣā,* the *Hastavalāprakaraṇa,* the *Sāmānyalakṣaṇaparīkṣā,* the *Yogāvatāra,* and the *Trikālaparīkṣā.* These analyze cognition and the theory of "representation only." Dignāga's studies of logic were also important for later philosophers.

Dharmapāla is best known for his *Vijñaptimātratāsiddhi,* a commentary on Vasubandhu's *Thirty Verses.* Dharmapāla admitted the reality of objects of cognition *(parikalpita) in one sense.* He also drew a distinction between "that which changes" and "that which is changed" in consciousness. In addition to introducing the notion of eight consciousnesses, he distinguished four aspects of consciousness: its subjective aspect, objective aspect, self-conscious aspect, and self self-conscious aspects. The first three aspects may have been admitted by his predecessors, but Dharmapāla clearly was responsible for the addition of the fourth. Dharmapāla also taught that things may exist, in a relative sense, in the objective aspect of consciousness. It was Dharmapāla's unique understanding of Yogācāra thought that became normative in East Asian Vijñānavāda.

The scholar Śāntirakṣita (c. 680–740) and his disciple Kamalaśīla (c. 700–750) revived the ideas of the Nirākāra-vijñānavāda school. The former wrote a voluminous tract, the *Tattvasaṃgraha,* to which the latter produced commentaries. Śāntirakṣita knitted together the Mādhyamika and Yogācāra doctrines; Kalamaśīla established this combination as a synthesis superior to either of the two independent traditions. Śāntirakṣita's idealistic views deny the assertion of the existence of external objects and see self-cognition *(svasaṃvedana)* as the unity of all cognition. Śāntirakṣita held, however, that every cognition is devoid of both "the cognized" and the "cognizer." [*See the biographies of Śāntirakṣita and Kamalaśīla.*]

The Mādhyamikas. Disputes between two great scholars of Mādhyamika after Nāgārjuna, Buddhapālita (470–540) and Bhavya (or Bhāvaviveka, c. 490–570), led to the formation of two schools, known by the names given them in the Tibetan tradition: the Prāsaṅgika school of Buddhapālita and the Svātantrika school of Bhavya. The best known of Bhavya's works are the *Prajñāpradīpa,* a commentary to the *Madhyamakakārikā;* the *Madhyamakahṛdayakārikā* and its autocommentary, the *Tarkajvālā;* the *Madhyamārthasaṃgraha;* and the *Karatalaratna.* Bhavya's school admitted degrees of reality and levels of insight that are dependent on spiritual maturity and the degree of *samādhi* achieved, arguing therefore that it is possible to make assertions about the existence of things from the standpoint of conventional truth. Bhavya held that all the works of the Buddha as they appear in the *sūtras* are *pramāṇa* (right knowledge) and do not require verification by reason *(yukti);* the function of *yukti* is a correct understanding of scripture *(āgama),* not a verification of it. Bhavya also tried to demonstrate *niḥsvabhāvatā,* or *śūnyatā,* by way of syllogism, a departure from the more common Mādhyamika view that all such assertions are ultimately self-contradictory *(prasaṅga).* His use of independent inference *(svatantra-anumāna)* in this respect gave his school of thought its name Svātantrika. Kamalaśīla inherited and developed this method and was instrumental in its transmission to Tibet. [*See the biography of Bhāvaviveka.*]

Buddhapālita, on the other hand, extended Nāgārjuna's use of the *prasaṅga* form of argumentation and denied the use of independent inference. His *Mūlamadhyamakavṛtti,* a commentary on the *Madhyamakakārikā,* is the sole extant treatise by his hand. Buddhapālita's thought was later championed by Candrakīrti (c. 600–650), who defended the *prasaṅga* method of reasoning against the attacks of Bhavya and hence is himself classed as a Prāsaṅgika by Tibetan sources. Candrakīrti is also known for his refutation of Yogācāra doctrines concerning the reality of consciousness and the Absolute. His major works include the *Prasannapadā,* a commentary on the *Madhyamakakārikā,* and the *Madhayamakāvatāra.* [*See the biographies of Buddhapālita and Candrakīrti.*]

Another important Mādhyamika thinker was Śāntideva (c. 650–750). In his *Bodhicaryāvatāra,* an introduction to the practices of the *bodhisattva,* he criticized the theory of self-consciousness *(svasaṃvid)* of mind *(vijñāna)* from an epistemological standpoint while admitting its temporary existence, a view he maintained without contradicting the notion of emptiness. An exponent of the Prāsaṅgika tradition, he also embraced the Nirākāravāda concept of mind. Other of Śāntideva's major works include the *Śikṣāsamuccaya* and the *Sūtrasamuccaya,* both anthologies of Mahāyāna scriptural passages. [*See the biography of Śāntideva.*]

TATHĀGATA-GARBHA THOUGHT

The notion of the *tathāgata-garbha,* or "womb of the Tathāgata," represents the tendency of some Mahāyāna scriptures toward a more kataphatic way of regarding ultimate reality. In contrast to the assertions of the Śūnyavādins, who spoke of the Absolute solely in terms of absence or lack of independent existence, advocates of *tathāgata-garbha* tended to see in all sentient beings an indestructible core of Buddhahood that is productive of both mundane and transcendental reality. By emphasizing an ontological basis for both everyday existence and enlightenment, Tathāgata-garbha thinkers were able to speak fruitfully of the ultimate identity of the two realms and therefore to assert not only the potential for enlightenment in every being but also the sense in which all things are fundamentally and originally enlightened. In Japan, this *hongaku* ("original enlightenment") theory was transmitted and developed within the Tendai school, and became one of the dominant religious and philosophical motifs of Japanese Buddhism. Tathāgata-garbha thought shows, especially in its later phases, a relationship with Yogācāra thought founded principally on the integration of the notions of *tathāgata-garbha* and *ālaya-vijñāna.*

Tathāgata-garbha literature developed in three major phases. In the first phase, represented by the *Tathāgatagarbha Sūtra* and the *Śrīmālādevī Sūtra,* no mention is made of *ālaya-vijñāna.* Texts of the second period, including the *Mahāyānasūtrālaṃkāra* and the *Fo-hsing lun,* mention both but fail to elaborate on their relationship. In the third period, the *ālaya-vijñāna* doctrine was incorporated into that of the *tathāgata-garbha* to produce a *tathāgata-garbha* theory of dependent origination. Such is the work of the *Laṅkāvatāra Sūtra* and the *Ta-sheng ch'i-hsin lun* (**Mahāyāna śraddhotpāda Śāstra,* attributed to Aśvaghoṣa but according to some scholars, produced in Central Asia or China itself). Other major works treating this notion include the *Ratnagotravibhāga Śāstra* and the *Mahāyānāvatāra,* both perhaps the work of Sāramati, who is often credited as the systematizer of Tathātgata-garbha thought.

The *Ta-sheng ch'i-hsin lun* became particularly important in East Asia Buddhism, where it was widely read and commented upon, particularly in the Hua-yen tradition. This highly sophisticated and intricate text explores the nature of "original enlightenment" in its aspects as both "substance" *(t'i)* and "function" *(yung).* By substance, the text refers to the underlying and unchanging enlightenment that is the nature of all sentient existence; by function it refers to the way in which this fundamental enlightenment is present in the world—the interplay between original enlightenment, nescience *(avidyā),* and the experience of enlightenment as replacing ignorance in the consciousness of the religious practitioner. The text thus demonstrates the reliance of nescience, the source of our false imputation of independent reality to phenomena, on fundamental mind itself. [*See also* Tathāgata-garbha.]

THE LOGICIANS

Logical methods came to be emphasized in Buddhist thought as an outgrowth of the need to provide greater rigor for the epistemologies of the Mahāyāna tradition, particularly in defending their positions against proponents of non-Buddhist schools such as the Nyāya. [*See* Nyāya.] Incipient forms of Buddhist logic can be identified in the *Saṃdhinirmocana Sūtra,* in Maitreya's *Yogācārabhūmi,* and Asaṅga's *Abhidharmasamuccaya.* Vasubandhu is regarded as the progenitor of Buddhist logic, although the discipline was given its first full formulation by Dignāga. Vasubandhu's logical works include the *Vādaviddhi,* the *Vādavidhāna,* the *Vādakauśala,* and the *Tarkaśāstra* (although the provenance of this last work is disputed).

Working from this beginning, Dignāga created a new Buddhist logic. The "old" logic of the Nyāya school employed a five-step syllogism: (1) proposition *(pratijñā);* (2) reason *(hetu);* (3) example *(dṛṣṭānta);* (4) application or recapitulation of the cause *(upanaya);* and (5) conclusion *(nigamana).* For example: (1) a word is impermanent; (2) it is impermanent because it is produced by causes; (3) a word is like a pot [for]; (4) a pot is produced by causes and is impermanent [just as words are]; (5) therefore, a word is impermanent. Another famous example is as follows: there is fire on the mountain for the mountain is smoking; wherever there is smoke there is fire, as is the case on a kitchen hearth; the mountain smokes, therefore, there is fire on the mountain. Dignāga omitted the fourth and fifth steps of this scheme, giving it a concision and simplicity comparable to the Aristotelian syllogism. He also set forth a theory of nine types of valid and invalid arguments. The fifth type corresponds to the fallacy of irrelevant conclusion, but Dignāga called it "inconclusive," on the basis of the Buddhist assumption of "neither being or nonbeing" as a logical mode different from "being" and "nonbeing." Dignāga's theories of knowledge appear in his *Pramāṇasamuccaya,* while his *Nyāyamukha* deals with the forms of argumentation. Also by Dignāga are the *Hetucakranirṇaya* and the *Hetucakraḍamaru.* Śaṃkarasvāmin's *Nyāyapraveśaka,* a brief introduction to Dignāga's logic, was widely studied by East Asian students of Buddhist logic.

Dignāga's fusion of logic and epistemology was elaborated upon by Dharmakīrti (c. 600–650), whose major works include the *Nyāyabindhu,* the *Pramāṇavārttika,* a treatise on Dignāga's *Pramāṇasamuccaya* in which he admits two kinds of valid knowledge, direct perception and inference (Dharmakīrti also regarded the Buddha as a source of valid knowledge), and the *Pramāṇaviniścaya,* an epitome of the *Pramāṇavārttika.* According to Dharmakīrti, every being is transitory; what is assumed to be the continuous existence of an individual is nothing but a sequence of moments; the person is merely a construct of our imagination and discriminative thinking *(vikalpa).* Objects of inference are for Dharmakīrti universals, whereas objects of perception are individual, nothing but moments. [*See the biography of Dharmakīrti.*]

Later logicians include Śāntirakṣita and Kamalaśīla (both eighth century), Śubhakara (c. 650–750), Dharmottara (c. 730–800), Paṇḍita-Aśoka (ninth century), Jitāri (940–980), and Jñānaśrībhadra (fl. 925). Śāntirakṣita and Kamalaśīla adopted Dignāga's three-point syllogism, refuting the traditional five-point syllogism of the Nyāya school. Śāntirakṣita also defended Dharmakīrti's analysis of three characteristics of reason *(hetu)* against the attacks of Pātrakesari. Śubhakara, who was probably Dharmottara's teacher, composed the *Bāhyārthasiddhikārikā,* which attempted to prove the objective reality of external things, thus refuting Buddhist idealism *(vijñānavāda).* Major works of these later scholars include Dharmottara's *Apohaprakaraṇa,* Paṇḍita-Aśoka's *Avayavinirākaraṇa* and *Sāmānyadūṣaṇadikprasāritā,* Jñānaśrībhadra's *Laṅkāvatāravṛtti* and *Sūtrālaṃkāra-piṇḍārtha,* and Jitāri's *Jātinirākṛti* (in which he sets forth the controversy on universals between Buddhists and the Vaiśeṣikas, the Mīmāṃsākas, and the Jains) and *Hetutattvopadeśa.*

The eleventh-century scholar Jñānśrīmitra, a follower of the Dharmakīrti school at Vikramaśīla University, wrote twelve treatises on logic. Ratnakīrti, who flourished at about the same time, proved the existence of other minds from the standpoint of relative truth in his *Īśvarasādhanadūṣaṇa,* but denied it from the standpoint of highest truth in *Saṃtānāntaradūṣaṇa.* This latter work is particularly interesting because it unreservedly declares that solipsism is the final goal of idealism. Ratnakīrti's other works include *Apohasiddhi,* two works entitled *Kṣaṇabhaṅgasiddhi,* and *Sthirasiddhidūṣaṇa.* Ratnākaraśānti (fl. 1040), a scholar of the Nirākāra-vijñānavāda school, is the author of the *Antarvyāptisamarthana.* Mokṣākaragupta (c. 1050–1202) wrote an introductory work based on Dharmakīrti's *Nyāyabindu* entitled *Tarkabhāṣā.* Other noteworthy scholars of this period include Haribhadra (fl. 1120), author of the *Anekāntajayapatākā,* and Ravigupta, who advocated the theory of momentary flux *(kṣaṇikatva).*

Social and Political Thought

Expressions of political and social idealism are evident in a variety of Mahāyāna texts. Some appear in the form of letters from monks to kings. Mātṛceṭa's *Mahārājakanikalekha,* Nāgārjuna's *Ratnāvalī* and *Suhṛllekha,* the *Wang-fa cheng-li lun* (T.D. no. 1615), attributed to Maitreya, and the thirteenth chapter of the *Suvarṇaprabhāsa Sūtra* are among the important works that address rulers and proper rule. Other texts, such as the *Cittaviśuddhiprakaraṇa* by Āryadeva and the *Vajrasūcī,* advocate equality. The latter, a direct attack on the Brahmanic caste system, is attributed to Dharmakīrti by the Chinese.

Mahāyāna political and economic theories reflect the conditions in which they developed, when India consisted of many major and minor kingdoms. Some texts call upon subjects to overthrow kings who do not rule according to the ideals of *dharma.* Kings are directed to rule with clemency toward both men and other living things; they must also assure peace for their kingdoms (with military force, if necessary), increase national production, provide necessities in times of calamity, maintain social order, and promote education—all through their allegiance to and support of Buddhism. Āryadeva, on the other hand, asserted that the prestige and authority of kings is fictitious.

The spiritual leaders of Mahāyāna were monks who led otherworldly lives; they never engaged in the economic activities that they denounced. But some held that the worldly economic life was also of religious significance. Material charity was encouraged, and the abolition of poverty was espoused. However, certain vocations, such as cattle-raising, slave trading, and sales of liquor, were utterly condemned.

The problem of taxation also came under Mahāyāna scrutiny. Out of sympathy for the people, Mahāyānists called upon kings to minimize their exercise of the right to collect tribute and dispose of it at will. It was proposed that taxes be limited to one sixth of production, and it was argued that low taxes would stimulate production and fulfill this additional duty of the king. Kings were encouraged to distribute their treasures among their subjects to promote happiness, which would in turn increase the king's income. Thus, a rudimentary form of redistributive finance was proposed.

Advice was also offered on the use of force, the goal of which should be to protect the needy and to maintain tranquillity in the state. Although the guilty must be punished, clemency should be applied in the assignment of penalties. Capital and corporal punishments of all degrees were forbidden. If attacked, the king was obligated to protect his subjects and to repulse invaders. Hence, defensive war was recognized, but maintenance of pacificism was upheld as the ideal.

The king was also expected to be as virtuous in his private life as he was diligent in his administration of the state; sensual enjoyments and sexual dalliance were condemned. He was encouraged to choose advisors and subordinates wisely and to promote on the basis of merit. The state's goal should be to guide each subject to salvation. If the king administers the state according to divine law, he will bring benediction upon it and the state will flourish. Both he and his subjects will be happy, and his rebirth in heaven will be assured.

Above all, altruism was stressed, based on the virtue of compassion. A sense of human solidarity shaped Mahāyāna thought and governed its ethics: the refusal to give alms was regarded as the gravest of sins. Men were taught to help one another in the belief that no single man has the strength to sustain his own life, the highest sense of the idea of Buddhist solidarity.

[*See also* Buddhism, *article on* Buddhism in India; Soteriology, *article on* Buddhist Soteriology; *and* Buddhist Philosophy. *For further discussion of the development of Mahāyāna literature, see* Buddhist Literature, *article on* Survey of Texts.]

BIBLIOGRAPHY

Burtt, Edwin Arthur. *The Teachings of the Compassionate Buddha.* New York, 1955.

Conze, Edward. *Buddhist Thought in India: Three Phases of Buddhist Philosophy* (1962). Reprint, Ann Arbor, 1970.

Conze, Edward, ed. and trans. *Buddhist Scriptures.* Harmondsworth, 1959.

Conze, Edward, et al., eds. *Buddhist Texts through the Ages.* New York, 1954. A comprehensive collection of Indian Mahāyāna texts.

Cowell, E. B., et al., eds. *Buddhist Mahāyāna Texts.* Sacred Books of the East, edited by F. Max Müller, vol. 49. Oxford, 1894; reprint, New York, 1969.

Dayal, Har. *The Bodhisattva Doctrine in Buddhist Sanskrit Literature* (1932). Reprint, Delhi, 1975.

Dutt, Nalinaksha. *Aspects of Mahāyāna Buddhism and Its Relation to Hīnayāna.* London, 1930.

Frauwallner, Erich. *Die Philosophie des Buddhismus.* 3d rev. ed. Berlin, 1969.

Glasenapp, Helmuth von. *Der Buddhismus in Indien und im Fernen Osten.* Berlin, 1936.

Hamilton, Clarence H., ed. *Buddhism: A Religion of Infinite Compassion; Selections from Buddhist Literature.* New York, 1952.

Hirakawa Akira. "The Rise of Mahāyāna Buddhism and Its Relationship to the Worship of Stūpas." *Memoirs of the Research Department of the Tōyō Bunko* 22 (1963): 57–106. A well-documented analysis of a crucial topic in the history of Buddhism.

Hirakawa Akira. *Indo bukkyōshi.* 2 vols. Tokyo, 1974–1979. This comprehensive survey of Indian Buddhism contains extensive bibliographies of Japanese secondary sources.

Lamotte, Étienne. *Histoire du bouddhisme indien des origines à l'ère Śaka.* Louvain, 1958. Extensive footnotes and a comprehensive index make this work an invaluable reference tool.

Lamotte, Étienne, trans. *Le traité de la grande vertu de sagesse.* 5 vols. Louvain, 1944–1980. A translation from Kumārajīva's Chinese translation *(Ta chih-tu lun)* of the Sanskrit *Mahā-*

prajñāparamitā Śāstra, a commentary on the *Pañcavimśatisāhasrikā-prajñāparamitā.* the original Sanskrit commentary, sometimes attributed to Nāgārjuna, is no longer extant.

La Vallée Poussin, Louis de. *Bouddhisme.* Paris, 1909.

McGovern, William Mongomery. *An Introduction to Mahāyāna Buddhism.* New York, 1922.

Radhakrishnan, Sarvepalli. *Indian Philosophy,* vol. 1. 2d ed. London, 1927. A lucid introduction for the beginning student.

Schayer, Stanislaw. *Vorbereiten zur Geschichte der Mahāyānistischen Erlösungslehren.* Munich, 1921. Translated by R. T. Knight as *Mahāyāna Doctrines of Salvation* (London, 1921).

Stcherbatsky, Theodore. *Buddhist Logic* (1930–1932). 2 vols. Reprint, New York, 1962.

Suzuki, Beatrice Lane. *Mahāyāna Buddhism* (1938). 3d ed. New York, 1959.

Suzuki, D. T. *Outlines of Mahāyāna Buddhism* (1907). Reprint, New York, 1963.

Thomas, Edward J. *The History of Buddhist Thought.* 2d ed. New York, 1951.

Thomas, Edward J., trans. *The Quest of Enlightenment: A Selection of the Buddhist Scriptures.* London, 1950. A brief anthology of Mahāyāna texts in translation with particular reference to the career of the *bodhisattva.*

Wassiljew, W. *Der Buddhismus.* Saint Petersburg, 1860.

The Way of the Buddha. Delhi, 1957. Published by the Publications Division of the Ministry of Information and Broadcasting, Government of India.

Wayman, Alex. *The Buddhist Tantras: Light on Indo-Tibetan Esotericism.* New York, 1973.

Wayman, Alex, trans. *Calming the Mind and Discerning the Real: Buddhist Meditation and the Middle View, from the Lam rim chen mo of Tson-kha-pa.* New York, 1978.

Winternitz, Moriz. *Der Mahāyāna-Buddhismus, nach Sanskrit- und Prākrittexten.* 2 vols. Tübingen, 1930.

Winternitz, Moriz. *A History of Indian Literature,* vol. 2, *Buddhist Literature and Jaina Literature* (1933). Reprint, New York, 1971. Even now, this work remains probably the best introduction to the subject.

13 ESOTERIC BUDDHISM

ALEX WAYMAN

Buddhist esotericism is an Indian movement obscure in its beginnings. Combining yoga and ritual, it calls itself the Diamond Vehicle (Vajrayāna)—where *diamond* means "the unsplittable"—or the Mantra Vehicle (Mantrayāna)—where *mantra* means "magical speech." The revealed texts of the tradition are called *tantra,* in contrast to *sūtra* (the generic name of the non-Tantric Buddhist scriptures), but both these words have the implication "thread" or "continuous line." In the case of the Tantras, the "continuous line" can be understood in various ways: the lineage of master-disciple, the continuity of vows and pledges in the practitioner's stream of consciousness, or the continuity of practice leading to a religious goal.

Much of Tantric literature is ritualistic in nature, manifesting Brahmanic influence by the use of incantations *(mantra)* and the burnt offering *(homa),* both of which were employed for magical purposes as far back as Vedic times. [*See also* Mantra]. Similarly, the notion of the "five winds" found in certain of the Tantras dates back to some of the Upaniṣads. Many of the hand gestures and foot stances of Buddhist Tantric practice are also found in Indian dance. [*See also* Mudrā.] However, as specifically Buddhist Tantras, such texts are colored both by Buddhist theories and practices and by the typical terminology of Mahāyāna Buddhism. These texts regularly employ such ancient Buddhist formulations as the triad body, speech, and mind, and draw upon such common Mahāyāna notions as the pair "means" *(upāya)* and "insight" *(prajñā).* [*See also* Upāya *and* Prajñā.] The Tantras accept the old Buddhist ontology of three worlds filled with deities and demons, and contribute the premise that one can relate to these forces by ritualistic manipulation of one's nature (body, speech, and mind), thereby attaining "success" *(siddhi)* in such mundane forms as appeasing the deities, or the supermundane success of winning complete enlightenment (Buddhahood), possibly in a single lifetime. The old Buddhist terminology "son or daughter of the family," here the Buddhist family, was extended to refer to Buddha families. Initially, the texts propose a triad of three Buddhas or Tathāgatas: Vairocana, Amitābha, and Akṣobhya. Later, Ratnasambhava and Amoghasiddhi are added to make up a family of five, and Vajrasattva to make a family of six. A supreme Buddha, referred to variously as Mahā-Vajradhara, Heruka, orĀdibuddha ("Primordial Buddha"), is also mentioned. But the texts do not use the term "Dhyāni Buddhas" that is sometimes found in Western books on the subject.

INFLUENCE IN TIME AND PLACE

Buddhist Tantrism appears to have originated in eastern India and to have been transmitted orally in private circles from around the third century CE. When we speak of the period of the origination of the tradition, however, we refer only to that era in which Buddhist Tantras arose in syncretism with an already extant lore non-Buddhist in character, and not to some hypothetic origin of Tantrism per se. The first textual evidence of this current is found in chapters bearing the title *dhāraṇī* (a kind of *mantra*)within certain Mahāyāna scriptures. The ninth chapter of the *Laṅkāvatāra Sūtra* (fourth century CE), for example, is devoted to magical formulas of supposedly meaningless sounds, which, when recited for one hundred and eight times, are claimed to ward off demons. The earliest Tantras are those that still give a leading role to Śākyamuni, the historical founder of Buddhism, perhaps placing him at the center of a *maṇḍala.* By comparing the names of the five Buddhas in the *Durgatipariśodhana Tantra* (i.e., Vairocana, Durgatipariśodhana, Ratnaketu, Śākyamuni, and Saṃkusumita) with those of the five Buddhas of the Mahākaruṇāgarbha Maṇḍala, which is derived from the *Vairocanābhisaṃbodhi Tantra* (i.e., Mahāvairocana, Dundubhinirghoṣa, Ratnaketu, Amitāyus, and Samkusumitarāja) and with the five of the Vajradhātu Maṇḍala, derived from the *Tattvasaṃgraha Tantra* (i.e., Mahāvairocana, Akṣobhya, Ratnasambhava, Amitābha, and Amoghasiddhi), we can observe that the name Śākyamuni is still employed in the earliest Tantras but is later replaced by the name Amitāyus, and finally by Amitābha, resulting in the standard set of Buddha names of later times.

Between the third and the eighth centuries, these cults, with their "revealed" scriptures, were transmitted secretly from master to disciple, but by the eighth and ninth centuries a remarkable change had occurred in the fortunes of Buddhist Tantrism. Evidence of the growing influence of the movement may be seen in the fact that a king called Great Indrabhūti of Uḍḍiyāna is said to have been initiated into the Tantric mysteries at about this time. Other important evidence of the growth of the tradition is found in the texts of the period. Whereas the revealed Tantric works of earlier centuries were written in strict anonymity and attributed to divine authorship, now historical figures begin to attach their names to commentarial literature. Buddhaguhya (second half of the eighth century) wrote learned commentaries on the three Tantras mentioned above. A host of commentaries also arose on the *Guhyasamāja Tantra* and the *Śrī-Cakrasaṃvara Tantra* cycles by such celebrated writers as Saraha and the Tantric Nāgārjuna (author of the *Pañcakrama*). While some Tantric works had been translated in Chinese earlier, it was not until the eighth century that Tantrism would take hold in China, owing largely to the efforts of the monk Vajrabodhi and his disciple Amoghavajra. Their kind of Tantrism was transmitted to the talented Japanese monk Kūkai (posthumously called Kōbō Daishi, 774–835), who introduced to Japan an elaborate cult based on the "two Tantras," the *Vairocanābhisaṃbodhi* and the *Tattvasaṃgraha.* This cult, a fusion of art, mysterious rituals, colorful costumes, religious music, and handsome calligraphy, would have a great cultural impact on Japan.

In this period certain Tantras were also translated into Tibetan. Tibet eagerly embraced these cults, and in time would produce native works on the most popular Tantras. While a vast number of Tantric texts was translated into Tibetan, a lesser amount was preserved in Chinese translation. Chinese Buddhism generally disliked the Tantras, partly for their intricate ritualism, but more for the sexual symbolism, offensive to the Chinese mind, found in Tantras such as the *Guhyasamāja.* In Java, construction of the Borobaḍur monument, begun in the eighth century, shows Tantric influence in its use of *maṇḍalas* at its central stupa. It is also known that Atīśa, who arrived in Tibet in 1042 and became a towering figure in Tibetan Buddhism, had earlier studied for twelve years in the celebrated Tantric college of Śrīvijaya (now part of Indonesia). Thus it is clear that after the eighth century, Buddhist Tantrism was strongly entrenched in eastern India from Bengal north, had advanced to Nepal and Tibet, flourished for a time in China, became highly influential in Japan, and would establish a great school in the "Golden Isles" (Indonesia).

Tibet became an extraordinary center for Tantrism as well as the major storehouse of Tantric literature. The Indian *guru* Nā-ro-pa (956–1040?) was an important link in this development. It was Nā-ro-pa who transmitted Buddhist esotericism to the translator Mar-pa, who in turn taught it to the poet Mi-la-ras-pa. [*See the biographies of Nā-ro-pa, Mar-pa, and Mi-la-ras-pa.*] Thereafter, from this lineage arose the Bka'-brgyud-pa school, continuing the Great Seal *(mahāmudrā)* teachings andthe six yoga doctrines that had been taught by Nā-ro-pa. In modern times, the Tibetan tragedy has resulted in a number of Tibetan monk refugees transplanting their Tantric lineages to Europe and the United States.

BUDDHIST TANTRIC LITERATURE

The Tibetan canon classifies the Tantras into four groups, the Kriyā Tantras, the Caryā Tantras, the Yoga Tantras, and the Anuttarayoga Tantras. The translations of the revealed Tantras were included under the four headings in a section of the canon called the Bka'-'gyur (Kanjur); the commentaries are grouped in a section of exegetical works called the Bstan-'gyur (Tanjur). The Sino-Japanese canon does not so group them. In the Tibetan canon, the two chief works of the Japanese Tantric school (Shingonshū), the *Vairocanābhisaṃbodhi* and the *Tattvasaṃgraha,* are the principal works of the Caryā and Yoga Tantras, respectively. The *Hevajra Tantra* and the *Guhyasamāja Tantra,* works well known to Western scholars, belong to the Anuttarayoga Tantra class, and are respectively a "Mother" and a "Father" Tantra of this class. The status of the popular *Kālacakra Tantra,* definitely an Anuttarayoga class text, has been disputed. There is also a host of small works called *sādhana,* which set forth methods of evoking a given deity. The *Sādhanamālā* is a well-known collection of such works. Since in the Tantric tradition deities are arrayed in designs called *maṇḍala*s, there are also treatises devoted to *maṇḍala*s and their associated rituals. [*See also* Maṇḍalas.] The *Niṣpannayogāvalī* is a work on twenty-six of these *maṇḍala*s. During the last period of Buddhism in India the popularity of Tantrism gave rise to a group of Tantric heroes called *mahāsiddha*s ("great adepts"), and tales were compiled concerning their superhuman exploits. Their Tantric songs are collected in a work called the *Caryāgīti.* Other well-known Tantras include the *Mañjuśrī-mūla-kalpa* (a Kriyā Tantra), the *Sarvadurgatipariśodhana* (a Yoga Tantra), and the *Mañjuśrī-nāma-saṃgīti,* which was commented upon both as a Yoga Tantra and as an Anuttarayoga Tantra.

The editor of the Tibetan canon, Bu-ston (1290–1364), arranged the Tantras in their respective four classes according to a theory that in order for a Tantra to be a Buddhist one, it should be in some Buddhist family, headed by one of the Buddhas. In the case of the Anuttarayoga Tantras, the Mother Tantras were classified under one or another of seven Buddhas, in order: "Teacher" (Tib., *ston pa,* probably referring to Vajrasattva), Heruka (i.e., Akṣobhya), Vairocana, Vajraprabha (i.e., Ratnasambhava), Padmanarteśvara (i.e., Amitābha), Paramāśva (i.e., Amoghasiddhi), and Vajradhara. The *Śrī-Cakrasaṃvara* and the *Hevajra* were included under Heruka. The Father Tantras were classified under six Buddhas, identical to those used to classify the Mother Tantras except that the first, "Teacher," is omitted. The *Guhyasamāja Tantra* was classified under Akṣobhya and the *Yamāri* (or *Yamāntaka*) *Tantra* under Vairocana. The *Mañjuśrī-nāma-saṃgīti Tantra* and the *Kālacakra Tantra* were not included in this classification, presumably because they were classed under Ādibuddha, "Primordial Buddha."

In the case of the Yoga Tantras, the basic scripture, called *Tattvasaṃgraha,* is itself divided into four sections corresponding to four Buddha families. Explanatory Tantras of the Yoga Tantra class could thus be classed in one of those four sections or families, or could emphasize either "means" *(upāya)* or "insight" *(prajñā).* For example, the *Paramādya* is classed chiefly as an "insight" scripture.

The Caryā Tantras were classified under three Buddha families, the Tathāgata family (under Vairocana), the Padma family (under Amitābha), and the Vajra family (under Akṣobhya). The *Vairocanābhisaṃbodhi* is classed under the Tathāgata family; the *Vajrapāṇyabhiṣeka* is classed under the Vajra family; but the Padma family has no corresponding text among the Caryā Tantras.

The arrangement of the Kriyā Tantras is rather complicated. Using the same three families that govern the Caryā Tantras, the Kriyā Tantras make further subdivisions for the Lord of the Family, the Master, the Mother, Wrathful Deities, Messengers, and Obedient Ones. In addition, the Tathāgata family is subdivided into Uṣṇīṣa, Bodhisattvas, and Gods of the Pure Abode. For example, the *Suvarṇaprabhāsottama,* which was also quite popular as a Mahāyāna *sūtra,* is included under the Mother of the Tantras family. The Kriyā Tantras also include a category "Worldly Families" as well as "General" Kriyā Tantras, a category that includes the *Subāhuparipṛcchā*.

Naturally, there was always a considerable degree of arbitrariness in such categorizations; in fact, certain Tantras had a disputed status. The traditions carried to Tibet also classified the four divisions of Tantras according to their respective deities and according to the preferences of the human performers. When classed in terms of deities, the division reflects degrees of courtship: laughing for the Kriyā Tantras, mutual gazing for the Caryā Tantras, holding hands for the Yoga Tantras, and the pair united for the Anuttarayoga Tantras. When arranged according to human performers, the respective preference for outer ritual or inner *samādhi* is the determining factor. Kriyā Tantras appeal to those with a preference for ritual over *samādhi.* In the Caryā Tantras, ritual and *samādhi* are balanced; in the Yoga Tantras *samādhi* prevails over ritual; and in the Anuttarayoga Tantras *samādhi* alone is the requisite practice. An unorthodox explanation of these four classes is found in Smṛti's commentary on the *Vajravidāraṇā-nāma-dhāraṇī* (Kriyā Tantra, Master of the Family class). This author claims the four classes correspond to four kinds of Buddhist followers and the way in which they "cleanse with voidness." For the *śrāvakas* (i.e., Hīnayāna monks) external cleansing purifies the body. For the *pratyekabuddhas* (*ṛṣis*, "seers") inner cleansing purifies speech. For the Yogācāras (the Mind Only school) secret cleansing purifies the mind, and for the Mādhyamikas "reality cleansing" with a diamondlike *samādhi* unifies body, speech, and mind. [*See also* Samādhi.]

THE LANGUAGE OF BUDDHIST ESOTERICISM

Opponents of the Tantras have based their condemnations on what they read in such works. Since works of the Anuttarayoga Tantra class, the *Hevajra* and *Guhyasamāja Tantras* in particular, are still preserved in the original Sanskrit, modern scholars have consulted these for their conclusions about Tantrism and are usually unable to consult the Tibetan or Sino-Japanese versions of a wide range of Tantras. Some scholars accordingly have referred to Buddhist Tantrism by names such as the Vāmācāra ("left-handed path") or the Sahajayāna ("together-born path"), but the Tantras themselves do not use such terms, and in fact such designations fail to throw light on their contents. It should be recognized that the followers of the Tantric cults, including many Tibetan monks, would *never* presume to interpret a Tantra from the language of the revealed text alone. These invariably require the assistance of a commentary, perhaps one written by their *guru*. On such grounds a number of Tantras translated into Tibetan have traditionally been considered "off-limits" precisely because they were not transmitted with their "lineage," the authoritative explanation, or with "permission" *(anujñā)* to evoke the deity of the Tantra. Commenting on the *Guhyagarbha Tantra,* the Tantric Līlavajra observes that the literal interpretation of Tantric texts is the basis for misunderstanding them and practically admits that some of his contemporaries not only misunderstand the texts but also appeal to them in order to justify their own corrupt practices. In the same way, modern authors who are outsiders to the cult assume that the literal meaning is the only meaning, and thus wrongly explain fragments of Tantras available to them.

A commentary on the *Guhyasamāja Tantra* by the Tantric Candrakīrti sets forth four kinds of explanation of the sense of a given passage (cf. Wayman, 1977, pp. 116–117): (1) the invariant sense *(akṣarārtha),* or literal meaning; (2) the shared sense *(samastāṅgārtha),* or sense of the text that is shared either with non-Tantric traditions or with Tantras of the three lower classes; (3) the pregnant sense *(garbhyartha),* by which is meant a meaning that either clarifies the doctrine of lust *(rāgadharma),* reveals conventional truth *(samvṛtisatya),* or considers the three gnoses (*jñānatraya;* i.e., Light, Spread of Light, Culmination of Light); and (4) the ultimate sense *(kolikārtha),* or the one that clarifies the Clear Light *(prabhāsvara)* or reveals the paired union *(yuganaddha).*

Equally important, the Tantras frequently use language that is deliberately obscure. In the Anuttarayoga Tantras this kind of arcane language is called *sandhyābhāṣā,* frequently rendered "twilight language" or "intentional language." In this highly metaphoric idiom the term "Diamond Body" *(vajrakāya)* is used to refer to menstrual blood, "Diamond Speech" *(vajravāk)* to refer to semen, and "Diamond Mind" *(vajracitta)* to refer to scented water. Clearly, Tantric language does not conform to our expectations of ordinary expository writing, where the clearer text is considered "better." In no other Buddhist tradition do the texts strive deliberately to conceal their meaning. But the Tantras have a synthetic character that combines such standard, and non-esoteric, practices as the contemplation of voidness *(śūnyatā)* with special secret practices all their own. The most basic meaning of "secret" in the Tantric tradition is that its theories and practices should be kept secret from those who are not fellow initiates, that is, from those who have not obtained initiation *(abhiṣeka)* or taken vows *(samvara)* and pledges *(samaya).* When these works explain the term "secret" (usually *guhya* in Sanskrit), they apply it to certain things that owe their secrecy to being inward or hidden, like the secret of female sexuality.

A list of secret topics in this literature would comprise states of yoga, the circle of deities, and other experiences that are not accessible to ordinary consciousness and cannot be appreciated by the thoroughly mundane mind. Accordingly, it was never maintained that a person with initiation into a Tantric cult had thereby experienced such esoteric matters. Rather, it continues to be held that someone who had gone through such a ritual establishes a bond with a *guru* who will supply the lore of the particular Tantra and guide the disciple in its practice. Tantric language shares with many other Indian works a difficulty of interpretation. The compact style of Indian philosophical treatises, for example, is the cause for much dispute over their meaning. The Tantras compound this difficulty by the very nature of their contents, making interpretation of the texts all the more difficult. [*See also* Language, *article on* Buddhist Views of Language.]

TANTRIC PRACTICE AND ANALOGICAL THINKING

Tantric practice aims at relating man to supramundane forces or deities. In so doing, it makes use of two widely disparate systems of analogy. One procedure associates man and the divine by means of rules applicable to all practitioners. The other procedure assigns persons to one or another Buddha family according to the dominant personality traits of the individual practitioner. In terms of the four divisions of the Tantras, the first two, the Kriyā and Caryā, make use of the first system. The latter two, the Yoga and Anuttarayoga, generally employ the second. Each approach has its supporters who claim that it provides a way to become a *saṃbuddha* ("complete Buddha").

A preeminent Tantra of the first kind is the *Vairocanābhisaṃbodhi.* This Tantra stresses the basic triad Body, Speech, and Mind—the "three mysteries" of the Buddha—and the prescribed practices by which certain attainments may be generated. Here, the human performer affiliates with the Body by means of hand gestures *(mudrā);* with the Speech by means of incantations *(mantra);* and with the Mind by means of deep concentration *(samādhi),* especially on the *maṇḍala.* In this Tantra, the transcendental Buddha is Mahāvairocana, and the human Buddha is Śākyamuni. This correspondence agrees with the division of the bodies of the Buddha into *dharmakāya* and *rūpakāya* that is found in early Mahāyāna Buddhism. In the same light, Kūkai, the founder of the Japanese Shingon school, explicitly identifies Mahāvairocana with the *dharmakāya.* It is noteworthy that the practice in the Caryā Tantra, in fact the practice based on the *Vairocanābhisaṃbodhi,* has a twofold basis: "yoga with images" and "yoga without images." In the former, one contemplates the inseparability of "self reality" *(ātmatattva)* from "deity reality" *(devatātattva),* and in sequence the performer meditatively generates himself into Vairocana with one face and two hands, making the *samāpatti mudrā* ("seal of equipoise"). The process is called the "subjective ground." The performer then contemplates the Buddha Vairocana, like himself, in front of himself. This step is termed the "objective ground."

In the "yoga without images" the mind is understood to have two sides, one mundane-directed (the *manas* face), the other supramundane-directed (the *buddhi* face). Upon reaching the limit of "yoga with images" one perceives as though before the eyes a configuration of the body of the deity on the mundane-directed side of the mind. The practitioner then follows this with a contemplation in which the deity body appears as a bright illusion on the supramundane-directed side of the mind.

Through this process one achieves the same result as do practitioners of the early Buddhist meditations on "calming the mind" *(śamatha)* and "discerning the real" *(vipaśyanā).* This approach is directed to an ultimate goal indicated by the term "arising of the Tathāgata," and chapters bearing this title are found both in the *Vairocanābhisaṃbodhi* and in the Mahāyāna scripture collection called the *Avataṃsaka Sūtra.* The multiple Buddhas in this tradition of Tantric analogies are on the mental level; they may also be understood to refer indiscriminately to "all Buddhas" rather than to particular Buddha families.

The fasting cult of Avalokiteśvara, which uses the *mantra* "Oṃ mani padme hūṃ," employs a similar system of analogies. [*See also* Avalokiteśvara.] The famous six-syllabled formula is correlated with six Buddhas, six colors, and six realms of sentient beings. It is also recited during six times of the day and the night. The individual performer must pass ritually through the six syllables. The situation is comparable to the youth Sudhana's tenure of study under many different teachers in sequence, as portrayed in the *Gaṇḍavyūha Sūtra* (part of the *Avataṃsaka*).

The second analogical system is formulated in the Yoga Tantra *Tattvasaṃgraha.* It consists of four sections. Persons of different predominant vices in their stream of consciousness are affiliated respectively with these sections, each presided over by a Buddha, as shown in table 1. The commentator Buddhaguhya explains that the fourth of these sections results from a merger of the Ratna family (as agent) and the Karman family (as the fulfilling action), but for convenience, the *Tattvasaṃgraha* usually mentions only Ratnasambhava as the presiding Buddha here. The correlation of persons with particular Buddha families indicates which of the predominant mind-based vices is to be eliminated by the "purification path" of the particular Buddha family. Each of the four paths in turn requires four kinds of *mudrā* ("seal"), but each path emphasizes one of the four and subordinates the other three. The first path emphasizes the Great Seal *(mahāmudrā);* the second, the Symbolic or Linkage Seal *(samayamudrā);* the third, the Dharma Seal *(dharmamudrā);* and the fourth, the Action Seal *(karmamudrā).* The paths have been expanded by the addition of four corresponding *maṇḍalas*, as shown in table 2.

According to Mkhas-grub-rje's *Fundamentals of the Buddhist Tantras* the practice of these purificatory paths commences with an effort by the practitioner to generate the Symbolic Being, the practitioner's own symbolization of the deity with whom he has established a link or bond. One then draws in (usually through the crown of the head) the Knowledge Being *(jñānasattva),* the deity in the absolute sense, who

TABLE 1. Analogical Correspondences according to the *Tattvasaṃgraha*

SECTION OF FUNDAMENTAL TANTRA	BUDDHA FAMILY	PRESIDING BUDDHA	PREDOMINANT CONSCIOUSNESS
1. Diamond Realm	Tathāgata	Vairocana	lust
2. Victory over the Three Worlds	Vajra	Akṣobhya	hatred
3. Training the Living Beings	Padma	Amitābha	delusion
4. Achieving the Objective	Ratna / Karma	Ratnasambhava / Amoghasiddhi	avarice

TABLE 2. Correspondence of the Four Maṇḍalas according to the *Tattvasaṃgraha*

Mandala	Seal *(mudrā)*	Object Symbolized	External Symbolizer	Internal Symbolizer
1. Great *(mahā)*	Great Seal of Body	Form of the deity's body	Hand gesture[1]	Identification of oneself and the deity
2. Memory *(dhāraṇī)* or Linkage *(samaya)*	Symbolic Seal of Mind	Knowledge of deity's mind	Hand symbol[2]	Identification with deity and his knowledge
3. Doctrinal Syllables *(dharma)*	Dharma Seal of Speech	Elegancies of deity's voice	Syllables imagined in deity's body	Identification with deity and with an array of interior syllables
4. Action *(karman)*	Action Seal of Wondrous Action	[not stated]	[not stated]	[not stated]

[1]Hand gesture refers to such well-known gestures as "giving confidence" or "meditative equipoise."
[2]Hand symbol refers to material emblems (e.g., the lotus [*padma*] or arrow) held in the hand.

is usually said to emanate "from the sky." Mkhas-grub-rje explains: "The purpose of executing the seals of the Four Seals is to merge and unify the body, speech, mind, and acts of the Knowledge Being with the body, speech, mind, and acts of the Symbolic Being. There would be no foundation for merger if either were present by itself."

The Japanese school of Tantra called Shingon is based on the *Vairocana* scripture (mainly its first chapter) and the *Tattvasaṃgraha* (mainly its first section, "The Diamond Realm"). Thus, this school ignores the real clash between these two scriptures. Shingon employs two *maṇḍala* realms, that of the Vajradhātu Maṇḍala (Jpn., Kongōkai), an unchanging "diamond" knowledge realm derived from the *Tattvasaṃgraha,* and that of the Mahākaruṇāgarbha Maṇḍala (Jpn., Taizōkai), the changing realm of becoming that makes possible the "arising of the Tathāgata." This latter *maṇḍala* is derived from the *Vairocana* scripture. In the terminology of Tibetan Tantrism, this theory and practice of becoming a Buddha is classified as Caryā Tantra because the scripture from which the Mahākaruṇāgarbha Maṇḍala derives is so classified. This is so because there is no attempt here to relate performers to particular Buddha families according to dominant fault as is the case in the Yoga Tantras. The Yoga Tantra *Tattvasaṃgraha* serves here to add a further dimension of knowledge in the form of commentarial additions and related practices, so as to preserve consistency between the two *maṇḍala* (Jpn., *mandara*) cycles.

The Anuttarayoga Tantras continue the procedure of the Yoga Tantras, and, in the Father Tantras, allot distinct character to the five Buddhas for the purpose of a fivefold correspondence with five different kinds of persons. The Mother Tantras of this class raise the correspondences to six. The Anuttarayoga Tantras also have a basic division into two stages, a stage of generation *(utpattikrama)* and a stage of completion or consummation *(saṃpannakrama).* Indeed, the stage of generation overlaps the Yoga Tantra by way of what it calls the "three *samādhis*," named "preliminary praxis," "triumphant *maṇḍala,*" and "victory of the rite." Tsoṅ-kha-pa's *Sṅags rim chen mo* (Great Treatise on the Mantra Path) elucidates the stage of generation in terms of six consecutive members, each of which corresponds to one of the three *samādhis*, as shown in table 3. These three *samādhis* can be used as a classification in Yoga Tantra practice as well. In fact, when generalized, the three are the three parts of every Buddhist Tantric ritual: the preliminaries, the main part, and the concluding acts.

The second stage of the Anuttarayoga Tantra, the "stage of completion," deals with more concrete matters like the centers in the body (*cakras*) and five mysterious winds (first mentioned centuries earlier in the *Chāndogya* and other Upaniṣads). This stage comprises a six-membered yoga *(ṣaḍaṅgayoga),* also classified in five

TABLE 3. The Stages of Generation according to Tsoṅ-kha-pa's *Sṅags rim chen mo*

MEMBERS	SAMĀDHI	BUDDHA FAMILY	ACTIVITY	REASON FOR THE FAMILY
1.	Preliminary Praxis	Vairocana	Contemplation of the palace that is the Buddha's dwelling place	Because Vairocana is the nature of the material aggregate *(rūpa-skandha)*
2.	Preliminary Praxis	Vajrasattva	Generation of the symbolic circle *(samayacakra)* and the knowledge circle *(jñānacakra),* followed by the generation of passion via the divine Father-Mother	Because Vajrasattva uses passion to "materialize" the *maṇḍala* deities from the *bodhicitta* ("thought of enlightenment") of the Father-Mother pairs
3.	Triumphant *Maṇḍala*	Akṣobhya	Initiation *(abhiṣeka)* conferred by the *vidyā* ("wisdom") goddesses	Because Akṣobhya is the essence of the water initiation
4.	Victory of the Rite	Amitābha	Enjoyment of the ambrosia *(amṛta)*	Because Amitābha is the "diamond of speech" that satiates the devotee
5.	Victory of the Rite	Amoghasiddhi	Making offerings	Because Amoghasiddhi is the progenitor of the Karma family, with power over offerings made to the Buddha and over acts on behalf of sentient beings
6.	Victory of the Rite	Ratnasambhava	Praise of the Buddhas[1]	Because praise extols merits, and Ratnasambhava ("arising of jewels") is the arising merits of Body, Speech, and Mind

[1]Some other formulations conclude the "victory of the rite" with the acts of dismissing the deities, along with a burnt offering *(homa).*

Table 4. Correspondence of the Six Yogic Stages with Goddesses (Ḍākinīs) according to the *Ocean of Ḍākinīs*

Member	Name of Member	Ḍākinī	The Five Steps	Comment
1.	*pratyāhāra* ("withdrawal")	She the Crow-faced		Withdrawal, i.e., interiorization of the ten sense bases (five subjective and five objective)
2.	*dhyāna* ("meditation")	She the Owl-faced		Meditation on the nature of the five Tathāgatas
3.	*prāṇāyāma* ("control of the winds")	She the Dog-faced	Diamond Muttering	Control of the winds in five colors by means of "diamond muttering" *(vajrajāpa)*
4.	*dhāraṇā* ("retention")	She the Boar-faced	Purification of Mind Personal Blessings	Manifestation of the five signs by means of purification of mind *(cittaviśuddhi)* and personal blessings *(svādhiṣṭhāna)*. Movement to the Clear Light via the Three Gnoses
5.	*anusmṛti* ("recollection")	She, Yama's Messenger	Revelation-Enlightenment	Recollection, so as to proceed in the reverse order, by means of revelation-enlightenment *(abhisaṃbodhi)*. Movement from the Clear Light via the Three Gnoses
6.	*samādhi* ("consummation")	She, Yama's Cremation Ground	Pair United	The consummation of knowledge by means of *yuganaddha*, "the pair united"

steps *(pañcakrama).* The five steps are accomplished in members three through six, while the first and second members represent a link with the stage of generation. Table 4 shows the six members and how they were identified with goddesses (*ḍākinīs*) in the *Tantra Śrīḍākārṇava-mahāyoginī-tantra-rāja* (Ocean of Ḍākinīs).

The Anuttarayoga Tantras also contain passages on the "higher initiations," the practice of which includes elements often referred to by modern writers as "sexo-yogic." Briefly speaking, these have to do with worship of the female, and, perhaps, a rite of sexual union in which the male performer does not emit semen. Before attempting any explanation of this topic, it would be well to mention that historically there were lay as well as renunciant Tantrics, just as there were lay as well as renunciant *bodhisattvas* in the Mahāyāna tradition. Among the Tibetan sects that practice Tantrism, it is only the Dge-lugs-pa that observes the Vinaya code of monastic morality. This does not mean, however, that the Dge-lugs-pa practices a "cleaned-up" Tantrism with the objectionable passages expurgated from the texts. As we have noted before, it is not necessary to read the Tantras in the literal manner without benefit of commentaries, as some modern scholars are wont to do.

The four initiations *(abhiṣeka)* of the Anuttarayoga Tantras begin with the "initiations of the flask," rites taken in common with the three lower classes of Tantras. To this is added a "secret initiation," an "insight-knowedge initiation," and an initiation known as the "fourth" (also called *akṣara,* denoting "syllable" or "the incessant"). The secret initiation involves a mysterious "red and white element," an experience of "bliss-void," and the implication that the initiation takes place in the *cakras* of the body (those centers ranged along the spine but said to exist as well in a subtle body). Treatises such as that by Mkhas-grub-rje distinguish between a *karmamudrā* (the female partner) and a *jñānamudrā* ("seal of knowledge"). The insight-knowledge initiation involves a sequence of four joys *(ānanda)* associated with the downward progress of the "melted white element": descending from the forehead to the neck there is joy; descending to the heart there is "super joy" *(paramānanda);* descending to the navel there is the "joy of exhaustion" *(viramānanda);* and upon reaching the sex center there is "together-born joy" *(sahajānanda),* on which occasion the element is not to be emitted. If we are to assume that the element in question is indeed semen, how was it able to descend from the forehead?

There is also an Anuttarayoga Tantra explanation of the "four seals," but it differs from that found in the Yoga Tantras. In the Anuttarayoga Tantra, two separate sequences of *mudrā* are employed, one for the stage of generation, the other for the stage of completion. These are discussed in chapter 36 of the Mother Tantra *Śrīcakrasaṃvara* and in Tsoṅ-kha-pa's commentary to this text, the *Sbas don.* For the stage of generation the sequence is as follows:

1. *Karmamudrā:* one imagines the external *prajñā* woman in the form of an attractive goddess.
2. *Dharmamudrā:* sacred seed syllables such as *hūṃ* are imagined in that body.
3. *Samayamudrā:* the radiation from the seed syllables is drawn back together in the circle of the completed *maṇḍala.*
4. *Mahāmudrā:* one imagines oneself as having the body of the principal deity.

The version for the stage of completion reverses the position of the *samayamudrā* and the *mahāmudrā,* as shown in table 5.

Table 5. **Correspondence of the Four Seals according to the Anuttarayoga Tantras**

Mudrā ("seal")	Path	Buddha Body
karmamudrā	The external *prajñā* woman, because by the four acts of courtship she confers joy.	*nirmāṇakāya*
dharmamudrā	The central channel *(avadhūtī)* and its inner *prajñā* woman	*dharmakāya*
mahāmudrā	The *bodhicitta* of great bliss *(mahāsukha),* which is the fruit of those two *mudrās* (above)	*saṃbhogakāya*
samayamudrā	Manifestation of a variety of divine images	*mahāsukhakāya,* with *bodhicitta* of bliss-void

Particularly worthy of note in conjunction with table 5 is the difference in the description of the *prajñā* woman in the stage of generation and in the stage of completion. In the former, the practitioner approaches the *prajñā* woman only through his imagination, that is, he imagines that she is a goddess with radiating germ syllables in her body. He imagines drawing back the radiation into his own body as a *maṇḍala,* and finally imagines himself as the chief deity. In the stage of completion this woman can confer concrete joy in the four degrees of courtship previously mentioned in correlation with the four classes of Tantras (laughing, mutual gazing, holding hands, the two united). But there is also another *prajñā* woman, the one of the central channel (among the three said to be in the position of the spine). When the texts speak of a *prajñā* consort, which one is intended? Nā-ro-pa has some important information about this in his commentary on the *Hevajra Tantra.* He cites a verse from the *Mañjuśrī-nāma-saṃgīti* (10.14) referring to the four *mudrās*, and gives their order in agreement with the stage of completion described above, substituting *jñānamudrā* for *dharmamudrā.* He then makes this revealing statement:

> *The* karmamudrā [*i.e., the external woman*] *is the causal one, being initial, from which there is the together-born* [sahaja] *non-transiting joy. While this is indeed a truth* [satya], *there are two truths* [*conventional and ultimate*], *and* [*the* prajñā *woman of the* karmamudrā] *is true in a conventional sense, like a reflection in a mirror, but is not true in the absolute sense. Thus, one of keen intelligence should not embrace the* karmamudrā. *One should cultivate the* jñānamudrā *by such means as purifying the personal aggregates* [skandhas], *elements* [dhātus], *and sense bases* [āyatanas] *into images of deities, as the ritual of the* maṇḍala *reveals. By working them with continual friction one ignites the fire of wisdom* [jñāna]. *What is to be attained is the Great Seal* [mahāmudra]. *How is it attained? Through that fire when the* haṃ *syllable is burnt* [*as is stated in the final verse of chapter 1 of the* Hevajra Tantra]. *The Great Seal is like a dream, a hallucination, and the nature of mind. One should embrace this* [*the Great Seal*] *until one realizes directly the Symbolic Seal* [samayamudrā], *which is not a perishing thing.*
>
> (Vajrapada-sāra-saṃgraha-pañjikā, *Peking Tanjur, Jpn. photo ed., vol. 54, p. 2-4-8 to 2-5-5)*

Nā-ro-pa thus acknowledges that some male Tantrics (presumably laymen) resort to the concrete woman as both "initial" (mother) and "together" (wife) in this part of the stage of completion. But he goes on to insist that one of keen faculty, striving for the high goal, will skip this *mudrā* and go directly to the inner *prajñā* consort, the ignited "fire of wisdom" that brings on the Great Seal. Staying on this Great Seal, which introspects mental processes as a hallucination, one realizes directly the *samayamudrā,* the *mahāsukhakāya,* or "body of great bliss."

The above remarks should lend a more benign interpretation to the Tantras than has been the case in the past, when judgments such as "ghastly" were often passed on this literature. The style, of course, is quite unlike that of the older Buddhist scriptures.

RITUAL IN THE TANTRAS

The *maṇḍala* rites of the *Guhyasamāja Tantra* cycle may be seen in outline form in the following sequence:

1. Rites of the Site: clearing the site; seizing (contemplatively) the site; elimination of the obstructing demons
2. Preparatory Acts: pitching the (initial) lines (in the *maṇḍala*) with chalk; preparing the flask (i.e., placement of the flask by the *maṇḍala*); beseeching the gods; preparation of the disciple
3. The Main Rite, beginning with *maṇḍala* construction: placement of the five colored threads (representing the five Buddhas); putting in the colors (in the colored areas of the *maṇḍala*); invitation of the gods (to take residence in the *maṇḍala*)
4. Initiations of the Flask: drawing the disciple into the *maṇḍala;* diadem initiation; diamond initiation; mirror initiation (=water initiation); name initiation; emblem initiation (=bell initiation)
5. Offerings: offerings to the gods; offerings to the guru
6. Permission and Drawing Together: conferral of permission on the disciple to invoke the deity; drawing together of the deities who are in the *maṇḍala*
7. Concluding Acts: release of the magic nail, that is, dismissal of the deities along with a burnt offering *(homa)*

In order to work, each of these rituals must be accompanied by an intense awareness, referred to as *samādhi,* that could also be termed *yoga.* By "working" is meant that at all times the performer maintains a connection with the divine, as is confirmed by the *mantra* "Samayas tvam" ("You are the symbol").

These rituals are replete with details that would take much space to set forth properly. A few details can be given about one that is especially interesting, the disciple's entrance into the *maṇḍala.* The first phase is divided into "entrance outside of the screen" and "entrance inside of the screen." While outside the screen, the disciple ties on a red or yellow blindfold. This is not removed until later in the ceremony, when the initiate receives a superintending deity by throwing a flower into the *maṇḍala,* after which it will be proper to view the complete *maṇḍala.* The preceptor tells the disciple to imagine in his heart a *vajra,* thereon a sun, and on this a black *hūṃ* syllable. He is then to imagine in his throat a lotus, thereon a sun, and on this a red *āḥ* syllable; and in his head a wheel, thereon a moon, and on this a white *oṃ* syllable. He should also imagine that rays from those syllables make his body full of light. The preceptor guides the disciple to the east gate of the *maṇḍala.* Now, in the phase inside the screen, the disciple recites *mantras*. He begins with the east gate, reciting to both the deity of the center and the deity of the east gate. The east gate deity is addressed in order to empower oneself; the south gate deity, to confer initiation on oneself; the west gate deity, to turn the wheel of the Dharma for oneself; and the north gate deity, to make the ritual acts effective. He also bows at each gate: for the east, he bows with all the limbs, the diamond palms (i.e., adamantine and thus unassailable by demons) advanced; for the south, he bows with the forehead, the palms joined at the heart; for the west, he bows with the mouth, the diamond palms joined at the top of the head; for the north, he touches the earth with the head, the diamond palms having been lowered from the top of the head and placed at the heart. Then at the east gate, the preceptor sets forth the pledge(s), contacting the disciple by taking his hand, or else by touching the disciple on the head with the *vajra,* and saying, "Today you may enter the family of all the Tathāgatas," in recognition of the fact that entrance into the *maṇḍala* makes one their progeny; and that having seen the *maṇḍala* means the deities are revealed to the initiate.

The disciple is not to disclose the rituals he has undergone to others who have not entered the *maṇḍala.* Dire consequences are threatened for violating the pledge; guarding it yields magical success. Among the pledges is one requiring that the initiate avoid the fourteen transgressions, especially the first one, disparaging one's master, and the seventh one, revealing the secrets to immature persons (that is, persons who have not been initiated). Both are transgressions of Dharma. After taking the pledge, the officiant goes through an imaginative process, the aim of which is to have the gnosis deity *(jñana-sattva)* descend from the sky into the disciple. It begins with the officiant imagining the disciple in voidness, then generating him into a Buddha from a germ syllable, and then going through a sequence of *sādhanas* (evocations) in which he imagines the disciple's body filled with light. The disciple is induced to circumambulate the *maṇḍala* carrying a *vajra* in his right hand and doing a dance. The second phase is entering, in the sense of viewing, the *maṇḍala.* Still wearing the blindfold, the disciple is directed to throw a flower onto an area with five pictures representing Buddha families. The throwing of the flower constitutes entrance into the *maṇḍala.* The deity on whom the flower then falls is the superintendent deity *(adhideva)* for the disciple. The preceptor imagines that the Diamond Being is opening the Diamond Eye of the disciple; the disciple performs the same act of imagination and removes the blindfold, reciting the *mantra* "Oṃ jñānacaksuḥ Hūṃ Āḥ Svāhā," where *jñānacakṣuḥ* denotes the eye of knowledge. Then the preceptor says, "Now, by virtue of faith, may you see the reality of this *maṇḍala!* May you be born in the family of the Buddha, be empowered by *mudrā* and *mantra,* be endowed with all *siddhi*s (magical success), be the best pledge *(samaya)!* May you realize the *mantra*s with the sport of the *vajra* and lotus!" Thus the disciple is given the "initiation of the flower wreath," a process that establishes whether the disciple should receive other initiations. When it is the case of conferring permission on the disciple to evoke a particular deity, a different procedure is followed. Such evocations are undertaken after examining dreams and other omens.

The burnt offering is among the concluding acts of the ritual. There are four kinds of burnt offering, each corresponding to a different type of magical art: the worldly aims of appeasing the deities *(śāntika),* winning material prosperity *(pauṣṭika),* subduing demons *(vaśīkaraṇa),* and overpowering enemies *(abhicāruka).*

Judging from these various indications, one may conclude that Buddhist esotericism has considerable appeal to Buddhists who find fulfillment in ritual participation, who prefer a secret life that is religiously motivated, and who believe that by exercising all avenues of one's being (body, speech, and mind) one is speeding up the progress to enlightenment. The performer must be strong in imagination of images and in belief, and resolute in daily service to the presiding or tutelary deity.

[*For the place of Esoteric Buddhism within the larger Tibetan context, see* Buddhism, *article on* Buddhism in Tibet. *The Tantric lineages of Tibet are discussed in* Mahāsiddhas. *Tantric literature is treated in* Buddhist Literature, *article on* Survey of Texts. *For Esoteric Buddhism in China, see* Chen-yen, *and in Japan, see* Shingon-shū.]

BIBLIOGRAPHY

Bhattacharyya, Benoytosh. *The Indian Buddhist Iconography.* 2d ed., rev. & enl. Calcutta, 1958.

Chou, Yi-liang. "Tantrism in China." *Harvard Journal of Asiatic Studies* 8 (March 1945): 241–332.

Eliade, Mircea. "Yoga and Tantrism." In his *Yoga: Immortality and Freedom,* pp. 200–273. New York, 1958.

Evans-Wentz, W. Y. *Tibetan Yoga and Secret Doctrines.* 2d ed. London, 1967.

First Panchen Lama. *The Great Seal of Voidness.* Prepared by the Translation Bureau of the Library of Tibetan Works and Archives. Dharamsala, 1976.

George, Christopher S., ed. and trans. *The Caṇḍamahārośaṇa Tantra, Chapters 1–8.* American Oriental Series, vol. 56. New Haven, 1974. In English and Sanskrit.

Guenther, Herbert V., ed. and trans. *The Life and Teachings of Nāropa.* Oxford, 1963.

Guenther, Herbert V., ed. and trans. *Yuganaddha: The Tantric View of Life.* Chowkhamba Sanskrit Studies, vol. 3. 2d rev. ed. Varanasi, 1969.

Hakeda, Yoshito S., ed. and trans. *Kūkai: Major Works.* New York, 1972. With an account of his life and study of his thought.

Kvaerne, Per. "On the Concepts of Sahaja in Indian Buddhist Tantric Literature." *Temenos* (Helsinki) 11 (1975): 88–135.

Kvaerne, Per. *An Anthology of Buddhist Tantric Songs.* New York, 1977.

Lessing, Ferdinand D. *Yung-ho-kung: An Iconography of the Lamaist Cathedral in Peking.* Stockholm, 1942.

Lessing, Ferdinand D. and Alex Wayman, eds. and trans. *Fundamentals of the Buddhist Tantras.* Indo-Iranian Monographs, vol. 8. The Hague, 1968. A translation of Mkhas-grub-rje's *Rgyud sde spyi'i rnam par bźag pa rgyas par bśad pa.*

Snellgrove, David L., ed. and trans. *The Hevajra Tantra: A Critical Study.* 2 vols. London Oriental Series, vol. 6. London, 1959.

Tajima, Ryūjun. *Étude sur le Mahāvairocana-sūtra.* Paris, 1936.

Tajima, Ryūjun. *Les deux grands maṇḍalas et la doctrine de l'esoterisme Shingon.* Paris, 1959.

Tsuda, Shin'ichi. *The Saṁvarodaya-tantra: Selected Chapters.* Tokyo, 1974.

Tsuda, Shin'ichi. "A Critical Tantrism." *Memoirs of the Research Department of the Tōyō Bunkō* 36 (1978): 167–231.

Tucci, Giuseppe. "The Religious Ideas: Vajrayāna." In *Tibetan Painted Scrolls,* vol. 1, pp. 209–249. Translated by Virginia Vacca. Rome, 1949.

Wayman, Alex. *The Buddhist Tantras: Light on Indo-Tibetan Esotericism.* New York, 1973.

Wayman, Alex. "The Ritual in Tantric Buddhism of the Disciple's Entrance into the Maṇḍala." *Studia Missionalia* 23 (1974): 41–57.

Wayman, Alex. *Yoga of the Guhyasamājatantra: The Arcane Lore of Forty Verses.* Delhi, 1977.

Wayman, Alex. "Reflections on the Theory of Barabuḍur as a Maṇḍala." In *Barabuḍur: History and Significance of a Buddhist Monument,* edited by Hiram W. Woodward, pp. 139–172. Berkeley, 1981.

Wayman, Alex. "The Title and Textual Affiliation of the Guhyagarbhatantra." In *Daijō Bukkyō kara Mikkyō e* [From Mahāyāna Buddhism to Tantra: Honorary Volume for Dr. Katsumata Shunkyō], pp. 1320–1334 (Japanese order), pp. 1–15 (English order). Tokyo, 1981.

Wayman, Alex, ed. and trans. *Chanting the Names of Mañjuśrī: The Mañjuśrī-nāma-saṃgīti (Sanskrit and Tibetan Texts).* Boston, 1985.

14 THE SCHOOLS OF CHINESE BUDDHISM

STANLEY WEINSTEIN

In any discussion of the schools of Chinese Buddhism it is important to bear in mind that the widely used English term *school* is simply the conventional translation of the Chinese word *tsung*. As we shall see, the practice of equating *school* and *tsung* has resulted in some persistent misconceptions about what actually constitutes a school in Chinese Buddhism. The root of the problem lies in the word *tsung,* for which dictionaries list as many as twenty-three separate definitions. In Buddhist texts, however, it is used primarily in three different senses: (1) it may indicate a specific doctrineor thesis, or a particular interpretation of a doctrine; (2) it may refer to the underlying theme, message, or teaching of a text; and (3) it may signify a religious or philosophical school.

TSUNG AS DOCTRINE

Tsung in the sense of doctrine or thesis is frequently encountered in fifth-century texts in such phrases as *k'ai-tsung,* "to explain the [basic] thesis," or *hsü-tsung,* "the doctrine of emptiness." Especially common was the use of the term *tsung* to categorize doctrinal interpretations of theses enumerated in a series. In the 470s, for example, the monk T'an-chi wrote the *Ch'i-tsung lun* (Essays on the Seven Interpretations), which presented the views of seven different monks on the meaning of nonsubstantiality as found in the *Po-jo ching* (*Prajñāpāramitā Sūtra;* Sutra on the Perfection of Wisdom). A few years later the renowned Buddhist lay scholar Chou Yung wrote an influential tract entitled *San-tsung lun* (Essays on the Three Theses), which examined the complementary Buddhist concepts of absolute truth and empirical truth from three perspectives. In neither case should *tsung* be understood as denoting an institutionalized school.

The term *tsung* was also used to designate the major categories of Buddhist doctrines, particularly when they were arranged in a scheme commonly known as *p'an-chiao* (classification of teachings), in which the doctrines were ranked in relation to each other. Although there were classifications that reduced the Buddhist teachings to two, three, four, five, six, and ten types of doctrine *(tsung),* the most influential were the four-doctrine classification devised by Hui-kuang (468–537) and the ten-doctrine classification established by Fa-tsang (643–712). Hui-kuang divided the

Buddhist teachings into four essential doctrines *(tsung),* none of which refers to an institutionalized Buddhist school: (1) the doctrine that phenomena arise in accordance with preexisting causes and conditions *(yin-yüan tsung),* the basic teaching of the Abhidharma, advanced in refutation of the non-Buddhist view of spontaneous production; (2) the doctrine of the *Ch'eng-shih lun* that phenomena were no more than empirical names *(chia-ming tsung)* insofar as they could not exist independently of the causes and conditions that produced them;(3) the doctrine proclaimed in the *Po-jo ching* and the *San-lun* (Three Treatises) that even empirical names are deceptive *(k'uang-hsiang tsung)* insofar as there are no real or substantial phenomena underlying them; and (4) the doctrine taught in the *Nieh-p'an ching (Mahāparinirvāṇa Sūtra), Hua-yen ching* (*Avataṃsaka Sūtra;* Flower Garland Sutra), and other such *sūtras* that the Buddha nature is ever abiding *(ch'ang tsung)* and constitutes the ultimate reality.

The doctrinal classification devised by Fa-tsang was far more ambitious in that it delineated ten types of Buddhist doctrines *(tsung),* of which the first six corresponded to the teachings of specific schools of Indian Hīnayāna. Of the remaining four types of doctrines, each of which represented a different variety of Mahāyāna teaching, only the last, the Hua-yen, can be identified with a specific school of Chinese Buddhism. [*See the biography of Fa-tsang.*]

THE EMERGENCE OF THE EXEGETICAL TRADITIONS

The arrival of the translator Kumārajīva (d. 409) in Ch'ang-an from Kucha in 401 marked a turning point in the development of Chinese Buddhism. [*See the biography of Kumārajīva.*] Well versed in Chinese and Indic languages, Kumārajīva created an extensive terminology that made it possible to transmit Buddhist ideas with a degree of accuracy and clarity that had not been achieved by his predecessors, who had often used Taoist terms to express Buddhist concepts. But Kumārajīva's contribution to the development of Chinese Buddhism was not simply that of a translator. He involved large numbers of native Chinese monks in the translation process, generally lecturing on the text he was translating before audiences numbering in the hundreds or even thousands. His leading disciples wrote prefaces or postfaces for the newly translated texts or produced commentaries on them. It was around these disciples that the first exegetical traditions developed.

The approximately thirty-five texts selected for translation by Kumārajīva belong to the three major categories of Chinese Buddhist scriptural writings: Sūtra (purported discourses of the Buddha), Vinaya (the disciplinary codes covering the clergy), and scholastic discourses, which include both treatises and commentaries on the *sūtras*. Although not all the texts translated by Kumārajīva were of equal importance or had equal appeal, a surprisingly large number came to be regarded as basic scriptures of East Asian Buddhism. Of the ten texts most commonly studied during the fifth century in South China, seven had been translated by Kumārajīva. These included four *sūtras*, *Fa-hua ching* (*Saddharmapuṇḍarīka;* Lotus of the Good Law), *Wei-mo ching* (*Vimalakīrtinirdeśa;* Teaching of Vimalakīrti), *Po-jo ching* (in two versions), and *Shih-chu ching* (*Daśabhūmika;* Ten Stages [of the Bodhisattva]); the recension of the Vinaya called in Chinese *Shih-sung lü,* which was used by the Sarvāstivāda school; and two works belonging to the category of scholastic discourses, *Ch'eng-shih lun* (Treatise on the Perfection of Truth) and *San-lun* (Three

Treatises), which, as the name indicates, actually refers to three distinct, but closely related treatises that are usually studied together. The three other major texts studied in South China during the fifth century were the *Nieh-p'an ching,* translated by Dharmakṣema in 421, the *Tsa o-p'i-t'an hsin lun* (Treatise on the Essence of the Abhidharma; popularly referred to as *P'i-t'an*), translated by Saṃghavarman around 435, and the *Sheng-man ching* (*Śrīmālāsiṃhanāda Sūtra;* Sutra on the Lion's Roar of Śrīmālā), translated by Guṇabhadra in 436.

Dynastic wars in the 420s and 430s, followed by a harsh suppression of the Buddhist religion in the 440s, led to a precipitous decline in Buddhist scholarship in the North during much of the fifth century. When the traditional scholarly activities of the clergy—lecturing on scripture and writing commentaries—were finally resumed in the North in the last decades of the fifth century, monks for the most part focused their attention on texts that were different from those that were the mainstays of southern Buddhism. Although northern monks of the sixth century did occasionally lecture on the texts popular in the South (the *Nieh-p'an ching* is a conspicuous example), their main focus was on texts that had either been ignored in the South or were newly translated. In the former category were the *Hua-yen ching,* translated by Buddhabhadra in 420, the *P'u-sa-ti-ch'ih ching* (*Bodhisattvabhūmi Sūtra,* Sutra on the Bodhisattva Stages), translated by Dharmakṣema in 418, and the *Ssu-fen lü* (Four Part Disciplinary Code), the Vinaya recension used by the Dharmaguptaka school of Indian Hīnayāna.

Of the many new translations appearing in the North during the first half of the sixth century, the one that excited the most interest was the *Shih-ti ching lun* (Commentary on the Sutra of the Ten Stages; commonly called *Ti-lun*), translated by Bodhiruci and others in 511. Similarly, two new translations caught the attention of learned monks in South China in the second half of the sixth century: the *She ta-sheng lun* (*Mahāyānasaṃgraha,* Compendium of Mahāyāna; commonly called *She-lun*) and the *O-p'i-ta-mo chü-she shih lun* (*Abhidharmakośa,* Treasury of the Abhidharma), both translated by Paramārtha in 563. Finally, to complete the list of the major scriptural texts of Chinese Buddhism used during the fifth and sixth centuries, mention should be made of the *Ta chih-tu lun* (Commentary of the Sutra on the Perfection of Wisdom; popularly called *Ta-lun*), translated by Kumārajīva in 405. This work was largely ignored until the second half of the sixth century, when its study was taken up by scholars in the San-lun tradition.

Unlike most monks of the fourth century, who tended to interpret Buddhism through Taoist concepts, the learned clergy of the fifth and sixth centuries were aware that Buddhism and Taoism were two distinct systems that differed fundamentally from each other and hence sought to understand Buddhism on its own terms. Although monks during this period were generally well versed in a number of scriptures, there was a growing tendency to specialize in a specific text, which was often viewed as representing the highest teaching within Buddhism. We might cite as typical examples of such monks Pao-liang (444–509), who during the course of his life is said to have lectured on the *Nieh-p'an ching* eighty-four times, the *Sheng-man ching* twenty-four times, the *Wei-mo ching* twenty times, the *Ch'eng-shih lun* fourteen times, and the *Po-jo ching* ten times, and Chih-tsang (458–522), who lectured and commented on the *Po-jo ching, Nieh-p'an ching, Fa-hua ching, Shih-ti ching,* and *P'i-t'an,* among others. Yet despite their familiarity with such a broad range of scripture, each was recognized by his contemporaries as being a specialist in a particular text: for Pao-liang it was the *Nieh-p'an ching;* for Chih-tsang, the *Ch'eng-shih lun.*

TSUNG AS THE UNDERLYING THEME OF A TEXT

When commenting on a particular text, the exegetical scholars of the fifth and sixth centuries were of course interested in the definition of terms and the explanation of difficult passages. But their principal concern was to identify and expound the text's *tsung,* that is, its underlying theme or essential doctrine. Scholars who devoted themselves to the comparative study of the Sūtra literature as well as those who became expert in a single *sūtra* were known by the broad designation *ching-shih* ("*sūtra* masters"), whereas monks specializing in a particular treatise were generally referred to by the name of the treatise that they expounded. Thus, an exponent of the *Ch'eng-shih lun* was called a *Ch'eng-shih shih* (*Ch'eng-shih* master); an exponent of the *Ti-lun* became a *Ti-lun shih* (*Ti-lun* master). In addition to these two types of treatise masters, we also find references to *San-lun shih* (or *Chung-lun shih,* the *Chung-lun* being the most important treatise of the *San-lun* group), *P'i-t'an shih, She-lun shih,* and *Ta-lun shih.* Since the *Ta-lun,* which attracted scholarly attention only in the latter half of the sixth century, was closely related in doctrine to the *San-lun,* we can speak of five basic exegetical traditions centered on the treatise literature, those of the *Ch'eng-shih lun, Ti-lun, San-lun, Pi-t'an,* and *She-lun.*

It is highly questionable whether these exegetical traditions can properly be termed "schools" as is done in much of the contemporary scholarly writing on Chinese Buddhism. That the *Nieh-p'an ching,* the two recensions of the Vinaya, and the five treatises (or groups of treatises) mentioned above were studied intensively by several generations of scholars and had their staunch partisans cannot be disputed. But a school, as we shall explain below, implies something more than a group of scholars who study a particular text, even if they exalt that text above all others. While we do encounter in fifth- and sixth-century primary sources occasional references to *Ch'eng-shih tsung, Nieh-p'an tsung, P'i-t'an tsung,* and others, a careful reading of these sources shows that the term *tsung* when following the title of a text does not mean "school," as it has often been mechanically interpreted, but rather the "underlying theme" or "essential doctrine" of the text in question.

Although it is misleading to refer to the various exegetical traditions as schools, it is clear that by the end of the sixth century "study groups" *(chung)* specializing in particular texts were accorded formal recognition by the government. We note, for example, that in the years 596 and 597 Emperor Wen of the Sui dynasty appointed eminent monks to head the *Ti-lun, Vinaya, Ta-lun, Nieh-p'an* and *Treatise* (i.e., the *Ta-lun*) study groups at the Ta-hsing-shan Ssu, the main state temple in Ch'ang-an.

TSUNG AS A FULL-FLEDGED SCHOOL

The term *tsung* should be translated "school" only when it refers to a tradition that traces its origin back to a founder, usually designated "first patriarch," who is believed to have provided the basic spiritual insights that were then transmitted through a unbroken line of successors or "*dharma* heirs". This definition is derived from the original meaning of *tsung,* which signified a clan that was descended from a common ancestor. Although later patriarchs often expanded the insights of the founder in response to new challenges from rival traditions, they viewed themselves essentially as guardians of an exclusive orthodoxy to which no other tradition could lay claim. Competing traditions were thought to have only varying degrees of validity compared to one's own school–hence the need to engage in *p'an-chiao,* the relative ranking of the different teachings within Buddhism.

Judged by these criteria, none of the exegetical traditions of the fifth and sixth centuries, with the possible exception of the San-lun tradition, can be regarded as a school in the proper sense of the word. Although the *Nieh-p'an, P'i-t'an, Ch'eng-shih, Ti-lun, She-lun,* and the two recensions of the Vinaya were studied by generations of scholars, no founder's name is associated with any of these traditions, nor were these traditions transmitted through an exclusive lineage. A careful examination of the master-disciple lineages that have been reconstructed for the fifth and sixth centuries reveals that there was no consistent transmission of specific interpretations of texts, nor indeed was the disciple necessarily expected to specialize in the same text as his master.

San-lun stands midway between the exegetical traditions of the sixth century and the full-fledged schools of the T'ang dynasty (618-907). The notion that the San-lun tradition constituted an orthodox transmission that passed through a clearly defined lineage seems to have been first espoused by Chi-tsang (549–623), its *de facto* systematizer, who repeatedly cited the "succession on Mount She" *(She-ling hsiang-ch'eng)* as the source of his authority. [*See the biography of Chi-tsang.*] According to Chi-tsang, the San-lun teaching was transmitted from India to China by Kumārajīva, whose Chinese spiritual heir, Seng-lang, settled in the Ch'i-hsia Monastery on Mount She in Kiangsu Province. From Seng-lang the San-lun *dharma* was passed in an unbroken line to Chi-tsang, who was the third generation successor to Seng-lang. It is difficult, however, to view San-lun as a genuine school because the lineage to which Chi-tsang belonged became extinct around 650 with the death of Yüan-k'ang, his successor in the second generation. If the San-lun is to be considered a school, it is one that barely survived its founder.

It is only in the eighth century that we encounter full-fledged schools with founders, lineages, supposedly orthodox transmissions of doctrine, and large numbers of followers. Three such schools made their appearance during the second half of the T'ang dynasty: Ch'an, T'ien-t'ai, and Hua-yen. The early history of Ch'an is too complex to be dealt with here; I shall simply mention that by the late eighth century there were five or six competing Ch'an lineages, almost all claiming descentthrough a mutually recognized line of patriarchs. The pivotal position in this line of patriarchal descent was held by Bodhidharma, a semilegendary figure who was believed by Ch'an Buddhists to be the twenty-eighth, and last, patriarch of Indian Buddhism in a line that extended back to Śākyamuni Buddha himself. By proclaiming in China the "true law," the Ch'an teaching, to which he alone was the rightful heir, Bodhidharma became the first patriarch of Chinese Ch'an and the ultimate source of legitimacy. It is of little consequence that the historical reality concerning the origins of Ch'an in China are at variance with the Bodhidharma legend; what matters is the perception that all Ch'an orthodoxy must pass through Bodhidharma. [*See the biography of Bodhidharma.*]

Historical evidence indicates that the first true Ch'an monastic community was the one founded by Tao-hsin (580–651), who in later Ch'an legend was counted as the fourth patriarch in a direct line from Bodhidharma. Moreover, the designation *Ch'an-tsung* ("Ch'an school") was not in fact used until the ninth century, when it replaced the earlier designations *Tung-shan tsung* ("East Mountain school") and *Tung-shan fa-men* ("East Mountain doctrine") Tung-shan being the site of Tao-hsin's monastic establishment in Hupei.

A similar discrepancy between legend and fact is also found in T'ien-t'ai. The *de facto* founder and systematizer of this school, Chih-i (538–597), did not see himself as the creator of a new tradition but rather as the inheritor of a doctrine that had been transmitted through a lineage that extended from Śākyamuni Buddha to Nāgārjuna in an unbroken succession of Indian masters. [*See the biography of Chih-i.*] Chih-i believed that the Chinese spiritual heir of Nāgārjuna was the relatively obscure monk Hui-wen, whose disciple, Hui-ssu, had been Chih-i's teacher. Believing that his teachings were an outgrowth of this transmission and nothing less than *the* true Buddhism, Chih-i did not give a specific name to the elaborate doctrinal system that he fashioned.

The designation *T'ien-t'ai tsung* ("T'ien-t'ai school") was first used by Chan-jan (711–782), a successor to Chih-i in the fifth generation, who wrote lengthy commentaries on Chih-i's major works. Active in the latter half of the eighth century, when other schools of Buddhism, notably Ch'an and Hua-yen, had already appeared, Chan-jan was forced to take note of their doctrines, particularly when they were in conflict with the position of T'ien-t'ai. He asserted the superiority of his own school over the rival Ch'an, arguing that the T'ien-t'ai lineage counted the eminent scholiast, Nāgārjuna as its first patriarch, whereas the first patriarch of Ch'an, Bodhidharma, was merely one of many Indian masters who settled in China.

The third major school of Chinese Buddhism to appear under the T'ang dynasty was the Hua-yen, which, according to traditional accounts, was founded by Fa-shun (557–640). In fact, however, as in the case of the T'ien-t'ai school, its real founder/systematizer was not the so-called first patriarch but the monk who was subsequently designated third patriarach, Fa-tsang (643–712). Like his T'ien-t'ai counterpart, Fa-tsang did not apply a sectarian name to the elaborate doctrinal system that he formulated, although he was keenly conscious of his spiritual debt to his predecessors in the study of the *Hua-yen ching*. The designation *Hua-yentsung* ("Hua-yen school") occurs for the first time in the writings of Fa-tsang's third generation disciple Ch'eng-kuan (738–839). The orthodox Hua-yen lineage was, in turn, fixed by Ch'eng-kuan's disciple Tsung-mi (780–841), who drew up a list of patriarchs in which Fa-tsang figured as the third. Later Hua-yen sources designated Ch'eng-kuan and Tsung-mi the fourth and fifth patriarchs respectively.

BUDDHIST SCHOOLS AS REFLECTED IN THE SUNG CHRONICLES

The frequent polemics in the eleventh century between Ch'an and T'ien-t'ai, in which each side attacked the legitimacy of the other's lineage, led scholars of these two schools to produce chronicles that sought to establish the validity of their own traditions. The two surviving T'ien-t'ai chronicles from the Sung dynasty (960–1279), the *Shih-men cheng-t'ung* (1237) and the encyclopedic *Fo-tsu t'ung-chi* (1269), offer us valuable information regarding how the schools of Buddhism were actually viewed in the thirteenth century.

Both works recognized five schools under the heading *tsung:* Ch'an, Hua-yen, Tz'u-en, Mi (or Yü-ch'ieh Mi), and Lü (or Nan-shan Lü). In addition, the two chronicles also provided a lengthy account of the T'ien-t'ai lineage, which, however, was not included among the *tsung* but followed immediately after the biography of Śākyamuni Buddha, thus showing that T'ien-t'ai was not merely one among several schools but rather a unique lineage that stemmed from the Buddha himself.

Whether the Tz'u-en, Mi, and Lü actually constituted full-fledged schools during the T'ang period is open to question. Tz'u-en (commonly called Fa-hsiang in modern times after its Japanese counterpart, Hossō) was an important doctrinal system based on Hsüan-tsang's translations of Yogācāra texts and the commentaries and treatises on these by his disciple Chi (632–682), later known as K'uei-chi or Tz'u-en (hence the name of this doctrinal system. [*See the biography of K'uei-chi.*] The Yogācāra teachings transmitted by Hsüan-tsang and systematized by Chi were intensively studied during the eighth and ninth centuries and exerted some influence on the development of T'ien-t'ai and Hua-yen thought. Nevertheless, these teachings did not evolve into a truly independent school because their premise that enlightenment was reserved for a predestined elite ran counter to the ideals of Chinese Buddhism. It is not surprising, therefore, that the Sung chronicles listed only two Chinese "patriarchs": the translator Hsüan-tsang and his disciple Chi. Unlike T'ien-t'ai, Hua-yen, and Nan-shan Lü, which all had their eminent exponents in the Sung and later periods, the Tz'u-en teachings were virtually ignored until the twentieth century, when its long lost treatises and commentaries were retrieved from Japan.

Equally dubious is the classification of the Mi (Esoteric) teaching as a school. The *Fo-tsu t'ung-chi* lists three patriarchs, but two of these, Vajrabodhi (671–741) and Amoghavajra (705–774), are simply translators of Esoteric (i.e., Vajrayāna) texts. The third, Hui-lang, who was a disciple of Amoghavajra, had already become a totally obscure figure by the time the *Fo-tsu t'ung-chi* was compiled. Virtually nothing is known about him, nor do any of his writings survive. Although a large number of Vajrayāna texts were translated into Chinese and many Esoteric practices eventually incorporated into Chinese Buddhist ritual, no attempt was made in China to develop a comprehensive system of Esoteric Buddhism, as had been done in Japan.

The Nan-shan Lü school has its origins in the exegetical traditions of the fifth and sixth centuries that focused on two Chinese recensions of the Vinaya, the *Shih-sung lü* and the *Ssu-fen lü.* By the beginning of the T'ang dynasty the *Ssu-fen lü* had effectively displaced the *Shih-sung lü,* gaining universal acceptance by the clergy, which recognized it as the supreme authority in ecclesiastical matters. Of the three outstanding seventh century scholars who wrote commentaries on the *Ssu-fen lü,* the most influential was Tao-hsüan (596–667), also known by his sobriquet Nan-shan, who, in addition to being the author of what are now regarded as the definitive treatises and commentaries on the *Ssu-fen lü,* was also a church historian and bibliographer of the first rank.

Although Tao-hsüan was the systematizer of the *Ssu-fen lü* tradition, he did not regard himself as the founder of a new school. This role was assigned to him by his successor in the fourteenth generation, Yüan-chao (1048–1116), who was the leading *Ssu-fen lü* scholar of the Sung period and the author of numerous commentaries on Tao-hsüan's major writings. While it is doubtful that a Nan-shan Lü school existed under the T'ang dynasty in any meaningful sense, it is clear that such a school had taken shape in Sung times. The *Fo-tsu t'ung-chi,* in its account of the Nan-shan Lü, counts Tao-hsüan as the ninth patriarch in a lineage that begins in India with Dharmagupta, the reputed compiler of the *Ssu-fen lü.* The Nan-shan Lü lineage has been perpetuated down to our own day by the monks who staff the large monasteries where most ordinations are conducted.

It is important to note that neither of the Sung dynasty chronicles cited above included Pure Land among the Buddhist schools. Although an entire section of the *Fo-tsu t'ung-chi* consists of biographies of Pure Land devotees, the Pure Land faith was not recognized as a distinct school; rather, it was considered a type of devotional practice that pervaded all segments of the Buddhist community. The *Fo-tsu t'ung-chi* lists among its devotees patriarchs of the various schools, eminent monks and nuns, members of Pure Land societies *(she),* and devout laymen and laywomen.

BUDDHIST SCHOOLS IN MODERN CHINA

Although a number of independent schools arose under the T'ang dynasty, occasionally quarreling with each other about points of doctrine or wrangling over the legitimacy of their respective lineages, it should be remembered that some monks sought to reconcile the seeming differences between the schools in the hope of preserving what they considered to be the essential unity of Buddhism. Since a monk often studied with several masters, each belonging to a different school, it was not uncommon for a single monk to appear in lineages of different schools. Just as the independent sectarian lineages of the T'ang dynasty tended to crisscross under the Sung, so too were many of the finer points of doctrine lost on monks of later periods because of the interruption of oral transmissions and the destruction of much of the commentarial literature in the wars that attended the collapse of the T'ang. Although T'ien-t'ai, Hua-yen, and to a lesser extent Fa-hsiang, have survived into the modern period as doctrinal systems *(fa-men),* they no longer command the exclusive allegiance of groups of monks nor maintain even a fictive lineage that goes back to T'ang or even Sung times. By the Ming period (1368–1644) the pre-eminence of Ch'an had been so firmly established that almost the entire Buddhist clergy were affiliated with either its Lin-chi or Ts'ao-tung lineages, both of which claimed descent from Bodhidharma.

It has been customary since the Sung dynasty to divide Buddhism into three major traditions (*men,* "gateways"): lineal traditions *(tsung-men),* doctrinal traditions *(chiao-men),* and the disciplinary tradition *(lü-men).* The term *lineal traditions* refers to the two previously mentioned Ch'an lineages that have come down to the present. Virtually every monk in China today belongs to one of these two lineages. A monk's formal affiliation with a lineage is established when he is tonsured and granted a religious name by his master at the latter's temple. The designation *doctrinal traditions* is applied to the T'ien-t'ai, Hua-yen, Fa-hsiang, and other formal systems of Buddhist thought, any one (or several) of which would be studied by a monk with scholarly interests, regardless of his lineal school affiliation. The teacher who instructs a monk in a particular doctrinal system is usually different from the master who tonsured or ordained him. *Disciplinary school* is another name for the Nan-shan Lü school, to whose lineage belong the monks who carry out most ordinations. Thus, the present-day Chinese monk typically will belong to a Ch'an lineage *(tsung-men),* will probably have studied in some detail a particular doctrinal system *(chiao-men),* and will have been ordained by a master who stands in the lineage of one of the branches of the Nan-shan Lü school *(lü-men).* In addition, his daily devotions are likely to be derived from the Pure Land teaching.

[*For discussion of some of the traditions discussed in this article, see* T'ien-t'ai; Hua-yen; Chen-yen; *and* Ch'an. *San-lun and Fa-hsiang doctrines are treated in* Mādhyamika *and* Yogācāra, *respectively.*]

BIBLIOGRAPHY

The single most important study of the concept of school in Chinese Buddhism is T'ang Yung-t'ung's "Lun Chung-kuo fo-chiao wu shih tsung," *Hsien-tai fo-hsüeh* 4 (1962): 15-23. Also of value, although in some ways superseded by the preceding study, is the same scholar's *Sui T'ang fo-chiao shih kao* (Peking), which was written in the late 1920s but not published until 1962. The treatment of the schools in post-T'ang Buddhist literature is surveyed in detail in Yamanouchi Shinkei's *Shina bukkyōshi no kenkyū* (Kyoto, 1921). For a comparative study of the rise of schools in India, China, and Japan, see Mano Shōjun's *Bukkyō ni okeru shū kannen no seiritsu* (Tokyo, 1964). Hirai Shun'ei's *Chūgoku hannya shisōshi kenkyū* (Tokyo, 1976) is primarily a study of the San-lun tradition, but it also contains a valuable discussion of the definition of school in Chinese Buddhism (pp. 25–57). A traditional account in English of the doctrines of the various schools is given in Takakusu Junjirō's *The Essentials of Buddhist Philosophy*, edited by Wing-tsit Chan and Charles A. Moore (Honolulu, 1947). The most reliable account of the role of schools in twentieth-century China is found in Holmes Welch's *The Practice of Chinese Buddhism, 1990–1950* (Cambridge, Mass. 1967).

15 THE SCHOOLS OF JAPANESE BUDDHISM

Araki Michio

Prior to its official introduction into the court in 552 CE, Buddhism had been brought to Japan by Chinese and Korean immigrants and was presumably practiced widely among their descendants. According to the *Nihongi,* an envoy of the king of Paekche presented Buddhist statues, *sūtras*, and other artifacts to the Japanese court in 552 (other sources give 538). The official introduction of Buddhism exacerbated the antagonism that had been developing between the internationalist Soga clan, which supported the court's recognition of Buddhism, and the more parochial clans, which considered the Buddha a *banshin* (foreign deity). To avoid further dissension, the court entrusted the administration of Buddhism to the Soga clan. The Buddhism promulgated by the Soga was primarily magical. However, aristocrats and court nobles were initially attracted to Buddhism as an intrinsic part of the highly advanced continental (i.e., Chinese and Korean) culture and civilization, which also encompassed Confucianism, Taoism, medicine, astronomy, and various technological skills. As it developed on the continent, Buddhism was not exclusively a religion, for it was also associated with a new, esoteric culture that included colorful paintings, statues, buildings, dance, and music.

Although Japanese understanding of Buddhism was superficial and fragmented in the early stages of assimilation, it gained religious depth through the course of history. The rise of Japanese Buddhism and the growth of schools or sects were closely related to and influenced by the structure of the state bureaucracy, which was itself in the initial stages of development. Yōmei (r. 585–587) was the first emperor officially to accept Buddhism, but it was his son, the prince regent Shōtoku (574–622), who was responsible for creating Japan's first great age of Buddhism. Although the sources provide very little precise information about his activities, Shōtoku is said to have been a great patron of Buddhism. In addition to building many Buddhist temples and sending students and monks to study in China, he wrote commentaries on three texts—the *Saddharmapuṇḍarīka* (Lotus) *Sūtra,* the *Vimalakīrti Sūtra,* and the *Śrīmala Sūtra*—and is supposed to have promulgated the famous "Seventeen-Article Constitution" based on Buddhist and Confucian ideas. Later, Shōtoku was worshiped as the incarnation of the *bodhisattva* Avalokiteśvara. His promotion of Buddhism fell strictly within the bounds of the existing religio-political framework of Japanese sacral kingship: he upheld the imperial throne as the central authority and envisioned a "multireligious system" in which Shintō, Confucianism, and Buddhism would maintain a proper balance under the divine authority of the emperor as the "son of Heaven." Shōtoku's religious policies, his indifference to the doctrinal and ecclesiastical divisions of Buddhism, his dependence on the universalistic soteriology of the *Lotus Sutra,* and his emphasis on the path of the lay devotee significantly influenced the later development of Japanese Buddhism. [*See the biography of Shōtoku Taishi.*]

BUDDHISM IN THE NARA PERIOD

During the Nara period (710–784) the Ritsuryō state, based upon the principle of the mutual dependence of imperial law *(ōbō)* and Buddhist law *(buppō),* recognized Buddhism as a state religion and incorporated it into the bureaucratic system of the central government. Under these conditions Buddhism enjoyed royal favor, and temples and monks became wealthy. However, the state's sponsorship of Buddhism was not entirely altruistic. Throughout the Nara period the government was concerned with the political power held by the Buddhists. The state promoted Buddhism as a religion that could civilize, solidify, and protect the nation. Monks were encouraged to engage in the academic study of Buddhist texts, probably in the hope that they would settle in the government-controlled temples. These temples were presumably subordinate to the state and functioned as an intrinsic part of the state bureaucracy: priests were expected to perform rites and ceremonies to ensure the peace and order of the state, and monks and nuns were ordained under the state authority and thus were considered bureaucrats. The Ritsuryō government prohibited monks from concerning themselves with the needs and activities of the masses. However, those who were not granted official status as monks became associated with folk Buddhist activities. Movements of *ubasoku* (Skt., *upāsaka;* laymen), *hijiri* (holy men), and *yamabushi* (mountain ascetics) emerged spontaneously, integrating indigenous Shintō, Buddhist, and other religious and cultural elements. At the center of these movements were unordained magician-priests who lived in mountainous regions and who had acquired, through ascetic practices, shamanistic techniques and the art of healing. Later, these groups were to inspire powerful popular movements and would influence the development of Japanese Buddhism. [*See* Hijiri.]

Prior to the Nara period Buddhism had remained nonsectarian. However, as the study of texts and commentaries on the *sūtra*s became more intense and sophisticated, groups of scholar-monks organized themselves into schools or sects. Here, the term "sect" *(shū)* does not refer to an organized school but, rather, to a philosophical position based on the various *sūtra*s. Differences between the sects were based solely on the particular text chosen as the focus of study: the ecclesiastical, doctrinal, or religious orientations of the individual sects were not mutually exclusive. Often, these sects were housed in a single temple and, under the restrictions imposed by the Ritsuryō government, they remained dependent on both the state and each other.

Of the six most noteworthy sects of Nara Buddhism, two were affiliated with the Hīnayāna tradition and four with the Mahāyāna tradition. In the first category were the Kusha, based on Vasubandhu's *Abhidharmakośa* (Jpn., *Kusharon;* Treasury of Higher Law), and the Jōjitsu, based on Harivarman's *Satyasiddhi* (Jpn., *Jōjitsuron;*

Completion of Truth). The Mahāyāna-affiliated sects included Sanron (Chin., *San-lun*), based on the *Mādhyamika Śāstra* (Jpn., *Chūron;* Treatise on the Middle Way) and on the *Dvādaśadvāra* (Jpn., *Jūnimon;* Treatise on Twelve Gates), both of which were written by Nāgārjūna, as well as on the *Śataśāstra* (Jpn., *Hyakuron;* One Hundred Verse Treatise), written by Āryadeva; the Hossō sect (Skt., Yogācāra), principally based on the *Vijñaptimātratāsiddhi* (Jpn., *Jōyushikiron;* Completion of Mere Ideation) by Dharmapāla; the Kegon sect, based on the *Avataṃsaka Sūtra* (Jpn., *Kegongyō;* Flower Garland Sutra); and the Ritsu sect (Vinaya), based on the so-called Southern Mountain tradition of Chinese Vinaya studies, represented chiefly by the work of Tao-hsüan (596–667). In the early years of the Nara, the most prominent and prestigious of these sects was the Hossō, which was transmitted by Dōshō, a Japanese monk who had studied in China. The prestige of the Hossō gradually waned, to be replaced by the Kegon sect under the leadership of Rōben. The Ritsu sect provided the codes and external formalities of monastic discipline. The remaining three sects represented, for the most part, academic and political alternatives to the more powerful temples. [*See also* Mādhyamika; Yogācāra; *and* Hua-yen.]

SCHOOLS OF THE HEIAN: TENDAI AND SHINGON

The government's decision to move the capital from Nara to Kyoto was motivated in part by the need to regain the power held by the large, wealthy Buddhist temples. Toward the end of the Nara period, the effort to integrate Buddhism and temporal politics resulted in the accumulation of wealth and the acquisition of large tracts of private land by the Buddhist temples and the involvement in state politics by the more ambitious monks. This trend culminated in the so-called Dōkyō incident, which was, in effect, an attempt to make the religious authority of Buddhism supreme. Under the sponsorship of Empress Kōken (later, Shōtoku), Dōkyō, a monk in the Hossō sect, was promoted rapidly through the ranks of the state bureaucracy. In 766 Dōkyō was appointed "king of the Law" *(hō-ō),* and several years later he attempted to usurp the throne, an action that was quickly crushed by the court aristocracy. The government responded to this affair by once again affirming Buddhism's subordination to the state and enforcing traditional Buddhist discipline. Throughout the Heian period (794–1185), Buddhism continued to be promoted as the religion that would ensure the safety of the state *(chingo kokka).* The sects that arose in the Heian, however, were considerably different from the six Nara sects. Like their predecessors, the Heian sects depended on teachings recently brought back from China as a source of their religious authority. But rather than relying on Japanese and Chinese commentaries, as had their Nara counterparts, Heian-period monks began to focus their study on the actual *sūtra*s, allegedly the words of the Buddha himself. In addition, the schools of the Heian were established by individuals who were considered de-facto "founders" of sectarian lineages. They also tended to be centered in the mountains, that is, at a symbolic distance from political authority, and had their own systems of ordination. The two most important schools of this period were Tendai (Chin., T'ien-t'ai) and Shingon (Chin., Chen-yen). Both stressed the importance of learning, meditation, and esoteric cults and mysteries. Most significantly, however, both schools attempted to establish a united center for Buddhism that would encompass all sects and unite Buddhism and the state.

Tendaishū. The founder of this sect, Saichō (767–822, also known by his posthumous title, Dengyō Daishi), was a descendant of Chinese immigrants. In his youth, Saichō was trained in the Hossō, Kegon, and Sanron traditions; at the age of nineteen he was ordained at Tōdaiji in Nara. Thereafter, he withdrew from the capital city and opened a hermitage on Mount Hiei. Here, he began to study the writings of Chih-i, the systemaizer of Chinese T'ien-t'ai. [*See* T'ien-t'ai *and the biography of Chih-i.*] During his travels in China, Saichō received the *bodhisattva* ordination *(bosatsukai)* from Tao-sui, was initiated into *mantra* practices *(mikkyō)* by Shun-hsiao, studied Zen (Chin., Ch'an) meditation under Hsiao-jan, and trained in the Chinese Vinaya traditions. Upon his return to Japan, Saichō established a Tendai school that synthesized these four traditions within the framework of the *Lotus Sutra.* Saichō adhered to the T'ien-t'ai doctrine that recognized universal salvation, that is, the existence of the absolute nature of Buddhahood in all beings, and stressed the meaning and value of the phenomenal world. These teachings stood in opposition to the standard philosophical position of the Nara schools, best represented by the Hossō doctrine that claimed that Buddhahood was accessible only to the religious elite.

Saichō's ecumenical approach won the approval of the court. With the death of his patron, Emperor Kammu, and the rise of Kūkai and the Shingon sect, Saichō's influence at court diminished. One of his dreams—that the court approve the establishment of an independent center for Tendai ordination—was granted only after Saichō's death. The Tendai sect continued to exercise a profound influence on Japanese Buddhist life for centuries after the death of its founder. Under Ennin (794–864), a disciple of Saichō, the full flowering of Tendai Esotericism (Taimitsu) took place. Ennin was also responsible for the transmission of the Nembutsu cult (i.e, the practice of invoking the name of Amida Buddha) from China. Enchin (814–891), another prominent Tendai monk, also propagated the Taimitsu tradition and was responsible for the formation of the so-called Jimon subsect of Tendai, a group that vied for ecclesiastical power with Ennin's Sanmon subsect. Additionally, many of the most prominent Buddhist figures of the Kamakura period studied at the Tendai monastic center on Mount Hiei, including Hōnen of the Pure Land sect, Shinran of True Pure Land, Eisai of Rinzai, Dōgen of Sōtō Zen, and Nichiren, whose school bears his name. Through them the Tendai legacy was firmly, is subtly, maintained in Japanese Buddhism. [*See also* Tendaishu *and the biographies of Saichō, Ennin, and Enchin.*]

Shingonshū. Kūkai (774–835, also known by his posthumous title, Kōbō Daishi), the founder of the Shingon school, was originally a student of Confucianism and hoped to enter government service. According to various legends, he experienced a compelling desire to leave the capital and live in the mountains, where, it is said, he trained with shamanistic Buddhist priests. He was inspired by the *Mahāvairocana Sūtra* (Jpn., *Dainichikyō;* Sutra of the Great Sun Buddha), which eventually led him to the tradition of Esoteric Buddhism (Vajrayāna). Between 804 and 806 he traveled in China, where he studied under Hui-kuo, the direct disciple of the Tantric master Amoghavajra. [*See the biography of Amoghavajra.*] On his return to Japan he began to promote Shingon (i.e., Tantric) doctrine. At this time he wrote the *Jūjūshinron* (Ten Stages of Religious Consciousness), in which he systematized the doctrines of Esoteric Buddhism and critically appraised the existing Buddhist teachings and literature. Under the patronage of Emperor Saga, Kūkai established a monastic center of Mount Kōya and was appointed abbot of Tōji (Eastern Temple) in Kyoto, which was granted the title Kyōō Gokokuji (Temple for the Protection of the Nation). In return for these favors, Kūkai performed various rites for the court and aristocracy.

According to the Shingon teachings, all the doctrines of Śākyamuni, the historical, manifested Buddha, are temporal and relative. Absolute truth is personified in the figure of Mahāvairocana (Jpn., Dainichi), the Great Sun Buddha, through the "three secrets"—the body, speech, and thought—of the Buddha. To become a Buddha—that is, to bring one's own activities of body, speech, and thought into accord with those of Mahāvairocana—one depends on *mudrās* (devotional gestures), *dhāraṇī* (mystical verse), and *yoga* (concentration). The Shingon school developed a system rich in symbolism and ritual, employing *maṇḍalas* and icons to meet the needs of people on all levels of society. Like the Tendai sect, Shingon produced many outstanding monks in subsequent generations. [*See* Chen-yen, Shingonshū *and the biography of Kūkai.*]

Owing to the support of the court and aristocracy, the Esoteric Buddhism of Tendai (Taimitsu) and Shingon (also called Tōmitsu; "Eastern Esotericism," after its chief monastery, Tōji) prospered. While each school had its own principle of organization and its own doctrinal position, both sought the official authorization and support of the court. Therefore, as the power of the state declined, Tendai and Shingon evolved into religions associated solely with the elite, for whom they offered various magico-religious rites.

BUDDHIST SCHOOLS IN THE KAMAKURA PERIOD

The decline of the Ritsuryō system and the rise of military feudalism brought many changes to the organization and practice of Buddhism, although the basic ideology of the Ritsuryō persisted until the Ōnin War (1467–1477). It has been argued that the new Buddhist schools that emerged in the Kamakura period (1185–1333) transformed Buddhism in Japan into Japanese Buddhism. Unlike the schools of the Nara and Heian, which identified the religious sphere with the national community, the schools of the Kamakura attempted to establish specifically religious societies. The earlier schools had never seriously questioned the soteriological dualism that divided the path of monks from that of the laity, nor had they developed an independent community governed by normative principles other than the precepts. In spite of its otherworldly beliefs, Buddhism, as practiced in Nara and Heian Japan, was a religion grounded firmly in this world. The founders of the new schools in the Kamakura period had all studied at the Tendai center on Mount Hiei but had become dissatisfied with the emphasis on ceremonies and dogma, the perceived corruption of monastic life, and the rigid transmission of ecclesiastical office. In their stead, these religious leaders stressed personal religious experience, simple piety, spiritual exercise, intuition, and charisma. In many respects the practices and doctrines of the new schools reflect the eschatological atmosphere that had emerged toward the end of the Heian, when the country had experienced a series of crises, including famine, epidemics, war, and a deadlock of economy and politics. This sense of apocalypse found its expression in the widespread belief in *mappō,* the notion that Buddhism and society as a whole had entered an era of irreversible decline, and in the resultant popularity of the cult of Amida, which offered a religious path expressly intended to provide for beings living during *mappō.* In one way or another, these popular beliefs were incorporated into the most representative schools of the Kamakura period—Jōdoshū (Pure Land school), Jōdo Shinshū (True Prue Land school), Nichirenshū, and the Rinzai and Sōtō schools of Zen. [*See* Mappō.]

Jōdoshū. Prior to Hōnen (1133–1212), the founder of the Jōdo sect, most Buddhist schools incorporated the belief in the Pure Land and the practice of Nembutsu as adjuncts to their other practices. It was only with Hōnen, however, that absolute faith in Amida (Skt., Amitābha) Buddha became a criterion for sectarian affiliation. [*See* Amitābha *and* Nien-fo.] Like many of his contemporaries, Hōnen had become disillusioned with his early training in the Nara and Tendai schools. He turned to the charismatic teachings of such masters as Eikū, who promoted the belief in *mappō* and the efficacy of the cult of Amida. Under their tutelage, Hōnen came to realize the impossibility of attaining salvation and sanctification through the practice of precepts, meditation, and knowledge. Instead, Hōnen held that one must seek the path to salvation in the Pure Land and the saving grace of Amida. In this, Hōnen was much influenced by Genshin's *Ōjōyōshū* (The Essentials of Rebirth, tenth century), a work that provides the theoretical basis for faith in the Pure Land. [*See the biography of Genshin.*] However, in his own work *Senchaku hongan nembutsushū* (Collection of Passages on the Original Vow in which Nembutsu Is Chosen Above All), Hōnen clearly departs from earlier forms of the cult of Amida. Here, Hōnen claims that one's salvation depends exclusively on one's "choice" (i.e., one's willingness) to place absolute faith in the salvific power of Amida Buddha. The community Hōnen established in the capital city was structured on the notions of egalitarianism and faith and, thus, was able to transcend the social distinctions of kinship and class. Such organizing principles made Hōnen's school a paradigm for the later development of Buddhism. [*See also* Jōdoshū *and the biography of Hōnen.*]

Jōdo Shinshū. Little is known of the formative influences in the life of Shinran (1173–1262), the founder of the Jōdo Shin school, except that he entered the Tendai monastery on Mount Hiei at the age of eight. When he was twenty-nine, Shinran met Hōnen, with whom he studied for six years. Shinran's notion of Amida Buddha's salvific power went far beyond that of his master. In holding that one's faith in Amida must be absolute, Shinran denied the efficacy of relying on one's own capacity to bring about redemption. His teachings went to the extreme of claiming that the recitation of the Nembutsu was an expression of gratitude to Amida rather than a cause of one's salvation. Shinran further stated that it is not man who "chooses" to have faith in Amida, but that it is Amida's Original Vow that "chooses" all beings to be saved. Therefore, even those who lead lives of crime and sin are saved.

Shinran's teachings represent a radical departure from traditional Buddhist doctrine. He reduced the Three Treasures (i.e., Buddha, Dharma, and Sangha) to one (i.e., Amida's Original Vow) and rejected the accepted methods of spiritual exercises and meditation as paths to enlightenment. He was critical of the government's persecution of Hōnen and argued that the secular authority of the state was subordinate to the eternal law of the Dharma. In the religious communities that surrounded Shinran, distinctions between the clergy and laity were eliminated; Shinran himself was married and had children. Although Shinran never formally established an independent sect, his daughter began to build a True Pure Land sectarian organization.

This was the first time in the history of Buddhism in Japan that the continuity of a school was based on heredity. [*See* Jōdo Shinshū *and the biography of Shinran.*]

Nichirenshū. Nichiren (1222–1282), eponymous founder of the sect, is perhaps one of the most charismatic and prophetic personalities in Japanese history. In the time he spent on Mount Hiei between 1242 and 1253, Nichiren came to believe that the *Saddharmapuṇḍarīka Sūtra* (Lotus Sutra) contained the ultimate and complete teaching of the Buddha. In many respects, Nichiren's thought is based on Tendai doctrine: he upheld the notion of *ichinen sanzen* (all three thousand spheres of reality are embraced in a single moment of consciousness) and advocated universal salvation, urging the nation to return to the teachings of the *Lotus Sutra.* However, Nichiren was also a reformer. Rather than accept the traditional concept of the transmission of the *Lotus Sutra* through ecclesiastical offices, Nichiren argued that it was transmitted through "spiritual succession." Thus, he saw himself as the successor to the transmission that began with Śākyamuni and passed to Chih-i and Saichō. He also identified himself as the incarnation of Viśiṣṭacāritra (Jpn., Jōgyō), the *bodhisattva* to whom the Buddha is said to have entrusted the *Lotus Sutra.* Other of his reforms included the attempt to discredit the established Buddhist sects, in particular, Pure Land and Zen. At the same time, however, Nichiren incorporated many of their key notions and practices. With Shingon he shared the use of the *maṇḍala* and the concept of *sokushin jōbutsu* ("becoming a Buddha in this very body"), and with Pure Land he shared the practice of chanting (in this case, the title of the *Lotus Sutra*) and the concept of the salvation of women and people whose natures are evil. Although Nichiren promoted the doctrine of universal salvation, his school developed into the most exclusivist and often militant group in Japanese religious history. Several modern Japanese movements trace their inspiration to Nichiren. [*See* Nichirenshū; New Religions, *article on* New Religions in Japan; *and the biography of Nichiren.*]

Zen Buddhism. In the Nara and Heian periods, Zen (Chin., Ch'an) meditation was a spiritual and mental discipline practiced in conjunction with other disciplines by all Buddhist sects. It was not until the Kamakura period, when the Lin-chi (Jpn., Rinzai) and Ts'ao-tung (Jpn., Sōtō) schools of Ch'an were brought from Sung-dynasty China, that Zen emerged as a distinct movement.

Rinzaishū. The establishment of Rinzai Zen in Japan is associated with Eisai (1141–1215). Discouraged by the corruption of Buddhism in the late Heian, Eisai was initially concerned with the restoration of the Tendai tradition. He traveled to China, first in 1168 and again between 1187 and 1191, hoping to study the true Tendai tradition. In China, Eisai was introduced to the Lin-chi school of Chinese Ch'an. At that time Ch'an was noted for its purist approach—its emphasis on a transmission that stood outside the classical Buddhist scriptures and what is termed the "direct pointing to the mind and perceiving one's own nature." In addition, the Ch'an monks in Sung China refused to pay obeisance to the secular authorities. Eisai, however, was more conciliatory. He studied the practices, ceremonies, and texts of other schools and willingly paid obeisance to the Kamakura regime, which in return favored him with its patronage. Eisai strongly believed that one of the central tasks of Buddhism was to protect the nation and that Zen was a state religion. Far from approaching the common people, Eisai's form of Zen was elitist. Rinzai was established by Eisai's followers as an independent school, and while it remained an elitist group throughout the Kamakura period, its contributions to the cultural life of Japan were significant. [*See* Zen *and the biography of Eisai.*]

Sōtōshū. Dōgen (1200–1253), the transmitter of the Ts'ao-tung school of Chinese Ch'an to Japan, entered the Tendai monastery on Mount Hiei when he was thirteen years old. His intense search for the certainty of attaining Buddhahood drove him from Mount Hiei, first to a Pure Land teacher and later to Myōzen, a disciple of Eisai. Finally, in 1223, Dōgen traveled to China, where he attained enlightenment under the guidance of Ju-ching, a Ch'an master of the Ts'ao-tung school. In 1227 Dōgen returned to Japan and began to expound Sōtō doctrine, eventually establishing an independent sect. As a student of the Ts'ao-tung sect, Dōgen emphasized the gradual attainment of enlightenment through the practice of *zazen* (sitting in meditation), a meditative discipline that entailed sitting without any thought or any effort to achieve enlightenment. Dōgen's notion of *zazen* (also called *shikantaza*) stood in marked contrast to Eisai's use of the *kōan* as a means to attaining sudden enlightenment.

In spite of his adherence to Ts'ao-tung tradition, Dōgen is known for his independence and self-reliance. He was convinced that the truth of Buddhism is applicable to everyone—regardless of sex, intelligence, or social status—and that enlightenment could be attained even in secular life. This doctrine is best expressed in Dōgen's dictum that all beings *are* the Buddha nature. Dōgen also rejected the theory of *mappō* popular among other Kamakura Buddhists. He held that the "perfect law" of the Buddha was always present and could be attained by a true practitioner at any time. Dōgen's emphasis on faith in the Buddha represents yet another departure from traditional Zen teachings that stress self-realization. Because he claimed that the Zen practitioner must have faith not only in the Buddha but also in scriptures and one's masters, Dōgen's school is often characterized as sacerdotal and authoritarian. However, after his death, Dōgen's school was institutionalized and grew to be one of the most politically and socially powerful movements in later periods. [*See the biography of Dōgen.*]

BUDDHISM IN THE MODERN ERA

As a result of the Ōnin War and the Sengoku period (a period of incessant wars among feudal lords), the political system was destined to undergo formal changes. Oda Nobunaga (1534–1582), Toyotomi Hideyoshi (1536–1598), and Tokugawa Ieyasu (1542–1616), the three men who unified the nation, rejected the Ritsuryō system's principle of the mutual dependence of imperial and Buddhist law. The Tokugawa regime (1600–1868) instead adopted Neo-Confucianism as the guiding principle of the nation, manipulating Buddhist institutions to strengthen its systems and policies. It maintained strict control over the development, organization, and activities of religious sects. The Tokugawa government continued to recognize and support all the Buddhist schools including those that the Muromachi government had deemed official religions. However, many of its policies toward Buddhism were stimulated by its persecutions of Christianity and its adoption of Confucianism as the state ideology. New sects and doctrinal developments were prohibited, forcing new movements, such as folk Nembutsu to go underground or suffer suppression. Existing schools forfeited their autonomy, and temples, monks, and nuns were institutionalized and routinized within the political structure. In many temples and local temple schools, particularly those associated with Zen, monks studied and taught the Confucian classics.

Along with political and economic modernizations, the Meiji restoration of 1868 brought significant changes to religious institutions. The Meiji government (1868–1912), which attempted to restore the actual ruleof the emperor in a modern context, rejected some aspects of the religious policies of the feudal Tokugawa. It rejected the religious institution of Buddhism as a state religion and devised the hitherto nonexistent State Shintō as a "nonreligious" national cult. The loss of government patronage and the decline in prestige, power, and security experienced by institutionalized sects of Buddhism forced them to cooperate with the government. The various sects worked within the structure of the imperial regime by performing ancestral and life-cycle rituals. However, the absence of government favor also brought about a spiritual awakening within Buddhism. Buddhist intellectuals attempted to integrate Buddhist thought and tradition into the newly acquired Western culture and technology. Throughout the Meiji and into the Shōwa period (1912–), popular Buddhism continued to thrive. [*See* New Religions, *article on* New Religions in Japan.] Such movements as Kokuchūkai (Nation's Pillar Society), led by the ex-Nichiren priest Tanaka Chigaku, gained popularity in the nationalist fervor of the 1890s. Another folk movement to grow out of Nichiren was the Honmon Butsuryūkō (Association to Exalt the Buddha), founded by the former monk Ōji Nissen and concerned primarily with faith healing. The increased popularity of new religions and lay Buddhist associations such as Sōka Gakkai, Reiyūkai, and Risshō Kōseikai continues in post–World War II Japan.

[*See also* Japanese Religions, *overview article, and* Buddhism, *article on* Buddhism in Japan.]

BIBLIOGRAPHY

Anesaki Masaharu. *History of Japanese Religion* (1935). Reprint, Tokyo and Rutland, Vt., 1963.

Ienaga Saburō, Akamatsu Toshihide, and Tamamura Taijō, eds. *Nihon bukkyōshi.* Kyoto, 1972.

Kitagawa, Joseph M. *Religion in Japanese History.* New York, 1966.

Saunders, E. Dale. *Buddhism in Japan.* Philadelphia, 1964.

Takakusu Junjirō. *The Essentials of Buddhist Philosophy.* Edited by Wing-tsit Chan and Charles A. Moore. Honolulu, 1947.

Tsuji Zennosuke. *Nihon bukkyōshi.* 10 vols. Tokyo, 1944–1955.

16 — THE SCHOOLS OF TIBETAN BUDDHISM

David L. Snellgrove

The various sects or schools of Buddhism in Tibet are probably best referred to as "religious orders" in that most of them are in many ways analogous to Christian monastic orders in the West, namely Benedictines, Dominicans, and so forth. Thus, not only do they accept as fundamental the same Tibetan Buddhist canon (finally compiled in the thirteenth century and consisting almost entirely of works translated from Buddhist Sanskrit originals), but many of them were founded by outstanding men of religion, just as the various Christian orders were established, and so far as doctrine and religious practice is concerned there are no considerable differences between them. Conversely, the various sects or schools of Indian Buddhism were clearly distinguishable at two levels: first, they began to separate according to their various diverging versions of the traditional "monastic rule" (Vinaya), attributed by all of them to Śākyamuni Buddha himself; second, ever greater divergences developed from the early centuries CE onward as some communities adopted philosophical views and religious cults typical of the Mahāyāna, while other communities held to the earlier traditions.

Distinctions of these kinds do not exist in Tibetan Buddhism, since all Tibetan religious orders have accepted unquestioningly the monastic rule of one particular Indian Buddhist order, namely that of the Mūlasarvāstivādins, who happened to be particularly strong in Central Asia and in northern India, and it was in these circles that the Tibetans found their first Indian teachers. Moreover, the form of Buddhism which became established in Tibet represents Indian Buddhism in its late Mahāyāna and Vajrayāna form, with the result that the earlier sects, known collectively as Hīnayāna, have left no impression on Tibetan Buddhism and are known in Tibet only in a historical and doctrinal context. These considerations inevitably lent an overall unity to Tibetan Buddhism that was lacking in India. It follows, however, that such divergences as do exist between the various Tibetan orders are special to Tibet, being largely the result of the many historical vicissitudes which have conditioned the gradual introduction of Buddhism into Tibet—a long process which lasted from the seventh until the thirteenth century. Thus their differences, which from the Tibetan point of view may appear appreciable, can only be explained against a historical context. Moreover, having compared Buddhist religious orders with Christian ones, one must emphasize that whereas monastic orders are in a sense accidental to Christianity, which can operate quite well without them, monastic orders are fundamental to Buddhism in all its traditional forms. Once the monasteries have been destroyed or "laicized," it ceases to exist as a effective cultural and religious force.

Yet another distinction must be drawn, one which is important for an understanding of Tibetan religious life in general and which affects profoundly the relationships between one Tibetan religious order and another. The idea of a religious lineage, that is to say, of a particular religious tradition, usually involving special kinds of religious practice, which is passed in succession from master to pupil, is not altogether unknown in the West, but it is absolutely fundamental in Tibetan thought, and it is precisely this idea which gives coherence to their various religious orders and explains the many links which may exist between them. As distinct from a "lineage," which is bound up with the personal relationships of those involved in the various lines of transmission, who may often belong to different religious orders, we may define a "religious order" (or sect) as one which is to outward appearances a separate corporate body distinguished by its own hierarchy and administrative machinery, by the existence of its various monastic houses, and by its recognized membership. It is precisely in these respects, as well as in the manner of its foundation, that some Tibetan orders may be said to resemble Christian ones. However, religious lineage remains so important in Tibetan Buddhism that some supposed religious orders exist rather as a group of lineages than as an order in any understandable Western sense. This can be made clear only by dealing with them in a historical sequence.

From the time of the foundation of the first monastery in Tibet (Bsam-yas) toward the end of the eighth century until the mid-eleventh century there was no separately named religious order in the country. It had been ordained by royal decree that the Vinaya of the Mūlasarvāstivādins should be followed, and as more monasteries were founded there was no need in the early period for distinctions of any other kind to be made. However, the breakup of the Tibetan kingdom in 842 and the disappearance of any central control resulted in a kind of free-for-all in the matter of maintaining or winning the support of people in Tibet for the new religion, and the conditions of proselytization varied greatly from one part of the country to another. Contacts were certainly maintained with the Tun-huang region in eastern Central Asia, whence Chinese Buddhist influences had already made themselves felt during the royal period, while Indian teachers and Tantric yogins continued to remain easily available across the western and southern borders of the land. Through lack of aristocratic patronage many temples and monasteries fell into decay, but religious lineages were maintained and new ones initiated, and as circumstances became more favorable old monastic sites were brought to life again and fresh ones were founded. According to later Tibetan accounts, this period was one of almost total disruption; but if one judges by what emerged later, this is certainly not the whole truth.

Toward the end of the tenth century, a new royal dynasty began to assert its authority in western Tibet, and the rest of the country gradually became stabilized under the rule of local chieftains. There is now no sign of opposition to the new religion, which certainly made itself felt during the earlier period, and thanks to the royal and aristocratic support which became available once more, religious life began to be organized again under some semblance of control. The vast work of translating Sanskrit Buddhist literature into Tibetan was a continuing priority, and monasteries and literary centers began to flourish. It was in this context that the famous Indian scholar Atīśa (more properly, Atiśa) was invited to Tibet in 1042, remaining there until his death in 1054. He was one of many such teachers, but is especially important in the present context, because his chief Tibetan disciple, 'Brom-ston (1008–1064), established with his master's support the first distinctive Tibetan religious order with the founding of Rwa-sgreṅ Monastery in 1056. Known as the Bka'-gdams-pa ("bound to the [sacred] word"), this new order was intended to bring a proper measure of organized monastic discipline into the professed religious life. A few years later, in 1073, another monastery was founded in the principality of Sa-skya by Dkon-mchog Rgyal-po of the 'Khon family, who was one of the disciples of a remarkable scholar-traveler known as 'Brog-mi (a name meaning simply "the nomad," 992–1072).

This later period, from the later tenth century onward, is known as the "second diffusion" of Buddhism in Tibet; it differed from the earlier period in that the influences were now exclusively Indian, earlier contacts with Central Asia and China having been very largely forgotten. While the same level of scholarly activity, which typified the earlier royal period, was encouraged primarily by the religious rulers of western Tibet, much the same kind of free enterprise which had characterized the hundred years and more of the politically unstable period which had followed continued to account for much of the progress which was now made.

Another successful entrepreneur, who seems to have had no aristocratic support at all, was Mar-pa (1012–1096), who made several journeys to eastern India, studying with various Tantric yogins and especially with his chosen master, Nā-ro-pa (956–1040). The most famous of Mar-pa's pupils is Mi-la-ras-pa ("the cotton-clad Mila"), renowned for his life of extreme asceticism. It is interesting to note how the practice of sexual yoga, in which Mar-pa was adept, could be associated in this particular lineage with the strictest abstinence. Mi-la-ras-pa transmitted Mar-pa's teachings, derived from those of famous Indian sages and yogins, to Sgam-po-pa (1079–1153), who founded the monastery of Dwags-lha-sgam-po, where the teachings continued to be passed on, although it never became the center of a distinct religious order. However, Sgam-po-pa's direct disciples established six famous schools, which developed subsequently into the various branches of the now well-known Bka'-brgyud order, all of whom trace their traditions back through Sgam-po-pa, Mi-la-ras-pa, and Mar-pa, to the Indian yogin Nā-ro-pa and his master Ti-lo-pa, who are placed in immediate succession beneath the supreme Buddha Vajradhara. The so-called Bka'-brgyud order therefore represents an interrelated group of suborders, which are effectively religious orders in their own right, in that they have developed from the start separate hierarchies and administrative organizations with some quite distinct traditions. [*See the biographies of Mi-la-ras-pa, Mar-pa, Nā-ro-pa, and Tilo-pa.*]

The greatest of Sgam-po-pa's disciples was probably the Lama Phag-mo-gru (1110–1170) who founded the first important Bka'-brgyud monastery, that of Gdan-sa-mthil. It is interesting to record that he started this later-flourishing establishment as a simple hut in which he lived, while disciples gathered around building huts of their own. It was soon transformed into a wealthy monastery, however, thanks to the patronage of the wealthy Rlaṅs family, which thereafter provided the religious head as well as the chief administrative officer. This close relationship between an important religious hierarchy and a local ruling family also has characterized the Sa-skya order. As may be expected, both of these religious orders have been involved in national politics, and they may be said to foreshadow in their organization the later religious form of government which became the Tibetan norm.

Special mention must also be made of the Karma-pa order, founded by another of Sgam-po-pa's disciples, namely Dus-gsum-mkhyen-pa (1110–1193), who founded the monastery of Mtshur-phu in 1185. This order is probably named after the monastery of Karma Gdan-sa, which he had earlier founded in eastern Tibet, whence he had come. This order has the distinction of being one of the first to use the reincarnation system for the discovery and identification of successive head lamas, and its hierarchy has continued right down to the present day. Other Bka'-brgyud-pa orders adopted the same system, especially those that were not subject to aristocratic patronage, in which cases the controlling family would normally keep the succession within its own ranks. The practice was presumably adopted by these early Bka'-brgyud-pas from the circles of Indian Tantric yogins, with whom they were so closely connected in their origins and where such reincarnations were traditionally believed to occur. Gradually, the practice was adopted in other religious orders, of which the best-known examples are the reincarnating heads of the Dge-lugs-pa order, the Dalai and Panchen lamas (see below), but they are but two of many later hundreds.

It should be added that the name *Karma-pa* is explained traditionally in another way. According to this interpretation, an assembly of gods and *ḍākinīs* is believed to have bestowed upon the founder of the order knowledge of the past, present, and future (viz., the whole chain of karmic effects) as well as a magical black miter, woven from the hair of a myriad of *ḍākinīs*. This has resulted in the nickname "Black Hats" for this order as distinct from the later "Red Hat" lineage, which branched off after a certain Grags-pat-seṅge received special honors, including a fine red hat from one of the Mongol emperors of China. We shall refer to such political involvements briefly below.

Returning to Sgam-po-pa's disciples, one recalls a third important one, Sgom-pa (1116–1169), who founded the suborder known as Mtshal-pa from the name of the district where his first monastery, Guṅ-thaṅ, was established. Three other Bka'-brgyud orders are second-generation foundations, in that they were started by disciples of the great lama Phag-mo-gru. These are the 'Bri-guṅ-pa, named after 'Bri-guṅ Monastery, which was founded by 'Jig-rten-mgon-po (1143–1212); the Stag-luṅ-pa, also named after its chief monastery; and the 'Brug-pa, named after the monastery of 'Brug in central Tibet, although it was Rwa-luṅ which became in effect its chief monastery. Whether one refers to these various Bka'-brgyud-pa branches as orders or suborders is a matter for choice, depending upon their later historical vicissitudes. Important ones surviving to this day are the Karma-pa, which is well established now in exile, the 'Bri-guṅ-pa, which survives in Ladakh, and the 'Brug-pa, which has been all-powerful in Bhutan since the seventeenth century and which is also well represented in Ladakh.

Noting that Bka'-brgyud (Śaṅs-pa-bka'-brgyud) has the more general meaning of "lineage of the (sacred) word," one may draw attention to the Śaṅs-pa-bka'-brgyud, a separate order founded by Khyuṅ-po-rnal-'byor around 1100 (dates uncertain). Having begun his religious life studying Bon and Rñiṅ-ma doctrines, this remarkable scholar later traveled in northern India, where his chief teacher was the extraordinary *yoginī* Ni-gu-ma, the sister of Nā-ro-pa. Having studied with her and other Tantric teachers, he established himself at Źaṅ-źuṅ in Śaṅs, after which his school was named. The lineage of his teachings has continued to the present, but internal dissensions later brought his school to an end as a separate order.

These various Bka'-brgyud traditions, whether linked as most were with Mar-pa's line of transmission or not, and also the traditions of the Sa-skya order, all have related origins in the late Mahāyāna and Tantric Buddhism of northeast India from the tenth to the early thirteenth century. It is exactly the same form of developed Indian Buddhism, which varies only insofar as their original Indian masters preferred slightly varying Tantric traditions. The Bka'-gdams-pa order differed only in its far stricter adherence to the monastic rule, while the others permitted noncelibate as well as monastic religious life. However, wherever there were monasteries, it was always the same ancient Indian Buddhist monastic rule, namely that of the Mūlasarvāstivādins, that was followed. High standards of scholarship were of the order of the day, for it was precisely during this period that the great enterprise of transferring all that remained of Indian Buddhism onto Tibetan soil was achieved. One should mention in particular the considerable works of translation of the great Rin-chen-bzaṅ-po (958–1055) of western Tibet and of his collaborators and successors, who may be associated with the Bka'-gdams-pa order from the time of its foundation, and later the impressive scholarship of the great Sa-skya lamas during the twelfth and thirteenth centuries. Scholars of all orders contributed in their various ways to the eventual formation of the Tibetan Buddhist canon, consisting of well over a hundred volumes of doctrine attributed to Śākyamuni Buddha himself or his accredited representatives and over twice as many volumes of commentaries and exegetical works by Indian masters.

THE RÑIṄ-MA-PA AND BON TRADITIONS

All the various orders so far discussed were founded during the eleventh and twelfth centuries in a country where Buddhist traditions had been more or less active since the eighth century, if not before. In the earlier period there had been religious lineages of the kind described above, but no religious orders with separate hierarchies and distinctive traditions as already defined. However, it is quite understandable that those who continued to represent the earlier teachings, which were still being transmitted, should begin to band together in order to protect them, the more so as the new orders tended more and more to challenge their orthodoxy. Thus, the "Old Order" (Rñiṅ-ma) and Bon as another clearly constituted order gradually appear on the scene from the twelfth century onward. The latest to achieve recognized existence, they preserve the oldest Buddhist as well as pre-Buddhist traditions, while at the same time benefiting from the teachings accumulated during the later period.

Neither the Rñiṅ-ma-pas nor the Bon-pos are religious orders in the precise sense defined above, but rather groupings of related lineages, where certain high lamas (like many other orders, they came to adopt the reincarnation system) have achieved particular eminence. By their very nature they have no clearly distinguishable historical founder, as do the later orders, although the Rñiṅ-ma-pas claim in retrospect the yogin-magician Padmasambhava, who visited Tibet in the later eighth century, as their founder, while the Bon-pos attribute their teachings to the mythical teacher

Gśen-rab, who came from the country of Ta-źig, a vague region beyond western Tibet (the same name occurs in Tadzhik S.S.R.) in the remote past. While they hold many religious teachings in common, there is one fundamental difference between them. Although the later orders rejected some of the teachings of the Rñiṅ-ma-pas as unorthodox (thus inducing them to make their own special collection of Rñiṅ-ma Tantras), they have never doubted their credibility as reliable Buddhist teachers; thus, they unquestioningly form part of the whole Tibetan Buddhist tradition.

On the other hand, the Bon-pos have put themselves beyond the acknowledged Buddhist pale by insisting that their teachings, very largely Buddhist in content as they undoubtedly are, have come not from India but from Ta-źig or Shambhala, a totally mythical land, and maintaining that while Gśen-rab is a genuine Buddha, Śākyamuni is a counterfeit one. I suspect that their earliest Buddhist traditions go back to the period before the seventh century, when Indian religious teachings were already penetrating ancient western Tibet from the far northwest of India and from Central Asia, and that subsequently they would never have accepted the undoubted historical origin of similar teachings when they were later imported into Tibet under royal patronage. Much pre-Buddhist Tibetan religion has been formally incorporated into their teachings, but their whole way of life from the time they appear in Tibet as an organized body from the twelfth century onward has been modeled on that of the recognized Buddhist orders and, in recent centuries, especially on the Dge-lugs-pa, in whose great monastic schools they had no hesitation in studying. Since the recognized Buddhist orders have also adopted many non-Buddhist cults at a popular level of practice, the Bon-pos have lost even that separate distinction. Seemingly unaware of the overwhelmingly Buddhist content of Bon-po teachings, orthodox Tibetan writers have identified them retrospectively with all those who opposed the introduction of the new religion into Tibet during the seventh and eighth centuries. All in all, the Bon-pos are a most curious religious phenomenon. They survive now in exile together with the other Tibetan religious orders that have succeeded in rebuilding their fortunes abroad after the organized destruction of religion in Tibet from 1959 onward.

In their transmitted teachings the Rñiṅ-ma-pas have much in common with the Bon-pos because they have preserved teachings which were developed in Tibet under Central Asian and Chinese Buddhist influence from the eighth century onward. Most distinctive of these is the Rdzogs-chen ("great fulfillment") tradition, which can be traced back through eighth-century Tibetan teachers to Central Asian and Chinese masters. The loss of contact with the Indian originals, inevitably involved in such long lines of transmission, led scholars of the later orders, who could so easily obtain Indian originals directly from Nepal and northern India, to challenge in good faith many Rñiṅ-ma-pa teachings, although it must be added that in some cases the Rñiṅ-ma claim has since been vindicated by the discovery of Sanskrit originals. At the same time, none of the later schools deny the great importance of Padmasambhava, often incorporating rituals that center upon him as a recognized Buddha emanation.

Both Rñiṅ-ma-pas and Bon-pos have resorted to the practice of rediscovering "hidden treasure" *(gter ma),* namely religious books, really or supposedly deposited in some secret place by an earlier renowned teacher, often in times of persecution, real or imagined, so that they might be rediscovered at an appropriate later date by those who are skilled in the task. Some of these works are in a prophetic form and (like the *Book of Daniel*) can be dated more or less by the later events to which they refer. The Rñiṅ-ma and the Bon traditions represent the most complex and interesting of Tibetan religious orders.

OTHER LATER RELIGIOUS ORDERS

We may refer briefly to later Tibetan orders of the fourteenth and fifteenth centuries, which were constituted after the completion of the formative period of Tibetan Buddhism described above and which are therefore more or less relatable to the already existing orders, although their leaders often appealed directly to Indian Buddhist sources in justification of their teachings. The Jo-naṅ-pas emerge as a distinct school in the fourteenth century as the result of the precise form given certain teachings on the nature of the absolute by a renowned scholar, Śes-rab-rgyal-mtshan of Dol-po (1292–1361), although similar views can be traced back to earlier teachers, certainly to the Indian Yogācārins to whom this Tibetan school appeals. It was named after the monastery of Jo-mo-naṅ, founded by Śes-rab-rgyal-mtshan's own teacher. It would seem to be a rare example of a Tibetan order of which the distinctive characteristic was a particular philosophical doctrine, namely the real existence of Buddhahood in an ontological sense. Like some of their Yogācārin forebears, they were accused of being "Buddhist brahmans," and the order was formally proscribed by the fifth Dalai Lama after he came to power in 1642, but probably more for political than philosophical motives.

Yet another totally innocuous order was started by the disciples of the great scholar Bu-ston (1290–1364), who had been largely responsible for bringing the work on the Tibetan canon to a successful conclusion. Named Źwa-lu-pa after his monastery Źwa-lu, this small order had close associations with the then powerful Sa-skya order. [*See the biography of Bu-ston.*] In the fifteenth century, a great Sa-skya scholar, Kun-dga'-bzaṅ-po (1382–1444), founded the monastery of Nor E-vam-chos-ldaṇ, and based on this foundation there developed a new Sa-skya suborder known as Nor-pa, which, like other surviving Tibetan schools, exists nowadays in exile in India.

Left for final consideration is the very important order of the Dge-lugs-pa, nicknamed the "Yellow Hats," founded by the great scholar-reformer Tsoṅ-kha-pa (1357–1419). Having studied with teachers belonging to several of the already established orders, Mtshal, Sa-skya, Phag-mo-gru, Źwa-lu, and Jo-naṅ, he joined the great Bka'-gdams-pa monastery of Rwa-sgreṅ, founded by Atīśa's disciple 'Brom-ston. After he founded his first monastery of Dga'-ldan near Lhasa in 1409, his school was referred to as the "New Bka'-gdams-pa," since he insisted on the same strict monastic discipline as had his great predecessor Atīśa. His flourishing order certainly won early esteem on account of its superior moral virtues, but to the detriment of such qualities it eventually achieved political power during the reign of the fifth Dalai Lama by the same method of calling upon foreign aid as had been used earlier by other religious orders.

POLITICAL INVOLVEMENTS

The history of Tibet is so bound up with its religious orders and, prior to 1959, its form of government was so peculiarly religious in structure, that some brief summary of these political involvements is required. Tibet was strong and independent as a self-constituted united country of Tibetan-speaking peoples from approximately 600 CE until the fall of the last of the line of Yar-kluṅs kings in 842. Thereafter, although disunited it remained free from foreign interference until the Mongols, united under Chinggis Khan, took possession of it during the first half of the thirteenth century. Looking for a notable local representative whom they could hold responsible for Tibetan submissiveness, they lighted upon the grand lamas of Sa-skya as the most suitable in the absence of any obvious nonreligious choice. The Sa-skya order began to benefit greatly from this connection, especially when Khubilai Khan became the first Mongol emperor of China and established Peking as his capital (1263). Jealous of the wealth and power that Sa-skya enjoyed, other orders, the Karma-pa, the Mtshal-pa, and the 'Bri-guṅ-pa, also sought for Mongol patrons. Thus from 1267 until 1290 the monasteries of Sa-skya and 'Bri-guṅ waged war with one another, resulting in the destruction and burning of 'Bri-guṅ. However, the Karma-pas maintained a profitable interest at the Chinese court, lasting beyond the Mongol (Yüan) dynasty into the Ming without such untoward results.

Sa-skya preeminence was brought to an end by one of its own monks, Byaṅ-chub-rgyal-mtshan of the Rlaṅs family, which was affiliated with the Phag-mo-gru order, and for one hundred thirty years Tibet was ruled by him and his successors as an effectively independent country. Their rule was then replaced by that of their powerful ministers, the princes of Rin-spuṅ, and they in turn by the rulers of Gtsaṅ, both of these families being supporters of the Karma-pa order, which duly benefited. With the destruction of the supremacy of Gtsaṅ by the fifth Dalai Lama and his new Mongol supporters, the Karma-pas suffered most from his displeasure. It was probably as much due to the patronage which the Jo-naṅ-pas had also previously enjoyed as a result of their good relations with the Karma-pas, which led to their proscription by the fifth Dalai Lama, as to any unorthodox views which they may have held.

Scarcely any country throughout its history has been as tolerant in the religious sphere as Tibet, but vengeance has been terrible wherever political interests were involved. It is significant that the Rñiṅ-ma order, which might well be judged even more unorthodox, has survived more or less unscathed throughout the centuries, thanks to its lack of political involvement; the same is true of the Bon-pos, whose views must surely be interpreted as totally heretical so far as the person of Śākyamuni Buddha himself is concerned. The Karma-pas survived the displeasure of the fifth Dalai Lama and have since lived gentle lives remote from the political scene. However, their "Red Hat" incarnation came to a sad end in 1792 as a result of his treacherous involvement with the newly established Gorkha regime in Nepal. Largely at his personal instigation, the Gorkhas invaded Tibet in 1788 and sacked Bkra-śis-lhun-po, against which he harbored a particular grudge. When the Gorkhas were later defeated by a Chinese army he committed suicide and was duly forbidden by the Tibetan government to reincarnate in future.

The last victim of Tibetan political intrigue was the Incarnate Lama of Rwa-sgreṅ Monastery (the original Bka'-gdams-pa foundation) in 1947, an event that was surely disastrous for the whole country, just when it was threatened with foreign Communist occupation. Whatever benefits the Tibetans have gained in spiritual well-being from their religious orders, they have suffered correspondingly politically as a result of the built-in weaknesses of such a religious form of government. Quite apart from sectarian jealousies, the reincarnation system leaves long periods of interregnum between the decease of one ruling lama and the time when his successor becomes old enough to attempt to regain power from the regents who have been operating in his stead.

[*See also* Buddhism, *article on* Buddhism in Tibet; Tibetan Religions, *overview article*; Bon; Dge-lugs-pa; Mādhyamika; *and* Yogācāra.]

BIBLIOGRAPHY

Kapstein, Matthew. "The Shangs-pa bKa'-brgyud: An Unknown Tradition of Tibetan Buddhism." In *Tibetan Studies in Honour of Hugh Richardson*, edited by Michael Aris and Aung San Suu Kyi, pp. 136–143. Warminster, 1979.

Kvaerne, Per. "The Canon of the Bonpos." *Indo-Iranian Journal* 16 (1974): 18–56, 96–144.

Kvaerne, Per. "Who are the Bonpos?" *Tibetan Review* 11 (September 1976): 30–33.

Li An-che. "Rñin-ma-pa: The Early Form of Lamaism." *Journal of the Royal Asiatic Society* (1948): 142–163.

Li An-che. "The bKa'-brgyud-pa Sect of Lamaism." *Journal of the American Oriental Society* 69 (1949): 51–59.

Petech, Luciano. "The *'Bri-guṅ-pa* Sect in Western Tibet and Ladakh." In *Proceedings of the Csoma de Kőrös Memorial Symposium*, edited by Louis Ligeti. Budapest, 1978, pp. 313–325.

Richardson, Hugh E. "The Karma-pa Sect: A Historical Note." *Journal of the Royal Asiatic Society* (1958): 139–165 and (1959): 1–18.

Richardson, Hugh E. "The Rva-sgreng Conspiracy of 1947." In *Tibetan Studies in Honour of Hugh Richardson*, edited by Michael Aris and Aung San Suu Kyi. Warminster, 1979.

Ruegg, David S. "The Jo-naṅ-pas: A School of Buddhist Ontologists According to the *Grub-mtha' śel-gyi-me-loṅ*." *Journal of the American Oriental Society* 83 (1963): 73–91.

Sperling, Elliot. "The Fifth Karma-pa and Some Aspects of the Relationship between Tibet and the Early Ming." In *Tibetan Studies in Honour of Hugh Richardson*, edited by Michael Aris and Aung San Suu Kyi, pp. 280–287. Warminster, 1979.

Snellgrove, David L., and Hugh E. Richardson. *A Cultural History of Tibet* (1968). Reprint, Boulder, 1980.

Tarthang Tulku. *A History of the Buddhist Dharma*. Crystal Mirror, no. 5. Berkeley, 1977.

Tucci, Giuseppe. *The Religions of Tibet*. Translated by Geoffrey Samuel. Berkeley, 1980.

FOUR

DIMENSIONS OF RELIGIOUS PRACTICE

17

THE BUDDHIST SAMGHA

HEINZ BECHERT

The word *saṃgha* (or *saṅgha*) is a common noun found in Sanskrit, Pali, and the various Prakrit languages, meaning "multitude" or "assemblage." For Buddhists it became the technical term for their religious community, and the term in this sense was also adopted by followers of Jainism and of other contemporary religious groups.

The Buddhist *saṃgha* in the wider sense of the word consists of four "assemblies" (Skt., *pariṣad;* Pali, *parisā*); they are the monks (*bhikṣu;* Pali, *bhikkhu*), the nuns (*bhikṣuṇī*; Pali, *bhikkhunī*), the male lay followers *(upāsaka),* and the female lay followers *(upāsikā).* A similar wider understanding of the term "fourfold *saṃgha*" is also known from Jain sources. In the narrower sense of the word, *saṃgha* is the community of monks and nuns only.

The Buddhist *saṃgha* was established by the Buddha himself when he accepted as his first disciples five men before whom he had preached his first sermon in a park near Varanasi. During his lifetime, the community grew considerably, and the Buddha is credited with having regulated its life and organization in a very detailed manner.

SOURCES

The law book for the Buddhist *saṃgha* forms the first part of the Buddhist scriptures. This collection, called the Vinaya Piṭaka (Basket of Monastic Discipline), has been handed down in a number of different recensions, each belonging to a particular "school" *(nikāya)* of early Indian Buddhism. The rather close similarity of the main parts of these texts clearly points to a common source. The complete text of the Vinaya Piṭaka of the Mahāvihāra (the main tradition of the Theravāda school) has been preserved in Pali. Most other versions were originally composed in Sanskrit, but only parts of the original texts are preserved. Several complete recensions are available in Chinese translation, and the Mūlasarvāstivāda version is available in Tibetan translation. In Chinese translation we possess more or less complete Vinaya Piṭakas of the Sarvāstivāda, Mūlasarvāstivāda, Dharmaguptaka, Mahīśāsaka, and Mahāsāṃghika schools. Parts of the Vinaya texts of the Lokottaravāda, Kāśyapīya, and

Sammatīya schools and of the Abhayagirivihāra subschool of the Theravāda tradition are also extant.

All versions of the Vinaya Piṭaka consist of three main sections: the *Vinayavibhaṅga,* the *Skandhaka* (Pali, *Khandhaka*) or *Vinayavastu,* and the *Parivāra.* The most ancient part of the *Vinayavibhaṅga* is represented by the group of rules known as the Prātimokṣa (Pali, Pātimokkha), injunctions regulating the behavior of monks and nuns; all of them are believed to have been issued by the Buddha himself. Their number is slightly different for each of the various early Buddhist schools, ranging from 218 rules for the Mahāsāṃghikas to 263 rules for the Sarvāstivādins. These rules are also handed down as a separate work serving as the confession formula to be recited at the regular confessional ceremonies of the *saṃgha.* In the *Vinayavibhaṅga,* all these rules are listed along with an account of the occasion on which the Buddha issued each one, casuistry, and additional explanations. The work is divided into two parts, one listing regulations for monks and the other giving rules for nuns. Since each rule is an injunction whose transgression is followed by a particular sanction, the *Prātimokṣa* and *Vibhaṅga* represent a compendium of the penal laws of the *saṃgha.*

The *Skandhaka,* or *Vinayavastu,* functions as the procedural law of the *saṃgha.* Here, detailed regulations are given for admission to the order, the confessional ceremony, and various aspects of monastic life, such as the behavior prescribed for monks and nuns during the rainy season, what possessions they are permitted, the use of medicines, and so forth. Most versions of this text contain as an appendix an account of the first two Buddhist councils. The *Parivāra* contains additional material in the form of mnemonic summaries, explanations, and so on.

RULES AND PROCEDURES

Admission to the *saṃgha* was a rather informal process during the Buddha's lifetime, but detailed formalities were instituted later on. Two steps are required in the complete transformation of a layman to a fully ordained monk. The first step is *pravrajyā* (Pali, *pabbajjā*), the "going forth" by which a candidate becomes a novice (*śrāmaṇera;* Pali, *sāmaṇera*). The second step is *upasaṃpad* (Pali, *upasampadā*), the "obtaining" of ordination, whereupon the novice is admitted as a *bhikṣu,* a full-fledged member of the *saṃgha.* Admission as a *śrāmaṇera* requires a minimum age of eight years. The novice remains under the guidance of a preceptor and a spiritual master even after ordination, for which the minimum age is twenty years. *Śrāmaṇeras* and *bhikṣus* are expected to follow the respective rules of monastic discipline *(vinaya).* The novice obeys ten precepts (*śikṣāpada;* Pali, *sikkhāpada*), whereas a *bhikṣu* is expected to obey all injunctions listed in the Prātimokṣa. These regulations are divided into seven groups according to the seriousness of offenses against them. Violation of the four *pārājika* injunctions, which forbid sexual intercourse, theft, the intentional taking of human life, and falsely or self-interestedly claiming superhuman powers, is cause for permanent expulsion from the *saṃgha.* A monk who transgresses the rules of the second group is subject to temporary demotion in the *saṃgha.* For minor offenses, confession is considered sufficient.

Further procedures of the *saṃgha* include the *poṣadha* (Pali, *uposatha*), or confessional ceremony, which is held on the days of the new moon and the full moon, during which time the Prātimokṣa is to be recited. All procedures must strictly follow the established rules in order to be valid. They must be performed by a complete *saṃgha* within an established "boundary" *(sīmā)* by using the particular *karmavācanā* (Pali, *kammavācā*), or prescribed formula; all monks living within a particular place defined by boundaries that have been fixed for a formal act of the *saṃgha* must meet and act together exactly in the prescribed way. The minimum number of monks who may perform valid "acts of Vinaya" *(vinayakarma* or *saṃgha-karma)* is four, but for particular acts a larger number is prescribed; for example, ten monks are required for the performance of an ordination in India, but only five are required in the "borderlands." For most formal acts, unanimous decision is necessary; for less important decisions, a majority vote may be permissible.

The term *saṃgha* may be used in a general sense denoting "the *saṃgha* of the four directions" (i.e., the Buddhist monastic communities as a whole), but in the context of the juridical prescriptions of the Vinaya Piṭaka, it designates the *saṃgha* of a particular place that may perform a "Vinaya act." If the *saṃgha* of a particular place fails to assemble in full, or if it cannot agree, *saṃghabheda* ("division in a *saṃgha*") has occurred; such a schism was considered a grave offense. The first *saṃghabheda* was created by Devadatta, the adversary of the Buddha, who unsuccessfully tried to make himself the head of the Buddhist community.

The community of nuns was organized in a similar way, but additional regulations make their *saṃgha* dependent on that of the monks.

LIFE OF THE MONKS

The early *saṃgha* was a community of mendicants. Upon leaving worldly life, the candidate gives up all possessions and thenceforth depends on the laity for his subsistence. The number of requisites he owns is prescribed. He lives on the food that is placed in his begging bowl during his daily alms round. He is also allowed to accept personal invitations for meals, but he should not eat after midday.

The *saṃgha* as a community was allowed to accept most kinds of donations, including property, and generous contributions to the *saṃgha* by laity were considered highly meritorious acts. In this way, some monastic communities became wealthy, and the way of life of their members came to differ from original doctrinal and canonical ideals. Therefore, the application of the formal rules of monastic discipline grew more imperative, and the degree of strictness in the fulfillment of these regulations was considered a measure for the standard of a Buddhist monastic community.

The original *saṃgha* had practically no hierarchical organization. During his lifetime, the Buddha was the highest authority, but he declined to appoint a successor, saying that his doctrine alone should guide his followers. The only hierarchical principle accepted by the early *saṃgha* was that of seniority, counting from the day of ordination. An elder monk is called *sthavira* (Pali, *thera*). In principle, all monks had equal rights and equal obligations. However, particular monks would be elected by the *saṃgha* to serve in various functions, including the solution of disputes, the resolution of cases of ecclesiastical jurisdiction, and various administrative duties in the monastery. The importance of these responsibilities grew with the transformation of the *saṃgha*s from groups of mendicants into residential monastic units.

THE PLACE OF THE SAṂGHA IN THE TEACHINGS OF THE BUDDHA

If we consider the structure of the *saṃgha* as described above we realize that it was defined by formal regulations that might characterize it as a legal system. We know, however, that the Buddha stressed that all of his teachings were proclaimed for the exclusive purpose of guiding his disciples on their way to final enlightenment. The texts make it clear that monastic discipline and the *saṃgha* represent only the outer form, which was created in order to give people the opportunity to abandon their secular responsibilities and worldly connections in order to concentrate on enlightenment. Monastic discipline is the formal aspect of morality *(śīla,* Pali, *sīla),* which is the right mode of mind and volition and, as such, the first foundation of the way to liberation. Morality in this sense is practiced through self-restraint; thus the observance of the Vinaya is an integral part of the spiritual training of the Buddha's disciples.

In relation to the laity, a member of the *saṃgha* is legitimized as a disciple of the Buddha by his adherence to the laws of Vinaya. The *saṃgha* is worthy of respect and donations because it follows and perpetuates the Buddha's law, thereby embodying the "highest field of merit." On the other hand, the existence of the *saṃgha* is a precondition for the continuation of Buddhism inasmuch as it hands down the teaching of the Buddha. The Buddha ordered his monks to preach his Dharma, but in a decent, restrained manner, and only if asked to do so.

HISTORY OF THE SAṂGHA

Immediately after the death of the Buddha, a first "council" *(saṃgīti* or *saṃgāyanā)* of Buddhist monks is said to have assembled in Rājagṛha and collected the words of the Buddha, thereby compiling the Buddhist scriptures. Although the extant scriptures are of later origin, the ancient record seems to reflect a historic event. It is likely that the earliest version of the Prātimokṣa was collected during this meeting. A second council is said to have assembled at Vaiśāli one hundred years later to resolve certain disputes on monastic discipline. The division of the Buddhist tradition into various schools or groups *(nikāyas),* which are often wrongly termed "Buddhist sects," began at this time. In the first period, the formation of these groups was based mainly on the geographic diversification of local *saṃghas* and on different views about details of monastic discipline. The texts were handed down orally; their written codification began only in the first century BCE. In most cases, the formation of the "schools" took place in such a way as to avoid the formal violation of the above-mentioned injunction against *saṃghabheda.*

The *nikāyas* handed down separate recensions of the scriptures, and they also organized additional councils or convocations for the task of collecting and correcting them. The collections of the scriptures arose in different parts of India and were originally transmitted in Middle Indo-Aryan dialects. Most of them were translated later into Sanskrit, with the exception of the scriptures of the Theravāda school, which remained in Pali, a dialect originating from central India.

Historical accounts of several schools contain traditions on a third council at the time of King Aśoka (272–231 BCE), but from the rather contradictory accounts it becomes clear that the diversification of the schools was already far advanced by that time. [*See* Councils, *article on* Buddhist Councils.]

When, around the beginning of the common era, Mahāyāna Buddhism came into existence, the organization of the early *nikāyas* was unaffected, precisely because the *nikāyas* were differentiated by their acceptance of a particular version of the Vinaya texts and not by dogmatic opinions. Therefore, in some instances monks holding Śrāvakayāna or Hināyāna views could live together and perform *vinayakarmas* together along with followers of Mahāyāna. In contrast, monks belonging to different *nikāyas* would not form a common *saṃgha,* though they might accept similar dogmatic views. In the course of time, new *nikāyas* were also formed on the basis of dogmatic dissensions. All Buddhist monks, whether Hināyāna or Mahāyāna, accept and (at least theoretically) follow one particular recension of the Vinaya Piṭaka, and thus can be connected with one of the *nikāyas* of early Buddhism.

THE SAṂGHA IN THERAVĀDA BUDDHISM

The validity of a monk's ordination depends on an uninterrupted line of valid ordinations going back to the Buddha himself. Since *pārājika* offenses incur mandatory expulsion from the order, the validity of the succession can be assured only if the monks who belong to the particular *saṃgha* lead an irreproachable life. Whenever the discipline in the *saṃgha* deteriorated, its legal existence was in danger, whether the transgressors continued to wear the monks' robes or not.

Originally, the Buddhist *saṃgha* was an autonomous body; interference by the laity was not provided for in its original laws. In this respect the Jain order was different, because there the laity exercised a considerable degree of control over the *saṃghas*. However Aśoka acted in order to achieve a purification of the Buddhist *saṃgha,* but he did so in conformity with Vinaya rules. This tradition shaped the history of Theravāda Buddhism in Sri Lanka from the time of its introduction during the reign of King Aśoka. Several purifications of the Sinhalese *saṃgha* under royal patronage are recorded. Later, additional law books termed *katikāvata* were enacted to regulate the affairs of the *saṃgha,* and a hierarchical system was established. Parallel developments can be observed in the history of the *saṃgha* of the other Theravāda communities in Burma, Thailand, Laos, and Cambodia. A characteristic feature of Buddhism there is the introduction of ordination traditions from other countries that were deemed superior to the local tradition on the occasions of *saṃgha* purification. Royal patronage over the monastic institutions went far beyond the role played by ancient Indian rulers and in some countries (e.g., in Thailand) the administration of the monasteries developed into a kind of government department. After the breakdown of royal patronage of the *saṃgha* in Burma and in Sri Lanka, these two countries witnessed the interference of monks in secular affairs during the colonial and in the early postcolonial era. In Burma, a new effort to form an autonomous hierarchical organization of the *saṃgha* under the patronage of the government has been made since 1978.

However, the old tradition that the *saṃgha* should be devoted to its spiritual aims only has also survived in Theravāda countries. To this end, monks formed groups of "forest dwellers" *(araññavāsin).* In the course of time, such groups were integrated into the structure of the official *saṃgha* organization, while other monks decided to leave the established ways of fully organized monasticism and go into solitude.

Membership in the *saṃgha* always implies, of course, certain minimal relations with other monks so that the prescribed *vinayakarmas* may be performed.

The history of Theravāda has seen the formation of new schools *(nikāya)* at various times. In ancient Sri Lanka the Abhayagirivihāravāsin formed a separate *nikāya* in the first century BCE, as did the Jetavanavihāravāsin in the fourth century CE. In the twelfth century, the three *nikāyas* were ordered to reunite and the Mahāvihāra tradition was declared authoritative by King Parākramabāhu I. Since the beginning of the nineteenth century, the *saṃgha* of Sri Lanka has split into a number of *nikāyas* again. In Burma, the first great schism arose when Chapaṭa and his disciples established the Sīhaḷa Sangha (based on a tradition of ordination introduced from Sri Lanka), in contrast to the local Mrammasangha. From the early eighteenth century until a royal decision of 1784, the *saṃgha* of Burma was divided over the correct way of wearing the monastic robes. During the nineteenth century, a number of new *nikāyas* were established there. In Thailand and in Cambodia, the *saṃgha* currently comprises the Mahānikāya and the reformist Dhammayuttikanikāya (founded in 1864 by King Mongkut while he was still a *bhikkhu*). These divisions prevent monks belonging to different *nikāyas* from performing *vinayakarmas* together but do not prevent them from cooperating in many other ways, including performing other rituals. Most of these divisions have arisen not from dissensions about dogma but from controversies about the validity of *vinayakarmas*. For the Buddhist laity, such divisions are largely irrelevant.

Typically, the *saṃgha* became involved with communal life in many ways, particularly in areas where almost the whole population identified themselves with Buddhism. The study of the holy scriptures *(pariyatti)* and the realization of the road to salvation *(paṭipatti)* remained the traditional tasks of the monks, but religious practice largely concentrated on the gaining of merit, which is accomplished through the cooperation of monks and laymen. The everyday relationship between *saṃgha* and laity is characterized by copious gifts from laymen to the monks and monasteries, and invitations to take part in important functions, such as funerals. The monks give religious addresses, readings of sacred texts, and ceremonial recitations of *paritta* texts, thus providing protection from evil forces and disaster. Until the creation of modern school systems, monks also acted as teachers, giving general education to the laity in their monasteries. A highly sophisticated system of monastic schools and ecclesiastical examinations and titles still functions in Sri Lanka, Burma, and Thailand.

However, there have always been monks who have concentrated almost exclusively on asceticism and meditation, and a living tradition of meditation masters is maintained in a number of Burmese and Thai monasteries. In recent years, meditation centers headed by famous monk-teachers have also been opened for interested laity in these areas.

THE SAṂGHA IN MAHĀYĀNA BUDDHISM

Many of the ancient *nikāyas* survived in India until the final destruction of Buddhism by Islamic conquerors. Their monasteries housed Hināyāna and Mahāyāna monks, and the situation was similar in eastern Turkestan. Mahāyāna Buddhism prevailed in China, Korea, Japan, and Tibet, but the *saṃgha* as an institution continued to be based on one of the old Vinaya traditions. The Chinese monks follow the Vinaya of the Dharmaguptaka school, and this has been adopted in other countries where Buddhism was introduced from China, including Vietnam. The Tibetans follow the Mūlasarvāstivāda tradition, and this version of the Prātimokṣa is still recited today in their monasteries. Mahāyāna and Vajrayāna Buddhism encompass other forms of religious initiation, and religious communities outside the structures of traditional monasticism came into existence. But the histories of Chinese and Tibetan Buddhism recount several successful efforts to revive the ancient monastic discipline, and the formal distinction between monks and laity is still observed. This, however, does not apply to all forms of East Asian Buddhism. Particularly in Japan, the ancient monastic tradition has lost much of its original importance, and a majority of Buddhist schools there no longer form monastic communities.

The central role of the *saṃgha* for the Buddhist religion is still acknowledged by most Buddhist communities, both Therāvāda and Mahāyāna. In 1966, an international *saṃgha* organization, the World Buddhist Sangha Council, was created in Colombo by delegates from Sri Lanka, Vietnam, Malaysia, Taiwan, Hong Kong, Nepal, Cambodia, Korea, Pakistan, India, Singapore, Thailand, England, and Laos, and a special delegation of the Tibetan *saṃgha* in exile. In a declaration made at its third congress (Taipei, 1981), this organization stated that there are more than one million Buddhist monks in the world today.

[*For further discussion of the monastic ordinances, see* Vinaya. *The historical development of monastic communities in Buddhism is treated in* Monasticism, *article on* Buddhist Monasticism. *The role and function of Buddhist clerics is the subject of* Priesthood, *article on* Buddhist Priesthood.]

BIBLIOGRAPHY

The Theravāda Vinaya Piṭaka in Pali was edited by Hermann Oldenberg as *The Vinaya Piṭakam,* 5 vols. (London, 1879–1883), and has been translated by I. B. Horner as *The Book of the Discipline,* 6 vols., "Sacred Books of the Buddhists," vols. 10–14, 20, and 25 (London, 1938–1966). For a complete bibliography of the Vinaya literature of other Buddhist schools, see Yūyama Akira's *Vinaya-Texte: Systematische Übersicht über die buddhistische Sanskrit-Literatur,* pt. 1 (Wiesbaden, 1979). An excellent study of the growth of Vinaya texts is Erich Frauwallner's *The Earliest Vinaya and the Beginnings of Buddhist Literature* (Rome, 1956). Further information on the early Buddhist *saṃgha* and early Buddhist schools is provided in the relevant chapters of the standard work by Étienne Lamotte, *Histoire du bouddhisme indien: Des origines à l'ère Śaka* (Louvain, 1958). On *karmavācanā,* see Herbert Härtel's *Karmavācanā: Formulare für den Gebrauch im buddhistischen Gemeindeleben* (Berlin, 1956); on the problem of *saṃghabheda* and *nikāyabheda* and Aśoka's reform of the *saṃgha,* see my essay "The Importance of Aśoka's So-Called Schism Edict," in *Indological and Buddhist Studies: Volume in the Honour of Professor J. W. de Jong,* edited by L. A. Hercus and others (Canberra, 1982). A survey of all available versions of the Prātimokṣa is found in Wang Pachow's *A Comparative Study of the Prātimokṣa* (Shantiniketan, 1955). Unfortunately, the existing monographs on the early *saṃgha* are of limited use only, because their authors, who have not understood the rules of Vinaya as a legal system, concentrate on historical aspects and often propose problematic theories. Some titles of this nature are Sukumar Dutt's *Early Buddhist Monachism, 600 B.C.–100 B.C.* (London, 1924), Gokuldas De's *Democracy in Early Buddhist Saṃgha* (Calcutta, 1955), Charles S. Prebish's *Buddhist Monastic Discipline* (University Park, Pa., 1975), and Rabindra Bijay Barua's *The Theravāda Saṅgha* (Dacca, Bangladesh, 1978). Important sources from Sri Lanka are edited and translated by Nandasēna Ratnapāla in his *The Katikāvatas: Laws of the Buddhist Order of Ceylon from the Twelfth Century to the Eighteenth Century* (Munich, 1971). For the relation of *saṃgha* and state in later Theravāda Buddhism, see my *Buddhismus: Staat und Gesellschaft in den Ländern des Theravāda-Buddhismus,* 3 vols. (Frankfurt, 1966–1973). For *saṃgha* in Jainism, see Shantaram Bhalachandra Deo's *Jaina Monastic Jurisprudence* (Varanasi, 1960) and his *History of Jaina Monachism, from Inscriptions and Literature* (Poona, 1956).

18 SAMGHA AND SOCIETY

H. L. SENEVIRATNE

The Sanskrit word *saṃgha* (Pali, *sangha*) denotes the Buddhist monastic order, although in its early usage (c. 500 BCE) in North India the word referred to the gatherings of the tribal republics of the time. The *saṃgha*'s relationship to society can best be prefaced with a consideration of its historical origins. Since the *saṃgha*'s significance is inseparable from that of Buddhist thought and philosophy, this will include a consideration of the social origins of that philosophy as well.

The details of ancient Indian history are controversial, but the major outlines are generally accepted. Accordingly, we can focus on the material and social background immediately preceding the rise of Buddhism in the region of its birth, the area known as the Middle Country *(madhyadeśa),* in northeastern India. The eastward-moving Aryans, who entered India around 1500 BCE, seem to have established themselves in the region by the sixth century BCE, the time of the Buddha's birth. The demographic picture, however, is far from simple, for the area also seems to have been populated by people who were of Tibetan and Burmese extraction. This period was one of extensive development of settled agriculture, a change from the nomadic type of existence ascribed to the predominant Aryans. Along with other developments such as crafts and industry, this economic progress led to surpluses, the rise of cities, and changes in political organization from ancient tribal republics to monarchies. Six great cities figure prominently in the Buddhist texts: Sāvatthi (Śrāvastī), Sāketa, Kosambi (Kauśāmbī), Kāśī (modern Vārāṇasī), Rājagaha (Rājagṛha), and Champa (Campā). Smaller cities such as Kapilavastu, Mithilā, Vesālī (Vaiśālī), and Gayā are also mentioned frequently. The cities seem to have had high population densities and to have developed a complex division of labor.

The replacement of the collective rule of the tribal republics by a monarchial form of rule reflected the centralization of power in one person, the rise of cities, and the division of labor, which emphasized the worth of the individual specialist. These factors are understood by some scholars to be indicative of a fundamental change in the evaluation of the individual within society. From a status of submergence in the group the individual gradually achieved a relative independence somewhat analogous to that of the individual in the modern West. Furthermore, many hold that the rise of the individual during this period, with the complementary need to competitively foster that individuality, set in motion potentially anomic forces that tended to minimize traditional social values of mutuality in favor of an egoistic construction of the self.

It therefore comes as no surprise that Buddhism, a tradition that is conspicuous for its early association with urbanism, should conceive of the problem of existence as one caused by an exaggerated notion of the ego or "self." The visible, tangible misery caused by excessive individualism in the realm of politics or economics (or wherever competitiveness and the display of egoism are dominant) is easily translated into the sphere of the transcendental as the idea that the malaise of the individual being is the exaggeration of the ego or the individual self. According to this analysis, the source of tranquillity must be sought in a devaluation of that self. This step is accomplished by the philosophical formulation that the self is an illusion. It is not that those who adopt this view attempt to reduce Buddhist philosophy, in particular its central doctrine of *anātman* (Pali, *anatta,* "no-self"), to a sociological phenomenon; rather, what is suggested is merely a correspondence.

If man's suffering stems from his exaggerated perception of an ego and from clinging to its desires, then suffering can be alleviated only by the denial of that ego and its desires. Just as the ego grew out of all proportion within the social context, the same social mechanism can be used to vitiate it, to realize that there is no immutable soul, but only process created by the perceiving aggregates. This realization must ultimately be a personal one, but it is facilitated by social organization. That facilitating social organization is the *saṃgha,* a unique idea in Indian religious thought. Groups of wandering ascetics existed before and after the founding of the Buddhist *saṃgha,* but none was so organized and institutionally complex. Unlike previous groups, the *saṃgha* was structured around a sophisticated code of discipline and monastic etiquette, the Vinaya. [*See* Vinaya.] Although the pursuit of mental cultivation by withdrawal to the forest or cave persisted, it appears that this "rhinoceros [i.e., solitary] ideal" was a survival from pre-Buddhist practice. Religious quest within a well-organized social group, the *saṃgha,* was a specifically Buddhist innovation. Although the ideals of the *saṃgha* were spiritual, its nonegoistic, socialistic, and republican features made it a model for a secular society at peace with itself, just as the uncompromising commitment of the renouncer was a virtue to be emulated by the individual layman. [*See also* Monasticism, *article on* Buddhist Monasticism.]

THE ECONOMIC LIFE OF THE SAṂGHA

Although some Western interpreters have maintained that Buddhism is concerned with the salvation of the individual renouncer, from its inception the tradition also clearly had a ministerial component. The Buddha's instruction to the seekers who heard his message was to carry it far and wide "for the good of the many, the comfort of the many." Yet alongside this purely missionary function grew functions of a pedagogic and parish nature arising out of the *saṃgha*'s scholastic bent and the instructional needs of the laity. Thus in the *saṃgha* two divisions grew, the "bearing of contemplation" *(vipassanā dhura),* or meditative development of one's own spirituality, and the "bearing of the books" *(gantha dhura),* the scholastic and parish functions. Eventually, the latter would gain in valuation, indicating the close relation the *saṃgha* was expected to maintain with society. At the same time, society took on the obligation to support and maintain the *saṃgha.* This arrangement, however, can be considered a consequence, albeit an early and a necessary one, of the rise of Buddhism within a social context.

There was a more basic reason why the economic life of the *saṃgha* could not exist apart from the munificence of the laity. An individual member of the *saṃgha,* the *śramaṇa* (f., *śramaṇā*), or renouncer, renounced what belonged to him or her in order to tread the path of purity and spiritual release. Providing such renouncers with their needs was an excellent opportunity for those who must remain within the bounds of household life to gain stores of merit *(puñña)* that would bear them fruit in the form of good fortune and good future births. The poverty of the *saṃgha* thus perfectly suited a laity in search of opportunities to perform good deeds *(puñña kamma;* Skt., *puṇya karman),* for it was held that no deed was so good in its potential for generating merit as the support of the *saṃgha.* The *saṃgha*'s economic dependence on the laity for subsistence is, therefore, no mere necessity, but, as more than one scholar has observed, an outward token of the renouncer's abandonment of personal resources to depend on those of the community that he serves. Thus, early in the development of Buddhism, the renouncer's needs were confined to the *catu paccaya* ("four requisites"), namely food, clothing, shelter, and medication. An individual monk ideally owns nothing privately but the *aṭṭha parikkhāra* ("eightfold items"), robes, begging bowl, and other basic personal accoutrements.

During the historical development of Buddhism, especially in the Buddhist kingdoms of Sri Lanka, Thailand, and Burma, the economic life of the *saṃgha* went through radical transformations. Extensive monastic properties grew, paradoxically arising from the sacred poverty of the *saṃgha.* Similarly, it was the fundamentally nonhierarchical nature of the *saṃgha,* among other reasons, that led to its being closely allied with the political order. In Sri Lanka, Buddhism was established as the state religion from its very inception: according to tradition, the king was the first Buddhist. Thus it was incumbent upon the king to endow the *saṃgha* generously, as did successive kings of all Buddhist polities, to bring under the purview of the *saṃgha* vast properties in the form of land. The king's act was exemplary and was followed by his patrimonial bureaucracy, down to the petty chiefs. Thus, paralleling the political hierarchy grew a hierarchy of monasteries owning vast stretches of property. The ideal of monastic poverty, however, was never abandoned, even though individual monks may have had access to considerable economic resources. This ideal was maintained in two ways. First, although land grants were made to the monasteries, their administration was separated from them and entrusted to lay officials. Second, lands granted to the monasteries, especially by the king, could in theory be taken away, although in fact this hardly ever occurred. However, in Sri Lanka sectarian schisms occasionally prompted monarchs to transfer properties of one monastic sect to another. The policy of making large-scale land grants contributed enormously to the longevity of the *saṃgha* and to its ability to survive economic adversity. In those agricultural societies that depended on the vagaries of rainfall for the cultivation of crops, especially the staple rice, prosperity could not be taken for granted, and often war and famine made it difficult for the laity to continue unbroken their pious donations. Indeed, the Sinhala term for famine, *durbhikṣa,* literally means the "absence of shares [i.e., food given as alms]." Thus the wealth of the monasteries can be considered to have played no small role in the viability of the *saṃgha* in the Buddhist polities of South and Southeast Asia.

The king's munificence toward the *saṃgha* served a politically legitimizing function. In addition, the land grants had a more direct political use, arising from the king's choice of their location. The king in Sri Lanka, for example, sometimes donated areas of property located in a province too distant for his immediate control (and hence potentially rebellious) and placed it under the control of a loyal subordinate. The tract of land thus demarcated, often extensive in size, essentially constituted a pocket of royal authority that acted as a counterforce to the threat posed by the provincial ruler.

A related point of great interest is the argument that monastic properties gave rise to monastic social structures. This intriguing theory has an important kernel of truth, especially when viewed in the context of the absence of hierarchical organization in the *saṃgha.* It can plausibly be argued that certain monastic social structures are indeed a function of the management of properties. The weakness of the theory lies in its very limited explanatory potential. Monastic properties, although in theory granted to an idealized *saṃgha* unbounded by time and space, are in fact granted to actual worldly institutions. It is in the context of particular space- and time-bound social structures that such properties must be understood. Even here it is doubtful whether the holding of property preceded evolution of the social structure, for the simple reason that it was an existing institution that received the property, an institution whose sociological structure could, of course, be modified by virtue of the new acquisition. At the broadest levels, and in the long run, it is difficult to maintain the materialist view that social structures are the product of property relations, although certain dynamic interrelations between the two are undeniable.

SAṂGHA AND POLITICAL AUTHORITY

One of the striking contrasts presented by early Buddhism is that whereas the *saṃgha* was ordered according to the political principles of the ancient tribal republics of India, its preferred political ally was clearly the monarchy. This may be explained by several factors. As I have indicated, Buddhism has been viewed as a reaction to a spirit of individualism that it perceived as the cause of social and individual suffering. Since the rise of the monarchical principle epitomizes that same individualism, it would seem appropriate for the *saṃgha* to organize itself on nonindividualist, nonmonarchical, nonhierarchical lines. However, Buddhism, always realistic in spirit, seems to have accepted the likelihood that the propagation of its message would be better facilitated by good relations with the monarchy. It must not be supposed, however, that this was a one-way process. The benefits were mutual. As Buddhism was from its very inception a movement that appealed most to urban strata, the task of controlling the powerful urban centers and sub-centers was rendered easier for the political authority, the monarch, once he espoused the religious ideology of the socially and economically dominant urban strata.

The affinity of Buddhism and its *saṃgha* to kingship is expressed in diverse ways, including myths and symbols of Buddhist kingship. Buddhist literature and lore have elevated the Buddha's father, the Śākyan ruler of a small kingdom, to the status of a monarch of imperial stature. The close relations between the Buddha and the kings of the Middle Country such as Kośala and Bimbisāra are no doubt characterized by some literary embellishment, but the historicity of the Buddha's affinity with contemporary monarchs of the region cannot be doubted. The most elaborate correlations between Buddhism and kingship are perhaps those in the symbolic sphere, in particular the identity between the Buddha and the *cakravartin* ("wheel turner"), the universal monarch. The auspicious bodily marks of the Buddha and the *cakravartin* are considered in Buddhist lore to be the same. The *cakravartin* turns the wheel of political conquest while the Buddha turns the wheel of the Dharma, the philosophy of Buddhism as well as its moral law of righteousness. The obsequies of the Buddha are considered in Buddhist literature to be those appropriate to a *cakravartin.* [*See* Cakravartin.]

The absence of hierarchy in the *saṃgha* has already been noted. Although this does not by any means make the *saṃgha* a democracy in the modern political sense—distinctions of senior and junior, teacher and pupil, ordained and novice are definitely observed—the *saṃgha* had no effective encompassing organization with laws, edicts, and codes smoothly flowing down a hierarchy of *saṃgha* officials. Since the *saṃgha* had no effective coercive authority within the bounds of its own organization, it had to look elsewhere for the sustenance and objectification of its moral and political integrity and for the adjudication of its conflicts. The preeminent repository of these functions was the king. Thus the *saṃgha* was politically as well as economically dependent on the king. This dependence most often took the form of "purification of the order" *(śāsana viśodhana;* Pali, *sāsana visodhana),* that is, by the staging of periodic purges of the *saṃgha* to free it from monks who violated the code of discipline. In addition, the purifications signified public reaffirmation of the *saṃgha*'s purity, on which depended its high esteem in society. The general public welcomed the purges because they guaranteed a virtuous and exemplary *saṃgha,* donations to which surpassed, in popular belief, all other acts of merit. The purifications were thus generally beneficial to all parties. Hence it is possible that these were regularly staged in Buddhist polities, as the historical record illustrates, whether or not an objective purificatory need existed. Apart from purifications, the king's organizational role in relation to the *saṃgha* was also manifest in the codification of doctrine and other acts that would enhance the *saṃgha*'s collective integrity. Historically, then, the king was indispensable to the *saṃgha.* Today, in Buddhist societies bereft of monarchy, this role is performed by the state.

Often, the integration of the *saṃgha* was historically effected by a hierarchy, imposed on it by the king, a hierarchy that duplicated the hierarchy of his secular patrimonial bureaucracy. The effectiveness of such imposed hierarchy, however, depended on the king's firm exercise of authority. At such times, the *saṃgha* may be considered to have had a more-than-usual political integration. In fact, it is more accurate to say that at all other times the *saṃgha* was merely a collection of politically disparate and inarticulate local communities. A king, however, was only able to integrate the *saṃgha* if he were an able ruler who integrated the secular polity itself, which in these systems was in a chronic state of tension between centripetality and centrifugality. Thus the king's integration of the *saṃgha* by the imposition of a hierarchy was no more than an extension of the integration of his secular power. Paradoxically, when the *saṃgha* was most politically integrated, and therefore most powerful, it was most dominated and regulated by the secular authority. At the same time, the king, while dominating the *saṃgha,* dared not alienate the monastic order lest it strike at the source of his legitimacy. Acceptance by the *saṃgha* was politically crucial for the king. It was part of the general cultural ideology of the Buddhist polity that the religion was the true sovereign over the land. Thus in Sri Lanka, kingship was described as being conferred by the *saṃgha* in order to maintain the religion. Kings periodically enacted symbolic abdication in favor of the Three Jewels (Buddha, Dharma, and Sangha), and the *saṃgha* "in keeping with custom" restored the kingship to the king, accepting in return a token of its overlordship, such as a land grant made on the occasion by the king.

One of the fundamental dilemmas of the association between kingship and the *saṃgha* is their respective ideal representation of two divergent realms, the temporal and the spiritual. The tension between the two spheres becomes reality when, as is the case with the Buddhist polity, righteousness is declared the foundation of the state. Statecraft necessitates not only the maintenance of internal law and order ultimately backed by coercive means but also the suppression of external enemies by bloodshed, not to mention more covert Machiavellian (or, the Indian context, Kautilyan) acts by means of which the state's ends are maintained. Such practices are far from "righteous."

Two resolutions of this dilemma are discernible in the history of Buddhist polities. First, the ruler's reign is divided into two periods, an unrighteous period followed by a righteous period, with the implication that the sins of the former are washed away by the pure waters of the latter. The empirical prototype of such a king, and indeed of all Buddhist kingship, is Aśoka (268–231 BCE), who, as Caṇḍāśoka ("Aśoka the cruel"), ruthlessly expands the empire bequeathed him by his Mauryan ancestors; his reign climaxed in the bloody conquest of Kaliṅga. Later, as Dharmāśoka ("Aśoka the righteous"), he proclaims the end of conquest by the sword and the dawn of the reign of *dharma* alone. The emperor's inner transformation thus serves as the resolution of the might-versus-right conflict. [*See the biography of Aśoka.*]

The second resolution of the king's dilemma, like the first, is initiated by the personal remorse of the conqueror, although the process takes a less ethicized form. Apprehensive of the moral retribution that may befall him in future lives, the conqueror grows afraid of the demerit of bloody conquest overtaking the merit column of his moral balance sheet. The resolution of this conflict involves a diminution of the universal perspective, for it takes the form of personal reassurance granted the conqueror that the bloodshed he caused was for the purpose of protecting from alien threat the *dharma* and maintaining its dominance. Thus in the Sri Lankan chronicle *Mahāvaṃsa,* the hero Duṭṭhagāmaṇī is assured by the *saṃgha* that of the thousands massacred during the conquests, the number of human beings killed amounts to a mere one and a half (the rest being heathen whose extinction has little consequence for the king's moral state). This second resolution, in which elements less than universalist are apparent, can be further evaluated as ethically inferior in its relative valuation of human life (believers are truly human, heathens fit for slaughter). [*See the biography of Duṭṭhagāmaṇī.*]

This tension between the ideals of the *saṃgha* and those of the king are meaningfully characterized precisely because the two are in relation. Had they been fully and completely separate from each other, as in the case of a hypothetical fully secular king and an equally hypothetical forest-dwelling ascetic having no relations with the society of men, there would be no occasion for this dilemma to arise. However, in the actual world, the spiritual and the temporal, though ideally separate, are in fact coexistent. In the case of the Buddhist polity this "dialectical tension," as Stanley J. Tambiah has called it, is generated by the location of the *saṃgha* in society even while the *saṃgha* is not of the society. Such tension is based not so much on any social relationship between king and *saṃgha* or on the king's role as conqueror and converter of the heathen as on the indistinguishability of the spiritual and the temporal in the office of the sovereign as conceived in the Buddhist notion of kingship. Furthermore, this indistinguishability forces on the king the paradoxical obligation to deal with schisms in the *saṃgha.* This obligation involves the use of force against members of the *saṃgha* who are deemed offenders against orthodox purity. But such a judgment can by no means be objectively assured. Not infrequently in the history of the Buddhist polities "purges" of the *saṃgha* constitute a "unification" of the church, the meaning as well as durability of which may be dubious. Yet at least at the time of its accomplishment the act itself would appear to represent a victory both for the king and the section of the *saṃgha* he supported, and, in its "unified" sense, for the *saṃgha* as a whole. In principle, the king, now armed with the force of a purified and unified *saṃgha,* gains important political and religious prestige through his action, although such action presupposes considerable political power in the first place.

The relationship between kingship, that is, political authority, and the *saṃgha* has been so close in Buddhist polities that it is sometimes said that the existence of the *saṃgha* presupposes Buddhist kingship. The functional complementarity of the two parties centers around the *saṃgha*'s dependence on the king for economic and organizational sustenance and the king's need of the *saṃgha* to legitimize his authority. *Saṃgha*-society relations are, however, broader than *saṃgha*-king relations, for the whole of society includes a third crucial party that makes up the whole, the mass of the lay population. Thus, it has been observed that the Buddhist polity consists of a triadic relation between *saṃgha,* king, and people. In time, such a polity could develop a strong identity fortified further by a common language and a real or imagined common ethnicity. Such an entity could grow to possess considerable integrative potential submerged in its chronic tension between centripetality and centrifugality. This potential could manifest itself with vigor at times of crisis, such as the external threat of some alien religion, language, and/or ethnic group. At such times, an ordinarily dormant and structurally vague *saṃgha* might awaken, assume formidable solidarity, and inspire the people to heightened states of patriotic fervor. Characteristically, it would return to its structural somnolence at the abatement of the crisis. The Buddhist polity is thus capable of producing two remarkable phenomena: (1) a unification of the *saṃgha* from within, inconceivable during normal times, when unification is achieved only by state imposition, and (2) a sense of political unity and identity, rare in the traditional world, which becomes historically ubiquitous only with the rise of the modern nation-state. Clearly, this crisis-triggered phenomenon represents neither a true unification of the *saṃgha* nor political centralization.

SAṂGHA SECTS AND SECTARIANISM

It is sometimes observed that there are no doctrinally differentiated sects in Buddhism. Yet Theravāda and Mahāyāna can both be considered sects in this sense. So can the numerous schools that developed within Theravāda in the early period of Buddhism. But throughout most of the history of Buddhist kingdoms, sects in this sense did not survive. As the schisms, purifications, and unifications show, however, differences of opinion and their corresponding social manifestations as sects *(nikāya)* were an integral part of the history of Buddhist kingdoms.

It is possible to posit two kinds of sects as ideal types. First are those sects that have as their basis some doctrinal difference. Ideology here determines the social categorization. Second are *saṃgha* sects derived from or influenced by secular social organization. The term *ideal type* is used because empirically neither type is found in pristine form. The ideologically determined sects have social factors contributing to their genesis; the socially determined ones often have ideological differences (however hairsplitting they may be), or at least cover the social origins of their differences in ideological apparel. [*See also* Buddhism, Schools of, *overview article.*]

Present in both modern times and antiquity are sects that express the tension in the *saṃgha* between eremitical and cenobitic ideals, forest dwelling and village dwelling, "bearing of contemplation" and "bearing of the books." Although Buddhist liberation is an act of personal endeavor, I have noted above that from its inception Buddhism conceived of the greater facility with which this end can be reached within a community framework; hence the vast importance in Buddhism of the *saṃgha* as the "third jewel." At the same time, the pre-Buddhist orthodox means of salvation by resorting to solitary confinement in forest or cave, the rhinoceros ideal, continued to be followed by some, if only a minority. Perhaps because the very solitariness of the search suggested greater purity and commitment, free from any obligations either to fellow members of the *saṃgha* community or to the laity, the solitary ideal was always held in high esteem. Sects or breakaway groups in the history of the *saṃgha* that were founded on doctrinal differences exemplify the ascetic/monastic tension and have invariably proclaimed their departure from the fold of orthodoxy as a movement toward greater purity and a renunciation of the comforts and social involvement of monasticism. Undoubtedly, such proclamations are idealizations; the true picture is more complex and allied with less lofty causal variables. Nevertheless, in terms of the renouncing group's own conceptualizations, movements toward asceticism can be viewed as purifications generated within the *saṃgha* itself, as opposed to those imposed upon it by the political authority.

In the history of the *saṃgha* such rebel movements, often inspired by and centered upon charismatic leadership, have in time succumbed to the very monastic organizational structures (and their secular economic, political, and adulatory accompaniments) that they denounced to begin with. Eventually, they have been lured back to the fold of worldly monasticism within which they may either rejoin the original parent group, remain within it as a distinct subgroup, or form a new sect altogether. Whichever of these forms the newly returned group assumes, its organizational form will normally be identical with that of the established sects. This "routinization of charisma" is neatly expressed in microcosmic form in the rite of ordination, in which the neophyte takes extreme vows of asceticism and, at the end of the ceremony, emerges with a higher status in the monastic establishment. Just as the rite of ordination is no more than a reaffirmation of high and pure ascetic ideals, so ascetic movements are periodic reminders of the true path of renunciation.

When confronted with cases in which elements of the secular social order have played a decisive role in the formation of Buddhist sects (as was true of the role of the Sinhala caste structure in the formation of certain nineteenth- and twentieth-century sects), some sociological observers have seen no more in these movements than the intrusion of society into the *saṃgha.* While this view is not wholly without merit, to assert it unequivocally is to reduce to social form phenomena that are ideologically autonomous and irreducible to social or other causal factors. To have recourse to this deterministic view is also to ignore the role of symbolic classification in the generation of sects. The evidence from Sri Lanka in particular suggests that certain sectarian divisions followed successive binary differentiations.

SECTS, SAINTS, AND MILLENNIAL BUDDHISM

The forest dwellers, a group that either came into being as a result of the self-purifying tendency within the *saṃgha* or arose anew from the laity (a less likely possibility), symbolically represent physical distance from the established secular order. They also typify a politically peripheral status in their habitation of the traditional sanctuary of the politically rebellious, namely the untamed forest. Hence, their appeal to the established political center can be vast. Furthermore, forest dwelling is synonymous with virtue and purity, and in the Buddhist polities of East Asia in particular, forest dwellers are often attributed great miraculous powers. As Tambiah's study of Thai Buddhism illustrates, the forest saints not only exemplify true asceticism as described in the classic text on the subject, the *Visuddhimagga,* but are also sometimes considered by the laity to have actually reached liberation by achieving "the winning of the stream" in the voyage to *nirvāṇa* (Pali, *nibbāna*). The politically central personalities—kings, prime ministers, generals—are thus forced by both spiritual and temporal interests to recognize and pay homage to them, a task that temporarily forces them out of their central fortresses to make uneasy journeys to the physical and political periphery where saints coexist with rebels. In general the saints are not interested in politics; their concern is spiritual commitment and the spiritual welfare of their immediate disciples and votaries. Nor is it possible for the political center to devote its sole energy to the veneration of the saints. In Thailand a happy medium is struck in medallions and amulets blessed with the saint's miraculous powers. In these cultic metal objects, which are made available to those who inhabit and control the political center, spiritual and temporal interests are welded together in much the same way as they are in the saint of the forest, whose path of purification also leads to the cosmic mountain symbolic of world conquest.

Today as in the past, a group surrounding such a forest saint is a potential threat to the political center, a threat to which the latter typically reacts in either of two ways. First, as already observed, it can make peaceful and devoted overtures and invoke the power of the miraculous objects blessed by the saint. Second, if the group surrounding the saint turns hostile, the center may resort to military action, against which the rebels, armed more with millennial expectations than military hardware, are no match. The forest saint's implicit premise that the established *saṃgha* and polity are corrupt may become the rallying point of rebellion, although this need not necessarily be so. In the established realm, *saṃgha* and political authority are separate but bound in reciprocity and mutuality, whereas in millenarianism, one possible rallying point of which is the forest-dwelling exemplar, the roles of renouncer and ruler tend to fuse together. This brings back full cycle, however fragile and illusory, the ideal unification of world renunciation and world conquest.

[*See also* Kingship, *article on* Kingship in Southeast Asia; Priesthood, *article on* Buddhist Priesthood; *and* Buddhism, *article on* Buddhism in Southeast Asia. *For a historical discussion of the development of the* saṃgha *in Sri Lanka, see* Theravāda.]

BIBLIOGRAPHY

A concise yet lucid source of the social and ideological background of Buddhism and the incipient *saṃgha* is Trevor O. Ling's *The Buddha* (London, 1973). Further details on this early period and developments up to about 1200 CE, with more focus on the *saṃgha* than on the wider society, are found in Sukumar Dutt's two works, *Early Buddhist Monachism,* 2d ed. (Bombay, 1960), and *Buddhist Monks and Monasteries of India: Their History and Their Contribution to Indian Culture* (London, 1962). E. Michael Mendelson's *Sangha and State in Burma: A Study of Monastic Sectarianism and Leadership,* edited by John P. Ferguson (Ithaca, N.Y., 1975), discusses several aspects of *saṃgha* relations with society, including the tension between the *saṃgha* and the political order. Kitsiri Malalgoda's *Buddhism in Sinhalese Society, 1750–1900* (Berkeley, 1976) discusses the response of the *saṃgha* to colonial domination in nineteenth-century Sri Lanka and relates sectarianism to caste competition generated by the dynamism of the period. The economic basis of monastic social structures is argued with forceful subtlety by R. A. L. H. Gunawardhana in his *Robe and Plough: Monasticism and Economic Interest in Early Medieval Sri Lanka* (Tucson, 1979), a work notable for its painstaking scholarship. The *saṃgha*'s preeminent position in society and polity in ancient Sri Lanka is described in Walpola Rahula's *History of Buddhism in Ceylon* (Colombo, 1956). The towering achievement in the study of *saṃgha*-society relations remains Stanley J. Tambiah's trilogy based on Thai material, *Buddhism and the Spirit Cults in North-East Thailand* (Cambridge, 1970), *World Conqueror and World Renouncer* (New York, 1976), and *The Buddhist Saints of the Forest and the Cult of Amulets* (Cambridge, 1984). The first work illustrates the transformation of the *saṃgha* in the process of meeting village-level society. The second is a grand view of the relations between *saṃgha* and polity. As Tambiah demonstrates, while in the decentralized kingdoms of Sukhōthai, Ayutthayā, and early Bangkok the *saṃgha*'s relations with the polity were loosely articulated, in the centralized Thai polity dating from the mid-nineteenth century the *saṃgha* became a systematized order actively participating in and regulated by the polity. This work also traces the path of achievement available to monks, from the rural monastery to the metropolis. The third of the trilogy examines the polity's relations with the nonestablished *saṃgha,* the forest-dwelling saints. The high esteem in which the political center holds this peripheral order, and the issue of millennialism lurking in its shadow, are discussed with authority and insight. All three works display vast learning and contain excellent bibliographies. Among the modern masters of social thought, Max Weber alone dealt with Buddhism in *The Religion of India,* translated and edited by Hans H. Gerth and Don Martindale (1958; reprint, New York, 1967), where he characteristically constructs an ideal type of the early *saṃgha* as separate from society yet in time transforming itself to accommodate lay religious needs. Although many of Weber's views are disputed, most forcefully by Tambiah, whose sociological imagination and expository style are reminiscent of Weber's own, there is still a great deal of potency and suggestiveness in his observations. Bardwell Smith has edited two volumes, *Religion and Legitimation of Power in Thailand, Laos and Burma* and *Religion and Legitimation of Power in Sri Lanka* (both Chambersburg, Pa., 1978), that contain several useful articles on the subject.

The Mahāyāna monastic orders of Japan and Tibet are vastly different from the Theravāda *saṃgha*s of Sri Lanka, Thailand and Burma, which constitute data for the analysis presented in this article. For Tibet, there is little scholarly focus from a social science point of view, the bulk of the work being textual and religio-philosophical. Authoritative though brief discussions on Tibetan monasticism ("Lamaism") are found in Giuseppe Tucci's *The Religions of Tibet* (Berkeley, 1980) and Rolf A. Stein's *Tibetan Civilization* (Stanford, Calif., 1972). Daigan and Alicia Matsunaga's *Foundations of Japanese Buddhism,* 2 vols. (Los Angeles and Tokyo, 1978), deals with, among other things, the development of scholastic Buddhism as a magical agent of the Ritsuryō government, and the generalization of Buddhism from an aristocratic religion to one embracing all strata, and suggests the cyclically regenerative and reinterpretive nature of Japanese Buddhism. For a historically based discussion of the relationship of church and state in early Chinese Buddhism, see Erik Zürcher's *The Buddhist Conquest of China,* 2 vols. (Leiden, 1972).

19 BUDDHIST CULTIC LIFE IN SOUTHEAST ASIA

Richard F. Gombrich

Buddhist cultic life may seem to present a paradox. The Buddha taught that attachment to rituals and other externals of religion was one of the three main hindrances to spiritual progress. The doctrine he preached was for each individual to internalize; it had nothing to do with shrine, locality, or society. The Buddhist path to salvation is traditionally conceived to consist of morality, meditation, and wisdom, a formulation which seems to leave no place for devotion. Moreover, within the Theravāda tradition the Buddha is regarded as mortal, possessed of no power to aid others beyond exhortation and example; he cannot answer prayers. One's spiritual welfare can be affected by no external agency, only by the moral quality of one's own acts, a quality which resides inside one, in intention, not outside one, in effect; this moral development alone leads to a good rebirth and eventually to *nibbāna.* One's material welfare is not the proper concern of religion.

The religious life of Theravāda Buddhists, however, lacks neither external observances nor the sentiments of worship and devotion. It may even—like the practice of other religions—be not indifferent to worldly goods. But the Buddha's teaching has ensured that external observances are not allowed to appear as empty forms; they are accompanied by words which give them an orthodox rationale. Acts of devotion produce spiritual welfare because they are said to calm the mind, and thus constitute part of the same mental training as morality and meditation. They may even produce material welfare (although, to be sure, this is not the best motive for undertaking them) via the transfer of merit.

TRANSFERRING MERIT

The rationale for transferring merit is inherent in the doctrine that the moral quality of an act lies in the intention alone. Thus, to empathize with a good deed, to enter into the state of mind of the doer, may be as meritorious as actually performing the deed. Further, to draw attention to one's good deed is in itself good, since it gives others a chance to empathize and so share the merit. At the same time, this sharing results in no loss to oneself; it is like lighting one candle from another.

Buddhists believe that human beings have more opportunity than gods to do good; life in the heavens is too comfortable for awareness of universal suffering, so there is not much Buddhist activity there. Thus, when they have done a good deed Buddhists invite the gods to rejoice in it with them and thus share the merit. They hope that in return for this consideration the gods will look after them on earth. [*For further discussion, see* Merit, *article on* Buddhist Concepts.]

SCRIPTURAL AUTHORITY

Scriptural authority for most Theravāda cultic observances derives from a single canonical text, the *Mahāparinibbāna Sutta.* This account of the Buddha's last days and death appears in every recension of the Buddhist canon and probably dates back to the fourth century BCE. In the Pali version, the Buddha advises two ministers that when one has fed holy men one should dedicate that act to the local gods, who will return the honor done them by ensuring one's welfare (*Dīghanikāya,* Pali Text Society ed., 2.88–89). Later in the same text, the Buddha recommends the building of stupas (2.142–143) and prescribes pilgrimage (2.140–141). The text ends by describing the distribution and worship of his relics (2.164–167). The Buddha says that whoever puts flowers or incense or paint on one of his stupas, worships it, or derives from it the religious emotion of happy tranquillity, will long benefit (2.142); furthermore, anyone who feels happy and calm at the sight of the stupa of an enlightened person will go to heaven (2.143), as will anyone who dies on pilgrimage (2.141). If we add that the commemoration of the Buddha's death is a principal event in the liturgical calendar, and that Thai Buddhists also commemorate his funeral, we see how important a charter the above-mentioned text is for Buddhist practice.

INTERPRETATION OF RELIGIOUS BEHAVIOR

Like adherents of all religions, Buddhists profess various rationales for the same religious behavior. Interpretations will vary both with sophistication and with the context, individual or cultural. The more sophisticated interpretations, which generally coincide with the preservation of canonical orthodoxy, tend to be held by monks, though these days more and more laypersons are acquiring enough knowledge of Buddhist doctrine to manipulate its concepts and indulge in apologetics on their own account. To the sophisticated, "merit" (Pali, *puñña*) is just a term for doing good, while its "transfer" *(patti),* in and of itself an important source of merit, can be rationalized in the way that has been explained above. But for the unsophisticated, merit is something more like money, a spiritual voucher system which, like sacrifice in other religions, enables one to earn material rewards from the gods. This example should not be read to mean that there are only two levels of sophistication, or that the least sophisticated understanding necessarily has the logical or historical priority implied by talk of "rationalization." On the contrary, the unsophisticated devotee who thinks of *nibbāna* as a place at the top of the sky rather than as the ideal spiritual condition represents change in the opposite direction, a coarsening of originally subtle concepts.

Any religion is a structure of symbols, and it is hazardous to assume that these are interpreted literally, even by the unsophisticated. For example, the Buddha is often referred to, and his image treated, as a king. Again, justification for this is found in the *Mahāparinibbāna Sutta,* in which the Buddha says his body is to be treated like that of a supreme emperor (2.141). When kings of ancient Sri Lanka endowed Buddhist relics with emblems of royalty and even gave them sovereignty over the country, the symbolic nature of their reverent acts was clear. So if Buddhists now treat the Buddha image as if it were a king, that does not mean they believe it to be one. [*See also* Cakravartin *and* Kingship, *article on* Kingship in Southeast Asia.]

Variation in context is just as important as variation in sophistication, and may even override it. Most Buddhists are fully aware that the Buddha is dead and cannot help them, but in a crisis even a sophisticated Buddhist may pray to the Buddha for help, even if afterwards he is ashamed to admit it. Such variations in context may be culturally patterned. For example, in Sri Lanka, when a new Buddha image is to be installed in a shrine (traditionally a public shrine; domestic shrines are a modern innovation), there has to be a ceremony at which its maker completes it by painting in the eyes. He must be left alone with the image and paint in the eyes without looking at them directly, by using a mirror. The incipient gaze of the Buddha image is treated as if it were dangerous, but such an idea conflicts with the orthodox Buddhist view that the Buddha is not only dead and no longer active but, in any case, wholly benign. The ceremony could not have arisen had someone not believed otherwise, and perhaps the traditional craftsman still does. Monks will strongly deny that the gaze is dangerous and may even dismiss the custom as a superstition. In between are many who will attend the ceremony without asking themselves what they think about it. Thus a mere description of religious behavior can tell us nothing certain about the participants' motives, feelings, or ideology.

LAY RELIGIOUS STATUSES AND VOWS

This polyvalence of even verbal behavior is striking at the outset of any description of Theravāda observance. The layperson begins every public religious occasion, every private devotion, and in some societies every day in the same way. After reciting three times (in Pali), "Worship to the Blessed Arhat, the Fully and Supremely Enlightened One," he declares (again three times) that he "goes for refuge" to the Three Jewels of Buddhism: the Buddha, the Dhamma, and the Sangha. What does this mean? The Dhamma is necessarily present and the Sangha contingently still extant, but the Buddha? It is easy for orthodoxy to claim that the recitation is merely a way of declaring oneself inspired by the Buddha's example; but the devotee may feel the Buddha's presence in a more direct way. After the recitation of the Three Jewels, one takes the Five Precepts: not to kill, steal, be unchaste, lie, or take intoxicants. Most Buddhists are vividly aware that just to mouthe the words is nothing; one must mean them. Thus, the Buddha's insistence that good morals are the precondition for spiritual progress influences Buddhist ritual and daily life. The Sinhala service of Radio Sri Lanka begins every day with the Three Refuges and Five Precepts, intoned by monks for lay response as on public occasions. Although lay membership is rarely formalized, to take the Three Refuges and Five Precepts is to define oneself as a Buddhist.

The Buddhist liturgical calendar has lunar months. The quarter days of the lunar month *(uposatha)* are days of intensified observance. The full-moon day is the most important (most festivals occur then), followed by the new-moon day. Intensified observance mainly consists of visiting the temple and taking the Eight Precepts. These build on the basic five: the third is strengthened to exclude all sexual activity and one undertakes additionally not to take solid food after midday, not to watch entertainments, not to use adornments (in this formulation these last two form a single undertaking), and not to use grand beds. The person undertaking these abstentions behaves almost as if ordained, for the lower ordination or *pabbajjā* (novitiate) involves taking the Ten Precepts, which, treating the abstentions from entertainments and from adornments as separate injunctions, are the same as the Eight Precepts with an additional injunction against handling gold or silver (i.e., against using money). Taking the Eight Precepts on *uposatha* days is ideal conduct, but even at the full moon only a minority, predominantly women, do so.

One can also take the Ten Precepts without being ordained. This is done mostly by elderly and widowed people. Since the Theravāda order of nuns is extinct, the Ten Precepts represent the strictest formal category of observance attainable by women. Some women shave their heads, wear ocher robes, and live much like monks, their nearest male counterparts, in religious communities or as virtual hermits. They generally do not receive the same recognition as monks, although they usually lead ascetic lives and beg their food.

The minimum age for entering the order as a novice *(sāmaṇera)* is about seven. One can take the higher ordination *(upasampadā)* and so become a monk *(bhikkhu)* at twenty. Although anyone who feels unsuited to monastic life can leave at any time, in Sri Lanka it is always assumed that ordination is taken with lifelong intent. This is not so in other Theravāda societies. In Burma, every boy is supposed to enter the order temporarily as a novice, usually for at least a week. This temporary service has no bearing on whether he becomes a monk later in life. There is a similar system of temporary ordination, but one which is even more flexible, in Thailand. (Until the communist takeovers of the 1970s, Laos and Cambodia had similar Buddhist traditions and practices.) Even the king of Thailand spends one or more spells in monastic robes. The most common time for short-term ordination is the "rains retreat" (*vassa,* normally from July to October).

MERIT MAKING

An often cited Pali verse lists ten good acts that comprise all the ways of making merit: generosity, observing the precepts, meditation, transferring merit, empathizing with merit, serving (one's elders), showing respect, preaching, listening to preaching, and right beliefs. Several of these are discussed below.

Generosity. Generosity *(dāna)* is considered the foundation of all virtues. In practice, the term usually refers to generosity toward the monastic order (which is described in liturgy as "the best field in which to sow merit"), and in particular to feeding monks—so much so that the word for "generosity" in Sinhala *(dānē)* commonly means a monk's meal.

Meditation. Traditionally, the only forms of meditation in which laity engaged were the simple recitation of Pali verses and formulas (*gāthās*), usually undertaken at the temple as part of *uposatha* ("quarter-moon") observance; such recitation is culturally defined as "calming" *(samatha)* meditation but does not strike Western observers as having the intensity they associate with meditation. The commonest subjects for meditation are the qualities of the Buddha, kindness *(mettā),* and the constituents of the body. The more technical forms of meditation, whether "calming" or "insight" *(vipassanā)* meditation, have by custom been confined to the monastic order; but since about 1950 laypeople have become increasingly interested in meditation, and the more modernized sectors of society have seen the establishment of meditation centers (not necessarily in monasteries) at which laity take meditation courses, sometimes even under lay instruction. The most common technique now employed for teaching meditation to laity seems to be awareness of breathing. [*See* Meditation, *article on* Buddhist Meditation.]

Preaching. What is common to virtually all public occasions for making merit is that the laity feed monks and the monks respond by preaching. At the very least they preach a short sermon (which may be purely formulaic), instructing the laity to share the merit of this act and expressing the hope that it may help them to good rebirths and finally to attain *nibbāna* under the next Buddha, Maitrī (Metteyya; Skt., Maitreya). There are many other types of preaching, including sermons composed for the occasion and delivered in the local language. But the most distinctive form of Theravāda preaching is the recitation of a particular set of Pali texts called *paritta* ("protection, amulet"). *Paritta* recitation has the general aim of bringing good luck, not merely by the mechanisms which apply to all merit making but also by reminding potentially malevolent spirits, to whom some of the texts are addressed, of such Buddhist principles as kindliness. The recital can be done by anyone, but usually several monks participate; for long sessions they take turns at reciting in pairs in a style which aims at an uninterrupted flow of sound. The commonest form of traditional *paritta* ceremony lasts one night, although there are versions lasting up to a week. Another common version consists of the first three texts of the full form: the *Maṅgala Sutta,* the *Ratana Sutta,* and the *Metta Sutta,* poems from the canonical *Suttanipāta.* Every monk must know these three texts by heart. At traditional *paritta* ceremonies the chanting endows thread and water with protective properties, and laypeople afterwards wear pieces of the sanctified thread as amulets.

CYCLICAL CEREMONIES

The only life crisis solemnized by monks is death, unless we choose to regard the Burmese temporary ordination of boys as a puberty rite, which is not how the Burmese see it. Birth and marriage are themselves secular events, even if on these and other important occasions Buddhists naturally tend to make merit and seek religious edification. Monks must officiate at funerals; there is always a sermon, and the preacher is given cloth to use for robes, a surrogate for the shroud which was originally declared suitable stuff for a monk's robe. Death rites do not end at the funeral. The bereaved family must subsequently invite monks to be fed and to preach, and transfer the merit to the newly dead, in case he has been reborn as a hungry ghost *(peta)* who can only accomplish good (and so hasten to a better life) by empathizing with this merit. Sinhala Buddhists give a *dānē* after a period of seven days, again after three months, and then annually following a death; the ceremony at three months is normally a major occasion with *paritta* chanting all night.

Buddhist calendrical rituals vary greatly from country to country, even among Theravādins. All Theravādins regard the full moon of Visākha, which falls in late May or early June, as the anniversary of the Buddha's birth, enlightenment, and death; it is the Enlightenment which is the most commemorated. But in Burma that festival is far less important than the end of the rains retreat. The monastic rains retreat takes three months, and its beginning and end are marked by important festivals. During the three months, no monk is to be away for more than seven days from the monastery where he began the retreat. During the month after the retreat there is a major ceremony at which one monk in each monastery, chosen by the incumbent, is presented by the laity with a special robe, the *kaṭhina* robe. The *kaṭhina* ceremony is the only calendrical ceremony involving the laity for which there is authority in the Pali canon.

Monks play a part in lay festivals but also have private observances, which are much more important to them. Every fortnight, on the *uposatha* days of the new and full moons, the monks are enjoined to gather to recite their disciplinary code, the Pātimokkha, after first confessing to one another their transgressions against it. A special ceremony of this kind, the Pavāraṇā, is held at the end of the rains retreat; then the monks ask one another's forgiveness for any offense they may have caused. Higher ordination ceremonies are crucially important to the order. [*See also* Priesthood, *article on* Buddhist Priesthood.]

SACRED OBJECTS

Since Buddhists know that the Buddha is dead but wish that he were alive to help them, it is not surprising that they worship relics, objects which help to bridge the gap between his physical absence and his psychological presence. Relics are traditionally classified into three groups, in descending order of holiness: (1) physical parts of the Buddha or other saints; (2) objects used by the Buddha; (3) reminders of him. By a slight extension, places associated with his life are categorized along with objects used by him, and form the major centers of pilgrimage. The most common "object used" is a Bodhi Tree; others are the Buddha's robes and begging bowl. The Buddha's physical remains were put under burial mounds, known as stupas. Stupas usually serve to enshrine a physical relic. Their mere shape, however, makes them reminders, or what we might call visual symbols. A Buddha image is also a reminder relic, although it may contain physical remains as well. Scriptural texts, too, are sacred objects, perhaps because they embody the Dhamma, since, as the Buddha said, "He who sees the Dhamma sees me" (*Saṃyutta Nikāya* 3.120). Such texts are sometimes enshrined in stupas like physical relics. The offerings most commonly placed before relics are flowers, incense, and lights. [*See* Stupa Worship.]

Thai Buddhists commonly wear amulets, made by respected monks to bring safety and prosperity, or such sanctified objects as *paritta* thread, mentioned above. The sacredness of such objects derives from their association with a monk, better still a saint *(arahant),* best of all the Buddha. The main objects of veneration, both in theory and practice, are the monks themselves; even the most unworthy monk is a "son of the Buddha" and symbolizes Buddhist ideals.

[*See also* Saṃgha, *overview article;* Pūjā, *article on* Buddhist Pūjā; Pilgrimage, *article on* Buddhist Pilgrimage in South and Southeast Asia; *and* Buddhist Religious Year.]

BIBLIOGRAPHY

There is no one work covering Theravāda Buddhist practice as a whole. Perhaps the most useful broad survey is in a collection edited by Heinz Bechert and me, *The World of Buddhism* (London and New York, 1984). There are, however, detailed descriptions of traditional practice in separate countries. On Sri Lanka, see my *Precept and Practice: Traditional Buddhism in the Rural Highlands of Ceylon* (Oxford, 1971) and J. F. Dickson's "Notes Illustrative of Buddhism as the Daily Religion of the Buddhists of Ceylon, and Some Account of Their Ceremonies after Death," *Journal of the Royal Asiatic Society* (Ceylon) 8 (1884): 203–236 (the pagination is corrected by an erratum slip to pp. 297–330). On Burma, Melford E. Spiro's *Buddhism and Society: A Great Tradition and Its Burmese Vicissitudes* (New York, 1970) is fairly comprehensive; one may find its psychoanalytic interpretations too facile. On Thailand there are three excellent books. Kenneth E. Wells's *Thai Buddhism: Its Rites and Activities* (1939; reprint, Bangkok, 1960) and Jane Bunnag's *Buddhist Monk, Buddhist Layman* (Cambridge, 1973) both deal primarily with urban Buddhism in central Thailand, and are well complemented by the village study of Stanley J. Tambiah, *Buddhism and the Spirit Cults in North-East Thailand* (Cambridge, 1970), which takes a structuralist approach. Still the best translation of the *Mahā Parinibbāna Sutta* is by T. W. Rhys Davids and C. A. F. Rhys Davids, *Dialogues of the Buddha,* vol. 2 (London, 1910), often reprinted. The *Metta* and *Maṅgala Sutta* are translated in Walpola Rahula's *What the Buddha Taught,* rev. ed. (Bedford, England, 1967), a superb general introduction to Buddhism by a Theravādin monk.

20 BUDDHIST CULTIC LIFE IN EAST ASIA

TAITETSU UNNO

The abundance of rituals, ceremonies, and special observances among the great variety of schools and traditions of East Asian Buddhism precludes all but the most cursory survey of their cultic life, but for our purposes we may outline cultic practices under three major headings: those that are limited to, or primarily observed by, the clergy, generally in a monastic setting; those that involve lay participation and the wider public; and those that originated in Buddhist institutions but are now secularized. Although the practices I shall describe are more or less common to all East Asia countries, this article will focus on Japan, which has retained many of the traditional forms of Buddhist cultic life and remains the most active East Asian Buddhist culture.

Among the first group of cultic practices found among the monastic and priestly communities are rituals of ordination, accession ceremonies, religious disciplines (such as meditative and contemplative practices), monastic rituals (governing all aspects of the lives of the order), worship services, commemorative rituals, funeral and memorial rites, formalized lectures and debates, and Tantric rituals such as the *goma* and *kanjō* (consecration rites). Various other premodern observances expressed the Buddhist worldview. These rituals included ceremonies for the freeing of captured animals, prayer services for the imperial household, for peace, and for the prosperity of the state, observance of imperial birthdays, and rites of exorcism in times of danger to the person or the community.

Included in the second group of practices, those that involve mass participation and frequently integrate folk beliefs and local customs, are such cultic events as the New Year service and the midsummer Ullambana festival (sometimes referred to as All Souls' Day); the celebrations relating to the life of Śākyamuni Buddha—his birthday, his enlightenment, and his decease, or *parinirvāṇa;* vegetarian feasts and the honoring of Buddha relics; the observance of the spring and autumn equinoxes (primarily in Japan); the commemoration of the birth and death anniversaries of the Buddha, founders and successive masters of schools or lineages; daily home services before the family altar; wedding ceremonies, funerals, and memorial services; the taking of the formal vows of Buddhist life; the copying of scriptures and Buddha images and the sculpting of Buddhas and *bodhisattvas* as meritorious acts; pilgrimages and processions, and so on.

Among the third group are ritual traditions that originated in or were intimately connected with Buddhist institutions but have only nominal relations with them today: dance, theater, ballads, the arts of the tea ceremony and flower arranging, calligraphy, archery, and so forth. In this category we must also include the time-honored social practice (called *senbetsu* in Japanese) of giving envelopes containing money when a person leaves home on a voyage or for a more permanent sojourn, and a similar practice on occasions of marriage, birth, and death. This custom, emphasizing mutual help in times of need, is based on the Buddhist teaching of the interrelationship and interconnectedness of all life.

In many of these religious rituals the cultic ritual of chanting the scriptures is a central practice. The chanting of scriptures, chosen to suit the particular school and the occasion, fulfills several important functions: praise of the virtues of the Buddha and his teachings, expression of gratitude to the Buddha and all beings that make possible the deliverance from *saṃsāra,* repentance for past evils (which may be a separate ritual service by itself), the vow to attain supreme enlightenment, the celebration of the *dharma* lineage, and the wish to share the accumulated merits of religious practice with all beings on the Buddhist path. Functionally, the chanting intoned in various melodic and rhythmic patterns and punctuated with musical instruments—gongs, bells, wooden clappers, wind instruments, and so forth—creates the atmosphere of sacred space and time, preparing the participants to enter a religious mode of being.

No study of cultic rituals would be complete without mentioning the religious implements and icons used. These include the primary objects of worship—images in sculpture or painting of Buddhas, *bodhisattva*s, protective guardians, founding masters and their successors, as well as sacred tablets or scrolls with names of Buddhas or *bodhisattva*s or with *mantra*s written on them—and symbolic implements, such as the stupa or pagoda, the wheel of *dharma,* and various kinds of reliquaries, denoting the presence of the Buddha. The altar generally holds the standard implements of religious worship. The home altar has a set of three implements: a candle holder, a flower vase, and a censer. In temples, the altar holds a set of five implements: a pair of candle holders, a pair of vases, and a censer. The candle symbolizes the wisdom of enlightenment, the flower, impermanence, and the incense, purification. Fruits, rice, and vegetables are offerings made as expressions of gratitude.

The rules and regulations concerning the proper array of the clerical robe in accordance with ecclesiastical rank and religious occasion are also important aspects of ritual life. There are also religious implements that are unique to particular schools: the almsbowl and fly whisk *(hossu),* among other items, in Zen; the single- and three-pronged *vajra* and five-pronged *vajra* bell in Shingon; and extensive use of the rosary *(nenju)* in the Pure Land schools. We must also note the importance of the different musical instruments used especially to accompany chanting: gongs, bells, drums, wind and string instruments, and the *mokugyo,* the fish-shaped drum of hollow wood.

The range, variety, and complexity of Buddhist cultic practices limit our discussion to only a few selected examples of the major rituals (referred to by their Japanese names, since they are still observed today by the people). Unlike the Judeo-Christian tradition, which holds weekly religious services, the Buddhist life centers around annual and seasonal rites. While some are common to all schools of Buddhism, each school retains its own particular rituals and festivals. Many of them are observed both at temples and homes, and some on a national scale.

Common to all the various schools of Buddhism are the celebrations of the three major events in the life of Śākyamuni Buddha—birth, enlightenment, and decease. These are held on different days in countries dominated by Mahāyāna Buddhism, unlike the Wesak observance in the Theravāda tradition, which combines all three major events of the Buddha's life into a single religious holiday in May. The birthday celebration of the Buddha, which is known under a variety of names (Kanbutsu-e, Kōtan-e, Busshō-e), is said to have begun as early as the fourth century in China. The Chinese pilgrim Fa-hsien, who left China for India in 399 and returned in 414, reported seeing this event during his travels in Magadha and Khotan. Traditionally, it was held on the eighth day of the fourth lunar month as part of the monastic rituals. At one time it was elevated to an imperial ceremony in both China and Japan and at other times it was held in individual homes. Today it is observed on 8 April by the clergy and laity alike. The central altar is a flower-bedecked shrine, especially made for the occasion, with a figure of the infant Śākyamuni standing in a basin of sweet tea. The shrine, covered with spring flowers, symbolizes the garden of Lumbini, where the Buddha was born. The standing figure with one hand pointing to the heavens and the other to the earth depicts the legend surrounding the Buddha's birth, in which he is said to have taken seven steps to the east and proclaimed to the world, "Heavens above, heavens below, I alone am the World-Honored One." At that time, the legend continues, the earth shook, beautiful music resounded throughout the universe, and flower petals and sweet tea rained from the sky. Following the procession of monks or priests and the chanting of *sūtras*, the believers, both young and old, bow in obeisance to the Buddha image, pour sweet tea over it with a ladle, and receive flowers and sip sweet tea.

Local variations on this basic ritual include simultaneous lantern festivals, the drinking of the sweet tea made from herbs (thought to have a beneficial effect), prayer ceremonies for children's health and well-being, and the use of sweet tea to make ink for writing amulets as preventives against calamity. Basically, the birthday celebration is a festive occasion, a time for joyful springtime celebration, coinciding with the beginning of the agricultural cycle. Thus, in contemporary Japan it is referred to as the Festival of Flowers (Hanamatsuri). In some temples processions led by a white elephant (usually simulated on a float) carrying the flower-bedecked altar go through the village and towns, a legacy of ancient Indian practice.

The observance marking the Buddha's attainment of enlightenment (Jōdo-e), generally held on 8 December, is a far more solemn occasion. A religious service is held in remembrance of the Buddha's renunciation of the extremes of hedonism and asceticism and his forty-nine-day meditation under the Bodhi Tree that culminated in his supreme enlightenment. On occasion the painting depicting the Buddha descending a mountain (signifying his abandonment of asceticism) is shown as a reminder of the event. The Zen tradition holds an intensive training period, called *rōhatsu daisesshin,* from 1 through 8 December, emulating the enlightenment experience of Śākyamuni Buddha and culminating in an all-night sitting until the dawn of 8 December. A typical *sesshin* begins at 2:00 or 3:00 A.M. and is followed by a lengthy chanting service, alternate sitting and walking meditations throughout the day, mid-afternoon tea, lecture or *teishō* ("presentation of inner meaning"), and private interviews with the master, and meals. The sitting, eating, and sleeping are generally all observed on the mat *(tan)* assigned to the practitioner. The seven-day period is said to be the ideal length to take care of the successive and alternating moods of eagerness, dejection, doubt, boredom, resignation, and elation. The December training session is the most rigorous of all the *sesshin* held throughout the year.

The anniversary of the death of the Buddha, his *parinirvāṇa,* was traditionally commemorated on the fifteenth day of the second lunar month. The ritual, known as Nehan-e, was observed in India by the great pilgrim Hsüan-tsang (596–664), and in China it was held under imperial auspices as early as the sixth century, during the Liang (502–557) and Ch'en (557–589) dynasties. In Japan it is first mentioned during the reign of the empress Suiko, also in the sixth century. Today, it is observed on 15 February or 15 March. The ritual centers on the huge painting of the Buddha's deathbed scene: the reclining Buddha lies peacefully on his right side, surrounded by waiting monks and nuns with animals and birds of the forest forming the background. In some monasteries the cremation ceremony of Śākyamuni Buddha is reenacted, and the Buddha's last sermon is chanted as a regular part of the service.

All the above observances began in the monastic setting; later they were patronized by some imperial powers, and in more recent centuries they included participation of the lay public. Among the most popular of the rituals primarily for the laity is the Ullambana festival, known in Japan as Obon. Observed on 13–16 July, and sometimes in August, it began in the sixth century in China and soon after was introduced to Japan, where it incorporated many folk beliefs and local customs. At one time it was considered the most important Buddhist ritual sponsored by the state; an emperor would often order all the monasteries of the land to give lectures on the *Ullambana Sūtra* in honor of seven past generations of parents. The origin of the Ullambana ceremony is found in the legend of Moggallāna (Skt., Maudgalyāyana), who through transcendental vision saw his mother suffering in Avīci hell. In order to save her he followed the advice of Śākyamuni Buddha and practiced charity by feeding hundreds of monks. Through this selfless act, he was able to save his mother. Moggal's deed is extolled as a model of filial piety. In the major temples the ceremony was used to publicly display rare possesions, and frequently dramatic performances were held for the laity.

Today, the main purpose of Ullambana is to remember the dead and to honor the ancestors. Buddhist household altars are prepared to receive the spirits of the dead, and the family graves are cleaned and flowers newly placed. Belief in the returning spirits is not Buddhist but originates in folk religion. In some areas bonfires are made to serve as beacons for the visiting spirits; in other areas the seasonal flowers placed before the graves are thought to carry spirits with them; in still others, dragonflies are believed to be carriers of the dead spirits. During Ullambana, colorful dances with drums, singing, and lanterns entertain the returning spirits. These dances originated with the *odori nembutsu* (dancing while calling on the name of Amida Buddha) of the Heian period (794–1185). Among some sects, the spirits of the dead are sent off in miniature sailboats, carrying candles, into the rivers and oceans. The Obon festivals held throughout Japan today are concluded with dancing around a temporary tower holding singers and drummers. Handclapping, drums, gongs, flutes, and *shamisen* provide the rhythm and music. The local variations of Obon dances, which have become folk dances, are numerous and diverse. While much of the content of the Ullambana festival is non-Buddhist in origin, today the clergy holds services in both temples and homes and, while the chanting of *sūtras* and the remembrance of the dead is the primary ritual, the occasion is also used to instruct the people in the Buddha's teaching.

Another equally popular ritual, unique to Japanese Buddhism, is the Higan-e, the observance of the spring and autumn equinoxes. That it has become so much a part of the ritual life of the people is evident in the popular saying, "Winter cold and summer heat end at *higan* (the spring and winter equinoxes)." Originating in the Heian period, the Higan-e is observed for the three days before and after the equinox. The number of days of observance is said to have been based upon the six perfections *(pāramitās)*—giving, observance of the precepts, perseverance, effort, meditation, and wisdom—needed before one goes from this shore of *saṃsāra* to the further shore of *nirvāṇa* (the literal meaning of *higan* is "other shore"). The ritual includes repentance of past sins and prays for enlightenment in the next life. It also includes the remembrance of the dead and visits to the family graves. In some cases pictorial representation of hells are displayed, sermons on hell and paradise are given, and the people are exhorted to aspire to the Pure Land. The offerings for the services, including sweets, rice, vegetables, and so forth, are distributed to the congregation, friends, and neighbors. As with the Ullambana festival, the spring and autumn equinoxes are occasions for the clergy to hold services in private homes. It is thought that the spring and winter equinoxes, being the most temperate times of the year, are ideal moments to reflect on the meaning of life and hear the teaching of the Buddha.

Another popular Buddhist ritual is the New Year service. Special religious ceremonies are held close to midnight on New Year's Eve and early on the morning of New Year's Day. At midnight the temple gongs are struck 108 times, signifying the 108 kinds of blind passions (Skt., *kleśas*) that must be purified in the coming year. The New Year's Day service (Shūshō-e) was one of the most important observances in the imperial household in the Nara period (710–795). Although Shintō in origin and nature, it has become part of the Buddhist tradition, and in the temples it remains the first important ritual of the New Year. The service is held to express gratitude for the past year and to resolve to walk the Buddhist path in the coming year. It includes prayers for good health, success, and long life.

An important influence in the lives of East Asian peoples was the introduction of Buddhist funeral rites. After the advent of Buddhism, a number of rituals were observed to express gratitude to the dead, to console the spirits, and to channel the grief of the family and turn their thoughts to enlightenment. Funerary rites include the bedside service, wake, funeral, and cremation, as well as a series of memorial observances on the seventh, thirty-fifth, forty-ninth, and one-hundredth days, on the first, third, seventh, thirteenth, seventeenth, thirty-third, fiftieth, and one-hundredth years, and so on (some differences exist between the Chinese and Japanese practices). The determination of the memorial days and years is derived from a mixture of Buddhist ideas and ancestor worship. The most important of the memorial days is the forty-ninth, which, according to legend, is the length of time the spirit of the dead wanders before finding its final resting place.

When a person dies, the "last water" is applied to moisten the lips, the body is bathed and properly clothed, in some cases a knife is placed on the body to drive away evil spirits, and the wake service is observed. A posthumous Buddhist name is given to the deceased, a memorial tablet is placed on the altar, and people gather to present "incense money" *(kōden)* in memory of the deceased. This is an expression of mutual aid in times of distress and a demonstration of solidarity among relatives, friends, and neighbors. The funeral service consists of *sūtra* chanting, remembering and honoring the deceased, offering incense, and, as the conclusion to the rite, a vegetarian dinner during which sake and tea are served.

Major religious observances related to the funeral rites are found in the commemorative services for the founders and successive heads of each Buddhist school (birthday commemorations are also very important). The anniversaries observed every fifty or one hundred years are considered the most significant. These are occasions to renew one's commitment to the heritage, undertake the renovation of temple buildings, hold elaborate and colorful ceremonies, express gratitude to the teachers, and strengthen ties among the believers. An example of such a commemorative service is the case of Shinran (1173–1262), the founder of the Jōdo Shinshū branch of Japanese Pure Land Buddhism, whose seven-hundredth memorial anniversary was observed in 1962 and his eight-hundredth birthday celebration in 1973. Today there are ten subschools of Jōdo Shinshū, the largest being the Hompa Honganji, also known as Nishi Honganji, whose headquarters is in Kyoto, Japan. A monthly memorial service is held on the sixteenth day of each month, and in the Hompa Honganji a service, called Hōonko, is held every year from 9 January through 16 January to honor Shinran. (This service is held fom 21 through 28 November in the Higashi Honganji subschool). During Hōonko, members congregate in their respective temples for a seven-day period of religous services, consisting of chanting verses from Shinran's writings *(Shōshinge),* reading Shinran's biography *(Godenshō),* listening to sermons, and receiving the epistles of Rennyo, the eighth successor to Shinran and the principal preserver of the tradition. Traditionally, the followers ate only vegetarian meals for the seven days; in some areas all the shops were closed for the duration, since people went to the temples for services in the morning, afternoon, and evening and took some of their meals together there. As the most significant religious observance for Jōdo Shinshū believers, the memorial service is held not only to honor the founder, but to reinstill his religious message. Thus, devotees engage in praising the virtues of Amida (Skt., Amitābha) Buddha, listening to and discussing the teaching, and praying for the well-being of all people.

The true significance of Hōonko should be understood in the context of the historical evolution of Pure Land Buddhism. As early as the fifth century, Pure Land rituals consisted of five observances: worship, praise of Amida Budhha's virtues, aspiring for birth in the Pure Land, contemplative insight into reality, and turning over one's accumulated merit to all beings. The first three observances were elaborations of *śamatha* (preparation for meditation), and the fourth was the equivalent of *vipaśyanā* (insight into reality), which was the primary goal of the religious life. It was T'an-luan (475–542) who developed the basis of Pure Land thought centered around this fivefold practice.

Shan-tao (613–681) modified the ritual into the five true practices: (1) chanting and reading scriptures, (2) contemplation and meditation, (3) worship, (4) recitation of the name of Amida Buddha, and (5) praise consisting of obeisance as bodily act, singing as verbal act, meditation as mental act, aspiring to birth in the Pure land,

and transferring merits to all beings. For Shan-tao, the most important was the fourth, the recitation of the name of Amida.

By the time of Hōnen (1133–1212) in Japan the exclusive recitation of Amida's name (the Nembutsu) became the one and only practice of Pure Land Buddhists. For Shinran, the saying of the Nembutsu included the praise of Amida's view of salvation, gratitude for its blessings, repentance for one's karmic evil, wish for birth in the Pure Land, and prayer for the well-being of all people. Thus, in the Hōonko service the Nembutsu flows spontaneously from the lips of the faithful throughout the seven-day observance, like ocean waves rising and falling as the religious mood dictates.

In Jōdo Shinshū the entire ritual act of the believer, then, is to be contained in the recitation of the Nembutsu. Being a simple act, albeit expressing profound depths, it can be practiced by anyone, at any time, and under any circumstances. The primary goal of the Buddhist life, to sanctify everyday existence, is thus realized in this simple utterance.

Such is the ultimate goal of all Buddhist cultic life—celebrating this life and affirming its value—not only in Jōdo Shinshū but also in Zen, Nichiren, Shingon, and other schools. In Zen Buddhism the emphasis is not on the *satori* experience but rather its manifestation in "everyday mind," whether chopping wood or carrying water; in the Nichiren school this life is the arena of *bodhisattva* activity, calling for the transformation of the world, following the ideals of the *Lotus Sutra;* and in Shingon Buddhism one cherishes the five elements that constitute the universe—earth, fire, water, ether, and space—as the very body of the Buddha.

There are many other cultic practices that should be discussed, but space will permit us to mention only a few significant ones. A four-fold *samādhi* (meditation, trance) practice, originating in Chinese T'ien-t'ai and transmitted in Japanese Tendai, incorporated (1) sitting meditation, (2) chanting the name of Amitābha in circumambulation of the meditation area, (3) contemplation based on the *Dhāraṇī* and *Saddharmapuṇḍarīka sūtra*s, and (4) forms of meditative practice other than the preceding. The first influenced the formation of Zen, the second, the practices of Pure Land Buddhism, and the third came to be intimately connected with Shingon. Rituals of repentance, important in Tendai and Zen, among others, remind the practitioners of past and potential karmic sins. Shingon and Tendai Esoteric traditions, Tōmitsu and Taimitsu respectively, utilize sacred syllables *(mantra),* symbolic gestures *(mudrā),* and the cosmogram *(maṇḍala),* the essential characteristics of each handed down in secret oral transmission. The time-honored ritual of *sūtra* copying *(shakyō),* still popular among Jōdo, Shingon, and Tendai followers, is undertaken to bring repose to the spirits of the dead, accumulate merit for the practitioner, and deepen faith in the *sūtra* copied. Pilgrimages to holy sites, centered around the cult of Kōbō Daishi (Kūkai), founder of Shingon, have become a folk religious practice aimed at purifying the senses, cultivating self-awareness, and bringing a person closer to nature.

[*See also* Buddhist Religious Year; Meditation, *article on* Buddhist Meditation; Nien-fo; *and* Priesthood, *article on* Buddhist Priesthood. *The interrelationship of Buddhist practice and the fine arts and architecture in East Asia is treated in* Drama, *article on* East Asian Dance and Theater; Music, *articles on* Music and Religion in

China, Korea, and Tibet *and* Music and Religion in Japan; *and* Temples, *article on* Buddhist Temple Compounds.]

BIBLIOGRAPHY

No comprehensive study on Buddhist cultic life is available in any language, but a handy, brief reference is *Bukkyō gyōji to sono shisō,* edited by Matsuno Junkō (Tokyo, 1976). Kenneth Ch'en's *The Chinese Transformation of Buddhism* (Princeton, 1973) has a helpful chapter on Buddhist religious and social life. In it, he notes the pervasive influence of Buddhism: "In celebrating the festivals collectively, all classes of Chinese society . . . were drawn together by the unity and solidarity of a common faith. Such a feeling of communion may be traced to a great extent to the Mahāyāna emphasis on compassion and salvation for all sentient creatures" (p. 256). For cultic life in ninth-century China, see the translation by Edwin O. Reischauer, *Ennin's Dairy,* and its companion volume, *Ennin's Travels to T'ang China* (both, New York, 1955). The best description of the rituals and regulations in a Rinzai Zen monastery is in D. T. Suzuki's *The Training of a Zen Buddhist Monk* (Kyoto, 1934).

21 — BUDDHIST CULTIC LIFE IN TIBET

Robert A. F. Thurman

Traditional Tibetan religion, which exiled Tibetans still practice in the Himalayas, can be considered at once primitive, medieval, and modern. It is primitive in the sense that the majority of Tibetans believe in a supernatural order that animates natural phenomena at all levels. It can be considered medieval because the sacred subculture of monasticism still flourishes, and it is modern in the sense that since the mid-seventeenth century it has been vigorously nationalistic, centering its national life on a fully elaborated cult of the state. Calling itself the "integration of the Three Vehicles"—the monastic *(Hīna-)*, messianic *(Mahā-)*, and apocalyptic *(Vajra-)* Vehicles *(yāna)*—Tibetan Buddhism is a continuation of the form of Buddhism that gradually developed over fifteen hundred years in India. The Indian masters who came to Tibet as missionaries followed their usual practice of preserving the folk traditions they encountered, keeping them within "cultural sight" and symbolically incorporating them, in modified form, into the Buddhist universe. This Buddhist missionary strategy, variously described as assimilation, amalgamation, and syncretism, can be better understood as a process of transformation or transvaluation by which an old religious form is symbolically sublimated and directed to a new end.

Before Buddhist missionaries reached Tibet, the Źaṅ-źuṅ empire of western Tibet and Sinkiang followed the Bon religion, an amalgamation of Inner Asian religious ideas and, perhaps, Zoroastrianism and shamanism. When Buddhism began to flourish in Tibet, Bon adapted numerous Buddhist doctrines and institutions to its own ends. Following the early Tibetan Buddhist (later called the Rñiṅ-ma-pa) scheme of "nine vehicles"—the three traditional vehicles (Monk, Hermit, and Bodhisattva) and six Tantric vehicles (Action, Performance, Yoga, and Great, Greater, and Ultimate Tantras)—Bon developed its own scheme of Nine Vehicles. The Bon vehicles either syncretized and systematized the shamanistic practices of ancient Tibet or mirrored the Buddhist vehicles. [*See* Bon.]

Tibetan Buddhists sharply distinguish between their cultic life and that of Bon. They have also attempted systematically to suppress shamanism, which they consider misguided, tribalistic, and violent. Certain Tibetan Buddhist rituals, however, are related to the first four shamanistic Bon vehicles: Oracle Priest, Visionary Priest, Magician, and Healer. But there are basic differences in the Tibetan Buddhist attitude toward, and the practice and content of, such rituals, which they considered mundane rather than religious. For example, because of their doctrine of transmigration and its concomitant respect for animal life, the Buddhists do not engage in blood sacrifice. In place of animals they use ritual cakes and effigies as sacrificial offerings.

While the Tibetan Buddhists believe in all the ancient gods of their nation and the numerous spirits of the land, sky, and underworld, they consider them to be fellow wanderers in *saṃsāra.* They take the Buddhas and *bodhisattvas* much more seriously. Especially revered are the "precious incarnate lamas," who are considered the human incarnations and quintessential representatives of the Buddha and *bodhisattvas*. Thus, their faith is rooted in the historical presence of the Buddha Śākyamuni, his life teachings, and the monastic community (i.e., the Three Refuges); it flourishes by focusing on the celestial Tantric emanations of Śākyamuni, especially on the "terrific tutelaries" (such as Yamantaka and Hayagrīva); and the angelic *bodhisattvas*, especially sAvalokiteśvara, Mañjuśrī, Vajrapāṇi, and Tārā in all her forms; it culminates in their enjoyment of the presence of the Incarnations, especially the Dalai Lama. [*See* Avalokiteśvara; Mañjuśrī; Tārā; *and* Dalai Lama.]

The Tibetan mythic universe centers on the cycle of the *bodhisattva* of great compassion, Avalokiteśvara, who is believed to protect and cultivate the Tibetan nation. Most Tibetans firmly rely on his immanent presence in history. The great Dharma kings of Tibet—for example, the sixth-century monarch Sroṅ-btsan-sgampo and, more recently, the Dalai Lamas—are considered his incarnations. Geographically, the city of Lhasa, with its Jo-khaṅ Monastery built by Sroṅ-btsan, is the center of the blessed field of Avalokitśvara, but the *bodhisattva*'s most outstanding architectural symbol is the Potala Palace. This seventeenth-century palace, which stands on Red Mountain overlooking Lhasa, serves as an iconic memorial of the special covenant between the compassionate messiah and his people. All Tibetan Buddhist domestic shrines have a picture of this monumental edifice. The Potala, an ancient Inner Asian fort, a tomb for ancient kings, a temple, monastery, royal palace, and government bureaucracy, is also a *maṇḍala*—a heavenly palace of the perfect, pure land of the *bodhisattva* on earth. Inside, the ritual gateways to numerous other divine *maṇḍala*/universes are simultaneously upheld. The building itself is an excellent example of the complexities of the Tibetan faith.

According to the Tibetan Buddhist idea of spiritual evolution, two stores—the store of merit and the store of wisdom—must be gathered for a person to advance toward better rebirths and eventual Buddhahood. The simple person mainly concentrates on merit while vicariously gathering wisdom by supporting those who pursue study, reflection, and contemplation in order to gain wisdom. Merit can be accumulated by body, speech, and mind as these evolve toward the evolutionary consummation of body, speech, and mind that is Buddhahood. An important religious act of Tibetan laity and monastics is pilgrimage to, and circumambulation of, sacred sites. For Tibetans from all walks of life, the Potala and Lhasa are the hub of this devotional movement. [*See also* Merit, *article on* Buddhist Concepts *and* Pilgrimage, *article on* Tibetan Pilgrimage.]

The basic Tibetan religious service, whether one of solitary contemplation or public ritual, has seven branches: prostration/refuge, sacrifice/offering, confession/absolution, congratulation of others' merit, invocation of Buddhas to teach, prayer for the continuing presence of enlightened beings, and dedication of merit to benefit all beings. Tibetan pilgrims often spend months circumambulating Lhasa and the Potala, prostrating themselves in the road once every step, reciting their prayers, which they dramatize by making ritual gestures, and focusing their minds on the presence of the living messiah in his mansion. When not on pilgrimage, Tibetans chant the *mantra* wheel of the *bodhisattva,* his "heart *mantra,*" "Oṃ mani padme hūṃ," keeping the rhythm of their work or motion or following their fingers touring the 108-bead rosaries they carry. During these physical and verbal devotions, the mind is focused on simple devices of visualization, such as a luminous wheel of light made of the six syllables of the *mantra.* As they recite, the Tibetans visualize it turning, radiating rainbow light rays that drive away evil and fill them and all other beings with bliss and peace. As a reminder of this they often carry a *mani* prayer wheel. Tibetans also erect stupa monuments to represent the Buddha's mind, commission the printing and reading of texts to honor the Buddha's speech, and commission icons and statues to commemorate his body.

The monastics have other important ceremonies: rituals of ordination (for novices and fully ordained monks or nuns), monthly rituals of purification, summertime rituals of retreat, and rituals of accession to higher ranks and offices within the monastic hierarchy. In the Dge-lugs-pa, the largest Tibetan monastic order, a whole series of stages relate to education, practice, and attainment. For example, certain practices and fields of study, which take about twenty years, lead to the *dge-bśes (geshe)* degree. This is followed by passage into the nine-year program of the Tantric colleges, where the Esoteric study and practice intensify until one reaches the Vajra Master stage, involving a lengthy retreat. [*See* Dge-lugs-pa.] Then there is the process of transmitting what one has mastered to younger monks—through teaching, debate, composition, and in the ceremonial setting of initiation. The clergy performs many functions for the laity: they administer the refuges, supervise the entrance into Buddhism or renewal of the faith, give the *bodhisattva* vows and precepts, and conduct purification rites. Monks also consult oracles, give advice, dispense medicine, and in extreme cases, exorcise malignant influences. [*See* Priesthood, *article on* Buddhist Priesthood.]

The monastic government, centered in the All-victorious Dga'-ldan Palace, originally in 'Bras-spuṅs Monastery but since the seventeenth century located in the Potala, continually renews the sense of national millennium through a cycle of yearly festivals and performances. The most important of these is the Great Prayer Festival, held in Lhasa at the lunar new year in spring, from the new moon to the full moon of the first month. Founded in 1409 by Tsoṅ-kha-pa, the festival commemorates the fortnight when Śākyamuni Buddha performed triumphal miracles at Śrāvastī. The keys to the city are handed over to the abbots of the major monasteries and the entire city becomes a monastery for the two weeks. If we recall that monasticism itself is an institutional form of millennialism, a microcosmic society wherein individuals and their relations have been sanctified into a "pure land" millennial quality of goodness, then we can recognize in this yearly festival a renewal of the millennial sense of nationhood Tibetans enjoy as the chosen people of Avalokiteśvara. During the first celebration of this festival, Tsoṅ-kha-pa offered a heavenly crown and royal ornaments to the Śākyamuni image in the Jo-khaṅ Cathedral to symbolize Tibet's commitment to the vision of Śākyamuni's eternal presence on the subtle plane, affirming the apocalyptic core of Tibet's culture. [*See the biography of Tsoṅ-kha-pa.*] The fifth Dalai Lama and his colleagues and successors invested considerable effort in writing history, in sponsoring the national theater troupe, and in instituting fashions of dress connected with the national pageant, masquerade dances, butter-sculpture contests, and so on. They sought systematically to foster the cult of the nation as a link to the benevolent *bodhisattvas*, its service a form of the merit and altruism central to the religious practices of the monastic and messianic vehicles.

Many of the ritual practices that link the monastics to the laity are formalized in the three lower categories of Tantra: Action (Caryā), Performance (Kriyā) and Yoga Tantras. The important deities are the *bodhisattvas* Avalokiteśvara, Mañjuśrī, Vajrapāṇi, Tārā, and Uṣṇīṣavijayā, and such protectors as Mahākāla and Śrīdevī. For the lama's own spiritual progress, he concentrates on the Unexcelled Yoga Tantras (Anuttarayoga Tantra), wherein the highest practices are taught and studied. The major cycles of these Tantras are Guhyasamāja, Cakrasaṃvara, Yamantaka, Hevajra, Hayagrīva, Vajrakīla, and Kālacakra. These tutelary forms of Buddha are at the core of the culture, key to the study, personal practice, realization, identity, and activity of the most learned lamas, the reincarnations who are central within the national cult.

In practice, the Unexcelled Yoga Tantras are divided into two stages: creation and perfection. The creation stage centers on the discipline of the imagination known as "purification of perception." Here the yogin systematically envisions a perfect self-identity and a perfect environment, training himself to enter at will a fully elaborated alternative reality, more or less heavenly in quality. Its sequence is called the "conversion into the Three Bodies." The ordinary life cycle of death, between-state *(antarābhava),* and birth/life is converted into the perfection of the Buddha bodies of Truth, Beatitude, and Emanation, respectively. When the yogin can completely withdraw from all perceptions of ordinariness into a universe of aesthetic perfection, the creation stage is over.

The perfection stage, with its six-branch or its five-stage (depending on the system) yoga, now begins. Here the yogin goes beyond merely imagining the death, between, and rebirth stages and enters into trance states during which outer breath ceases and the coarse five sense-consciousnesses are dissolved. He or she enters inner, subtle states of death and bliss, with the subtle consciousness directed toward achieving a conscious ability to control the subtlest biological processes. The famous "six yogas of Nā-ro-pa"—those of heat, magic body, dream, between-state, clear light, and transference—all involve the yogic technology of the perfection stage.

Whatever the reality underlying the depth psychology of these Unexcelled Yoga Tantras, the highest Tibetan lamas are considered masters of the Tantras and regarded with awe. Most Tibetans are aware of the existence and nature of these yogas and believe that the lamas are able to master the death and rebirth process and will return, through reincarnation, to bless and guide their people. These Tantras also have elaborate liturgies for bringing to fruition religious aims in the world. The goals of the Tantras are called "accomplishments" *(siddhi)* and are classified as either transcendent or mundane. The "transcendent accomplishment" is simply Buddhahood, which automatically contains all lesser accomplishments. And the most important liturgical forms—such as the Esoteric anointment or initiation *(abhiṣeka)* rites—lead to this accomplishment. Elaborate rites are needed to construct the *maṇḍala* palace and to transform the ordinary body, speech, and mind of the initiate into divine, or Buddha, body, speech, and mind. The yogin carefully integrates the patterns of these rites and reenacts them later during contemplation.

There are also numerous rites, which we might call magical in nature, performed to attain mundane accomplishments. These rites fall into four main categories: (1) pacification rites (to pacify, bless, and heal); (2) augmentative rites (to increase lifespan and good luck and to generate bounty and wealth); (3) empowering rites (to enhance control of divine and human individual and social forces, to tame and discipline); and (4) terrific rites (to protect against evil and remove obstacles; exceptionally, these rites may involve the taking of sentient life).

Interestingly, the functions of the Bon vehicles of oracle, visionary, magician, and healing priests are here assumed by the highest Buddhist leaders within the transcendentalistic framework of one of the Anuttarayoga Tantra cycles. Oracular functions fit in the third category, visionary in the second, and magical in all but especially the fourth; life-enhancing functions belong to the first and second.

There are so many elaborate ceremonies that it is impossible to deal with them in any detail. One of these is linked to the cult of the state oracle maintained at the Gnas-chuṅ Monastery, originally next to 'Bras-spuṅs near Lhasa, and now rebuilt at Dharamsāla. Pe-har, Tibet's major tribal deity, was tamed by Padmasambhava, the eighth-century apocalyptic Buddhist missionary. He was not destroyed but was bound by oath to give up the sacrificial cult with which he was previously worshiped. Instead, he was to be offered the sacrifice of egotism by people devoted to the Buddhist Dharma; in exchange, he would protect and counsel them. Thus, a ritual connected to the cycle of Hayagrīva, the major terrific form of Avalokiteśvara, was created. It was performed by specially trained monks who would evoke Pe-har's chief "minister" angel, as the deity himself was too potent to be evoked safely. This angelic minister, Rdo-rje-drag-ldan, would possess one particular monk, able to serve as medium, who would then demonstrate supernormal powers to prove the presence of the deity and, more importantly, provide information to the state, respond to questions, give warnings of impending danger, and so on.

During every New Year festival, the oracle monk, dressed in ceremonial garb, is brought before the Dalai Lama in public. While in a trance state, he blesses the state and the people, stalks about among the ministers of state in case there are any unworthy ones, and, to roars of public approval, shoots a symbolic arrow at the heart of the scapegoat effigy in which all the evil of the previous year is magically entrapped. The effigy, made of butter and flour, is then burned in a spectacular bonfire.

This ceremony contains the most primordial energies from the deepest recesses of the Tibetan tribal consciousness, yet it is fully integrated with the national devotion to Buddhism. It expresses the Buddhist ideals of compassion, selflessness, national nonviolence, and persistence in the monastic disciplines, which have as their aim self-transformation—the highest possible end of human life.

[*See also* Buddhism, Schools of, *articles on* Tibetan Buddhism *and* Esoteric Buddhism; Buddhism, *article on* Buddhism in Tibet; Tibetan Religions, *overview article; and* Maṇḍalas, *article on* Buddhist Maṇḍalas.]

BIBLIOGRAPHY

Avedon, John F. *In Exile from the Land of Snows.* New York, 1984.

Beyer, Stephen. *The Cult of Tārā: Magic and Ritual in Tibet.* Berkeley, 1973.

Govinda, A. *Foundations of Tibetan Mysticism according to the Esoteric Teachings of the Great Mantra Oṁ Maṇi Padme Hūṃ.* London, 1959.

Gyatso, Tenzin. *My Land and My People* (1962). Reprint, New York, 1983. The autobiography of the fourteenth Dalai Lama.

Nebesky-Wojkowitz, R. de. *Oracles and Demons of Tibet* (1956). Reprint, Graz, 1975.

Stein, Rolf A. *Tibetan Civilization.* Stanford, 1972.

22 BUDDHIST MEDITATION

Winston L. King

Meditation as a means of religious discipline and spiritual attainment is not unique to Buddhism, but in its character and in its irreplaceable centrality to the gaining of ultimate salvation Buddhist meditation has a distinctive nature all its own. Basically, meditation is here conceived as a regimen of carefully structured steps of concentration on chosen objects, which concentration is designed to lead in the end to a "going out" *(nirvāṇa)* from the eternally recurring cycle of birth and death *(saṃsāra)* in which every sentient creature is enmeshed.

The meditative quest of Gautama (Pali, Gotama) under the Bodhi Tree, by which he became an enlightened one, or a Buddha (from *bodhi,* "enlightening knowledge"), remains the classic archetype of the discipline and experience. In the Theravāda (Pali canon) account, Gotama thereby discovered that attachment to individualized existence *(taṇhā)* was the cause of rebirth; in the Mahāyāna account, he discerned that the Buddha nature is inherent in all sentient beings.

ORIGINS

The precise historical origins and components of the Buddhist meditative techniques are difficult to pin down. The Pali canon portrays Gotama as having vainly sought deliverance from *saṃsāra* by means of then-current Indian ascetic and meditative methods. These he ultimately rejected as wrong and insufficient in their extreme asceticism and in their goal of distinctionless union with the absolute *(brahman).* But although Buddhism denied the reality of the Upaniṣadic Self *(ātman),* and although the stated purpose of the new Buddhist meditation was to gain an existential realization of the *un*reality of the self *(anattā)* and to transcend an existence characterized by impermanence *(anicca)* and suffering, or innate unsatisfactoriness *(dukkha),* the aim of Buddhist practice remained spiritually kin to the Upaniṣadic quest of the Self: "The Self, which is free from evil, ageless, deathless, sorrowless, hungerless, thirstless, whose desire is the Real. . . .He should be searched out." [*See* Upaniṣads.]

Substitute *nirvāṇa*—the going out of, or from selfness and thirst for continued being—for the Upaniṣadic Self, and one has a good description of the thrust toward the Buddhist goal, as well as an intimation of its methodology. So too, though the

Yoga system developed independently of Buddhism and remained within the Brahmanic-Hindu fold, the yogic methodology that was developing during the early Buddhist period certainly contributed techniques, and probably followers, to the spreading Buddhist movement. [*See* Yoga.]

THERAVĀDA STRUCTURE

Theravāda Buddhism has sought to fashion its meditational theory and practice in faithful adherence to the model provided by Gotama in his attainment of Buddhahood. This model is set forth most extensively in the *Majjhima Nikāya* (Middle-length Sayings), but owing to their analytic depth and rigor, the anonymous *Vimuttimagga* (The Path of Freedom) and Buddhaghosa's massive *Visuddhimagga* (The Path of Purification; both c. 500 CE) became the orthodox manuals of Theravāda meditation. [*See the biography of Buddhaghosa.*]

In these sources, meditation is presented as the only successful means to attain full and final release from the endless round of birth and death. The essence of the method is to so existentialize and internalize an awareness of the inherent nature (impermanent, unsatisfactory, lacking a permanent self) of all existence that the meditator becomes both intellectually and emotionally free from attachment to existence, thereby destroying the desire-driven karmic propulsion into ever new forms of space-time being.

Meditation is envisaged as a progression through three organically interdependent stages. *Sīla,* or morality, is the foundation and thus is intrinsic to the whole process. Only the morally earnest person can meditate properly. As spiritual development takes place, the central ethical values become progressively refined, stengthened, and internalized until they become fully dispositional. The five moral precepts (avoiding killing, stealing, lying, illicit sex, and intoxicants) and five further abstemious, but not ascetic, regulations are the core of *sīla.* The monk's life, originally geared almost exclusively to meditation, gradually acquire an elaborate superstructure of regulations built on this base. [*See* Vinaya.]

The second level or factor is the development of the power of attention *(samādhi)* until it can attain to one-pointed concentration on a single subject *(cittasya ekāgratā)* for long periods of time. The third and highest level of attainment is the fruit of the proper use of this one-pointed concentration of mind, called *paññā* (wisdom). In this state, the fully developed understanding of the true nature of *saṃsāra* results in enlightenment, the attainment of *nirvāṇa.* [*See* Samādi *and* Prajñā.]

BASIC THERAVĀDA TECHNIQUES

Solitude—that is, freedom from disturbance by distracting sounds and sights—is essential for the beginner. The classic "lotus" posture is standard: legs folded beneath the torso, with each foot, sole upward, resting on the inner thigh of the opposite leg. The hands rest in the lap, palms upward, left hand underneath. The spine and neck are to be kept in a straight, but not strained, almost erect position. This mode of sitting provides a solid position that can be mainetained without undue fatigue for extended periods. The lower centers of sensation, sphincteral and sexual, are thereby quieted and neutralized. The eyes are either half or totally closed.

There are some forty traditional subjects for meditation. They are classified in two ways: in terms of the types of persons for whom they are suitable, and in terms of the kind and level of meditative attainment their use can produce. Five types of personal character are recognized: devotional, intellectual, sensual, choleric, and dull. Meditation on the Buddha, the *sangha* (the Buddhist order), peace, and benevolence fit the devotional type; repulsiveness-of-food themes fit the intellectual type; cemetery meditations fit the sensual type; attention to breathing is recommended for the angry (choleric) type; and the dull type should meditate on the four "illimitables": loving kindness *(mettā)*, compassion *(karuṇā)*, joy in others' joy *(muditā)*, and equanimity *(upekkhā)*. Meditation on specified shapes and colors *(kasiṇas)* suits all types.

In terms of level of attainment, there are two types of results: jhanic and vipassanic. The jhanic (trance) states, representing the Yogic-Upaniṣadic inheritancce of Buddhism, are eight in number (or by some counts nine): the four *jhānas* (Skt., *dhyānas*), through which the Buddha is portrayed as passing to gain enlightenment; and four succesive states based on contemplation of formless subjects—infinity of space, infinity of consciousness, nothingness, and neither perception nor nonperception. All of these, according to the Pali cannon, Gotama rejected in his search for the right method. Typically, these are to be produced on a *kasiṇa*-type base that is progressively refined and dematerialized in its perception until the meditator reaches the attenuated eighth stage, in which "subject" and "object" are barely distinguishable. Theravāda holds that such attainments per se do not constitute nirvanic experience however; that is reserved for the vipassanic type of technique. [*See also* Cosmology, *article on* Buddhist Cosmology.]

Vipassanā (insight) meditation is the quintessentially Buddhist element in the meditational structure. It is devoted exclusively to the intensification of the awareness of all visible-tangible realities, including the totality of the meditator himself, as intrinsically impermanent *(anicca)*, unreal *(anattā)*, and painful *(dukkha)*, the essence of *saṃsāra*. Certain of the forty subjects of meditation seem especially suited to vipassanic concentration. Meditation on the repulsiveness of food (the digestive process), the decaying states of a dead body, the analysis of the body into its thirty-two components, and on the sensations, emotions, and thought process of one's own body-mind lend themselves naturally to the *anicca, anattā, dukkha* analysis. All these component elements and processes are perceived to be atomistic aggregates dependent on each other for achieving existent form, a prime example of dependent origination *(paṭicca samuppāda)*, with no real or permanently self-identical "self" or "soul" present in any part or in the whole. [*See* Pratītya-samutpāda *and* Soul, *article on* Buddhist Concepts.]

The *vipassanā* level of concentration scarcely rises above the jhanic preliminary access concentration. (Access concentration is an "approach road" to the truly jhanic [tance] depths; it is a lightly concentrated state in which ordinary sounds can still be heard but are no longer at the center of attention or distractive to it.) But by its nature, *vipassanā* insight is the *sine qua non* of deliverance from *saṃsāra*, whether formalized as a method or not—although in the end *vipassanā* did become an independent method. Classically, it was used in conjunction with the jhanic type, whose *jhānas*—"peaceful abidings," Buddhaghosa calls them—must be subjected to vipassanic scrutiny lest the meditator become attached to them and consider them nirvanic attainment. But they too are still within the samsaric domain.

The experiential quality of *vipassanā* is not, however, purely negative or neutral; at its higher levels it too produces a jhanic-like result: path awareness, or the direct awareness of the unconditioned *nirvāṇa.* When this path awareness is first experienced it comes as a fleeting, flashing moment of sensing the nirvanic essence directly, brief but unmistakable. The meditator then knows he has reached the level of "stream enterer" *(sotāpanna),* with only seven more rebirths awaiting him. Then in succession come the stages of "once returner to rebirth" *(sakadāgāmin),* "nonreturner to human birth" *(anāgāmin),* and "*nirvāṇa* attainer" *(arahant).* The mere flashes of path awareness have now been developed until they come more frequently and sustainedly. [*See* Arhat.]

There is a crowning experience that Buddhaghosa says is possible only for *arahants* and *anāgāmins* who have also perfected the mastery of the eight jhanic trances. It is called *nirodha-samāpatti* ("complete cessation of thought and perception") and is the fullest, most intense, and longest (up to seven days) maintainable experience of nirvanic bliss that can be attained in this life. It is not, however, essential to after-death *nirvāṇa,* which may be achieved by *vipassanā* alone.

MAHĀYĀNA DEVELOPMENTS

That vast and varied development of Buddhist doctrine and institutions known as Mahāyāna, beginning late in the pre-Christian era, inevitably resulted in significant changes in the goals and methods of meditation. The basic techniques of posture and of breath, body, and thought control were retained, as were many of the meditational terms. But the inner meaning of the latter was radically changed, and the whole discipline was restructured in the light of new Mahāyāna doctrines. [*See* Buddhism, Schools of, *article on* Mahāyāna Budhism.]

Relevant Doctrinal Changes. Four overlapping and interacting developments of doctrine and practice in Mahāyāna tended to modify the meditational pattern as well. First was the transformation and extention of the Buddha ideal from that of an exalted human who sought and gained immortality in the fifth century BCE to a transcendent being, exemplified variously by the Eternal Buddha of the *Saddharmapuṇḍarīka Sūtra* (Lotus Sutra), the eternally saving Buddha of Limitless Life (Amitāyus) of the Pure Land scriptures, the absolute Buddha essence *(dharmakāya),* or the impersonal "emptiness" *(śūnyatā)* of the *Prajñāpāramitā* and other Mahāyāna scriptures. [*See* Śūnyam and Śunyatā.] Second, the Lotus Sutra also taught that the ultimate goal of all human beings was to become Buddhas—implying the later doctrine of the Buddha nature impliit in all beings. Thus the ideal of bodhisattvahood, the selfless serving of others by repeated voluntary rebirths in order to serve and save them, replaced that of the *arahant* seeking release in *nirvāṇa.* The great *bodhisattvas* of compassion and power, absorbing the characteristics of indigenous deities along the way, became prime objects of popular devotion in many Mahāyāna cultures. [*See* Celestial Buddhas and Bodhisattvas.]

Third, the consequence of all this was the laicizing of Buddhist values. Thus the *Vimalakīrti Sūtra* relates how a pious layman of that name, fully involved in secular activity, surpasses all the heavenly *bodhisattvas* in spiritual attainments. But though these doctrines and ideals would seem to guarantee the genuine and effective opening up of the heights of spiritual realization (Buddhahood) to all people, this democratizing tendency was almost completely undercut by the simultaneous multiplication and complication of ritual and meditative techniques in some traditions. Ch'an (Jpn., Zen), with its demeaning of scripturalism and tradition, was one attempt to break through to greater simplicity; Chinese and Japanese Pure Land, with its repetition of the name of the Buddha Amitāyus (Jpn., Amida), was another.

Fourth, the Confucian-Taoist influence fundamentally altered East Asian Mahāyāna. The concept of Heaven, which embraaced man in an organic relation, and the notion of the Tao as that infinite primordial formlessness out of which flows all the forms of the universe, both fused in many instances with such central Buddhist concepts as the *dharmakāya* (absolute Buddha essence) and *śūnyatā* (emptines). Functionally, these became the Buddhist forms of the Tao.

Variant Forms of Mahāyāna Meditation. These Taoist characteristics were especially influential in the formation of Ch'an/Zen meditational patterns. The Taoist language of intuitive as opposed to rationalistic awareness, its viscerally sensed oneness with reality, its assertion of vacuity as true fullness, of silence as eloquence, of deepest truth as verbally unstatable, and of conceptual absurdities as revelatory of highest wisdom, were all adopted by Ch'an/Zen and made the basis of its meditational method and philosophy. The silent sitting and formless, objectless meditation (Jpn., *shikantaza*) of Japanese Sōtō, and Rinzai's use of the absurd, nonsensical, paradoxical *kōan* are thoroughly Taoist in nature.

Zen. The styles and methods of meditation in Sōtō and Rinzai monasteries vary considerably despite their common heritage. The *kōan* plays only a limited role in Sōtō, even though it has not been totally absent from its tradition. Dōgen, the great thirteenth-century master and founder of the Sōtō sect in Japan, allowed that some persons have gained enlightenment while using *kōan,* but that the true agent of that enlightenment had been their silent sitting in meditation *(zazen).* [*See the biography of Dōgen.*] He asserted that this was indeed the teaching of the Buddha himself. Hence, the role of the meditation master *(rōshi)* in Sōtō is minimal. Sudden, flashing enlightenment experiences are not deliberately sought; in their placce, a quieter and more natural inner-outer harmony of thought, feeling, and action is observed. To sit is to be a Buddha; continued and faithful sitting gradually transforms one's life, enabling one to find and develop one's innate Buddhahood and to encounter one's *kōan* in life situations.

For Rinzai, the *kōan* replaces the Theravāda *kasiṇa,* so to speak. Rinzai meditation does not seek to create either an attenuated luminous form before the eyes of the state of cessation. Rather, it has as its goal a state of full, visceral oneness with the *dharmakāya,* an awareness that one's own mind is the Buddha mind and a sense of unity, although not blank undifferentiated oneness, with the universe and others, which Rinzai calls enlightenment (Jpn., *satori*). In this sense of "unity-with," one lives and does all one's work. This transition is seen as the great death of the concept-bound, self-bound, habit-bound individual and the transformation of that individual into a full, spontaneously free self in which the inner-outer, conscious-subconscious, self-other, holy-profane dichotomies are organically unified.

To achieve this transformation, Rinzai utilizes the *kōan*. Originally stemming from informal repartee, the interchanges between famous masters and their disciples were called *kōan* (public records or cases), and finally were collected into the Rinzai texts. There are some 1,700 in one famous collection. Jōshū's *mu* ("No!"—that is, there is no Buddha nature in a dog) and Hakuin's "the sound of one hand clapping" are famous ones, often used for beginners in meditation. Each student-monk is given a *kōan* by his master after some preliminary training. Once or twice a day he must present himself to his *rōshi* with his *kōan* and his "answer." The answer may be a word or phrase, a look, a gesture, an action. On the basis of that, the master judges the meditator's progress toward true understanding of the Buddha mind. When the answer shows such intuitive insight that the master is convinced of its authenticity, he pronounces the *kōan* solved. (The meditator's own subjective sense that he has had a *satori* experience will not suffice; the master may judge it to be delusive.) The meditator is then encouraged to expand and deepen this awareness through other *kōans*, which still further break down the person's sense of dualistic separation from his world or division within himself, and to apply this new "Buddha-mindedness" to wider areas of his life. [*See also* Ch'an.]

T'ien-t'ai. Of course, other forms of meditation, basing themselves on various *sūtras* and adopted by various sects, developed in the Chinese and Japanese contexts. The *Śūraṃgama Sūtra,* for example, sets forth a method of concentrating on the various basic sense data and their related sense organs in turn, several types of consciousness, and the component elements of existence.

The sect known as T'ien-t'ai (Jpn., Tendai), being highly inclusive in its doctrinal and practice structures, also developed various meditative techniques. Its basic scriptural warrant was the twenty-fourth chapter of the *Lotus Sutra,* the sect's main scripture, in which sixteen types of *samādhi* (meditation-induced mental concentration) are mentioned.

In T'ien-t'ai, four ways of attaining *samādhi* were recognized: (1) a ninety-day period of exclusive meditation on any proper subject; (2) exclusive invocation of Amitābha's name for ninety days; (3) a seated and walking meditation directed against bad *karman;* (4) a concentration on seeing ultimate reality as (a) empty substantive actuality *(chi-k'ung),* (b) having immediate but provisional existence for thought and action *(chi-chia),* (c) climactically being *both* empty and existent *(chi-ch'ung)*—again a Taoist-influenced awareness.

Especially important for T'ien-t'ai was the direction given to it by Chih-i (538–597), the school's third patriarch. [*See the biography of Chih-i.*] He emphasized the necessity for balance in meditation and taught the fourth of the methods described above. Chih-i spoke constantly of the necessary presence of two factors at all times: *chih* (Skt., *śamatha*) and *kuan* (Skt., *vipaśyanā*). *Chih* is the stopping and calming of thought. This meditative mode produces an awareness of sheer emptiness *(śūnyatā),* the realization of the great void in an inner stillness, but by itself too nirvanic-passive and withdrawn. *Kuan,* or introspective attention to the workings of one's own mind (not unlike Teravāda *vipassanā*), leads to the awareness of illusory quality of mind, a sense of its relativistic dependence on exterior objects, and embodied *bodhisattva* compassion. The proper combination of the two at all stages of meditation gives rise to a compassionate wisdom in which all things and situations are seen as neither totally real nor unreal. Japanese Tendai, introduced to Japan by Saichō in the ninth century, soon adopted Esoteric techniques in competition with Shingon, and was also modified by Zen. [*See* T'ien-t'ai.]

Pure Land. The Pure Land schools also had their forms of meditation, and for some devotees, a system of visualization based on the *Kuan wu-liang-shou ching* (Amitāyus Meditation Sutra). Beginning with the attention focused on the setting sun (in the direction of the Western Paradise), the meditator successively visualized sun (with both open and shut eyes), water, ice, lapis lazuli (fundament of the Pure Land),

and the Pure Land glories as described in the *sūtra,* climaxing in a vision of Amitābha himself and his two flanking *bodhisattvas.* In Japan, success in this was sometimes linked with the number of invocations of Amida's name. No doubt T'ien-t'ai's second method was influenced by these Pure Land practices.

Still another type of meditative visualization is set forth in the *Pratyutpanna-buddha-saṃmukhāvasthita-samādhi Sūtra,* an early Mahāyāna work possibly intended for the laity. The meditator who would achieve this *samādhi* must prepare for it by scrupulous adherence to the precepts, the study of scripture, and a continual effort to see the Buddhas everywhere and in everything. This is to be capped by a period of intensive meditation. The *sūtra* promises that if one meditates continuously for seven days and nights he will assuredly see the Pure Land and Amitābha. Other possible objects of concentration are also mentioned. On meditates on some particular Buddha, or perhaps on the Buddhas as a whole, and in the ensuing *samādhi* all the Buddhas and their attendants will present themselves before him. One interpretation of this language is that the meditator travels, by visualization, to the lands of the Buddhas and hears them expound the Dharma directly. The *sūtra* promises that these visualizations will be "as in a dream." In the *samādhi* that ensues, the meditator will not be sensible of day or night, inner or outer, or of any distinction of any sort, "not seeing anything." Some see this as an effort to bridge the gap between the burgeoning Pure Land cult of seeing the Buddha Amitāyus and the Prajñāpāramitā "emptiness" *(śūnyatā)* philosophy. [*See* Amitābha; Pure and Impure Lands; *and* Nien-fo.]

ESOTERIC BUDDHISM

The so-called Mantrayāna and Vajrayāna methods that developed in Tibet and that have taken a somewhat similar form in Japanese Shingon are considered to be generally Mahāyāna, yet they have distinctive freatures. Tibetan practice, which includes Tantric and pre-Buddhist Bon elements, strongly emphasizes visualizations and *mantra* repetition. Although these induced visualizations—in which *maṇḍalas* are used as a base and *mantras* as a ritual aid—are ostensibly visual representations of various demons, gods, Buddhas, and *bodhisattvas,* they are in fact only visualized froms of the basic psychic forces, good and bad, within the meditator himself. These the meditator must project into full consciousness, in part by the use of those *mantras* containing divine-name power, and then overcome or appropriate them. Considerable attention and effort are expended on the control of the flow of vital energy into the various *cakras* (psychosomatic centers) in the body, and on the transmutation of the lower forms of energy into the higher. A very important part of the various Tibetan methods, often combined with other visualizations, is the strengthening of the meditator's Buddha awareness by consciously visualizing the inclusion of the Buddha's characteristics into himself, so that in the end he himself is in some measure a Buddha, and of visualizing the whole world as Buddha-filled and offering it to the Buddha in its maṇḍala form. But again, the crowning realization is that of the ultimate emptiness [*See also* Buddhism, Schools of, *article on* Esoteric Buddhism; Maṇḍalas, *article on* Buddhist Maṇḍalas, *article on* Buddhist Maṇḍalas; Mantra; *and* Cakras.]

Japanese Shingon has an elaborate, esoteric ritual structure for its adepts in which various deities are invoked and their power solicited. Visualization here begins at least with the visualization of a luminous disk (reminding one of the liminous circular *kasiṇa* form of Theravāda meditation) into which, one by one, are projected various sacred Devanāgarī (Hindu script) characters, whose power the meditator this gains. The final goal is to become Buddha in this very body and this very life. [*See* Chen-yen *and* Shingonshū.]

In few of these forms did Mahāyāna fulfull the apparent potential of its *bodhisattva* ideal of "every being a Buddha," and of a meditative discipline within the range of the ordinary person's capacities, permeating everyday life and work. Zen has offered meditation to the laity, but real progress toward enlightenment has usually been understood to necessitate a monastic life. The popular recitation of the Nembutsu ("Namu Amida Butsu," "Reverence to Amida Buddha") of the Japanese Pure Land sects was the nearest approach to a daily lay meditative technique. Sometimes among the Japanese *myōkōnin* (Nembutsu pietists), Amida-consciousness reached a nearly mystical sense of oneness with Amida. And perhaps the Nichiren repetition "Namu Myōhōrengekyō" ("Adoration to the Lotus Sutra") as a mantric chant has become something of a popular meditative practice.

MODERN TENDENCIES

In general, and especially in Zen and Theravāda, the trend in modern meditational teaching has been one of simplification and adaptation of techniques to contemporary conditions and to wider lay practice. In Theravāda, this has taken the form of an almost exclusive emphasis on the less technically demanding *vipassanā* technique. In particular, attention is given to breath and to body-mind processes, as well as to *vipassanā*'s practicality for daily life in the world. Efforts are being made to bring Zen out of the monastery and into lay life by modifying the strictness of its regimen and relating its orientation to the "ordinary mind," which after all is the Buddha mind. And in both traditions there was been a notable missionary penetration of Europe and America in the form of meditation centers and temporary short-term meditation sessions. Some have also incorporated Zen elements into various psychosomatically oriented self-development and self-realization techniques.

[*See also* Soteriology, *article on* Buddhist Soteriology; Nirvāṇa; *and* Buddhism, *article on* Buddhism in India.]

BIBLIOGRAPHY

Buddhaghosa, Badantācariya. *The Path of Purification.* 2d ed. Translated by Bhikkhu Ñyāṇamoli. Colombo, 1964. The comprehensive manual of Theravāda meditation, considered authoritative by Theravādins.

Chang, Garma C. C. *The Practice of Tibetan Meditation.* New York, 1963. One of the few reliable and specific treatments, including text and methodological sections.

Chang, Garma C. C., trans. and ed. *The Teachings of Tibetan Yoga.* New Hyde Park, N.Y., 1963.

Chang, Garma C. C. *The Practice of Zen.* New York, 1970. A clear and knowledgeable exposition of Zen practice for Western readers.

Conze, Edward. *Buddhist Meditation* (1956). Reprint, New York, 1969. A collection of Buddhist meditation texts from *The Path of Purification* and various Sanskrit and Tibetan sources, with a brief introduction.

King, Winston L. *Theravāda Meditation: The Buddhist Transformation of Yoga.* University Park, Pa., 1980. A systematic analysis of *The Path of Purification* pattern, the Indian-Yogic origins, and the dynamic structure of Theravāda meditation, with a chapter on contemporary Burmese forms.

Kornfield, Jack. *Living Buddhist Masters.* Santa Cruz, Calif., 1977. The best overall exposition of a wide variety of contemporary forms of Theravāda meditation in Southeast Asia.

Luk, Charles (K'uan Yü Lu). *The Secrets of Chinese Meditation.* London, 1964. Detailed description of several lesser-known meditational techniques, based in part on the author's own experiences.

Nyanaponika Thera, trans. *The Heart of Buddhist Meditation.* New York, 1975. A clear, authentic discussion and exposition of contemporary Theravāda Buddhist meditation theory and practice. Centered on the vipassanic "bare-attention" type.

Suzuki, D. T., Erich Fromm, and Richard De Martino. *Zen Buddhism and Psychoanalysis.* New York, 1960. An interesting and penetrating discussion of the Zen and psychological interpretations of Zen meditation.

Tucci, Giuseppe. *The Theory and Practice of the Maṇḍala.* Translated by Alan Houghton Broderick. London, 1969. Illuminating discussion of the Indo-Tibetan *maṇḍala* as a "psychocosmogram."

Vajirañāṇa Mahāthera, Parahavahera. *Buddhism Meditation in Theory and Practice.* Colombo, 1962. Clear, systematic exposition of the classic orthodox Theravāda system and theory of meditation in the traditional terminology of the Pali canon.

23 BUDDHIST ICONOGRAPHY

SIMONE GAULIER and ROBERT JERA-BEZARD

Translated from French by Ina Baghdiantz

In the course of its development and diffusion, Buddhism has expressed itself through an abundance of visual forms, but in order to understand them, one has to take into account the profound evolution of Buddhist doctrine over time and space, notably the changes brought into the fundamental doctrines of early Hīnayāna ("lesser vehicle") Buddhism by the Mahāyāna ("great vehicle").

ŚĀKYAMUNI BUDDHA

The fundamental image around which the cult has developed is that of its founder, the Buddha, represented in the essential moments of his religious career. These moments are often evoked solely through the language of gestures (*mudrās*) and postures (*āsanas*) devoid of all context. [*See* Mudrā.] Nonetheless, his image did not figure at all in the earliest, anecdotal presentations preserved on bas-reliefs. Because the Buddha as a personality was deemed to have passed outside of history altogether at his *parinirvāṇa,* or death, his presence was instead symbolized by such motifs as the rich turban of the prince Siddhārtha, the throne of the Blessed One, his footprints marked with the Wheel of the Law (see figure 1), the begging bowl *(pātra),* or the Bodhi Tree (the Enlightenment). Similarly, the First Sermon among the monks in Banaras is evoked by the *triratna* ("three jewels," a three-pointed motif representing the Buddha, his Law, and his Community) surmounted by the Wheel (symbolizing by its movement the transmission of the dogma) and surrounded by deer. Most important of all, the *parinirvāṇa* of the Buddha is recalled by the stupa, the domical shrine believed to have contained the precious relics of the Master. Together with the image of the Buddha, the stupa, as an actual monument or an iconic representation (and through such transformations as the *dāgoba,* or step-pagoda, and the Tibetan *chorchen;* see figure 2) remains at the center of the cult and its visual imagery. [*See* Stupa Worship.]

From the outset of Indian Buddhist art (third–second centuries BCE), the legendary accounts of the Buddha's previous incarnations and earthly life *(jātaka* and *avadāna)* are reflected in sanctuary paintings and bas-reliefs representing the palace life of the young prince Siddhārtha. These depict scenes from the moment of his miraculous conception as a white elephant visiting Queen Māyā (his mother) to the

FIGURE 1: The Wheel of the Law.

time of his "Great Departure" from the life of a householder, mounted on his horse, Kaṇṭhaka. As the Buddha came to assume a supernatural aspect, the figure of the Great Departure sometimes appeared as an astral figure (clearly solar, as seen on the central medallion of the ancient sanctuary cupolas). Bedecked with princely garments, jewels, and an elaborate headdress, the future Buddha is often difficult to distinguish from other *bodhisattvas*, such as Maitreya.

The representation of the Buddha that rapidly became universal probably originated in Gandhāra or Mathurā between the first century BCE and the first century CE; it shows the monk wearing the robe and mantle of the *bhikṣu* (mendicant), with his head encircled by a nimbus, probably the result of Hellenistic influences. Among the thirty-two auspicious marks (*lakṣaṇas*) that designate a Buddha, the most characteristic ones are the *ūrṇā,* the circular tuft of hair on his forehead; the *uṣṇiṣa,* the bump in his skull that looks like a bun of hair; the distended earlobes; the wrinkles on his neck; his webbed fingers; and his gold skin coloring. His posture, the serenity of his features, and his half-closed eyes suggest the depth of his meditation and detachment from the exterior world. This body language rapidly became conventionalized (see figure 3), although, as seen especially in the *maṇḍalas* of the Esoteric (Vajrayāna) tradition in Tibet and East Asia, it hardly remained free of complexity.

FIGURE 2: Stupa and Pagoda.

FIGURE 3: **Seated Buddha.**

Two of the major events following the Great Departure are the Buddha's Enlightenment under the Bodhi Tree and his First Sermon among the monks in the Deer Park in Banaras. But the ultimate evocation of his earthly life is the symbology of the *parinirvāṇa,* where the Master is shown lying on his right side upon a cushion in the presence of the Malla princes, the *bodhisattva* Vajrapāṇi, and his own disciples, all of whom are in mourning.

By the fifth century CE, representations of the Blessed One, standing, seated, or reclining as described above, attained colossal dimensions in a variety of media: chiseled in cliffs or modeled in clay, cut into stone or cast in bronze. From then on he is portrayed as monarch of the world *(cakravartin),* with the "seven jewels" as his attributes (the attendant, the general, the beautiful woman, the horse, the elephant, the wheel, and the pearl or gem). This concept had been expressed earlier with images of the Buddha seated majestically on a lion throne, sometimes in the European fashion or wearing his royal attributes (crown, jewels, cloak with three points) over his monastic dress. Most often, however, he is shown seated in the

Indian manner, his legs crossed more or less tightly, either on a "grass throne" (during the attack of Māra, the Evil One, immediately preceding his Englightenment) or on a stepped throne possibly symbolizing Mount Meru, axis of the world. Alluding to the Great Miracle of Śrāvastī, when the Buddha multiplied his presence in the form of little Buddhas seated on lotuses, he also appears, seated or standing, on a lotus base.

THE TRANSCENDENT BUDDHA

With the Mahāyāna, the supernatural vision heralded in the Great Miracle of Śrāvastī culminates in the myriad Buddhas of the universe, which began to appear in the third and fourth centuries CE and were subsequently painted over and over on sanctuary walls and sculpted or modeled on temples and stupas. This concept of the Buddha's omnipresence is often combined with that of the lotus as cosmic image: each lotus petal constitutes a world, and each torus is occupied by one of the myriad Buddhas, evoking the universe past, present, and future.

The emphasis on this supernatural power manifested itself concretely in both painting and sculpture with images of the Buddha Vairocana, monarch of the universe. These transcendent Buddhas, their bodies covered with images of Mount Meru, the stupa, the sun and moon, aquatic subjects and the lotus, the *vajra* (thunderbolt), wheel, *triratna,* and other signs and symbols, are encountered very early along the path of penetration of the Great Vehicle into China. The doctrine, once evolved, expresses itself in even more elaborate forms in Southeast Asia's mountain temples (Borobudur, Java) and in the temples of faces (Bayon of Angkor Thom, Cambodia). The human character of the Buddha, so evident in the older works, is totally overshadowed in the concept of his three bodies *(trikāya):* the formless body of the Law (*dharmakāya,* which is visually untranslatable); the pleasure body *(saṃbhogakāya),* or body of glory (supraworldly); the transformation, or human, body (*nirmāṇakāya;* i.e., the historical Buddha). From this point on, his retinue *(parivāra)* is enriched with a whole Buddhist pantheon. The eminent helping figures of this new religion of salvation, the Great Vehicle, are added to the monks, the holy patriarchs, the anonymous followers, and the princely donors: first the *bodhisattvas*, personalized as the Buddhas of the future, then the five Jinas ("victors") and their descendants, each one evoking an attitude of Śākyamuni Buddha.

MONKS AND PATRIARCHS

The monks are often dressed in the tattered monastic robes prescribed by the Buddha himself. The robe is attributed to certain of the ten disciples of Śākyamuni, among whom the youngest, Ānanda, and the oldest, Kāsyapa, often appear as acolytes in representations of the historical Buddha. The *arhat* (Chin., *lo-han*) are ascetics who have attained the highest degree of sanctification possible in Hīnayāna soteriology and are the designated protectors of the Law; they are portrayed as old men with pronounced features. Among the "eminent monks" and patriarchs, two groups are distinguished by their wild appearance, very close to that of the sorcerers: the five Masters of the Law as well as the *mahāsiddhas* ("perfected ones"), eighty-four of whom, according to Tibetan tradition, haunt the cemeteries where the adepts of Tantrism complacently thrive. The *bla-ma* (lama, teacher in the Tibetan tradition), by contrast, is depicted serenely.

BODHISATTVAS AND MINOR DEITIES

The *bodhisattva* Maitreya has played a very significant role since the beginning of the Christian era, and for this reason he was rapidly designated in sculpture by specific attributes and often by his posture as well. Like the other *bodhisattva*s he wears the lavish garb of the Indian princes but frequently carries the water vase of the brahmans *(kamaṇḍalu)* in his left hand, while in his right hand he either holds the long-stemmed blue lotus or makes the gesture of instruction *(vitarka);* sometimes he carries a miniature stupa in his tiara and can be seated in European fashion, with his legs crossed in front of his chair. In painted sanctuary decoration he is often depicted enthroned in the Tuṣita Heaven, from which he must descend in order to reincarnate himself as Śākyamuni's successor.

The image of Avalokiteśvara (Kuan-yin in China, Kannon in Japan) also emerges early on, although his powers and therefore his iconography gain more precision with the texts of the Mahāyāna. At first he can be confused with Maitreya since they both carry a flask containing the elixir of life *(amṛtakalaśa)* and a lotus (see figure 4). His relationship with Amitābha Buddha is indicated by the presence of a little meditating Buddha in his tiara; as an assistant to Amitābha, he appears in the triad with the *bodhisattva* Mahāsthāmaprāpta and is included in the great painted scenes of the paradise of Amitābha. Avalokiteśvara is shown with little Buddhas of transformation in his aureole. According to the *Saddharmapuṇḍarīka Sūtra* he is the protector one invokes against the ten perils (snakes, ferocious beasts, robbers, poisons, storms, and so forth); these are often depicted with him on bas-reliefs and paintings.

Of the many forms he can take in both painting and sculpture, some, influenced by the Indian pantheon, are very particular: that of Avalokiteśvara "who faces all" with his eleven heads arranged in a pyramid above his shoulders in order to extend his protection to all directions (the towers of faces in Bayon at Angkor Thom convey the same concept). Reflecting another aspect of his multiple powers as Lord of the World (Lokeśvara), he is portrayed with four, six, or eight arms indicating a *mudrā*. The same aspect is summoned by Kuan-yin "of a thousand hands and a thousand eyes" that encircle him in an aureole; each hand, with an eye marked on the palm, holds a significant attribute: the stupa, rosary, jewel, flask, lotus, and so forth. In Far Eastern art, Kuan-yin comes to assume female forms.

With the diffusion of the Mahāyāna texts, other personalities of the *bodhisattva*s of salvation also appear as statues, on bas-reliefs, or in paintings decorating constructed and rock-cut sanctuaries, as well as in the illustrations of votive tablets and manuscripts. Mañjuśrī and Samantabhadra can often be identified by the animals they ride, generally the golden lion and the white elephant respectively. To the youthful Mañjuśrī one can attribute the book, as to the master of the word, with the gesture of instruction. Devotion to the *bodhisattva* Kṣitigarbha has widely diffused his image in art: as a monk, standing or seated with shawl, ringing stick *(khakkhara),* and pilgrims' bowl, he is enthroned, usually in the midst of the kings of the hells, as master of the six paths of rebirth.

OTHER CELESTIAL ATTENDANTS

Vajrapāṇi, the faithful companion of the Blessed One, was present in all the scenes of the Buddhist legends of the Lesser Vehicle from the very beginnings of the religion. He rapidly abandoned the aspect of the Herculean athlete (the Gandhāra re-

FIGURE 4: Avalokiteśvara.

liefs), however, for the costume and armor of a knight carrying the thunderbolt (*vajra;* see figure 5), the symbol of his protective power, received from Indra. The esoteric forms of Tantric Buddhism were to give Vajrapāṇi a terrifying aspect that multiplied itself into many ferocious *vajradhāras*. Alongside the Blessed One and presiding more or less visibly over his destiny are the titular divinities of Hinduism, Indra and Brahmā, one wearing his characteristic diadem, the other with his bun in a tiara. Later, with the evolution of the Mahāyāna, Śiva was to join them in his terrible aspect as Maheśvara.

The guardian-kings of the four directions (*lokapālas*) appear quite early in the entourage of the Master, in the episode of the offering of the four bowls after the Awakening. In the older paintings and reliefs they are often present up to the *pari-nirvāṇa,* shown in a princely aspect, with aureoles like the other figures of the

FIGURE 5: Vajra.

Buddhist pantheon; soon, however, they appear as warriors wearing armor. The best known among them is Vaiśravana, guardian of the North and master of a host of animal-headed *yakṣas*. Dhṛtarāṣṭra, guardian of the East, leads the *gandharvas*, celestial musicians like the *kinnaras*, half-human, half-bird. In the same fashion Vrūpākṣa (West) and Virūḍakha (South) reign over the graceful, flying *apsaras* and over the dwarf *gaṇas*, all of them celestial beings from Hinduism. They are often depicted as mounts or pedestals under the feet of the guardian-kings. The guardians of the doors (*dvārapālas*) were to retain their athletic physiques but rapidly took on the terrifying aspect commonly adopted by protective divinities to vanquish and convince, which was further accentuated by Tantrism. Also figuring among the supernatural spirits and guardians are the ten *devarājas*, or celestial kings, and the guardians of the Law, the most famous of which is probably Mahākāla, the "big black," who is shown in his monstrous Tibetan-Nepalese form with his lips curled back to show his menacing teeth.

Prajñā and Tārā, female counterparts of these divinities, soon made their appearance, and their powers were rapidly defined. Their complementary energies can often be seen in the representation of divine couples embracing on paintings and bas-reliefs, especially in Nepal and Tibet. Among the protective divinities, Dākiṇī and other tutelary goddesses with fierce aspects can be found on portable paintings (*tankas*); the terrifying Lha-mo appears on Tibetan bronzes, where she wears a necklace of skulls and rides on a bloody human corpse.

The ancient Hindu myth of the bird Garuḍa fighting the serpents to steal their soma, the elixir of life, has been adopted along with other Buddhist myths about hybrid beings as a theme of rebirth: Garuḍa can be an eagle, a falcon, a bird with a human head, or a man with a falcon's beak. The *haṃsa* (wild goose or duck) can evoke for the adept an intermediary state of the transmigrating soul. The Nāgarāja (king of the *nāgas*, or water serpents) in his princely aspect, his head capped or encircled by a hood of serpents, is found in all of the representations and legends dealing with the domain of the waters; in the Far East, the serpents become dragons.

EVOCATIONS OF THE SUPERNATURAL

As in the ancient religions, the representation of water, symbol of fertility, occupies an important place in iconography. Water bears the most expressive image of this fertility, the lotus, which appears everywhere, painted and sculpted on domes, walls, cupolas, and ceilings, to the point that it expresses the innumerable worlds of the cosmos. The lotus, also a symbol of purity, becomes the bearer of the most eminent figures of Buddhism as well as of the little reborn souls *(putti)* of the *bodhisattva*s of the Pure Lands. [*See* Lotus.]

It is through the theme of the waters peopled with aquatic figures, and through those of the flying musician spirits, that the artists have attempted to suggest supernatural visions and certain cosmic concepts: life-giving earth and elaborate heavens, which are, following sophisticated mental constructions, arranged in superimposed worlds. Mount Meru depicted as a conical pillar, as a stepped pyramid, or as an hourglass tied at the center with *nāga*s, constitutes the expressive symbol of the axis of the world plunging into the primordial ocean. Even the plan of the stupa, based on the square (earth) and the circle (heaven), with its structure combining the cube and the dome, develops into more and more elaborate buildings. Nonetheless, they always follow the rules inspired by the symbolism of forms and subject to an axial principle, the cosmic axis. This principle commands the elevation of multistory pagodas and is even found in the rock-cut sanctuaries, where the cult image of the Buddha is placed against the pillar of the encircling hall. In the decoration, the flying figures of the *apsara*s and the celestial musicians (*gandharva*s, *kinnara*s, or *kinnari*s) transpose these scenes to a supraterrestrial realm.

The evolution of the historical Buddha toward transcendence, already visualized in the multiplication of the Buddha images, was subsequently organized and systematized in the representation of the five transcendent Buddhas, the Tathāgatas or Jinas. Vairocana, the supreme Buddha, appears at the center, surrounded by the four cardinal points (this concept is found in the plan of certain sanctuaries or in *maṇḍala*s). Amitābha, the ruler of the West, was to achieve particular success in the Far East. His cult has produced numerous images, especially painted ones, where he is enthroned in the center of a multitude of *bodhisattva*s in his "Pure Land of the West," represented as a Chinese palace with terraces and a pond covered with lotuses, where the adepts hope to go through rebirth as pure souls. This paradise has its counterpart in the "Pure Land of the East" of the Buddha Akṣobhya. The transcendental evocations are completed symmetrically with the representations of the Pure Land of Maitreya and that of Śākyamuni preaching on the Vulture's Peak.

The five Jinas appear together or separately on painted or sculpted images or on liturgical ornaments (the five-pointed tiara). Generally surrounded by attendants, they can be distinguished from one another by their specific ritual gestures, some of which are inherited from the *mudrā* tied to the principal events of the historical life of the Buddha Śakyamuni, and by the specific colors attributed to each of them and to their respective lineages.

In Esoteric Buddhism, the Jinas and the divinities can be represented by conventional symbols, such as the *vajra* in its diverse forms, by a Sanskrit formula, or even by a "seal" *(mudrā)*. The five Jinas each have ferocious aspects as counterparts, the "kings of sciences of great virtue" (*ming-wang* in Chinese, *myōo* in Japanese): surrounded by flames, they assume menacing postures, often have a number of faces with grimacing features, and brandish weapons and other symbolic attributes in their multiple hands.

With the widespread diffusion of these Esoteric forms, the more or less fantastic representations of the evolved Buddhist pantheon multiplied alongside the images of the serene Buddha. These fantastic forms appear not only as great cult images painted or sculpted in sanctuaries, on banners of silk or hemp in the Far East, and on Tibetan *tanka*s, but also as small statues of painted wood, bronze, carved stone, or semiprecious materials (jade, amethyst, chalcedon, quartz) destined for offerings and domestic altars. Before the end of the first millennium CE, block prints contributed to the diffusion of the images of the most venerated figures in addition to manuscript illuminations. Even on the humblest of materials, such as the rough wood or modeled clay of Afghanistan or Central Asia, gold leaf is generally used along with paint, especially to cover the visible flesh of the Blessed One.

At this degree of complexity in the representations of Esoteric Buddhism, only the initiated could decipher the interpretation. For the majority of adepts, however, such doctrinal problems did not play a major role. The Chinese pilgrim I-ching reports that in India until the seventh century the institutional distinction between the adepts of the Hīnayāna and the Mahāyāna was not precise; the former recited the *sutra*s of the Lesser Vehicle, the latter, those of the Great Vehicle, all in the same sanctuary. It is, however, through the concreteexpressions of iconography as well as through the texts that we are able to trace the ascendancy and evolution of beliefs, beliefs that have been profoundly penetrated by the magic power of painted or sculpted images, for centuries objects of veneration for the faithful.

[*See also* Temple, *article on* Buddhist Temple Compounds.]

BIBLIOGRAPHY

Alfred Foucher's *L'art greco-bouddhique du Gandhāra,* 3 vols. (Paris, 1905–1923), remains one of the basic sources for the origins of Buddhist iconography. Foucher's *The Beginnings of Buddhist Art and Other Essays on Indian and Central Asian Archeology,* rev. ed. (Paris, 1917), may also be consulted. A different and complementary point of view is expressed in Ananda K. Coomaraswamy's *Elements Of Buddhist Iconography* (Cambridge, Mass., 1935). *The Image of the Buddha,* edited by David L. Snellgrove (Paris, 1978), is a collective work with broad coverage and abundant illustrations.

Étienne Lamotte's *Histoire du bouddhisme indien: Des origines à l'ère Śaka* (Louvain, 1958) provides a historical context for the religion. On the cosmology of the stupa from its origins to its most complex forms, see Paul Mus's *Barabudur* (1935), edited by Kees W. Bolle (New York, 1978). A good initiation into the Tantric pantheon is found in Marie-Thérèse Mallmann's *Introduction à l'iconographie du tântrisme bouddhique* (Paris, 1975).

For regional studies, see *Buddhism in Afghanistan and Central Asia,* by Simone Gaulier, Robert Jera-Bezard, and Monique Maillard, 2 vols. (Leiden, 1976), which analyzes the evolution of images along the Silk Route; E. Dale Saunders's *Mudrā: A Study of Symbolic Gestures in Japanese Buddhist Sculpture* (New York, 1960), which treats the symbolic language of ritual and iconography; and two museum catalogs: *Bannières et peintures de Touen-houang conservées au Musée Guimet,* 2 vols., compiled by Nicole Vandier-Nicholas et al. (Paris, 1974–1976), and Roderick Whitfield's *The Art of Central Asia: The Stein Collection in the British Museum,* vol. 1, *Paintings from Dunhuang,* 2 vols. (Tokyo, 1982–1983).

24 FOLK BUDDHISM

DONALD K. SWEARER

Religious traditions are, by their very nature, complex. On the one hand, they symbolize the highest aspirations of the human mind and spirit; on the other, they sanctify and give meaning to the most ordinary and commonplace human needs and activities. The complexity of religion and its functions have been analyzed in various ways. There has been a tendency, however, to distinguish between those aspects created by and appropriate to the educated elites, for example, priests and rulers, and those that help the uneducated, common folk cope with the uncertainties and exigencies of life. Scholars have sometimes referred to this distinction as obtaining between "great" and "little" traditions or between "elite" and "folk" traditions. It must be kept in mind that these formal distinctions do justice neither to the multiplexity of religious traditions nor to the organic unity that characterizes them, even though such categories may serve a useful analytical function.

"Folk" Buddhism may be understood as a persistent, complex, and syncretic dimension of the Buddhist tradition characterized by beliefs and practices dominated by magical intent and fashioned with the purpose of helping people cope with the uncertainties and exigencies of life. Its varied expressions emerge along the wide spectrum between the normative Buddhist ideal represented quintessentially but not exclusively by the Buddha and the concept of *nirvāṇa,* and the indigenous magical-animistic and shamanistic traditions of the given culture in which Buddhism becomes institutionalized. Consequently, some aspects of folk Buddhism (e.g., the figure of the Buddha, the person of the monk, and the practice of meditation) appear to be closely affiliated with the normative ideals of Buddhism, while others are barely distinguishable from native, non-Buddhist religious forms. Folk Buddhist institutional structures, religious practices and practitioners, and oral and written literatures reflect this variation.

Buddhism has had a folk or popular dimension since its inception. Early Buddhist scriptures challenge the view of a "golden age" of pure monastic practice dedicated to the pursuit of *nirvāṇa* unencumbered and undisturbed by the needs and expectations of a simple, uneducated laity. That the Buddha and his followers were supported by laypersons for reasons of material gain and magical protection, as well as for spiritual benefit, cannot be denied. Even meditation, the *sine qua non* of monastic practice, was perceived as leading not only to equanimity and enlightenment but also to the acquisition of magical power. The *Mahāvagga* of the Theravāda Vinaya Piṭaka depicts the Buddha not simply as an enlightened teacher, but as a yogin who wins followers through his magic. Moreover, although the source is later commentary, it is significant that the future Buddha, just prior to his enlightenment, was said to have been offered food by a woman who mistook him for a tree deity. In general, Buddhist scriptures readily intermesh doctrinal exposition with magical and animistic figures and elements ranging from *deva*s (gods) to *mantra*s (sacred utterances).

To be sure, folk Buddhism became a more dominant aspect of Buddhist institutional and cultural life as the religion grew in size and cultural significance throughout Asia. In India, Aśoka's strong support of the Buddhist monastic order in the third century BCE proved to be crucial to its growth and diffusion, and the appropriation of folk elements from different cultures was a means by which Buddhism spread and accommodated itself to the cultures of Asia from at least the beginning of the common era. Indigenous folk religions, therefore, were the major media through which Buddhism became a popular religion not only in India, but in Southeast, Central, and East Asia as well. The fact remains, nevertheless, that the folk element within Buddhism has been a part of the tradition since its inception, and has persisted in different forms to the present.

Folk Buddhism has several different facets that reflect various modes of interaction between normative, doctrinal-institutional Buddhism and native religio-cultural traditions. In some cases, the normative Buddhist tradition made only inconsequential adjustments; in others, Buddhism emerged as a thinly veiled animism. The major ingredient of folk Buddhism is usually referred to as animism or magical-animism, that is, the belief in benevolent and malevolent supernatural powers and the attempt to avoid them or to enlist their aid. These powers range from spirits of the living and the deceased to deities of regional or even national jurisdiction associated with non-Buddhist (e.g., Brahmanic) pantheons. The dialectical relationship between Buddhism and indigenous animism such as the Bon of Tibet led to the parochialization of Buddhism, but also changed the face of those native traditions encountered in Tibet, Korea, Japan, and elsewhere. For example, Shintō, rooted in an autochthonous animism, developed in Japan in competition with the more sophisticated traditions of Chinese Buddhism, just as religious Taoism in China institutionalized, at least in part, in response to Indian Buddhist influence.

The complex nature of folk Buddhism can be analyzed in various ways, but the method should do justice to its common or generic elements as well as the uniqueness of distinctive religio-cultural environments. Folk Buddhism as an essentially syncretistic phenomenon can be seen in terms of three types or modes of interaction between Buddhist and non-Buddhist elements: appropriation, adaptation, and transformation. These categories are intended to characterize particular historical instances as well as describe general types. Although they have overlapping qualities, they point to the variety within folk Buddhist belief and practice as well.

APPROPRIATION

In many cases, folk Buddhism merely appropriated and subordinated indigenous symbols, beliefs, and practices with very little change in meaning. This is particularly true in the incorporation of a wide range of supernatural beings and powers into the Buddhist system. Generally speaking, these supernaturals, whether gods or spirits, malevolent or benevolent, were subordinated to the dominant Buddhist symbols and motifs. Most often they played a protective role, standing guard at a sacred Buddhist precinct, be it temple or *maṇḍala,* or functioned in an appropriately subordinate way in relationship to the Buddha. In Sri Lanka, for example, a kind of divine pantheon evolved, a hierarchy of gods and spirits ranging from the most localized guardian spirits of village and field to the suzerainty of regional gods the likes of Skanda and Viṣṇu with the entire structure under the sway of the Buddha. In Tibet the gods of the everyday world *('jig rten pa)* became protectors of the *dharma,* obeying the commands of the great teachers. While they are so numerous and indeterminate as to defy a fixed ordering, they generally are divided according to the traditional Indian tripartite cosmology of heaven, earth, and the intermediate realm. In Burma the indigenous *nat* spirits are incorporated into Burmese Buddhism as *deva*s. Thagya Min, for instance, is assimilated into Sakka (the Brahmanic Indra), and resides in Tāvatiṃsa Heaven as king of the *deva*s, but is also said to be ruler of the "thirty-seven *nat*s." [*See* Nats.] In Thailand various supernaturals including *devatā, cao,* and *phī* have a complex relationship to Thai Buddhism involving linkage, hierarchy, and instances of both opposition and complementarity. In Japan, Buddhism absorbed native Japanese deities or *kami.* In many cases the *kami* are taken as manifestations of Buddhas or *bodhisattva*s (the theory of *honjisuijaku*), although a uniform set correspondence did not develop. [*See* Honjisuijaku.] A similar story can be told for Buddhism in China, Korea, and other parts of Asia. While the specific list of supernaturals appropriated into the Buddhist system varies from culture to culture, these beings represent a hierarchy of powers and suzerainties dependent on, under the authority of, or even in tension with, Buddhist figures, symbols, and motifs.

These supernaturals have been assimilated into the Buddhist cultus as well as into Asian Buddhist worldviews; they are amalgamated into orthodox ritual activity or become a distinct ritual subset. Throughout Buddhist Asia the guardian spirits of a temple precinct, such as the *phī* in Thailand or the *kami* in Japan, may be propitiated prior to an auspicious ceremonial event. In Tibet, Tantric ritual has provided a framework for customary religious practices in which Tibetan deities exist side by side with Indian Buddhist ones. In Sri Lanka, devout Sinhala Buddhists paying respects to the Buddha at the famous sanctuary of Lankatileke outside of Kandy will make offerings before images of the Hindu deities enshrined in *devale*s around the perimeter of the building. In Thailand, Brahmanic deities (e.g., Viṣṇu) may be invoked during a customary Buddhist ritual, and offerings are made to the guardians of the four quarters as part of the New Year celebration at a Buddhist monastery *(wat).*

Of special significance in folk Buddhism have been the belief in the soul (the existence of which is scarcely maintained in scripture), or spirit element(s), of the individual, and various rituals associated with this belief, especially life-crisis or life-transition rites. The role of Buddhism in the conduct of mortuary and death anniversary rites for the souls of the dead in China, Korea, and Japan is well known. In Japan, the Obon festival celebrated in the seventh month honors the return of the souls of the dead. Graves at Buddhist temples will be cleaned in preparation for the spirits' return, and the household altar *(butsudan)* will be decorated with flowers, lanterns, and offerings of fruit. In Burma, mortuary rituals are performed to prevent the soul of the deceased from remaining in its former haunts and causing trouble. In Thailand, soul-calling *(riag khwan)* rites are performed at life-transition times such as weddings and even as part of ordination into the monkhood.

ADAPTATION

In assimilating indigenous magical-animistic and shamanistic religious beliefs and practices, Buddhism itself has changed. This process of adaptation and parochialization has been part of the Buddhist tradition from its outset: the Buddha as teacher but also miracle-worker, meditation as the vehicle for the attainment of insight and supernatural powers, the monk as *nirvāṇa*-seeker and magician. In the Theravāda traditions of Sri Lanka and Southeast Asia the miraculous power of the Buddha is attested to not only in supernatural feats of magical flight, prognostication, and the like, but also in the cult of Buddha relics and Buddha images that typifies ritual practice in this region. The Mahāyāna and Tantryāna traditions elaborated the salvific function of the Buddha through the proliferation of Buddhas and *bodhisattvas*. In China, Tao-an (312–385) popularized Buddhism by promoting Maitreya as a savior Buddha, the god of Tuṣita Heaven, an earthly paradise accessible to all. Hui-yüan (334–416) did for Amitābha Buddha and his Pure Land (Sukhāvatī) what Tao-an did for Maitreya and Tuṣita Heaven. Both Maitreyism and Amidism became fundamental to folk Buddhism. In Japan, one of the specific adaptations was the assimilation of popular elements into the figure of the *bodhisattva* Jizō (Skt., Kṣitigarbha), who thereby came to occupy an even more important place than did his Chinese counterpart, Ti-tsang. Not only does Jizō deliver souls from hell, but he also helps women in childbirth and, like Kannon (Chin., Kuan-yin), another popular savior, is seen as the giver of healthy children and a guide to the Western Paradise of Amida. [*See* Celestial Buddhas and Bodhisattvas; Kṣitigarbha; *and* Avalokiteśvara.]

The supernormal powers associated with meditation adepts has a close association with shamanism. Monks have become famous for their skills as alchemists, for their ability to communicate with the spirit world, and for their prognostication of future events, activities that conflict with the Vinaya. The biographies of such Tantric adepts as Padmasambhava and Mi-la-ras-pa attest to this type of parochialization, and even the lives of the Ch'an (Zen) patriarchs are not exempt from supernatural hagiographic elaboration. [*See also* Mahāsiddhas.] In Sri Lanka, ascetic monks are revered not only for their piety but for their magical prowess as well, and in Thailand a significant cult of monk-saints has developed. Popular magazines attest to their extraordinary deeds, their advice is sought for everything from lottery numbers to military ventures, and their amulets are worn for protection against danger and disease. [*See* Arhat.]

TRANSFORMATION

Buddhism appropriated magical-animistic and shamanistic religious forms and adapted its own beliefs and practices to this type of cultural milieu. The degree to which assimilation and adaptation has occurred has led to profound transformations of the tradition. While decisive turns in the development of Buddhism have taken various forms, popular sectarian movements have provided one of the most fruitful contexts for this kind of transmutation. Examples abound throughout Buddhist Asia. In Burma and Thailand messianic Buddhist groups emerged in the modern period centered around charismatic leaders often claiming to be Maitreya Buddha. In China, Buddhist sectarian groups led by "rebel monks" split off from monasteries in the Northern Wei kingdom (386–535) as early as the fifth century. The best known is the White Lotus movement, a complex of rebel eschatologies active from the twelfth to the nineteenth century. Other major sects include the Maitreya, White Cloud, and Lo, or Wu-wei. These groups were lay-based, heterodox, and syncretistic, and were often politically militant. The White Lotus sect developed its own texts, a married clergy, hereditary leadership, and by the mid-fourteenth century a full-blown eschatology derived from both the Maitreyan tradition and Manichaeism. By the late sixteenth century the principal deity of the White Lotus groups was a mother goddess. Eventually, by the late nineteenth century, the Buddhist elements were so extenuated that they had become congregational folk religion rather than a distinctive form of folk Buddhism. [*See* Millenarianism, *article on* Chinese Millenarian Movements.]

In Japan as early as the Heian period (794–1185) holy men *(hijiri)* developed a folk Buddhism outside the orthodox ecclesiastical system. [*See* Hijiri.] In the tenth and eleventh centuries Amida *hijiri* and Nembutsu *hijiri,* preeminent among whom was Kōya, a layman of the Tendai sect, taught universal salvation through the repetition of the Nembutsu (the formulaic recitation of the name of Amida Buddha). The Nembutsu came to be seen as a powerful form of protection against the spirits of the dead and evil spirits *(goryō)* and a means to release them into Amida's paradise. [*See* Nien-fo.] While the founders of the orthodox Pure Land sects, Hōnen and Shinran, rejected the animistic and magical aspects of the Nembutsu, the attitudes of the common folk did not substantially change. The Amida *mantra* was considered a causally effective means to attain the Pure Land after death as well as a magical spell for sending evil spirits to Amida. Popular sectarianism has continued to develop into the contemporary period. Some of the so-called new religions *(shinkō shūkyō)* in Japan represent a unique form of folk Buddhism. Arising in the nineteenth and twentieth centuries in a period of political and social crisis, these religions, which developed around strong, charismatic leaders, are syncretistic and often utilize magical ritual practices. Two of the best known are Risshō Kōseikai and Sōka Gakkai. Both are indebted to the *Lotus Sutra*-Nichiren tradition. Through its political wing, Sōka Gakkai has become a sometimes militant force in Japanese politics. [*See* New Religions, *article on* New Religions in Japan.]

The Buddhist encounter with folk religion, which has taken the forms of appropriation, adaptation, and transformation, has not occurred without conflict. In Southeast Asia stories abound of the Buddha's encounter with indigenous supernatural beings who are only eventually subdued and made to vow their allegiance to the *dhamma.* Other heroic figures exemplify a similar pattern. Especially noteworthy is Padmasambhava's propagation of the *dharma* in Tibet. The key to his success, in contrast to the previous failure of the great teacher Śāntirakṣita, was Padmasambhava's magical prowess in subduing the powerful Tibetan deities. Such conflict may be mirrored in Buddhist ritual as well as in myth and legend. In northern Thailand, for example, offerings of buffalo meat to the guardian spirits *(phī)* of Chiang Mai are made as part of the New Year celebration; however, this ritual activity has no formal connection with the elaborate ceremonies occurring at Buddhist sanctuaries in the area.

The practitioners of folk Buddhism likewise present a great diversity. Those most closely tied to the autochthonous animism may be likened to shamans, for they function in a shaman-like manner. They have the power to enter into the realm of the supernaturals, an act often symbolized by magical flight; they may also become possessed by supernatural beings or function as a medium between the supernatural and human realms, and have the knowledge to enlist or ward off their power. In Tibet, *mdos* rituals are performed by wandering lamas (Tib., *bla mas*) or exorcists *(sṅags pa)* for protection against dangers, hindrances, injuries, illness, and obstacles caused by evil powers. The person who carries out exorcistic rituals *(gto)* must be an expert in meditating on his *yi dam* or tutelary divinity. The *yamabushi* or mountain ascetics of Japan, while affiliated with the Tendai and Shingon sects, perform exorcisms and function as village magicians. The Chinese shaman *(wu),* who exorcised spirits of evil and illness and danced and chanted to ward off disasters, influenced the popular conception of the charismatic leadership of folk Buddhist sects in China. Often, lay Buddhists are the principal practitioners of the folk traditions, especially because many of the magical practices associated with folk Buddhism are either forbidden or discouraged by the orthodox Vinaya. In the Esoteric schools of Buddhism (e.g., Shingon), as well as in sectarian movements, the differentiation between mainstream beliefs and practices and those of the folk dimension are more difficult to perceive. Even in the Theravāda countries of Southeast Asia, however, actual monastic custom and practice may be far removed from the strict ideal of monastic discipline, which discourages fortune telling, alchemy, and the like.

The texts of folk Buddhism also reflect the ways in which the normative tradition has appropriated, adapted, and been transformed by indigenous folk religion. An important genre of folk literature is the miraculous tale, often purporting to be an episode from the life of the Buddha or a famous Buddhist figure such as Maudgalyāyana or Vimalakīrti. Included in this literary genre are the Jātakas, which are themselves examples of the appropriation of folktales, mythic accounts of heavens and hells (e.g., *Petavatthu*), legendary elements in chronicles, lives of the saints in various Buddhist traditions, and vernacular collections such as the Chinese *pien-wen* (texts of marvelous events). Other texts, such as the *paritta* (scriptural passages which, when chanted, are said to have apotropaic power) in the Theravāda tradition, function in a magical manner in Buddhist ritual, even though the content reflects the highest ethical and spiritual ideals of the normative tradition. The *Bar do thos grol* (Tibetan *Book of the Dead*), although at the center of the Tantric technique of liberation, certainly incorporates shamanistic elements. Another type of folk Buddhist literature includes those texts specifically related to the practice of astrology, fortune telling, and animistic rituals.

In the final analysis, folk Buddhism should not be seen as a later degeneration of the normative Buddhist ideal. Rather, it is a complex dimension of the tradition, present from its origin, that has provided the tradition with much of its vitality and variation from culture to culture.

[*See also* Priesthood, *article on* Buddhist Priesthood; Chinese Religion, *article on* Popular Religion; Japanese Religion, *article on* Popular Religion; *and* Worship and Cultic Life, *articles on Buddhist cultic life.*]

BIBLIOGRAPHY

In recent years studies of folk or popular Buddhism have been greatly enhanced by the work of anthropologists, especially those working in Southeast Asia. These descriptive and analytic studies provide an important complement to the work of cultural historians and historians of religion. Notable of mention for the Theravāda Buddhist cultures are the works of Stanley J. Tambiah, in particular his *Buddhism and the Spirit Cults in North-East Thailand* (Cambridge, 1970). While this work is a micro-study, like many anthropologists Tambiah offers a more comprehensive interpretation of the religious system in northeast Thailand. Tambiah's structuralist-functionalist approach contrasts with the social-psychological perspective (as found, for instance, in the works of Abram Kardiner) of Melford E. Spiro's *Buddhism and Society: A Great Tradition and Its Burmese Vicissitudes,* 2d ed. (Berkeley, 1982). A dominant theme in anthropological studies is the nature of the interrelationship between the folk or "little" tradition and the "great" tradition. In various ways this theme is addressed in Michael M. Ames's "Magical-animism and Buddhism: A Structural Analysis of the Sinhalese Religious System," in *Religion in South Asia,* edited by Edward B. Harper (Seattle, 1964), pp. 21–52; Gananath Obeyesekere's "The Great Tradition and the Little in the Perspective of Sinhalese Buddhism," *Journal of Asian Studies* 22 (February 1963): 139–153; Manning Nash's *The Golden Road to Modernity: Village Life in Contemporary Burma* (New York, 1965); and A. Thomas Kirsch's "Complexity in the Thai Religious System: An Interpretation," *Journal of Asian Studies* 36 (February 1977): 241–266. This theme figures in studies of the religious systems in Central and East Asia as well. See, for example, J. H. Kamstra's *Encounter or Syncretism: The Initial Growth of Japanese Buddhism* (Leiden, 1967), Alicia Matsunaga's *The Buddhist Philosophy of Assimilation: The Historical Development of the Honji-Suijaku Theory* (Rutland, Vt., and Tokyo, 1969), and Christoph von Fürer-Haimendorf's *Morals and Merit: A Study of Values and Social Controls in South Asian Societies* (London, 1967).

Popular Buddhist millenarian movements constitute another theme addressed by recent studies of folk Buddhism. For Southeast Asia, E. Michael Mendelson's "The King of the Weaving Mountain," *Journal of the Royal Central Asian Society* 48 (July–October 1961): 229–237, and Charles F. Keyes's "Millennialism, Theravāda Buddhism, and Thai Society," *Journal of Asian Studies* 36 (February 1977): 283–302, are particularly noteworthy. For China, Daniel L. Overmeyer's *Folk Buddhist Religion: Dissenting Sects in Late Traditional China* (Cambridge, Mass., 1976) is definitive.

Studies dealing with folk Buddhism that do not take a particular thematic perspective abound. Francis L. K. Hsu's *Under the Ancestors' Shadow; Chinese Culture and Personality* (New York, 1948) treats Chinese popular religion and the ancestral cult. H. Byron Earhart's *A Religious Study of the Mount Haguro Sect of Shugendō* (Tokyo, 1970) deals with the Shugendō sect, a popular movement combining Esoteric Buddhism with Japanese folk religious beliefs. René de Nebesky-Wojkowitz's *Oracles and Demons of Tibet: The Cult and Iconography of the Tibetan Protective Deities* (The Hague, 1956) treats popular Tibetan protective deities. For folk Buddhism in Japan, see also Hori Ichirō's *Folk Religion in Japan; Continuity and Change,* edited and translated by Joseph M. Kitagawa and Alan L. Miller (Chicago, 1968).

FIVE

THE PATH TO ENLIGHTENMENT

25 THE ARHAT

Donald K. Swearer

The Sanskrit term *arhat* (Pali, *arahant*) derives from the root *arh (arhati)* and literally means "worthy" or "deserving." The term is especially important in Theravāda Buddhism, where it denotes the highest state of spiritual development, but it also has pre-Buddhist and non-Buddhist applications.

HISTORY AND DEVELOPMENT OF THE TERM

In Vedic and non-Vedic contexts, the noun *arhat* and the verb *arhati* applied generally to persons or gods whose particular status earned for them the characterization of "worthy" or "deserving of merit." The terms also denoted "being able to do," or "being capable of doing." For example, in *Ṛgveda* 1.94.1 Agni is addressed in a song of praise as "the worthy one" *(arhat).* The term *arhat* does not appear in the Upaniṣads, but the verb *arhati* occurs there five times with the sense of "being able." The ten occurrences of the verb in the *Bhagavadgītā* convey a similar general meaning.

In the Jain *sūtras* the term is often used in a sense closer to that found in Buddhist writings. Here the *arhat* is described as one who is free from desire, hatred, and delusion, who knows everything, and who is endowed with miraculous powers. While these characterizations are consistent with the Buddhist use of the term, it should be noted that the Jains applied the word exclusively to the *tīrthaṃkaras* or revealers of religion, whereas in Buddhism arhatship is an ideal to be attained by all serious religious strivers, especially monks and nuns. [*See* Tīrthaṃkaras.]

In the Pali scriptures of Theravāda Buddhism *arahant/arahati* shares with Vedic, Hindu, and Jain sources the same general meanings "worthy, able, fit." In a more specific usage, but one that is not yet part of the most prevalent formulas found in the Sutta and Vinaya Piṭakas, the term is applied to those who have supernatural powers or who practice austerities.

PLACE IN BUDDHIST SOTERIOLOGY

In its most typical usage in Theravāda Buddhism, however, the term *arahant* signifies persons who have reached the goal of enlightenment or *nibbāna* (Skt., *nirvāṇa*). In the Pali canon the *arahant* emerges not simply as the revealer of the religion or the person worthy of receiving gifts but as one who has attained freedom of mind and heart, has overcome desire and passion, has come to true knowledge and insight, has crossed over the flood (of *saṃsāra*) and gone beyond *(pāragata),* has destroyed the *āsavas* (deadly attachments to the world), is versed in the threefold knowledge *(tevijja)* of past, present, and future, has achieved the thirty-seven factors of enlightenment, and who has attained *nibbāna.*

In the Vinaya, the concept of the *arahant* appears to be connected with the concept of *uttarimanussa* ("further being, superhuman being"). Here, the *arahant* is said to possess one or more of the four trance states *(jhāna),* one or more of the four stages of sanctification, mastery of the threefold knowledge and the sixfold knowledge *(chaḷabhiññā),* which includes knowledge of previous rebirths, and to have achieved the destruction of the *āsavas,* or "cankers." Indeed, it may be that the notion of *uttarimanussa* constitutes the earliest beginning of a more elaborated and refined concept designated by the term *arahant.*

It is in the Nikāyas, however, that the concept of the *arahant* achieves its mature form. In the first volume of the *Dīgha Nikāya* ten of the thirteen *sutta*s deal almost entirely with this theme; the other three are indirectly related to it. In these texts arhatship is extolled as the highest of social ranks, the only form of sacrifice worth making, the best asceticism, and the true form of *brahmacariya* (Skt., *brahmacarya*). Clearly, the term *arahant* signifies the Buddhist transvaluation of terms applied to the most worthwhile aspects of life. In the *Majjhima Nikāya* the *arahant* is said to recognize things as they really are, to have eliminated the *āsava*s, to be far removed from evil, and to be beyond birth, decay, and death.

There are several *arahant* formulas in the Pali Tipiṭaka. Perhaps the best known is the following:

> *Rebirth has been destroyed. The higher life has been fulfilled. What had to be done has been accomplished. After this present life there will be no beyond.*
>
> (Dīgha Nikāya *1.84 and elsewhere)*

Other formulas emphasize the attainment of the emancipation of mind, the transcendence of rebirth, the realization of jhanic states, knowledge of the Four Truths, the overcoming of the *āsava*s, and the gaining of salvation and perfect knowledge. The term also appears in the formulaic phrase characterizing the Buddha: "A Tathāgata arises in the world, an *arahant,* a fully enlightened one perfect in knowledge and conduct, a wellfarer, a world-knower, unsurpassed driver of men to be driven, a teacher of *deva*s [gods] and mankind, A Buddha, an Exalted One."

Arhatship figures prominently into the Theravāda notion that the salvific journey is a gradual path *(magga)* in which one moves from the condition of ordinary worldly attachments governed by ignorant sense desires to a state of liberation characterized by utter equanimity and the knowledge of things as they are. As Buddhagosa put it in his *Visuddhimagga* (Path of Purification), the classic synopsis of Theravāda doctrine, the *arahant* has completed all of the purities derived through the observance of the moral precepts, *(sīla),* meditational practice *(jhāna),* and the purity of knowledge *(paññā-visuddhi).* The *sine qua non* of this path is meditation, which leads to extraordinary cognitive states and stages of consciousness *(jhāna)* and, allegedly, to the acquisition of various supernormal "powers" *(iddhi).* These attainments became fundamental to the cult of saints, an important aspect of popular

Theravāda Buddhist practice. This popular aspect of arhatship has not always been easy to reconcile with the classical notion, which emphasizes the acquisition of what Buddhagosa refers to as the "analytical knowledges," for example, the analysis of reality in terms of its conditioned and co-arising nature *(paṭicca-samuppāda;* Skt., *pratītya-samutpāda).*

In the classical formula of the four stages of sanctification one becomes an *arahant* after first passing through three preceeding stages: "stream-enterer" *(sotāpanna;* Skt., *srotāpanna),* "once-returner" *(sakadāgāmin;* Skt., *sakṛdāgāmin),* and "never-returner" *(anāgāmin).* These stages are described in terms of a karmic/cosmic pattern of rebirth in which the *arahant* transcends all states within *saṃsāra* (the cycle of life and death). In the *Milindapañha* (Questions of King Milinda) only the self-enlightened Buddhas *(paccekabuddha)* and the completed Buddhas *(sammāsambuddha)* are designated as higher stages of attainment; but these are so rare that the *arahant* is held up as the goal of the renunciant life.

Both the Theravāda *Kathāvatthu* (Points of Controversy) and Vasumitra's *Samayabhedoparacanacakra* (History of the Schisms, a Sarvāstivāda work) give ample evidence that during the first few centuries following the death of the Buddha there were frequent disputes within the order concerning the nature and attributes of the *arhat.* The greatest challenge to the *arhat* ideal, however, came from the Mahāyāna tradition, which proclaimed the career of the *bodhisattva* to be superior to that of the *arhat.* Texts such as the *Saddharmapuṇḍarīka* and *Vimalakīrti Sūtras* criticize the *arhat* for pursuing, in their view, an unacceptably self-centered soteriological path.

THE ARHAT AS CULT FIGURE

In popular Buddhism the *arhat* has become a figure endowed with magical and apotropaic powers. In Burma, the *arahant* Shin Thiwali (Pali, Sivali), declared by the Buddha to be the foremost recipient of gifts among his disciples, is believed to bring prosperity and good fortune to those who petition him. The *arahant* Upagupta, who tamed Māra and converted him to Buddhism, is thought to have the power to prevent storms and floods as well as other kinds of physical violence and unwanted chaos. Customarily, Buddhist festivals in Burma and northern Thailand are initiated by an offering to Upagupta in order to guarantee the success of the event. In Burma, offerings are made to the Buddha and the eight *arahant*s (Sāriputta, Moggallāna, Ānanda, Revata, Upāli, Koṇḍañña, Rāhula, and Gavampati) as part of a long-life engendering ceremony in which each *arahant* is associated with one of the eight days of the Burmese week and with a special planet. Piṇḍola Bhāradvāja, one of the sixteen great *arhat*s (Chin., *lo-han*), was particularly venerated as the guardian saint of monasteries' refectories in China and Japan (where he is known as Binzuru), and was also worshiped as a popular healing saint.

The *arhat,* as one who has realized the *summum bonum* of the spiritual path, is worshiped on the popular level as a field of merit *(puṇy akṣetra)* and source of magical, protective power. Some, such as Upagupta and Piṇḍola, became in effect protective deities believed to have the power to prevent violence and illness. Offerings to their images or symbolic representations of their presence constitute cultic practice in both domestic and public rituals. However, *arhat*s other than those associated with the Buddha during his lifetime or the sixteen *arhat*s enumerated in

Nandimitra's *Record of the Abiding of the Dharma* (T.D. no. 2030) have served as sources of power. Claims of arhatship are continuously being made on behalf of holy monks in countries like Sri Lanka, Burma, and Thailand. Devoted laypersons seek them out for boons and wear protective amulets bearing their image or charred remains of their hair or robe. They may be venerated as wizards (Burm., *weikza*) with magical skills in alchemy, trance, and the like. Elaborate hagiographies tell of extraordinary natural signs announcing their birth and detail careers characterized by the performance of miraculous deeds. Their monasteries, in turn, may become holy pilgrimage centers both during and after their lifetime.

In short, the *arhat* embodies one of the fundamental tensions in the Buddhist tradition between the ideal of enlightenment and equanimity and the extraordinary magical power concomitant with this attainment. This tension, while present in the texts, is further heightened in the light of popular Buddhist attitudes and practices regarding the figure of the *arhat.*

[*For further discussion of the notion of the* arhat *in Buddhist soteriology, see* Soteriology, *article on* Buddhist Soteriology, *and* Nirvāṇa. *The career of the* arhat *is contrasted with that of other religious figures in* Bodhisattva Path *and in* Mahāsiddhas. *For a cross-cultural perspective, see also* Perfectibility.]

BIBLIOGRAPHY

The classic study of the *arahant* in the Theravāda tradition is I. B. Horner's *The Early Buddhist Theory of Man Perfected* (London, 1936). In recent years both historians of religion and anthropologists have studied the Buddhist saint. Nathan Katz has compared the *arahant* concept in the Sutta Piṭaka to the concepts of the *bodhisattva* and *mahāsiddha* in the Mahāyāna and Tantrayāna traditions in his book, *Buddhist Images of Human Perfection* (New Delhi, 1982). George D. Bond's "The Problems of 'Sainthood' in the Theravāda Buddhist Tradition," in *Sainthood in World Religions,* edited by George Bond and Richard Kieckhefer (Berkeley, 1984), provides a general analysis of the Theravāda *arahant* while Michael Carrithers's *The Forest Monks of Sri Lanka* (New York, 1983), and Stanley J. Tambiah's *The Buddhist Saints of the Forest and the Cult of Amulets* (Cambridge, 1984) offer anthropological analyses of the Theravāda saint in the contexts of modern Sri Lanka and Thailand, respectively. John S. Strong reminds us that the *arhat* receives approbation in the Mahāyāna as well as the Theravāda tradition in "The Legend of the Lion-Roarers: A Study of the Buddhist Arhat Piṇḍola Bhāradvāja," *Numen* 26 (June 1979): 50–87.

26 THE CAREER OF THE BODHISATTVA

NAKAMURA HAJIME

The English term *bodhisattva path* translates the Sanskrit *bodhisattvayāna,* "vehicle of the *bodhisattvas*," or, more frequently, *bodhisattvācāryā,* "the practice of the *bodhisattva,*" terms widely employed in Mahāyāna Buddhist texts. In Pali literature the word *bodhisattva* appears quite often, but the Pali equivalents of the aforementioned Sanskrit words do not, reflecting the quite different conception of the *bodhisattva* enjoyed by Hīnayāna and Mahāyāna Buddhism.

Etymologically, *bodhisattva* is a term compounded out of *bodhi,* meaning here "enlightenment [of the Buddha]," and *sattva,* denoting "living being." Thus, *bodhisattva* refers either to a person who is seeking *bodhi* or a "*bodhi* being," that is, a being destined to attain Buddhahood. Another interpretation, "one whose mind *(sattva)* is fixed on *bodhi,*" is also recognized by the tradition.

In early Buddhism and in conservative schools such as the Theravāda, the term *bodhisattva* designates a Buddha-to-be. It refers in this context merely to one of a very limited number of beings in various states of existence prior to their having attained enlightenment. Its principal use was thus confined to the previous lives of the Buddha Śākyamuni; however, the existence of other *bodhisattvas* in aeons past was acknowledged, as was the bodhisattvahood of the future Buddha, Maitreya. Śākyamuni's previous existences as a *bodhisattva* are the subject of the Jātaka literature, which illustrates the religious career of the future Buddha as he perfects himself in his quest for enlightenment.

HISTORY AND DEVELOPMENT OF THE TERM

In early and Pali Buddhism the idea of the *bodhisattva* was especially popular among the laity. A large number of the Jātakas, accounts of the prior births of the Buddha, were based on popular stories, including animal tales, current in the traditions of the time. These were transformed to more didactic ends as the *bodhisattva* idea was later woven into the Jātaka narrative structure as a whole. Beyond this, however, the notion of the *bodhisattva* underwent little further elaboration until the rise of Mahāyāna Buddhism around the beginning of the common era. It was the Mahāyāna, with its vastly altered understanding of Buddhahood and the path of spiritual sanctification, that transformed the notion from its very limited initial application to a vehicle of universal salvation.

Early Buddhism maintained that there was only one Buddha in any one epoch within our world system. The career of the being destined to become the Buddha Gautama was held to have begun with a vow *(praṇidhāna)* to attain enlightenment taken before another Buddha (Dīpaṃkara) ages ago. This vow was confirmed by a prophecy *(vyākaraṇa)* by Dīpaṃkara that at such-and-such a time and such-and-such a place the being who had taken this vow would become the Buddha for our particular world age. During countless subsequent births the future Buddha labored to perfect himself in a variety of virtues (*pāramitā*s, "perfections"), principal among which were wisdom *(prajñā)* and selfless giving *(dāna)*. This mythic structure was also held to obtain for Buddhas in other epochs, all of whom had uttered a vow, undertaken religious practices *(bhāvanā)*, and perfected themselves in various ways prior to their enlightenment. This religious path, then, was conceived as the exclusive domain of a very small number of beings (eight or twenty-five by the most common reckonings), whose appearance in the world as Buddhas was deemed metaphorically "as rare as the appearance of the *udumbara* blossom." In early Buddhism, the liberation of beings other than Buddhas seems to have entailed insight into the same truths as those discovered by the Buddhas, that is, the tradition initially appears to have discerned little difference in the content or depth of their awakening. However, profound differences remained in the religious *paths* taken by the respective practitioners. The path of those who merely heard the Buddha preach, the so-called *śrāvaka*s, or "listeners," was held to culminate not in Buddhahood but in the attainment of arhatship. Unlike a Buddha, an *arhat* (Pali, *arahant*) comes to the Dharma through hearing it preached by others; he does not participate in the cosmic drama that results in the appearance of a Buddha in the world.

Mahāyāna Buddhism, on the other hand, developed a radically different view of the path of religious practice, a view that embodied a critique of the *arhat* ideal. Our sources suggest that within a century or so of the death of the Buddha the *arhat* was viewed by some Buddhists, notably the Mahāsāṃghikas, as embodying a distinctly less exalted spiritual state than that of a Buddha. Accounts of the first schism in the *saṃgha* credit the Mahāsāṃghikas with maintaining that the *arhat* is subject to doubt, is plagued by remnants of desire, specifically sexual desire, and retains vestiges of ignorance on nonreligious topics. Although there is no direct evidence linking the Mahāsāṃghikas to the origins of the Mahāyāna community, it is clear that the critique of the *arhat* was a contributing factor in the development of alternate religious paths in the Buddhist community. [*See* Mahāsāṃghikas.]

The Mahāyāna probably had its origins in groups of clergy and laity outside of the formal *nikāya*s who took as their base the stupas (Skt., *stūpa*), or reliquary mounds of the Buddha. Members of these "orders" appear to have centered their practice on devotion to the Buddha and to have referred to themselves as *bodhisattva*s. [*See* Stupa Worship.] Although we know little of these early groups, the movement they spawned emerged by the second century of the common era with a literature that championed a much different view of the *bodhisattva*. For the Mahāyāna, the path of the *arhat* is one characterized by a self-centered concern for personal salvation and a distinctly less than complete insight into the nature of things. Here, in other words, the enlightenment of the *arhat* is held inferior to that of Buddhas.

Mahāyāna texts propose that the end of religious practice properly conceived is nothing less than the universal insight achieved by the Buddha, that is, that the goal of religious practice ought to be Buddhahood itself. They further insist that it is ultimately meaningless to speak of the liberation of an individual alone, for enlightenment inevitably entails a wholly selfless compassion for others *(karuṇā)* that mandates concern for their spiritual welfare. [*See* Karuṇā.] For the Mahāyāna, all those who, like the Buddha Śākyamuni, commence their religious career with a vow to become a Buddha and to work tirelessly for the enlightenment of others are by definition *bodhisattva*s, and the career of the *bodhisattva* is conceived here as open to any and all beings who undertake with right resolve to become Buddhas. What is more, some Mahāyāna texts proclaim, the career leading to Buddhahood is in fact the only real path preached by the Buddha. All other soteriologies, these texts aver, are merely strategies employed by the Buddha against those whose understanding was not sufficiently developed for the Mahāyāna teachings. It is this new and more universal soteriology that lent to the movement its self-designation *Mahāyāna,* the "Greater Path" to salvation.

Ultimately then, by the early centuries of the common era the tradition recognized the existence of at least two distinct paths of religious practice: the *śrāvakayāna* (as the Mahāyānists termed it) and the *bodhisattvayāna.* The former expounded a practice that emphasized self-liberation; the latter embraced a more socially-oriented ideal that stressed the salvation of others. Believing that the salvation of one entails the salvation of all beings, Mahāyāna *bodhisattva*s vow to postpone their own liberation and to remain in the world as Śākyamuni did following his enlightenment, exercising compassionate concern for others until all beings have been saved.

As Mahāyāna Buddhism developed doctrinally it came to propose an elaborate Buddhology (notions concerning the nature of the Buddha) to explain how Buddhas and *bodhisattva*s function in the world to save sentient beings. In brief, these doctrines held that Buddhas and *bodhisattva*s, through their long aeons of spiritual practice, had accumulated vast funds of religious merit that they could freely transfer to others in order to help them to salvation. The mechanism of this transfer of merit *(pariṇāmanā)* varied over the tradition, but in general it was believed that at a certain point in the stages *(bhūmi)* of the path a *bodhisattva* could assume a form at will in any of the realms of being, there to exert a beneficent effect on the course of the beings inhabiting them. [*See* Merit, *article on* Buddhist Concepts.] A *bodhisattva* could, if he chose, be born in one of the various hells to be a boon to its denizens. On their part, sentient being were encouraged in many texts to pay homage to various Buddhas and *bodhisattva*s by meditating on them, making offerings to them, and reciting their names. Consonant with this was the cult rendered certain great or "celestial" *bodhisattva*s, figures with distinct personalities in the Buddhist pantheon who were believed to be *bodhisattva*s of the very highest attainment. Chief among these frankly mythological figures were Avalokiteśvara, Mañjuśrī, Maitreya, and Kṣitigarbha, all of whom enjoy significant cultic followings throughout Buddhist Asia. These *mahāsattva*s, or "great beings," became the subjects of an elaborate iconography that emphasizes their majesty, insight, and concern to save others. [*See* Iconography, *article on* Buddhist Iconography.]

Often, the *bodhisattva* path is held to be one of three vehicles to liberation: the path of the *bodhisattva,* the path of the *arhat,* and a path that culminates in a Buddhahood attained by one who has never heard the Dharma preached, but who by his own efforts naturally comes to an understanding of *pratītya-samutpāda* (the doctrine of causality). Because of the special circumstances under which these *pratyekabuddhas*, as they are called, achieve enlightenment, they are held incapable of transmitting the Dharma to others. This threefold formulation is very early; both the Sarvāstivādins and the Theravādins recognized the existence of three distinct soteriologies. The Pali *Upāsakajanālaṅkāra,* for instance, speaks of three types of liberation: *sāvaka (śrāvaka) bodhi, pacceka (pratyeka) bodhi,* and *samyaksaṃbodhi* (that of a fully enlightened Buddha), although their understanding of the three terms is naturally incommensurate with the Mahāyāna view. Various Mahāyāna texts treat the relationship between the vehicles, but the most radical view is that of the *Saddharmapuṇḍarīka Sūtra* (Lotus Sutra), which holds that the Buddha preached the *śrāvakayāna* and the *pratyekabuddhayāna* as mere expedients *(upāya)* designed to draw beings of varying spiritual capacities to the Dharma. [*See* Upāya.] For the *Lotus,* the three vehicles are in reality one vehicle *(ekayāna),* which is Buddhahood itself. The *Lotus* is famous for its insistence that all beings who hear the Dharma and conceive of faith and confidence in its message will eventually become Buddhas.

BODHISATTVA PRACTICE

The career of the *bodhisattva* is traditionally held to begin when the devotee first conceives the aspiration for enlightenment *(bodhicitta)* and formulates a vow to become a Buddha and work for the weal of all beings. The uttering of this vow has profound axiological consequences for the *bodhisattva:* henceforth, it will be the vow that will be the ultimate controlling factor in one's karmic destiny, inaugurating one on a path of spiritual perfection that will take aeons to complete. The specific contents of this vow vary from case to case: all *bodhisattvas* take certain vows in common, among which, of course, are the resolve to postpone one's own enlightenment indefinitely while endeavoring to save others, to freely transfer merit to others, and so forth; but the *sūtras* also record vows specific to the great figures of the Buddhist pantheon. Amitābha, for instance, while the *bodhisattva* Dharmākara, is said to have formulated a series of vows in which he resolves to create a "Pure Land" where beings can be reborn to hear the Dharma preached by a Buddha. [*See* Amitābha.] The *Daśabhūmika Sūtra* enumerates ten "great aspirations" *(mahāpraṇidhāna)* of the *bodhisattva,* among which are the resolve to provide for the worship of all Buddhas, to maintain the Buddha's Dharma, to bring all beings to spiritual maturity, and to practice the *pāramitās*. Similarly, Queen Śrīmālā and the *bodhisattva* Samantabhadra are each said to have given issue to ten vows.

Ultimately, the *bodhisattva* path calls for the practitioner to perfect a series of six or ten virtues called *pāramitās*, "perfections." The (probably earlier) enumeration of six virtues, found in such texts as the Prajñāpāramitā Sūtras or the *Lotus,* consists of *dāna* ("giving"), *śīla* ("morality, the precepts"), *kṣānti* ("patience, forbearance"), *vīrya* ("effort"), *dhyāna* ("contemplation"), and *prajñā* ("transcendental insight"). Later texts such as the *Daśabhūmika Sūtra* add *upāya* ("skill in means"), *praṇidhāna* ("resolution," i.e., the *bodhisattva* vow), *bala* ("strength"), and *jñāna* ("knowledge"). [*See especially* Prajñā *and* Jñāna.]

The *pāramitās* were meant as an explicitly Mahāyāna counterpart to the older scheme of spiritual development—*śīla, dhyāna,* and *prajñā*—that prevailed among the Hīnayāna practitioners, but lists of *pāramitās* are not unknown to the Hīnayāna scriptures. For instance, enumerations of *pāramitās* were used in all traditions as a scheme for interpreting the Jātaka tales, now regarded as instances of the Buddha's accomplishment of the Perfections. The *pāramitās* as a systematic outline of *bodhisattva* practice are treated *inter alia* in Śāntideva's *Bodhicaryāvatāra.* [*See* Pāramitās.]

Another enumeration of *bodhisattva* practices is afforded by the thirty-seven so-called *bodhipakṣya dharmas*, or "principles conducive to enlightenment." These comprehend four *smṛtyupasthānāni,* or "states of mind fulness"; four *prahāṇāni,* or "abandonments"; four *ṛddhipādāḥ,* or "elements of supernatural power"; the five *indriyāṇi,* or "moral faculties"; five *balāni,* or "moral powers"; seven *bodhyaṅgāni,* or "components of perception"; and the Noble Eightfold Path. This list the Mahāyāna holds in common with the Hīnayāna, save for the fact that the Mahāyāna adds to it the practice of the *pāramitās* and the enumeration of ten *bodhisattva* stages, known as the *bodhisattva bhūmis*.

The classic enumeration of the *bhūmis* occurs in the *Daśabhūmika Sūtra,* although a variety of alternate schema also exist. Here, the *bodhisattva* path is conceived of as an ascent through levels of spiritual accomplishment that, in this text at least, are symmetrically linked with the practice of the ten *pāramitās*. The list clearly betrays an older enumeration of but seven *bhūmis*, as is evidenced by the fact that at the seventh *bhūmi* the practitioner is held to have undertaken those disciplines sufficient to win *nirvāṇa,* although his vow constrains him to remain in *saṃsāra.* Traditionally, the seventh *bhūmi* is also regarded as the stage at which no spiritual retrogression is possible: from this level the enlightenment of the *bodhisattva* is inevitable.

The *bodhisattva bhūmis* of the *Daśabhūmika* are as follows:

1. *Pramuditā* ("joyful"). Rejoicing in *bodhi* and in the fact that he shall succor all beings, the *bodhisattva* perfects himself in *dāna.*
2. *Vimalā* ("pure"). Perfecting himself in morality *(śīla),* the *bodhisattva* is free from all impurities.
3. *Prabhākarī* ("light giving"). The *bodhisattva* brings the light (of his insight) to the world and perfects himself in *kṣānti.*
4. *Arciṣmatī* ("radiant"). Perfecting himself in *vīrya* and in the thirty-seven *bodhipakṣya dharmas*, the *bodhisattva*'s practice burns away ignorance.
5. *Sudurjayā* ("difficult to conquer"). Endeavoring to perfect himself in *dhyāna* and in the practice of the Four Noble Truths, the *bodhisattva* is not easily conquered by the forces of Māra, the tempter of the Buddhas.
6. *Abhimukhī* ("face to face"). Perfecting himself in *prajña* and insight into *pratītya-samutpāda,* the *bodhisattva* stands "face to face" with *nirvāṇa.*
7. *Dūraṃgamā* ("far-going"). With this stage, the practical aspects of the *bodhisattva*'s career are brought to fruition. Able now to comprehend reality just as it is, the *bodhisattva* stands at the "basis of existence" *(bhūta-koṭivihāra)* and is said to perfect himself in *upāya,* the "skillful means" necessary to help beings to salvation (although the text also calls for the *bodhisattva* to cultivate all ten *pāramitās* at this stage).
8. *Acalā* ("immovable"). The *bodhisattva,* unmoved by thoughts either of emptiness or phenomena, cause or non-cause, cultivates *praṇidhāna* and manifests himself at will throughout the various levels of existence.

9. *Sādhumatī* ("stage of good beings"). The *bodhisattva* acquires the four *pratisaṃvids* (analytical knowledges) and perfects himself in *bala.*
10. *Dharmameghā* ("cloud of the Dharma"). Just as space is dotted with clouds, so is this stage dominated by various trances and concentrations. The *bodhisattva* acquires a radiant body befitted with gems, and works miracles for the aid of beings. Perfecting himself in *jñāna,* he obtains the ten "deliverances" of the *bodhisattva.*

The *Daśabhūmika* maintains that the *bodhisattva* enters the first *bhūmi* immediately upon giving rise to *bodhicitta.* Other schemes, however, call for variety of intervening stages. One popular outline consists of fifty-two *bodhisattva* stages: ten degrees of faith, ten "abodes," ten degress of action, ten degrees of "diversion" (alt., the transfer of merit), the ten *bhūmis*, and two subsequent stages of highest enlightenment. Then again, some schools, particularly in East Asia, decried the tendency to divide the path into ever finer increments and insisted on the suddenness of the enlightenment experience. The Ch'an and Zen sects, for instance, virtually ignore the formal outline of the *bhūmis* in their insistence that enlightenment is a sudden, radical break in consciousness. The Esoteric traditions as well, while still prescribing a rigorous and detailed path of spiritual training, insist that Buddhahood can be attained "in this very body"; they thus minimize the importance of the traditional *bodhisattva* path, with its inconceivably long period of spiritual preparation necessary to attain Buddhahood.

BODHISATTVA DISCIPLINES

The formation of Mahāyāna did not entail a total rupture of the Buddhist community. Monks who professed the Mahāyāna soteriology did not necessarily leave the monastic compounds of the Hīnayāna *nikāyas* and, indeed, continued to be ordained according to their Vinayas. [*See* Vinaya.] Because of the nature of their practice and aspirations, however, practitioners of Mahāyāna did come to formulate guidelines for their life as a community, particularly for clerical life. These guidelines did not reject the Vinaya precepts so much as they did provide for supplemental practices and attitudes consistent with the altruistic spirit underlying Mahāyāna thought. The greater flexibility and liberality of Mahāyāna practice and doctrine also tended to create a role of enhanced importance for the laity, for the Mahāyāna typically rejected the assertion, prominent in Hīnayāna texts, that only as a cleric was one able to fulfill the religious life and win liberation. Thus, Mahāyāna ethics continued to endorse the legitimacy of lay life as a field of religious action and to provide religious sanction for the duties and obligations incumbent upon householders.

The disciplines of the *bodhisattva* are set forth in the *Bodhisattvabhūmi,* traditionally ascribed to Maitreyanātha. Here are described the so-called Threefold Pure Precepts of the *bodhisattva: saṃvaraśīla,* or adherence to the Prātimokṣa, aims at suppressing all evil acts on the part of the practitioner; *kuśaladharma samgrāhakam śīlam,* "practicing all virtuous deeds," aims at cultivating the roots of virtuous acts *(karman)* of body, speech, and mind; *sattvārtha-kriyā śīlam,* "granting mercy to all beings," aims at inculcating in others the practice of compassion and mercy toward all beings. The latter two practices comprise the specifically Mahāyāna component of the *bodhisattva* discipline, emphasizing as they do not merely the suppression of unwholesome acts but the positive injunction to do good on behalf of others. Another text, the *Brahmajāla Sūtra* (Sutra of Brahma's Net), was widely esteemed in East Asia as a source of precepts for *bodhisattvas*. Although in China monks continue to be ordained according to the Vinaya of the Dharmaguptaka school, in Japan, the *Brahmajāla Sūtra* provided a set of Mahāyāna precepts (Jpn., *bonmōkai*) observed by Tendai ordinands in lieu of the Vinaya altogether. Other Mahāyāna precepts appear in the *Bodhisattvaprātimokṣa Sūtra* (identical with the *Vinayaviniścaya-upāliparipṛcchā*) and the *Śrīmālādevī Sūtra*. The vows of Queen Śrīmālā in this latter work constitute a discipline all their own, prohibiting transgressions against morality, thoughts of anger, covetousness, jealousy, and disrespect toward others, and enjoining liberality, sympathy, help to those in need, and faith and confidence in the Dharma.

[*See also* Buddhism, Schools of, *article on* Mahāyāna Buddhism; Celestial Buddhas and Bodhisattvas; Soteriology, *article on* Buddhist Soteriology; *and* Buddha.]

BIBLIOGRAPHY

Dayal, Har. *The Bodhisattva Doctrine in Buddhist Sanskrit Literature* (1932). Reprint, Delhi, 1970.

Kajiyama Yūichi. "On the Meaning of the Words Bodhisattva and Mahāsattva." In *Indological and Buddhist Studies: Articles in Honor of Professor J. W. de Jong,* edited by L. A. Hercus et al., pp. 253–270. Canberra, 1982.

Nakamura Hajime. *Indian Buddhism: A Survey with Bibliographical Notes.* Osaka, 1980.

27 CELESTIAL BUDDHAS AND BODHISATTVAS

David L. Snellgrove

The term *bodhisattva* occurs frequently in early Buddhist literature, usually referring to Śākyamuni Buddha prior to the time of his enlightenment, which he achieved as he sat under the famous Bodhi Tree (Skt., *bodhivṛkṣa,* "tree of enlightenment") a few milessouth of Gayā in modern Bihar. *Bodhisattva* means literally "enlightenment being," or, according to a theory that *bodhisattva* is a slightly mistaken Sanskrit spelling of the early dialectical form *bodhisatta* (as preserved in Pali), it could have originally meant "intent upon enlightenment." Whatever the literal meaning (and most scholars would favor the first one), a *bodhisattva* is a living being, usually human but not necessarily so, who has set out on the long path toward Buddhahood, which in accordance with the general Buddhist acceptance of the Indian theories concerning continual rebirth (or transmigration) was calculated to lead the aspirant through a very long series of different lives.

Large collections of such legendary life stories *(jātaka)* were made in the early Buddhist period, illustrating the heroic self-sacrifice of the future Buddha Śākyamuni in his progress toward his last life (also told in legendary style), when his purpose was finally revealed to the world. As Śākyamuni was never regarded as the one and only Buddha, but rather as one in a whole series (seven are named in early texts, but the number is gradually much extended), each of whom appears in a separate world age, it was inevitable that his followers should come to expect a future Buddha for the next world age. Thus, a new *bodhisattva,* Maitreya ("loving kindness"), appears as the first of the many other "great beings," who later extend the Buddhist pantheon to infinity. The cult of Maitreya is certainly attested among the followers of the early Buddhist sects, later referred to disparagingly as Hīnayānists, and his appearance seems to mark the beginning of the considerable devotion that came to be directed toward these celestial beings.

It should be borne in mind that the distinctions between the so-called Mahāyānists and Hīnayānists were not so clear-cut in the early centuries CE as they appear to be later. The same mythological concepts concerning the nature of a Buddha and a *bodhisattva* (a future Buddha) remain fundamental to Buddhism in all its forms, and it can easily be shown that all the later extravagant developments of the Mahāyāna are traceable to tendencies inherent in the earliest known forms of Buddhism. The

Mahāyānists differed in their philosophical assumptions and the manner in which they applied the *bodhisattva* theory to normal religious life. For them, the *bodhisattva* career was the only genuine path toward enlightenment, which they distinguished from the goal of *nirvāṇa,* interpreted by them as the limited selfish aspiration of the early disciples. At the same time they followed the same forms of monastic discipline (Vinaya) as their Hīnayāna brethren, often living together in the same monastic compound until doctrinal disputes led them to set up separate communities of their own. Thus freed, the Mahāyānists began to go their own way, but there would appear to have been no very noticeable iconographic changes in their monasteries until several centuries later.

The well-known caves of Ajantā were probably occupied by Buddhist communities up to the eighth century CE, and there is scarcely any image or painting there that might displease a determined adherent of the older sects. The only celestial *bodhisattva* apart from Maitreya to be painted at Ajantā is Avalokiteśvara ("the lord who looks down in compassion"), and he may be quite convincingly interpreted as the future Buddha Śākyamuni, who looked down in compassion from the heaven called Tuṣita ("joyful") before finally agreeing to be born in our world for the benefit of its inhabitants. None of the many Buddha and *bodhisattva* images surviving at Ajantā in carved stone can be identified as particular celestial Buddhas and *bodhisattva*s. Numerous *bodhisattva*s are named in Mahāyāna *sūtra*s from the first century CE onward, but a rather more limited number achieved generally accepted iconographic forms, namely those who were especially popular as distinct beings and those who were fitted into *maṇḍala*s and related iconographic patterns.

The earliest iconographic pattern, which resulted in the eventual appearance of three leading *bodhisattva*s, is probably the triad of images representing Śākyamuni Buddha flanked by two attendants. According to early accounts, Śākyamuni was attended by Indian divinities at his birth. Originally, these two attendants may have been thought of as Brahmā and Indra, but they came to be accepted as Buddhist divinities by the simple method of giving them new Buddhist names. They thus become identified as Padmapāṇi ("lotus-holder") and Vajrapāṇi ("*vajra*-holder"). Padmapāṇi comes to be identified with Avalokiteśvara, who also holds a lotus flower, and thus becomes a great *bodhisattva* in his own right. Vajrapāṇi's rise to fame is very much slower, since through the earlier Mahāyāna period he continues to be regarded as Śākyamuni's personal attendant, his function and duties merely being extended to protect all other *bodhisattva*s.

It is not until we reach the early Tantric period as represented by the *Mañjuśrīmūlakalpa* that Vajrapāṇi appears as a powerful *bodhisattva* in his own right, but still as a member of a triad. By this time (perhaps the fifth to the sixth century CE) many non-Buddhist divinities were being spontaneously accepted into the Buddhist fold; they were being accepted for the straightforward reason that those who became supporters of the monks or who even became Buddhist monks themselves did not need to renounce their devotion to other divinities, whose existence and capabilities were never denied either by Śākyamuni himself or by his followers. Local divinities decorate Buddhist stupas (Skt., *stūpa*s) from at least the second century BCE onward, and as already noted, the great Hindu divinities were soon incorporated as Buddhist "converts." This process continued throughout the whole history of Indian Buddhism and goes far to explain the existence of so many celestial beings in the ever more elaborate Buddhist pantheon.

In the *Manjuśrīmūlakalpa* these divinities are grouped into various "families," of which the three chief ones are those of the Buddha or Tathāgata, the Lotus, and the Vajra. Divinities who were already accepted as fully Buddhist were placed in the Buddha's family, while gentle divinities due for conversion were placed in the Lotus family under the leadership of Avalokiteśvara; fierce divinities, whose conversion was supposed to be troublesome, were placed under the command of Vajrapāṇi, who was able to subdue them with his powerful *vajra* ("thunderbolt"). Since it was suitable that the original Buddha family should be headed by a *bodhisattva* just like the other two, this position was assigned to Mañjuśrī ("gentle and glorious one," also known as Mañjughoṣa, "gentle voice"), who appears in early Mahāyāna *sūtra*s as Śākyamuni's chief spokesman. His origin is obscure but it is significant that he is later linked with Sarasvatī, the Hindu goddess of speech, taking her *mantra* ("Oṃ vāgīśvari muṃ") as his own. It must be emphasized that none of these great *bodhisattva*s has a "history" in the modern sense: they are all mythological creations.

CELESTIAL BUDDHAS

While the cult of a celestial *bodhisattva* as a Great Being of heavenly associations clearly has its roots in the early cult of Śākyamuni, who was appealed to as both Buddha and *bodhisattva*, its full implications were developed from approximately the first century CE onward by those who began to adopt specific Mahāyāna teachings. Śākyamuni was traditionally acclaimed as the one and only Buddha of our present world age, and early legends tell how he made the vow, when he was a brahman boy named Megha or Sumegha, before a previous Buddha, Dīpaṃkara, to follow the self-sacrificing *bodhisattva* path toward Buddhahood. It must be emphasized that the later concepts never had the effect of negating the earlier ones, and despite the change of viewpoint that I am about to explain, the cult of Buddhas of the past, as well as of the future, was never abandoned. The "Buddhas of the three times" (past, present, and future) are frequently mentioned in Mahāyāna literature and their cult has continued in Tibetan Buddhism to this day.

The change that takes place in Mahāyāna theories results from their perhaps more realistic view of the nature of the cosmos. The early Buddhists viewed the world as a closed system, comprising four main island-continents arranged around a central sacred mountain, known as Meru, identified with Mount Kailāśa in western Tibet. Mahāyāna teachings, on the other hand, were greatly affected by views that envisaged the universe as whole galaxies of world systems, extending endlessly throughout all the directions of space. It followed logically from this that there should also be Buddhas operative in all these other world systems. [*See also* Cosmology, *article on* Buddhist Cosmology.] One of the earliest disputes that arose between Mahāyānists and those who held to the earlier views concerns precisely the problem of whether there can be more than one Buddha at a time, and it is clear that they argue against different cosmological backgrounds. Mahāyāna ideas on the nature of such myriads of world systems may be learned from the reading of any of the Mahāyāna *sūtra*s, where Buddhas, surrounded by *bodhisattva*s, continue to preach simultaneously in their various "Buddha fields" *(buddhakṣetra)*.

Not all such worlds are fortunate enough to have a Buddha at any particular time. Those that do are divided generally into two classes, known as "pure" or "impure." The pure fields contain only those beings who are on the way to Buddhahood, that is, *bodhisattvas*, while the impure fields contain beings of all kinds at all stages of spiritual advance and decline. The manner in which *bodhisattvas* may travel miraculously from one Buddha field to another is well illustrated in the important Mahāyāna *sūtra*, the *Vimalakīrtinirdeśa* (The Teaching of Vimalakīrti), where the question is understandably raised as to why Śākyamuni should have elected to be born in an impure field rather than a pure one. His superiority is acknowledged by visiting *bodhisattvas* from a pure field, who exclaim: "The greatness of Śākyamuni is established; it is wonderful how he converts the lowly, the wretched and the unruly. Moreover, the Bodhisattvas who are established in this mean Buddha-sphere (i.e., our world) must have inconceivable compassion" (Lamotte, 1976, pp. 204–218). [*See also* Pure and Impure Lands.]

Śākyamuni's essential identity with all other Buddhas is often asserted, sometimes subtly, sometimes quite explicitly, as in chapter 15 of the *Saddharmapuṇḍarīka Sūtra* (Lotus of the True Law Scripture). In another *sūtra*, the *Śūraṃgamasamādhi* (Lamotte, 1965, pp. 267–270), the *bodhisattva* Dṛḍimati asks Śākyamuni how long his life will last. Śākyamuni tells him to go and ask another Buddha named Vairocana ("resplendent one"), who presides over a world system named Well Adorned, which is to be reached in the eastern direction by crossing over thirty-two thousand Buddha fields. Having traveled there he is told by that Buddha: "My length of life is exactly the same as that of the Buddha Śākyamuni, and if you really want to know, the length of my life will be seven hundred incalculable world ages." Returning to Śākyamuni, the inquiring *bodhisattva* says: "In so far as I understand the words of the Lord, I would say that it is you, O Lord, who are in the world-system named Well Adorned, where with another name you work for the happiness of all living beings."

So many different kinds of Buddha manifestations are taken for granted in the Mahāyāna *sūtras* that scholarly efforts have been made to reduce them to some order. The best account of such attempts will be found in Louis de la Vallée Poussin's translation of the *Ch'eng wei-shih lun*, Hsüan-tsang's compilation of ten major commentaries to Vasubandhu's *Triṃśikā* (La Vallée Poussin, 1929, vol. 2, p. 762).

The simplest scheme, which gradually gained general acceptance, envisages an "Absolute Buddha Body" (the *dharmakāya* of early Buddhist tradition) manifesting itself as various "glorious bodies" (*saṃbhogakāya*, "body of enjoyment") to high-ranking *bodhisattvas* in celestial spheres, and as various "human bodies" (*nirmāṇakāya*, "manifested body"), which need not necessarily be human but are usually conceived as such, in impure Buddha fields like our own world. Later Tantric tradition suggests the existence of a fourth, supreme body, known as *svābhāvikakāya* ("self-existent"), but earlier this is used as an alternative name for the Absolute Body (*dharmakāya*). We shall note later the tendency to arrive at ever-more-transcendent states of Buddhahood, when a sixth, supreme Buddha is placed above the set of five cosmic Buddhas. To these we must now give attention as the production of later Mahāyāna speculation and as the foundation of the whole class of *tantras* known as Yoga Tantras.

Just as Buddha manifestations, conceived in a diachronic time sequence in accordance with the earlier conceptions of Buddhahood, came to be represented by a triad of Buddhas, referred to as the Buddhas of the Three Times, namely Dīpaṃkara, Śākyamuni, and Maitreya (in this later context he is referred to as Buddha and no longer as *bodhisattva*), so those other Buddha manifestations, conceived synchronically as existing simultaneously in all directions throughout space in accordance with later Mahāyāna conceptions of the universe, came to be symbolized by the Five Buddhas of the cosmos, representing the center and the four cardinal points. These have been popularly referred to as *dhyāni-buddhas* ("meditational Buddhas"), a term that Brian Hodgson (1800–1894) seems to have heard used locally in Nepal but that appears to have no traditionally established justification. In the few *sūtras* and the many *tantras* and their commentaries in which they are referred to, they are known simply as the Five Buddhas *(pañcabuddha)* or the Five Tathāgatas *(pañcatathāgata)* with no other ascription. If such is required, then the term *Cosmic Buddhas* seems appropriate, in that their primary function is to represent Buddhahood in its cosmic dimension, as symbolized in the fivefold *maṇḍala.*

As may be expected, this set of five Buddhas evolved gradually, and we find at first various sets of names, some of which become gradually stabilized. Two fairly constant ones from the start are Amitābha ("boundless light") or Amitāyus ("boundless life") as the Buddha of the West, and Akṣobhya ("the imperturbable") as the Buddha of the East. It has been suggested with great plausibility that the Buddha of the West was first accepted as an object of devotion by the Buddhists of the far northwest of the Indian subcontinent as a result of Persian cultural and religious influence, since light and life are essential characteristics of the chief Zoroastrian divinity, Ahura Mazdā. This hypothesis is borne out by the very special devotion shown to this particular Buddha in Central Asia and especially in China and Japan, where a particular constellation of sects (known generically as Pure Land) is devoted to his cult. There is no indication that any such special cult developed elsewhere in India, where Amitābha/Amitāyus remains simply one of the Five Buddhas. Judging by the very large number of images found, the most popular Buddha, certainly in northeastern India, where Buddhism survived until the early thirteenth century, is Akṣobhya, the Buddha of the East. Iconographically he is identified with Śākyamuni Buddha, who was challenged at the time of his enlightenment by Māra, the Evil One (the Satan of Buddhism), to justify his claim to Buddhahood. Śākyamuni called the earth goddess to witness his claim by tapping the ground with the fingers of his right hand, and she duly appeared to give testimony, to the total discomfiture of Māra. A Buddha image formed in this style became the typical image of Bodh Gayā (south of Gayā) in eastern India, where Śākyamuni showed himself imperturbable *(akṣobhya)* despite the assaults of the Evil One.

The geographical choice of this particular Buddha (Akṣobhya) as the Buddha of the East in the later formulation of the set of five is not difficult to understand, being the obvious one because of his popularity in the eastern region. The central Buddha came to be identified with the Buddha image, which must have been typical of another famous place of pilgrimage, the Deer Park (now known as Sārnāth, a few miles from Vārāṇāsī), where Śākyamuni was believed to have preached his first sermon. The gesture of preaching is symbolized by the two hands linked in front of the chest in order to suggest a turning wheel, the "wheel of the doctrine," which Śākyamuni is said to have turned, just as the chariot wheels of a universal monarch (*cakravartin,* "wheel-turner") turn throughout the world.

A Buddha's supremacy in the religious sphere was equated in very early Buddhist tradition with the supremacy of the quasi-historical but mainly mythological concept of a "universal monarch," with the result that a *bodhisattva* is generally idealized as a kind of crown prince; thus it is in princely garments that he is generally portrayed.

In particular, Mañjuśrī, Śākyamuni's spokesman in early Mahāyāna *sūtras*, is referred to specifically as the prince *(kumārabhūta).* It is not surprising that as central Buddha of the set of five, the preaching Śākyamuni comes to be referred to as Vairocana ("resplendent one"), the very Buddha of vast age with whom he claims identity in the *Śūraṃgamasamādhi Sūtra.* The full name of that particular Buddha is in fact Vairocana-raśmipratimaṇḍita-vikurvanarāja ("resplendent one, adorned with light-rays, transformation-king"). The remaining two Buddhas, placed to the south and to the north, become generally stabilized in this configuration as Ratnasambhava ("jewel-born"), presumably symbolizing Śākyamuni's boundless generosity, and Amoghasiddhi ("infallible success"), symbolizing his miraculous powers.

Summarizing these various kinds of Buddha manifestations, one may make the following observations:

1. The state of Buddhahood is essentially one and only, or, to use a safer term, nondual, and nonmanifest in any way whatsoever: such is the Absolute Body of Buddhahood.
2. The various stages at which this Absolute Body may assume apparently manifested form have been explained as various grades of Buddha bodies, of which the Glorious Body, or Body of Enjoyment, and the Human Body, or Manifested Body, are the other two terms in more general use.
3. According to the earliest Buddhist beliefs, Buddhas manifest themselves in a kind of historical sequence, each one presiding over a different world age.
4. According to the later Mahāyāna theories, Buddhas are manifest all the time in all the directions of space, presiding over their individual Buddha fields.

These various concepts, which may appear to an outsider as in some measure conflicting, are retained by those who were responsible for the later formulations, while in general the "historical" Buddha Śākyamuni continues to hold the center of the stage.

BODHISATTVAS AND GODDESSES

Large numbers of *bodhisattvas* are mentioned in the Mahāyāna *sūtras* as residing in various Buddha fields, but very few of these come to receive a special cult as great individuals. The three primary ones, Mañjuśrī, Avalokiteśvara, and Vajrapāṇi, have already been mentioned. These are later identified as the "spiritual sons" of the three primary Buddhas, Śākyamuni (alias Vairocana), Amitābha, and Akṣobhya. The concept of Five Buddhas causes the number of Buddha "families," previously three, to be extended to five, and thus two more leading *bodhisattvas* are required to complete the set. They are known as Ratnapāṇi ("jewel-holder") for the Jewel family of Ratnasambhava, and as Viśvapāṇi ("universal holder") for the Sword or Action family of Amoghasiddhi. Both these are latecomers and their artificial nature is suggested by their names.

In the early Mahāyāna *sutras* we find various *bodhisattvas* named, such as the student Sadāprarudita ("always weeping"), whose story is told in the Perfection of Wisdom literature, or Dṛḍhamati ("firm-minded"), who is the main spokesman in the *Śūraṃgama Sūtra,* or again the *bodhisattva* Dharmākara ("expression of the *dharma*"), who sets the conditions for his own Buddha field through a long series of vows, the fulfillment of which is a precondition for his becoming the Buddha

Amitābha. None of these achieves individual fame except for the last as the Buddha Amitābha, of whom he is little more than a formative shadow, like the brahman boy Megha who eventually became the Buddha Śākyamuni. Vimalakīrti, already mentioned above, gains a popular following in Central Asia and in China. Of others so far not mentioned there is the one-time *bodhisattva* Bhaiṣajyarāja ("king of medicine"), named in *The Lotus of the True Law* (see Kern, 1963, pp. 378ff.), whom we find soon elevated to the rank of Buddha with the name of Bhaiṣajyaguru. In certain sets of divinities, the *bodhisattva* Ākāśagarbha ("womb of space") replaces Ratnapāṇi as chief of the Jewel family; neither of these leading *bodhisattvas* appears to attract any special cult. Paralleling Ākāśagarbha, at least in name, is the *bodhisattva* Kṣitigarbha ("womb of the earth"). Perhaps by the mere chance form of his name, Kṣitigarbha achieved enormous success in Central Asia and China as the one who controls the welfare of the dead. By far the most popular of all the "great gods" of Buddhism is Avalokiteśvara, who also assumes the name of Lokeśvara ("lord of the world"), normally Śiva's title in Hindu tradition. It is possible that his name was a deliberate parody of Śiva's title, with the syllables changed sufficiently to give the new meaning of "lord who looks down (in compassion)." It remains doubtful if any image of him can be identified specifically before the sixth century, unless we include the lotus-holding (Padmapāṇi) attendant by Śākyamuni's side, already referred to above. However, by the sixth century his cult is well established, as attested by an entire *sūtra,* the *Kāraṇḍavyūha,* compiled in his honor. It is here that the well-known *mantra* "Oṃ maṇipadme hūṃ" ("O thou with the jeweled lotus") can be firmly identified for the first time. This *mantra,* like the one of Mañjuśrī, is in the form of a feminine vocative for reasons that should become immediately clear.

Feminine divinities first appear within the Buddhist pantheon as handmaidens of the great *bodhisattvas*, whom they accompany in much the same way that Indian princes were usually depicted with a small circle of lady companions. Thus we may note that in the *Mañjuśrīmūlakalpa* (Macdonald, 1962, pp. 107ff.) Avalokiteśvara is surrounded by Pāṇḍaravāsinī ("white-clad"), Tārā ("savioress"), Bhrukuṭi ("frowning"), Prajñāpāramitā ("perfection of wisdom"), Tathāgata-locanā ("Buddha-eye"), and Uṣṇīṣarājā ("lady of the wisdom-bump"). We shall meet with some of these again within the scheme of the fivefold *maṇḍala,* but already two and possibly three look forward to devotional cults of their own, since they become the great goddesses of Buddhism. The goddess Prajñāpāramitā represents the fundamental wisdom of Mahāyāna philosophy, as a divine concept corresponding in many respects to Sancta Sophia of Christian tradition. Even more popular is Tārā, whose flourishing was assured by the salvific assurance conveyed by her name. She was soon recognized as the feminine counterpart (not a partner in the Tantric sense) of Avalokiteśvara. Tārā is his feminine expression, just as Sarasvatī becomes the feminine expression of Mañjuśrī. Thus we may note that since the *mantra* of a great divinity is also his expression (his *vidyā* or special knowledge, as it is often called), his *mantra* too assumes a feminine form. Tārā became so important that many other feminine divinities came to be regarded as her various forms. Thus she appears as Bhrukuṭi when she wishes to show her displeasure, or in the triumphant form of Uṣṇīśasitātapatrā ("lady of the wisdom-bump with the white parasol") when she becomes manifest with a thousand arms and a thousand heads, arranged in paintings so as to appear as a high, elaborate headdress, so that she is in no way grotesque. Here, she corresponds to the eleven-headed, thousand-armed form of Avalokiteśvara.

These more complex forms may clearly be related to subsequent Tantric developments, where the central divinity of the *maṇḍala* may be conceived of as comprising in his person all his various directional manifestations, from four to a thousand. Fluctuation in sex is not uncommon in the early stages of elaboration of this vast and complex pantheon; as is well known, in later Chinese Buddhist tradition Avalokiteśvara (Kuan-yin) merges with Tārā so as to become a feminine divinity. Returning to the *Mañjuśrīmūlakalpa,* we may note that just as Avalokiteśvara is surrounded by benign goddesses (except possibly for Bhrukuṭi), so Vajrapāṇi is surrounded by fierce ones, named Vajrāṇkuśī ("lady of the *vajra* hook"), Vajraśṛṅkhalā ("lady of the *vajra* fetter"), Subāhu ("strong-armed one"), and Vajrasenā ("lady of the *vajra* army"). It is sometimes difficult to draw a line between *bodhisattvas* and great goddesses, but Tārā in her various manifestations is as great as the greatest of *bodhisattvas*. She is saluted as the mother of all Buddhas, and in time Śākyamuni's human mother was duly seen as one of her manifestations.

The travelogue of the famous Chinese pilgrim Hsüan-tsang, who visited monasteries throughout Central Asia and the Indian subcontinent between 629 and 645, well illustrates the extent of popular devotion accorded the images of certain great *bodhisattva* figures during the seventh century CE. Himself a scholarly Mahāyāna philosopher, Hsüan-tsang was nonetheless pleased to hear of the miraculous powers of such images, mentioning in particular those of Maitreya, Avalokiteśvara, and occasionally Mañjuśrī and the great goddess Tārā; on many occasions he offered devout prayers to them on his own account. One may also mention that Hsüan-tsang was equally interested in the cult of *arhats* ("worthy ones"), those early disciples of Śākyamuni Buddha, who, having achieved *nirvāṇa,* were often believed to continue in some kind of suspended existence in remote mountain places. More wonderful tales of *arhats*, tales certainly learned from his Mahāyānist brethren in India, are retold in his account than stories about *bodhisattvas*. In fact, the continuing cult of *arhats* (Chin., *lo-han*), which spread through Central Asia to China, survives in a set of sixteen or eighteen Great Arhats well known to Tibetan Buddhists. [*See* Arhat.] These earlier traditions provide an interesting link, all too often ignored, between Hīnayānists and Mahāyānists. Thus, the Buddhist world of the early centuries CE was peopled with a large variety of celestial beings, among whom certain favorite *bodhisattvas* were only just beginning to come to the fore.

Tantric Buddhism, at least in its higher aspirations, may be described as a system of practices, either of ritual *yoga* or of physical and mental *yoga,* by means of which the practitioner identifies himself with his tutelary divinity, who is identified both with the practitioner's own teacher and with the goal of final enlightenment. One of the main means toward such an objective is the *maṇḍala* or mystic circle of divinities who symbolize existence at all its various levels, the essential sameness of which the pupil must learn to experience through the guidance of his teacher *(guru). Maṇḍalas* are described in earlier *tantras*, where a "three-family" arrangement predominates, but it is not until the so-called Yoga Tantras, with their fivefold arrangement of *maṇḍalas*, begin to appear that the new symbolism can be worked out effectively.

In the earlier Tantras there is a gradation of importance in the various families: the Buddha or Tathāgata family predominates; the Lotus family with its gentle divinities comes next; the Vajra family of Vajrapāṇi and his fierce children comes last. However, in the Yoga Tantras Vajrapāṇi comes right to the fore as the chief representative of Śākyamuni, alias Vairocana. He is also called Vajradhara ("holder of the *vajra*") and Vajrasattva ("*vajra* being"), names that at a later stage of Tantric development refer exclusively to a sixth, utterly supreme Buddha. The main *tantra* of the Yoga Tantra class is the *Sarvatathāgatatattvasaṃgraha* and here the chief *maṇḍala* is known as the Vajradhātu Maṇḍala, the Maṇḍala of the Adamantine Sphere, where *bodhisattvas* with Vajra names, all essentially manifestations of Vajrapāṇi, form circles around the Five Buddhas and the four Buddha goddesses. (See figure 1.) Although *maṇḍala* means circle, the main divinities may also be arranged around a central square within the main circle, since this square, which is usually provided with four elaborate doorways, represents the sacred palace in which the main divinities dwell. (See figure 2.)

Next in importance after the Five Buddhas are the four Buddha goddesses, who occupy the subsidiary directions of space, namely Locanā, Māmakī ("my very own"),

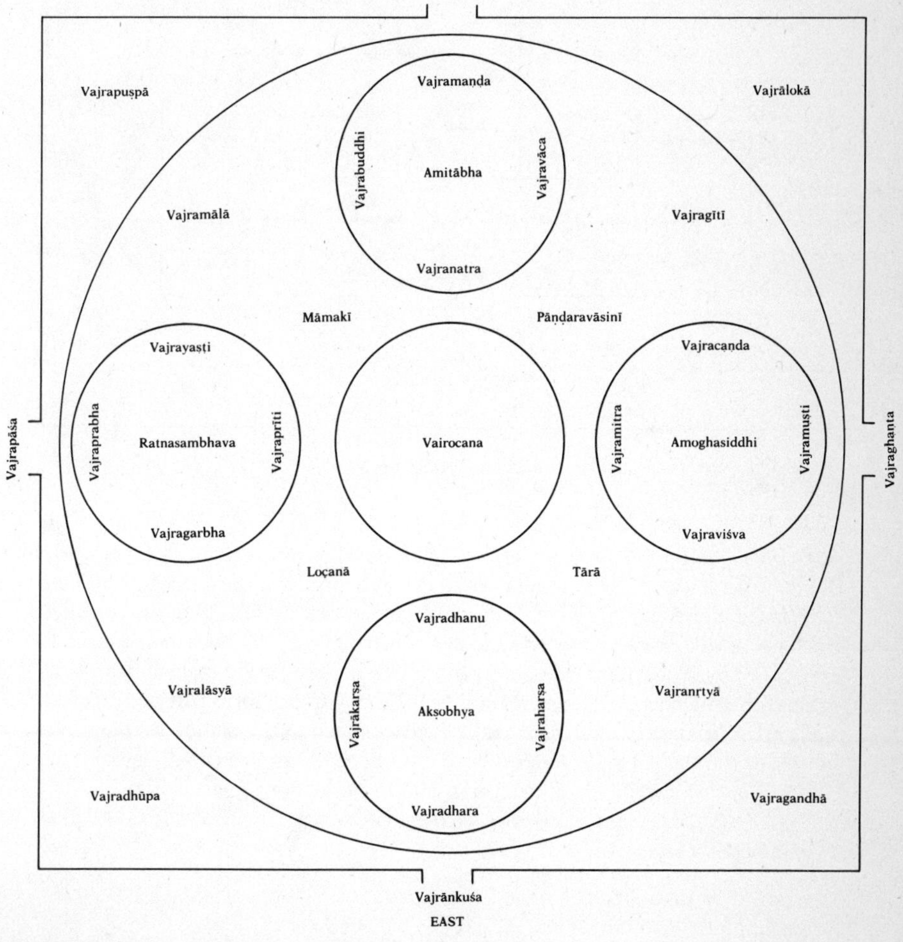

FIGURE 1: The Vajradhātu Maṇḍala, Alternate Rendering 1

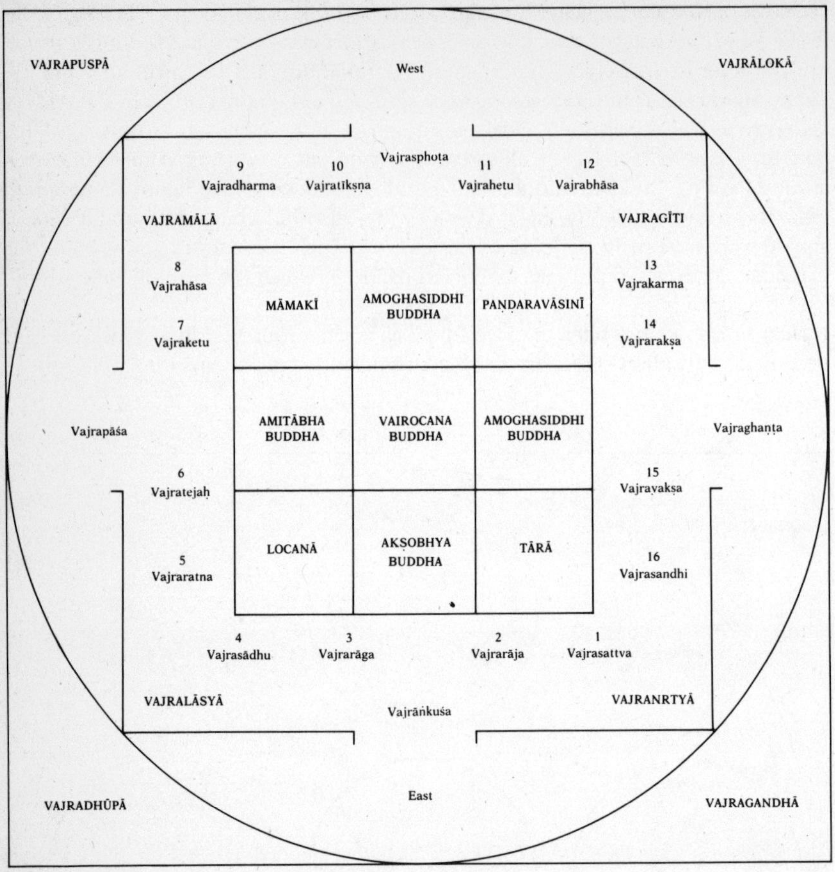

FIGURE 2: **The Vajradhātu Maṇḍala, Alternate Rendering 2**

Pāṇḍaravāsinī, and Tārā. They are usually interpreted as symbolizing the four main elements (earth, water, fire, and air), while the fifth (space) coalesces with supreme Buddhahood at the center. In later *tantras* a fifth, central Buddha goddess is named Vajradhātvī śvarī ("lady of the adamantine sphere"), but she does not appear in *maṇḍalas* of the Yoga Tantra class normally, since these coupled male-female divinities (known as *yab-yum,* "father-mother" in Tibetan) do not form part of their symbolism. Apart from the sixteen Great Bodhisattvas, all with Vajra names, we may draw attention to the eight lesser goddesses of the offerings, arranged farther out from the center in the intermediate directions, and the four door guardians at the four main entrances. The eight goddesses of the offerings are mere symbols, as their names indicate at once:

1. Vajralāsyā, or Vajra Frolic
2. Vajradhūpā, or Vajra Incense
3. Vajramālā, or Vajra Garland

4. Vajrapuṣpā, or Vajra Flower
5. Vajragīti, or Vajra Song
6. Vajrālokā, or Vajra Lamp
7. Vajranṛtyā, or Vajra Dance
8. Vajragandhā, or Vajra Scent

The names of the four door guardians, beginning with the eastern one, may be interpreted as Vajra Hook, Vajra Noose, Vajra Fetter, and Vajra Bell.

The possible variations within this fundamental pattern are considerable. Thus, the sixteen *bodhisattvas* fall into four groups of four, being allocated in these sets to the four directional Buddhas. The leaders of these four groups are directly identifiable with the chief *bodhisattvas*, already mentioned above, as well as with others who have not yet been mentioned. (See table 1.) Such names are generally interchangeable within the Vajrafamily, which in the Yoga Tantras is closely associated with the so-called family of All Buddhas. Among the names not met before in this article we draw attention especially to Samantabhadra ("all good"), from whom Vajrapāṇi is said to arise. Since it is also used as a title of Vairocana, the central Buddha, it is not surprising that it is used later as one of the names of a sixth, supreme Buddha.

TABLE 1. The Four Families of Yoga Tantras

FAMILY	ASSOCIATED DEITIES		
Vajra	Vajrasattva or Vajradhara	Vajrapāṇi	Samantabhadra
Jewel	Vajragarbha	Vajraratna	Ākāśagarbha
Lotus	Vajradharma	Vajranetra	Avalokiteśvara
Karma	Vajraviśva	Vajrakarma	Viśvavajra

Other *tantras* of the Yoga Tantra class, while generally retaining all the Buddha goddesses, the sixteen *bodhisattvas*, and lesser divinities, introduce different names and iconographic forms for the Five Buddhas themselves. As devised by Tantric masters in India (presumably from the seventh century onward) from a wide choice of names, to which others could be added as one pleased, the combinations, at least in theory, are infinite. Mañjuśrī in a four-headed and eight-armed manifestation may replace Śākyamuni at the center, and a highly complex *maṇḍala,* which includes the eight Uṣṇīṣa Buddhas as well as the four directional Buddhas together with the sixteen Great Bodhisattvas and a host of lesser divinities, is known as Dharmadhātu Maṇḍala, or the Maṇḍala of the Dharma Sphere, of which a fine example survives in the eleventh-century monastery of Sumda in Zangskar.

HORRIFIC BUDDHAS

As a result of Śaiva influence transmitted through Tantric yogins of northeast India, celestial Buddhas of horrific appearance become acceptable tutelary divinities in Mahāyāna communities from perhaps the ninth century onward. Most of the *tantras* that describe these divinities provide their own special *maṇḍalas*, with Heruka, Hevajra, Śaṃvara, Caṇḍamahāroṣaṇa, and other such horrific figures clasping their equally horrific feminine partners as they dance on corpses at the center of their circle of *yoginīs*. *Bodhisattvas* are rare in such company. Of the strange Buddha figures just named, only Caṇḍamahāroṣaṇa has male divinities in the four directions, who are all manifestations of Acala ("imperturbable"), a variant of Akṣobhya's name. Claiming superiority over all previous *tantras*, their propagators asserted the existence of a sixth, supreme Buddha, who subsumed the fivefold set, and with whom their particular tutelary divinity is identified. He is usually given the name of Vajrasattva ("*vajra* being") or Vajradhara ("*vajra*-holder"), both of which are titles of Vajrapāṇi in the earlier Yoga Tantras, as has already been noted.

Special mention should be made of the *Guhyasamāja* ("secret union") *Tantra*, for although this *tantra* was later grouped together with the others just mentioned as a so-called Anuttarayoga Tantra ("*tantra* of supreme yoga"), it adheres much more firmly to the fivefold scheme, and although Akṣobhya is made central Buddha of the set of five, the sixth, supreme Buddha is known as Great Vairocana (Mahāvairocana). *Tantras* of the "Old School" (Rñiṅ-ma-pa) of Tibetan Buddhism are to a large extent based on the fivefold scheme of Yoga Tantras with the addition of fierce divinities of the Heruka type. Their supreme Buddha, as in the case of those heterodox Tibetan Buddhists, the Bon-pos, is named Samantabhadra, a title also earlier closely connected with Vajrapāṇi.

FINAL SURVEY

While we have pointed out that far too stark a contrast is often drawn between Mahāyāna Buddhism of the early centuries CE with the already developed Buddhism accepted by their Hīnayānist brethren, there is no doubt that the contrast must have been very stark indeed during the last few centuries of Buddhist life in northern India (from the tenth to the twelfth century), concentrated mainly in Kashmir in the far north west and in Bihar, Bengal, and Orissa in the east. While the monasteries continued to practice the same ancient monastic rules, one of which was adopted by the Tibetans from the eighth century onward (namely that of the order known as Mūlasarvāstivāda, particularly strong in Central Asia and northern India), the cult of Buddhas, *bodhisattvas*, greater and lesser goddesses, and various attendant beings had developed in the manner described above, introducing many new iconographic forms into the temples and covering the walls with murals of the kind that now only survive in the old temples of Ladakh and western Tibet (tenth to thirteenth century). Although no such murals survive in India (those of Ajantā up to the eighth century are the only ones remaining), the close relationship between the early Tibetan paintings and the original Indian ones, now lost, is proved by the many that still can be seen in the form of miniature paintings on manuscripts of the Pāla dynasty, which ruled in eastern India during the last Buddhist period. These have survived in Nepal and Tibet, where they were subsequently carried.

It would seem that it was not so much the Mahāyāna that was responsible for the great divergence that develops between the cults of the "early" schools (Hīnayāna) and later Buddhism, despite the very important role that celestial *bodhisattvas* play in Mahāyāna *sūtras*. As noted already, very few of these can be identified iconographically before the sixth or even the seventh century, namely Maitreya, Avalokiteśvara, Mañjuśrī, the great goddess Tārā, and finally Vajrapāṇi, who begins to come to the fore only at the end of this Mahāyāna period. Vajrapāṇi has the best-documented "career" of all Buddhist divinities and it is he (or rather his cult) that results in the Vajrayāna. He appears together with Padmapāṇi ("lotus-holder"), flanking Śākyamuni in several surviving iconographic examples, and the identification of Padmapāṇi with the favorite *bodhisattva* Avalokiteśvara must have suggested a higher status for Vajrapāṇi as well. This he receives in the earliest *tantras*, but he still heads the lowest of the three families, for it is clearly taught that those who receive consecration in his Vajra family cannot perform rites in the two higher families.

It is only in the Yoga Tantras, which become well-known from the eighth century onward, that Vajrapāṇi comes fully to the fore as the leading *bodhisattva,* for all the *maṇḍalas* are based on the Vajradhātu Maṇḍala, even those of the Buddha (or All Buddhas) family. It is thus from this time on that one may correctly speak of a Vajrayāna, as distinct in many ways from the Mahāyāna. All the later *tantras*, which came to be classed as Tantras of Supreme Yoga, belong effectively to the Vajra family. It is even said that Vajrapāṇi himself taught them on the instructions of Śākyamuni Buddha, for although the Yoga Tantras and all earlier ones together with all Mahāyāna *sūtras* are explicitly taught as the word of the Buddha (i.e., Śākyamuni) himself, there was some understandable hesitancy in attributing the Yoginī Tantras, as they were earlier called, directly to him. Moreover, as related above, the sixth, supreme Buddha of these *tantras* is named as Vajrasattva or Vajradhara, titles that are applied exclusively to Vajrapāṇi in the Yoga Tantras. Thus with these exclusive titles and with a slightly developed iconographic form he attains the highest possible rank in the Buddhist pantheon. It has already been pointed out that no later development ever nullifies earlier ones, with the result that Vajrapāṇi continues to fulfill all the roles described above.

Mañjuśrī also becomes the representative of supreme Buddhahood in the Dharmadhātu Maṇḍala; later he receives a form expressing the union of "means" *(upāya)* and wisdom in that he clasps his feminine partner to his breast in the manner of all the great Tantric divinities of this class of *tantra.* Known as Mañjuvajra, he is in essence identical with Vajradhara/Vajrasattva. On the other hand, Avalokiteśvara remains the most popular of the great *bodhisattvas*, especially in his triumphant eleven-headed thousand-armed form. But despite his close relationship with Tārā, his feminine counterpart, neither he nor she is even thought to have lost their virginity. It is interesting to note how all the great *bodhisattvas*, despite iconographic changes, preserve their most essential attributes throughout the whole history of Buddhism. Being a powerful queller of the foe, it is Vajrapāṇi who forcibly converts the great gods of Hinduism, thus becoming their leader and finally the representative of all terrible divinities who are raised to high Buddhist rank. Mañjuśrī remains the representative of pure Buddhist teaching (despite his aberrational form as Mañjuvajra): when the followers of Tsoṅ-kha-pa (1357–1419) look for a suitably holy lineage for the leader of the reformed Tibetan Dge-lugs-pa ("yellow hat") order, they identify him as an incarnation of this particular *bodhisattva.* Avalokiteśvara remains popular for his unbounded compassion for the sufferings of all living beings. In order to save living beings, he is prepared to be born in any of the wretched places of existence, among suffering animals or tormented spirits, and even in the regions of hell. It was thus not difficult to suggest that he might also deliberately appear on earth as a recognizable incarnation. Since the Tibetans, in accordance with their pre-Buddhist beliefs, accepted their early kings (those from the sixth to the ninth century) as divine representatives from the heavens, it is not at all surprising that the king during whose reign Buddhism was first introduced into the country (namely Sroṅ-brstan-sgam-po, d. 650?) should have been retrospectively regarded as an incarnation of the *bodhisattva* Avalokiteśvara.

When the fifth Dalai Lama reunited Tibet under his rule in 1642 this same distinction was claimed for him, and since then all succeeding Dalai Lamas, while being theoretically reincarnations of their predecessors, are at the same time honored as incarnations of Avalokiteśvara. Other interesting high incarnations are those of the Grand Lama of Bkra-śis-lhun-po (Tashilhunpo), who is identified traditionally with the Buddha Amitābha, and the abbess of Bsam-sdings Monastery (now presumably destroyed), near the Yar-'brog (Yamdrok) Lake, who is identified with the boar-headed partner of the horrific Tantric Buddha Cakrasaṃvara, known as Vajravārāhī ("adamantine sow"), a sufficient indication that such "converted" Hindu divinities were in practice accorded *bodhisattva* rank.

From the above comments it should be clear that it is difficult to draw distinctions in late Indian Buddhism and in Tibetan religion, which inherits the greater part of Indian Buddhist traditions, between *bodhisattvas* and other divinities who are effectively raised to *bodhisattva* rank. Thus, to my knowledge the position of the four chief goddesses, Locanā, Māmakī, and so forth, as well as that of the feminine partners of the great Tantric divinities (who are themselves manifestly accorded full Buddha rank) is scarcely definable in traditional Buddhist terms. They are all said to be manifestations of the Perfection of Wisdom, at least according to the later Tantric theories, and thus an associate Buddha rank must be assumed for them. Clearer distinctions, however, continue to remain between Buddhas and *bodhisattvas*, in accordance with the ideas prevalent during the earliest Buddhist period. According to purist theories, once a *bodhisattva* achieves enlightenment and thereby becomes a Buddha ("enlightened") he effectively passes beyond the realm of imperfect living beings. The fact that Śākyamuni Buddha continued to work for the good of others during the forty-five years that elapsed between his enlightenment at the age of thirty-five and his decease *(parinirvāṇa)* at the age of eighty created a philosophical problem for the philosophers of the early schools. Only as *bodhisattva* can there be no doubt of his ability to respond to the needs of lesser beings. It may be for this reason that some early Buddha images are inscribed as *bodhisattva* images, for Śākyamuni in the earliest period could be regarded as both Buddha and *bodhisattva*.

The cult of Maitreya as future Buddha soon supplied the need for a *bodhisattva,* who could still assist living beings so long as he had not entered the impassive state of Buddhahood. His cult was followed by that of Avalokiteśvara, the "lord who looks down (in compassion)," doubtless suggested by Śākyamuni's previous existence in the heavens, when as *bodhisattva* he had looked down on suffering living beings. The whole *bodhisattva* doctrine represents a remarkable aspect of Buddhist religion, expressing a degree of compassionate concern for others that is either far less developed or lacking altogether in other Indian religious traditions. The distinction between a Buddha who represents an ideal state still to be achieved and a *bodhisattva* who assists one on the way there remains fairly clear throughout the whole history of Buddhism. Only rarely can a Buddha become an object of prayer and supplication. One well-known exception is Amitābha, the Buddha of the West. But one may note that his cult, so strong in China and Japan, is based upon the *Sukhāvativyūha Sūtra,* which lists the many aspirations of the monk Dharmākara toward achieving Buddhahood in a Buddha paradise, where he may still be available for the solace of living beings in the most marvelous manner possible. This particular Buddha cult may therefore be regarded as exceptional.

[*For further discussion concerning the nature of the Buddha, see* Buddha *and* Tathāgata. *The career of the* bodhisattva *is treated in* Bodhisattva Path. *The larger cultic and doctrinal contexts of these figures are treated in* Buddhism, Schools of, *articles on* Mahāyāna Buddhism *and* Esoteric Buddhism; Soteriology, *article on* Buddhist Soteriology; *and* Nirvāṇa. *See also* Maṇḍalas, *article on* Buddhist Maṇḍalas. *For discussion of the particular figures referred to here, see especially* Amitābha; Avalokiteśvara; Bhaiṣajyaguru; Kṣitigarbha; Mahāvairocana; Maitreya; Mañjuśrī; *and* Tārā.]

BIBLIOGRAPHY

References

Beal, Samuel, trans. *Si-yu-ki: Buddhist Records of the Western World* (1884). Reprint, Delhi, 1969.

Conze, Edward, trans. and ed. *Buddhist Scriptures.* Harmondsworth, 1959.

Conze, Edward, trans. *The Large Sūtra of Perfect Wisdom.* Berkeley, 1975.

Dayal, Har. *The Bodhisattva Doctrine in Buddhist Sanskrit Literature* (1932). Reprint, New Delhi, 1975.

Hodgson, Brian H. *Essays on the Languages, Literature and Religion of Nepal and Tibet* (1874). Reprint, New Delhi, 1972.

Kern, Hendrik, trans. *Saddharmā-Puṇḍarīka, or The Lotus of the True Law* (1884). Reprint, New York, 1963.

Lamotte, Étienne, trans. and ed. *La concentration de la marche héroïque.* Brussels, 1965. A translation of the *Śūraṃgamasamādhi Sūtra.*

Lamotte, Étienne, trans. *The Teaching of Vimalakīrti.* London, 1976. A translation of the *Vimalakīrtinirdeśa Sūtra,* rendered from Étienne Lamotte's *L'enseignement de Vimalakīrti* (Louvain, 1962).

La Vallée Poussin, Louis de, ed. and trans. *Vijñaptimātratāsiddhi: La Siddhi de Hiuan-tsang.* 2 vols. Paris, 1928–1929.

Macdonald, Ariane, trans. *Le maṇḍala du Mañjuśrīmūlakalpa.* Paris, 1962.

Skorupski, Tadeusz. *The Sarvadurgatipariśodhana Tantra: Elimination of All Evil Destinies.* Delhi, 1983.

Snellgrove, David L. *Indo-Tibetan Buddhism, Indian Buddhists and Their Tibetan Successors.* Boston and London, 1986.

Snellgrove, David L., and Tadeusz Skorupski. *The Cultural Heritage of Ladakh.* 2 vols. Warminster, 1977–1980.

Tucci, Giuseppe. *Indo-Tibetica.* 4 vols. Rome, 1932–1941.

Further Reading

Bhattacharyya, Benoytosh. *The Indian Buddhist Iconography* (1924). 2d. rev. ed., Calcutta, 1958.

Getty, Alice. *The Gods of Northern Buddhism* (1914). Reprint, Oxford, 1963.

Mallmann, Marie-Thérèse de. *Introduction à l'iconographie du tântrisme bouddhique.* Paris, 1975.

Snellgrove, David L., ed. *The Image of the Buddha.* London, 1978.

Tucci, Giuseppe. *Tibetan Painted Scrolls.* 2 vols. Translated by Virginia Vacca. Rome, 1949.

28 THE MAHASIDDHA

REGINALD RAY

The Buddhist *mahāsiddha* ("fully perfected one"), or simply *siddha* ("perfected one"), is the central enlightened ideal of Tantric or Vajrayāna Buddhism, the last major developmental phase of Indian Buddhism and particularly prominent on the subcontinent between the eighth and twelfth centuries CE. Best known are the list of eighty four of the greatest Buddhist *siddha*s (as enumerated by the twelfth-century Indian author Abhayadatta) and the grouping of *siddha*s into seven lineages (by the Tibetan author Tāranātha). Like the Buddha for earliest Buddhism, the *arhat* for the pre-Mahāyāna tradition, and the *bodhisattva* for the Mahāyāna, the *siddha* stands as the preeminent model of an accomplished person for the Vajrayāna tradition. And like those earlier ideals for their traditions, the *siddha* embodies in his person the particular character and ideals of the Vajrayāna, with its emphasis on meditation, personal realization, the master-disciple relationship, and the nonmonastic ways of life of the householder and the wandering yogin.

SOURCES

Our knowledge of the Buddhist *siddha*s comes from a considerable amount of biographical material that survives chiefly in Tibetan texts, which are either translations of, or are based directly or indirectly on, Indian written and oral tradition. These biographies of the *siddha*s, which vary in length from a few lines to hundreds of pages, tell the "liberation story" *(rnam thar)* of their subjects, recounting their individual journeys from the ordinary human state to one of full awakening.

The biographies of the *siddha*s are especially characterized by strong mythological, symbolic, and magical overtones. As in the case of the Buddha Śākyamuni in his biographies, but to a much greater degree, the *siddha*s are depicted as beings whose lives are charged with the transcendent and supernatural. At the same time, the *siddha*s are shown as real men and women with specific connections to the everyday, historical world. Their stories depict them as coming from particular places, belonging to certain castes, and following this or that occupation. Their teachers, Tantric practices, and lineages are carefully noted. The greatest among them figure as great teachers, lineage founders, monastic officials, and prolific authors of extant Tantric texts. Many *siddha*s are known historically to have played important roles in the transmission of the Vajrayāna from India to Tibet, China, and Southeast Asia, and are part of the social and political history of those countries. This confluence of the mythological and transcendent on the one hand, and the historically tangible and specific on the other, is one of the particular marks of the *siddhas* and of the Vajrayāna in general.

STRUCTURE OF THE SIDDHA IDEAL

The *siddhas* are depicted in their biographies both as particular individuals and as members of a common type: their lives share a certain general structure or pattern, resumed here, that marks them as Buddhist *siddhas*.

Before Enlightenment. The *siddha*'s life story generally begins with his birth, sometimes in the great Tantric areas of Kāmarūpa (northeast India), Uḍḍiyāna (northwest India), or Nāgārjunikoṇḍa (southeast India), sometimes in some other region. There typically follow details of caste status. In contrast to earlier Buddhism, where the higher castes are implicitly regarded as preferable, the *siddhas* come not only from the high castes *(brāhmaṇa* and *kṣatriya)* but as often from the low; some of the greatest *siddhas* were originally hunters, fishers, herdsmen, weavers, cobblers, blacksmiths, prostitutes, and even thieves. This diversity of social origins gives particularly vivid expression to the classical Buddhist insistence that caste and social distinctions are not spiritually rooted or inherent in reality, and that enlightenment can occur equally in any conditioned situation, whatever its conventionally stated social value.

The *siddhas* are typically depicted at the beginning of their careers as ordinary people who possess some often unspecified longing. They are men and women, monks and laypeople, privileged and destitute, but they all share a sense of unavoidable dissatisfaction and circularity in their lives. They reach a critical point in their religious career when they encounter a Tantric teacher who presents them with the possibility of a spiritual path—of meditation, of the shedding of habitual patterns, and of awakening. Their response is often a mixture of attraction and fear, but they share a feeling of connection with the teacher and with the message he articulates. Following this encounter, the future *siddhas* begin a demanding course of training under their *gurus*. The importance of the teacher-disciple relationship in each *siddha*'s biography reflects the Vajrayāna emphasis on the primacy of individual awakening and of the necessity of a realized, personal teacher to that process.

There follows in each *siddha*'s life a period of study with a teacher, whom the pupil sometimes attends for many years, and sometimes meets only periodically for new instructions. Formless meditation and liturgical Tantric practice *(sādhana)* are unremitting parts of the student's training, but so is activity "in the world"; many of these later-to-be-*siddhas* are instructed to carry out caste occupations and to marry. Some are instructed to perform tasks that are anathema to their former identities, such as the *brahmans* Bhadrapa and Lūyipa, who are told to make their living cleaning latrines and serving a prostitute, respectively. In general, hard tasks and humiliation of previous ego ideals marks the testing and training of the *siddhas* during their student days and their journey toward classic Buddhist realization of egolessness.

Siddhas as Enlightened Figures. After many years of arduous training, the *siddhas* emerge as fully enlightened people. In contrast to the Buddha, who was regarded as one of a kind thus far in our world age, to the *arhat,* whose enlightenment was seen as less than the Buddha's, and to the *bodhisattva*, who is enjoined to postpone his full awakening, the *siddhas* are depicted as having attained full awakening, thus fulfilling the Vajrayāna intention to make possible "enlightenment in this very lifetime."

As enlightened figures, the *siddhas* manifest a lively individuality as householders, yogins, or monks. Although the *siddhas* represent a basically nonmonastic ideal, they not infrequently turn up as followers of monastic discipline outwardly, but realized *siddhas* within.

The classical Vajrayāna understands itself as a development of the Mahāyāna; the *siddhas* are depicted as *bodhisattvas* whose primary motivation is to work for the benefit of others. Thus, the realized *siddhas* are all primarily teachers of others. Later Tibetan tradition explains the great diversity of origins, training, and teaching methodologies of the *siddhas* as a fulfillment of the Mahāyāna *bodhisattva* vow to help sentient beings in all stations and conditions by adopting their way of life.

This compassionate motivation is also given in explanation of the *siddhas'* undeniable unconventionality. As I have already noted, teachers sometimes send their students into situations conventionally forbidden to their caste. The *siddhas* themselves often break social and religious taboos as part of their teaching. The depiction of such unconventional activity is intended to reinforce the Tantric insistence that genuine spirituality cannot be identified with any particular external social form. Here, the *siddhas* give characteristic expression to the ancient dictum of the Buddha: awakening is a matter of seeing the conditioned structure of the world as such, not of slavishly identifying with a particular way of life or religious norm.

Magical Elements. Magic also plays an important role in the lives of the realized *siddhas*. On one level, the *siddha* biographies articulate the traditional Buddhist (and pan-Indian) belief that spiritual awakening puts one in possession of miraculous powers. In this sense, the *siddha* carries on a motif present in the depiction of the Buddha, of some of the *arhats*, and of the *bodhisattvas* of higher attainment. But in the *siddhas'* lives, magic plays a more prominent role than it does in the earlier hagiographical traditions. This greater prominence is probably due to a combination of (1) the great emphasis in the Vajrayāna on practice and realization; (2) its alignment with nonmonastic, and thus yogic and lay, life; and (3) its bent toward breaking what it sees as the conservatism and stolid fixations of earlier Buddhism.

Some accounts of magic appear to be metaphorical, such as when *siddhas* turn others into stone, "petrifying" them with their unconventional teaching. Other feats, such as the production of jewels from a worthless substance, are perhaps psychological, indicating the way in which the *siddhas* can, through their insight, transform apparently worthless passions of the personality into the highest prize of enlightenment. Other examples of magic, such as Saraha's walking on water, may illustrate the *siddhas'* freedom from cause and effect. In all these examples the *siddhas'* use of magic points to the basic Vajrayāna (and classical Buddhist) teaching that the commonsense world is not as definite and fixed as it appears, but in fact contains unlimited freedom, power, and sacredness.

A final characteristic of the realized *siddha* is his passing away, which is understood not as a death in the ordinary sense but as a passing into a state that is invisible, but nevertheless real and potentially available. The *siddhas*, we are told, do not die, but rather go to a celestial realm from which they may appear at any time.

HISTORICITY AND THE SIDDHA BIOGRAPHIES

The historical concreteness of the *siddha* biographies, the existence of texts, songs, and lineages they created, their social and political impact, and the existence of the Vajrayāna itself leave little doubt that the *siddha*s were historical individuals. But to what extent are their stories simple historical accounts and to what extent do they represent a gathering of originally disparate elements around a particular figure?

Study of the Vajrayāna biographies themselves shows that it would be a mistake to take them simply as accounts of single individuals, at least in the ordinary sense. Many sometimes different, sometimes apparently contradictory accounts are given in the same and different texts about a single *siddha.* In addition, one finds the same motifs and even entire stories appearing in the lives of several different *siddha*s. In light of these factors, one perhaps best understands the *siddha*s' lives as sacred biographies, some elements of which undoubtedly emerged originally in the lives of those individuals, and others of which originated from elsewhere. These became the general property of the tradition, to be used and reused to clarify the nature of the *siddha* ideal itself through the medium of specific biographies.

Does this rather flexible approach to writing history reflect a lack of historical awareness on the part of Vajrayāna biographers? The temptation to answer this question in the affirmative must be resisted, at least until the particular Vajrayāna attitude toward history is clearly understood. The lives of the *siddha*s do not restrict themselves to what we in the West have typically understood as the legitimate domain of a person's "life," beginning with birth and ending with death. The "life" of a *siddha* may include "events" that precede birth and postdate death, and may also include dreams, visions, and supranormal experiences other respected persons may have had of those *siddha*s before, during, and after their human lives. This more inclusive attitude taken by the Vajrayāna toward a *siddha*'s life is due not so much to its lack of historical awareness, but rather to the particular understanding of history that it possesses. The *siddha*s are real people who are significant precisely because they embody cosmic, timeless, and universal dimensions of human reality. They may express themselves equally from their ordinary human as well as their transhuman aspects. For the tradition itself, contradictory stories about a *siddha* may simply indicate multiple manifestations of that person, while the repetition of the same stories in several lives may just mean a later *siddha* is teaching according to an earlier, typical pattern. Such elements are considered in the Vajrayāna not only a legitimate but a necessary part of proper historical writing about the *siddha*s.

Finally, it is necessary to mention the important impact of liturgy and of certain later Tibetan Tantric masters' lives on the understanding of the *siddha*s' biographies. What is understood as the universal and timeless essence of the *siddha*s makes it possible to invoke the living and tangible presence of the *siddha*s through liturgy. Moreover, many of the most famous *siddha*s are understood to be present, in later incarnations, in the persons of Tibetan *tulku*s (incarnate lamas). The living example of the *tulku*s and the invocation of the presence of the *siddha*s in ritual contribute significantly to the making present and interpreting of the *siddhas* whose lives and teachings can be read in the texts.

HISTORICAL ROLE OF THE SIDDHAS

The major historical legacy of the *siddhas* is the tradition they represented and the Vajrayāna lineages they helped build, many of which are alive today. On a more restricted front, the *siddhas* were the authors of a great many Tantric works, hundreds of which survive in Tibetan translation. The most characteristic compositions of the *siddhas* are perhaps their *dohās* ("enlightenment songs"), which survive in independent collections, in biographies, and in the Tantras themselves. These songs are supposed usually to have been composed in liturgical situations to express the individuality and sacredness of that moment of awakened experience. The *siddhas* also composed other varieties of texts, including commentaries on the *tantras*, biographies of great masters, liturgical texts, and so on. A list of some six hundred works by Indian *siddhas* is given in the Tantric section of the Tibetan Bstan-'gyur (Tanjur); works of the *siddhas* are also included in other parts of the Tanjur and in Tibetan collections of Indian Buddhist texts.

The *siddhas* also played an important part in the history of Indian and Asian Buddhism. In India, the *siddhas* were the prime carriers of the Vajrayāna for a millenium, in its early formative period (pre-eighth century CE), during the time of its prominence (eighth to twelfth century CE), in the several centuries following the Islamic decimation of monastic Buddhism at the end of the twelfth century, through the sixteenth century, when contemporary Tibetan accounts give a first hand picture of a strong and vital Vajrayāna tradition in India. In the history of Tibetan Buddhism, it was the *siddhas* who carried the Vajrayāna to that land. All four of the major surviving schools, and many that did not survive, ultimately derive from Indian *siddhas*: the Bka'-brgyud-pa from Ti-lo-pa (988–1069) and Nā-ro-pa (1016–1100); the Rñiṅ-ma-pa from Padmasambhava and Vimalamitra (both eighth century); the Sa-skya-pa from 'Brog-mi (922–1022); and the Dge-lugs-pa from Atīśa (982–1054), who, while not himself a *siddha,* inherited some of their traditions). [*See* Dge-lugs-pa.]

Siddhas such as Śubhākarasiṃha, Vajrabodhi, and Amoghavajra, all of whom journeyed to T'ang China in the eighth century, were responsible for bringing the Vajrayāna to that land. [*See* Chen-yen.] Although their unconventional and wonderworking activity proved ultimately discordant with the Chinese outlook, and although the Vajrayāna they brought did not long survive in China, their activity provided the foundation for the transmission of the Vajrayāna to Japan by Kūkai (774– 835), who founded the Shingon school there. [*See* Shingonshū.] The *siddha* ideal played an indirect role in the religious history of the Mongols as well, following Mongol appropriation of Tibetan Buddhism in the thirteenth century.

Finally, the *siddhas* carried the Vajrayāna to Southeast Asia, where there is evidence of their activity in Java, Sumatra and Kamboja from the early ninth century onward. The Vajrayāna continued there until the sixteenth century at least, when the Indian Vajrayānist Buddhaguptanātha visited that area and gave firsthand accounts of the Tantric tradition there.

[*For further discussion of soteriological paths in Buddhism, see* Soteriology, *article on* Buddhist Soteriology; Arhat; *and* Bodhisattva Path. *See also the biographies of*

Padmasambhava, Ti-lo-pa, Nā-ro-pa, Mar-pa, Mi-la-raspa, Tsoṅ-kha-pa, Śubhākarasiṃha, Vajrabodhi, Amoghavajra, and Atīśa.]

BIBLIOGRAPHY

Abhayadatta's *Caturśīti-siddha-pravṛtti* (History of the Eightyfour Siddhas), the most important extant Indian text on the *siddhas*, has been translated from the Tibetan by James B. Robinson as *Buddha's Lions* (Berkeley, 1979). The extended Tibetan biographies of two of the most important Indian *siddhas*, Padmasambhava and Nā-ro-pa, are given respectively in W. Y. Evans-Wentz's *The Tibetan Book of the Great Liberation* (Oxford, 1954) and *The Life and Teachings of Naropa,* translated by Herbert Guenther (Oxford, 1963). Per Kvaerne's *An Anthology of Buddhist Tantric Songs* (Oslo and New York, 1977) analyzes an important collection of the Indian *siddhas*' songs. Shashibhusan Dasgupta's *Obscure Religious Cults,* 3d ed. (Calcutta, 1969), attempts to see the Indian *siddhas* in their larger religious context; my "Accomplished Women in Tantric Buddhism of Medieval India and Tibet," in *Unspoken Worlds,* edited by Nancy A. Falk and Rita M. Gross (New York, 1980), pp. 227-242, discusses Indian women *siddhas*. Several works provide useful summaries of the role of the Indian *siddhas* and of the Vajrayāna outside of India. For Tibet, see David L. Snellgrove and Hugh Richardson's *A Cultural History of Tibet,* (New York, 1968; reprint, Boulder, 1980), pp. 95–110 and 118ff.; for China, see Kenneth Ch'en's *Buddhism in China* (1964; reprint, Princeton, 1972), pp. 325–337; for Japan, see Daigan and Alicia Matsunaga's *Foundation of Japanese Buddhism* (Los Angeles, 1974), vol. 1, pp. 171–200; and for Southeast Asia, see Nihar-Ranjan Ray's *Sanskrit Buddhism in Burma,* (Calcutta, 1936), pp. 12–14 and 62–99.

29 NIRVANA

THOMAS P. KASULIS

About twenty-five centuries ago in northern India, Siddhārtha Gautama achieved *nirvāṇa.* That event ultimately changed the spiritual character of much of Asia and, more recently, some of the West. That something indeed happened is an indisputable fact. Exactly what happened has been an object of speculation, analysis, and debate up to the present day.

Nirvāṇa is both a term and an ideal. As a Sanskrit word (*nibbāna* in Pali), it has been used by various religious groups in India, but it primarily refers to the spiritual goal in the Buddhist way of life. In the broadest sense, the word *nirvāṇa* is used in much the same way as the now standard English word *enlightenment,* a generic word literally translating no particular Asian technical term but used to designate any Buddhist notion of the highest spiritual experience. Of course, Buddhism comprehends a diverse set of religious phenomena, a tradition with sacred texts in four principal canonical languages (Pali, Sanskrit, Tibetan, and Chinese), and a spiritual following throughout the world. Not surprisingly, then, when referring to the ultimate spiritual ideal many Buddhist groups prefer to emphasize their own distinctive terms instead of *nirvāṇa.*

NIRVĀṆA IN THE EARLY BUDDHIST AND ABHIDHARMA TRADITIONS

In the Pali Nikāyas and Chinese Āgamas, works first written down or composed two or three centuries after the death of the Buddha, there is little philosophical discussion about the nature of *nirvāṇa.* Indeed, on technical points such as the enlightened person's status after death, the *sūtras* admonish that such metaphysical speculation is only an obstacle to achieving the ultimate goal. In a famous story found in the *Majjhima Nikāya,* for example, Māluṅkyāputta asked the Buddha several metaphysical questions, including whether the Buddha continues to exist after death. The Buddha responded that such questioning is beside the point; it would be comparable to a man struck by a poison arrow who worried about the origin and nature of the arrow rather than pulling it out.

> *Whether there is the view that the Tathāgata both is and is not after dying, or whether, Māluṅkyāputta, there is the view that the Tathāgata neither is nor is not*

> *after dying, there is birth, there is ageing, there is dying, there are grief, sorrow, suffering, lamentation and despair, the suppression of which I lay down here and now.*
>
> *(Horner, 1954–1959, vol. 2, pp. 100–101)*

In short, the early Buddhist texts primarily approached *nirvāṇa* as a practical solution to the existential problem of human anguish. Specifically, they maintained that by undertaking a disciplined praxis the Buddhist practitioner can achieve a nondiscursive awakening *(bodhi)* to the interdependent nonsubstantiality of reality, especially of the self. With that insight, it was believed, one could be released from the grips of insatiable craving and its resultant suffering.

In most cases *nirvāṇa* is described in negative terms such as "cessation" *(nirodha),* "the absence of craving" *(tṛṣṇākṣaya),* "detachment," "the absence of delusion," and "the unconditioned" *(asaṃskṛta).* Although in the Nikāyas and subsequent Abhidharma school commentaries there are scattered positive references to, for instance, "happiness" *(sukha),* "peace," and "bliss," and to such metaphors of transcendence as "the farther shore," the negative images predominate. Indeed, the word *nirvāṇa* itself means "extinction," and other words used synonymously with it, such as *mokṣa* and *mukti,* refer to emancipation. One difficulty with the early texts, however, is that they were not always clear or unequivocal about *what* was extinguished and *from what* one was emancipated. One prominent tendency was to understand *nirvāṇa* as a release from *saṃsāra,* the painful world of birth and death powered by passion, hatred, and ignorance. According to the early texts, the Eightfold Path leading to *nirvāṇa* is the only way to break free of this cycle and to eliminate the insatiable craving at its root. The Path is not merely a set of moral exhortations, but rather, a program of spiritual reconditioning that liberates one from the pain of *saṃsāra.* [*See* Eightfold Path.]

The Buddhist view of *saṃsāra* developed as the notion of rebirth was taking root in ancient India. So enlightenment came to be understood as the extinction *(nirvāṇa)* of what can be reborn, that is, as the dissolution of any continuing personal identity after death. This led to the need to distinguish between (1) the enlightenment of the person who has transcended in this world the suffering caused by craving, and (2) the perfect *nirvāṇa* achieved only when that person dies and is fully released from *saṃsāra,* the cycle of birth, death, and rebirth. The Pali texts, therefore, distinguished "*nirvāṇa* with remainder" *(saupādisesa nibbāna)* from "*nirvāṇa* without remainder" *(anupādisesa nibbāna),* or even more simply, enlightenment *(nibbāna)* from *complete* enlightenment *(parinibbāna;* Skt., *parinirvāṇa).*

The Abhidharma traditions interpreted the distinction in the following way. After many lifetimes of effort and an overall improvement in the circumstances of rebirth, the person undertaking the Path finally reaches the stage at which craving and its attendant negative effects are no longer generated. This is the state of "*nirvāṇa* with remainder" because the residue of negative karmic effects from previous actions continues. The enlightened person still experiences physical pain, for example, as a consequence of the mere fact of corporeality, itself a karmic "fruit." Once these residues are burned off, as it were, the person will die and achieve the perfect "*nirvāṇa* without remainder."

An ambiguity in the distinction between *saṃsāra* and *nirvāṇa* is whether the contrasted terms refer to psychological or ontological states. That is, are *saṃsāra* and *nirvāṇa* states of mind or kinds of existence? If *saṃsāra* refers to the psychological worldview conducive to suffering, then the transition from *saṃsāra* to *nirvāṇa* is simply a profound change in attitude, perspective, and motivation. If, on the other hand, *saṃsāra* refers to this pain-stricken world itself, then *nirvāṇa* must be somewhere else. Here the ancient metaphor of *nirvāṇa* as "the farther shore" could assume a metaphysical status. In effect, *nirvāṇa* could be understood as a permanent state of bliss beyond the world of birth, death, and rebirth. The reaction against such an interpretation influenced the Mahāyāna Buddhist views of enlightenment.

NIRVĀṆA IN THE INDIAN MAHĀYĀNA BUDDHIST TRADITIONS

Indian Mahāyāna Buddhists minimized the opposition between *nirvāṇa* and *saṃsāra,* renouncing the suggestion that *nirvāṇa* was an escape from the world of suffering. Instead, they thought of enlightenment as a wise and compassionate way of living in that world. The adherents of the two major Indian branches of Mahāyāna philosophy, Mādhyamika and Yogācāra, each developed their own way of rejecting the escapism to which, it was thought, the Abhidharma interpretation led.

The Perfection of Wisdom and Mādhyamika Traditions. One Mahāyāna strategy was to undercut the epistemological and logical bases for the sharp distinction between the concepts of *nirvāṇa* and *saṃsāra.* Without *nirvāṇa* there is no *saṃsāra,* and vice versa. How then could one be absolute and the other relative? This question was most clearly raised by the Perfection of Wisdom (Prajñāpāramitā) literature and philosophically analyzed in the Mādhyamika school founded by Nāgārjuna (c. 150–250 CE).

In effect, Mādhyamika thought radicalized the Buddha's original silence on this critical issue by trying to demonstrate that any philosophical attempt to characterize reality is limited by the logical interdependence of words or concepts. Assuming an isomorphic relationship between words and nonlinguistic referents, Nāgārjuna reasoned that the interdependent character of words precludes their referring to any absolute, nondependent realities. To the very extent we can talk or reason about *nirvāṇa* and *saṃsāra,* therefore, they must depend on each other. Neither can be absolute in itself.

For the Mādhyamikas, the real cause of human turmoil is that through naming and analyzing we try to grasp and hold onto what exists only through the distinctions imposed by the conventions of language. From this perspective, Buddhist practice frees one from this attachment to concepts by cultivating *prajñā,* a nondiscursive, direct insight into the way things are. Once one recognizes that the substantialized sense of ego is based on a linguistic distinction having no ultimate basis, an enlightened attitude develops in which one actively shares in the suffering of all other sentient beings. In this way, the wisdom of *prajñā* can also be considered a universal form of compassion, *karuṇā.* This *prajñā-karuṇā* ideal eventually became a major paradigm of enlightenment within the entire Mahāyāna tradition in India, Tibet, and East Asia. [*See* Mādhyamika; Prajñā; Karuṇā; *and the biography of Nāgārjuna.*]

Nirvāṇa in the Idealistic and Yogācāra Traditions. The typical approach of such idealistic texts as the *Laṅkāvatāra Sūtra* and of its related philosophical school, Yogācarā, was to assert that *nirvāṇa* and *saṃsāra* had a common ground, namely, the activity of the mind. The terminology varied from text to text and thinker to thinker, but the thrust of this branch of Mahāyāna Buddhism was that the mind was the basis of both delusion (understood as *saṃsāra*) and enlightenment (understood as *nirvāṇa*). For many in this tradition, this implied that there is in each person an inherent core of Buddhahood covered over with a shell of delusional fixations. Sometimes this core was called the *tathāgata-garbha* ("Buddha womb, Buddha embryo," or "Buddha matrix"); in other cases it was considered to be part of a store-consciousness *(ālaya-vijñāna)* containing seeds *(bīja)* that could sprout either delusional or enlightened experience. In either case, Buddhist practice was seen as a technique for clarifying or making manifest the Buddha mind or Buddha nature within the individual. This notion of mind and its relation to Buddhist practice influenced the later development of Mahāyāna Buddhism, even the schools that first flourished in East Asia, such as T'ien-t'ai, Hua-yen, and Ch'an (Zen). [*See* Tathāgatagarbha *and* Ālaya-vijñāna.]

A problem raised by this more psychological approach to enlightenment was the issue of universality. Is the inherent core of enlightenment in one person the same as in another? Is it equally present in everyone? With such questions, the difficulty of the ontological status of enlightenment once again emerged. That is, if both *nirvāṇa* and *saṃsāra* are dependent on the mind in some sense, the problem for the Yogācāra philosophers was to explain the objective ground for *nirvāṇa*. Otherwise, truth would be merely subjective. Yogācāra thinkers such as Asaṅga (fourth century CE) and his brother, Vasubandhu, approached this problem by asserting a transindividual, mental ground for all experience called *ālaya-vijñāna*. Other Yogācāra thinkers such as Dignāga, however, rejected the existence of such a store-consciousness and tried to establish the necessary ground for objectivity within mental cognition itself, while denying the substantial reality of any object outside cognition. In general, the former approach persevered in the transmission of Yogācāra's philosophy into East Asia, where the idea of the ground of enlightenment or of the Buddha nature would become a major theme. [*See* Yogācāra *and the biographies of Asaṅga, Vasubandhu, and Dignāga*.]

Buddhahood in Devotional Mahāyāna Buddhism. *Nirvāṇa*'s ontological or metaphysical nature was also a theme in Mahāyāna religious practices quite outside the formal considerations of the philosophers. This development was associated with the rise of the notion that the historical Buddha who had died in the fifth century BCE was actually only an earthly manifestation of an eternal Buddha or of Buddhahood itself. This line of thought developed into the construction of a rich pantheon of Buddhas and *bodhisattvas* living in various heavenly realms and interacting with human beings in supportive ways. These heavenly figures became the objects of meditation, emulation, reverence, and supplication. [*See* Celestial Buddhas and Bodhisattvas.]

The evolution of the Buddhist pantheon was consistent with the general Mahāyāna principle that a necessary component of enlightenment is compassion. The Buddha, it was believed, would not desert those who had not yet achieved *nirvāṇa* and were still in a state of anguish. Whereas the physical person of the Buddha was extinguished, the compassion of his Buddhahood would seem to endure. Following this line of reasoning, the historical Buddha was taken to be only a physical manifestation of enlightened being itself. This interpretation made moot the question of *nirvāṇa* as the release from the cycle of birth, death, and rebirth. If Buddhahood continues even after the physical disappearance of the enlightened person, enlightenment must be more *manifested* than achieved. This way of thinking was conducive to Mahāyāna Buddhism's transmission into East Asia.

NIRVĀṆA IN EAST ASIAN BUDDHIST TRADITIONS

The Mahāyānists were generally more interested in the truth to which enlightenment was an awakening than the pain from which it was a release. This emphasis on the positive aspect of enlightenment also caused to be diminished the importance of *nirvāṇa* as the release from rebirth. This perspective was well suited to Chinese thought. Since the Chinese had no indigenous idea of the cycle of rebirth, release from that cycle was not the existential issue in China it had been in India.

A second Mahāyānist idea readily accepted by the Chinese was that enlightenment is available to anyone in this very lifetime. The Abhidharma traditions generally assumed the path to enlightenment would take eons, and that the last rebirth in this progression of lifetimes would be that of a monk blessed with the circumstances most conducive to concentrating on the final stages of the Path. This view led to a distinction between the spiritual development of monastics and laypersons: laypersons were to support monastics in their religious quest; such support would, in return, give the laypersons meritorious *karman* leading to successively better rebirths until they too were born into circumstances allowing them to reach the final stages of the Path.

The Mahāyāna ideal, on the other hand, was that of the *bodhisattva*, the enlightened (or, more technically, almost enlightened) being who chooses to be actively involved in alleviating the suffering of others by leading them to enlightenment. In other words, the *bodhisattva* subordinates personal enlightenment to that of others. Both Abhidharma and Mahāyāna Buddhism aim for the enlightenment of everyone, but whereas in the Abhidharma view enlightenment is achieved by one person at a time and the group as a whole pushes upward in a pyramid effect, supporting most the spiritual progress of those at the top, in Mahāyāna Buddhism the *bodhisattva*s at the top turn back to pull up those behind them until everyone is ready to achieve enlightenment simultaneously. Ultimately, the Mahāyāna model dominated in East Asia, partly because the collectivist viewpoint was more consistent with indigenous Chinese ideas predating the introduction of Buddhism. [*See* Bodhisattva Path.]

When Buddhism entered China around the beginning of the common era, Confucianism and Taoism were already well established. Confucianism placed its primary emphasis on the cultivation of virtuous human relationships for the harmonious functioning of society. This emphasis on social responsibility and collective virtue blended well with the Mahāyāna vision of enlightenment. [*See* Confucian Thought, *article on* Foundations of the Tradition.]

Compared to Confucianism, Taoism was relatively ascetic, mystical, and otherworldly. Yet its mysticism was strongly naturalistic in that the Taoist sage sought unity with the Tao by being in harmony with nature. In Taoism, as in Mahāyāna Buddhism, the absolute principle was completely immanent in this world, accessible to all who attune themselves to it by undertaking the proper form of meditation and self-discipline. Since one of the root meanings of the term *tao* is "path," the Chinese found parallels between the Buddhist sense of the Path and the Taoist understanding of achieving oneness with the Tao. [*See also* Taoism, *overview article.*]

Nirvāṇa in the T'ien-t'ai and Hua-yen Schools. Eventually there arose new forms of Mahāyāna Buddhism distinctive to East Asia, schools either unknown or only incipient in India. The term *nirvāṇa,* possibly because it carried connotations of a foreign worldview replete with such ideas as rebirth and the inherent unsatisfactoriness *(duḥkha)* of existence, tended to lose its privileged status in favor of such terms as "awakening" *(chüeh)* and "realization" *(wu).*

The Chinese T'ien-t'ai and Hua-yen traditions formulated their own sophisticated philosophical worldviews out of ideas suggested by Indian *sutras*. Both schools emphasized the interpenetration of all things. In T'ien-t'ai terminology as developed by such philosophers as Chih-i (538–597), all the "three thousand worlds" are reflected in a single instant of thought. Reality's underlying, unifying factor was understood to be mind. [*See the biography of Chih-i.*] For T'ien-t'ai followers the fundamental mind is itself always pure and does not contain, as most Indian Yogācārins held, both delusional and enlightened seeds.

The T'ien-t'ai assumption of an underlying, inherently pure, mind had two important consequences. First, the goal of its primary contemplative practice, known as "cessation and discernment" *(chih-kuan),* was explained as immersion into, rather than the purification of, mind. By ceasing to focus on the surface flow of ordinary phenomena, one can discern the underlying single mind at the source of all things. Second, since the underlying mind is pure or enlightened, it follows that all things, even inanimate ones, are endowed with Buddha nature. This corollary was first proposed by the ninth patriarch of the tradition, Chan-jan (711–782), who clearly articulated the view that the entire world, as it is, is already somehow enlightened. The goal, then, is to realize, awaken to, or manifest that enlightenment in one's own life. The relationship between inherent and acquired enlightenment became a central problematic in the T'ien-t'ai tradition and a major theme behind the development of the various schools of Japanese Buddhism in the Kamakura period (1185–1333) as well.

Chinese Hua-yen Buddhism also affirmed the interdependence among, and harmony within, all things. Unlike the adherents of T'ien-t'ai, however, the Hua-yen philosophers did not think of mind as the underlying, unifying entity. Fa-tsang (643–712), for example, preferred to deny any single unifying factor and used the phrase "the nonobstruction between thing and thing" *(shih-shih wu-ai).* In other words, each phenomenon itself was thought to reflect every other phenomenon. Tsung-mi (780–841), on the other hand, favored the phrase "the nonobstruction between absolute principle and thing" *(li-shih wu-ai).* Thus, he regarded principle (*li*) as the fundamental unifying substrate, even the creative source, of reality. [*See the biographies of Fa-tsang and Tsung-mi.*]

In all these T'ien-t'ai and Hua-yen theories we find a recurrent, distinctively East Asian, interpretation of *nirvāṇa.* Just as the Confucians sought harmony within the social order and the Taoists harmony within the natural order, the T'ien-t'ai and Hua-yen Buddhists understood enlightenment in terms of harmony. Rather than emphasizing the painful aspect of the world and the means to emancipation from it, the T'ien-t'ai and Hua-yen Buddhists focused on recognizing the intrinsic harmony of the universe and feeling intimately a part of it. [*See* T'ien-t'ai *and* Hua-yen.]

Nirvāṇa in the Ch'an (Zen) School. Ch'an (Kor., Sŏn; Jpn., Zen) is another school with roots in India, but it developed into a full-fledged tradition only in East Asia. It is distinctive in its de-emphasis of the role of formal doctrine and religious texts in favor of a direct "transmission of mind" from master to disciple. Ch'an focused most on the interpersonal aspect of the enlightenment experience. Enlightenment was considered a stamp embodied in a particular lineage of enlightened people going back to the historical Buddha, and the personal encounters of great masters and disciples were recorded in order to serve as the object of meditation for future generations.

One topic of debate about enlightenment in the Ch'an school concerned the issue of whether enlightenment was "sudden" or "gradual." The Northern school emphasized the inherent purity of the mind and, therefore, advocated a practice intended to remove delusional thoughts covering over that intrinsically undefiled core. Then, it was assumed, the inherent enlightenment of the mind could shine forth ever more brilliantly. According to the *Platform Sutra,* a text of the Southern school, this position was expressed in a poem by Shen-hsiu (606–706) as follows:

> The body is the Bodhi tree,
> The mind is like a clear mirror.
> At all times we must strive to polish it,
> And must not let the dust collect.
> (Yampolsky, 1967, p. 130)

The members of the Southern school, on the other hand, accused their Northern school counterparts of reifying enlightenment into an independently existing thing. In the expression of Hui-neng (638–713) also recorded in the *Platform Sūtra*:

> Bodhi originally has no tree,
> The mirror also has no stand.
> Buddha nature is always clear and pure;
> Where is there room for dust?
> (ibid., p. 132)

In other words, enlightenment should be manifest at all times in all one's activities. It is not a separate state or seed to be nurtured or cared for. The goal for the Southern school, therefore, was to make enlightenment manifest while going about one's daily affairs. [*See the biography of Hui-neng.*] This viewpoint eventually led some Southern masters, especially those in the lineage of Ma-tsu (709–788), to de-emphasize simple meditation in favor of the shock tactics of shouting, striking, and using the ***kung-an*** (Jpn., ***kōan***). These special techniques were all ways of making the disciple realize and manifest Buddha nature in a sudden manner.

Another approach to the sudden/gradual issue was originally taken by the previously mentioned Hua-yen (and Ch'an) master Tsung-mi, and later developed extensively by the great Korean Sŏn master, Chinul (1158–1210). Their view was that the Southern school (which eventually dominated for political as much as religious or philosophical reasons) was correct in maintaining that enlightenment, the awakening to one's own Buddha nature, had to be a sudden realization. Yet Tsung-mi and Chinul also maintained that realization had to be gradually integrated into one's life through a continuously deepening practice of spiritual cultivation. Thus, their position is known as "sudden awakening/gradual cultivation," rather than "sudden awakening/ sudden cultivation." This distinction exemplifies the importance Ch'an philosophers accorded the need to define as precisely as possible the relationship between practice and enlightenment. [*See the biography of Chinul.*] Dōgen (1200–1253), the founder of the Japanese Sōtō Zen tradition, addressed the problem of how enlightenment could be inherent and yet practice still necessary. That is, if people are already primordially enlightened why should anyone bother to sit in meditation? Dōgen understood practice to be enlightened activity itself: one does not sit in meditation in order to achieve enlightenment, but rather, one's enlightenment is expressed as one's sitting in meditation. [*See the biography of Dōgen.*]

For virtually all the Ch'an (and Sŏn and Zen) traditions, enlightenment is more than an insight or even a sense of harmony. It is also a mode of *behavior* to be continuously enacted and tested in everyday life. Much of the interpersonal dynamics between master and disciple is designed to challenge the person to make *nirvāṇa* manifest in such ordinary activities as talking, working, eating, and washing, as well as meditating. [*See* Ch'an *and* Zen.]

Nirvāṇa in the Pure Land Traditions. All forms of Buddhism discussed up to now have assumed that one can only achieve *nirvāṇa* through years (or even lifetimes) of concentrated practice. The Pure Land tradition, especially as developed by Shinran (1173–1262) in Japan, radically reinterpreted the notion of Buddhist practice, however.

Pure Land Buddhism is another Mahāyāna tradition that had its basis in Indian *sūtra*s but that only fully blossomed in East Asia. It began with a rather otherworldly orientation: the present period of history was considered so degenerate that it was thought to be no longer possible for human beings to practice genuine Buddhism and to achieve *nirvāṇa.* A *bodhisattva* named Dharmākara (Hōzō in Japanese), however, vowed not to allow himself to achieve full Buddhahood if people who called on his name with faith were not reborn in a Pure Land, a place ideally suited for Buddhist practice. In that Pure Land, people could attain enlightenment and even come back into the world as *bodhisattva*s to aid in the spiritual progress of others. The Pure Land *sūtra*s go on to explain that Dharmākara became the Buddha Amitābha/Amitāyus (Jpn., Amida). Therefore, he must have fulfilled his vow, and thus if people can call on that Buddha's name with complete faith in his compassion and power to help they will be guaranteed rebirth in the Pure Land.

The major lesson in this account for Pure Land Buddhists like Shinran was that human beings today cannot achieve *nirvāṇa* by their "own power" *(jiriki).* Rather than help themselves through the practice of calculated, self-conscious actions (*hakarai*), people should simply resign themselves completely to the "power of another" *(tariki),* that is, the power of Amida's compassionate vow. Even this act of the "entrusting heart and mind" *(shinjin)* must itself be an expression of Amida's vow and not an effort on one's own part. In this way, Shinran maintained that enlightenment could ultimately only be achieved by first releasing oneself to the spontaneousness "naturalness" *(jinen hōni),* the active grace of Amida's compassion as this world itself. "Amida Buddha is the medium through which we are made to realize *jinen*" (Ueda, 1978, pp. 29–30). By subordinating even Amida and his vow to the principle of spontaneous naturalness in this way, Shinran removed the otherworldly traces in Pure Land teaching, making it more suitable to its East Asian, particularly Japanese, context. [*See* Amitābha *and the biography of Shinran.*]

Nirvāṇa in the Esoteric Traditions. The Esoteric, Vajrayāna, or Tantric forms of Buddhism can be generally viewed as extensions of Mahāyāna. In general, however, Esoteric Buddhism was most permanently influential in Tibet (including the Mongolian extensions of Tibetan Buddhism) and in Japan. In both cases, Esotericism merged its practices and doctrines with the indigenous shamanistic, archaic religions of, respectively, Bon and Shintō.

In terms of their understanding of *nirvāṇa* the Esoteric traditions added an important dimension to their otherwise generally Mahāyānistic outlook, namely, that enlightenment should be understood as participation in the enlightenment of the Buddha-as-reality (the *dharmakāya*). From this viewpoint, sacred speech (*mantras*), sacred gestures (*mudras*), and sacred envisioning (*maṇḍalas*) constitute a Buddhist ritualistic practice having an almost sacramental character. That is, in performing the rituals outlined in the Tantras, the Esoteric Buddhist believes that one's own speech, action, and thought become the concrete expression of the cosmic Buddha's own enlightenment.

This notion found a particularly clear formulation in the Japanese Shingon Buddhism established by Kūkai (774–835). According to Kūkai, the fundamental principle of Shingon practice and philosophy is that of *hosshin seppō,* "the Buddha-as-reality [*dharmakāya*] preaches the true teaching [*dharma*]." In making this claim, Kūkai rejected the exoteric Buddhist notion that only a historical Buddha *(nirmāṇakāya)* or a heavenly Buddha *(saṃbhogakāya)* can preach. All of reality in itself, according to Kūkai, is the symbolic expression of the *dharmakāya* Buddha's enlightened activity and, as such, is the direct manifestation of truth. The way to grasp this symbolic expression is not to be an audience to it, but rather to take part in it directly through Esoteric rituals. The individual's own enlightenment was considered an aspect of the cosmic Buddha's enlightened activity. Kūkai identified the Buddha-as-reality or the cosmic Buddha as the Great Sun Buddha, Dainichi Nyorai (Skt., Mahāvairocana). [*See* Mahāvairocana.]

Kūkai's view of enlightenment was, therefore, summarized in the phrase "attaining Buddha in and through this very body" *(sokushin jōbutsu).* Through the ritualized, physical participation in the world, the person could become a concrete expression of Dainichi Buddha's enlightened action. Kūkai expressed this intimacy between the individual and Dainichi Buddha as "the Buddha enters the self and the self enters the Buddha" *(nyūga ganyū).* In effect, the Mahāyāna Buddhist's identification of *nirvāṇa* with the world was taken to its most radical conclusion. That is, from the Shingon perspective, this very world *is* the Buddha Dainichi. This means that enlightenment is not inherent in the world, but rather, the world itself is the experience of enlightenment. [*See* Buddhism, Schools of, *article on* Esoteric Buddhism; Chenyen; Shingonshū; *and the biography of Kūkai.*]

CONCLUSION

As this article has shown, there is no single Buddhist view of *nirvāṇa*. The Buddhist ideal varies with the culture, the historical period, the language, the school, and even the individual. Still, we do find in the Buddhist notions of *nirvāṇa* what Ludwig Wittgenstein would have called a "family resemblance," that is, a group of characteristics that no single family member entirely possesses but that all members share to such an extent that the members of one family are distinguishable from the members of another. In this case, the Buddhist conceptions of *nirvāṇa* share a set of qualities that can be summarized as follows.

1. *Nirvāṇa* is the release from ignorance about the way the world is. Because we do not understand the nature of human existence and the laws affecting human life, we live in either a state of outright suffering or in a state of disharmony. *Nirvāṇa* is ultimately acknowledging and living by the truths of our world. In that respect, its orientation is this-worldly.
2. The knowledge achieved by *nirvāṇa* is not merely intellectual or spiritual. *Nirvāṇa* is achieved through a process of psychological and physical conditioning aimed at reorienting and reversing ego-centered forms of thinking and behaving. *Nirvāṇa* is achieved through and with the body, not despite the body.
3. One is not alone on the Path. There is support from texts, philosophical teachings, religious practices, the Buddhist community, the examples of masters, and even the rocks and trees. Most of all, there is the power of compassion that one receives from others and that grows stronger the more it is offered to others.
4. *Nirvāṇa* is achieved by penetrating and dissolving the slashes or virgules separating humanity/nature, self/other, subject/object, and even *nirvāṇa/saṃsāra*. The particular pairs of opposition vary from place to place and time to time as Buddhism attacks the special dichotomies most destructive in a given culture during a specific period. *Nirvāṇa* entails a recognition of the inherent harmony and equality of all things.
5. *Nirvāṇa* has an intrinsically moral aspect. By eliminating all egocentric ideas, emotions, and actions, the enlightened person approaches others with either complete equanimity (wherein self and others are treated exactly the same) or with a compassionate involvement in alleviating the suffering of others (wherein self is subordinated to the needs of those less fortunate). Morality can be considered the alpha and omega of *nirvāṇa*. That is, the Path begins with accepting various rules and precepts of behavior, whereas *nirvāṇa* culminates in the open, moral treatment of other people and things.
6. Although in any given context, one viewpoint is emphasized over the other, generally speaking, *nirvāṇa* can be understood from either a psychological or ontological perspective. Psychologically viewed, *nirvāṇa* is a radical change in attitude such that one no longer experiences the negative influence of egocentric thinking. If this perspective is misunderstood and overemphasized, however, it leads to a psychologism that holds that truth is simply in the mind without any connection to an external reality. The remedy for this distortion is to assert the ontological aspect of *nirvāṇa*.

Ontologically speaking, *nirvāṇa* is the affirmation of the inherent goodness of the world and even of human nature. In this sense, *nirvāṇa* is not merely a kind of experience (as depicted by the psychological view) but is also the content or even *ground* of an experience. If this ontological viewpoint is overemphasized, on the other hand, it can lead to the distorted idea that diligence and practice are arbitrary or even unnecessary. The remedy is, conversely, to neutralize that distortion with more emphasis on the psychological side of *nirvāṇa*.

In short, both the psychological and ontological views contain truths about the nature of *nirvāṇa*, but if either position is developed in such a way as to exclude the other, the result is a distortion of the Buddhist Path. For this reason, the two views coexist throughout Buddhist history, one view always complementing the other and checking any distortions that might arise out of a one-sided perspective.

[*See also* Buddhist Philosophy; Buddhist Ethics; Buddhist Literature, *article on* Exegesis and Hermeneutics; Language, *article on* Buddhist Views of Language; *and* Soteriology, *article on* Buddhist Soteriology.]

BIBLIOGRAPHY

As the fundamental ideal of Buddhism, *nirvāṇa* is discussed in a wide variety of works: *sūtras*, commentaries, and secondary critical works by scholars of various traditions. Any bibliography must be, therefore, incomplete and, at best, highly selective. The following works have been chosen for their particular relevance to the issues discussed in the foregoing article.

Nirvāṇa in the Indian Buddhist Traditions. Of the many references to *nirvāṇa* in the early Indian texts, certain passages have traditionally received the most attention. For example, in the Pali scriptures, the status of the Buddha after death (*parinibbāna*) is handled in various ways. Most prominent, undoubtedly, is the traditional account of the Buddha's passing away described in chapter 6 of the *Mahāparinibbāna Suttanta.* A translation of this text by T. W. Rhys Davids is readily available as *Buddhist Suttas,* volume 11 of "The Sacred Books of the East," edited by F. Max Müller (1881; reprint, New York, 1969). An interesting feature of this account is its clear distinction between the Buddha's *nirvāṇa* and his meditative capacity to cause the complete cessation (*nirodha*) of perceptions, thoughts, and feelings. This passage is often quoted, therefore, against any claim that the early Buddhist view was simply nihilistic and world-renouncing. Notably absent in this text, however, is any detailed treatment of the classic distinction between *nirvāṇa* with remainder and *nirvāṇa* without remainder. That distinction is more clearly presented in *Itivuttaka,* edited by Ernst Windisch (London, 1889), esp. pp. 38–39. An English translation by F. L. Woodward is in the second volume of *Minor Anthologies of the Pali Canon,* edited by C. A. F. Rhys Davids (London, 1935).

Another commonly analyzed theme is the Buddha's own reticence to describe the status of the enlightened person after death. On this point, there are two particularly provocative textual references. One is the above-mentioned story about Māluṅkyāputta in *Majjhima-Nikāya,* 4 vols., edited by Vilhelm Trenckner, Robert Chalmers, and C. A. F. Rhys Davids (London, 1887–1925), *suttas* 63–64; the other is in *The Saṃyutta-nikāya of the Sutta piṭaka,* 6 vols., edited by Léon Freer (London, 1884–1904), vol. 3, p. 118. English translations of these two complete collections are, respectively, *The Collection of the Middle Length Sayings,* 3 vols., translated by I. B. Horner (London, 1954–1959), and *The Book of Kindred Sayings,* 5 vols., translated by C. A. F. Rhys Davids and F. L. Woodward (London, 1917–1930).

As already mentioned, descriptions of *nirvāṇa* are for the most part posed in negative terms; the interested reader can find a multitude of examples by consulting, for example, the excellent indexes in the collections of early Pali texts cited above. One particularly striking exception to this rule, however, is found in *The Saṃyutta-nikāya,* vol. 4, p. 373. This passage gives a rather lengthy string of mostly positive equivalents to *nirvāṇa,* including terms that mean "truth," "the farther shore," "the stable," "peace," "security," "purity," and so forth. Such positive characterizations of *nirvāṇa* are found elsewhere, but never in quite so concentrated a list.

On the issue of the transcendent, mystical, or metaphysical aspect of *nirvāṇa* in the early Buddhist tradition, a pivotal textual reference is in *Udāna,* edited by Paul Steinthal (London, 1948). An English translation also occurs in volume 2 of Woodward's *Minor Anthologies,* cited above. On pages 80–81 of *Udāna,* we find an indubitable reference to a state of mind or a place beyond birth and death, beyond all discrimination and ordinary perceptions. Controversy still continues over the proper interpretation of the passage. In Rune E. A. Johansson's *Psychology of Nirvana* (London, 1969), for example, there is a sustained discussion of the enlightened state of mind as being a mystical, transempirical, nondifferentiated state of consciousness. The passage from *Udāna* naturally figures prominently in Johansson's argument. On the other hand, this viewpoint is severely criticized in David J. Kalupahana's *Buddhist Philosophy: A Historical Analysis* (Honolulu, 1976), chap. 7. By interpreting this passage as referring to the state of cessation (*nirodha*) just prior to the Buddha's death but not to ordinary *nirvāṇa* in this world, Kalupahana argues that early Buddhism consistently maintained that the achievement of *nirvāṇa* does not require, or entail, any transempirical form of perception. In this regard, Kalupahana is expanding on the theory that early Buddhism was primarily empirical in outlook, an interpretation first fully developed in Kulitassa Nanda Jayatilleke's *Early Buddhist Theory of Knowledge* (London, 1963).

Another controversial issue among modern scholars is the relationship between early Buddhism and the contemporary form of Hinduism. Whereas Kalupahana's approach sharply distinguishes the early Buddhist view of *nirvāṇa* from the contemporary Hindu ideal of the unity of *ātman* with *brahman,* Johansson tends to see a common mystical element in the two. A generally more balanced and convincing position on this point can be found in the thorough discussion of Kashi Nath Upadhyaya's *Early Buddhism and the Bhagavadgītā* (Delhi, 1971).

A good introduction to the modern view of *nirvāṇa* from the standpoint of the only living tradition of Abhidharma, the Theravāda, is Walpola Rahula's *What the Buddha Taught,* rev. ed. (Bedford, England, 1967), chap. 4. This small work is highly regarded for its ability to explain the gist of centuries of Abhidharmic analysis in a straightforward, accurate, and yet nontechnical manner. On the way *nirvāṇa* actually functions today as an ethical ideal in Theravāda daily life, see Winston L. King's *In the Hope of Nibbana: An Essay of Theravada Buddhist Ethics* (La Salle, Ill., 1964). For a more historical and specialized approach to the development of the early Abhidharma views of *nirvāṇa,* see Edward Conze's *Buddhist Thought in India* (1962; reprint, Ann Arbor, 1970), esp. sections 1.5 and 2.3. Although this book is poorly written and organized, it still contains some information not readily available in English elsewhere.

For Nāgārjuna and the Mādhyamika school, the *locus classicus* is Nāgārjuna's discussion in chapter 25 of his *Mūlamadhyamakakārikā.* The complete Sanskrit original and English translation of this work with extensive commentary is found in David J. Kalupahana's *Nagarjuna: The Philosophy of the Middle Way* (Albany, 1985). A good discussion of Nāgārjuna's basic position with respect to *nirvāṇa* also appears in Frederick J. Streng's *Emptiness: A Study in Religious Meaning* (New York, 1967), pp. 69–81.

For studying the Yogācāra and idealist position, the reader may wish to consult *The Laṅkāvatāra Sūtra,* translated by D. T. Suzuki (1932; reprint, Boulder, 1978). The identifications of *nirvāṇa* with the pure *ālaya-vijñāna* or the *tathāgata-garbha,* as well as with the mind released from delusional discriminations are particularly discussed in sections 18, 38, 63, 74, 77, and 82. For the more systematically philosophical developments of the Yogācāra tradition, the reader may refer to the following works. Asaṅga's *Mahāyānasaṃgraha* has been translated and edited by Étienne Lamotte in *La somme du Grand Véhicule d'Asaṅga,* vol. 2 (Louvain, 1939). Translations of Vasubandhu's *Viṃśatikā* and *Triṃśikā* by Clarence H. Hamilton and Wing-tsit Chan, respectively, can be found in *A Source Book in Indian Philosophy,* edited by Sarvepalli Radhakrishnan and Charles A. Moore (Princeton, 1957). Sylvain Lévi's *Matériaux pour l'étude du système Vijñaptimātra* (Paris, 1932) remains the definitive discussion on Vasubandhu's writings. For an analysis of Dignāga's thought, see Hattori Masaaki's *Dignāga, on Perception* (Cambridge, Mass., 1968).

For a straightforward and detailed discussion of Indian Buddhist theories of *nirvāṇa,* see Nalinaksha Dutt's *Mahāyāna Buddhism* (rev. ed., Delhi, 1978), chap. 7. Although sometimes biased against the Abhidharma traditions, his account of the differences among the Indian Buddhist schools is very good. For a thorough and fascinating discussion of the attempts of Western scholars to interpret the idea of *nirvāṇa* as found primarily in the Pali texts, see Guy R. Welbon's *The Buddhist Nirvāṇa and its Western Interpreters* (Chicago, 1968). Welbon includes a good bibliography of works in Western languages. His book culminates in the famous debate between Louis de La Vallée Poussin (1869–1938) and Theodore Stcherbatsky (Fedor Shcherbatskii, 1866–1942). Both were noted as first-rate commentators on Mahāyāna Buddhism, but their own personalities and temperaments led them to take distinctively different views of Buddhism and its intent. Thus, in examining the same early Buddhist texts, the former emphasized the yogic and religious aspects whereas the latter favored the philosophical. Despite their limitations, however, La Vallée Poussin's *Nirvāṇa* (Paris, 1925) and Stcherbatsky's *The Conception of Buddhist Nirvāṇa* (Leningrad, 1927) remain classic works on this subject.

East Asian Traditions. For the reasons given in the essay, the idea of *nirvāṇa* is not discussed as explicitly in the East Asian as the South Asian traditions. When *nirvāṇa* is analyzed by East Asian Buddhists, the sharply etched distinctions among the various Indian Mahāyāna schools are softened. A clear example of this is D. T. Suzuki's *Outlines of Mahayana Buddhism* (New York, 1963), chap. 13. In this chapter, and indeed throughout the book, Suzuki approaches the ideas of Mahāyāna Buddhists as coming from discrete traditions but involving an underlying common spirit.

For the view of the T'ien-t'ai school as developed by Chih-i, the most thorough discussion in English is Leon N. Hurvitz's *Chih-i (538–597); An Introduction to the Life and Ideas of a Chinese Buddhist Monk* (Brussels, 1962). For the impact of the T'ien-t'ai idea of inherent enlightenment on Japanese Buddhism in the Kamakura period, see the comprehensive study in Tamura Yoshirō's *Kamakura shinbukkyō shisō no kenkyū* (Tokyo, 1965).

Like T'ien-t'ai, the Hua-yen tradition has not yet been comprehensively studied in Western works. One of the better philosophical overviews of Hua-yen theory in relation to enlightenment is the discussion about Fa-tsang in Fung Yu-lan's *A History of Chinese Philosophy,* translated by Derk Bodde (Princeton, 1953), vol. 2, chap. 8. Fa-tsang is also central to the analysis in Francis D. Cook's *Hua-yen Buddhism: The Jewel Net of Indra* (University Park, Pa., 1977). Essays on the history of Hua-yen practice are included in *Studies in Ch'an and Hua-yen,* edited by Robert M. Gimello and Peter N. Gregory (Honolulu, 1984).

On the theory of the four realms of reality *(fa-chieh),* the culmination of which is the "nonobstruction between thing and things," a key text is Ch'eng-kuan's *Hua-yen fa-chieh hsüan-ching,* a translation of which is found in Thomas Cleary's *Entry into the Inconceivable* (Honolulu, 1983). One noteworthy point about the translation, however, is that it translates *li* as "noumenon" and *shih* as "phenomenon," a rendering popular in earlier English translations, but now usually replaced by terms less speculative and philosophically misleading, such as, respectively, "principle" and "event" (or "principle" and "thing").

On the Ch'an distinction between sudden and gradual enlightenment, the exchange of poems by Shen-hsiu and Hui-neng is recorded in the first ten sections of the *Liu-tsu t'an-ching,* a good translation of which is Philip B. Yampolsky's *The Platform Sutra of the Sixth Patriarch* (New York, 1967). For Tsung-mi's view of sudden enlightenment and gradual cultivation, as well as Chinul's elaboration on this point, see the discussion in *The Korean Approach to Zen,* translated by Robert E. Buswell, Jr. (Honolulu, 1983). For Dōgen's view of the oneness of cultivation and enlightenment, see Hee-Jin Kim's *Dōgen Kigen: Mystical Realist* (Tucson, 1975), chap. 3, and my *Zen Action/Zen Person* (Honolulu, 1981), chaps. 6–7.

For an overview of the Pure Land tradition and, in particular, Shinran's view that enlightenment is unattainable through any efforts of one's own, see Alfred Bloom's *Shinran's Gospel of Pure Grace* (Tucson, 1965), still the only major objective study of Shinran in English. There are two good translation series of Shinran's works: the "Ryūkoku Translation Series" and the "Shin Buddhism Translation Series," both of Kyoto, Japan. Neither series is complete but, between the two, most of Shinran's works have been adequately translated. The quotation in the foregoing essay is from the first volume of the latter series, namely, *The Letters of Shinran: A Translation of Mattōshō,* edited and translated by Ueda Yoshifumi (Kyoto, 1978).

For Kūkai's view on the distinctiveness of Esoteric Buddhism, a key text is *Benkenmitsu nikyō ron* (On Distinguishing the Two Teachings—Exoteric and Esoteric). On the role of ritual in enlightenment, see his *Sokushin jōbutsu gi* (On Achieving Buddhahood with This Very Body) and *Shōji jissō gi* (On Sound-Word-Reality). English translations of these works and others can be conveniently found in Yoshito S. Hakeda's *Kūkai: Major Works* (New York, 1972).

CONTRIBUTORS

ARAKI MICHIO, Tsukuba University
ANDRÉ BAREAU, Collège de France
HEINZ BECHERT, Georg-August-Universität zu Göttingen
ROBERT EVANS BUSWELL, JR., University of California at Los Angeles
RONALD ERIC EMMERICK, Universität Hamburg
SIMONE GAULIER, Collège de France
RICHARD F. GOMBRICH, Balliol College, University of Oxford
LUIS O. GÓMEZ, University of Michigan
HERBERT GUENTHER, University of Saskatchewan
CHARLES HALLISEY, Loyola University of Chicago
WALTHER HEISSIG, Rheinische Friedrich-Wilhelms-Universität Bonn
ROBERT JERA-BEZARD, Collège de France
THOMAS P. KASULIS, Northland College
WINSTON L. KING, Vanderbilt University (emeritus)
NAKAMURA HAJIME, Eastern Institute, Tokyo
REGINALD RAY, Naropa Institute
FRANK E. REYNOLDS, University of Chicago
H. L. SENEVIRATNE, University of Virginia
DAVID L. SNELLGROVE, School of Oriental and African Studies, University of London (emeritus)
DONALD K. SWEARER, Swarthmore College
TAMARU NORIYOSHI, University of Tokyo
ROBERT A. F. THURMAN, Amherst College
TAITETSU UNNO, Smith College
ALEX WAYMAN, Columbia University
STANLEY WEINSTEIN, Yale University
ERIC ZÜRCHER, Rijksuniversiteit te Leiden

FINDING LIST OF ARTICLE TITLES

The following table lists the article titles (in parentheses) as they originally appeared in *The Encyclopedia of Religion.* Titles not listed below are unchanged.

Buddhist Religion, Culture, and Civilization (Buddhism: An Overview)
The Buddha (Buddha)
Buddhism in India (Buddhism: Buddhism in India)
Buddhism in Southeast Asia (Buddhism: Buddhism in Southeast Asia)
Buddhism in Central Asia (Buddhism: Buddhism in Central Asia)
Buddhism in China (Buddhism: Buddhism in China)
Buddhism in Korea (Buddhism: Buddhism in Korea)
Buddhism in Japan (Buddhism: Buddhism in Japan)
Buddhism in Tibet (Buddhism: Buddhism in Tibet)
Buddhism in Mongolia (Buddhism: Buddhism in Mongolia)
Hīnayāna Buddhism (Buddhism, Schools of: Hīnayāna Buddhism)
Mahāyāna Buddhism (Buddhism, Schools of: Mahāyāna Buddhism)
Esoteric Buddhism (Buddhism, Schools of: Esoteric Buddhism)
The Schools of Chinese Buddhism (Buddhism, Schools of: Chinese Buddhism)
The Schools of Japanese Buddhism (Buddhism, Schools of: Japanese Buddhism)
The Schools of Tibetan Buddhism (Buddhism, Schools of: Tibetan Buddhism)
The Buddhist Saṃgha (Saṃgha: An Overview)
Saṃgha and Society (Saṃgha: Saṃgha and Society)
Buddhist Cultic Life in Southeast Asia (Worship and Cultic Life: Buddhist Cultic Life in Southeast Asia)
Buddhist Cultic Life in East Asia (Worship and Cultic Life: Buddhist Cultic Life in East Asia)
Buddhist Cultic Life in Tibet (Worship and Cultic Life: Buddhist Cultic Life in Tibet)
Buddhist Meditation (Meditation: Buddhist Meditation)

SYNOPTIC OUTLINE

A synoptic list of articles on Buddhism in *The Encyclopedia of Religion*

PRINCIPAL ARTICLES

Buddhism
- An Overview
- Buddhism in India
- Buddhism in Southeast Asia
- Buddhism in Central Asia
- Buddhism in Mongolia
- Buddhism in Tibet
- Buddhism in China
- Buddhism in Korea
- Buddhism in Japan
- Buddhism in the West

Buddhist Studies

SCHOOLS OF THOUGHT

Buddhism, Schools of
- An Overview
- Hīnayāna Buddhism
- Mahāyāna Buddhism
- Esoteric Buddhism
- Chinese Buddhism
- Japanese Buddhism
- Tibetan Buddhism

Ch'an
Chen-yen
Ching-t'u
Dge-lugs-pa
Hua-yen
Jōdo Shinshū
Jōdoshū
Mādhyamika
Mahāsāṃghika
Nichirenshū
Reiyūkai Kyōdan
Risshō Kōseikai
Sarvāstivāda
Sautrāntika
Shingonshū
Sōka Gakkai
Tendaishū
Theravāda
T'ien-t'ai
Yogācāra
Zen

SUPPORTING ARTICLES

Ālaya-vijñāna
Arhat
Bodhisattva Path
Buddhist Ethics
Buddhist Literature
- Canonization
- Survey of Texts
- Exegesis and Hermeneutics

Buddhist Philosophy
Buddhist Religious Year
Cakravartin
Celestial Buddhas and Bodhisattvas
Cosmology
- Buddhist Cosmology

Councils
- Buddhist Councils

Dalai Lama
Dharma
- Buddhist Dharma and Dharmas

Eightfold Path
Enlightenment
Folk Religion
- Folk Buddhism

Four Noble Truths
Gozan Zen
Iconography
- Buddhist Iconography

Karman
- Buddhist Concepts

Karuṇā
Language
- Buddhist Views of Language

Mahāsiddhas
Maṇḍalas
- Buddhist Maṇḍalas

Mappō
Martial Arts
- Buddhist Martial Arts

Hsüan-tsang
Hui-neng
Hui-yüan
I-ching
Ikkyū Sōjun
Ingen
Ippen
Jien
Kamalaśīla
Keizan
Kōben
Kōya
K'uei-chi
Kūkai
Kumārajīva
Liang Wu-ti
Lin-chi
Malalasekera, G. P.
Mar-pa
Mi-la-ras-pa
Moggaliputtatissa
Mongkut
Musō Soseki
Nāgārjuna
Nanjō Bunyū
Nā-ro-pa
Nichiren
Nikkō
Padmasambhava
Paramārtha
Rennyo
Saichō
Śāntideva
Śāntirakṣita
Seng-chao
Shan-tao
Shinran
Shōkū
Shōtoku Taishi
Śīlabhadra
Sthiramati
Śubhākarasiṃha
Suzuki, D. T.
Suzuki Shōsan
T'ai-hsü
Takakusu Junjirō
T'ang Yung-t'ung
T'an-luan
T'an-yao
Tao-an
Tao-ch'o
Tao-sheng
Ti-lo-pa
Tsoṅ-kha-pa
Tsung-mi
Tu-shum
Vajrabodhi
Vasubandhu